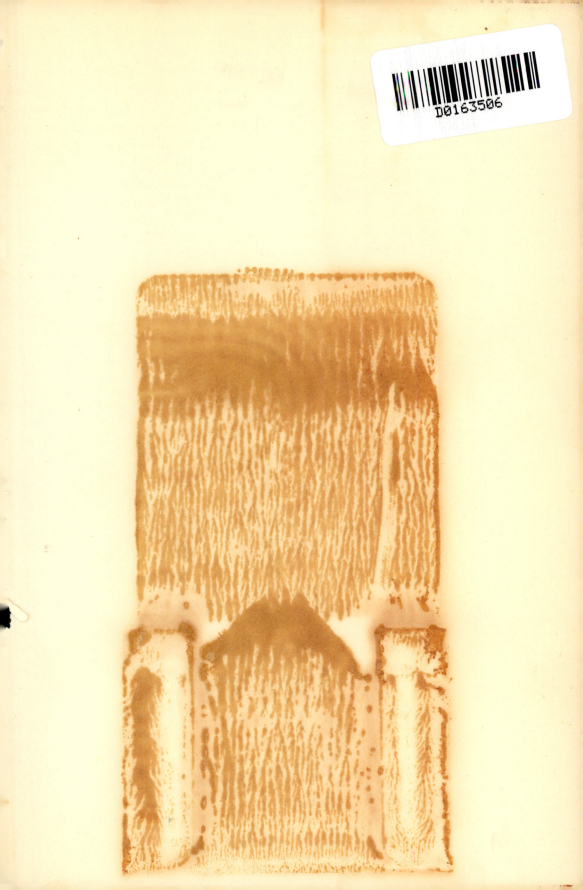

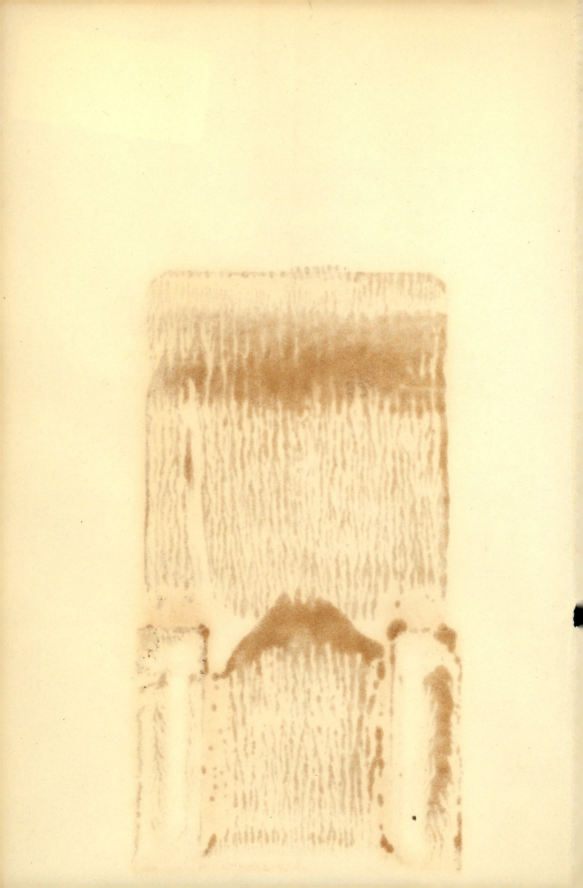

POLITICS AND CULTURE IN INTERNATIONAL HISTORY

POLITICS AND CULTURE IN INTERNATIONAL HISTORY

BY ADDA B. BOZEMAN

PRINCETON, NEW JERSEY
PRINCETON UNIVERSITY PRESS
1960

Publication of this book
has been aided by the Ford Foundation program
to support publication,
through university presses, of works in the humanities
and social sciences.
✧
Printed in the United States of America
by Princeton University Press, Princeton, New Jersey

TO ANYA BOZEMAN

ACKNOWLEDGMENTS

Work on the present volume was begun with the aid of a grant from the Carnegie Endowment for International Peace and a research fellowship from Sarah Lawrence College. It was greatly furthered through contacts with the students at the College, who gave me the opportunity to test the material selected for inclusion in this book. The staffs of various libraries, especially Mrs. Elisabeth Seely of Sarah Lawrence College, were helpful in arranging for inter-library loans.

A number of friends and authorities have very kindly read chapters and offered detailed criticisms that considerably altered and improved my original intentions, and I wish to acknowledge their kindnesses with profound thanks; notably, Drs. Mary and Arthur F. Wright through whose suggestions many new insights were contributed to the section dealing with China and Indo-Chinese relations; Sir Hamilton A. R. Gibb, who read the chapter on the Islamic realm; and Dr. H. H. Fisher, whose inspiration and moral support gave me the courage to undertake this enterprise and who then gave particular attention to my chapter on Byzantium. Dr. Philip C. Jessup read a good half of the manuscript and sent me several pages of notes. My thanks go also to Dr. Helen McMaster for her reading and discussion of a number of chapters and to Dr. Arne Barkhuus, who went through a large portion of the galleys. Special gratitude is due to Mr. Joseph Campbell, who read the whole manuscript, made numerous editorial suggestions and, for the Indian chapter, supplied valuable bibliographical advice.

A. B. B.

CONTENTS

ix

CONTENTS

CONTENTS

PART III

CHRISTIANITY AND ISLAM

PART IV

INTERNATIONAL HISTORY AND THE
WORLD SOCIETY TODAY: A RECONSIDERATION OF
REALITIES AND MYTHS

CONTENTS

POLITICS AND CULTURE IN INTERNATIONAL HISTORY

INTRODUCTION

I

THE IMAGE of the world as a physically indivisible entity was formulated slowly in the history of mankind as the continents were discovered and explored. It acquired new dimensions of meaning with the steady improvement of communications between the once isolated regions of the earth. The acceleration of contacts between the world's various peoples that followed in the wake of these developments suggested a transposition of the image of wholeness, in the sense that the world could now be viewed as the abode of men whose various destinies were inextricably intertwined. This spiritual, as well as physical, version of unity received further definition when it became evident that certain ideas and institutions, first tested and defined in Europe and North America, had a universal appeal.

Most of the peoples outside the Atlantic community of nations accepted the standards of intellectual and material achievement that Occidental thought and enterprise represented, subscribed to the vocabulary of political symbols that had been composed in the West, adopted the forms of government that Europeans and Americans had devised, and acknowledged the validity of the tenets of international intercourse long associated with the European system of states. They thus came to see both their present and their future in terms of Western aspirations and achievements and, since the historical records of most Asian and African peoples were first compiled and analysed by Occidental scholars, even viewed their past in the mirror of Western historiography.

This widespread diffusion of the Western legacy, which was attended by an intense propagation of the literate knowledge accumulated in Europe and America, had the undeniable effect of providing the modern society of nations with a unifying structure. It was instrumental also in fostering the assumption that all peoples participate in a world culture and constitute a world community.

However, in the first half of the twentieth century, a cluster of totalitarian doctrines of statecraft, exalting with a flourish of new ideals the old principles of despotic power and aggressive nationalism, shook not only the political but even the cultural foundations upon which European civilization rests and which the new societies of

3

Asia and Africa appeared to share. An atmosphere of general faith and trust was temporarily restored when the short-lived German, Italian, and Japanese empires were defeated in the great military combat that they had themselves provoked, and a synchronistic evolution of the peoples of the earth to higher levels of mutual understanding than had been reached before was again taken generally for granted when the United Nations Organization was established in 1945 and universally acclaimed as the highest embodiment of the image of a unified family of man.

Serious doubts whether all peoples were in genuine agreement as to the paramount values projected by the new world constitution developed only when the Russians asserted a totally different concept of human destiny and global order. The theme of conflict and diversity implicit in this statement had actually been present long before the promise of the One World image had become legally substantiated in its present organizational form, for it is deeply anchored in the political doctrine of communism which had been formulated in Western Europe in the mid-nineteenth century in opposition to the prevailing Occidental value system before it was taken over by the Soviet Union as its guiding principle. As relayed by the governing communist elites of the contemporary scene, this world view puts forth an image of mankind gathered, on the one hand, in the peace-loving camp of socialism under the patronage of the Soviet Union, and, on the other, in the degenerate camp of capitalism under the leadership of the Western democracies. In the context of this divisive doctrine neither unity nor lasting peace is to be envisaged until the camp of socialism is coextensive with the world. The communist challenge, projected upon the world arena and its many subsidiary stages in the form of political and psychological warfare, has thus had the effect of disestablishing the halcyon myth of unity and of setting in its place the rival image of a bipolar world.

This rendition of reality controls the scene of world affairs today. For not only does it inform the policies of the principal antagonists, but it also has persuaded people everywhere that they must interpret their destinies in terms of one or the other of these alternative ways of life, and that it is possible to reduce all tensions in international and intercultural relations to the measure of the conflict in which the protagonists of the Western and the communist value systems are engaged. Indeed, it must be conceded that in its recognition of the motif of strife and dissonance the principle of the two worlds is more realistic than the principle of the one. Nevertheless, in its trite and summary treatment of the deeply various causes of strife and dissonance it is no less mythical than the latter. For each of the regions of the earth— whether regarded as a province of one great world society, or as a pawn in the struggle between two—has its own traditions of life and thought, which antedate, in many cases by millenniums, both the conception of the one world and that of the two.

Most of these indigenous patterns of life and thought became blurred during the centuries of European supremacy, when they were being integrated in the Occidental scheme of things. Many were officially discarded because they seemed to impede the attainment of the political and social goals associated with the cause of progress, as suggested by voluntary or involuntary contacts with the West. Others simply withered away with the social structures to which they had given support. However, when the non-Western peoples began to assume their places as modern political communities in the world so largely shaped by Western thought, it became increasingly apparent that the Western ideas were not the exclusive mainsprings of their political attitudes and actions. Whether in India, Egypt, or Nigeria, men have been generally stimulated by the spread of literacy and the growth of nationalism to probe their own pasts and to resurrect the realities and myths that antedated their knowledge and acceptance of the Western ways. Behind the screen of an official accord upon Occidental interpretations of such values as tyranny and freedom, power and law, ignorance and knowledge, discords grew in the field of intercultural relations. The Africans and Asians proceeded, both consciously and unconsciously, to reinstate their native modes of thought and behavior, while continuing to pay obeisance to Western words and forms. The Europeans and Americans, meanwhile, hearing their words employed in senses strangely foreign to long-familiar definitions, began to realize that not only their transplanted words but also their institutions had come to stand for practices and attitudes that differed greatly from the parental norms. An intense, albeit little-noticed, dialogue between substratal or residual non-Western values on the one hand, and the classical Occidental on the other, had thus been in progress for some time when the encounter of civilizations was further complicated by Russia's propagation of the communist doctrine.

Each nation, each culture, each region is thus today a separate stage upon which local, communist, and Western European systems of reference and belief interact; and, barring the contingency of an ultimate obliteration of one or the other by conquest, each is likely to evolve its own syncretic system for the ordering of life within its contours and the projection of its interests abroad. In other words, the realities of world affairs today are not adequately rendered when conveyed in the simple myth of a bipolar world; for between the poles of the contemporary cultural and political map of the world there are numerous well-defined civilizations as well as many others that are just beginning to define themselves.

The world order that the Occidental nations projected during the centuries of their intellectual and political supremacy when they assumed that the world was likely to become a macrocosm of their own realm is thus in issue, not only because it is being contested by the communists but also because it is not easily compatible with the traditional local orders that are being revived in Africa and Asia. Some examples may illustrate this point.

One of the basic concepts in modern international politics is the sovereign democratic nation-state which acquired its connotations in the histories of Western Europe and America. Since groups of people in all continents have willingly identified their collective aspirations with this norm of organization by claiming the right to self-determination, declaring their independence from former authorities and agreeing to constitutions that recognize the individual as the bearer of civic rights, it was generally understood that the modern state had actually superseded older, local forms of government. In the prevailing climate of egalitarian thinking, it is easy to forget that most communities in the Balkan and Black Sea regions had matured under the political tutelage of the monolithic Byzantine Empire, whose tenets of rule were quite at variance with those developed in the West; that India had not been a nation before it was unified by the British; that China's ancient systems of politics and ethics contained no analogues to modern democratic norms; that Islam had not evolved the kind of secular law from which civic rights could be derived; and that the various West African tribes now assembled in the nation state of Ghana were not united either by a common culture and language or by traditions of cooperation.

What is generally being overlooked today as the concept of the modern state and its allied principles of law and democracy undergo their various metamorphoses in non-Western environments, is that these norms originated in the most literate of known civilizations as highly complex legal abstractions. That is to say, the vocabulary of political ideas for which world-wide applicability is being claimed to-day was composed by successive generations of people who regarded the written word as the principal mode of expression and law as the principal source of all symbols denoting political achievements and objectives. Such an orientation had not evolved in the histories of other cultures. In the ancient civilizations of the Far and Near East, where the art of writing originated, literate knowledge never spread to the masses, since it was consistently viewed as the preserve of the intellectually and politically elect. The organized societies in these regions of the world thus developed symbols and institutions quite different from those of the generally literate Occidental nations for the conveyance of shared political understandings. Even greater deviations from the assumed agreement upon the form and substance of the presently current political language than those implicit in the contrast just noted can be found in the histories of completely nonliterate civilizations. Here, where the biographies of heroes and the histories of peoples were recited orally and remembered, not written or filed in archives; where trade was known to proceed silently; where peace was ratified by the smoking of a pipe, not by the signing and depositing of certificates of ratification; and where crime and injustice could be set aright to everyone's satisfaction through the appropriate gesture of a respected chief, the written word, let alone the legal term, cannot today become the trusted frame of reference, however intense its propagation among the now-living generations.

In the light of these relationships between politics and culture as well as between past and present, it appears that many Occidental instruments of government, such as written constitutions supporting parliamentary procedures on local, regional, and global levels of political organization, are fundamentally uncongenial to those peoples who have inherited non- or semi-literate forms for the expression of their political destinies and dispositions. Some of these indigenous symbols have been justly treated as anachronistic, and therefore expendable, by the architects of the modern world order, since they represent principles and values whose further maintenance would not ensure the well-being and development of the communities concerned. However, certain other non-Western modes of comprehending the incidents of government seem, on examination, to refer to precisely, or nearly, the same values that Western nations are now trying to convey through written paragraphs and clauses. In these cases it may not always have been wise to sever the original connection between symbol and substance. For example, if the essence of democracy is found to reside in government by consent and restraint of power rather than in certain types of written constitution establishing parliamentary forms of rule, then one would have to say that many nonliterate societies, such as those now comprised in the state of Ghana, had developed a number of rather solid democratic institutions long before the Western ideologies arrived, albeit under a protective shield of customs, rites, and symbols with which no literate European would readily identify his version of democracy.

As one reviews the present national and international systems, which certain particularly talented European nations have brought into constitutional forms through generations of revolutionary thinking and planning, one cannot avoid the realization that these nations in their overemphasis on the political and constitutional aspects of their social development have disregarded many sources of cultural strength, not only in their own civilization, but also in the realms that they came to dominate, and that, as a consequence, the world has been to this extent not only impoverished of its human heritage but also prevented from attaining the full measure of its possible cultural accords. It is, however, equally clear that by perfecting their own peculiar approaches to the relations between polities and cultures, these same Western nations have succeeded in unifying the world, at least rhetorically, and that this is in itself a remarkable achievement. However, the achievement has been made at considerable cost, for it has been attended by a steady weakening of the separate cultures that now are being called upon to support a world society.

In those non-Western parts of the world where an official acceptance of the unifying Western value system implied the deliberate or involuntary devaluation of the native norms of thought and behavior, it has fostered the development of what may be called split cultures, where societies, wavering between two frames of reference, have become so uncertain of their true attachments that they are approaching a state of sociological neurosis. Both at home, in their attempts to apply the most modern Western methods to immemorial local problems, and in the international field, where the terminology little accords with their actual ideals, they have affected attitudes and intentions that cannot be brought into accord with their inheritance. Meanwhile, the Western nations that produced the unitarian philosophy of intercultural relations have, in their turn, suffered effects of another kind; by overextending the radius of their culture realm to include peoples unable to achieve an organic relationship to its institutions, and by permitting a number of their most cherished values to receive alien connotations and inflections incompatible with their actual meanings, they have unwittingly contributed to a denaturing of their own civilization.

The effort to unify the world by the propagation of a common vocabulary has thus yielded considerable intellectual confusion both in national and in international affairs, for it is becoming increasingly apparent that the various peoples of the world are speaking of different things even while uttering the same words.

Many of the fallacies implicit in the early optimistic estimate of mankind's capacity for cultural and political coalescence are being exposed today as the Western and non-Western nations review the cultural realities of our time. However, most of the restatements that have been made are extremely limited in scope and nature. Not only do they continue to employ the old vocabulary of agreement, which has been discredited by recent history, but they are being addressed almost exclusively to the current manifestations of two rather recent historic processes. That is to say, every one of the problems faced by the non-Western peoples of the world is being reviewed either in terms of the impact that the West has had in the last few centuries upon their fortunes, or in terms of the new challenge tossed by the communists onto the stage of African and Asian affairs. Neither approach reaches the heart of any of the matters actually at issue in the non-Western areas. No less narrow bounds seem to restrict the self-analysis in which the Occidental nations themselves are engaged, since the validity and nonvalidity of Western values are being defined almost exclusively in counterpoint to communism and with reference to a competition for the loyalty and support of the so-called noncommitted nations.

This book does not refute the need for either of the analyses now in progress, but suggests that the real affinities and differences between the various cultural and political systems of the present world society can be uncovered only after a thorough exploration of the historic sources of all significant patterns of political thought and behavior. Only when one knows what meanings a particular nation has traditionally attributed to such prominent words in the current international vocabulary as peace, war, unity, authority, and freedom, or what other values and institutions, not included in this dictionary, it has recognized as major structural principles, can one test with any hope of accuracy the authenticity and worth of presently existing international arrangements and assumptions.

The answers to questions such as these can be found only in the separate histories of the separate culture forms. However, if such records are to yield the insights into local value systems requisite for an understanding of present international conflicts and accords, they must be read in the context of the region and the time to which they refer rather than in perspectives suggested by contemporary manifestations of international relationships. Non-Western systems should therefore be identified in their pre-Western incarnations, while the Western system should be reviewed as it existed before it was projected into foreign realms. Only when each of the disparate political systems presently represented in the world is recognized in its intrinsic substance will it be possible to understand the various patterns that their mutual relations have assumed.

The aim of this book, therefore, will be to bring the separate stories down to the critical epoch of their fusion, around A.D. 1500, when the caravels of Portugal and Spain opened the seaways of the new world.

II

The cumulative records of both literate and nonliterate civilizations support the view that myths, apart from being projections of indefinable culture dreams, are also major structuring principles of reality. It follows that the past and present of a given society cannot be even approximately understood until the historian has begun to reestablish as authentically as possible the interplay between reality and myth in the region's history. The same mandate holds for those who would review and analyse the cultural and political relations between societies. For the discords and agreements that mark such relations have always been determined in considerable measure by the particular conceptions of reality and myth that each of the involved societies has developed in the course of time.

Today reality and myth are commonly regarded as opposites. One seems to denote the realm of reason, the other that of the imagination; and whereas the former is supposed to include the sum total of rationally ascertainable facts, the latter is said to be inhabited by all those fictions and beliefs for whose existence scientific, or other rational, proof cannot be adduced. Poets, artists, and visionaries may dwell in the abode of myth; indeed, they are expected to adorn reality by cultivating the fancies and fictions that make for myth. Those who claim the mandate to order society, on the other hand, be they political thinkers, psychologists, or statesmen, are generally expected to secure the future of man by contracting the realm of myth and progressively expanding the domain of reason and reality. They may hold and develop political ideals, it is true, but their ideals must be rationally tenable and capable of realization; they may not be myths.

It would thus seem that myth and reality might be distinguished from each other objectively, if we could endow the two concepts with appropriate definitions, or identify their appeals for individuals of different callings. The tendency to arrange for such a separation is particularly great in an age such as the present, in which great trust is placed in both verbalization and professional specialization. However, it becomes clear upon reflection that most men have resources that cannot be subsumed in their vocations and that concepts such as those here in question have substances that cannot be bounded by fixed definitions. Since the individual mind is endowed with both reason and imagination, it is capable of responding to poetry as well as to politics. What is real and what mythical is therefore determined in the final analysis by the subjective images that a particular individual forms of his environment and in terms of which he acts.

Man's freedom to contrive such images, however, is conditioned by the time and place in which he finds himself. Distinctions between reality and myth that were convincing in the thirteenth century may be found inappropriate or even incomprehensible in the twentieth, and the conceptions of truth prevailing in Egypt at any given date may not be shared in the contemporary United States. Time and place thus inevitably influence all individual attempts to establish the correct relationship between illusion, dream, or desire on the one hand, and the facts that are known or knowable on the other. These are also the principal inhibiting factors for those who would set themselves the task of reconstructing the records of the past. What the beholder of the past is inclined to recognize as having been the real and rationally ascertainable part of human experience may have been to those whose lives he is reviewing inconsequential or unreal. Conversely, what today's historian tends to regard as a myth, or as a figment of the imagination unrelated to the facts of life that he has uncovered, may in its time have been experienced as the ultimate reality. Indeed, it is doubtful, to say the least, whether any generation in the epochs preceding the age of science and analysis has ever been as sensitive to the differentiating characteristics of the realms of myth and reality as the one that is fashioning society in the present century.

The following examples will serve to suggest some of the ambiguities that are implicit in all historical interpretations.

The unity of medieval Christendom can scarcely be treated as a verifiable fact in the context of presently valid tests of actuality. Belied by the institutions and policies to which the different component parts of the so-called Christian commonwealth subscribed, medieval unity appears, in our perspective, as a messianic dream to which man was beholden because he was convinced that a united world was indispensable if humanity was ever to achieve the divinely prescribed state of ultimate perfection. But this vision, nebulous as it may have been even in the consciousness of Byzantine or Western European Christians, was nevertheless, according to our most reliable accounts, the solid substance of all medieval life, with the result that—as Ernst Kantorowicz puts it—"the myth stands out and becomes almost reality."[1] Similar ambiguities attend our present historical treatments of such important themes as "peace" and "law," for each of these conceptions was acknowledged as a fact by medieval man, even though the twentieth century reviewer may be hard put to corroborate its actual existence in terms of modern standards of proof. Indeed, we today cannot extricate ourselves easily from the web of fact and fancy that our predecessors have woven, however adept we may have become in separating reality from dream. Even if the ancient notion of a peaceful harmonious *universitas* is regarded by us as an illusion, the fact is incontrovertible that it has generated images upon which statesmen as well as poets have never ceased to draw, and that it has supplied the fundamental ideas upon which Europe's major institutions have been built.

No less intricate relationships between reality and myth emerge from other cultures, whether literate or nonliterate. The myth of China's solitary universal power that controlled the minds of generations of Chinese was not borne out by physical evidence, yet it was the mainspring of the actual patterns of political organization with which China has been identified. The image of a politically unified Muslim community that dominated the Arabized peoples in the Middle East was gainsaid by the actual divisions of the Dar al-Islam into multiple sovereignties, yet it gave rise to a doctrine of indivisible union that is

[1] "The Problem of Medieval World Unity" in *The Quest for Political Unity in World History*, Stanley Pargellis, ed., American Historical Association, 1944, p. 33.

still being experienced widely as the conclusive reality. Even more poignant mythical interpretations of history are to be found among those numerous peoples who have committed their experiences of reality to memory rather than to writing. The nonliterate nations of West Africa, for instance, have formed separate tribal groupings throughout recorded time; but there was a mythical time, their legends tell us, in which many of them were joined in greater unions. These traditions, whether one terms them real or mythical, have been re-activated in the mid-twentieth century (albeit under the suggestive influence of French and English constitutionalism), when ethnic, linguistic, and cultural differences have been merged in the formation of such multitribal and multicultural societies as Ghana, the Ghana-Guinea Federation and the Mali Federation.

This book has been informed by these reflections. However, it does not pretend to incorporate the whole mythology and reality of all of the world's cultures and nations. It is neither a consecutive exposition of what has often been termed world history, nor a systematic study of the whole context of international and intercultural relations. It is devoted to, and accentuates, certain specific themes. Presenting a selection of records from a spectrum of civilizations, the following chapters suggest a panoramic view of recorded cultural traditions and invite the conclusion that all history constitutes an internationally shared fund of multifarious human experience. However, in tracing the confluences of separate histories and in exploring the evolution of the chief ideas and institutions to which transnational and transcultural significance can be attached today, the book emphasises those which have been conducive to peace and order. While analysing the development in time and space of these patterns of thought and behavior, it draws attention to the role that informed elites have played when they have been called upon to regulate encounters between their civilizations by dispelling conflict and establishing trusted terms of reference for the conduct of domestic and foreign relations. This focussed approach explains the concentration of the following chapters on norms of political organization on local, regional, and international levels. It explains also the stress placed upon the emergence of writing and the gradual diffusion of literacy throughout the world.

Ideas, symbols, myths, and institutions conducive to peace and order in a world whose reality would seem attuned to neither have been present in all epochs and all parts of the globe, as the following chapters are designed to show. But they disengaged themselves most emphatically, and—it is suggested—most instructively for us today, in the Mediterranean region between the twelfth and fifteenth centuries. A considerable part of the present commentary on international and intercultural relations has therefore been set aside for an analysis of the Byzantine, Muslim, Mongolian, and Western European systems of thought and symbol, which are here treated as the precursors of presently distinguishable political orders.

Conceived as an international history, this book will thus address itself to the intellectual and political crises that have ensued, and will continue to ensue, from the close encounter of the greatly different, often even antagonistic civilizations of the world, and to the need of locating principles of agreement that are more widely meaningful than the ones presently in use. It will do so by reviving and reactivating those collective memories of mankind that seem to be the most promising sources of international cooperation today, and by recapturing those moments in recorded time in which men of different continents and cultures succeeded in transcending their local environment.

PART I

THE ANCIENT NEAR EAST AND INDIA

CHAPTER 1

THE ANCIENT NEAR EAST
IN INTERNATIONAL RELATIONS

A. The Significance of Near Eastern History for the
Concept of International History

THE interdependence of all nations and cultures is generally taken for granted in the twentieth century world. It is usually seen in two perspectives of time. Contemporary generations have discovered, under the sudden impact of revolutionary forces set in motion by preceding generations, that the problems of the present and expectations of the future are essentially shared concerns throughout the world, however differently they may manifest themselves locally. A similar realization, however, has as yet not illumined their understanding of the past. In this perspective man's mind continues to move, consciously or unconsciously, in strictly local circuits. But since his memory feeds his view of the present and his vision of the future, all contemporary efforts to solve existing problems and realize future hopes in an internationally meaningful and effective way will fall short of their aim as long as they are not inspired by the awareness that history, too, is shared international experience.

Many circumstances make it difficult to come to this awareness. "Time," for instance, has not always or everywhere been clearly conceived in terms of past, present, and future. In the consciousness of nonliterate peoples in particular, these perspectives have often tended to merge in a wider but much less clearly defined experience of existence, and the local methods of recording this experience have not been easily intelligible to literate men whose very approach to time stimulated the invention of quite different methods of recording the events encompassed. Only after literacy had set the pattern for history as it is generally understood today did the more imaginative of literate men begin to reconstruct the chronologies of societies that to them seemed historically "lost." Since their own view of history frequently barred them from understanding the meanings attributed to the past in these other cultures, however, they did not always preserve the authenticity of local experience in their accounts.

Methods employed in reconstructing the past have also retarded the development of international history. In public understanding at least, history has come to mean the sum total of available and readable local chronologies. These chronologies are usually seen as running on separate tracks through time and space. Junctions are not really expected. They can, of course, not be ignored when they are obviously marked by such actual encounters as geographical contiguity, war, trade, or diplomacy. But the countless historical situations in which separate chronologies interlock through the diffusion of ideas become visible only to those who are willing to leave the accustomed local tracks in order to look for new ways of reliving the past.

Even nonliterate peoples at times dimly perceived junctions of this kind when, for instance, bards in the West African Sudan reached out through folklore and myth to incorporate the experiences of other nations into the stream of their own memories. And scholars locate them today in increasing numbers as they apply their technical skills across the boundaries of epochs and areas to uncover the many connections, cross references, synchronisms, and correlations that mark history as a continuous international experience.

The general attitudes and particular skills that have made it possible to think of the past in these terms originated between 4000-1500 B.C. in the Near East, India, and China. But for thousands of years the experiences there registered held no meaning for peoples in other regions of the world. Writing and literacy had to be diffused from their early Near and Far Eastern centers before Europeans, for instance, could share not only in the history of Egypt and Mesopotamia, but also in the experiences of all other nations that had succeeded in the course of time to the ancient heritage.

The forms of thought and action that literacy made possible led in the realm of government and politics to the evolution of a special kind of community organization known ever since as the state. The type for this associational design was first established during the formative period of the Near and Far East. The immediate causes for the evolution of particular states varied then as they have varied ever since. They can be traced, in some cases, to the need for organizing worship, in others to the need for regulating economic activities or for securing adequate defence. Then as now, states enclosed greatly differing social orders. Life in some communities was regulated by elaborate written laws, in others by a tradition of general understanding, in still others by a government's absolute power. Political jurisdiction might extend to city-states or cover a vast empire. Regardless of historical inception, size, power, or social content, however, the very existence of the state expressed in all cases agreement on the outer form of political organization.

As these agreements multiplied in the Near and Far East, the state became an internationally shared form. In this function it served both East and West (i.e., what was then considered West) as the chief agency of international communication and supplied a framework for the first regularized system of international relations. On this first rough draft of a society of nations that international history records, generations have been elaborating ever since.

For twentieth century men, hard pressed by revolutions that are world-wide in scope, the records of the ancient Near East hold a further meaning. They tell of the first great cultural revolution in the known annals of humanity. Inventions such as writing, concepts such as the continuity of history, and institutions such as the state were in their time radical departures from older patterns of life. The proper uses of literacy, history, and the state have remained the most challenging problems in contemporary international relations, and no definite answers to their challenge have as yet been found.

B. The Near Eastern States

No one can say with certainty precisely when men began living together in societies such as we today should recognize as antecedent to the modern state. But it so happens that the records of people who lived in the valleys of the Euphrates, the Tigris, and the Nile between the fourth and second millenniums B.C. have been reconstructed, and that all who make up the community of nations in the second millennium A.D. can find common roots in these civilizations of the ancient Near East. For all we know, this is where writing was invented and first used as a tool for a highly organized type of community life, and where intelligence strengthened by literacy began directing man to question and eventually to order his surroundings. By assigning definite meanings first to pictures, then to shorthand versions of pictures, and finally to various forms of simplified script, men in Mesopotamia and Egypt found out how to transmit human experience accurately and impersonally to their contemporaries and to posterity. Moreover, by creating systems of numerical notation and finding other social agreements on the meanings of symbols and the values of things, they generated exact sciences such as arithmetic, geometry, and astronomy. "Time" was given new significance and fitted into human planning when the Sumerians divided day and night into twelve double hours and devised the sundial and water clock for the measurement of the intervals, and when the Egyptians created the solar calendar. "Nature" was studied, evaluated, and subjected to human control when the inhabitants of the river valleys began, in the fifth millennium, to build canals, dikes, and irrigation systems. By 3000 B.C. writing was well developed, and the documents speak to us across the millenniums, telling of ancient man's relationship to the universe and to his fellow men.

These relationships, as well as the intellectual and artistic achievements that helped to form them, were in large measure determined by the natural environment in which the people lived. Although the Nile rose and subsided in a regular rhythm, convincing the Egyptians that the gods specially cared for them, the Tigris and Euphrates would flood without notice, break dikes, and submerge crops, continually reminding the Mesopotamian that his lot was insecurity. And whereas the desert and sea kept Egypt unified and isolated from other countries until the second millennium B.C., Mesopotamia was open to contact with others from her earliest beginnings. These are some of the geographical facts that help to explain why Egypt and Mesopotamia developed different images of the world, different attitudes toward foreigners, and different principles of government.

A. MESOPOTAMIA

The first development of urban centers in the history of mankind took place in the middle of the fourth millennium B.C. in Mesopotamia. Many villages in Sumer and Akkad expanded into cities; cities absorbed surrounding territories and became city-states. While each state relied on its own government, invoked the protection of its own gods through the mediation of its own priests, and remained forever suspicious of the governments and gods of the other states, the separate sovereignties were nevertheless unified in important respects. All were dependent on the same rivers and shared in the civilization that they had jointly created. All developed essentially identical forms of government. And in each the members of a priestly caste occupied a privileged position as advisers to the king, mediators between men and gods, and administrators of the temple estates. Apparently it was in response to their duties in these positions that they invented writing and ciphering, and developed schools in which their knowledge and monopoly over these secret crafts could be perpetuated through the education of suitable successors. Since every temple and school employed the same signs and conventions, the various priestly castes constituted, at least for intellectual and pedagogical purposes, a theological "international" across state boundaries. In the exercise of their political functions, however, they served their local deities and kings, for whose greater glory wars were fought incessantly. It is therefore no accident that the oldest legible documents are accounts of temple administrators and descriptions of frontier wars between neighboring cities.

Out of such shared realities a uniform Mesopotamian view of the world emerged on which political unification could later be founded. Since the view crystallized in the middle of the fourth millennium, along with Mesopotamian civilization itself, it was based on the forms with which men were then most familiar. It reflected the unity of the valleys, man's earliest traditions of government, his dread of certain natural forces, and his acceptance of power as the supreme arbiter of destiny. To the Mesopotamians the cosmos was a state—an ordered system of relationships—in which all powers, all beings, all inanimate matter, and all ideas were thought to be represented according to their intrinsic worth. The criterion of differentiation was power. Just as only free men were entitled to sit in the ancient village assemblies, so only gods and those natural forces that fill mortals with awe were full citizens of the Cosmic State, exercising a decisive political influence. In the Assembly of the Deities the God of the Sky, the source of all authority, ranked the highest. Second to him, men imagined the God of the Storm, personification of a dreaded cosmic force and executor of heaven's verdict and will. The name of the heaven-god was Anu; that of the storm, Enlil. A third deity, Ea or Enki, more sympathetic to man than either of the others and symbolized by the serpent, supervised the abyss.

Independent of any external control, the universal state appeared as the only truly sovereign polity, and the human society had to take its place as a secondary power structure within this polity. The earthly state was nothing more than the extension of the political domain of a god. A local deity serving as the deputy of Enlil administered its affairs and appointed a human steward who was in turn expected to delegate his power to lesser rulers. In man's imagination the cosmos, the empire, the city-state, and the village were in this way organically linked in a single all-embracing view of cosmic government.

Such a philosophy of politics was a standing invitation to human bids for power. Any invasion from without or insurrection from within could be rationalized as the execution of divine will. This explains why, in the course of Mesopotamian history, Enlil's authority was invoked effectively to justify rather different methods of conducting international affairs.

When Hammurabi subjugated all of southern Mesopotamia after ruling the small city-state of Babylon for thirty years, his success meant in cosmic terms that the city god of Babylon had been chosen by the Divine Assembly to administer the functions of Enlil, their chief executive, and that this city god had in turn delegated the functions to Hammurabi. As the great king himself explained in his famous Law Code, it was in execution of this authority that he had conquered and was now governing an empire. A millennium earlier, in the conflicts between Lagash and Umma, however, the gods had pursued a different policy. Since that boundary clash had been conceived to be a dispute between two divine landowners, the gods of Lagash and Umma, it had been taken to a divine court. Enlil, that is to say, imposed a form of arbitration through his delegate, the powerful King of Kish, who proceeded to draw the boundary line between the two city-states in a manner that had been revealed to him by his divine overlord.[1] Although the secular power of the arbitrating sovereign could have enforced compliance with this or any other award, we should not depreciate the significance of this first known case of international arbitration. On divine and human insistence a form of settlement had been chosen that played down the substance of power and achieved a solution that at least advertised the possibility of peacefully solving disputes.

The cities and states whose organization reflected the Mesopotamian world view were after all built by enterprising men in response to earthly needs and interests. Living in a country whose geographic position and natural properties invited relations with other people, the Mesopotamians had early taken to agriculture, industry, and trade as natural incidents of existence. In the pursuit of such secular objectives they regulated the flow of their rivers, found a generally valid system of weights and measures, produced merchandise for local consumption

[1] *The Cambridge Ancient History*, Cambridge, England, 1923-39, Vol. I, pp. 368ff., 380ff. See A. Poebel, "Der Konflikt zwischen Lagas und Umma zur Zeit Enannatums I und Entemenas," in *Oriental Studies*, published in commemoration of the 40th anniversary of Paul Haupt, Baltimore, 1926, pp. 220-267, for an analysis of the recurring boundary disputes between Lagash and Umma. See also the essays on general conceptions of law and government in Egypt and Mesopotamia in "Authority and Law in the Ancient Orient," *Supplement* to the *Journal of the American Oriental Society*, no. 17, 1924.

as well as for sale, and speculated about the uses of writing in the recording of treaties and laws. In the course of these activities, which brought them into relations with peoples outside the narrow limits of their states, they soon found that it was not prudent to trust only their gods. They found that they were often better off relying on their own definition of equity and mutuality and on such compromises of interest with foreigners as they could obtain through bargaining, than on the revelations of tradition. Out of the accumulation of their historical experiences many people began developing their own standards of ethics. These standards in turn made them impatient with the arbitrariness of authority in general. By the advent of the second millennium B.C., the expectations of "the good life" were in many quarters at variance with the earlier divinely imposed order of things, at least as interpreted by God's many stern representatives on earth.

A growing conviction that "justice" was not simply the favor of the powerful, but a human right, had already found an early expression in the Sumerian codes, and this conviction had been applied to the whole fabric of government during Hammurabi's "Golden Age" (c. 1728-1686 B.C.).[2] Ecclesiastical affairs were then delimited from secular concerns, judicial and executive powers were distinguished, criminal and civil law cases were treated differently, and real and personal property rights found separate consideration. The search for man's right place in the universe, which so long had engaged the Mesopotamian imagination and found expression in innumerable early myths, took a new turn at this time, one of disillusionment and quest. The Gilgamesh Epic tells of a revolt against death and an unsuccessful journey to obtain everlasting life. Gilgamesh, the legendary king, had failed in his personal quest; the actual god-kings of the period, locked in perennial competition for permanent dominion, were also meeting with stalemate and frustration. From the middle of the second millennium B.C. on, the city-states contended for ever higher stakes, and their interests collided in ever wider areas. The national wars had always been hard to win conclusively and local peace was always difficult to maintain. But as Babylonians, Hittites, and Egyptians were drawn into a cosmopolitan age that encompassed all of southwest Asia, the Levant, and northeast Africa, both belligerent and peaceful relations became infinitely complex and required consummate ingenuity to solve.

---

[2] Authorities differ on the exact dates of this rule: Albright: 1728-1686, Breasted: 1948-1905. Cf. *The Cambridge Ancient History*, Vol. I, pp. 49ff.

B. EGYPT

The same intellectual and economic revolution that shaped Meso-potamia into a political system of separate city-states vying with each other for supremacy as the best guarantee against insecurity, shaped Egypt into a culturally centralized and politically unified state. Sur-rounded by barren desert, the inhabitants of Egypt associated all fertil-ity and creativity with the flow of one river—their river—whose waters in a rainless land made all the difference between life and death, and equally with a blazing sun whose regular circuit over their valley was convincing proof that it was meant to shine for them alone. They found the obvious explanation for such privilege in the power and benevolence of the gods who had created the universe and made Egypt its center. In order to care properly for this privileged land the al-mighty Sun God had appointed his son as the God King of Egypt. The pharaoh was the link with the universe, the country's representa-tive among the gods. He was the good shepherd whose special function it was to keep God's special people in green pastures. Thus he was the God of all fertility and of all waters. Such a view of the universe nat-urally fostered a centrally governed state. It inspired consistent efforts to join the two rather disparate regions into which Egypt had from time immemorial been divided: Upper Egypt, which reaches into the desert and Africa, and Lower Egypt, which faces the Mediterranean and Asia. United both in their isolation from the rest of the world and in their dependence upon the Nile, the two Egypts were eventually brought together under the centralized rule and double crown of a single God King.

The sheltered and united Egyptians lived close together in villages and cities where they developed special skills and a way of semi-urban life, which, they observed, contrasted drastically with the desert exist-ence of their immediate neighbors. This recognition confirmed Egypt's natural isolation from other human societies and strengthened the view that the universe, nature, and the Egyptian state were made for each other and constituted the only balanced cosmic order. In this cos-mic order the Egyptians were the only chosen people and securely pos-sessed all the boons of life. According to Egyptian legend, this was an indisputable historical fact which all foreigners accepted. As a Syrian prince is said to have admitted to an Egyptian envoy: "For the (Im-perial) God Amon founded all lands. He founded them, but first he founded the land of Egypt, from which thou hast come. For skilled work came forth from it to reach this place where I am."[3]

Since the outside world offered Egyptians nothing that seemed desirable or necessary, and since their knowledge and skills were unequalled in adjoining areas, "foreigners" from Libya and Asia were approached with pity, condescension, and disdain. A peculiar brand of isolationism and nationalism grew out of these circumstances. It had little if anything to do with racism or chauvinism. It stemmed rather from the facts of geography religiously read and from pride in human achievement religiously inspired. It was the life in Egypt, not the race of Egyptians, which the gods had singled out and blessed. This explains why foreigners who settled in Egypt and accepted its civilization were readily accepted as members of "the people," and why foreign customs and ideas were received without rancor or chauvinism provided they could be painlessly assimilated. Cultural snobbery so understood permitted generosity of a kind. Egyptians felt sorry for all those who could not share in the abundant gifts of the Nile. After thanking the Rain God for his goodness to Egypt, an Egyptian worshipper went on in his praise to say: "Thou makest that whereon all distant countries live. Thou hast put (another) Nile in the sky, so that it may come down for them"[4]—"them" meaning foreigners and beasts. And a later text makes the King of the Hittites say that he must make overtures to the King of Egypt because the pharaoh not only controls the waters of Egypt but is also the rain maker for all foreign countries.[5] Such references do, of course, confirm Egyptian self-centeredness and conceit. But they also carry the acknowledgment that there are certain things in life, such as water, in which all people, whether chosen or neglected by the deities, ought to share, at least when the goods exist in abundance. And while this "ought" was never, in the ancient Near East, thought of as a right that people could claim, its formulation as an ethical adjunct to materialistic boasting did point the way, at least historically speaking, to the deliberate national and international recognition of such rights in later more developed systems of law.

Officially Egyptian public policy recognized no comity between nations. The Middle Kingdom (1991-1786 B.C.)[6] persisted in the same

---

[3] John A. Wilson, "Egypt," in *The Intellectual Adventure of Ancient Man*, Henri Frankfort, ed., Chicago, 1946, p. 31.

[4] *ibid.*, p. 38.

[5] *ibid.*, p. 80.

[6] *Relative Chronologies in Old World Archeology*, Robert W. Ehrich, ed., Chicago, 1954, p. 16.

isolationism that had characterized the Old Kingdom. It continued to trade for essentials with Somaliland, Nubia, and the Phoenician cities, and drew on Syria for its supplies of big timber, oil, and wine. But its relations with Babylonia, Elam, and Hatti during the 12th dynasty were comparable to those maintained by the Chinese emperor with the outer world of England, France, and Holland, before the wars of the eighteenth century A.D. proved to the "Empire of the Middle" what the Hyksos conquest proved to Egypt—namely, that the universe did not revolve around one untouchable center but included other major nations as well. Under the threat of invasion and the experience of occupation Egypt's central government disintegrated, the myth of her security and isolation destroyed. Where previously self-confidence had generated a permissive internationalism, a psychosis of fear now made for a new kind of patriotism. Expelling the Hyksos meant not only invading Syria, but building a bigger empire with safe frontiers.

As a result of a number of brilliant military campaigns in the Fertile Crescent (which incidentally charted invasion routes that were to be followed in the eighteenth century A.D. by Napoleon I and in the twentieth by General Allenby's British armies) Thutmose III (1501-1444 B.C.) laid the foundations for an imperial domain that stretched in the early fourteenth century B.C. from the Sudan to the Upper Euphrates. Within this empire cities were protected by Egyptian garrisons, sea lanes were guarded from pirates by marine police, and caravans were safely convoyed through vassal territories. Within the sphere of this system of security cultural and commercial exchanges quickened. "Barbarian" vassals received their education at the pharaoh's court, Phoenician merchants established themselves in Egypt's trading cities, and Semitic gods found a place in the Egyptian pantheon. Egypt's Sun God became officially the World God, but, as a corollary, constant intercourse with foreign nations forced the pharaoh to step down from his exalted position in the cosmic order to engage in more mundane relations with his neighbors in Babylonia and the land of the Mitanni. In short, the facts of empire deeply influenced Egypt's view of the world.[7] During the reign of Ikhnaton (1375?-1358? B.C.) the developments precipitated a religious revolution. As proclaimed by this remarkable monarch in hymns and other texts, God is the father of all men irrespective of race, nationality, or residence, and since His existence transcends all earthly power realms, it does not have to be justified or strengthened through the extension of political frontiers,

[7] See *The Cambridge Ancient History*, Vol. II, p. 87.

the destruction of enemies, and the dethronement of local gods. In fact, God can be worshipped in a variety of equally acceptable ways in the broad world of changing human fortunes.

The monotheism and universalism implicit in these doctrines were the intellectual property of a small clique of priests and other royal advisers. Since these doctrines neither influenced nor reflected "public opinion" in Egypt, and since this "revolution" was an isolated event in the age, it remained a rather ineffective suggestion for the practical conduct of contemporary international relations. Its immediate impact on Egypt's position in the world was disastrous. For while the government engaged in metaphysical speculations and beheld a totally new perspective of world events, the empire slipped from its control. Hittites and Hebrews broke into the imperial domain. Asian allies appealed for help against forces of disorder and aggression. Trade was interrupted and caravans were plundered. Ikhnaton's lofty theories seemed refuted by stern political realities, and a new Egyptian government, branding Ikhnaton as a traitor, returned to the more traditional and time-tested patterns of Egyptian thought.[8]

C. International Relations in the Near East in the Second Millennium B.C.

A. THE POLITICAL SYSTEM OF STATES

In a low brick room, which had served as Ikhnaton's foreign office in Amarna, archaeologists found toward the end of the last century more than three hundred and fifty cuneiform letters and dispatches, through which we can trace Egypt's intercourse with the rulers of Asia and her gradual disintegration as an empire. These and certain other records, found both in Palestine and in formerly Hittite territory, convey at least an impression of the system of international politics that was functioning in the Near East in the second millennium B.C.

The many nations whose interaction brought about the early international society of this area were unequal in power. Their political fortunes underwent frequent changes. National identities were gained, bartered, and lost. States were built on different cultural and political foundations, and empires were acquired and maintained by different means. Of the great Near Eastern centers of government Egypt retained her influence the longest. Her most successful adversaries in the

---

[8] See *The Cambridge Ancient History*, Vol. II, p. 206; Vol. III, p. 127, for rather heroic views of Ikhnaton's philosophy. For a contrary estimate, see Alan W. Shorter, *An Introduction to Egyptian Religion*, London, 1932.

period here considered were the Hittites of Asia Minor, who dominated a vast territory by limiting their direct control to adjoining provinces and exercising only supervisory powers in a surrounding belt of federal client states. Beyond these clients lay other states, which the Hittites considered within their sphere of influence and from which they expected tribute, passage rights, and supplies as price for immunity from aggression.[9] Different, however, from both the Egyptian and the Hittite empires, and illustrating the institutional variety on which this Near Eastern states system rested, was a third center of power, the Cretan Federation with its system of alliances. This had grown out of the maritime power of many trading cities. For the merchant princes on the Mediterranean island of Crete had known not only how to capitalize commercially and culturally on their own strategic location in relation to Egypt, Western Asia, Cyprus, and Greece, but also how to develop political strength through intercity federations and interstate understandings with their neighbors.[10]

These three great nations then, together with Babylonia, Elam, Mitanni, and Assyria, were the chief members of the ancient states system, and with the exception of Crete they were essentially agricultural, self-sufficient communities. Their interests clashed mostly on the periphery of their empires and spheres of influence in that middle zone between the Euphrates and the Nile where each was striving for advantage and security. It was here that the great power conflict periodically lifted lesser states out of obscurity into political prominence.

With satellite states of varying strength moving in different power orbits, and with these orbits shifting as drives for empire and supremacy alternated with policies to maintain a balance of power, this society assumes, in retrospect, many characteristics of the Concert of Europe which influenced world relations so decisively in the nineteenth and twentieth centuries. Only in the latest stages of the duel between the chief contenders for supremacy, when incessant warfare had exhausted both the Egyptians and the Hittites, did the institutional and diplomatic defences of the whole international system crumble, and the Assyrians find it possible to make their bid for an essentially different world order, based exclusively on the military superiority of one nation.

[9] *The Cambridge Ancient History*, Vol. II, p. 229. See O. R. Gurney, *The Hittites*, London, 1952, pp. 73-76. See M. I. Rostovtzeff, *History of the Ancient World*, Oxford, 1926, Vol. I, pp. 79-110.
[10] Forced under Egypt's 18th dynasty to become tribute paying, Crete suffered another calamity in 1600 B.C. when it was partially destroyed.

B. COMMUNICATIONS BETWEEN STATES

1. The Development of an International Language and its Unifying Effects. Before the world was seen in the military terms of a bipolarity, various peoples in the Near East had developed interests and ideas within the context of their own culture and economy and in the pursuit of their own goals which they nevertheless shared in common, however bitter their feuds and divisions. A specialized skill, scientific invention, political institution, or ethical idea could become internationally significant because the people of that time had already developed reliable means of conveying their interests and ideas. When words had been generally accepted as the chief bridge of thought, and when speculation about the power and function of words had led to the invention of writing and to the systematic pursuit of knowledge, deliberate and systematic communications between nations had become possible. Experts in the cuneiform script had settled in the cities of Assyria, Syria, Asia Minor, Phoenicia, and lastly, Egypt, where they had brought native clerks in touch with Sumerian learning. The native lore of new peoples—the Hittites, Aryans, Cretans—was being transcribed, translated, and thus diffused. The written word became the main bond between the otherwise competitive member nations of the system when Babylonian was generally accepted as the Near East's *lingua franca* in the middle of the second millennium B.C. As an internationally valid language of diplomacy it thereafter served all governments until it was replaced by Aramaic about a millennium later. Aramaic was the *lingua franca* of the Persian Empire, much as French was long the generally accepted medium of communication in the modern European states system.

The uniform use of writing not only stimulated similar intellectual pursuits in widely separated national sectors of the international society, it also created similar habits and forms. Land registers and accounts were kept by Hittites and Egyptians, and laws were codified in Crete as well as in Babylonia. And while it is true that the various local land registers, contracts, and codes of law recorded different sorts of particulars, they nevertheless expressed, through their form, identical approaches to identical general concerns.

Clay and silver tablets carrying many kinds of information crossed frontiers and found their ways to the policy centers of the ancient world. They were written by scribes who had to satisfy similar requirements for office and to execute similar functions in widely distant courts. They were carried and interpreted by messengers who shared professional problems, such as the responsibility to know geography, to understand their instructions, to give oral explanations of letters with elusive references,[11] and to be familiar with all diplomatic idioms and terms. Moreover, the routine services of this "civil service" were supplemented by ambassadors who circulated between the great courts on the Euphrates and the Nile, and by agents or friends who represented the interests of the lesser states in the capitals of the great. The safety of all these diplomats soon became a matter of international concern. Their persons were considered inviolate, they travelled frequently with armed escorts, and they carried safe-conduct passes. It was further assumed that kings would implement these international understandings at home by punishing all insults to foreign diplomats that occurred in their territory.[12]

What were the contents of the tablets and papyri and the subjects that occasioned so much communication, representation, and discourse? Haunted by the spectre of war, this world expected feuds and hostilities of one kind or another. Not surprisingly therefore, the kings and their agents were frequently negotiating offensive and defensive alliances or securing their boundaries by other big deals. In the service of their national interests the contending monarchs were giving subsidies to some potentates and gifts to others. They were personally involved in numerous trading transactions. They were marrying off their daughters, often making sure by treaty that such royal pawns of diplomacy would be treated respectfully in the alien court. They were fomenting unrest among their rivals' subjects. They were also visiting each other in great pomp and ceremony. Throughout the collection of the so-called "Amarna letters," monarchs appear to be solicitous about ill health, death, or other grief in their families. They greet each other habitually as "brothers" and their wives engage in cordial correspondence. The Egyptian pharaohs and Babylonian kings even speak officially of the need to introduce a true spirit of brotherhood into the relations between nations.

Probably all of these contacts were deliberately planned to promote to the utmost the power of the national states concerned. But when a monarch lent the "technical assistance" of his outstanding physician, builder, or divining priest, he not only collected returns in increased prestige. He also engaged, however unwittingly, in mutual aid and cultural collaboration.

[11] *The Cambridge Ancient History*, Vol. II, p. 333.
[12] G. S. Goodspeed, *A History of the Babylonians and Assyrians*, New York, 1902, p. 147.

The variety of goals and motivations that seems to have characterized Near Eastern policy is strikingly illustrated by a treaty between
the Egyptians and the Hittites. Inscribed on a silver tablet, and probably brought to Egypt by Hittite envoys in 1272 B.C.,[13] this "Good
Treaty of Peace and Brotherhood" was intended to establish eternal
peace between the contracting parties. After reviewing their former
relations, both rulers renounced all projects of conquest against each
other, reaffirmed existing treaties, and set up a defensive alliance involving assistance against each other's enemies. These arrangements
were obviously made because neither the Egyptians nor the Hittites
could, at that time, afford to continue their traditional hostilities.
Ramses II recognized the failure of his effort to restore Egypt's domination over northern Syria and the Hittites were beginning to fear
the ascendancy of Assyria. But the remaining clauses of the treaty, as
they have been pieced together, are a reflection on other shared concerns. In expressing the hope that their respective subjects, too, should
live in peace with each other, and in promising to extradite political
fugitives and immigrants and to guarantee these people humane treatment, both absolute monarchs admitted that their individual authorities, as well as their mutual relations, depended very much on the
behavior of the common people of their realms.

Since this particular treaty seems to have been kept in good faith
by both parties, and since the ancient archives as a whole reveal quite
an astonishing degree of internationalism in this divided war-torn society, we may well ask, what were the deeper sources out of which any
degree of international good faith could grow?

The nations were not held together by a code of international law,
however similar many of their national laws might have happened to
be. Apart from some largely ceremonious protestations and admonitions, they saw little in the notion of the brotherhood of man. Nor did
they rally around the same religion. Ikhnaton's concept of a universe
held together by one God before whom all nations were equal never
displaced the earlier Egyptian and Near Eastern conviction that there
were many different national gods who protected their own people
only, and who derived glory through the defeat of other people and
other people's gods. All that can be said in this respect is that the states
agreed on religious nationalism and that the separate religious forms

---

[13] This treaty may have actually been concluded 50 years earlier, under Harmhab,
the predecessor of Ramses II. See *The Cambridge Ancient History*, Vol. II, p. 133;
Louis Le Fur et Georges Chklaver, *Recueil de Textes de Droit International Public*,
Paris, 1928, p. 1, for text.

were sufficiently similar to permit mutual understanding. The official sanction of the treaty of 1272 B.C., for instance, was linked to the benevolence and watchfulness of both the Hittite and the Egyptian gods, who appeared in equal numbers as witnesses to the good faith of the monarchs.

Although these nations were essentially independent of each other, they formed a loose concert of states whose national interests were in all cases, except within the Cretan Federation, defined and defended by absolute monarchs. For all intents and purposes there existed a fairly constant pattern of government and a common view of the world. This meant that the rulers, however antagonistic their foreign policies, understood each other's way of making policies. They agreed that there was nothing higher than the national interest and no more effective implement of the national interest than power. As an "international of monarchs" they developed an international code not so much of ethics as of procedure, agreeing on such norms as the need for adequacy in the exchange of gifts. Finding that tributes could be collected more easily when they were accepted as gifts, and that support from inferior powers was more easily forthcoming when negotiations were conducted on the basis of conventional equality, they frequently went out of their way to uphold the fiction of equality in their ranks. That is what the pharaohs did, for instance, when they had to protect their newly won empire in Syria by alliances with "lesser" nations in that strategic vicinity.

In short, the Near Eastern states, over the centuries, cooperated in creating a system of communications and a framework of forms within which they could operate independently and through which they could convey disagreement in agreed ways.

2. *The Impact of Trade on the Near Eastern States System*. International politics in the second millennium B.C. presented Near Eastern governments with a wide area of choice. Alliances could be avoided, concluded, or broken. Existing methods of diplomatic communication could be ignored, used, or expanded. Political frontiers could be advanced or contracted. But on another plane of their coexistence the choices were more limited. In varying degrees all Bronze Age communities depended for their industrial equipment on relatively uncommon and somewhat expensive metals or alloys of metals.[14] Hence, although commerce was not an absorbing pursuit among any of these essentially agricultural societies, their dependence on special materials

[14] Gordon Childe, *What Happened in History*, New York, 1946, p. 123 and ch. VII.

and luxuries had presented them throughout the third and second millenniums B.C. with similar problems, to which they had found similar solutions through urban organization, economic enterprise, and extended foreign contacts. Both the Babylonians and the Egyptians had often resorted to conquest and other forms of economic imperialism in order to control the sources of their needed supplies, developing like techniques in pursuit of their military ends. But the mutuality of their economic interests and needs had expressed itself even more strikingly in the innumerable individual transactions of a small commercial class common to the whole international order. A complex commercial system, with receipts and contracts baked on clay tablets, had developed in ancient Mesopotamia, to be eventually recognized in Hammurabi's monumental codification of laws. In addition to shedding light on the commercial practices of the day, this recorded story of Mesopotamia's law merchant shows for the first time in history that in all great matters relating to commerce legislators have copied, not dictated.[15] The rising class of the merchants was generating a new kind of interdependence, not only among the various states of the Near East, but the Near East, Farther Asia, North Africa, and Europe.

Bronze Age civilizations essentially similar to those of the Near East had emerged before 2500 B.C. in the floodplains of the Indus and its tributaries, and about the middle of the second millennium B.C. in the valley of the Yellow River. Both in India, where this civilization perished soon after 1500 B.C., and in China, people had achieved social agreements in relation to their respective conventional scripts, systems of numerical notation, and standardizations of weights and measures. They had developed populous cities and highly skilled industries. Their economic dependence upon each other vitalized the affinities between the Near Eastern and Farther Asian cultures. Regular imports of gold, silver, tin, lead, and precious stones reached Mesopotamia from Iran, Syria, northern Aghanistan, and Europe. Manufactured articles from Indian cities were sold on the Tigris and Euphrates, and foreign merchants even established factories and colonies in the urban centers of the Near East, where they enjoyed many special privileges.

While Mesopotamia's commerce seems to have been largely a matter of private or semiprivate enterprises, Egypt's generally more centralized system made for a state control of trade relations. To obtain foreign materials such as copper from Sinai, gold from Nubia, cedars

---

[15] J. B. Condliffe, *The Commerce of Nations*, New York, 1950, p. 32.

from the Lebanon, ebony, perfume, and spices from Arabia and Somaliland, and lapis lazuli and other gems from Asia, the pharaohs dispatched expeditions under military protection. The records also show, however, that Phoenician traders bartered in Egyptian villages along the Nile; that Phoenician sailors were employed to carry out a pharaoh's great project of circumnavigating Africa; and that foreign merchants enjoyed special quarters and immunities in such Egyptian trading cities as Memphis.[16] Nevertheless, although the foreign merchants and sailors could enter Egypt freely in the expectation of decent treatment, the Egyptians as a people do not seem to have been either very curious about the unknown parts of the world or very much interested in maintaining regular communications with the known. Their essentially receptive and permissive attitude toward commerce sprang from their economic self-sufficiency. They knew, after all, that the Nile valley could nourish them without the benefit of trade. And there was a second reason for their passivity, namely, the social system of the time. Commerce, in the sense of freedom to come and go, and buy and sell, could not develop very far in any of these great ancient states because their rigid social structures severely restrained all human movement and initiative. Only a few members of such societies could become really enterprising, intellectually and commercially.

On the other hand, in the less sheltered regions of the ancient world, where the geographic location alone often challenged individual initiative, the survival of the whole nation frequently came to depend on the social approval of greater individual liberties and people had more opportunity to move. In Crete, where a literate culture had developed about 2600 B.C., commerce attracted priest-kings and private traders alike. By the eighteenth century B.C. their combined trading ventures had reached mainland Greece, Cyprus, the Syrian coast, and Egypt. After 1400, when Crete was incorporated by the much lower Mycenaean culture of the Greek mainland, Mycenaean trade and migration penetrated not only Asia Minor but also Sicily and southern Italy. Many lesser insular and coastal communities in the eastern Mediterranean, such as the Phoenician cities, found outlets for their individual energies and compensation for their nation's political weakness in economic operations of this kind. Spearheaded or supported by piracy, such exploits often helped to curb the military power of the great and improve the bargaining position of the weak.

All communications in this expanding world, whether undertaken

16 See Thomas G. Williams, *The History of Commerce*, London, 1926, pp. 18-24.

freely or at the bidding of kings, were seriously hampered by transportation problems. Journeys by sea and land were then, as they have been until very recently, extremely risky and tedious ventures. Throughout the past millenniums it has been only by a process of very gradual evolution that existing industrial skills have been employed to build faster ships and equip safer caravans. The greatest crisis in the early stages of this development came with the taming and saddling of the horse. Use of the horse furthered the cause of interdependence more decisively than any human invention before the nineteenth-century power-driven machine. After its introduction all communications were immeasurably accelerated. In fact, the relative stability of the later Assyrian, Hittite, and Egyptian empires was largely due to the speed with which imperial overseers and soldiers could traverse their domains in light horse-drawn chariots.

3. Summary. During the second millennium B.C. the geographical area of human contact was greatly extended. Within this extended area the centers of power and influence in China and the Near East were linked to each other and to the rest of the known world in many new relationships. Before one can appreciate the historical significance of these relationships, however, one must remember that the dominant societies of the age shared certain characteristics that set them apart from other contemporary societies and were precisely the characteristics that have been regarded ever since as the chief attributes of "civilized" societies generally.

The political organization of the leading communities was based on residence, not on kinship. As a consequence of similar economic revolutions within their various domains, life in all of them was concentrated in cities. In all, moreover, men produced goods not simply for the satisfaction of their immediate individual needs but for surplus and exchange. There were specialists in knowledge and in technical skills. Also, following strikingly similar intellectual revolts against the arbitrariness of natural and supernatural forces, minorities in all of these states were discovering that life could be made more attractive by rational planning, that experience could be exchanged and transmitted reliably, and that the frontiers of knowledge were not fixed.

Nevertheless, in all four centers of this synchronous revolution—India, China, Mesopotamia, and Egypt—emancipation from the hazards and fears of existence was possible for only very few. Literacy, and the avenues of thought and achievement to which literacy leads, remained closed mysteries to the many. These majorities, therefore, were in no position to revise their views of the world and of each other. They could not question the arbitrariness of their gods, of nature, or of their more privileged and powerful fellow men. And this meant, in the realm of international affairs, that effective international communication—whether of interests, ideas, or goods—was bound to remain extremely limited.

The currents from China, Egypt, and the Near East, nevertheless, were gradually penetrating outlying areas. The continents were becoming tenuously joined, and the nonliterate peoples of Asia, Europe, and Africa were being gradually drawn into extending realms of literacy. By the time the Bronze Age abruptly ended in the Near East, around 1200 B.C., ". . . the pools of civilization . . . had merged into one broad, continuous lake from the Tigris to the Nile and the Adriatic and from the Black Sea coasts to the Persian Gulf."[17]

D. The Pattern of Empire in the Ancient Near East in the First Millennium B.C.

A. ASSYRIA AND CHALDEA

The political foundations of the Near Eastern culture area were radically altered when the Assyrian city-state in northeastern Mesopotamia expanded into a strong national state. With boundless ambition, this nation gained power so steadily in the course of about six hundred years that, despite a few temporary setbacks, it subdued all of its politically weakened neighbors and inherited their accumulated wealth and culture. After Egypt had been defeated in the seventh century B.C., the Assyrian domain extended from the Nile and the Mediterranean coasts to the mountainous countries north and east of the Tigris. The empire so established by military and commercial aggression set a precedent for international organization emulated ever since by countless aspirants to universal power.

The governing principle of Assyria's imperial administration was physical force, applied by kings who despised cities and regarded no man.[18] Invoking the universal jurisdiction and absolute sanction of the Assyrian gods, they abused the deities of subject races, broke covenants, oppressed vassals, and mercilessly exterminated beaten enemies. Armies with horse-drawn chariots and heavy offensive weapons were constantly on the move. They guarded against rebellion and invasion

[17] Childe, p. 167.
[18] Isaiah 33:8.

by deporting citizens, transplanting whole communities,[19] and rigorously policing boundaries and trade routes. This absolute government as practiced by the Assyrians existed, by virtue of force, only for the glory of the monarch and the enrichment of the governing classes. It could offer the subject peoples few, if any, material benefits in mitigation of their political degradation. It suggested no supranational ideology or promise for the future as compensation for the inflictions of past cruelty and present discomfort. When, in 612 B.C., it was weakened by inner dissension and revolt and threatened by invasions from abroad, it collapsed under attack: its mercenary soldiers and officials disappeared, its capital of Nineveh was destroyed, and its exhausted people vanished from history. For the brief spell of another one hundred years, however, the old Near East was then reunited under similar principles of government by the conquerors, another Semitic race, the Chaldeans.

As represented in such contemporary narratives as those of the Old Testament, the age seems to have been one of unmitigated horror. In the perspective of history, on the other hand, the Assyrians and Chaldeans appear not simply as oppressors of men; they were also the guardians of civilization. For although their own creative talents were largely drained off or thwarted by military pursuits, they compensated for this by appropriating whatever seemed new, attractive, or useful in the arts and sciences of foreign cultures. Their odd combination of savagery toward men and sensitivity for ideas appears strikingly in the biographies of some of their great kings. Ashurbanipal the Assyrian (669-628), for example, is notorious for having converted conquered Babylon into a wasteland, but has won even greater fame as a collector of books. The 20,000 tablets of his precious library, which archaeologists have uncovered, are a rich harvest of early scientific, as well as literary and religious, thought. Our modern historians of medicine owe most of their knowledge of Mesopotamian medicine, as it had developed through the centuries, to information gleaned from this collection,[20] and practically all studies of ancient religion have to begin with the library of Ashurbanipal.

[19] The practice of carrying peoples off en masse was probably initiated by Ashur-nasir-pal in the ninth century. It became the usual practice by the middle of the eighth century. King Sargon subdued Andia in Armenia and transported the inhabitants to the cities of Syria and Commagene. Later he carried off the tribes of Gandum and Carchemish to Ashur. After the fall of Samaria he reduced the Israelites to slavery and conveyed them to Assyria, while conquered Arab tribes were sent to Samaria. There are scenes representing some of these transactions in the Nineveh reliefs.

[20] Henry E. Sigerist, *A History of Medicine*, New York, 1951, Vol. I, p. 389. George Sarton, *A History of Science*, Cambridge, Mass., 1952-59, Vol. I, pp. 154ff.

Similar incongruities characterize the reign of the Chaldean Nebuchadnezzar (c. 605-562 B.C.). This monarch perfected the Assyrian policy of maintaining the tranquillity of subjugated peoples by forcibly transferring unreliable elements of their populations, a device that was to find many imitators in the nineteenth and twentieth centuries A.D. For example, in order to destroy the power of Jewish resistance, he removed the official leaders from Jerusalem, as well as all men capable of bearing arms. Contrary to the practices of modern despots, however, he went to considerable trouble to repair and put in order the places that were to receive the captives. Moreover, when Jerusalem was destroyed, the transportation was carried out in rather orderly fashion. The contemporary Jewish prophets alternately exalted and denounced the Chaldean as a necessary scourge of God. In the pageant of the time the "Babylonian Captivity"—so portentous a fact in Jewish history—was but one of many comparable episodes attendant on the mighty conquests of Assyria and Chaldea.[21]

Nebuchadnezzar know how to destroy Jerusalem, but he also knew how to rebuild Babylon in such splendor that historians continue to list it, on the testimony of the ancient Greeks, as one of the world's seven great wonders. Furthermore, though feared as ravagers of the subject earth beneath them, the Chaldeans were still highly esteemed as gazers at the stars above them long after their empire had crumbled into dust. Their celestial quests issued, it is true, from religious rather than from scientific motivations and led, for this reason, to astrology rather than to astronomy.[22] Nevertheless, when people such as the Greeks were ready to distinguish the goals of science from those of religion, it was found that many methods of research employed originally in the service of the Chaldean doctrines of divination could stand the new tests of purely scientific experimentation.

The dissemination of astrological and other ideas and the distribution of such goods as the cotton plant, which the Assyrians had originally imported from India, did more to unify the Near Eastern area and extend its influence in less developed adjoining territories than any of the bids for political dominion. In spite of the pattern of absolute rule under which it took place, the dispersal of these goods and ideas affected the population in greater depth than had any comparable improvements in previous centuries, because it coincided with the eco-

[21] See Wilfrid T. E. Castle, *Syrian Pageant, The History of Syria and Palestine 1000 B.C. to A.D. 1945*, London, pp. 21ff., 32ff., for Jewish life under these empires.
[22] Sigerist, p. 393.

nomic supremacy of iron, the development and diffusion of various alphabets, and the invention of coined money.

The use of iron affected the entire way of life in the Near East. It was not simply that an early monopoly in iron weapons had practically guaranteed Assyria's early military successes over nations equipped with weapons of bronze, thereby setting the stage for a wholly new political order; more important, by replacing expensive and scarce bronze tools, the cheaper and more readily available iron implements gave a new impetus to peaceful industrial and agricultural pursuits. With their help new ground could be cleared for cultivation and cheaper and better vessels and vehicles could be built. Transportation costs were thus generally reduced. In social terms, the introduction of the new metal meant that the small farmer and artisan now could achieve a more secure existence; in fact, such a man even had the chance of becoming independent. Internationally, the economic revolution quickened economic activities and interchanges everywhere, especially after 1200 B.C. when the use of iron spread to Western Asia and Greece, whence it was then carried still further westward by the Phoenicians and Etruscans.[23]

The idea of the alphabet travelled in similar fashion. Some time between 1300-700 B.C. the Asiatics passed it on to the Greeks. By 700 B.C. literacy had ceased to be a monopoly of the chosen few and was available to all classes. East and West could now share the knowledge that a few had collected and retained to themselves in the course of the past millenniums. By 200 B.C. a zone of alphabetically literate societies extended continuously from the Atlantic coasts of Spain to the Jaxartes in Central Asia and the Ganges in India, and from southern Arabia to the northern coasts of the Mediterranean and the Black Sea.[24]

A third invention that radically affected human intercourse in this period was coined money. The Egyptians and Babylonians had carried on their trade negotiations in terms of standardized weights and measures of staple commodities. Currency in the modern sense was, according to Herodotus, invented by the Lydians. Precisely when they hit upon this device he does not say, but we know that metal coinage began to circulate around the eastern end of the Mediterranean during the seventh century B.C. and that the Greeks were particularly active

[23] Childe, p. 184. Just how and when ironworking spread to India and China is still uncertain.
[24] Childe, p. 181.

in its diffusion. The Chinese, who issued stamped blocks of gold, may have invented coined money earlier than the Aegean peoples and a diffusion of the idea from the Far East to Lydia in that period is by no means an impossibility. In any case, the international significance of the invention rests in the properties of precious metals. They are naturally uniform—one ounce of gold is like another. Metals can be cast into units of standard size and weight. These are portable and easily concealed. They are nearly imperishable and resist wear. Metals are somewhat difficult to obtain and limited in quantity, and this means that a small coin can be worth much in commodities. Moreover, the market value of metal fluctuates less than that of perishable commodities.[25] And finally, in addition to these practical attributes, coined money seems to have commended itself to trading peoples for aesthetic reasons. The international history of coinage indicates that, on many occasions, efforts to make a coin attractive were followed by its general acceptance as an international medium. It has been suggested, for instance, that Athens' success in capturing Aegina's trade in the sixth century B.C. was very much due to the introduction of an appealing coinage.[26]

The increasing use of the alphabet, money, and iron immeasurably enriched the life and prospects of the average man. Also, these developments stimulated more intimate and diversified contacts among the various peoples that made up the known world. In this international society of the first millennium B.C. there were certain nations in particular that acted as carriers of international contact. The Hebrews, Phoenicians, Cretans, Greeks, and Etruscans constituted minor states in the accepted power scale of the day, but in the long-range estimation of their influence on international relations they rise to a place of major importance. Phoenicia, for instance, as a country occupied a narrow strip of coast between the mountains of Lebanon and the sea, about a dozen miles wide for the most part and one hundred to two hundred long.[27] As a nation the Phoenicians founded no empire and engaged in no belligerent military activities. But in the life of their cities the riches of the universe seemed gathered. The twenty-seventh chapter of the Prophecy of Ezekiel gives a vivid picture of Tyre at the height of her commercial greatness in the sixth century B.C.,

[25] E. D. Chapple, and C. S. Coon, *Principles of Anthropology*, New York, 1942, pp. 644-647.

[26] *The Cambridge Ancient History*, Vol. IV, p. 129.

[27] Its frontiers were almost exactly those of the twentieth century Lebanese Republic.

when she was threatened by the power of Nebuchadnezzar. In this luxurious city, which was "a merchant of the people for many isles," ships were built from the fir trees of Senir, the cedars of Lebanon, and the oaks of Bashan, and sails were made of "fine linen with broidered work from Egypt." The vessels carried goods which the Tyrians collected from and distributed to the four corners of the world. Nor were the bold voyagers merely commercial intermediaries. They traded also in ideas and they taught others—albeit often unwillingly—how to process certain merchandise, how to navigate, and how to use an improved phonetic alphabet. Their trading stations in the Black Sea, the Aegean Sea, and later in the western Mediterranean, marked the pioneering spirit of this people whose skills and curiosity brought them eventually to the Pillars of Hercules (Gibraltar), into the Atlantic Ocean, and northward to Cornwall and the Baltic. Moreover, their voyages were not guided by chance. Charted with the aid of the stars, they were planned to link the various trading ports, factories, and colonies that had been established at convenient points during the long course of Phoenician expansion.

From Ezekiel's Prophecy we learn something also of the vast extent of the contemporary land traffic, which carried merchants from as far as India and China to the great fairs of Mesopotamia and Arabia. Here they traded in precious stones and metals, horses, mules, lambs, rams, goats, fine linens and other rich cloths, embroideries, spices and the "persons of men." A thousand years or so before the doom of Tyre was pronounced, for example, there passed through Gilead that company of Ishmaelites, or Midianites, with their camels bearing spices, balm, and myrrh, who bought the youth Joseph for twenty pieces of silver and sold him in Egypt later to Potiphar at an unknown price.

Most of the cities founded by the Phoenicians in support of their trading activities were permitted to become politically autonomous within the framework of a loosely organized all-Phoenician trade confederation. Indeed, it was under these terms of possible political emancipation that such former dependencies as Carthage became independent states and exerted a decisive influence on world politics in their own right. New patterns of government, international organization, and policy-making emerged, speeded by the recognition that the commerce and the human talents that had gained wealth could gain political power as well.

The application of power so conceived varied with the circumstances. In relations with nations of equal or comparable strength,

Tyrian power and technical skill were transformed into instruments of regional peace and cooperation. The First Book of Kings includes, for example, a very interesting agreement between King Hiram of Tyre and King Solomon of Israel. The Jewish monarch wished to build a temple, but needed Lebanese timber and Lebanese specialists; "for thou knowest," he told King Hiram, "that there is not among us any that can skill to hew timber like unto the Sidonians."[28] When Hiram agreed to provide both, he was sent additional crews of ten thousand Jewish workers a month, as well as deliveries of wheat and oil from Solomon's domains. Not only did this working partnership between Solomon's and Hiram's builders continue for many years until the temple was finished, but "there was peace between Hiram and Solomon, and they two made a league together."[29]

But peace and security could not be seen in terms of mutual assistance when it came to dealings with aggressive military empires. In these enterprises Phoenician power and skill were employed with daring ingenuity and considerable success to taunt and divide the great powers of the Near East. This kind of diplomacy boomeranged, however, when regional vanity and the unbridled pursuit of local wealth led to treachery and division within the Phoenician commonwealth itself. Instances such as Sidon's alliance with Assyria against her sister state of Tyre lent some justification to Ezekiel's indictment: "Thou hast corrupted thy wisdom by reason of thy brightness."[30] The Assyrian Nebuchadnezzar's overthrow of Tyre briefly interrupted the Phoenician activities, but their trade soon revived, to be finally crushed only by the destruction of the city at the hands of Alexander the Great in 332 B.C.[31]

The plain truth of the matter, recognized by many Assyrian and Chaldean rulers, was that the glory and wealth of Babylon derived principally from its position as the center of a great complex of Asiatic commerce. Such a position could be maintained only as long as the rulers of the city respected the trading nations that carried the goods to and from its markets. This meant, in view of the international division of labor that had gradually come into being, that Babylon usu-

---

[28] I Kings 5:6.

[29] ibid., 5:12.

[30] Ezekiel 28:17.

[31] Wyndham Bewes, *The Romance of the Law Merchant*, London, 1923, pp. 99ff. For a description of the caravan routes in the days of Tyre and Sidon, see H. G. Rawlinson, *History of Phoenicia*, London, New York, 1889, ch. x; see also W. S. Lindsay, *The History of Merchant Shipping and Ancient Commerce*, London, 1874-76, Vol. I, pp. 86ff.

ally molested neither the caravan traffic of the Arabians, Syrians, and Hebrews, nor the maritime trade of the Phoenicians in the Persian Gulf and the Bahrein Islands. So secured, Babylon's greatness—eloquently described by Herodotus—outlasted even its later subjugation by the Persians and the Greeks.[32]

B. PERSIA

1. The Foundations of the Persian World State. By the opening of the sixth century B.C. the tyranny of empires and the cupidity of cities had loosened the fabric of community life everywhere. Within the established boundaries of practically all the Near Eastern states, there was dissent and revolt. At this moment in history an Aryan people, the Persians, made their dramatic appearance in the Near East. All but unknown before, they succeeded in the course of thirty years in establishing the political center of the world.

Led by Cyrus, and later by Cambyses, these newcomers defeated their close relatives, the Medes, in 549 B.C., the Lydians in 546, Babylon in 538, and Egypt in 525. Campaigns in Africa established Persian supremacy over Ethiopian dynasties that ruled parts of what today constitutes the state of Sudan.[33] But in that continent the Persians failed to achieve their ultimate objective, the creation of an African empire as extensive as their Asian domain, largely because the subjugation of Carthage presented insurmountable obstacles. When the Punjab and Sind were annexed to the east, and Thrace and Macedon to the west, Persian rule extended from the Nile and Aegean to the Indus and Jaxartes, and from the desert of Africa to the icebound borders of China.[34] When Darius ascended the Persian throne, all these states, provinces, and territories, which conquest had loosely joined, were splendidly consolidated.

The empire that was so created in the course of one generation endured undivided for two hundred years. It was not only vaster than any preceding empire west of China, but was more stable and peaceful. Small wonder, therefore, that the Persian achievement has radiated suggestions to posterity ever since. It stimulated the imagination of conquerors like Alexander the Great. It supplied a fund of experience

[32] Williams, pp. 22-24.

[33] Early references to "Ethiopia" are misleading. The area that is included in the modern kingdom of Ethiopia was never controlled by the Persians.

[34] See on the history of Persian conquests, *The Cambridge Ancient History*, Vol. IV, pp. 10ff., and Sir Percy Sykes, *History of Persia*, London, 1921, Vol. I, pp. 169ff. Also Donald N. Wilber, *Iran, Past and Present*, 4th ed., Princeton, 1958.

to Arab and Turkish administrators when they were faced, centuries later, with the necessity of converting the conquered Near East into a secure possession. But the astounding history of Persia's accumulation of power tends to conceal the equally, if not even more, impressive processes which created the policies and institutions that lent this empire its remarkably cosmopolitan character. For, as organized by Darius, Achaemenian Persia was not simply a strong national state. It was the first deliberate attempt in history to unite heterogeneous African, Asian, and European communities into a single organized international society. Although this area is only one of the many regional realms in the world today, its coalescence in the sixth century B.C. established an important precedent in the history of international peace and organization. One might well ask, therefore, how and under what circumstances, were the Persian goals of unity set and attained?

As indicated earlier, there was much in the political climate of the time that facilitated the making of such a state. Persia's empire embraced many races and civilizations and an infinitude of differing customs and traditions, yet it did not have to cope with "nationalism" in the modern sense of the word. That is to say, the people of that time were, on the whole, not obsessed with the idea that the identity of a local language, religion, or set of customs, could be maintained only to the extent to which the people themselves were politically effective as a separate nation. This is one reason why the conquered communities were not greatly upset when they witnessed the demotion of their local political representatives, whether mayors or kings, within the framework of the new, superseding, imperial administration. A second reason for such complacence was the schism that commonly separated the rulers from the ruled. Cyrus and his conquering armies were everywhere assisted by dissident and revolutionary elements within the population. He won the throne of Babylon with the acquiescence—if not actually on the invitation—of a large segment of the inhabitants, who greeted him as the liberator from a rule that had long forfeited their allegiance. His successor Cambyses was aided similarly in the conquest of Egypt by treachery from within.

But these occasions of native endorsement do not make the Persian accomplishment the less noteworthy. They do not eliminate, for example, such questions as the following: How did the Persians succeed in attaining a seemingly genuine international consensus while resorting to the application of force? How did they reconcile their centralized administration with the continuing diversity of local traditions? Where did they find the common denominator in the separate Asian, African, European, and Near Eastern societies so suddenly joined? And whence did they derive the insight that enabled them not only to influence, but in large measure to satisfy, the many human expectations that had survived the original act of violent conquest?

When the history of nations is associated as dramatically as it is in the case of Persia with the biographies of great men, it is tempting to look for answers in the heroic qualities of superkings such as Cyrus and Darius. Such commonplace shortcuts to historical understanding seem indeed to commend themselves in this case for two reasons. Not only do the objective records indicate that Cyrus and Darius were, in fact, farsighted and talented statesmen, who knew how to size up situations, introduce acceptable principles of rule, and carry them out in a generally acceptable way, but also the subjective versions of the historical events, recorded by the heroes themselves, lend credence to this view. The reader of Persian history will look in vain for carefully phrased policy papers or blueprints of international organization. He will find instead seemingly impulsive, but carefully recorded, royal boasts of grandeur and outlines of unbridled ambition. Cyrus prided himself on being the Lord of all Asia and he admitted universal dominion to be his aim. Xerxes told his nobles that he would extend the Persian territory as far as God's Heaven reaches, and that he would pass through Europe from one end to the other, making of all the lands that it contains, one country.[35]

Yet to accept these exhortations on their face value as adequate explanations of the Persian goals and policies would be a mistake. Such documents are helpful for an understanding of the Persian state only when they are read in connection with certain less obvious evidences of thought and behavior.

The earliest literate nations in Egypt and Mesopotamia created their civilizations, as it were, out of themselves. Hence, though their specialists developed an interest in recording some of the processes of their own creativity, they had for obvious reasons no particular interest in studying the past. When we come to sixth century Persia, however, things are different. Like the upper class Assyrian to a lesser extent before him, the upper class Persian was fully aware of his dependence on past human accomplishment. This revolutionary realization deci-

---

[35] *The History of Herodotus*, M. Komroff, ed., George Rawlinson, tr., New York, 1928, Book VII, p. 358. (Referred to hereafter as *Herodotus*.)

sively influenced his attitude toward both history and the wider contemporary environment. It made him eager to imitate and preserve all
that seemed worthwhile of the past, and it prompted him to record
every contemporary event as fully and precisely as he knew how.[36]
History-mindedness of this kind accounts for many of the exaggerated
statements about Persia's place in the universe. It also goes far toward
explaining why most Persian statesmen did not lose themselves in the
triumph of the moment, or in dreams of the future, but were, on the
contrary, capable of planning a measured and durable political achievement.

As it manifested itself in sixth century foreign policy and international government, the Persian view of the world was strongly influenced by definite standards of ethics and religion. In this sphere the
Persians were not content simply to inherit the ideas of the Semites
and Sumerians, absorb Egyptian and Mesopotamian mythology, and
permit the interpenetration of all existing religions. On the contrary,
Iran had a very old religion of its own, which departed significantly
from the other creeds of the time by exalting one great God, Ahura-
Mazda. In fact, the intensification of religious thought in Iran between
the tenth and fifth centuries B.C. resulted (at some unknown date within
this span of time, probably in the sixth century) in the most forceful
statement of ethics that the Near Eastern world had yet received. In
the words of the prophet Zoroaster: "The two primal spirits who revealed themselves in vision as twins are the Better and the Bad in
thought, word and action and between these two the wise knew to
choose aright, the foolish not so."[37] This revolutionary doctrine ordered
man to accept Good and Evil as the only existing deities and to reject
all other gods. It was the first religion in history that required each
mortal to make a personal moral choice between the powers of light
and the powers of darkness, and take his stand voluntarily against
the whole world of treachery. Zoroaster's realistic acceptance of Evil
as a major life force grounded his religion in dualism. But in prophesy-
ing that the kingdom of perfect happiness and immortality would follow the last ordeal and the renovation of the world, he not only in-
jected the idea of ultimate salvation but anticipated religious monotheism.

Obviously, this doctrine, which took hold of all Iran, held immediate
relevance for the conduct of government and politics. By inviting man

---

[36] Rostovtzeff, Vol. I, p. 132.
[37] *Encyclopaedia of Religion and Ethics*, James Hastings, ed., New York, 1908,
Vol. XII, p. 864.

to *act* in behalf of his conviction, Zoroastrianism showed the way to the immediate secular realization of the good life. It implicitly gave the state the mandate of fighting for the good cause.[38] Zoroastrianism became in this way the ideal religion for a national state with cosmopolitan aspirations. It had universal appeal insofar as it conferred upon the king as representative of the state the task of ruling the world in the interest and defence of the Good. Darius's statement, "By the grace of Ahura-Mazda, I am king; Ahura-Mazda gave me the kingdom," therefore does not simply reflect egotistical feelings. It manifests also the religious conviction that the Persian king is the mandatory of Ahura-Mazda, the power of Good, to administer in his name the countries of the earth.[39] In the estimation of Persians and subject nations alike, the title "King of Kings" expressed, consequently, less the relation of the Great King to the petty vassals than the uniqueness of his particular kingship. Even to his independence-loving Greek subjects in Anatolia he was Basileus, the one and only real King in the world.

2. Principle and Expediency in Persia's Imperial Policy. There is no doubt that Persian religious universalism was a deep source of Persian imperial policy, and that all contemporary religious currents in the Near East were specially suited to make people receptive to the theme of secular universalism, whether in government, trade, or cultural exchanges. But in retrospect we cannot determine what was the precise causal relationship between religious or ethical doctrine and policy formation, and it is doubtful whether this could have been determined at the time. Again the Persian story introduces into international relations a new motive on which the international history of foreign relations has been developing variations ever since, the conflict between expediency and ideology.

The tenets of Western civilization, in particular those developed in the twentieth century, seem to impel students of foreign affairs to analyse the motivations underlying all policy decisions. Some argue that foreign policy is, and should be, determined exclusively by national interest, commonly understood as an accumulation of material power. They are challenged by other scholars and statesmen to whom foreign policy decisions seem defensible only when they do not contradict or offend the moral and ethical traditions that the policy-making country stands for. Many professional observers of the political scene go even further. They are not satisfied with the mere coincidence, if

---

[38] Compare this to the development of the Indian faith out of the same original data toward non-dualism, mysticism, and universal tolerance.

[39] William S. Haas, *Iran*, New York, 1946, p. 71.

a particular policy happens to be successful in the service of the national interest as well as fitting, logical, or consistent in terms of the ideology professed by the policy-making country. Before giving their approval to such a doubly successful policy, they want to know which of the two sets of reference provided the real motive for the particular decision or policy line. Were the Western Allies in World War I and World War II, for instance, really and earnestly thinking of liberation and self-determination when they freed the nations that had been subjugated by their adversaries? Or were the avowed goals merely a smoke screen behind which they were engaging in the pursuit of selfish gain? To these and similar questions unequivocal answers are often sought. But they have rarely been found even in our century, despite the availability of ample source material and diligent research methods, because motivations in this most complex field of human relations must of necessity merge and contaminate each other; they will do so as long as there is no international consensus, defining and acknowledging the values that ought to determine the foreign-policy-making process.

The issue between expediency and ethics was, to our knowledge, first clearly defined by fifth century Athens in her relations with her satellites and allies. Thucydides' analysis of this dilemma in the Melian Dialogue is, perhaps, still its most impressive presentation. Since Greece and Persia were in close touch with each other, and since Thucydides wrote his masterful account of the Peloponnesian War at about the time that similar issues were confronting the Persians, it is reasonable to assume that the leading Persians were not unaware of the ethical problem. In the absence of adequate Persian documentation, however, we do not know what kind of cogitation and intellectual disputation actually entered into the policy-forming process in Iran. One can, of course, always argue that the actual political situations must have required some such political answers as were in fact given, or that the same answers could and would have been given anywhere, without any reference to ideology, in the daily course of good statesmanship. But in the case of Persia, as in many other historical instances, a close connection between ethics and politics can nevertheless be presumed. By the time that Darius was systematizing the Empire's administration, Zoroastrianism was already a well developed, clearly stated, and generally accepted ideology or faith in Greater Persia.[40]

[40] It has been noted that Zoroaster himself made no reference to the Achaemenians, and that neither the Achaemenian kings nor Herodotus made any mention of the prophet. This fact together with the uncertainty of Zoroaster's chronological place

Under religious influences a definite world view had emerged which had accustomed the Persians to the need for making moral decisions. Furthermore, it is likely that this need was kept before their minds by their constant association with politically and intellectually sophisticated non-Persians who would be readier to accept pragmatically effective policies if they could be shown to be ethically defensible.

These suppositions are borne out by a review of Persia's attitudes toward foreign civilizations and non-Persian subjects. Nothing is quite so striking about this record, especially when one compares it with what went before, as the evolution that it shows of the Persian recognition of the value of tolerance. The Achaemenians had a great and consistent respect for the traditional life and customs of their diverse groups of subjects and did not, as a rule, impose either their religion or their language on the conquered. In fact, in many instances local institutions and beliefs were not only tolerated but deliberately supported and defended. But here again the merger of motivations eludes precise analysis; for although tolerance became a part of the Persian world view, it was not, strictly speaking, indicated in the religious traditions that helped to form this world view. Since Zoroaster argued that infidels, Turks, and nomads should be fought as part of the campaign to convert the whole world into the domain of the Good, this Persian policy of tolerance probably was suggested by the statesmanship rather than by the religious ethics of the sixth century B.C.

Wherever possible the Persian monarchs established themselves as the legitimate successors of the native kings. Cyrus publicly appeared in Babylon as the devoted servant of the religion of the conquered and accepted the throne as the gift of Babylon's own god Marduk. Similarly, when Cambyses and Darius reached Egypt, they took names claiming relationship with Egypt's god Re. All of these monarchs engaged, furthermore, in the policy of returning and reestablishing exiled human beings and local gods. Here again one might well argue that the tolerance that inspired such measures was less an ethically held value than a political device designed to gain the favor of the people while eliminating the threat of their local dynasties. In other words, Persian "liberation" was really "subversion." And were it not for the many known manifestations of national and cultural diversity in the Persian satrapies, one might be tempted to suggest, similarly, that Cyrus did not have to carry on the Assyrian and Babylonian method

---

in history indicates, in the opinion of some authorities, that Cyrus and Cambyses were not really familiar with the new gospel. See *Encyclopaedia of Religion and Ethics, loc.cit.*

of deporting conquered populations to distant places because the earlier deportations had already broken the national spirit of the peoples of whom he was now the king.

No case study of the motivations and sources of Persian behavior toward satellite or subject groups could illustrate these issues better than the history of Persia's relations with the Jews. It is a historical fact that Cyrus liberated the Jews; but it is not certain why he did so. According to Isaiah, the Jewish God commissioned the Persian king to free the exiles and subdue all other nations. According to Ezra, when Cyrus made the proclamation throughout his empire, putting it in writing that "the Lord God hath given me all the kingdoms of the earth, and he hath charged me to build him a house at Jerusalem," he was stirred by the Lord. According to this view, the later Persian policies transporting the Jews back to Jerusalem, returning the vessels of their temple which Nebuchadnezzar had taken, conveying timber for the temple from Lebanon to the Sea of Joppa, rehabilitating all their settlements, and instituting far-reaching local autonomy among them in judicial matters, would have been the logical and consistent consequences of an original moral decision.[41] But the same circumstances of liberation when seen in their immediate setting of practical international politics permit the view that this was the only expedient policy to adopt, and that it had little if anything to do with moral choice or intellectual consistency. For what, after all, did Cyrus do except support the dissident Jewish subjects of his enemy, the Assyrians, and set them up as a puppet state? This precedent has been followed by all prudent conquerors ever since. For example, in their campaign against the Western powers during World War II, the Japanese freed and rehabilitated the Indonesians and other colonial subjects of their adversaries.

And yet, even after expediency has been given its due as the main and usual motivation in diplomacy and imperial administration, the fact remains that the Persians realized what had never occurred to the Assyrians and the other imperialist powers of that age: that national interest does not have to express itself solely in vindictiveness, that it is not necessarily impaired by respect for lesser national interests, and that tolerance pays off. It must, furthermore, be borne in mind that before a governing administration can decide in what measure to tolerate, respect, or promote the laws and creeds of differing culture groups under its control, it must have developed both the incentive

[41] See on this subject: Ezra 1:7, 3:7, 4:3, 5:13, 7:25; Isaiah 44:28, 45:1; Daniel 1:21, 6:28, 10:1.

and the ability to understand those differing cultures. Perhaps it is not too farfetched to assume that the Persians were able to develop such capacities precisely because they were inspired by a definite ideological orientation.[42]

Additional light is shed on the sources of Persian policy-making when one regards it from the point of view of the foreign peoples to whom it was addressed. For example, one may study its effect upon the Jews. What was it, one may ask, about Persia, and about Cyrus in particular, that recommended itself to the Jewish prophets and fed the visions of the Jewish people? Was it only that Cyrus had stilled their despair about the present and fear of the future? Harassed and terrorized for centuries by the earlier Near Eastern empires, torn by constant internecine divisions and quarrels, the Jews had long cherished dreams of a righteous kingdom, which God himself had promised to establish for his Chosen People through instruments of his selection. Long before they came to associate the realization of this vision with Persia, the Jews had inherited much from Mesopotamian mythology and Egyptian monotheism: they were a people used to hearing and responding sympathetically to exalted spiritual appeals. At the crucial moment of their relations with Iran they were especially alert, therefore, to the ethical values of Zoroastrianism, with its belief in progress and the eventual victory of the Good.[43] Thus spiritually attuned to Persia, they must have been persuaded by the moral appeal implicit in Persian policy, no less than by Persia's power, which had been applied to their advantage and so could be readily justified through Jewish lore.[44]

To conclude, in all situations in which a dynamic foreign policy is conducted against the background of a widely accepted national ideology it is difficult, if not impossible, to identify the exact point at which ideology and interest interact, or determine each other; or, put differently, at which the recognition of national interest ends and obedience to moral principle begins. The Persian case, which presented this issue for the first time in historically known terms, is no exception. Iran's imperial system was certainly not a direct outgrowth or reflection

[42] But see the violation of these norms in Egypt during the campaign of Cambyses. This has been explained as due to the King's nervous breakdown. Cf. *The Cambridge Ancient History*, Vol. IV, pp. 22ff.

[43] The Jews were eventually to depart in significant respects from Zoroastrianism, notably by associating the cause of all evil with man himself.

[44] See Max Radin, *The Jews among the Greeks and Romans*, Philadelphia, 1915, pp. 56ff., for a general discussion of Jewish life in the Persian Empire.

of her dominant faith, yet it came into being through policy decisions so broadly formulated and attractively presented that non-Persian subjects could accept them without feeling threatened in their allegiance to locally cherished traditions. And this general approval of Persian principles yielded a margin within which imperial statesmanship could operate in the strictly Persian interest and yet be accepted by non-Persians.

3. The Administration of the Persian State. In consequence of Iran's policy of tolerance her economy came to be characterized by an interesting division of labor along ethnic lines. Treasury tablets from Persepolis show that the twenty-four distinct skilled trades recruited their specialists from many distant places. In Persepolis Egyptians served as woodworkers, Carians did the gold work, and Egyptians and Ionians were the cup-carriers. Similarly, in Susa, Babylonians moulded the bricks; Ionians and Sardians wrought the stone; Medes and Egyptians wrought the gold and adorned the walls; Sardians and Egyptians applied the inlays. Cedar timber was brought by Assyrians to Babylon, whence Carians and Ionians conveyed it to Susa.[45] Apparently the Persians not only respected the past and present circumstances of their innumerable subject groups, but also knew how to influence the expectations of peoples by offering them opportunities for improving their livelihood. This, in fact, was the attitude that made it possible for the Anatolian Greeks, who were Persian subjects, to develop their own culture. And it explains the notable advance at that time in Jewish literature, as well as the great prosperity of the Phoenician and Aramaean cities.[46]

It is a further example of the ingenuity of the Persians as international administrators that within some of their provinces they permitted the continuation of older and local forms of government. The Phoenician city-states continued to be governed by their kings; the Egyptians had their nome chiefs; the Jews had their high-priestly government and the Anatolian Greeks their city-states. In the light of these facts it might be asserted with a good deal of justification that the Persians were the first to recognize the "nation" as a cultural entity.[47] The Persian administrators interfered only when peace and order were threatened. Herodotus reports, furthermore,[48] that deputies from

---

[45] Carleton S. Coon, *Caravan*, New York, 1951, p. 76, quoting from Cameron, *The Persepolis Tablets*, Vol. LXV.

[46] M. Rostovtzeff, Vol. I, p. 153.

[47] William S. Haas, "Center of Creation, Radiation, and Mediation," *Background of the Middle East*, in E. Jackh, ed., New York, 1952, p. 26.

[48] *Herodotus*, Book VI, p. 321.

all the Ionian Greek cities were summoned and compelled to enter into agreements not to harass each other by force of arms but to settle their disputes in peace.

On the whole, the facilities, benefits, and promises so clearly associated with Persian overlordship made men acquiesce in a strong central administration. The pivotal point in this administrative system was the king. When Darius, as after him Xerxes and Artaxerxes, claimed in his inscriptions that he was the "king of many," or the "king of this great earth far and wide," he could justify his pretension by pointing to the great variety of the subject nations, the universality of his domination which united them, and his unshared and undisputed supremacy over them all.[49] Moreover, since both the Persians and the conquered people—even the highest dignitaries—were alike considered to be his slaves, as individuals they were all equal, if only in the negative sense of their submission to the king. This status was secured by a well-organized judicial system, likewise anchored in the king as source of all law, which became famous throughout the ancient world for the equity of its principles and methods.[50]

Just as his legal functions were in actuality delegated by the King of Kings to local judges, so were his administrative functions assigned to the provincial governors, the satraps. In each of the twenty to twenty-eight satrapies into which the Empire was at different times divided, the satrap was charged with keeping the peace and collecting tribute in cash, or in kind, as fixed by Darius in conformity with the particular riches and possibilities of the area. Gold dust came from India, the twentieth satrapy, which, being more densely populated than any other, paid the highest tribute; wheat came from Egypt; sheep and mules from Media; myrrh and frankincense from Yemen; and special gifts from Ethiopia. Usually the satrapies were formed by a joining together of nations that were neighbors; occasionally, however, Darius "passed over the nearer tribes and put in their stead those which were more remote."[51] Another device in this policy of divide and rule, to which the great king resorted in order to forestall unified rebellion, was the introduction of a regime of separation of powers within each satrapy. This meant that each of the officials in charge of the major governmental departments was obliged to report directly to the central administration.[52] This prevented him from arriving at any decisive agreements with the head of any other department.

[49] *The Cambridge Ancient History*, Vol. IV, p. 185.
[50] Coon, p. 79.   [51] *Herodotus*, Book III, p. 181.   [52] Sykes, Vol. I, p. 162.

The chief order-enforcing agency, however, was no doubt the long-invincible Persian army. When Herodotus had occasion to describe its operations during Xerxes' ill-fated expedition against Greece, it had already passed its zenith and was demoralized, impressive only as the most cosmopolitan host that any country had ever, in the history of the world, put into the field.[53]

The mobility of this army, as well as the collection of taxes and the execution of Persian policies generally, depended upon a reliable system of communications. The Assyrians had been road conscious for strategic reasons; but the Persians were the first whose record indicates a clear realization that the diversity of provincial life could be made to harmonize with the principle of imperial unity only by means of carefully developed technical facilities. And the principal instrument of this kind upon which the Persians elaborated masterfully were the roads that intersected the empire from east to west, and from north to south. Of these great arteries of trade, travel, and cultural exchange Herodotus has left a glowing description. He was impressed by their safety,[54] the speed (90 days) that marked the passage from Sardis to Susa on the Royal Road (1700 miles), the numerous and comfortable rest houses that punctuated the journey from Babylon and Susa to Persepolis, and above all, by the Persian messengers, who travelled as fast as "nothing mortal."[55] Along the whole line of the road, he writes, men are stationed with horses in number equal to the number of days which the journey takes, allowing a man and a horse to each day in each season or weather. Thus borne from hand to hand, like the light in the torch race of his Greek compatriots, dispatches bearing the royal will were carried to the remotest imperial outpost.

However, the royal will was implemented also by such elaborate networks of police and espionage that the Persian king was said to have "his eyes and his ears everywhere." These and other features of the regime point up what must appear to most twentieth century students of internationalism as the greatest failing of the Persian concept of empire, namely, its disregard of the individual. In apology for this lacuna in applied ethics and politics, it can be said that within his national or cultural group, which was more fully recognized by the Persians than by any other great power, the individual seems to have

[53] Cf. *Herodotus*, Book VII, pp. 365ff., for a vivid description, of over eight pages, of the many national contingents in their native fighting attire.

[54] Private travel and correspondence was strictly supervised and inspected by imperial guards. See also *Nehemiah* 21:7.

[55] *Herodotus*, Book VIII, p. 461.

been free to follow his calling and engage in his speculations, and that it was only in relation to the pivot of the whole cosmopolitan structure—the imperial administration itself—that no rights were presumed to inhere in man. Furthermore, the larger concept of the personality as endowed with definite political rights does not seem to have been developed either by any of the great contemporary or any of the preceding societies of the ancient world. Internationally it was unknown until the Greeks, who were destined to become Persia's most successful adversaries, introduced it into their civil government and thereby into international relations.

4. Persia's Relations with Other States and International Societies. It was natural that this technically and politically effective union of the cultured states of the Near East into one splendidly organized community should have given enormous impetus to international exchanges with the non-Persian countries. The golden Daricus—the monetary emblem of the indivisible Persian Empire—penetrated to the far corners of the Mediterranean. In the Orient Persian trade established connections with China and India, and the artistic influences that emanated from Persia in this period can be traced in both Chinese and Indian sculpture. Nor do the records leave any doubt that Darius and his successors desired even wider fields of international activity and trade. While the Hellespont was bridged for largely strategic reasons, the Persian planners never stopped dreaming up projects for closer commercial contacts with India and Egypt, for oceanic trade, and for direct sea routes around Arabia to Africa and through the Red Sea to the Mediterranean.[56] A sort of Suez Canal, connecting the Nile with the Red Sea, was in fact completed, only to decay when Egypt regained her independence. And after a Persian expedition led by the Greek admiral Scylax descended the Indus, explored the Indian Ocean, found its way into the Red Sea, and finally arrived, so the records indicate, in the neighborhood of Suez,[57] water communications between India and Persia, as well as between Egypt and Persia, were maintained for a considerable span of years.

For the development of these relations the Persians relied heavily on a group of peoples whose independence they were unable to curb for any length of time—the Arabs. Since this Semitic nation controlled the gateway to Egypt in particular, treaty relations resulting in a League of Friendship[58] were finally substituted for the earlier attempts

---

[56] M. Rostovtzeff, *Caravan Cities*, D. & T. Rice, trs., Oxford, 1932, p. 19.
[57] *The Cambridge Ancient History*, Vol. IV, p. 201.
[58] *Herodotus*, Book III, p. 180.

at political subjugation. Persia's trade with the West, which was at all times more extensive than its Oriental trade, was spearheaded by Phoenicians and Anatolian Greeks. It reached the city-states of the Greek mainland, the Black Sea coasts, Italy, Sicily, and the Phoenician colonies in northern Africa. Through these trade-minded communities, which made a handsome profit in their function as intermediaries between East and West, a Persian-sponsored trade in such commodities as perfume, ornaments, precious woods, and stuffs dyed in purple, reached southwestern and northern Europe[59] and the numerous tribes north of the Caucasus, where, as Herodotus remarks, "no one fears the Persians."[60]

These are only some of the known ways through which Persia's international state communicated with other separately organized regional realms. But research in comparative government, religion, literature, and art-forms points to much closer and more varied contacts between the different international societies of that historical epoch than can be definitely established through available documentation. For example, the Persian idea of the "world state" as represented by the "King of Kings" as well as techniques of government and statecraft were carried not only westward, where they influenced the Macedonians and the Romans, but also eastward, where they influenced state-building in India,[61] and perhaps even China.

[59] Rostovtzeff, *Caravan Cities*, p. 20.
[60] *Herodotus*, Book III, p. 183.
[61] See *The Cambridge History of India*, Cambridge, England, 1922, Vol. I, ch. XIV, on Persian dominions in northern India to the time of Alexander's invasion, particularly pp. 329ff. and pp. 341ff.

CHAPTER 2

THE PLACE OF GREECE
IN INTERNATIONAL HISTORY

AN INTRODUCTION TO INTERNATIONAL RELATIONS
BETWEEN "EAST" AND "WEST"

A. The World Community and the Study
of Greek History

INTO the bewildering profusion of mankind's major historical records many have tried to bring order and clarity by proposing theories of world history that explain the course of human events as indivisible, while distinguishing the histories of particular nations or civilizations and accommodating them to the general pattern. They have constructed their theories by ascribing a definite meaning to history as such, by delimiting the purposes of the study of history, by defining the relationship between past and present, and by discovering criteria that should permit, on the one hand, a delimitation of separate civilizations and, on the other, the recognition of connections between civilizations. The rich variety of the records, as read by countless scholars of various nations with differing insights, has naturally resulted in many conflicting approaches to that perplexing process called history. Indeed, although the evolution of literacy has everywhere tended to propose objectivity and detachment as the general goals of historical research, it is difficult, if not impossible, to divorce the particular views of the various scholars from the times and places in which they were set forth. The history of ancient Greece and Rome, for instance, exercised a great attraction for Europeans and Americans in the eighteenth and nineteenth centuries and was readily incorporated into the general theories, whereas the histories of such regions as Bactria and the West African Sudan, which have held no such allure for the intellectual leaders of the West, have been omitted.

The historian whose primary interest is the world community must admit his dependence on time and place. Like the nationalist historians, he, too, is influenced by the problems of the present. He is not usually interested in the history of international relations simply for the sake of preserving or completing records. His interest in the past stems, rather, from the expectation that his work may elucidate the contemporary scene, and he may be inclined to emphasize epochs and occurrences that feed his hopes for the eventual emergence of a transcendent human culture.

Like other scholars, the international historian is attracted to certain local scenes. But unlike most national historians, whose function and purpose it is to uncover the antecedents of particular communities or civilizations by searching local records, considering international or foreign data only if they are locally relevant, the international historian must not permit himself to become caught in the local records to the loss of his world perspective.

In nineteenth and twentieth century Europe, the time and place in which so much of the world's past was pieced together and studied, many influential historians proposed bridges between the past and the present, and between the local and the universal, by suggesting that world history was a kind of continuous argumentation between competitive local histories, constantly pleaded and adjudicated before the bar of history itself. In the absence of a generally recognized arbiter of all human destiny, this meant that the contemporary scene was the place of judgment and contemporary society the court of last resort. Since neither the present nor the past holds any common significance for the various generations that make up the modern world, it meant furthermore that the process of history was actually judged in each separate society in accordance with locally or individually preferred criteria of evaluation. The resultant views of mankind's past were open invitations to judge and measure local histories on the basis of "success." Civilizations that lasted longer than others, states that covered greater areas than others, ideas that were more popular than others, were acclaimed victorious, while the less obviously prominent or successful remained, as it were, outside the province of historical remembrance, to attract, at best, the attention of only a few specially dedicated scholars.

Dialectic views of humanity's past are dynamic and therefore attractive for the living. They may also have their place in a comparative history of civilizations. But they will not do as approaches to international history. International history is neither a comparison of national or regional histories, nor a series of success stories around the theme of survival and defeat. It is humanity's joint adventure, whether amply or sparsely recorded, whether marked by failure or success, whether immediately relevant to the present or not. Only after adopting what may be called a democratic approach to the countless constituents in whose behalf he writes, can the international historian indulge his own bias in the selection of the data that seem to him relevant to his search for common human foundations. In the international perspective the historically significant moment may have endured ten, five hundred, or one thousand years, and the historically significant scene may have been Ghana, Athens, China, or the entire world.

Before the political record of a particular nation or period can yield its internationally valid elements, it must be separated from the uses to which it has been put in the context of any specific civilization. This problem is best and most acutely illustrated by the relationship that has gradually grown up in the course of two thousand years between the past of ancient Greece and the continuing present of Western civilization. The relationship shows clearly that any rewarding study of international matters must reach backward into time in a broad way— even if understood entirely in terms of contemporary affairs. For example, most people in the twentieth century are in some way particularly concerned about the complex of relations between East and West. But what is the origin of the assumed clearcut division between "East" and "West"? Part, though by no means all, of the answer can be found by identifying the place that Western scholarship has assigned to the history of ancient Greece. So conceived and rendered, the heritage of Greece has shaped Western attitudes toward the East for centuries. Most historical treatments of Western literature, art, science, philosophy, and government begin their story there, where the family tree of Western civilization is supposed to root, thence to proceed to the Hebrews and the Romans, until coming to rest in Christianity. Indeed, the recitation of these antecedents has become virtually an act of faith for those who claim membership in Western civilization. With John Stuart Mill, most of us believe that the Greeks were not only the most remarkable people who have ever existed, but "the beginners of nearly everything, Christianity excepted, of which the modern world makes its boast . . ." since they were "the founders of mathematics, of physics, of the inductive study of politics, of the philosophy of human nature and life."[1]

Now the internationally relevant aspect of our relation to the ancient Greeks is not so much our admiration of their achievement as our claim—deduced, so it seems, from cultural kinship, historical discovery, and rights of usufruct—to *own* Greek history, and our jealousy

---

[1] *Dissertations*, ii, p. 283, as quoted by R. W. Livingstone, in *The Legacy of Greece*, Livingstone, ed., Oxford, 1921, pp. 251f.

to retain this possession as uniquely "ours." It is, for instance, interesting that a great twentieth-century scholar and scientist, who has done much toward putting the record straight between East and West, can still say, in speaking about the beginnings of science, that "we must necessarily restrict ourselves to *our own* [italics mine] ancestry"; that "early Hindu and Chinese science are generally left out not because they lack importance, but simply because they lack significance for us Western readers"; and that *"our own"* [italics again mine] culture of Greek and Hebrew origin is the one that interests us the most, if not exclusively, because ". . . our thinking has been deeply influenced by Hebrew and Greek thoughts, hardly any by Hindu or Chinese ones."[2] This is no doubt a correct statement of the situation, as far as it goes, and it would be futile to quarrel with the circumstances that have favored such a differentiated relationship to the past.[3] However, our chief concern at the present point in world history is not to controvert the traditional bases of Western (or any other) civilization, but to appraise the internationally relevant consequences of this Western emphasis upon Greece. For while it is reasonable to assume that considerations of national interest will long continue to divide the world in which we live, it is unreasonable to persist in applying the principles and practices of the separate present nations to our understanding of the whole reach of the historical forces of the past. *World* history, at least, ought not to be divided into spheres of exclusive national or cultural influence; it should, instead, be rendered as humanity's indivisible inheritance.

The particular world orientation to which the West was brought in the course of its history has led us to overstress those aspects of Greek civilization that have seemed particularly relevant to us, and to neglect others that do not fit so snugly into our picture. In our overemphasis on reason as a gate to knowledge, for instance, we have been inclined to overlook Greek susceptibilities to the mystical, sensual, and irra-

[2] George Sarton, *A History of Science. Ancient Science through the Golden Age of Greece*, Cambridge, 1952, p. x. Sarton adds that it would be wrong and evil to claim superiority for "our" culture because that kind of attitude is the main source of international trouble in the world.

[3] The Greeks occupied this preferred place in our thinking about history because 1) they were by all standards a remarkably creative people; 2) they had a "modern" sense for history equalled perhaps only by the Chinese; 3) they knew how to convey their history in terms meaningful to posterity; 4) their legacy remained accessible while that of other nations did not; 5) their experiences were directly relevant to history-conscious Western peoples; 6) their "discovery" was psychologically satisfying because the West could in this way come to an identifiable father and establish a continuity of existence.

tional elements in life. Ignoring the superstitions that accompanied the emergence of Greek science, our historians have failed even to give its due to the victory of Greek rationalism over superstition.[4] We have, in short, on many occasions read our own bias into Greece and have, to that extent, misread Greek history.

And having been to such an extent absorbed in but one sector of humanity's past, we have been rather insensitive to those other sectors, whose relevance to ourselves has not been so easy to establish. For not only are the records of the peoples east and south of Greece difficult to assemble and difficult to read, but Western minds, by the nineteenth century, were disinclined to find affinities in the histories of India, China, Persia, or Africa; the more so, since the contemporary societies of those regions seemed to diverge completely from the life patterns to which the West had become accustomed.

While the originality of Greek thought has been demonstrated in many instances, we know today that science, to take one example, did not begin in Greece, but that the Greek "miracle" was prepared for by millenniums of work in Egypt, Mesopotamia, and possibly in other regions. It also becomes clearer, as the records are assembled, that many inventions, discoveries, and ideas for which the West used to credit the Greeks exclusively were also—often simultaneously—developed in India and China. The Indians, as well as the Greeks, drew on Chaldean and Assyrian knowledge of medicine, borrowed heavily from Persia, and gradually infused scientific thinking into their approaches to the phenomena around them.[5] Speculations about the nature of the universe in which the scientists of Ionian Greece are supposed to have pioneered, were being matched elsewhere at the same time. The Jainas in India, for example, based their concept of progressive reincarnation on an elaborate systematization of the forms of life, which is said to represent a fundamentally scientific conception of the world.[6]

In the field of government, too, certain parallel developments have been noted. While the emergence of Greek democracy was revolutionary in many respects, the city-state as such had long been known

---

[4] Sarton, preface ix, pp. 6-8, 112ff. Eric R. Dodds, *The Greeks and the Irrational*, Berkeley, 1951.

[5] Henry E. Sigerist, *A History of Medicine*, 1951, Vol. I, p. 494.

[6] "The 24th Jaina Tirthankara, Mahavira, was roughly a contemporary of Thales and Anaxagoras, the earliest of the standard line of Greek philosophers; . . . the systematization of the features of nature which his teaching took for granted was already centuries old. It had long done away with the hosts of powerful gods and the wizard-magic of the still earlier priestly tradition. . . ." Heinrich Zimmer, *Philosophies of India*, New York, 1951, pp. 277-279.

in the Near East. Many institutions that we associate with the Athenian democracy of Solon in the seventh century B.C. may have been adaptations of earlier institutions, which the Greeks had seen in operation in Asia Minor. The secret ballot, for instance, was probably used one thousand years earlier among the Sumerians; it may have been known also to Indians of northern India at about the time when it was being brought to the Greek mainland by way of the Ionian cities.[7]

Since we have looked so steadily at "our" Greece only, we have taken scant notice of the close ties that bound Greece to eastern lands. As a consequence, we have been blind to the possible links between the ancient Eastern and Western societies. For not only were the Greeks indebted to previous discoveries made in the Near East, but being as rational and objective as we have found them to be, they acknowledged their legacy. This is made evident by the frequency with which the Greek scientists and philosophers explicitly referred to their Oriental forbears and colleagues, the extended sojourns of men like Thales of Miletus in Egypt,[8] the readiness with which Greece accepted the alphabet from West Asia and papyrus from Egypt (borrowings, by the way, that made Greek history available to the modern West), and the hospitality of Greek religion to foreign cults and deities. Nor does Greek history reflect its relations to the Oriental world merely through these and similar processes of diffusion. It reveals, especially in the sixth and fifth centuries, constant physical contact with Eastern peoples. That is to say, contrary to the popular understanding, the Greeks did not come *after* the Egyptians, Chaldeans, and Persians. These nations co-existed and their continuous exchanges made for a rich and lively international society.[9] The Greeks, on the one hand, and the Egyptians and Asians, on the other, engaged not merely in technical but also in intellectual communications. They were able to share many values, and their political differences did not prevent the development of sympathy and understanding between them. Indeed, the only Near Eastern

[7] W. C. MacLeod, *The Origin and History of Politics*, New York, 1931. See pp. 492ff. and 495 for the author's references to Indian sources of information, according to which Buddhist monks are known to have employed this device.

[8] Francis M. Cornford, *Before and After Socrates*, Cambridge, 1950, pp. 5ff.; Sarton, pp. 168-173.

[9] Relations between the Greeks and Egyptians were particularly intense between 663-625 B.C. and during the Persian regime. See Sarton, p. 112. The Greeks and Indians were in contact from the earliest recorded times. See H. G. Rawlinson, *India, A Short Cultural History*, London, 1952, pp. 53ff., and *Intercourse between India and the Western World from the earliest times to the fall of Rome*, Cambridge, 1916. Also Jawaharlal Nehru, *The Discovery of India*, New York, 1946, pp. 141-146.

folk with whom the Greeks had hardly any contact at this time were the Jews,[10] the people, curiously enough, with whom the West habitually has so closely linked them.

The crossroads of all these comings and goings in the sixth century was a province of the Persian Empire, the western coast of Anatolia, whose Ionian harbors were the terminals of countless sea lanes and caravan roads that spanned the eastern Mediterranean region and connected it with the whole of Asia.[11] Here, under the protection of Persian power and policy, a prosperous, culturally mixed civilization developed, its economic and intellectual leadership held by the Greek settlements.[12] Their mediating function in the sixth and fifth century world which they shared with the western Greeks, already suggests the relevance of their general history to any serious study of East-West relations. Compared with the history of ancient Egypt or China, that of the Greek cities was brief and directly affected only a very small area. Nevertheless, it had a greater influence on subsequent generations in the Orient, as well as in the Occident, than any other single set of national annals.

The special relevance of Greek history to any study of international history must be acknowledged, because the Greeks gave history, as such, a new meaning. They recognized the separateness of the past, the present, and the future, but did not lose their sense of the unity of experience through time. They were acutely aware of the significance of the past for the present, and yet did not permit remembrance to interfere with the pleasure of existence. A knowledge of the past was cultivated not for its own sake (as was to become the fashion in the later West) but in the service of the present and the future. In this way the Greeks preserved doggedly what Nietzsche has called an unhistorical sense. And this became the main source of their strength in the period of their greatest creativity.[13]

The Greeks also knew that not everything in history could be rationally ascertained or explained. Since they recognized both reason and intuition as sources of wisdom, their men of science were quite

[10] Sarton, p. 184; the best of the Jews and the best of the Greeks were pursuing their own purposes independently. It was two or three centuries later in Alexandria that they were brought together in consequence of Alexander's policies; see also Max Radin, *The Jews among the Greeks and Romans*, Philadelphia, 1915.

[11] Sarton, p. 162, for a descriptive analysis.

[12] M. I. Rostovtzeff, *A History of the Ancient World*, Oxford, 1926, Vol. i, pp. 189.

[13] Friedrich Nietzsche, *The Use and Abuse of History*, New York, 1957, p. 24.

ready to accept the myths as poetical descriptions of things that were not susceptible of scientific explanation.[14] During the following centuries mankind lost this sense for a measured dualism in perception. The nations east of Greece, such as India, relied so much on intuition and individual wisdom as the main sources of understanding that they were inclined to underestimate the possibilities of finding generally valid and rationally tested explanations, while those west of Greece lost touch with the sensual world of experience in their all too energetic pursuit of scientific definitions.

The Hellenic approach to history was further significant because it was tied up with new uses of literacy. Whereas Egypt and Mesopotamia before, and India and China afterward, regarded knowledge as a secret teaching to be jealously guarded by the literate elect and the specialized guilds, the Greeks made their knowledge as widely accessible as possible. By putting literacy into the service of both intuitively and rationally guided perception, they were able to convey life in all its richness not only to the learned but also to the unlearned, not only to Greeks but also to non-Greeks, and not only to contemporaries but also to posterity. Such a use of literacy also explains why they were more successful than the Indians and Chinese in identifying what was generally valid in the insights that they gained, as well as in applying the knowledge so found to the affairs of men in general. As a Chinese scholar has put it: "The intellectual quality of the Hellenic genius was to seek the general truth in [the previous Asian, Babylonian, and Egyptian] sciences by generalizing and formulating their principles. . . . For the Greeks there were two worlds: the world of the senses and the world of reason." It is this quality of the Greek mind, he continues, which marked the striking contrast between ancient Chinese and Greek thought and determined the divergence in the development of Eastern and Western civilizations.[15]

By transposing history, as it were, to a new key and by suggesting new uses for literacy, the Greeks laid the foundation of international history. Of this consequence the Athenian historian Thucydides seems already to have been aware. For when he offered the world his *History of the Peloponnesian War*, he said that he had written his work, not as an essay that is to win the applause of the moment, but as a possession for all time.

14 Sarton, pp. 194ff.
15 Chiang Molin, *Tides from the West*, New Haven, 1947, pp. 245f., as quoted in F. S. C. Northrop, *The Taming of the Nations*, New York, 1952, pp. 135f.

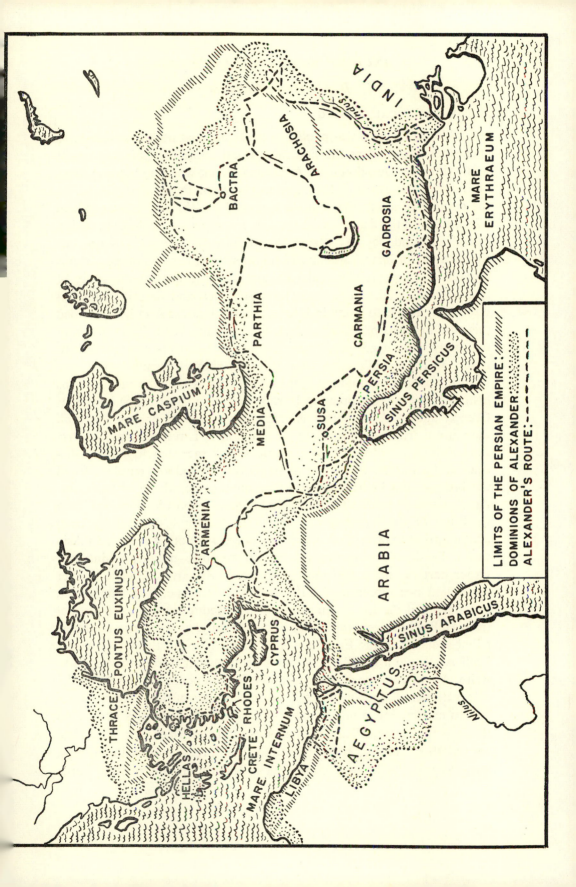

INDIA

BACTRA

ARACHOSIA

MARE ERYTHRAEUM

GADROSIA

CARMANIA

PARTHIA

PERSIA

SINUS PERSICUS

MARE CASPIUM

SUSA

MEDIA

ARMENIA

ARABIA

PONTUS EUXINUS

THRACE

CYPRUS

RHODES

CRETE

HELLAS

MARE INTERNUM

LIBYA

AEGYPTUS

SINUS ARABICUS

NILUS

LIMITS OF THE PERSIAN EMPIRE: ///////
DOMINIONS OF ALEXANDER: ::::::::
ALEXANDER'S ROUTE: -·-·-·-

B. The Greek City-States

A. THE HISTORICAL SETTING

In 430 B.C. a book was published in Greece that literate people have ever since regarded as the first methodical effort to relate history. It was written by Herodotus, an Anatolian Greek who had made Athens his home. It dealt with the relations between Persia and Greece in the context of a war that had commenced in 490 B.C. and ended, in 478 B.C., with the defeat of the Persian ambitions in the Aegean region and the ascendancy of Athens. Apart from its general and obvious significance for historiography, Herodotus' work has two other perhaps less obvious aspects that make it especially relevant for the study of international affairs. The "first historian" saw and described his environment as a case study in international relations. And he described this case in terms of a conflict between East and West. The latter motive, thus introduced into history, remained a more or less permanent fixture in the world's subsequent thinking about international affairs.

In his opening paragraph Herodotus explains that the theme of his history is the conflict between Europe and Asia. By Europe he means Greece, and by Asia, Persia as created by Cyrus. "For Asia, with all the various tribes of barbarians that inhabit it, is regarded by the Persians as their own, but Europe and the Greek race they look on as distinct and separate. . . ." The methods that Herodotus employed and the insights and interpretations of events that he advanced were outdated a few decades after he made his great exposition. Indeed, as a rendition of the international scene, the "history" could have been challenged at the time it was written. There were other nations in Asia which Persia did not even pretend to control—notably China, the larger part of India, and most of Arabia. Moreover, Greece neither controlled nor represented all of inhabited Europe. The Phoenician settlements of the European shores of the Mediterranean were distinct from Hellas both geographically and culturally, as were also countless tribal societies in the European hinterland. Nor did the Greek world itself constitute a readily identifiable realm when Herodotus began to write. Apart from the city-states on the Balkan peninsula, Greek settlements dotted all known shores. Using the islands of the Aegean Archipelago as stepping stones, emigrants from the Greek cities had sailed through the Dardanelles, the Bosporus, and the Black Sea. They had carried their culture, commerce, and civic organizations to Miletus, Susa, Smyrna, Ephesus, Samos, Chios, Rhodes, and many other ports.

And it was from these Greek Asiatic cities that the westward rebound had taken place. The colonists had spread to the most distant shores of the western Mediterranean, with the result that there existed, around 600 B.C., Greek settlements in southern Italy, Sicily, at Marseilles (Massalia), Malaga, and along the coast of Africa. Miletus alone was the mother city to no less than forty colonies. That is to say, the Greeks whom Herodotus introduces as Europeans could also be found in Asia. In fact it would seem that it was already difficult in the fifth century to draw a convincing boundary between East and West, or to identify satisfactorily what was Asia and what Europe. Nor do the records indicate that conflict was the rule in relations between the Greeks and Persians, or Europeans and Asians. The Greeks of Anatolia led a prosperous existence, first under the Lydians, and subsequently, after Cyrus defeated Croesus of Lydia, under the Persians, in full enjoyment of local autonomy in political and cultural matters. Many Asian peoples had been absorbed into their community life, and conversely, many Greeks had merged with other nations in Asia Minor.

It was only after Persia had conquered the Ionian islands, Thrace, and Macedon, thereby penetrating the Aegean, that she encountered rival Greek interests and had to evolve a definitely aggressive policy in lieu of her former permissive attitude—if for no other reason than to establish a connection by land and sea between the old and new parts of her empire. For when Athens supported an Ionian revolt (which seems to have originated in local causes rather than in Panhellenic aspirations[16]) and refused to acknowledge the supremacy of the King of Kings by the customary procedure of sending earth and water, the Persian policy-makers decided upon a show of force. The Ionian revolt was crushed and the city of Miletus burnt. A multinational army, estimated by Herodotus to have included 1,700,000 men, (although according to the estimate of J. A. R. Munro, in *The Cambridge Ancient History*, Vol. IV, pp. 271-273, the army may have included only 180,000 actual combatants) descended upon Greece. Led first by Darius (who died in 485 B.C.) and later by Xerxes, it laid Attica waste and destroyed Athens twice. But the chief battles, by land and by sea, were brilliantly fought and won by the mere handful of Greeks at Marathon, Salamis, Plataea, and Mycale. Herodotus' account ends with a report of the abandonment in 478 B.C. of the Persian plans to conquer Greece.

[16] Rostovtzeff, Vol. I. pp. 253ff.

The span of approximately fifty years that separates the battle of Plataea from the beginning of the Peloponnesian War witnessed the rise of Athens to power and greatness. With the help of a confederacy of Ionian states, later converted into an Athenian empire, the Athenian navy succeeded in expelling the Persians from the Aegean Sea. The Hellespont and the Sea of Marmora became Athenian waters. Athenian supremacy in the Mediterranean was for a time contested only by the Phoenicians, who retained their hold on Cyprus in spite of all efforts to dislodge them. But then finally it was in Greece itself—where the neighboring city-states, led by the Peloponnesian land power of Sparta, had become resentful and jealous of the Athenian ascendancy—that the great issues of fifth century international relations were decided in a protracted war. Brought on by political, economic, and ideological divisions, this Hellenic conflict compelled the Athenians to make peace with Persia.

The Peloponnesian War, with Athens and Sparta as the chief protagonists, began officially in 431 B.C. Interrupted by occasional truces and peace parleys when the parties reached exhaustion, it dragged on for twenty-seven years. Its causes, incidents, and consequences have been recorded, in their full complexity and timeless relevance for human affairs, by an Athenian contemporary patriot and general, Thucydides, who had the intelligence, vision, and moral strength to transcend his own and his city's involvement and recount the particular story of this localized military conflict in the general terms of tragedy.[17] When military danger prompted the radical faction in Athens to attempt to enlist new allies in Sicily by coercion, treachery and demoralization on the part of the individual leaders foiled the execution of the campaign plans and the city's political future was doomed. In 413 B.C. the ill-fated Sicilian expedition resulted in the total destruction of the Athenian forces.

Throughout this tragic struggle, Persian diplomacy, supported by an astute dispensation of Persian gold, succeeded where Persian arms had twice failed. By deliberately fostering division within Greece, the Persian policy-makers precipitated the political disunity of the Greek commonwealth and the end of an era that had started promisingly for Greece with victory and unity after the Persian Wars. Sparta was officially the victor. And yet she had neither the fleet nor the money to sustain her triumph. The peace that she dictated in 404 B.C. clearly

[17] Thucydides, *The Peloponnesian War*, Francis R. B. Godolphin, ed., in *The Greek Historians*, Benjamin Jowett, tr., New York, 1942, Vol. I.

reveals the influence of Persian power and policy. Moreover, all the later efforts of Sparta to rid herself and her associates of Persian dominance ended in failure. The city succeeded in retaining her own independence, but this was accomplished by bartering away the freedom of the Greek cities in Asia Minor. Then, under the terms of the "King's Peace" of 386 B.C., all the other Greek communities were given autonomy by the Persian king, except the cities in Asia which became subject to Persia, and the islands of Lemnos, Imbros, and Scyros, which were left to Athens.[18]

The efforts of Sparta to resist Persian power were no less paralyzed by inter-Greek feuds than those of Athens had been before. A Spartan defeat at the hands of Thebes, and Thebes' subsequent inability to turn the victory into an organized Hellenic peace, left Greece politically leaderless in the conduct of broader Aegean politics. The cultural and commercial life of the separate cities flourished, but war and revolution were endemic. In fact, during the eighty-five years that divided the Peloponnesian War from the conquest of Greece by Macedon, fifty-five considerable wars were waged by one Greek state against another. The record shows[19] that every Greek city experienced at least one war, or one internal revolution, every ten years.

Such anarchy in such a coveted region was naturally an open invitation for foreign intervention. However, the Persian Empire, which has done its best to create this condition, was by this time itself subject to disintegrating forces.[20] Its component kingdoms and satrapies, tempted by the promise of economic prosperity that free participation in the Greek-controlled international trade seemed to imply, had begun to resent the imperial fetters and were staging revolutions. And in these world circumstances the Macedonians, a rich and largely Hellenized European nation, rose to power in the fourth century. Their policy, decisively prepared by Philip following his ascension to the throne in 360 B.C., called first for the unification of Macedonia, next for the unification of all Greece, and ultimately for the conquest of the Persian Empire.

Caught between the expansive policies of these two great powers, most of the Greek states were more fearful of the imminent Macedonian threat to their political and commercial freedoms than of the remoter, already tottering Persian danger. Led again by Athens, where

[18] Rostovtzeff, Vol. I, pp. 312ff.
[19] Rostovtzeff, Vol. I, p. 322.
[20] Similar developments seem to have occurred in Central Asia at this time.

Demosthenes was admonishing his fellow citizens not to buy national unity at the price of political liberty, and supported by Persia, whose money was now being spent freely to bolster every possible anti-Macedonian faction, the Greeks resisted Macedon's superior forces valiantly and for some time, but were unequal to the task. Their effort ended in 338 B.C. with a total Macedonian victory in Chaeronea. The second and third objectives of Philip's program were then attained when a number of Greek states formed a general alliance under Macedonian leadership and the combined armies, commanded by Philip's son Alexander, destroyed the Persian army in 331 B.C. The new empire, thus founded by the Hellenized Macedonian king, united the two areas of the world that Herodotus had separated as Europe and Asia.

B. GREEK APPROACHES TO INTERNATIONAL RELATIONS

Most Near Eastern empires had relied on conquest as the foremost guarantee of security. They had maintained their vast dominions by means of military vigilance and by developing—at least in some outstanding instances—techniques for the peaceful administration of what they had forcefully acquired. Measured according to this scale of achievement, the ancient Greeks were a total failure. Their records show neither successful empires nor effective systems of international administration. Nevertheless, their experiences in the conduct of international relations are of timeless significance, because they furnish an entirely new measure for the evaluation of international policies. The Greeks made it possible to think of international affairs as essentially human affairs.

The emergence of this new orientation was, in terms of Greek history, a corollary of certain general intellectual trends. The early Greek thinkers had overcome tradition, fear, and ignorance by studying the natural world and questioning the supernatural world. Their moral courage emancipated reason, and set other Greeks free to speculate about the nature of man himself. Following the maxim "know thyself," they determined the respective spheres of the intellect and intuition, and so established man in the full complexity of his rational and sensual self as the measure of all life. This understanding led them to a definition of the qualities that should constitute the "excellent" man—the whole individual—as well as to a formulation of certain norms whose cultivation would help man to the attainment of his ideal form. Furthermore, since these philosophers had found freedom to be the indispensable condition for the evolution of reason, and since they believed that reason alone could bring knowledge of the true self, they logically regarded freedom as the chief value and interest in human life.[21]

But the observation of human existence had also convinced the Greeks at an early time that self-sufficiency was beyond the range of human nature. This meant that community life had now to assume a form which would permit all men to pursue the goals of life disclosed by reason. The Greeks found the model for this ideal organization in their own "polis," the small city-state in which every inhabitant could hear the town crier's voice. Such a pattern of communal existence was normal for Greece, since it was indicated by geography, the land being split into numerous sections, each secluded from the others by natural barriers. Furthermore, it was indicated by history, since Mesopotamian politics had for thousands of years revolved around city-states. There was, consequently, nothing particularly original about the polis as such. Where the Greeks were original was in their association of the polis with new purposes. Since the city was an extension of man and his faculties, the Greeks felt that it was his property, not the manor of the city's god as the Mesopotamians had explained it. Their ideal polis was the place in which all men were to develop their potentialities for excellence.

In order to permit this use of the state, a principle of order had to be found that would assure an adjustment between individual and collective interests. This led to an elaboration of the idea of justice as the chief bond between men. The hold of justice on Greek thinking is already indicated in Homer's writings and becomes fully recognizable in Solon's reforms of the Athenian constitution. That is to say, it was an activating idea long before it found classical expression in the teaching and writings of Socrates, Plato, and Aristotle.[22] For if the achievement of a harmony between the sensual and the rational worlds, and of a balance between individual and communal interests, are the natural purposes of human endeavor and the true sources of happiness, then it follows, obviously, that man must never overreach himself in his pursuits. Since the Greeks were remarkably logical and consistent in following through concepts that they had once accepted as valid, they soon established justice and restraint as the chief measures of hu-

[21] See Cornford, p. 51, for a discussion of the quest into the purposes of human life. While Socrates was the first Greek to ask these questions in their ultimate consequence, the direction of the search had been indicated much earlier in Greek history.

[22] See Charles Norris Cochrane, *Christianity and Classical Culture; a Study of Thought and Action from Augustus to Augustine*, Oxford, 1940, p. 74, and Cornford, pp. 59-61.

man thought and action, and conversely, they regarded wanton in-solence or excess (*hubris*) as the greatest social or personal crime of which any Greek could be guilty. In the early period, these precepts for living were counselled over all Greece by priests, through the means of oracles, and by statesmen, through social reforms. But nowhere was their general validity more consistently tested than in fifth century Athens. There these great themes were dramatized by the tragic and comic poets, discussed in political assemblies, and experienced con-stantly in the lives of representative men.

The cultivation of this Hellenic view of life led to the acceptance of democracy as the ideal form of government for the polis, and this rea-soned preference for a particular political protection of generally ac-cepted moral values suggested, necessarily, a definite orientation toward foreign affairs. If all community business was to be an extension of the individual and a reflection of his worth, then, clearly, the com-munity's foreign relations, which are just another aspect of its life, had to be similarly related to man's moral aspirations. The Athenians were obligated morally, by virtue of being logical and just Athenians, to apply identical standards in their conduct of foreign and domestic affairs.

Now all Hellenes were conscious of being in many respects a special breed of men, and the Athenians were particularly proud of being Athenians. Greek thought, however, whether expressed in philosophy, in literature, or in practical politics, never permitted the particular to overshadow the general, or the local to dominate the universal. Since it was generally understood that concepts were true only insofar as they were generally applicable, man and mankind had to remain the fundamental concern of all Greeks. But this orientation to the world around them was a distinct departure from traditional views. It intro-duced the proposition that international relations are human relations, and foreign policies human actions. It followed that decisions in this field, as in all other fields, could be only as good or as bad as the people who made them. We read, therefore, in Plutarch,[23] that because Aris-teides was a just Athenian and Cimon a moderate Athenian, the Greek allies respected the Athenian state and requested Aristeides to lead their combined armies, in preference to the available Spartan generals, whose community had permitted them to become corrupted in the enjoyment of unbalanced power.

[23] *Lives of Illustrious Men*, John Dryden and others, trs., 3 vols., New York, Vol. I, p. 521.

The Greek city-states, particularly Athens, were called upon to test their life orientation in the actual conduct of foreign affairs on the fifth century B.C. international stage set centuries earlier by older Near Eastern states, whose world view had allowed for the primacy of foreign policies without insisting upon their compatibility with a definite value system.[24] Some examples may illustrate this point. As did most other Greeks, the Athenians liked wealth just as much as the Phoenicians, and they acquired it by very similar trading practices. But whereas the Phoenicians seem to have had no particular political ideals and to have considered wealth to be an end in itself, the Athenians of the sixth and fifth centuries continually reminded themselves that it was the ultimate purpose of wealth to protect cities dedicated to the liberty of man.[25] Neither were the Athenians different from the other Mediterranean peoples in liking peace. But here again they associated the enjoyment of a desirable condition with the realization of purposes that were largely incomprehensible to their neighbors. "Peace," to Athens, was a meaningless and rationally indefensible proposition if it did not permit the pursuit and amplification of man's chief aspiration in life: the progress toward liberty. On these grounds the city disavowed its ambassadors, who had been ready to treat with the Persians, preferring war and uncertainty, as payment for freedom, to offers of peace and prosperity, as rewards for submission. In fact, since the issue between Athens, later supported by most of Greece, and Persia was clearly and deliberately joined on ideological, not on racial or economic,[26] grounds, the Persian War can well be considered to have been the first great war fought by an entire nation for the sake of its ideals.[27] That this was a new kind of conflict in human experience seemed already clear to contemporaries, friends and foes alike. For it was not simply pride in the victory of his adopted city, but keen observation of the international scene, which made Herodotus declare that while under the rule of tyrants the Athenians were not a whit more valiant than any of their neighbors, but no sooner free than they became de-

[24] Some aspects of Persian policy indicate a different relationship between principles and policies; see preceding chapter on Persia.

[25] See Thomas G. Williams, *The History of Commerce*, London, 1926, pp. 32ff.

[26] The prospect of economic gain was certainly envisioned, but only as a consequence of freedom.

[27] See also Spengler's suggestion that the Greeks in fighting for ideas were history's Don Quixote, whereas the Romans, who fought, in his opinion, mainly for wealth, are comparable to Sancho Panza, in *Der Untergang des Abendlandes*, München, 1923, 2 vols., Vol. I, p. 48. *The Decline of the West*, C. F. Atkinson, tr., 1 vol. ed., New York, 1932, p. 36.

cidedly the first of all.[28] Next to the gods, he therefore asserts, the Athenians were those who repulsed the invader, in calculated estimation of the worth of liberty.[29]

Thus it was that individually and locally tested ideals had been introduced successfully by Athens into her relations with other states, both Greek and non-Greek. When confronted with a threat of national extinction, the citizens had realized that they could retain their way of life at home only if they were ready to defend it through processes of foreign policy that in a time of emergency had to include war. In other words, the requirement of the Athenians of consistency in their domestic and foreign policies had expressed itself in their defence of their own freedom. As argued and defined in Athens, the concept of "freedom" was not evolved from Greek or Athenian, but from human nature. Nevertheless, while the Athenian actions during the Persian Wars could be regarded by contemporaries as a historical advertisement of the international validity of the Athenian view of life, they did not actually illustrate—and in their very nature could not have illustrated—the Athenians' readiness to apply their original insights into human nature to the treatment of people outside their own community.

For this failure many mitigating circumstances can be cited. Short of embarking on an offensive crusade in behalf of their ideals, it was obviously useless from the Athenians' point of view to approach officially foreign nations, such as Persia, which had shown their disregard or misunderstanding of Greek ideas, with draft covenants or other policy formulations of human rights. In the very nature of the international situation the Athenian view of these issues could register, if it was to register at all, only in the Athenian attitude toward foreigners as persons, rather than as representatives of foreign powers.[30] In the fifth century, the Greek attitudes toward foreigners naturally reflected a consciousness of Greek difference and isolation, fear of foreign aggression, and pride in Greek victory in the Persian Wars. Indeed, it was this understanding of their place in the world, rather than any preconceived notion of racial or cultural superiority, that supplied meaning to the term "barbarian," which Greeks so frequently employed when speaking of non-Greeks.[31] For although the Persians continued

[28] *The History of Herodotus*, M. Komroff, ed., George Rawlinson, tr., New York, 1928, Book v, p. 78. (Referred to hereafter as *Herodotus*.)

[29] *ibid.*, Book VII, 478 and Book VIII.

[30] The Greeks, as most other Near Eastern nations, had a fully developed system of diplomatic immunities.

[31] The connotation that "barbarian" means uncultured or uncouth accrued to the term much later.

for a long time to be their arch enemy, few if any Greeks can actually have believed that a person such as Darius was their "inferior" in character or endowment.[32] It seems clear also that the Greeks did not apply any rigid cultural or psychological measure for the testing of differences. In their relations with foreigners abroad, as in their relations with slaves at home, the lines of separation were forever fluctuating. Perhaps it is this peculiarly Greek trust in movement, when guided by reason, which Sir Henry Maine intended to identify as the "progress" that he found endemic in the Greek nation only.[33]

Existing notions of superiority were offset also by the constant stream of information that reached the ever-curious Greeks from distant lands,[34] and by their growing realization of their indebtedness to foreign, i.e., "barbarian" peoples. But the first group of individuals to question directly the logic of any distinction between Greek and foreigner were the Greek scientists, who were soon convinced by their physiological studies that the physical attributes and natural endowments of all people must be presumed to be the same.[35]

To insights gained from experience, necessity joined others. All the Greek states were dependent on each other and on foreign areas for their livelihood; Greek merchants could be found everywhere on the shores of the Mediterranean and the Black Seas, and foreign traders were welcome in Greek markets. As a result of this swiftly expanding commerce, the legal position of the alien, to take only one aspect of the problem, was greatly changed. Many legal disabilities of the alien resident in Greek towns disappeared as general international inter-

---

[32] See also Radin, p. 51.

[33] In speaking about "that bundle of influence which we call progress," Sir Henry Maine points to the Greeks as the only society in which progress was endemic. To this small people, he said, it was given to create the principle of progress. The other so-called progressive nations could not have brought forth any of their intellectual excellencies, had they been left to themselves in isolation. (*Village Communities in the East and West*, New York, 1880, p. 238.) See Coleman Phillipson, *The International Law and Custom of Ancient Greece and Rome*, 2 vols., London, 1911, Vol. I, chs. v to VIII, on Greece and foreigners.

[34] See the anthropological accounts in the writings of Herodotus, and the long descriptions of foreign geography in Aeschylus' tragedies, notably *The Suppliants*.

[35] Hippocrates was perhaps the first to raise the issue. He explains in his treatise on *airs, waters, places* that the physician should pay full attention to the climate of each locality, and to the variations of that climate caused by changeable seasons, by different exposures, by the nature of the available water and food, and so on. The second part of the book (chs. 12-24) deals with the effect of climate upon character, and is a kind of anthropological discussion of history. What is the difference between Europe and Asia, or between the Hellenes and the barbarians? Hippocrates ascribes those differences chiefly to physical (geographic) causes. So did his contemporary Herodotus, who put that teaching in the mouth of Cyrus, the king of Persia, and thus gave to his *History* the most significant ending. See Sarton, p. 369. See also E. Barker, *Greek Political Theory*, London, 1918, pp. 69ff.

course increased, and with it litigation. The alien suitor no longer had to plead through the agency of the proxenus (a sort of consul), but was allowed, in actual practice and despite strict theory to the contrary, to appear before the court in person or to instruct advocates to plead for him.[36]

Certain international traditions in confirmation and support of a transcendent human sympathy also proved stronger than national pride. The Greeks shared with many other literate and nonliterate folk, for example, such institutions as guest friendship and asylum. The right of asylum had first been systematically developed by the Egyptians, Assyrians, and Israelites.[37] The Greeks, however, knew how to elaborate upon the ideas in a special way, if only because they had so many highly literate and persuasive recorders. The epic adventures of the disguised beggar Odysseus, who was honored by his host with the best of food, and the tragedy of the fugitive Orestes, who sought and found asylum, forever reminded the Greeks that the validity of their most cherished moral convictions in the last resort hinged on the treatment accorded the nameless stranger. The suppliant, the fugitive, or the guest, whether known or unknown, noble or humble, was morally entitled to rely upon his host as his chief defender, banker, and provider. Thus understood, guest-friendship became an intercultural institution of great importance, facilitating trade and promoting the diffusion of goods and ideas.[38] All could consult the Oracle at Delphi.[39] All could attend the Olympic Games.[40] And all could profit, consequently, from the convenience of the neutralized roads and truces of God that were proclaimed and maintained for the duration of the festivals.[41]

In view of these customs and institutions, it is not surprising that the Greeks should have shown little hesitancy in "admitting" Lydians and Macedonians to Hellenism, or inviting Egypt to participate in a peace congress; that factions in Greek cities frequently called upon foreign nations for help against their own countrymen; and that

[36] Phillipson, Vol. I, pp. 208ff.

[37] See *ibid.*, pp. 349-354. Sometimes a number of states agreed to regard certain temples and indeed entire towns as enjoying a permanent privilege of affording protection to fugitives. Teos, for instance, was recognized by 25 states as such an asylum. Rome adhered to this convention in 193 B.C. and exempted Teos from tribute.

[38] Walter Miller, *Greece and the Greeks*, New York, 1941, p. 202.

[39] The Lydians and Persians had frequent recourse to oracles; see *Herodotus*, Book I, 1-10, for illustrations.

[40] Actual participation in the contests was limited to Hellenes.

[41] See Phillipson, Vol. II, pp. 284ff.

Athens had no scruples in supporting Egypt in her rebellion against Persia. When reason indicated that continued enmity with Persia was ruinous, Athens was ready to revert to a policy of peace and commerce, and under the terms of a treaty signed in 448 B.C. the two arch enemies became friends. The Greek waters were fixed as extending from the Bosporus entrance of the Black Sea to the Chelidonian Islands, off the coast of Lycia, and no Persian ships ventured into this area, which was considered to be a Greek sphere of influence. For a period relations were amiable and undisturbed, the nationals of the two countries spoke each other's language, and Athenian missions to Susa became so frequent as almost to assume the character of a standing legation.[42] Before the outbreak of the Peloponnesian War, therefore, experience, knowledge, necessity, tradition, and sympathy had pointed to a cosmopolitan orientation in relations with foreigners. This orientation was shaped into a positive policy by Pericles. Athens, he advised, should mix freely with mankind.[43]

C. HELLENIC UNITY

1. Retention of the city-state as an independent unit. In explaining to the Spartan envoys why they would not dream of making a deal with the Persians, the Athenians called attention to the common temples, language, and character, as specific rallying points of Hellenic unity, which demanded a joint defence of Greek culture everywhere.[44] And indeed, historical records confirm the belief that the Greeks, however divided politically, were so acutely aware of the many ties that linked them that they were always ready to fraternize in matters of social, religious, recreational, intellectual, and aesthetic concern. The Greeks in all parts of the Near Eastern world derived inspiration from shared literary forms, such as the drama, and from shared religious institutions, such as the mysteries and oracles. Also, in the realm of politics they agreed essentially that peace was the ideal condition of human existence, and the city-state the political institution most suited for the Greek way of life.

During the course of their common history the Greeks found the means to implement most of their shared values. The only goal that eluded concerted realization was peace, and the chief reason for this failure seems to have been the very success of the city-state. Since the

---

[42] Sir Alfred E. Zimmern, *The Greek Commonwealth*, Oxford, 1931, p. 371.
[43] *Thucydides*, Book II, ch. 38.
[44] *Herodotus*, Book VIII, p. 144.

generally accepted function of the polis was to secure a good life for the people in terms of individual development, and since the realization of this aim was deemed to be possible only if a city did not exceed a certain size, peace through political unification was actually inconsistent with the primary purpose of political association as understood by the Greeks. Moreover, the division into numerous small states meant, of course, that the periphery of each was exceedingly long in relation to its area,[45] and it is this situation more than any other that explains the prevalence of war in ancient Greece. Except in the period of the later Athenian Empire, the Greeks did not engage in expeditions for the deliberate conquest of other nations, but they did engage incessantly, as Thucydides has shown, in local border quarrels. And for the sake of the record it must also be stated that this inter-Greek warfare was characterized by practically unlimited ruthlessness[46]—despite a constant flow of reminders and admonitions that such practices were hardly compatible with the ideals otherwise professed.[47]

A realistic appraisal of the contemporary political scene convinced most Greeks that any hope for permanent peace between so many independent states was at best wishful thinking. This led them, however, to develop three limited approaches to the problem of peace and security. They tried to mitigate the destructiveness of war once it had broken out;[48] to prevent the outbreak of general wars by maintaining a balance of power between states (an approach that led to the conclusion of alliances, leagues, and confederations); and to settle disputes peacefully wherever possible (which led to the development of arbitration). The chief process for the attainment of all three of these objectives was diplomacy, and the chief instrument for registering agreement on any one of them, the treaty. Now there was, of course, nothing original about any of these devices; all had been employed before, and sometimes very successfully. But their use by the Greeks is interesting because it tested the international validity of two ideals that they took very seriously—equality and justice.

[45] Elias J. Bickerman, "The Greek Experience of War and Peace," in *Approaches to World Peace*, Lyman Bryson, ed., New York, 1944, p. 209.

[46] See M. Rostovtzeff, *The Social and Economic History of the Hellenistic World*, Oxford, 1941, Vol. I, p. 192; Phillipson, Vol. II, pp. 166ff.; Fustel de Coulanges, *La Cité Antique*, 1888, p. 244.

[47] See Aristophanes, *The Knights, Lysistrata*, and other plays; Euripides, *The Trojan Women*; and numerous comments in Thucydides.

[48] See Phillipson, Vol. II, pp. 210-273; Euripides, *Heracleidae*, where the poet contrasts Athenian humaneness toward captives with "barbarian" inhumaneness.

However unequal the actual distribution of power might be in a given case, the Greeks recognized but one form of treaty, that of an equal treaty between free and independent states. Usually such a treaty was concluded in order to regulate postwar conditions and to prevent aggression. The essence of the Greek treaty, therefore, might be said to have been a narrow-minded but precise definition of aggression, understood as a direct attack on national territory.[49] However, since this aggression clause was always part of a general settlement, it was binding only as long as the general settlement remained binding. Nonaggression, that is, was thought of as a temporary obligation. Consequently, along with all the other relationships between the states, it remained subject to the dictates of the balance of power.

The chief purpose of such a treaty was ostensibly negative and limited, yet it did not exclude more positive and far-reaching agreements. An alliance concluded for 100 years between Athens and the Argive Confederacy (420 B.C.), for example, involved so many parties and imposed so many obligations that it actually established an intricate system of collective security, rather than a temporary peace between two sovereignties. Whether concluded in anticipation or in settlement of war, most of the treaties, furthermore, expressed the Greek sympathy for the individual in clauses that provided for the decent treatment of prisoners, spies, hostages, and shipwrecked people; for the burial of the dead; for the protection of temples and other sacred sites, and the like. In the fourth century, when war and conquest had revealed the bankruptcy of the traditional Greek security system, Athens and Thessaly combined broad nonmilitary agreements with the customary military pact by concluding a perpetual alliance that permitted their respective citizens to intermarry, to hold property in both jurisdictions, and to participate reciprocally in religious ceremonies and other festivals. This agreement also regulated free trade, common access to sacred places and public games, and the fair treatment of heralds, envoys, and priests. Furthermore, the intensification of commercial and cultural contacts throughout the Greek world led to an interesting diplomatic elaboration of the recognized moral obligations of hospitality.[50] Treaties of public hospitality officially protected the in-

---

[49] Bickerman, pp. 204-209. This doctrine made pacts of nonaggression compatible with defensive alliances and with limited assistance to victims of attack. See also M. I. Rostovtzeff, "International Relations in the Ancient World," in *The History and Nature of International Relations*, E. A. Walsh, ed., New York, 1922, pp. 47-48.

[50] See Phillipson, Vol. I, pp. 221, 318, 382; M. Charles Calvo, *Le Droit International Théorique et Pratique*, 4 vols., Paris, 1880, Vol. I, p. 621, to the effect that the treaty first made its appearance in Greece in connection with the institution of hospitality.

terests of trading or sojourning foreigners, and attained their most developed diplomatic form in the institution of isopolity, which permitted citizens of the contracting states to intermarry and to hold property rights within both domains.[51]

Since none of these treaties—whether concluded in the pursuit of military or of civilian interests—encroached upon the political identity of the pacting states by creating new supranational authorities for the coordination of mutual rights and obligations, the principle of equality was never officially questioned in these instances. The case was somewhat different in the treaties establishing leagues and federations among states. The Greeks made many such attempts and experimented with a great variety of representative forms of government in interstate relations.[52] But most of these ventures were found wanting in the final analysis, either because they held fast to the principle of equality without regard to the actual distribution of power, or because they reflected the distribution of power without adequately safeguarding the rights of the weak against abuses on the part of the strong. This predicament is best illustrated by the Peloponnesian Confederation and the Delian League, two unions that had issued from permanent alliances or symmachies between theoretically autonomous states but that became, in time, instruments for the exercise of hegemony by the strongest member.

The Peloponnesian Confederation reflected both in its inception and in its organization the influence of earlier Mediterranean patterns of government. Brought about by Spartan conquest and influence, it included all the cities of the Peloponnesus, except Argolis and much of Achaea. Each member state, regardless of size, population, or strength, had one vote in the League assembly. Binding decisions were made through majority vote, but Sparta retained the exclusive privilege of introducing motions. This meant, on the one hand, that Sparta could not be forced into any action that she did not desire, and on the other, that she could not force the member states to any action of which the majority disapproved. Warfare was not excluded from relations between federated cities. It was prohibited only when the entire League was engaged in fighting a common enemy. If one of the member na-

[51] See Phillipson, Vol. I, p. 148; Rostovtzeff in Walsh, ed., p. 53; Calvo, Vol. I, p. 497 on the Greek institution of *proxenia* as the prototype of the modern consular system.

[52] For a review of this aspect of Greek history see *The Cambridge Ancient History*, Cambridge, England, 1923-1939, Vol. VII, pp. 732ff.; J. A. O. Larsen, *Representative Government in Greek and Roman History*, Berkeley, 1955.

tions attacked another in such an emergency, Sparta was empowered to punish the disturber by applying military sanctions. The combined forces of the League were commanded, furthermore, by Spartan generals.

The aim of the Delian League, which Athens organized as an offensive and defensive alliance against Persia in 478 B.C., was deliverance from Persia and protection from future aggression. Nothing was said about a possible withdrawal from the alliance once these objectives were attained. Each member state was separately bound by treaty to Athens, and the chief officers of the League—the presidents of the synods, the commanders of the fleet, and later the fiscal agents— were all Athenians. In spite of their recognition of Athenian preponderance, however, the individual communities were presumed to be equally free. They relied upon their equal representation in the synod and upon the Athenian promise, apparently not otherwise secured, that the big city would not tamper with the constitutions of the individual communities. In return for this assurance, and for the military protection they received, the members of the Delian League were to make annual payments either in money or in ships.[53] In the course of time this League became the Athenian empire.

On the whole it can perhaps be said that the Greeks did not succeed in finding a working relationship between the principles of equality and security as long as they professed to retain the political system of multiple independent states. They were much more successful in the conduct of international relations, on the other hand, when they attempted to relate national insistence on equality to national expectations of justice. This is indicated by their impressive record of interstate arbitrations, which stands comparison only with that of nineteenth century Europe and America.

The obvious explanation for the popularity among the Greeks of this method of settling conflicts was the intensity of the general contacts between the states, the frequency of these conflicts, and a natural reluctance to make each dispute a test of military strength. Another explanation, less obvious though no less important, is to be found in the general Greek interest in the idea of justice.

Greek arbitrations are reported regularly from the seventh century B.C. onward, and we have more or less complete evidence concerning eighty-one of the cases. Many of the older Near Eastern societies had

---

[53] G. W. Botsford and C. A. Robinson, Jr., *Hellenic History*, New York, 1946, pp. 119-121. See also Larsen, p. 53.

been familiar with the idea of arbitration. But it was these Greek arbitrations, as reported from the seventh century B.C., that set the basic pattern for the institution as we know it today. The more or less complete evidence of the eighty-one different transactions[54] indicates that this method of settling disputes was resorted to by states and leagues of all sizes. Among the cities, Athens seems to have done the most toward developing the institution by her willingness to submit cases, to persuade others to do likewise, and to act as arbitrator herself. Sparta was, on the whole, more reluctant to bind her freedom of action in this way; nevertheless, she too was respectful of the process. During the Peloponnesian War Spartan statesmen felt, for instance, that it was decidedly against the law to attack Athens since the Athenians had offered to arbitrate the conflict.[55] Many states, as they gained experience and observed the success of this international device, showed themselves ready to forego the customary attributes of independence by binding themselves to submit to arbitration all disputes that might arise out of the failure of either party to observe the terms of a treaty or confederate constitution. The issues that were thus lifted out of the sphere of military action were by no means negligible. The record shows a dispute between Athens and Mytilene over Sigeion, which amounted in effect to a contest for preponderant influence on the Hellespont; a dispute between Athens and Megara for possession of a strategically located island; and a dispute between Athens and Delos concerning the right to administer the sanctuary of Apollo, which gravely concerned the interests of both parties.[56]

The execution of arbitration agreements followed no rigid pattern. The arbitrators, for instance, were chosen in a variety of ways. Appeal was normally made to a disinterested Greek city; and that city, again, would often delegate its function to its local court. In some instances citizens from several states were called together as a body; in others, all the people of a particular town. The motives that determined these selections of arbitrators cannot be clearly ascertained. Writing about certain later cases, Polybius states that the Thebans and Lacedaemonians referred a dispute to the arbitration of the Achaeans, and to them alone among the Greeks, in consideration not of their power, for at that time they ranked almost lowest, but rather of their good faith

---

[54] J. H. Ralston, *International Arbitration from Athens to Locarno*, Stanford, 1929, p. 154. See also A. H. Raeder, *L'Arbitrage International chez les Hellènes*, New York, 1912, pp. 243ff.

[55] M. Niebuhr Tod, *International Arbitration amongst the Greeks*, Oxford, 1913, p. 177.

[56] See Raeder, pp. 247ff.

and moral excellence.[57] And there are many other references of this kind to moral standards as the chief prerequisites for the assignment of any judging functions. Without neglecting the power factor, which must have affected both the preparation and the execution of all arbitral agreements, the Greeks seem to have taken it generally for granted that the qualities usually associated with the "just" man ought also to be present in the arbitrator of international affairs. It was long remembered that Aristeides was so just in assessing taxes and contributions within the Delian League that none of his assessments was ever questioned by the member states.

The choice of arbitrators, no less than the general preference for arbitration, was determined by the particular expectations that the Greeks associated with this method of adjusting international relations. According to the available evidence, they looked, above all, for the re-establishment of friendship between the feuding states, not for a technically satisfactory liquidation of the official dispute. Since arbitration was thus in essence conciliation, their arbitrators were expected to think in terms of equity rather than of international law.[58] This view of their aim explains why the Greek arbitrators were given wide discretion in the interpretation of their functions. "Equity" and "discretion" are essentially moral terms. They imply the necessity of making moral decisions. Morally acceptable decisions can be made, however, only by morally respectable men. Therefore, since the Greeks were, on the whole, in agreement as to what constitutes a moral man, their ultimate reliance on human qualities, rather than on technical agreements, was, in the nature of the situation, their best practical approach to international disputes. And that this reliance was justified is indicated by the fact that refusal to accept an award when given was a rare occurrence.[59]

Now the political principles on which the much more extensive and complex modern Western world rested in the nineteenth century A.D. were very similar to those that informed the small Greek society of states in the sixth and fifth centuries B.C. They issued from certain broad moral agreements, included respect for multiple sovereignties and concern for a balance of power, and led to a frequent use of arbitration as the determinant of international conflict. But while the official record of these two societies is similar with regard to the peaceful settlement of their international disputes, the meanings and purposes

---

[57] See discussion in Tod, p. 86.

[58] It must also be remembered that the Greek world knew no codified international law in the modern Western sense of the term. See also Tod, pp. 123-130, 174.

[59] *ibid.*, p. 165.

ascribed by the two to arbitration would seem to be different. Beginning with ancient Rome, the Western nations have consistently engaged in the great quest for law as the measure of personal and governmental conduct. By the nineteenth century A.D., the results of this quest had greatly improved the lot of man in many parts of the world. By then, however, the Europeans were so richly blessed and burdened with their heritage of legal philosophy, jurisprudence, codes, constitutions, and treaties, that in many situations they were unable to recognize the fundamental purpose in behalf of which they had mustered so much of their talent and energy.

In the field of international relations, the basic goal of reaching an understanding through a conciliation of differences was frequently all but occluded by an overgrowth of legal definitions and technicalities. Modern international arbitration,[60] when compared with Greek arbitration, assumes the character of litigation. The arbitrators are usually instructed to concern themselves exclusively with the issue that is the immediate occasion for the dispute, rather than with the general set of relationships in the context of which the dispute originally arose. The West has tried to counteract this trend toward excessive legalism by distinguishing carefully between arbitration on the one hand, and more flexible devices, such as mediation and conciliation, on the other.[61] But its efforts cannot, in and by themselves, emancipate the concept and the cause of conciliation from the many ingenious processes that have been developed in its service through centuries of legal history.

Of this Western tendency to look, first of all, for legal remedies the Asians are well aware, since it contrasts with their own antipathy to the settling of disputes by recourse to laws and processes of litigation. To a Chinese scholar, Western justice means "justice in respect to the particular suit litigated upon. It is not justice reached after a consideration of all the past relationship between the litigating parties."[62] It

---

[60] As distinguished from labor arbitration where this development is not noticeable.

[61] See, for instance, Charter of the United Nations, ch. VI.

[62] Liu Shih-Fang, "Westernized Administration of Justice and Chinese Racial Characteristics," Alfred Wang, tr., pp. 1f., cited in F. S. C. Northrop, *The Taming of the Nations*, p. 124. Northrop finds similar criticisms of Western legal concepts in India. He concludes that Gandhi's non-Aryan Hinduism, Buddhism, and Confucianism regard laws and codes as the immoral way to settle disputes and something to be used only as a last resort (p. 142). Preference there is for mediation and for taking the middle way between the determinate theses of the disputants (pp. 56ff.).

See also Jean Escarra, *Le Droit Chinois*, Peiping, 1936, pp. 3, 17, 359ff. and Joseph Needham, *Science and Civilization in China*, 3 vols., Cambridge, England, 1954-59, Vol. II, pp. 519ff., 578ff., for comparisons between the Chinese and Western conceptions of law.

would seem, indeed, that many contemporary Asian societies are closer to ancient Greece in their general attitude toward the settling of international disputes than are most of the modern Western societies.[63] In other words, a study of international arbitration in the land that the West customarily regards as its own cradle, underlines the general conclusion indicated by a reading of Greek history: that Greek ways of life, far from being the great divide between East and West, are a meeting ground for modern men of all societies.

2. *Panhellenism—Voluntary and Enforced.* After referring to the links that made the Greeks a nation, Herodotus adds: "When we have finished with these barbarians [the Persians], let us form a common state."[64] Most of the Greeks were too realistic not to see that the system of the balance of power was sapping their collective energies and undermining their position in relation to the non-Greek world, in addition to being at variance with the spirit of fraternity that pervaded their nonpolitical relations with each other. However, plans for the political unification of all the states into one Panhellenic commonwealth presented great ideological and practical difficulties, largely because the state was, in the Greek view, not just a political convenience but the supreme expression of the concept of fellowship.

These difficulties did not deter the Greeks, however, from experimenting with the idea of unity. In their efforts to transcend the narrow framework of the polis they were most successful when the theme of unity suggested itself as an organic evolution from the reality of fellowship. This was the case, for instance, in the numerous Panhellenic councils that were formed from the eighth century onward (or perhaps even much earlier) for the administration of common religious concerns. In the most famous of these councils, the Delphic Amphictyony, twelve tribes agreed jointly to preserve and defend the Delphic territory with all its temples and shrines. And in the dispatch of this business, Athens, Sparta, and Thebes had no more influence than the

[63] C. J. N. Frank, *Courts on Trial; Myth and Reality in American Justice*, Princeton, 1949, pp. 378ff., to the effect that ancient Greek law, as opposed to ancient Roman, shared to a considerable extent the characteristic Indian and Chinese preference for equity and arbitration.

See also Sir Henry Maine, *Ancient Law*, 3rd American ed., New York, 1879, pp. 72ff. and John Henry Wigmore, *A Panorama of the World's Legal Systems*, (Library ed.), Washington, 1936, pp. 283-367 for analyses of the Greek approach to law; see especially pp. 324, 358, to the effect that emphasis in Greece was less on the strict rules of law than on the general justice of the case. Consult also Sir Paul Vinogradoff, *Outlines of Historical Jurisprudence*, Vol. II: *The Jurisprudence of the Greek City*, Oxford, 1922, and George M. Calhoun, *Introduction to Greek Legal Science*, Oxford, 1944.

[64] *Herodotus*, Book VIII, p. 144.

humblest Bœotian or Ionian city, since each constituent tribe was entitled to send two delegates to the council's assembly, where all deliberated and voted on the basis of strict equality. The amphictyonies had no official political jurisdiction, but since they were authorized to supervise the due execution of religious obligations, to wage sacred war on offenders, and to settle disputes, they were frequently successful in preventing the outbreak of general war. The member states were bound, however, by oath to refrain from destroying each other's cities and from interfering with each other's water supplies.[65]

Unification was also successfully stimulated after the Persian Wars, when many Greek states, in genuine admiration of certain Athenian institutions, agreed voluntarily to accept Athenian laws, courts, and currency in preference to their own less perfect arrangements of this kind. Here it was the strong appreciation of "excellence" as a measure of achievement, in which all Greeks shared, which proved stronger than the usual tender regard for particular local traditions. For as a result of her brilliant stewardship in the Hellenic defence against Persia, Athens was indeed recognized as an educator for all of Greece, and it was therefore not resented that she governed all the cities by the same laws. For the same reason Athens also assumed the chief responsibility for the organization of a military alliance of all the Aegean states, for clearing the adjoining seas of pirates, and for reviving Greek trade connections with the non-Greek world. While she was successful in rendering these services, she was ultimately unsuccessful in convincing the other states that her policies would further unification through compliance with accepted standards of excellence, or through a confirmation of the existing patterns of inter-Greek fraternity.

The Athenians spearheaded one interesting move which elicited widespread cooperation perhaps because it represented Athenian ideals at their best. They suggested the creation of an entirely new state at Thurii, dedicated to both liberty and Panhellenism. It was hoped that a new settlement, favorably situated at the crossroads of many trade lines, would not only become prosperous but contribute to the commerce of the cities in Greece. To the Athenians, a Panhellenic state

[65] See "Amphictyony" in *Encyclopaedia Britannica*, 1944, Vol. I; A. C. F. Beales, *The History of Peace*, New York, 1931, pp. 20ff.; Phillipson, Vol. II, pp. 3-12; Fustel de Coulanges, pp. 248-251, to the effect that none of the amphictyonies had any political jurisdiction worth mentioning; F. M. Stawell, *The Growth of International Thought*, New York, 1930, p. 22, to the effect that the Amphictyony can be regarded as the first "Council of Europe." See also E. A. Freeman, *History of Federal Government in Greece and Italy*, London, New York, 1893.

of this kind appeared as a living embodiment of the Athenian ideals of liberty and free intercourse, and they therefore invited all of Greece to participate in the great founding venture. Colonists streamed from everywhere. Poets and historians took a kindly interest. Protagoras, the Sophist, worked on Thurii's constitution. Yet within less than two years of its creation, the state's Panhellenic population had divided into the traditional forms of Hellenic tribal sectionalism.[66]

Like most Greeks, the Athenians were genuinely concerned with the limitation of intercity strife. Between 460-450 B.C. Pericles therefore propounded a plan for uniting all the Greek states on the continent, in Asia Minor, in Thrace, in Macedonia, and on the islands in one great league for the limited purpose of peacefully settling Greek disputes. To plan this union he sent to all the Greek settlements Athenian representatives, inviting them to a Panhellenic congress in Athens. But in his further planning he seems to have exceeded the originally limited purpose of the meeting by adding to the agenda projects for beautifying Athens, rebuilding Greek shrines, developing Greek shipping, and so forth. The representatives never assembled, and we know nothing more about the project,[67] except that some of the plans were subsequently carried out under the rather different auspices of the Athenian Empire. By that time Athens had ceased to cajole and had begun to dominate her weaker allies in the Delian League. The League's treasury had been transferred from Delos to Athens, and the member states were being forced to pay tribute, rather than persuaded to make contributions. When claims to excellence were dropped and references to power became frequent, all the Greeks realized that the noble, long sustained Athenian effort to project local liberties into Panhellenic strength had failed. This was officially confirmed by the events of the Peloponnesian War.

After the second Peloponnesian invasion in 430 B.C., the Athenian citizens were reminded: ". . . And do not imagine that you are fighting about a simple issue, freedom or slavery; you have an empire to lose, and there is the danger to which the hatred of your imperial rule has exposed you. Neither can you resign your power, if, at this crisis, any timorous or inactive spirit is for thus playing the honest man. For by this time your empire has become a tyranny which in the opinion of mankind may have been unjustly gained, but which cannot be safely surrendered."[68]

[66] Zimmern, p. 374.
[67] Plutarch, Vol. I, pp. 252ff.
[68] *Thucydides*, Book II, ch. 63; see also Book III, ch. 37.

When Athens decided, in 416 B.C., that the subjugation of Melos, a Spartan colony, was indicated by the necessities of the military situation, her own representatives realized to what extent their values had been perverted in the transaction of foreign affairs. "Well, then," we read, "we Athenians will use no fine words; we will not go out of our way to prove at length that we have a right to rule because we overthrew the Persians; or that we attack you now because we are suffering any injury at your hands. . . . But you and we should say what we really think, and aim only at what is possible; for we both alike know that into the discussion of human affairs the question of justice enters only where the pressure of necessity is equal, and that the powerful exact what they can, and the weak grant what they must."

The Athenians also heard the Melian reply: "Your interest in this principle [of justice] is quite as great as ours, inasmuch as you, if you fall, will incur the heaviest vengeance, and will be the most terrible example to mankind."[69]

Moral values, as defined and tested in the smallest community of men, the Greek polis, had, in the natural course of Athenian logic and consistency, been introduced into the conduct of foreign relations; but they had been found wanting in the larger context. In following the tragic course of this war, Thucydides observes, with his usual detachment and precision, that the whole Hellenic world was in commotion, and that war and revolution had brought upon the cities of Hellas terrible calamities, "such as have been and always will be while human nature remains the same." In peace and prosperity, he explains, both states and individuals are actuated by higher motives, because they do not fall under the dominion of imperious necessities; but war, which takes away the comfortable provision of daily life, is a hard master, and tends to assimilate men's character to their conditions. In such times "the meaning of words had no longer the same relation to things, but was changed by them as they thought proper. Reckless daring was held to be loyal courage; prudent delay was the excuse of a coward; moderation was the disguise of unmanly weakness; to know everything was to do nothing; frantic energy was the true quality of a man. A conspirator who wanted to be safe was a recreant in disguise. The lover of violence was always trusted, and his opponent suspected. He who succeeded in a plot was deemed knowing, but a still greater master in craft was he who detected one. . . . The cause of all these evils was the love of power."[70]

[69] *Thucydides*, Book v, chs. 89-90.   [70] *Thucydides*, Book iii, ch. 82-84.

Thucydides has handed to posterity the record of Athenian *hubris* in the conduct of foreign relations, as he saw it. And while he may have edited many of the speeches and debates that fill his "history," there is no reason to doubt, on the strength of all the evidence available, that most of his contemporaries were well aware of the course and causes of their moral and political calamity. Next to the events themselves that marked the ultimate miscarriage of Athenian attempts to relate their ideology to foreign relations, nothing is quite as fascinating about the Athenian story as the moral courage with which men "knew themselves" even in their total failure. Here are no attempts to excuse human action as destiny, as the will of providence, or as the fulfillment of Enlil's mandate.[71] Disaster is not blamed on fifth columns boring from within, or on international conspiracies guided from abroad. On the contrary, the Athenians appear to have consistently assumed that men are neither bystanders nor victims, but the makers of history, who must therefore accept the material, as well as the moral, consequences of all their actions. This explains the brutal frankness with which a perpetrator of "crimes against humanity," such as Cleon,[72] voluntarily identified his policies as deliberate violations of the accepted moral standards. The Athenians had no need to fear an international criminal court that might one day sit in judgment over their excesses; their own logic drove them to a constant practice of moral self-censorship. Indeed, one gets the impression from reading the contemporary comments as they appear in satire, philosophy, biography, and public debate, that the Athenians were more interested in preserving the integrity of their ideals by admitting that they had failed to live up to them, than in saving their egos by compromising on these ideals. While this Athenian awareness may have given small comfort to the living who authored this particular chapter in the world's history of international relations, it remains, in the greater perspective of some six thousand odd years of recorded human experience, an ironical triumph of idealism as directed by reason.

[71] See *supra*, ch. 1, "Mesopotamia."

[72] He planned the wholesale extermination of the Lesbian population but was restrained by the Athenian assembly.

CHAPTER 3

THE EMPIRE OF ALEXANDER THE GREAT
AND THE HELLENISTIC SYSTEM

A. Alexander the Great and the Outline
of a World State

A. THE SCOPE OF THE EMPIRE

WHEN Philip of Macedon defeated the Greek forces at Chaeronea in 338 B.C., a new dynamic power was set in motion. In the course of ten years under the leadership of Philip's son, Alexander, this power shaped an empire that included Greece, with all her leagues and cities; Persia, with her satellites and far eastern provinces; Phoenicia; Egypt; northwestern Afghanistan, Bactria, Sogdiana; and, in northern India, Punjab and Sind. The frontiers of this great state had not been determined in advance. They expanded and contracted with Alexander's shifting visions and fortunes. Since the young general was in the habit of keeping his plans largely to himself, contemporary records do not document adequately the emergence of his design. We know that he intended to conquer the civilized world, and that, like everyone else at that time, he identified the "civilized world" with the Persian Empire. But his image of the world and civilization changed as he advanced into Asia. When he reached India, he dimly perceived the existence of Farther India, China, and Siberia, and he made new plans for a voyage around Africa with Western Europe as its ultimate destination.[1] But the drafting of his projects was seriously hampered both by the abysmal ignorance of geography that had, by that time, descended upon Europeans and Asians[2] and by his own growing realization that the world was bigger and civilization more multifarious than he had supposed. His vision was further impaired by the painful discovery that the men on whom he had to rely for the execution of his dreams could often be unwilling to commit themselves to limitless uncertainty. Even when he was guided by knowledge and followed by men, he found that bounds were set to his ambition by the resistance of the peoples he

[1] C. A. Robinson, *Alexander the Great; the Meeting of East and West in World Government and Brotherhood*, New York, 1947, p. 194.

[2] Herodotus was no longer read. India was less well known to Greece in the fourth century B.C. than it had been a century earlier. See Robinson, p. 169.

meant to conquer. For instance, he was unable to reduce the Arabs to vassalage. In the end death, man's ultimate weakness, cancelled his further aspirations. The most famous man ever born[3] died in Babylon, in 323 B.C., at the age of 33.

The vast European, African, and Asian areas that Alexander's brief appearance had for a moment joined soon resumed their separate existences. Nevertheless, the imperial dream continued its hold on the remembrance and imagination of Western and Eastern peoples alike.[4] Often, where the Alexander of reality failed to conquer, the Alexander of romance took over. Peoples in Central Asia worship him as Iksander, the founder of cities, and many of their kings and rajas claim descent from him.[5] The Persian poet Firdausi introduced him to his countrymen as a half-brother to the Great Darius; Muslims deified him as Dulcarnain, the Lord of the Two Horns; the Jews regarded him as a propagandist of the Most High; and Christians used him as a model for the portrayal of Jesus. The nonliterate peoples of Europe and Asia tell romantic tales of him in many tongues, and the literate have incorporated his records in both profane and sacred literature. Rendered in twenty-four Western and Oriental languages,[6] the legend of Alexander has inspired posterity, since the day of his death.

B. THE ADMINISTRATIVE DESIGN OF THE EMPIRE

Alexander's Empire was built through conquest. His military campaigns were masterfully planned, and his battles are counted among the greatest ever fought. He won them all with a relatively small, but superbly equipped, army,[7] generally in encounters with numerically superior, highly disciplined forces. The victories, however, created an international situation that confronted him with two main problems. First, he had to find a general administrative scheme for his empire;

[3] Sir Percy Sykes, *A History of Persia*, London, 1921, Vol. I, p. 239. See also p. 282.

[4] Alexander's historian, Arrian, wrote: "For my own part, I think there was at that time no race of men, no city, nor even a single individual to whom Alexander's name and fame had not penetrated. For this reason it seems to me that a hero totally unlike any other human being could not have been born without the agency of the deity." (Quoted in Sykes, p. 283.) See also Arrian, *The Life of Alexander the Great*, Aubrey de Sélincourt, tr., Penguin, 1958, p. 256.

[5] Marco Polo found on his travels that the King of Badakshan boasted this ancestry and Sir Percy Sykes, travelling five hundred years later across the stupendous ranges of the Himalayas to Gilgit, heard a petty raja in the isolated valley state of Hunza announce similar claims. (*A History of Persia*, p. 239.)

[6] W. O. Botsford and Robinson, *Hellenic History*, N.Y., 1946, p. 253.

[7] The army that invaded Asia in 334 B.C. is supposed to have included 30,000 infantry and 5,000 cavalry. Its equipment dazzled contemporaries. See Robinson, p. 73.

second, he had to give the new world that he had created some kind of unity. Both tasks required a clarification of his own position in the world state.

Alexander's solution to the first of the two problems was not original. It recapitulated the wisdom of Darius in its understanding of the world's cultural diversity and respect for national differences. The official position that the young conqueror assumed in relation to his many new subjects varied in accordance with local needs and expectations. He was the King of Macedonia, commander-in-chief of the Corinthian League, ally of a number of Greek cities, the Great King of Persia, Pharaoh of Egypt, son-in-law of defeated kings, and the adopted son of Queen Ada of Caria. Following his decisive battle against Darius he was proclaimed King of Asia.

Being a master propagandist, he was able to gauge and influence people's morale. He pleased Babylon by sacrificing to Marduk and ordering the inhabitants to rebuild the temples that Xerxes had destroyed. Realizing that the military defence of Egypt's frontier would tax his available manpower too heavily, he subsidized local priests in Libyan border areas for the purpose of keeping the inhabitants pacified. He promoted domestic revolutions in behalf of democratic government in the Greek cities in Asia over which the Persians had set tyrants, and then, rather than permit the inclusion of these cities in the Greek League, proceeded to bind them to himself by treaty as free and independent allies. In what had been the Persian Empire he continued the Persian system of satrapies, but he used all manner of men —Macedonians, Greeks, and natives—as the satraps. And when he realized the size and complexity of India, he abandoned the system of satrapies in the Punjab in favor of a less centralized and more flexible association of allied powers, with himself as the dominant member. In fact, in King Poros of India Alexander recognized such greatness and dignity that he bade the Macedonian chiefs and Iranian princes regard Poros as their peer,[8] permitting him to govern his own kingdom as satrap under imperial overlordship.

C. THE VISION OF UNITY

Alexander's administrative patterns can be regarded only superficially as variations of principles earlier evolved by the Persians. On closer view they are seen to be different. They were new forms of international organization, inasmuch as their inception, as well as their

---

[8] *The Cambridge History of India*, Cambridge, England, 1922, Vol. I, p. 366.

application, had issued from Hellenism as modified by Alexander's own philosophy. The measure of their novelty is indicated by Alexander's continuous search for an answer to his second problem: how to give the Empire substantive unity. In the perspective of this search the administrative pattern became a framework, a set of necessary technical devices that were truly valid only if they could sponsor and support a spirit of empire-wide unity and concord.

Since Alexander was convinced by upbringing, tradition, and choice that Hellenic culture was superior to others, his international policies reflected many typically Greek values as a matter of course. Greek concepts of personality, virtue, and excellence decisively influenced his selection of international administrative personnel, his dealings with subject peoples, and his treatment of defeated leaders such as Darius and Poros.[9] And when he digressed from these standards through misjudgment[10] or loss of temper,[11] he was equally Greek in showing the capacity to repent of his errors.[12] The Hellenic heritage was evident also in his approach to knowledge. Thousands of scholars—engineers, geologists, hydrologists, botanists, historians, poets, and educators[13]—accompanied the host that he led to Asia. His military campaigns were paralleled by scientific field trips, and his negotiations with enemy commanders were interrupted by discourses with Indian sages.[14] Learning was used for the construction of fortifications, harbors, and wells; but it was also stored in newly founded universities and libraries, for the enlightenment of people from all cultures.

These attitudes and practices go far toward explaining the Empire's design. Alexander's quest for internationally effective principles of cohesion can be understood fully, however, only if it is remembered that he himself remained a student, always aspiring to know more. He had been educated by Aristotle, but was open to intellectual influences from many other quarters. We know, for instance, that in Egypt he was deeply impressed by Psammon, who taught that all mankind is under

[9] But compare his ruthless treatment of some of the Phoenician towns.

[10] As in his punishment of Thebes after the Greek rebellion. See *Plutarch's Lives*, Dryden, rev. ed., London, 1932, Vol. II, p. 472.

[11] See *ibid.*, p. 508, for an account of the banquet during which Alexander was provoked to stab a Macedonian.

[12] Cf. Arrian's remark that Alexander was the only one of the ancient kings who from nobility of character repented of the errors which he had committed. Robinson, p. 60; also Arrian, p. 136.

[13] He also arranged that 30,000 youths in Bactria should be taught Greek and trained in the use of Macedonian weapons. See *Plutarch's Lives*, Vol. II, p. 504.

[14] *Plutarch's Lives*, Vol. II, p. 520.

93

the kingship of God,[15] and that in India he took to himself as guru the Jaina saint Kalanos.[16]

In many ways, then, Alexander's personal life and imperial steward-ship exemplified the Greek ideal of continuous moral aspiration. Real-izing that Athenian law was more suited to guide man than any other legal system, that the Greek city was indeed the ideal school for the practice of equality and justice, and that the Greek language was the broadest avenue to the attainment of knowledge, Alexander set about diffusing these particular institutions throughout the areas under his control.[17] But Hellenization of this kind was, for him, a measure of internationalization, rather than an end in itself. Daily contact with thousands of non-Greeks, and wisdom variously gathered, convinced him that the Greeks did not hold a monopoly on truth. His appreciation of the timeless worth of certain Greek contributions was tempered by disdain for the smugness and snobbery of the Greeks in their relations with non-Greeks. Alexander, therefore, was always on the lookout for new ways of convincing both the Greeks and the "barbarians" that they were, in his estimation, partners in the Empire and equal as men. Plutarch explains,[18] for instance, how Alexander, in each of the prov-inces of his conquest, tried to accommodate himself in his way of living to that of the natives, and to bring them meanwhile as near as he could to the Macedonian customs. To maintain tranquillity, he hoped he might depend upon the good will that should arise from intermixture and association, rather than upon force and compulsion. By admitting Persians, Bactrians, and others to his army of Macedonians and Greeks, he made military service a school for the fusion of races. And by advocating mixed marriages (he set the example by twice marrying daughters of Asian kings) he hoped to create bonds between Asia and Europe that would prove stronger than the lifeless bridge across the Hellespont on which a Persian predecessor had relied.

Whereas these and other particular policies were successful within the limits of their operation, Alexander's search for over-all principles of unification remained inconclusive at the time of his death. This was so, perhaps partly because no generally valid formula was ever found to regularize his own position in the Empire. The record indi-cates that he was regarded as God by many of the subject peoples and that proposals to deify him officially were made from time to time. But we do not know to what extent, or in what sense, Alexander per-

---

[15] ibid., p. 484; also Arthur Weigall, *Alexander the Great*, London, 1933, pp. 214f.
[16] Heinrich Zimmer, *Philosophies of India*, New York, 1951, p. 507.
[17] According to tradition he founded 70 cities.
[18] *Plutarch's Lives*, Vol. II, p. 504.

sonally supported such moves. Plutarch writes[19] that Alexander did not have the vanity to think of himself as really a god, but merely intended to use his claim to divinity as a means of maintaining among other peoples the sense of his superiority. Such claims were easily acceptable, for example, to the Persians, who regarded prostration before a Great King as an act of etiquette rather than of worship. Nor were they really inconsistent with certain Greek traditions in which men had frequently been raised to the rank of gods. The loyalty of the Greeks and Macedonians to the imperial idea, however, had always been more brittle than that of the Asians. Whatever hope Alexander might have had that they would accept his divinity was certainly cancelled when his Macedonian veterans expressed their aversion to the whole idea by acts of mutiny.

In evaluating Alexander's Empire as an international state, two main points can perhaps be made. First, Alexander was the first agent in history to unite under one administration European, Asian, and African culture areas. The Persian Empire, by comparison, had been not only smaller but culturally and racially much less diversified. Second, Alexander's design for an international commonwealth was revolutionary in that it suggested new political bonds between men, a new relationship between the individual and the international community, and a new view of the world. The Persian Empire had been the first to project the notion of tolerance into international administration by permitting each of its component groups to pursue its own national life, and Alexander retained and developed these principles of international community living. Nevertheless, in his understanding an empire was infinitely more than a conglomeration of different groups. With him begins the idea of the inhabited world (the *oikoumene*) as a brotherhood wherein all men are the sons of one Father. In fact, it was the pursuit of this idea that inspired his schemes of secular government and made him pray, at a banquet of international reconciliation at Opis, for a union of hearts (*homonoia*), and for a joint commonwealth in which all peoples should be partners, not subjects.[20]

B. The Hellenistic System of States

A. MULTIPLE SOVEREIGNTIES

"Among the sayings of one Psammon, a philosopher, whom he heard in Egypt, Alexander most approved of this, that all men are governed

---

[19] *ibid.*, p. 488.
[20] W. W. Tarn, *Hellenistic Civilisation*, 3rd ed., London, 1952, pp. 79f.

by God, because in everything, that which is chief and commands is divine. But what he pronounced himself upon this subject was even more like a philosopher; for he said, God was the common father of us all, but more particularly of the best of us."[21]

Alexander had died leaving his Empire to the best. But since there was no agreement among his successors as to who was the "best," the imperial heritage was soon divided among three chief pretending dynasties: Egypt was under the Ptolemies; Macedonia under the Antigonidae; and Syria, which term included all of the eastern provinces of the Empire and some parts of Asia Minor, was under the Seleucids.

From these great states lesser sovereignties separated themselves in the course of time, beginning c.280 B.C. Syria, the most heterogeneous of the powers, lost Armenia, Cappadocia, Pontus, and Bithynia—all former tributary kingdoms of the Persian Empire—which became absolute monarchies with a strong Greek veneer. There also emerged such petty monarchies as Epirus in the Balkans, Pergamum, and the Bosporan Kingdom on the Black Sea; similarly in Africa, the Nubian Kingdom. In 248 B.C. the Parthians, a semi-nomadic people of Iranian stock, conquered the territory of the old Medo-Persian Kingdom in Central Asia and founded a strong state based on Iranian as well as Greek traditions. Bactria broke from Syria in 250 B.C. India recovered its independence under the powerful empire of the Mauryas, which dissolved soon afterward into a number of independent states. And within the Egyptian and Macedonian spheres several of the Greek city-states and two Greek leagues attained independence, but these remained under a constant threat from both Egypt and Macedon.

New states, meanwhile, were developing on the outskirts of this ancient world. In the north of the Balkan peninsula, Thracians and Celts became identifiable as political communities; in the steppes of south Russia, a Scythian kingdom arose, to be followed by several kingdoms of Sarmatians. In the western Mediterranean the strongest newcomers were Carthage, the Sicilian Greeks, various alliances of Italian clans (among which a league of Latin cities led by Rome was rapidly outdistancing all others in importance), and finally an alliance of Gallic or Celtic tribes in what is now France and north Italy.[22]

In this chaotic society of multiple sovereignties, each great power was trying to capture the leadership and establish a central control.

[21] *Plutarch's Lives*, Vol. II, p. 487.
[22] M. I. Rostovtzeff, *History of the Ancient World*, Oxford, 1926-1930, Vol. I, pp. 361ff.

And each lesser state was equally determined to retain its independence by keeping the international society decentralized. The mutually exclusive trends led to incessant strife and bickering for position. But, as in earlier periods when power could not be monopolized by a single great government, these conditions provided a fertile field for the growth of diplomacy and its related arts of winning friends and settling disputes. Arbitration, for instance, established a high water mark in the second century B.C. that has been surpassed, if at all, only in the nineteenth century of our own era.[23] Yet, oddly enough, in the fourth century B.C. the small country in which all of these Hellenistic trends and institutions of balance-of-power politics had first been really tested was reversing its traditional orientation. Within Greece itself the principle of autonomy seemed to be receding in favor of the principle of federalism.

Greek history in this period records numerous federal constitutions, having novel and rather effective provisions. The loose arrangement called isopolity, for instance, gave way in many of them to sympolity: a federal framework in which each person, while retaining citizenship in his home state, acquired double citizenship by becoming a citizen also of the federal community. The member cities of such an alliance were equal officially, but exercised their influence on federal affairs only in proportion to the number of their citizens.[24] The idea was carried still further in the constitution of the Thessalian Federation, according to which the constituents were not city-states, but territorial divisions that were themselves federations of cities.[25]

The Achaean League[26] of the third century B.C. was perhaps the most interesting of these new Greek federations. "Nowhere," writes Polybius, "could be found a system and a principle more pure and unalloyed of equality, freedom of speech, and, in a word, true Democracy

---

[23] Tod, p. 181, citing J. B. Moore, *The Nineteenth Century*, p. 24, to the effect that the nineteenth century witnessed one hundred and thirty-six completed arbitrations.

[24] E.g. the Chalcidian League in the fourth century. See Botsford and Robinson, *Hellenic History*, N.Y., 1946, p. 218, and J. A. O. Larsen, *Representative Government in Greek and Roman History*, Berkeley, 1955, for numerous references to this and similar leagues.

[25] See Moses Hadas, "Federalism in Antiquity," in *Approaches to World Peace*, Lyman Bryson, ed., New York, 1944, p. 33; Rostovtzeff, *Social and Economic History of the Hellenistic World*, Vol. I, p. 204, to the effect that these *sympolitai* were not, strictly speaking, economically unified.

[26] For the chequered history and intricate organization of this league see Kurt von Fritz, *The Theory of the Mixed Constitution in Antiquity, A Critical Analysis of Polybius' Political Ideas*, New York, 1954, pp. 4-10; Tarn, pp. 73ff.; T. R. Glover, *Democracy in the Ancient World*, Cambridge, 1927, pp. 135-149; Larsen, pp. 75ff., 86ff. and Appendix pp. 165-188 for a record of the meetings of the League's assemblies.

than among the Achaeans."[27] In his elaborate comments on the constitution of this union Polybius stresses above all the fact that, unlike the Delian and Peloponnesian confederacies of the fifth century, here was no dominating city. Whether they had belonged to the original League or had joined it only later, all the members were entirely on the same footing. However, all had to be democracies: the union, which included the majority of the Peloponnesian states, with the notable exception of Sparta,[28] did not admit tyrannical regimes or absolute monarchies. "By holding out the inducement of equality and freedom, by consistently making war on and crushing those who either on their own account or with the support of the kings tried to enslave their native cities, in this way and with this purpose they accomplished the work. . . . In return for the zealous aid they gave their allies, they bargained for nothing but the freedom of each state and the general concord of Peloponnesians."[29] On the basis of these principles the League formed a remarkably close-knit unit, having the same laws, weights, measures, and monetary system, and, in addition, a common government, a common deliberative assembly, and a common law court, so that in a way the whole territory of the League could be considered as belonging to one state.[30] This great venture in cooperative politics left an indelible mark upon the subsequent history of international administration, but its continuance as a going concern was not favored by the principal contenders for supremacy in the Mediterranean region. Deeply resented by Sparta, the League became in 222 B.C. a Macedonian protectorate and was eventually (146 B.C.) dissolved by Rome.[31]

[27] Glover, p. 137.

[28] In 192 B.C. Sparta seems to have become a member. But see von Fritz, p. 6 for qualifications.

[29] Glover, p. 138.

[30] Von Fritz, p. 4.

[31] The Romans were, on the whole, quite tolerant of regional leagues and federations, but they restricted these bodies in the exercise of political functions. The only league that continued to retain considerable political significance in the second century B.C. was the Lycian League of twenty-three cities in southwestern Asia Minor. The constitution of this federation has evoked great interest among commentators. It provided for a system of representation in proportion to population but distinguished also between three classes of cities, having one, two, and three votes each; and the same classification probably supplied the basis for the contributions of the cities to the confederate treasury. See W. W. Tarn, p. 77; Larsen, pp. 30, 99, 101; also W. C. MacLeod, *The Origin and History of Politics*, New York, 1946, pp. 365ff., who gives no sources for his information but sets out that the Lycian Assembly imposed a tax on all members in proportion not to population or wealth but to representation, adding that this is the first instance in history where the principle of no taxation without representation was recognized.

While the members of the great Hellenistic society of states had different forms of government and national interests, in varying degree all had been drawn into a single, Greek-inspired culture sphere. Within this sphere Greek had spread as an international language. The Persian roads, extended and improved by the Seleucids, led all the way to India, and continuous silk routes connected the Phoenician sea ports with Central Asia and China. A new seaway, from the Red Sea to China, was added to those previously used by Phoenicians, Cretans, and Egyptians. Trade and travel across these vast distances became safer as Hellenistic monarchies, Arabian states, and companies of merchants from all lands cooperated in the policing efforts.

The widely separated parts of the Hellenistic world were in this way linked not only with each other, but with the Far Eastern culture realms and the barbarian communities of the West. In no preceding age had so many races and countries been held together by mutual commercial interests. The Mediterranean area became a world market for perfumes, spices, drugs, ivory, and jewels from Central Africa, Arabia, and India; for gold, furs, and forest products from Siberia and Central Russia; for amber from the Baltic; and for metals from the British Isles and Spain. Among the most prized commodities of international trade were human beings. To the great international slave mart of Delos victims were brought from Britain, Ethiopia, south Russia, Morocco, Iran, and Spain. They were distributed to Seleucia, Antioch, Alexandria, Carthage, Rome, Athens, and Pergamum. Among them were not only laborers and prostitutes, but doctors, scientists, artists, and craftsmen, who carried their ideas, traditions, and skills along wherever they went. Then there were, of course, thousands of men who moved freely in the pursuit of their profession or out of curiosity. Alien merchant colonies could be found in every port. We read, for instance, of an Indian merchant, resident in Egypt, who actually held a priesthood there; of a guild of Syrian merchants who maintained a regular hostel on Delos providing lodgings, stock-rooms, a council chamber, and a chapel; of an Italiote bronze-worker who transferred his business from Lucania to Rhodes; and of a silk manufacturer from Antioch who died in Naples.[32]

This unparalleled freedom of intercourse naturally stimulated the interest of scholars everywhere. All of the Hellenistic successor states followed Alexander in supporting research and welcoming scientists and students from every part of the known world. Geographers gave

[32] Gordon Childe, *What Happened in History*, New York, 1946, pp. 232-233.

up studying the world according to national boundaries and developed, instead, Alexander's concept of the *oikoumene*—the inhabited world considered as a single unit.[33] Babylonian and Egyptian disciplines of thought united with those of classical Greece and the Orient, and institutions like the museum and library of Alexandria became meeting grounds for intellectuals from all cultures. The poets of Alexandria and Athens wrote for everyone in the Hellenistic society; the educated elite read the same books, admired the same plays, and listened to the same musicians and actors wherever they went on their cosmopolitan circuits.

In migrating from place to place, both the educated and the uneducated carried with them their various religious creeds and cults. Western beliefs penetrated deep into Central Asia, and Eastern deities found devout worshippers in the Mediterranean regions. These more or less spontaneous exchanges of faith were supplemented by deliberate missionary activities. For instance, the converted Buddhist emperor of India, Ashoka (c. 272-232 B.C.), accredited Buddhist missionaries to the courts of Egypt, Syria, and Macedonia. In practically all sections of the world mysticism, magic, alchemy, and astrology could be found competing with traditional religions for the loyalty of thousands of salvation-searching individuals. All these varied quests were tolerated practically everywhere.

B. THE INDIVIDUAL AND THE HELLENISTIC COMMUNITY

The culturally unified commonwealth that the Athenians of the fifth century had tried so hard to create in their limited Aegean world had virtually come about in the fourth and third centuries on a vastly extended stage. But in contrast to the Athenian society, the Hellenistic proved unable to evolve a protective organizational shell around its shared cultural substance. In extremities of political crisis or interest, the common culture was invariably adjusted to suit the purposes of separate governments. This meant, in the long run, that much of the shared cultural substance was devitalized and whittled away.

The disparity between cultural and political developments in the Hellenistic Age resulted partly because the common culture, with all its glittering attractiveness, had not—in its historically most decisive period—actually reached sufficient depth in human consciousness. It was consequently unable to generate the moral forces necessary to

[33] Hadas in Bryson, ed., pp. 30ff.; also *Hellenistic Culture; fusion and diffusion,* New York, 1959.

restrain war and support peace and unity. Indeed, wars were fought more bitterly and treaties broken more frequently than during any previous period of world history. This international society was perhaps further prevented from developing the moral strength that would have enabled it to survive because it was socially divided. While theoretically accessible to individuals from all civilizations and races, the culture, in all its cosmopolitan richness, was in practice open and meaningful only to the educated: the men who spoke Greek, and who liked to live the urban life that Greek culture had so eloquently advertised.

For there was a critical difference between the Greek and the Hellenistic societies. The Greeks, for the sake of making civilization meaningful to the majority, had clung to the polis as the cornerstone of their political existence, in the conviction that any greater political community would not adequately contain the kind of life that they had found to be most worth living. The polis, as such, had, of course, been widely diffused over the world by Alexander and his successors. But it had lost, irrevocably, its political relevance as the breeder and protector of *generally* shared values, because the actual Hellenistic political community had been immeasurably expanded to include every manner of group life. In short, the problem of finding a relationship between culture and politics had remained, but the circumstances in which the relationship was to be found had changed, and the Hellenistic statesmen—unlike their Greek predecessors in a former age—were incompetent to find an adequate contemporary solution. The common man, whether artisan, laborer, or tiller of the soil, felt lost and bewildered in the new world. He found no moral security in the babel of faiths growing around him, and he looked in vain for political security in a framework of government in which war and uncertainty had become endemic. This meant, quite apart from individual anguish and frustration, that the less educated were cut off as a group from the possibility of sharing the cultural and commercial values that compensated their more educated fellowmen for the many uncertainties of their cosmopolitan environment. Social tension, therefore, became another of the internationally unsettling factors in that originally so promising world.

The only philosophy from which the educated as well as the uneducated Alexandrian could hope to derive guidance and inspiration—and around which, therefore, the contemporary society, as such, could reform itself—was the rising new morality of universal aspiration. In probing the concept of justice, Socrates had concluded that no uni-

101

form meaning could be ascribed to this idea, since different people and communities, by virtue of their differing customs and traditions, interpreted the words "just" and "right" differently. But all humanity, he found, shares in the aspiration toward justice. In Plato's explanation of the Socratic theory, this meant that "justice" has indeed a universal meaning, which is independent of all the various things that are called just at various times and places.[34] The new morality was universal precisely because it implied spiritual self rule for each individual in the world, wherever located, however influenced by his environment, and irrespective of his intellectual limitations.

If the promise of moral comfort was to have any bearing on the reality of daily existence, however, it had to be accepted and redeemed by politically adequate institutions. Since it was universal in its spiritual appeal, it could not be limited by the boundaries of kingdoms, cities, or nations; instead, it invited and required a world-wide government, coextensive with the human race. This consequence was not seen clearly by Plato when he developed the Socratic philosophy. For Plato (and later, Aristotle) still thought in terms of the narrow polis as the actual political framework for man's various endeavors, even in spite of his obvious disillusionment with traditional Greek government.[35] With regard to a "new" and better form of government, Plato argued that the goal of justice, to which all men aspire, can in fact be known by an intellectual effort which only the best and most noble could undertake and sustain. Plato concluded that the rulers of the ideal commonwealth should be those few lovers of wisdom who have most nearly attained spiritual perfection.[36] Plato's scheme of government, therefore, did not suggest any lines along which Hellenistic society as a whole could politically reconstitute itself.

Disillusion in the failure of the city-state and other contemporary forms of government prompted many people to withdraw completely from active participation in community life, and to concentrate instead on their own private lives. Among the several schools of thought that offered these individuals new orientations in the troubled Hellenistic

[34] Francis M. Cornford, *Before and After Socrates*, Cambridge, 1950, pp. 59-61.

[35] It is interesting, for instance, that both ignored completely the brilliant experiments in federalism that were being carried through in many sections of Greece. These constitutional developments have led modern historians to express the wishful thought that, had not Rome intervened, Greece might with her sensitiveness and imagination have given the Mediterranean region not only a common culture but also a form of government that would have ensured unity, freedom, and permanence. See Robinson, p. 239.

[36] See Cornford's analysis of Plato's *Republic*, p. 59.

world by teaching the ideal of individual self-sufficiency, the Epicureans and the Cynics gained particularly wide popularity. Since moral rules and practices were found to be so different at various times and places, the Epicureans[37] argued against all intrinsic values and approved of social institutions only insofar as they were devices to secure the largest possible private good. Morality became for them a matter of expedience, on the assumption that the wise man would act justly because the fruits of injustice are not worth the risk of detection and punishment.[38] The Cynics, in their protest, went even further by disavowing all social institutions, including marriage and property. They recognized only the world as a socially relevant fact. And in this world all men were equal—whether rich or poor, Greek or barbarian, citizen or foreigner. However, since the Cynics surmised that most men were also fools, and therefore incapable of using their freedom and equality to full individual advantage, they had to conclude that only the wise could actually be cosmopolites and make the world their city.[39] While offering to the wise an intellectual escape from the troubles of the present, the Cynics left the less wise without any moral solace. Moreover, since the Cynics showed no concern for the acute dilemma in practical international politics, their philosophy could not contribute an answer to the chief problem of the age: how to translate the existing cultural consensus into positive principles of effective international administration.

The Stoics, on the other hand, as a consequence of their acknowledgment of direct ties between man and the world,[40] found a more positive meaning in the idea of a world-wide state. As the founder, Zeno, put it: "We do not dwell in separate cities or demes, each group bounded off by its own rules of justice; but we consider that all men are fellow demesmen and fellow citizens and that life is one and the

---

[37] The school was founded in Athens in 306 B.C.

[38] George H. Sabine, *A History of Political Theory*, New York, 1946, p. 135.

[39] Diogenes, leading proponent of Cynicism, may have been the first to use the word "cosmopolitan." Hadas, in Bryson, ed., p. 30, explains his statement: "I am a cosmopolite, a citizen of the world," as merely the proud assertion of an exile's consciousness of his own worth, in the face of a bourgeois society that scorned him. Max H. Boehm, in *The Encyclopaedia of Social Sciences*, Vol. IV, p. 457, defines "cosmopolitanism" as a mental attitude substituting for the attachment to a more immediate homeland an analogous relationship toward the whole world, which the cosmopolitan comes to regard as a greater and higher fatherland; it establishes through the symbol of citizenship an immediate union between the individual and mankind.

[40] Stoicism was founded in Athens sometime before 300 B.C. by Zeno, himself probably a native of Phoenicia.

universe is one."[41] In this cosmopolis men were brothers because they were all sons of God. Their relations with each other were to be governed ultimately not by local customs but by reason, for reason was not only the inherent attribute of God, but also a common human trait and therefore the ultimate source of all local customs. By thus holding up right reason as the all-pervading law of nature, Stoicism supplied not only an ideal of equity against which actual laws and customs could be measured, but an internationally valid goal toward which each individual could direct his moral aspiration.

In this and other respects the Stoic theory restated several concepts that had long been associated with Greek thought, reverting, in particular, to the original Socratic suggestion that men are linked with each other and God by their moral aspirations. But it must be noted that it was not only the Greek tradition that had influenced this new doctrine, giving it—among intellectuals at least[42]—such weight and prestige. The internationally persuasive appeal of Stoicism was derived, on the contrary, from its truly Hellenistic, oecumenical character. It reflected the close affinity that had gradually been established between Hellenic and Oriental thought. It fed, in particular, on the universal tendency toward religious monism. It was inspired most of all perhaps by the actuality of Alexander's world empire and his great vision that belief in one God required a world state based on the brotherhood of man.

The logic of these correlations and the memory of their political implementation were to influence international history decisively in the ensuing centuries by lending support to the Roman conceptions of empire as well as to the Christian views of the City of God, even though nothing could reverse or decisively modify the separatist forces that finally disrupted the outgoing Hellenistic Age. In spite of the historical collapse of the world of Alexander's vision, the philosophies advocating a cosmopolitan view had flourished under its inspiration. During the following centuries they contributed to the formulation of certain principles of international order in a pluralistic society which hold enduring interest for the cause of the world community. Their success at the time was limited and temporary, but their influence continues to the present.

[41] As quoted by W. Linn Westerman, "Greek Culture and Thought," in *The Encyclopaedia of the Social Sciences*, Vol. I, p. 36. See also p. 14.

[42] The Stoics, too, were impressed with the number of fools in the world and established wisdom as the requirement for citizenship in the world.

C. HELLENISTIC COSMOPOLITANISM IN LAW AND GOVERNMENT

In the Hellenistic Age, as in all other ages, only few people had the time, interest, or "right reason" to define the hopes and fears of man in abstract terms. The majority went on with the concrete business of living, sometimes hopefully, sometimes fearfully, doing the particular jobs that their station in life required of them at the moment. Since the Hellenistic "moment" had brought together citizens from many lands, however, the daily execution of many individual jobs assumed, as a matter of course, an international character. And in the process of such functional internationalism, definite world orientations were not only evolved, but in large measure also institutionalized. In other words, men's actual involvement in the life situations of the period brought some of the answers for which many philosophers had searched in vain.

The Greeks who settled in Bactria and India, for instance, did not escape life. They affirmed it, with all its uncertainties, by cooperating with Bactrians and Indians. Instead of waiting for the perfect unity of the entire human race, they concentrated on finding such syntheses between the Greek and Far Eastern ways of life as might enable their multinational governments to operate on the basis of popular acceptance and respect.

The citizens of Rhodes showed similar courage. They were too adventurous to permit insecurity to daunt their spirit of enterprise, and too busy ridding the Mediterranean region of its greatest scourge, piracy, to blueprint a perfect order for the cosmic state. Instead, the Rhodian jurists and merchants lowered their sights enough to tackle the most immediate international problem then challenging their interests and competence: they collected and systematized those laws of the sea which were generally observed, and they set about administering those laws as impartially as they knew how.

It is, of course, true that both of these operative international communities of interest were limited—to a specific area, in the case of Bactria and Northern India, and to specific functional pursuits, in the case of the Rhodian Sea Law. But in two respects both communities exceeded the boundaries within which the cosmopolitan theoreticians of the Hellenistic Age commonly kept their projects for better worlds to come. For since cooperation on the seas involved all who made maritime trade their calling (the educated as well as the uneducated), and since coexistence in Central Asian villages required mutual understanding on the part of all settlers (the wise and the not so wise), social divisions had little place in these communities of interest.[43] Secondly, while the philosophers' images of the cosmopolis were, by and large, reflections of the Hellenistic culture realm, the two functional communities here considered were not so narrowly confined. They regulated daily individual pursuits and developed international standards of behavior beyond the limits of the Hellenistic society, and thereby linked the latter to more distant communities in both the West and the East.

D. THE PLACE OF RHODES IN HELLENISTIC SOCIETY

As formulated by Alexander the Great and the Stoic philosophers, the concept of the cosmopolis had elicited the allegiance of the sophisticated individual but had left the average person unresponsive. The reality of the Hellenistic cosmopolis was so bewildering in the complexity of its new relationships that no one could really understand or define it in one great concept. Since the attempt to capture the total Hellenistic spirit in a single all-inclusive system of world organization had failed with the death of Alexander, it became the chief problem of the subsequent Hellenistic Age to develop whatever partial suggestions had been accumulated, whether through philosophical pronouncements or through practical experience, and relate them effectively to certain more limited but generally meaningful aspects of the great cosmopolis.

On the assumption that the Hellenistic spirit was characterized by individualism and materialism, as tempered by the realization of world-wide human interdependence, one can say that this spirit was most convincingly fulfilled in the pursuit of commerce. By participating in trading ventures of various sorts, the individual could express his personal interests while grasping the vastness of the world around him. He could find scope for individual courage and adventure while recognizing the stakes that he shared with other men. And this was particularly true in the maritime trade, where men moved outside of the accustomed national boundaries and along largely uncharted seas, uncontrolled by kings or local laws; where the perils of war, storm, and piracy had to be jointly faced by self-reliant individuals, regardless of their particular status, wealth, or creed; where one vessel, or one trading fleet, carried the hopes and the properties of people from different lands; and where one partnership comprehended extremely

---

[43] This does not mean that social divisions did not exist in other extensions of Bactrian and Rhodian life.

varied cosmopolitan and local interests. These circumstances help to explain why maritime trade in the ancient world was habitually treated as a series of joint adventures, and why a new ethic of international coexistence evolved, almost as a matter of course, from the regular recurrence of certain life situations. The pursuit of personal quests necessitated the stipulation of joint liability. The gratification of material ambitions demanded the cultivation of rules of fair dealing. The day-by-day reconciliation of many such incongruities resulted, in the course of time, in the establishment of an internationally valid maritime law.

Since the basic conditions of sea-borne commerce remained practically unaltered until about the thirteenth century of our era, and since maritime risks and promises have, in the larger terms of human expectations, remained the same through all the ages, the Hellenistic formulation of maritime law has a timeless significance. It was developed by several generations of Rhodian citizens, acting in this matter as the agents of the whole Hellenistic cosmopolis. Their residency was a small island in the eastern Mediterranean. Their state, once a part of the Persian Empire, had been restored as a democracy by Alexander the Great and subsequently transformed by him into an imperial city under his direct overlordship. When he died, the citizens declared their total independence. During the course of the Hellenistic era their small Aegean island became the chief clearing house for shipments from Phoenicia, Arabia, Egypt, Greece, Italy, and North Africa.[44] Thus at the crossroads of commercial, strategic, and political interests, equally accessible to the great and the secondary powers of three continents, the Rhodian state held a key position in the Hellenistic system of diplomacy.

In these circumstances the Rhodians realized early that their independence was inseparably connected with the freedom of international trade in the eastern Mediterranean, and that international trade could be free only as long as the high seas were kept clear of both piracy and great power imperialism. They made it therefore their business, with the aid of a small but superbly equipped navy, to police the adjacent waters and to maintain a balance of power among their powerful neighbors. And since their state was small and exposed to aggression on all sides, they pursued these bold policies by mobilizing

[44] The Rhodians traded mainly in wheat. Their customs revenues in 170 B.C. were a million drachmas as against 200,000 drachmas in the Athenian wheat trade of 401 B.C. Botsford and Robinson, *Hellenic History*, p. 314.

their human skills. The Rhodians became famous as traders, navigators, astronomers, jurists, and diplomats; they were respected as courageous defenders of national independence and human rights. But above
all, they were known to stand for the freedom of the seas. This meant
no privileges for anyone, the greatest possible security for all while
afloat, a minimum of taxes and duties, and the recognition of certain
general legal principles as governing maritime commerce.[45] In the pursuit of these policies Rhodes gained great influence and prestige—especially after she had withstood the attempted encroachments of the
larger powers, which culminated in a one-year siege. She was ultimately recognized by her contemporaries as the most important secondary state of the Hellenistic system and was trusted by all to act
both as the policeman of the Mediterranean and as the middleman of
international trade. When an earthquake destroyed vast sections of
the city, including its harbors and commercial installations (227 or
226 B.C.),[46] assistance came from all parts of the Hellenistic world—
from democracies and tyrannies alike. This gesture was no doubt ten-
dered in calculated recognition of Rhodian services, but it also reflected a genuine admiration for the beauty of the city and the accomplishments of its population. Continuous contact with the state's well-
informed citizenry had convinced contemporaries that the sources of
Rhodian skill and success lay in this people's love of learning and
scholarship, hospitality to foreign students, and generally cosmopolitan
orientation to the world. Special praise was always reserved for Rhodian
government, which experts found by far the best of all Greek governments.[47]

As general Rhodian history and these particular appraisals show,
the island state had, in many ways, inherited the legacy of Athens.
Not only did it occupy the international position that Athens had
vacated in the region, but its domestic constitution and foreign policies
rested on concepts that the Athenians had first clarified. The Rhodians,
like the Athenians, approached the subject of foreign affairs from the
inside: they brought their foreign policies into line with the basic
concepts on which they had chosen to build their home government,

[45] M. I. Rostovtzeff, *Social and Economic History of the Hellenistic World*, Oxford,
1941, Vol. I, p. 229.

[46] Also destroyed was the Colossus, a gigantic statue of Apollo, which the ancients
regarded as one of the seven wonders of the world.

[47] See H. van Gelder, *Geschichte der alten Rhodier*, Haag, 1900, p. 179, for the
testimony of a man such as Diodorus.

instead of stipulating for the absolute primacy of foreign affairs, in the fashion of most Near Eastern states.[48]

The Rhodians coupled deep concern for the welfare and security of their own city-state with both respect for the local autonomy of the many small islands and coastal communities that formed the expanding Rhodian commonwealth and a keen appreciation of the need to establish collective security among all independent states of the region. Rhodes had joined the Delian League as well as the Second Athenian Confederacy in 378 B.C. When the ties with Athens were severed in 357 B.C., she became the nucleus for a new league of republics, whose leadership she managed to retain by displaying the restraint and tolerance in confederate affairs for lack of which Athens had eventually come to grief.

Rhodes was equally prudent and considerate in exercising her protectorate over the nominally independent Temple Free State of Delos and the adjoining, strategically very important, Cyclades. Because she compensated Delos for its loss of domestic jurisdiction by patrolling the seas and protecting the sanctum from pirates and robbers, her supremacy endured here until the Romans transformed Delos into a competitive harbor for the deliberate purpose of ruining Rhodes. It was no doubt confidence in her judicious use of power that prompted the strong and the weak to request Rhodian advice, mediation, and arbitration. For instance, the Rhodians succeeded in settling a bitter feud between Byzantium and the neighboring Celtic tribes, which had practically paralyzed all shipping through the Bosporus, also in arbitrating a dispute between Priene and Samos that, for a long time, had seriously upset the entire Mediterranean world. In the latter case, the Rhodian award of 200 B.C. was considered so just that the Romans decided in 135 B.C. to retain it in its original Rhodian version.[49]

The record also shows that Rhodes did her best to keep peace among the Greeks. When the shadow of Rome was beginning to fall over the Mediterranean, she rallied all Hellenes under the leadership of Macedon, and when Greek factionalism threatened to undermine this concert, as it had so many earlier federations, Rhodes again exerted herself tirelessly, but this time unsuccessfully, in behalf of reconciliation.[50]

---

[48] See *The Cambridge Ancient History*, Cambridge, England, Vol. VIII, p. 621, to the effect that Rhodian greatness in international relations begins with the great reform in her constitution (407 B.C.) when three ancient communities were merged into one, and that ancient and modern historians agree in tracing the brilliant commercial development of Rhodes back to this fateful decision of some political genius.

[49] Van Gelder, p. 132.

[50] Between 209-206 B.C.

It was soon after the failure of this attempt that Rhodes reversed her traditional world policy and sided with ascending Rome. Frustrated by continued disunity among the Greek democracies, fearful of the imperialist ambitions of Macedon, and perhaps attracted by some of the manifestations of republicanism in the Roman state, the Rhodians seemed to realize that, under such changed circumstances, their diplomacy alone was no adequate defence of the system under which they had enjoyed their independence.

Finally the whole Hellenistic East was conquered by the Romans. Macedonia was defeated in 168 B.C. and became a Roman province in 147 B.C. Greece was utterly humiliated and subsequently attached to the province of Macedonia. Rhodes was stripped of her territory on the mainland of Asia Minor, deprived of her leadership in the Aegean, and annexed in 164 B.C. Thenceforward piracy steadily grew; by the end of the century it had developed into a plague that made commerce in the Aegean almost impossible.[51]

E. THE RHODIAN SEA LAW

In her punitive and aggressive expeditions against the states of the Hellenistic system, Rome wantonly destroyed many institutions that might have continued to serve the international community without impairing her own power. By displacing Rhodes as the international policeman of a great and important region, she automatically weakened the principles of law and order. It is therefore a testimony to the strength and vitality of these principles that we can trace the continued survival, across two millenniums and many continents, of the body of maritime law commonly known as the Rhodian Sea Law.

The Rhodians were neither the first to take to the sea nor the first to regulate their operations by reference to law. We know little about their predecessors in Egypt and Minoan Crete; we can read scraps of shipping documents in the Mesopotamian codes;[52] and we can only make conjectures about the contents of the Phoenician records, for the latter were mostly lost when the Phoenician cities were sacked and burnt. How old the custom is of assuming mutual liability, to give one example, we may never know. But readers of Demosthenes' speeches can find the first recorded instance of a kind of insurance, and the

---

[51] *The Cambridge Ancient History*, Vol. VIII, p. 631.

[52] The Code of Hammurabi contains probably the most ancient statement of shipping law in existence. See Wyndham Bewes, *The Romance of the Law Merchant*, London, 1923, pp. 70ff.

terms of this arrangement seem to have remained substantially the same until the thirteenth century A.D.[53]

By the time the Rhodians appeared as the chief navigators and traders of the Mediterranean region, Athenian law had, through borrowing and diffusion, become the basic civil law of the Hellenistic society. An international framework of legal agreement existed, therefore, into which innumerable preexisting maritime customs could fit themselves, anonymously but harmoniously, in the course of time. The Rhodians showed their genius by accepting this framework. They collected, elaborated, and restated the maritime customs that they found in use, and they provided, for the first time in the history of international maritime relations, the conditions in which these customs could be enforced regularly and over a large area. This first great collection of operative international law in the world has been identified ever since with the name of Rhodes. It included regulations, subsequently accepted universally, regarding copartnership, joint adventures, charter parties, and bills of lading. It established standards for the behavior of passengers while on shipboard, for the liability of commanders or seamen in cases of injuries to goods and carelessness or absence from duty; also it listed penalties for barratry (fraud or gross negligence), robbery of other ships, and careless collisions.[54] But since the written form in which the sea law has reached posterity was supplied between A.D. 500 and 800[55] by Byzantine jurists, no one will ever know with certainty in what precise conformation these legal concepts were applied during the Hellenistic Age, under the Rhodian aegis. Of the many extant provisions, only the law of jettison (*lex de iactu*)[56] has been definitely identified as originating in Rhodes.

The story of the uses to which the sea law has been applied in the contexts of different civilizations and particular legal systems may perhaps be said to illustrate two general propositions: one, that the date at which a statute receives its shape is not necessarily the date of the law that it contains, and two, that the law itself tends to remain unaltered as long as the conditions that gave rise to it remain unaltered.[57]

---

[53] For the speech of Demosthenes against Lacritos see Bewes, p. 64; also Walter Ashburner, *The Rhodian Sea Law*, Oxford, 1909, p. 209.

[54] V. Shaw Lindsay, *The History of Merchant Shipping and Ancient Commerce*, London, 1874-1876, Vol. I, pp. 183-184.

[55] There were also many forgeries of the sea laws. See Van Gelder, p. 426.

[56] The rules regulating the circumstances in which goods can be thrown overboard to lighten a ship in distress.

[57] For an analysis of the manuscripts see Ashburner, p. cxv.

When the Romans settled down to the business of administering the world that their arms had won, they were irresistibly drawn into the Hellenistic culture realm. Here they found many concepts that were not only intellectually persuasive to themselves as men living in a complex world, but extraordinarily useful as ideological supports for the world order that they were called upon to create. In Stoicism as a philosophy, Rome found a universally appealing concept of empire, and in Stoicism as applied in Hellenistic government and politics, she discovered the needed principles of order. But the chief center of Stoic philosophy at this time was the cosmopolitan state of Rhodes.[58] And so, in response to these attractions, the world-conquering Roman state became the debtor of the small Aegean confederation it had so crudely despoiled. The Rhodian Sea Law was praised by Cicero for its humaneness; its adoption throughout the Roman Empire was ordered by Augustus;[59] and its sovereignty was acknowledged by Rome's most outstanding Stoic emperor, Marcus Aurelius, when he responded to the appeal of a certain Eudaemon of Nicomedia, whose goods had been plundered when his ship had been wrecked: "I am the sovereign of the world, but the Rhodian law is sovereign wherever it does not run contrary to our statute law."[60]

We next hear of the Rhodian Sea Law when the law-conscious Emperor Justinian (A.D. 483-565) set about restating the Roman civil code. Among the monuments of Byzantine jurisprudence that have survived, perhaps none is to be found in more manuscripts than the little treatise on maritime law.[61] By this time, however, immemorial custom, Rhodian regulations, and Roman enactments had merged so completely that research cannot distinguish the various components. Essentially in this form the sea law was copied and handed down through the centuries in the Near East and in southern Italy. Although embodied in somewhat various forms and in different languages, it continued to represent the living law for both Eastern and Western communities from the tenth to the fifteenth centuries A.D. Its provisions were of particular importance in guiding the nautical and commercial adventures of Europeans in the Middle Ages. Indeed, we find them embodied in what is commonly regarded as the most interesting medieval sea statute, the *Constitutum Usus* of the city of Pisa (published in

[58] James Hastings, ed., *Encyclopaedia of Religion and Ethics*, New York, 1908, Vol. XI, p. 861.

[59] Van Gelder, p. 426, says that the sea *lex de iactu* in particular was so incorporated into Roman law.

[60] Lindsay, p. 183. [61] *ibid.*, pp. 501f.; also Ashburner.

1160),[62] as well as in the "rôles d'Oléron" (Gascony), the Statutes of Ragusa, and the practices of Venice, Genoa, and Amalfi. In the rendition of the roles of Gascony they formed the bases of the Laws of Wisby in Gotland and the ordinances of the Hanseatic League.[63]

While each of these later polities prided itself on its independence and referred to "custom" usually as "local custom," all were governed by practically identical laws when it came to matters of the sea. Within the framework of these long-tested principles of international order, leadership in the maritime community passed in modern times first to the Dutch and subsequently to the English. In assuming an international position for which Rhodes had set the precedent, these modern nations also became the trustees of the great legacy of international law that the Rhodians had first set up. Indeed, the authority of the Rhodian law was officially acknowledged in 1883 when an English judge (in *Burton v. English*) referred to the Rhodian law on jettison in the following words: "This [case] does not arise from any contract at all, but from the old Rhodian law which has become incorporated in the law of England as the law of the ocean. It is not a matter of contract but a consequence of the common danger, where natural justice required that all should contribute to indemnify for the loss of property which is sacrificed by one in order that the whole adventure may be saved."[64]

F. GREEK GOVERNMENT IN BACTRIA

The modern Western world has few culturally or politically meaningful contacts with the Central Asian area known today as northern Afghanistan. But to many of the people who are generally considered to have been the forbears of Western civilization, the region between the Hindu-Kush and the Oxus (then known as Bactria) and its extension between the Oxus and the Jaxartes (then known as Sogdiana) was home, even though they shared its possession with many different Eastern peoples. In that rich and fertile land, which the Greeks called the Jewel of Iran, at the crossroads of the Indian, Chinese, and Hellenic culture realms, where conquest was transmuted into coexistence, international history records one of its most fascinating chapters in

[62] The Pisans appointed special functionaries each year to judge matters of custom, and as there was great diversity in these judgments, they appointed another set of officials, the "constitutores," to write them down.

[63] See Bewes, pp. 72-76; and W. Cunningham, *An Essay on Western Civilization in its Economic Aspects*, Cambridge, 1913, Vol. I, p. 136.

[64] As quoted by P. Vinogradoff in his essay "Customary Law" in G. C. Crump and E. F. Jacob, eds., *The Legacy of the Middle Ages*, Oxford, 1926, p. 316; see n. 6.

cultural interpenetration and political cooperation. This particular achievement can be appreciated best if it is viewed in the general context of cultural relations between Greece and Asia.

Hellenistic history shows that the Greeks made a great impact on the peoples of Asia Minor and Syria, but failed to affect the civilizations of Babylon and Iran in any decisive way. The latter were too ancient and hard set to be modified. Babylonian law, for instance, was the one law in Western Asia that was untouched by Greek law,[65] and the strength of Iran showed itself in the obstinacy with which her social system withstood the Greek ideas of government. Alexander the Great had realized how critical these circumstances were for his program of imperial administration. Since he refused to acquiesce in the belief that Hellenism and Iranism were perpetual and instinctive enemies, he strove to include in one polity both the Greek city and the Iranian barony. Instead of following this lead, however, his Seleucid successors came down heavily on the side of the Greek city and in favor of their own nationals. As a result they never gained a tangible hold on Iran. This valuable possession fell away almost automatically the moment a new affiliation was suggested by the appearance of the Parthians, a small military aristocracy, which had adopted Iran's Mazdean religion and spoke a related tongue.

The Parthians were destined in time to become one of the most formidable Asian powers. They had no difficulty in securing the huge satrapy of Media. And yet they failed to acquire one foot of ground in Bactria, the rich, strategic region between the Oxus and the Hindu-Kush. In this easternmost portion of Iran, the Greeks had created a state based on partnership between themselves and the natives. That is to say, the Greeks in Bactria had succeeded where Alexander the Great had most desired to succeed, where the Seleucids had failed conspicuously, and where no Western statesmanship has ever since made any appreciable dent. The Bactrian story is incompletely documented; hence we cannot follow all the stages in the evolution of this remarkable object lesson in East-West relations. However, we do know that the Bactrian state, as established in the third century B.C., was pivotal in the cultural, commercial, and strategic relations of Western Asia, and that its governors knew how to use this position

[65] W. W. Tarn, *The Greeks in Bactria and India*, Cambridge, 1938, pp. 55-58. No Greek word has so far been found in the mass of Babylonian commercial documents of the Hellenistic period, though the Greek system of registration of documents was imposed upon or adopted by the Babylonians.

in the interests of both Bactria itself and the greater region. During the ensuing century it remained strong enough to ward off attacks by Parthians, rival Greeks, and a number of nomadic nations, while at the same time expanding eastward into India and southward into lower Afghanistan.

For these historical and geographical reasons Bactria has been cited as the perfect illustration of what Toynbee, in his discussion of "The Stimulus of Pressures," has called the "Marsh State."[66] It was a state on the boundary of the community to which by race and culture it belonged (in this case the Hellenistic community). As such, it acted as the shield of the interior against pressures from alien communities (in this case the seemingly inexhaustible reservoir of nomadic peoples in the northern steppes). If one uses the history of such a state in what has been a continuously crucial part of the world as a case study of regional and international relations, one may ask, what are the sources of Bactrian strength in domestic and foreign affairs? When the admittedly scanty source material is sifted, it leads us to a view, not of a general play of anonymous circumstances, but of certain Bactrian leaders and their policies. And this view is reinforced by the biographies of certain of the kings and by an impressive set of coins that bear the portraits of the Bactrian monarchs.[67]

Apart from their timeless and universal appeal as artistic masterpieces, these coins strongly support three chief impressions of Greco-Bactrian history. They show, first, that the various members of this dynasty were not ordinary men but seemed on the contrary born to rule. This becomes particularly clear when one looks at the heads of Euthydemus, a Greek from one of the Magnesias and the dynasty's founder (he died c. 189 B.C.) and his son Demetrius, later King of India. As W. W. Tarn suggests, "those who still believe in Greek decadence in the third and second centuries B.C. may find them (i.e., the faces on the coins) somewhat of a stumbling block."[68] The coins show, second, that the Euthydemids chose to rule Bactria by respecting the dual composition of their citizenry. For while the heads are un-

---

[66] A. J. Toynbee, *A Study of History*, 2nd ed., London, 1935, Vol. II, pp. 112-208. The classical instance of a marsh state in the Toynbee version was Brandenburg, long the Teutonic outpost against the Slavs.

Tarn, p. 409, suggests that both Macedonia and Bactria were such "marsh states," and that the story of Macedonia repeated itself, line upon line, in the Farther East: Euthydemus of Bactria was Philip II; Bactria was Macedonia; the derelict Maurya Empire was the Persian Empire, and Demetrius was a second Alexander.

[67] See *The Cambridge History of India*, Vol. I, plates III and IV for reproductions of the coins.

[68] p. 128.

mistakably Greek, their attire indicates that these kings were sufficiently wise to accept, or at least to respect, significant native forms.
Demetrius is shown crowned by a royal cap in the shape of the head
of an elephant; a certain Antimachus wears a flat kausia (cap); while
some of Menander's coins bear the Buddhist "wheel of the law."
Third, being artistic masterpieces, the coins suggest that Bactria's cultural and political dualism had in no way sapped the community's
general vitality and creativity.

As expressed in its foreign policy and in art, the vitality of Bactria
derived essentially from an over-all social consensus that enveloped,
rather than superseded, national and social diversity. It is certainly
highly unlikely that the Euthydemids could have accomplished what
they did without the support of the different groups of citizens whom
they ruled. The record seems to establish conclusively that their rule
was never contested by the native population. The national consensus
on which the Euthydemids were able to rely was not secured by military means, nor was it decisively determined by the central administrative policy, which the Greek kings developed and carried through so
successfully that it became, by the first century B.C., a favored pattern
in vast parts of Asia.[69] The genius of the Eastern Greeks showed itself,
rather, on the level of everyday local life, within each of the satrapies
into which Bactria-Sogdiana was divided. Euthydemus succeeded in
reconciling the Iranian barons, Greek settlers, and native serfs by
adapting Greek civic forms to Asian community life. His gradual transformation of hundreds of serf villages into organized quasi-autonomous
townships indicated the revolutionary nature of the Greek approach to
Central Asia. And as a result of his policy, the living conditions of the
mass of the population were immeasurably improved;[70] the country's
defences against the constant threat of nomadic raids were appreciably
strengthened (the villages were walled); and above all, a vigorous
communal spirit was generated, which lent strength and initiative to
countless centers of communal life.[71] Thus Bactria's cities of strength
could long stand in the gap when the end of Greek, and the imminence
of Asian, rule threatened the country with anarchy, and a Chinese
envoy who visited the country in the first half of the second century

[69] See Tarn, pp. 1-5, on the emergence of the "eparchy," which often corresponded
to a natural division of the country, as the general unit of organization in the "new"
Asia. See p. 113, on the division of Bactria-Sogdiana into satrapies.

[70] We do not know, unfortunately, on which terms the landholders agreed to this
reform.

[71] Cf. Tarn, p. 124.

B.C. could still report with amazement the effective operations of local government.[72]

While these Greco-Bactrian defences and institutions held good against the domestic "barbarians" (those alien peoples whom the Greek statesmen knew well), however, they crumbled under the onslaught of a hitherto unknown nomadic folk from the borders of China. These Central Asian people not only possessed irresistible numbers, but had perhaps been rendered desperate by a long failure to find any land in which they could settle in peace.[73] The Chinese records show that these so-called Yueh-chi, driven westward by the Huns c. 165 B.C., displaced the Shaka, who were inhabiting the country northeastward of Sogdiana and Bactria. The warlike Shaka pushed southward, occupied Bactria for a moment, but were in due course superseded by the great invasion of the Yueh-chi. And so the powerful Greek colony in the rich Indian sphere abruptly dissolved.

This Greco-Bactrian "land of the thousand cities" was not only a proving ground for the compatibility of Greek and Asian institutions. Until the very end of its political existence it was also a junction of the landroutes from China and India to the West and a meeting place of numerous and dynamic nations and cultures. As such, it was a filter through which artistic styles, religious forms, and political ideas radiated in all directions. In the first century B.C. Greek, Iranian, and Chinese products and art-motifs met in distant Mongolia. We know also that Hellenism exercised a certain artistic influence on the art of Siberia, and that the Greek calendar, as used in Bactria, swept Asia west of India.[74]

On the vaster stage of international relations the Greco-Bactrian state was a bridge, both geographically and culturally, between the Mediterranean and Far Eastern realms, notably China and India. The experiences in complex human relations which the Euthydemids had acquired by governing a rather primitive Asian people became the foundation for later Greek policies in India itself, where the talent of the Euthydemid conquerors was challenged by one of the oldest and subtlest civilizations of the ancient world. Had fortune allowed Demetrius to consolidate Bactria and Northern India into one empire, it might well have been strong enough to withstand even the Yueh-chi,

[72] See the report of Chang-kien, who visited the Yueh-chi in 126 B.C. after their conquest, in *Cambridge History of India*, Vol. I, p. 459; Tarn, pp. 212ff.

[73] Tarn, p. 413.

[74] See Tarn, p. 359. Most of these commercial and cultural encounters were initiated by an expedition that Euthydemus undertook into northern regions.

but the lot fell otherwise. At the very moment in history when a merger between East and West was in the making and Demetrius was breaking into India, the doom of this joint Eurasian adventure was already approaching—the western migration of the central Asian Yueh-chi had begun, and was to last from 165 to 125 B.C.[75] "The story of the Euthydemid dynasty," writes Tarn, "is then, in one sense, the story of a courageous experiment which failed, though there is nothing to show that it need have failed but for external interference. . . . One thing about that story is sure; win or lose, succeed or fail, it is the story of a very great adventure."[76]

C. Greece and India

A. THE ARTHASHASTRA AND BUDDHISM AS SOURCES OF INDIAN FOREIGN POLICY

Early reporters gave the Greeks the impression that a docile people of ideal goodness lived in a land at the extremity of the earth, and that nothing was impossible in that place called India.[77] But those Hellenes who reached the Orient somewhat later, as conquerors, scholars, and merchants, soon found that they could neither wholly subdue the Indian subcontinent nor really understand its intricate civilization. The great Seleucid attempt to penetrate the Farther East was frustrated by the Maurya King Chandragupta when Seleucus reached the Indus c. 305 B.C. Realizing then that the Greek and Indian powers were too evenly matched for him to risk a battle, the Hellenistic king agreed to a safe retirement of his military forces and the surrender of all of his dominions as far as the Kabul Valley. A matrimonial alliance between the rival courts capped this settlement, and diplomacy became in the ensuing period the cornerstone of a cordial relationship between the Indian and Hellenistic worlds.

This achievement deserves notice in the international history of diplomacy because it marked an adjustment not only between two competitive powers but also between two very different cultural systems. Moreover, the settlement assumes special interest in the context of Greek history, since the Indian kings who challenged the Seleucids

---

[75] Zimmer, p. 505.

[76] Tarn, p. 413. Tarn underestimates, however, the weakening effect of the inter-Greek struggles in the area, which resulted in a dynastic split between Bactria and India and an internecine war that was being hotly pursued at the very moment of the arrival of the Shaka and Yueh-chi.

[77] *The Cambridge History of India*, Vol. I, pp. 396-397.

were members of a new dynasty whose statesmen at that moment were engaged in supplying Indian statecraft with new meaning and techniques. The records of the period permit the inference that Seleucus and his successor were able to keep pace with the intellectual and political developments in India largely because they entrusted their diplomatic representation to a particularly astute and scholarly agent named Megasthenes. Through the reports of this envoy India became a reality to the Occidental world. Indeed, Megasthenes' reports, along with the books written by the earlier Greek scholars who had been in the entourage of Alexander the Great, created a conception of India that was so vivid that it endured in Christian Europe far into the Middle Ages.[78]

The Indian empire to which Megasthenes was accredited had been established during the years of trouble and confusion that immediately followed the death of Alexander the Great. It had been the work of Chandragupta Maurya (345?-300? B.C.) and his friend and counsellor, the Brahmin Chanakya Kautilya. These two remarkable men had employed their years of exile from the Nanda Kingdom of Magadha for the preparation of an ambitious scheme. Through a series of successful military and propagandist campaigns—which reflected, incidentally, a number of features acquired through contacts with Alexander and his legions—they assumed the leadership of native revolts, through which they finally eliminated not only the last of the Macedonian garrisons but also the native Nanda dynasty itself. Their new empire was later extended by the conquests of Chandragupta's grandson, Ashoka, until it covered the whole of North and Central India. Thus, for the first time in recorded history, a vast centralized Indian state arose, which stretched from the Arabian Sea to the Bay of Bengal and north to Kabul.[79]

Concerning the civil, social, legal, and fiscal organization of this state, we have not only the Greek records of Megasthenes but the far more profound expositions of the learned Chanakya. His masterwork, the *Arthashastra*, has been acclaimed as the greatest piece of literature surviving (in part at least) from the Maurya period, and its chapters on foreign policy are said to show the Indian genius for sys-

[78] *The Cambridge History of India,* Vol. I, pp. 398, 413, 425f.

[79] Vincent A. Smith, *History of India from the Sixth Century B.C. to the Mohammedan Conquest,* London, 1906, pp. 103f. (Vol. II in A. V. Williams Jackson, ed., *History of India*). See also B. G. Gokhale, *The Making of the Indian Nation,* Bombay, 1958; K. M. Panikkar, *A Survey of Indian History,* Bombay-Calcutta, 1954; A. L. Basham, *The Wonder That Was India,* London, 1954; H. G. Rawlinson, *India, A Short Cultural History,* London, 1952.

tematic exposition at its best.[80] As did his later Italian counterpart, Machiavelli (A.D. 1468-1527), the Indian chancellor addressed his manual to his sovereign, as a guide in the realistic pursuit of worldly power. In its brash and unscrupulous espousal of success as the true measure of statesmanship, the work is a reflection of India's long history of practically continuous war, strife, and division. It restates in the language of a systematic political philosophy the cold wisdom that India has traditionally rendered in its celebrated beast fables— where mice can survive the presence of cats only by dint of constant vigilance, resourcefulness, and treachery, and where little fish are the natural nourishment of big fish.[81]

In evaluating this fatalistic, sceptical, and realistic philosophy of life, one must remember that Indian political science distinguished between *dharma*, a concept carrying the broad general meaning of righteousness and best rendered in legal literature as the divinely ordained norm of good conduct,[82] and *artha*, which signifies utility and property. The sources of Indian political thought are thus essentially twofold: the dharmashastras, or treatises on law and political theory, among which the Code of Manu is the most renowned, and the arthashastras, which deal with practical politics on the national and international level. The realm of the latter was defined by Kautilya as "that science which treats of the means of acquiring and maintaining the earth. . . ."[83] All problems connected with the art of government and secular leadership thus fell within the purview of *artha*, and in this context it was understood that a king did not derive his right to rule from any divine source. He lacked both the prestige and the dignity, therefore, of the Mikado of Japan, the Pharaoh of Egypt, and the

[80] *The Cambridge History of India*, Vol. I, p. 474. There is some question as to whether this treatise can properly be attributed to Chanakya himself, whose deeds and reputation soon became legendary; but it is safe to assume that the ideas and institutions described in the work well represent those of the Maurya period.

[81] See Zimmer, pp. 87ff. Persian ideas seem to have exercised a considerable impact upon the political development of India. They are apparent in the style of King Ashoka's edicts and in expressions such as "the king's eye" and "the king's ear," which occur in the Arthashastra, and seem to furnish literary indications of the force of the concept of the King of Kings. See p. 97; *The Cambridge History of India*, Vol. I, pp. 323, 480, 494; also Jawaharlal Nehru, *The Discovery of India*, New York, 1946, pp. 137, 138, 140.

[82] This norm varied in accordance with class and caste. Indeed, the entire apparatus of the state and all operations of law are permeated by the distinction between castes. See J. H. Hutton, *Caste in India*, Cambridge, 1951, and authorities listed in *supra*, n. 79.

[83] See Donald Mackenzie Brown, *The White Umbrella, Indian Political Thought from Manu to Gandhi*, Berkeley, 1958, p. 17; also Basham, ch. IV, "The State."

Chinese Son of Heaven. Divinity in the Indian view was attached to one class of men only, the Brahmins—the interpreters of that Eternal Law (*dharma*) which it was the function of the king to enforce with his "rod of rule" (*danda*). Anointed by the Brahmin high priest, the king was an executive, but in himself, he was nothing. Indeed, in the vast Indian region there were many kings, and these, though enforcing dharma in the realms severally subject to their sway, were subject in their mutual relations only to the law of the fish. In other words, the ancient Indian system did not accommodate in practice either the concept of a family of nations or the idea of an international or transnational law.[84] "A king," we read in the *Mahabharata*,[85] "should display severity in making all his subjects observe their respective duties. If this is not done, they will prowl like wolves, devouring one another." Above the kings themselves there was no rod of rule. Hence their mutual relations were determined, of necessity, only by superior force and sensitive statesmanship. In Kautilya's words, power alone could bring peace between kings.[86]

In the resultant Indian jungle of competing bids for power, war was accepted as a continuance of policy and the ultimate arbiter of conflicting claims. Kautilya, however, in his explanation of its function, states that war should always serve the larger ends of policy and never become an end in itself. He argued forcefully (and successfully, as Chandragupta's relations with Seleucus were to show) against any war that might bring ruin to both contestants for power, and for the kind of statesmanship that instead of crushing an intelligent enemy would win him over. On the basis of such an arrangement the diplomatic relations of India with the Greeks continued to be cordial and commercially profitable for centuries. Strabo declares that the Oxus river formed a link in an important chain, along which Indian goods were carried to Europe by way of the Caspian and Black Seas. Other accounts indicate that Greek wine, Greek singing boys and maidens, even Greek sophists,[87] were in great demand at the Indian court, and that the scientists of the astronomical observatory in Central India knew how to keep in touch with their colleagues in Alexandria.[88]

[84] See Beni Prasad, *Theory of Government in Ancient India*, Allahabad, 1927, p. 362.

[85] *Mahabharata* 12. 120. 93, and again, 12. 140. 7. Cited by Zimmer, p. 121, n. 24.

[86] *Kautilya's Arthasastra*, R. Shamasastry, tr., Bangalore, 1915, p. 333.

[87] Antiochus filled other requests but replied that in "Greece the laws forbid a sophist to be sold." Nehru, p. 146.

[88] Greek astronomy superseded the native Indian system in the latter part of the fourth century B.C. *The Cambridge History of India*, Vol. I, p. 384.

Kautilya distinguished kings of equal, superior, and inferior power in the international society of states, and his instructions for their respective manners of behavior varied in accord with their status. But he expressly recognized the intrinsic fluidity of all existing power systems by sanctioning the breaking of agreements on the part of those who were rising in the power scale.[89] His outline for statesmanship revolved around the general proposition that each state must manipulate its relations with other states in such a way as never to allow itself to be overwhelmed. With this end in mind the wise king should make his realm the center of gravity in a series of concentric circles (*mandalas*) of kingdoms and regard the latter very much as the functioning elements of an international political wheel.[90] Within the sphere of the

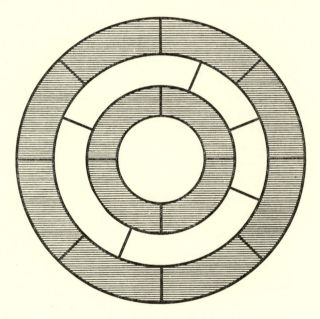

The Circle of States.

first ring, or mandala, surrounding him the monarch must expect to find his natural enemies, and in that beyond, his allies. Surrounding the second ring there is another of remoter danger, interesting primarily as supplying reinforcement to the enemy directly at hand. Within each ring, again, are subdivisions, signifying mutual natural animosi-

[89] Shamasastry, p. 385.

[90] S. V. Viswanatha, *International Law in Ancient India*, London, 1925, p. 90. See p. 50 to the effect that an order of seniority must have been observed among these kings in the royal assemblies which met for deliberations of interstate matters. On p. 11, Viswanatha compares Kautilya, on rather obscure grounds, to the seventeenth century European legalist Grotius.

ties, which have to be taken into account when arranging pacts.[91] Moreover, since each competing king must be presumed to be aware of his own mandala, a statesman operates, perforce, in an exceedingly complicated set of stresses and cross-stresses, always assuming his neighbor to be unfriendly, jealous, and aggressive, and always watching for his own time of surprise and treacherous attack.

In the continuous "white war of nerves" that resulted from this generally held concept of international politics,[92] an Indian king could hope for success only if he knew how to choose tactfully among the different classic manners of approaching neighboring states. He might, for instance, attempt the way of the snake charmer (*saman*), lulling his dangerous enemy into passivity by a nonaggression pact or a definition of spheres of influence. This kind of appeasement Kautilya contrasts with outright assault (*danda*), and with several variations of deceit and pretence (*maya*). In certain situations, for example, it is advisable to wear a mask, say, of religious righteousness, or to create other such traps, illusions, or appearances of things (*indrajala*).[93]

Kautilya's quasi-scientific rendition of foreign policy, which had some precedents in views earlier expressed,[94] found eloquent subscribers in the subsequent periods of Indian history,[95] and on the basis of their accumulated theories it is possible to conclude that the kings of ancient India were committed to the ruthless pursuit of national

---

[91] Zimmer, pp. 114f., describes and reproduces the chart. Shamasastry, p. 332 (reproducing Kautilya, Book VI, ch. 11). Viswanatha, p. 90, says that Kautilya distinguishes in this way four primary circles of states, twelve kings, sixty elements of sovereignty, seventy-two elements of states.

[92] Zimmer, pp. 111f.

[93] *ibid.*, pp. 120-122. The author compares these techniques with similar devices used by the Roman emperors, the Achaeminidae of Persia, the Muslim caliphates at Baghdad and Cairo, the Ottoman Empire, and modern totalitarian states, on pp. 111f.

[94] I.e., the *Mahabharata*. See Zimmer, p. 119, n. 22; Moriz Winternitz, *Geschichte der Indischen Litteratur*, Leipzig, 1920, Vol. III, p. 507.

[95] The last summing up of Hindu political thought is the Sukraniti, which borrows freely from the *Mahabharata*, Manu, and indirectly from Kautilya. This work was probably composed about the thirteenth century A.D. and received supplements in the sixteenth and seventeenth centuries. See Brown, p. 65. It should be remarked in this connection that the Muslim invaders of the eleventh and later centuries were unable to modify the traditional approaches to politics. "The influence of the Dharmashastras and the Arthashastras remained unspent in this (Muslim) epoch . . . at no period of our history has the influence of our ancient polity been quite moribund, and in this sense its persistence is one of the surest witnesses to the unity of Indian History." See K. V. Rangaswami Aiyangar, *Considerations on Some Aspects of Ancient Indian Polity*, Madras, 1916, as quoted by Brown, p. 8. The same view is expressed by K. M. Panikkar, p. 29: "If Indian administration of today is analysed to its bases, the doctrines and practices of Chanakya will be found to be still in force."

power. However, when one looks at the actual diplomatic record of the Maurya Empire, a somewhat different impression interposes itself. For not only did the Indian government engage in surprisingly co-operative practices in its relations with non-Indian governments, but the particular regional system of states that had developed on the Indian subcontinent itself revolved around a pattern of agreement on certain well-defined traditional categories of sovereignty and jurisdiction. For example, the Maurya government never lost sight of the fact that it did not actually control the area from the Hindu-Kush to Ceylon. This explains why Chandragupta's grandson, Ashoka, distinguished carefully between the following grades of control, while applying officially the traditional political theories:

a) The imperial dominions over whose kingdoms, vice-royalties, and provinces the emperor was supreme. Here he was the head of a great confederation of states, united under him for imperial purposes but retaining their independence in all other respects.

b) Beyond this domain, to the north, west, and south, the unsubdued border peoples whom the emperor regarded as coming within his sphere of influence. He was concerned with the welfare and good conduct of these in the interest of general peace, always patiently hoping that punitive expeditions or annexations would never be necessary.

c) Beyond the zone of these border peoples, realms of whose complete independence there was no question. With these remoter lands, which included, in the south, the ancient Dravidian kingdoms, the emperor's relations were merely such as might be expected to exist between friendly powers. We may note, by the way, that in the northwest Ashoka's sphere of influence ended at the frontiers of King Antiochus of the Seleucid dynasty.[96]

Indian ethics recognized implicitly that the rule of the fish, or of the jungle, as defined by Kautilya, should eventually be outlawed from human relations. Within each particular realm the king, as the policeman of *dharma*, had to see to it that cooperation and harmony obtained among the many component groups and individuals. While no hope was held out by theorists that this peaceful pattern should ever become transferred to the larger field of nations, people continued to hold fast to an ancient mythical ideal which represents a universal world-wide empire of enduring tranquillity under the Chakravartin, a just and virtuous world monarch. By virtue of their moral superiority

[96] *The Cambridge History of India*, Vol. I, pp. 514f.

his invincible armies were to put an end to the perpetual struggle of the contending states.[97]

Indeed, the Buddhist emphasis on the communion of the world, as contrasted with that of the race or nation, lent particular force and credence to the symbolic figure of a universal king. In this conception of the world, the Chakravartin became the secular counterpart of the all-redeeming Buddha—the temporal manifestation of the eternal and peaceful order of things which the Buddha's appearance heralded for the whole universe. When Ashoka, Chandragupta's grandson, was converted to Buddhism, the pre-Buddhist expectation of the Chakravartin appeared to have been briefly realized in India's political system. For this emperor was not only a devout disciple, but the official patron and effective propagator of the faith. Impressed with the horrors of war,[98] he preached abstinence from all violence and benevolence toward all living creatures, thus giving statesmanship a new function and *dharma* an extended jurisdiction. Immediately after his conversion a great series of edicts was set up in stone, under the terms of which war was outlawed as an instrument of Indian policy. These declarations had momentous effects, for their precepts were faithfully observed by the emperor throughout the remainder of his reign.

As a result of these developments Buddhism became not only a popular religion, but for a time the mainspring of India's foreign policy, thus either superseding or fundamentally complementing the mandates of the *Arthashastra*. A new moral law for the discharge of all official duties was proclaimed through imperial missives and edicts, and high officials were appointed for the express purpose of inculcating piety and redressing misfortunes in all situations—national and international—that came within the purview of imperial influence. Ashoka saw to it, for example, that medical aid was made easily available to both men and animals, not only in India and the neighboring states of South India, whether independent or dependent, but also in the northwestern territories and even in such foreign realms as the Greek kingdom of Antiochus.[99] Missionaries were sent forth to the utmost limits of the barbarian countries, to mingle among unbelievers and teach foreigners better things than those to which they were accus-

[97] The conception of the Chakravartin, "the superman turning the wheel," goes back to earliest Vedic and pre-Vedic, pre-Aryan traditions and is later reflected in various Buddhist, Jaina, and Hindu writings. Zimmer, pp. 127ff.

[98] He had waged an aggressive war against the Kalinga kingdom and the suffering there observed is said to have deeply stirred him.

[99] *The Cambridge History of India*, Vol. I, p. 499.

tomed. Taking advantage of the connection with the West, which had been maintained since the coming of Megasthenes, Ashoka sent teachers of the Buddhist *dharma* to Antiochus II of Syria, Ptolemy II of Egypt, Magas of Cyrene, Antigonus Gonatas of Macedonia, and Alexander II of Epirus;[100] to Ceylon, where the early Buddhist canon was committed to writing about 80 B.C.; and probably also to the Bactrian court.[101] In subsequent centuries Buddhism radiated from India to China, Japan, most of South Asia, and many Pacific islands, and became in this way a world religion. It is therefore no exaggeration to say that the moral decision of India's great ruler Ashoka had far-reaching consequences for all the subsequent generations of Asia.

B. THE FUSION OF STOICISM AND BUDDHISM IN THE GRECO-INDIAN GOVERNMENT OF DEMETRIUS AND MENANDER

Shortly after Ashoka's death his promising empire disintegrated, falling prey again to war and division, and it was then that the destinies of Indians and Greeks merged in a common Euro-Asian polity. Secure in their possession of Bactria, lured by the promise of what lay beyond, and committed perhaps to the memory of their great predecessor Alexander the Great, the Greeks (or Yavana, as their Indian neighbors called them) were able to extend their domain in the Orient beyond the bounds that had been reached by the first invasion.[102] The son of Euthydemus, Demetrius, and his successor, the great Greek general and king, Menander, established their mastery over the Indus valley. However, they were immediately harried in the rear, for a rival Hellenistic family, headed by Eucratides, succeeded in seizing power in Bactria and the resultant division of Greek power and continuous internecine war between the two Bactrian dynasties halted further Greek progress eastward. After 162 B.C. there were in India two royal houses of the Yavana and several branches of these two reigned at the same time in different kingdoms.

Now while it is clear that the Euthydemid conquest of India was conceived in connection with the dynasty's ultimate project of building a great empire in Asia, research indicates also that the Greeks were not in India for the purpose of Hellenizing the Indians. When it was realized that their chief purpose—conquest—was unattainable, they

---

[100] Zimmer, pp. 496ff.

[101] *The Cambridge History of India*, Vol. I, p. 499.

[102] The exact limits of this extension in India are somewhat in doubt. And it is also uncertain just how effective the Greek control over the wide expanse was under the successors of Demetrius. See *The Cambridge History of India*, Vol. I, p. 444.

stayed on to rule what they could.[103] In this situation they evolved a government that clearly reflected Alexander's ideas as elaborated by Euthydemus. A dual Greco-Indian state arose, comparable to that which had evolved from the Greco-Bactrian partnership. However, in Bactria the Greeks had come to terms with a people whose level of civilization was decidedly lower than their own, whereas in the Kabul Valley in India they were in contact with a culture very different from, yet certainly as advanced as their own, and much more ancient.[104]

Hellenistic policies in their encounter with this new and infinitely complex environment seem to have scored a considerable triumph. The sources of their success may be found in that peculiarly alert awareness to even the strangest realities that had so frequently marked the Greek approach to international relations. In the present instance, the Euthydemids accepted the fact that Indian civilization was strong enough to hold its own against invading values, and that the Indians neither took Greek names (as the people did in other parts of Asia) nor borrowed except in matters of external form.[105] And they realized, above all, that their own government would have no chance of operating at all in such a vast expanse of land unless it placed its chief reliance on the native element of the population. The well-developed Greek talent for sizing up any situation, however strange and awkward, was reinforced and guided furthermore—in Indian as well as in other experiences—by a strong disposition to pursue knowledge and look for truth in even the most unfamiliar surroundings. In India, it must be noted, the Hellenes, in this quest, seem to have been irresistibly drawn into the orbit of their host culture. In fact, scholars have found that a definite process of Indianization set in among the Greeks from about the first century B.C. onward[106] and that the process was particularly conclusive in the sphere of religion, where the Greeks were, thanks to their own hospitable creed, singularly free from any dogma or inhibition. It was in no way unnatural that many Greeks should have identified the Hindu deity Indra with Zeus and Shiva with Dionysus,[107] or that some of their official functionaries, such as the Greek ambassador to the Sunga court at Videsha, should have become worshippers of Vishnu.[108]

Menander, of all the Greek representatives in India, was without

---

[103] Tarn, p. 376.
[104] *The Cambridge History of India*, Vol. I, p. 545 for an analysis of this relationship.
[105] Tarn, p. 378.
[106] *ibid.*
[107] Zimmer, p. 504.
[108] Tarn, p. 378.

doubt the most fascinating. In his personality and his rule[109] the philosophies of Europe and Asia merged, and the partnership between Indians and Greeks, Stoics and Buddhists, which his leadership stimulated in such an inspiring way, ranks in the history of international adjustment as one of humanity's timeless achievements. The great general and king was himself either actually a member of the Buddhist order or so outspoken a benefactor that the local community looked upon him as one of their own.[110] He is the only Yavana, furthermore, who ever became celebrated in the ancient native literature of India;[111] for scholars have identified him with Milinda, the Yavana king of Chakala, who is one of the two leading characters in the work known as the "Questions of Milinda," a treatise dating from about the second century A.D. on the fundamental principles of Buddhist philosophy. In other words, in Asia Menander won for himself abiding fame rather as a philosopher than as a mighty conqueror. Indian history records that "as in wisdom, so in strength of body, swiftness and valour, there was found none equal to Milinda in all India."[112] Nor was his fame confined to the Orient. Some two centuries after his time, Plutarch recounted to the Western world the story of how, after Menander's death in camp, the cities of his realm contended for the honor of preserving his ashes and agreed on a division among themselves in order that the memory of his reign should not be lost—a tale that strikingly recalls the tradition of the distribution of the Buddha's ashes.[113]

It is perhaps symbolic that Stoicism, itself a synthesis of insights gained in the contexts of "Oriental" and "Occidental" civilizations, should have found its most persuasive exponents in the easternmost outposts of Hellenic culture. Those outposts, as held and used by their Greek organizers, became gateways through which the urban culture of the ancient Near East could pass to enrich the village life of Central Asia, there blending with the sophisticated culture of the Hindu and Buddhist societies of India, and thus making for increasingly meaningful adjustments between widely separated and differing worlds. It is significant, furthermore, for an evaluation of the mediating function

[109] His coins were distributed over a wider area than those of any other Greco-Indian ruler.

[110] Zimmer, p. 505.

[111] See Tarn, pp. 376, 408 for the circumstances in which Greek kings were taken up into the great Indian epic, the *Mahabharata*.

[112] *The Cambridge History of India*, Vol. I, p. 549.

[113] *ibid.*, p. 551. The cultural fusion between Buddhism and Hellenism found particularly vivid expression in the Gandhara school of art. See Tarn, p. 393; Zimmer, p. 132, n. 47.

of Hellenistic philosophy, as it was understood by the Greeks of Asia, that its influence did not register only in the isolated speculations or deeds of a few thoughtful men. Rather was it in the difficult sphere of organized government and practical statesmanship that the Greek adventure in Bactria and India came closest to a realization of Stoic ideals. Menander and the Euthydemids were, in fact, the only heirs of Alexander in the whole wide region of his conquest who continuously and consistently tried to translate his dream of international brotherhood into reality.

In India, as in Bactria, the Greeks were ousted, but not by the Asian peoples whom they ruled.[114] They were eliminated, or outflanked and isolated, in both regions by the relentless pressure of nomadic northern Asians: a series of invasions that brought first into Bactria, then into India, the Central Asian tribes known in China as the Yueh-chi.[115] As a result of these migrations, and of the Chinese Han Dynasty's temporary occupation of the Tarim basin in 115 B.C., the Far East gained direct geographical contact not only with India but also with the Near East, and international commerce was vitally affected. Henceforth the northern roads to China through Turkestan were clear for Indian trade. After 106 B.C. Chinese caravans were able to pass into Parthia by way of Bactria without the Greeks participating in any part in this traffic,[116] and the goods then went by the great landroutes of Persia to the Roman Empire.

It was Kanishka the Great (c. A.D. 78-123) whose dynasty united the five Yueh-chi tribes and entered India. This king then, like his Greek predecessors, was converted to Buddhism. With the Indian state system to the southeast, Han China to the northeast, and imperial Rome to the west, the flourishing Buddhist empire of Kanishka and his successors certainly occupied—until its overthrow in A.D. 236— a pivotal position in the political affairs of the civilized world, comparable to that previously filled by the Greco-Bactrians. Nevertheless, while the historically significant displacement of the Greeks as mediators between the cultures of the Far East and the Mediterranean region certainly led, in the very nature of things, to closer relations between India and China than had existed before, it may well have been a principal cause for the cultural estrangement in the subsequent relations between Mediterranean Europe and Asia generally, and Europe and

---

[114] Except in the extreme East of their Indian realm.
[115] In India, known as the Kushanas.
[116] See Tarn, p. 363; Childe, p. 234.

India in particular. It is difficult to estimate the long-range effects of the shift of rule upon the general development of cultural and political relations in the ancient world, but the evidence of the centuries that have since elapsed would seem to suggest that, following the establishment of the Kushana Dynasty, Mongolian and Indian societies became more closely related to each other (Buddhism, for example, spread into China), but India and the West became progressively estranged. The establishment of direct lines of communication between the Roman and Far Eastern civilizations was not necessarily synonymous with the creation of opportunities for a more intimate spiritual understanding. Indeed, it would seem that, apart from an isolated mission here and there, the great sovereignties of East and West reached something of a dead end in their contacts. A curtain fell between them—perhaps precisely because there was now no middleman, such as the Hellenistic society in Asia had been, to filter and interpret the heritage of the West to the East, and of the East to the West.

PART II

THE IMPERIAL SYSTEMS OF CHINA AND ROME

CHAPTER 4

THE PLACE OF THE CHINESE STATE
IN ASIA

A. *The Chinese System of International Relations*

THE contemporary image of "one world" has only recently begun to supersede the many separate world images that for a long time past have held the imagination of the world's different peoples. But its competitive chances to influence the formulation of national policies have been impaired unduly by our tendency to link its evolution exclusively to the political history and philosophy of Western Europe. In the interest of reconstructing the records of international history and appraising realistically the present worth of the "one world" theme, it is therefore necessary to understand those visions of the universe which non-Western peoples have held for thousands of years.

Just as medieval Europeans thought of themselves as constituting the center of world happenings, and as the Indians looked upon India as the chief country of the earth in relationship to which all other areas were uncivilized, so the Chinese regarded China as the sole world state and the center of all humanity. Every intellectual effort to understand the place of that "Middle Kingdom" in contemporary world affairs, be it as a member of twentieth century world organizations or as a participant in twentieth century Asian politics, should issue from a preliminary understanding of these views. Furthermore, Chinese interpretations of their place in the universe reflect certain incontestable facts. The record of Chinese history is longer than that of other existing states and it involves an immense expanse of land, a multitude of races, and many separate language groups.[1] China's achievement in state building is also unique in the annals of government because her people have known not only how to consolidate their empire but how to maintain it with a steadily increasing population as a continuously identifiable going concern. Given these circumstances, it is natural that the Chinese should have evolved their own system of international relations. And since the theories and practices thus formulated were ap-

[1] It should be noted, however, that the unity of the written language and literary tradition in the Chinese sphere was unbroken, even though there was a variety of dialects within the expanding Chinese realm.

plied successfully over several millenniums, it is certainly rash to suppose that China's comparatively recent entrance into the modern international state system as a single sovereignty co-equal with all present and prospective member nations, should have automatically cancelled the memory of generations, not only of Chinese but of other Asians, that China was herself, as far back as the dawn of human memory, a separate and self-sufficient world.

The ethical system that has largely determined the Chinese view of life, and therefore also the Chinese approach to foreign affairs, was already well established in its broad outlines in the first centuries of the Chou period, long before it was restated and amplified by Confucius in the sixth century B.C. It assumed a natural harmony between heavenly and earthly forces, and invited men to think of the entire universe as a peaceful world-embracing community, which Heaven governs in such a way that all human destinies can express themselves in ordered relationships on all levels of association, be it in the family, in the state, or in greater spheres. The thesis that Heaven is naturally superior to earth led to the further assumption that Heaven delegates its governing functions to a righteous ruler who thereby becomes the one and only Son of Heaven. The Chinese emperor was in a stronger position, therefore, than an Indian king. Furthermore, such was the importance traditionally attached in China to the practical realization of universal harmony that Chinese philosophical literature consistently reserved much more room for the treatment of actual politics than did any of the comparable philosophical writings in India.[2]

Universalist thought as it developed in China through the millenniums not only fostered the definite expectation that the great emperor of a united world would reflect through his personal character and official conduct the high moral principles that the heavenly order so forcefully suggests, but also indicated quite precisely the manner in which the divine mandate was to be exercised. Since early Chinese philosophers had proceeded from the premise of cosmic unity, they concluded logically that Heaven's only earthly administrator should exercise unlimited territorial jurisdiction. In the interest of practical statesmanship, however, gradations of actual control were admitted. The emperor was expected to rule his immediate environment in strict accordance with his moral mandate. Yet it was realized clearly that the more distant peoples could not be successfully governed as long as they did not understand the terms under which the emperor was exercising the will

[2] Helmuth von Glasenapp, *Die Fünf Grossen Religionen*, Düsseldorf, 1952, Vol. I, p. 163.

of Heaven. Chinese statesmanship was, therefore, charged with the preliminary task of educating the neighboring barbarians in the divinely sanctioned ways by inducting them gradually into the Chinese culture realm.

The moral conviction that the universe is one peaceful and harmonious community was strengthened by the widely accepted, albeit mythical, belief that the whole of Greater China had in very ancient times actually been under the rule of a single monarch. And after the Confucian philosophers had elaborated upon the ancient Chinese universalist creed, the national sentiments and traditions coalesced to constitute a concept of political unity that has, ever since, exercised a greater hold on the Chinese imagination than the actual record of belligerency, discord, and enforced unification which are characteristic of many periods of Chinese history. This unifying intellectual tradition has been of great moment in the development of Chinese affairs, for it has been responsible for a number of diplomatic experiments with confederations and leagues, as well as for certain general cultural offensives to attain greater regional unions. Indeed, a comparative study of the quests for political unity that have been carried on throughout the course of world history has revealed that the concept of unity is perhaps more highly developed in China than in any other country.[3]

Confucius' respect for the past caused him to lay special stress on the peculiarly patriarchal order that had characterized China's family life since time immemorial. As a consequence, the norms of behavior proper to such a family became, in due time, the only norms recognized in China as proper for political conduct—whether within the confines of the state itself, or in the sphere of humanity at large.[4] In other words, the Confucian system of government, as evolved from Confucian philosophy, regarded all men, including the emperor, and all communities, including the world state, as subject to the will of Heaven. It safeguarded this preordained order of natural harmony by teaching all mortals respect for the five fundamental human relationships: those between man and woman (or husband and wife), father and son, older and younger brother, friend and friend, sovereign and minister (or subject). When the timeless patterns of these associations were fully understood and realized, peace, order, and happiness were to prevail in the entire community, however great its scope.

[3] Homer Dubs, "The Concept of Unity in China," in *The Quest for Political Unity in World History*, Stanley Pargellis, ed., American Historical Association, 1944, pp. 8-19.

[4] Glasenapp, Vol. I, p. 185.

Now the essence of each of these relationships, with the possible exception of that between friends, is inequality. And just as it is Heaven's natural superiority over earth that ensures the cosmic order, so can order in human relations be maintained (so argued the Confucians) only if control is vested definitely in the party that is the best qualified socially to exercise it. The contrary ideal of equality, which was later to captivate so many generations of the Western world, held no promise or allure for those committed to Confucian thought, for it was identified by them with anarchy and barbarism. Indeed, until the late nineteenth and early twentieth centuries A.D., when their life orientations were unsettled by close contact with the West, the Chinese, for the most part, did their utmost to maintain the conditions of an ordered inequality as the best safeguard of harmony and peace.

B. Conflicting Chinese Theories
of International Relations and their Influence
on the Conduct of China's Foreign Policy

A true compliance with the hierarchical order was not as easy as the rigidity of the formal Chinese pattern of society might suggest, for it must be remembered that China's philosophers had pointed not only to order as humanity's ideal state, but also to concord and peace. These harmonious ends were expected to determine the methods employed for the attainment of the good life. In the very nature of human relations, superiors cannot expect automatic obedience from their inferiors. But since neither father nor husband, older brother nor emperor, was supposed to enforce subservience by reliance on the power that inhered in his superior status, the exercise of control was traditionally viewed as an art requiring consummate knowledge and skill. And this meant, in particular, that the socially privileged were to govern by virtue of reason and moral example.

Confucius taught that only men who are able to rule themselves can undertake the government of others, and that only those who can govern others can rule the kingdoms and families of the Empire.[5] As elaborated by his successor, Mencius (372?-289? B.C.), any king governing by goodness—and here Mencius identifies "goodness" with a definite series of social reforms—will become a True King, that is to say a monarch accepted by all China and dominating not by force but

[5] H. G. Creel, *Chinese Thought from Confucius to Mao Tsê-tung*, Chicago, 1953, p. 208, quoting from "The Great Learning." See also Lin Yutang, *The Wisdom of Confucius*, New York, 1943, pp. 80ff., and *Confucius, The Unwobbling Pivot and the Great Digest*, Ezra Pound, tr. N.Y., 1947, p. 20.

by his own goodness.[6] In the spirit of this ideal, many Confucians expected that workers would drift away from oppressive countries to the one where conditions were more to their liking, and that "bad" states would thus be depopulated while the good state would become so strong in numbers that it would finally dominate the whole of China.[7] In the context of Confucian thinking, then, government was, on all its levels, a matter of personal character and conduct, and character and conduct were proper when they conformed to traditional standards of goodness, rather than to any legal precepts of behavior.[8] As the Confucian creed developed during the Ch'in (255-206 B.C.) and Han (206 B.C. - A.D. 220) Dynasties, people were enjoined to believe that "From the Son of Heaven to the common man, all must consider cultivation of the person to be fundamental,"[9] and that the whole world can be peaceful only when all its states are properly governed.

During the Han Dynasty, Confucianism was strongly influenced by Lao Tzŭ (375? B.C.) and such later Taoists as Chuang Tzŭ (369?-286? B.C.), who held that the object of life should be the cultivation of inner powers rather than the pursuit of goodness in its strict Con-

---

[6] Arthur Waley, *Three Ways of Thought in Ancient China*, New York, 1940, p. 122.

[7] *ibid.*, p. 189. This theory could be evolved and exercise appeal because it was so deeply anchored in China's reverence for agricultural pursuits.

[8] These ideas were most clearly expressed by a later Confucian, Hsün Tzŭ (c.298-c.238 B.C.), in his book on "The Origins of Society and the State." In re-editing the Book of Rites (*Li Chi*), the same philosopher explains "li" as the mould imposed from without which will maintain men in the correct mean, i.e., the social gradations that are necessary if there is to be no conflict between man and man. So understood, "li" puts interdictions in advance of what is about to take place, whereas law makes interdictions on what has already occurred. (Fung Yu-Lan, *A History of Chinese Philosophy*, Derk Bodde, tr., Peiping, 1937, pp. 294, 338-340.)

For relation of "li" to law, see Jean Escarra, *Le Droit Chinois*, Paris and Peiping, 1936, pp. 70-78, to the effect that the very notion of law as understood in the West could not develop in China because the Chinese prefer the idea of a "model" and cannot distinguish law from morality. If law means anything to the Chinese, it means morality in action. See also pp. 435ff. On p. 17 Escarra explains: "There is no place for law in the Latin sense of the term. Not even rights of individuals are guaranteed by law. There are only duties and mutual compromises governed by the ideas of order, responsibility, hierarchy, and harmony. The prince, assisted by the sages, ensures the dominance of these throughout the realm. The supreme ideal of the *chin tzu* is to demonstrate in all circumstances a just measure, a ritual moderation, as is shown in the Chinese taste for arbitration and reciprocal concessions. To take advantage of one's position, to invoke one's 'right,' has always been looked at askance in China. The great art is to give way on certain points, and thus accumulate an invisible fund of merit whereby one can later obtain advantages in other directions."

Compare also Joseph Needham, *Science and Civilisation in China*, 3 vols., Cambridge, England, 1954-1959, Vol. II, pp. 521ff. on "Natural Law and Positive Law in Chinese Jurisprudence," especially p. 529 to the effect that responsibility is fixed not in terms of who has done something, but in terms of what has happened.

[9] Fung Yu-Lan, pp. 368, 365ff.

fucian meaning. "The Evolution of Li" in the *Li Chi* (Book of Rites ch. 7), states the following: "Confucius said: 'I have never seen the practice of the *Great Tao*. When the *Great Tao* was in practice, the world was common to all. . . . Therefore men did not love only their parents, nor did they treat as children only their own sons. . . . This was the period of Great Unity. Now the Tao has fallen into obscurity, the world has become (divided into) families. Each loves but his own parents. . . .' "[10] Caught in their own scale of graded love and compassion for fellow beings, Confucians could not quite reconcile the image of a Greater Unity with the reality of the familism they had created, and were therefore content to concern themselves exclusively with their own period of the "Small Tranquillity."[11] And within these limits, they concluded logically, any existing disorder in human relations—whether in the family, in the state, or in relations with other states—must have arisen organically from the failure of a governing individual or state to cultivate the necessary inner virtue. When, therefore, the state of Sung, in whose good government Mencius had once put all his hopes for the unification of China, was attacked by the two rival states of Ch'i and Ch'u, the philosopher was hard pressed to explain why his original prognosis that all the other states would range themselves voluntarily under Sung's leadership had not come true. He recounted stories of legendary ancient kings who had won the support of everyone under Heaven by putting into practice in their own small territory the humane precepts of Kingly Government, and he concluded that if Sung had failed to win such allegiance, it could only be because Sung "was not in point of fact practicing Kingly Government. . . . For if the King of Sung," he went on, "were indeed practicing such government, everyone within the Four Seas would raise his head and gaze

[10] *ibid.*, pp. 377f. See *The Sacred Books of China. The Texts of Confucianism*, James Legge, tr., Oxford, 1885, Part III, Book VII, The Lî Yun, sect. I, p. 364: "Confucius replied: 'I never saw the practice of the Grand course, and the eminent men of the three dynasties; but I have my object (in harmony with theirs).'
'When the Grand course was pursued, a public and common spirit ruled all under the sky; they chose men of talents, virtue, and ability; their words were sincere, and what they cultivated was harmony. . . . Now the Grand course has fallen into disuse and obscurity, the kingdom is a family inheritance. Every one loves (above all others) his own parents. . . . This is the period of what we call Small Tranquillity.'"
Louis Le Fur and Georges Chklaver in *Recueil de Textes de Droit International Public*, Paris, 1928, pp. 2f., render this chapter of the *Li Chi* as Confucius' outline for a perfect international association of all states. This interpretation seems erroneous. In speaking of the "Great Unity" the philosopher engages in a somewhat nostalgic reminiscence of times past, rather than in a casting of visions for the future.
[11] Fung Yu-Lan, p. 378.

toward him, wanting to have him and no other as lord and king. . . ."[12]
Similarly, when a king of Ch'i (319-301 B.C.) acquainted Mencius
with his ambition to dominate all the other states and requested advice on how best to realize this project, the learned adviser chose
to evade the question and told the king instead what "True Kingship"
really was. "Now the land that is within the Four Seas," said Mencius,
"has nine divisions, each a thousand leagues square. The territories
of Ch'i may, taken together, amount to as much as one of these nine
divisions. Is it not clear that one part has about as much chance of sub-
duing the other eight as Tsou (a very small state) has of beating Ch'u
(a very large state)? No, there is nothing for it but to go back to the
root of the matter. . . . If you were this day to set up a form of government founded on Goodness, at once all the officers under Heaven
would want to be enrolled in your court, all the ploughmen would want
to plough up your freelands, all the merchants and tradesmen would
want to bring their goods to your market, all travelers would want to
use your roads, and all those anywhere under Heaven who had griev-
ances against their ruler would want to lay their complaints before
you. . . ."[13]

Whatever the factual developments in Chinese politics between the
fourth and second centuries B.C., China's chief theorists—and it must
be remembered that most, if not all, were also active as political advisers—exerted themselves tirelessly and uncompromisingly in behalf
of peace and union as their country's chief political goals. And whereas
in certain other ancient lands (for example, India, where the realm
of politics could be strictly delimited from that of individual life) deceit, treachery, and aggression might be treated as legitimate means
of statecraft, such methods were explicitly condemned in the writings
of practically all the Chinese philosophers. Instead, they advocated a
rule by example and persuasion, and politics inspired by courtesy and
good faith.[14] The different schools of Chinese thought presented different arguments in support of the general pacifist philosophical position. The Taoist objection to war, for instance, was based not so much
on moral or humanitarian grounds as on the absolute insignificance

[12] Waley, p. 143. See also Melvin Frederic Nelson, *Korea and the Old Orders in
Eastern Asia*, Baton Rouge, 1945, p. 10.

[13] Waley, p. 149. For the entire dialogue see pp. 144-151.

[14] A comparative survey of internationalist thought reveals China as the unique
instance of a country in which practically all important philosophical opinion was
against war.
See *The Works of Hsüntze*, H. H. Dubs, tr., London, 1928, pp. 266f. For a full
discussion see also Elbert D. Thomas, *Chinese Political Thought*, New York, 1927.

and futility of the utmost that conquest can gain, or defence secure, when compared with the limitless inward resources of the individual.[15] And whereas Mencius, the Confucian, called those who boasted of their military skill "great criminals," and ministers who advised the use of force "robbers of the people,"[16] his rivals, the Mohists (adherents of Mo Tzŭ, 420 B.C.), considered the chief cause for the wars and dissensions that were at that time disuniting China to be the cherished Confucian doctrine that people are to be loved on a decreasing scale beginning with the parents. The Mohists countered this principle by suggesting that wars would cease if men loved the citizens of other states as much as their parents;[17] that is, if men would not insist on applying a double standard in their human relations.

However, even though the Confucian, Mohist, and Taoist philosophers were solidly ranged against recourse to belligerency, all made allowance for one type of warfare—the punitive action that Heaven might command to redress a great wrong. Even Mencius, the most extreme pacifist, believed that a "bad" nation or a state "badly" ruled[18] had to be chastised. He was in a great dilemma, however, when faced with the necessity of naming the ministrant who should execute Heaven's will, because at that time there was neither an indisputably sovereign emperor of all China nor a state that Mencius could have regarded as "worthy to act"—not even an interstate court to investigate the charges against an accused government.[19] In such a situation the "Righteous War principle" could be readily reduced to a moral cloak for the covering of wanton acts of sheer aggression.

In his discussion of these problems Arthur Waley suggests that it was this ostrich-like attitude toward "the actual facts of the world as it now exists" that brought Confucianism into discredit as a practical moral system and paved the way in China for a new, more realistic philosophy.[20] For China, after all, was a unity only in theory at the time when Confucius announced his political thesis. It was actually split into fifty-odd kingdoms and numerous peripheral tribes.[21] Moreover,

[15] Waley, p. 95.

[16] *Works of Mencius*, in Chinese Classics, Vol. II, pp. 316, 324-355; see comments in Nelson, p. 11.

[17] *The Ethical and Political Works of Motse*, Y. P. Mei, tr., London, 1929; see sections on Mohist doctrine of condemnation of offensive war. See also Waley, p. 174.

[18] *ibid.*, p. 152, on "the Yen episode."

[19] See *ibid.*, pp. 138ff., on the fabrication of atrocity stories for the incrimination of the state of Sung, which two other states wished to partition.

[20] *ibid.*, p. 143.

[21] See Thomas, pp. 12ff., 237ff. For a full discussion of the ancient political system see Richard L. Walker, *The Multi-State System in Ancient China*, New Haven, 1953.

China remained divided into at least six independent states with apparently rather different cultures as late as to the third century B.C.[22] From the middle of the fourth century until 221 B.C. Chinese politics were simply power politics. The states concluded defensive and offensive alliances, resorted to ruses and propaganda, engaged in warfare that devastated the country, and concluded truces and prepared systems of collective security by entering into greater unions. They were behaving in a manner suggestive rather of the cold, realistic principles of the Indian *Arthashastra* than of the idealism of the traditional Chinese books. A number of Chinese governments had entered into a covenant as early as 589 B.C., agreeing that the great states should not make raids on the small[23] and that there should be no crooked embankments to withdraw the water from one state and give it to another.[24] Nevertheless such precedents for cooperative relations were not persuasive guides to action in a period of unparalleled social and political confusion.

It was during those troubled centuries of "The Warring States," when it seemed impossible to reach a political equilibrium of forces, that the Chinese Legalists of the fourth and third centuries B.C. announced their new theories of government. These men, by and large, were realists of a type that ignored the individual and assumed that the chief object of any society was to dominate other societies. Since, according to them, it was the sole aim of a state to maintain, and if possible to expand, its frontiers, they laid special stress on power and authority, the concept of law as the sovereign's command, and the art of aggressive statecraft. In the coordinated version of their theories compiled by Han Fei Tzǔ (died 233 B.C.)—a work, incidentally, also drawing heavily on the doctrines of Lao Tzǔ and Hsün Tzǔ—the Legalists upheld the proposition that any state can be governed successfully only when these three emphases on power, law, and statecraft are properly developed.[25] The philosophers themselves had made it their business, therefore, to ingratiate themselves with the grasping war lords of the age by advising them how to gain power and enlarge their territories. Among those practicing philosophers, there was none who achieved a higher fame for ruthlessness than the Lord Shang, adviser of the state of Ch'in (between 359-330 B.C.). He taught his

[22] See Waley, p. 254, to the effect that no serious study has yet been undertaken as to the ways in which the cultures of these states differed from one another.
[23] Thomas, p. 278.
[24] *ibid.*, p. 268.
[25] Fung Yu-Lan, pp. 312ff., 321ff.; Waley, pp. 212-239.

prince how to roll up the empire like a mat, lift the whole world in his arms, and tie up the four seas in a sack.[26] And indeed, the western land of Ch'in succeeded subsequently in annexing Han in 230, Chao in 228, Wei in 225, Ch'u in 223, Yen in 222, and Ch'i in 221. The whole of China was thus brought under one command—and the books of the traditional philosophers were burned.

After just fifteen years of government, however, the Ch'in Dynasty collapsed, and the doom of the Law School was sealed with the fall of the royal house with which it had been so closely affiliated.[27] By a ruthless political realism the house of Ch'in had united a hopelessly sundered China—indeed, a larger China than that of the Early Chou Dynasty. The successful political institutions that Ch'in had fostered were not without influence on those later developed during the Han Dynasty, but the ideals of the Law School were outdated following the fall of Ch'in. Confucianism had been unable to unite China, but it revived in the newly unified China. In 136 B.C., it was made the orthodox philosophy of the Empire. Law was thus again made subservient to the traditional Chinese system of pacifist ethics.

The "Realist" interlude is instructive in many ways for students of international and comparative history. Among other matters, it illustrates the precariousness of all attempts either to identify general trends in a nation's thinking, or to compare one's tentative judgments of one culture with those abstracted from the records of other peoples. For example, when one is reading *The Book of the Lord Shang*, Kautilya's *Arthashastra* comes to mind, and therewith the thought that the Indian and Chinese views of politics were, after all, very similar, both featuring rather prominently the doctrine of expediency. Upon closer examination, however, the two expositions must be rated differently. Kautilya wrote a detached quasi-scientific treatise and argued his propositions out of the context of established and observed Indian traditions. Shang, on the other hand, indulged in so much personal vindictiveness and political opportunism that his manual cannot really be regarded as representative of a general Chinese tradition. To say the least, "expediency" was understood differently in India and China.

"Law" was another notion that the Realists introduced into China. A cursory view of its operations during the period of the Warring States and of Ch'in's supremacy would suggest that some of the

[26] Wei Yang, *The Book of Lord Shang*, a Classic of the Chinese School of Law, Dr. J. J. L. Duyvendak, tr., London, 1928, p. 2.
[27] *ibid.*, p. 126.

broader manifestations of law in China were analogous to certain effects habitually associated with the rule of law in Western Europe and the United States. Law was used in both cultures, for instance, to serve the cause of equality between men. But in the interpretation of the Chinese Legalists this function of law was a corollary of autocratic government. Law was the will of the sovereign, and the will of the sovereign had to be applied equally to all subjects. But such a linkage of force and law is at variance with Western constitutionalism, in the context of which law has been developed primarily as an alternative to government absolutism.

In these and in many similar situations, international understanding is not served by the mere recognition of identities or similarities between different civilizations. It is the historical process that evolved the ideology or institution, and the contemporary reasoning process that explains its operation, which must be studied if understanding and adjustment are to be attained.

As read by the Chinese, history had established their state as the pivot of all earthly affairs and the exclusive domain of world culture. It was therefore the Middle Kingdom's primary responsibility (so the argument ran) to introduce civilization into less privileged adjoining areas and thus prepare the barbarians for their ultimate inclusion in the world state. This task, it was felt, could be undertaken in a methodical way only after the "backward" nations had been brought to a full understanding and acceptance of the entire concept of "government through benevolence." But while China's statesmen were well aware of the need to adapt their policy of sinification to the level of culture of each region, they did not, as a rule, depart from the basic Confucian family principle. In educating "inferior" peoples the Middle Kingdom pretended to act either as a father in relation to a son, or as an elder brother in relation to a younger brother.[28] And in the course of two thousand years the Chinese created in this fashion a great power orbit, with a system for the conduct of relations with their hedge-guarding satellites that has proved to be more enduring and successful than the comparable order of any other historical nation.

China's relations with Korea are a case in point.[29] Until the end of the sixth century A.D., Korea did not qualify for inclusion in the Confucian world order. But when the peninsula was opened to Chinese

---

[28] It appears that the relationship of friend to friend did not suggest its equivalent in the world of international politics.

[29] See Nelson for a full treatment of this question.

civilization, its inhabitants recognized their own cultural inferiority and so permitted the gradual establishment of China's supremacy. It has been suggested that the Middle Kingdom was held in genuine respect by the Koreans as a culturally superior "Father" or "Elder Brother" nation.[30] This view would seem to be borne out by the fact that the Koreans resisted Sinification when it was administered by "barbarians" (the Mongol conquerors), but again acquiesced when a purely Chinese dynasty (the Ming) regained the throne.

During the Ming period the Sino-Korean relationship was defined in the following terms: "Kao-li is a small region in the far east, and is not under the rule of the Middle Kingdom. Let the Board of Rites inform it that so long as its rule is in conformity with the will of Heaven and in harmony with the hearts of men, and so long as it creates no strife on our borders, so long will its people be allowed to go and come and the Kingdom will enjoy happiness. . . ."[31]

This Sino-Korean family relationship remained substantially unaltered during the ensuing centuries, but was exposed to new influences when all of East Asia was forcibly drawn into the European state system, and came to an end when Japan conquered Korea in 1894. Throughout the crucial years of the late nineteenth century most Western statesmen seem to have misunderstood completely the relationship between Korea and her elder brother, China. The diplomatic correspondence that was exchanged after the United States manifested an interest in opening Korea, raised a question as to what rules—if any—of the Western legalists should be applied in defining and evaluating a relationship that the Western world found entirely perplexing. One eloquent document discusses, for example, the relevance of the views of Vattel (an eighteenth century European writer on International Law) on the status of dependent states with reference to foreign powers, and concludes that Vattel's text "has little application to countries which, in their history, antedate international law, of which, also, they never

---

[30] Nelson, p. 89: Before the seventeenth century, Sino-Korean relations were patterned on the family relationship of father and son. Under the Manchu dynasty China's attitude was more appropriately described as that of an "Elder Brother." It would be erroneous to refer to this arrangement as "Vassalage" in the Western sense of the word. Korea viewed her dependency upon China as an honor or mark of civilization to which barbarians could not attain (p. 91). Other inferior states regularly listed by the Chinese were: Liu-Ch'iu, Annam, Nan-Chang (Laos), Siam, Burma, Sula. Cf. pp. 102ff. for a discussion of Western misinterpretations of these relationships.

[31] *ibid.*, p. 70.

had any knowledge." And the document continues: "What unwritten law or tradition controls the relations of China with her dependencies remains unknown."[32]

Toward the close of the nineteenth century, and within a few years of the collapse of Korea, the *Chinese Times* (Nov. 3, 1890) supplied what, in retrospect, reads like an epitaph to the Confucian system of hierarchical world relations: "To establish such relations with their outlying neighbours as that the latter should almost feel proud of owning an allegiance to the Great Emperor which cost nothing, yet which on the one side secured the empire from attack and on the other supplied the stable force which kept chieftains in their seats and kings on their thrones, was not the work of children but of statesmen of the first class. To make policy accomplish the purposes of marching armies is the triumph of mind over matter which is the crown of statecraft, and probably no government ever attained such perfect results in this direction as China has done. . . ."[33]

From the theory that the Middle Kingdom was the center of world affairs and that all other regions and races were in varying degrees barbarian, it followed that isolation was, logically, the only attitude that China could adopt toward the rest of the world. And this was, in fact, her officially proclaimed policy—notably vis-à-vis Europe—until occurrences during the Manchu Regime (1644-1912) gradually forced upon her a drastic reorientation. The ancient view was expressed succinctly in a majestic letter from the Emperor of China to King George III of Great Britain:

"Swaying the wide world, I have but one aim in view, namely, to maintain a perfect governance and to fulfill the duties of the state. Strange and costly objects do not interest me. I . . . have no use for your country's manufactures. . . . It behooves you, Oh King, to respect my sentiments and to display even greater devotion and loyalty in the future, so that by perpetual submission to our throne, you may secure peace and security for your country hereafter. . . . Our Celestial Empire possesses all things in prolific abundance and lacks no products within our borders. There was, therefore, no need to import the manufactures of outside barbarians in exchange for our produce. . . . I do

---

[32] For this and other excerpted quotations see *ibid.*, pp. 190ff.
[33] *ibid.*, p. 203. This article on "Suzerainty" was included in a dispatch from Heard to Blaine: *Korea: Dispatches.* 22 vols., U. S. Department of State, Vol. VII, no. 125.

not forget the lonely remoteness of your island, cut off from the world by intervening wastes of sea, nor do I overlook your excusable ignorance of the usages of our Celestial Empire. . . . Tremblingly obey and show no negligence."[34]

C. The Influence of Buddhism on China's Relations with India: a Case Study in Cultural Adjustment

A. CHINA AND INDIA

In actual fact the Chinese were never quite as isolated as they professed and wanted to be. They had accepted wheat, cowry shells, and other articles from areas outside their realm at a very early time in their history. Such borrowings became more frequent from the fifth century B.C. onward, when China also began to show herself more receptive to foreign ideas and institutions.[35] Although many of the barriers that separated China from other civilizations were in the course of time broken down, the Confucian government officials consistently regarded commerce as an "inferior" occupation and an occurrence that could not easily be reconciled with the cherished image of China as a self-sufficient nation. Whenever possible, therefore, they identified it with "tribute bearing," the assumption being that the trading interests that brought "barbarians" to seek intercourse with China were in fact an overt recognition of the overlordship of the Son of Heaven. And this rationalization remained China's official attitude throughout the T'ang and Sung Dynasties, when the profits derived from commerce were so great that foreign merchants were explicitly invited to visit the Middle Kingdom, and even during the Ming Dynasty, when the emperors were finding it advantageous to dispatch their trading fleets in all directions. The Muslim court official who commanded a number of these expeditions (it has been suggested that the choice of a Muslim who was also a eunuch for the imperial services was itself indicative of the ambivalent character of the Chinese approach to trade)[36] could testify quite credibly, in 1431, his mission having been accomplished, that the Imperial Ming Dynasty had unified the seas and continents and that all countries beyond the horizon and at the ends of the earth had now become Chinese subjects.[37]

---

[34] Thomas, p. 289, n.17.

[35] L. Carrington Goodrich, *A Short History of the Chinese People*, rev. ed., New York, 1951, pp. 27f. for an account of borrowings that influenced her language, art, crafts, military science, etc.

[36] J. J. L. Duyvendak, *China's Discovery of Africa*, London, 1949, p. 27.

[37] *ibid.*, pp. 28f.

Nevertheless, even though the trade between China and the West was quite lively in certain historical periods—for instance, during the Mongol occupation of Asia—it apparently did not alter in any material way the Chinese attitude toward international commerce. This rather curious circumstance may help us, in some measure, to explain why commercial trading has never served as a bridge for the Chinese toward a fuller understanding of other nations. Indeed, though one may condemn the methods by which Europe "opened" China in the nineteenth century, still it is certain—or at least more than likely—that China's general reaction to any approach of Europeans seeking trade would have been strongly conditioned beforehand by an ambivalent view of such contacts, no matter what their form. And the record of China's relations with that other great Asian "world" which is India conveys an essentially similar, if less clear-cut impression. For the early Sino-Indian borrowings and exchanges never really dented the walls of aloofness and reserve that separated these two vast nations. Their relations remained remote until Buddhism was introduced from India into China.

On the other hand, the process of cultural approximation that was initiated when the gospel of Buddha entered China marks a most suggestive chapter in the general history of international adjustment. Its study seems particularly relevant in the mid-twentieth century for two chief reasons. First, China and India not only were great powers during the period of the Chinese Han and T'ang Dynasties, when their relationship to each other was so radically transformed, but each, at the time, was claiming exclusive greatness, both politically and culturally. And second, these two great and ancient culture spheres, not only self-contained but also fundamentally different in their political organizations, passed from long-standing isolation, first to contact and then to intense intellectual exchanges. This was surely an especially remarkable achievement, for while the conflicting claims to world supremacy and the two images of an exclusive central location in world politics were analogous, they had been shaped in accordance with different ethical premises and historical references. Compare Hindu India's approach to international politics as illustrated by Kautilya's *Arthashastra* with the pre-Buddhist views of world affairs in Confucian and pre-Confucian China. Whereas the Chinese insisted on modelling their norms of political behavior on the patterns of personal conduct observed in the family circle, the Hindus carefully distinguished between levels of personal and political relations. China and India were, in short, great and different powers. They had coexisted for thousands of years in virtual ignorance of each other, denying the need and even spurning the possibility of any closer cultural or political rapprochement, until an originally Indian faith was studiously adapted to Chinese needs to become eventually a popular Chinese religion.

At a time such as the present, when the imagination of statesmen is being severely tested in the search for bridges between seemingly irreconcilable political systems, it is instructive to turn back to this early phase of the Sino-Indian relationship in order to review the process that led in a few generations to close intellectual understanding between the two separate worlds. The fact that this great regional effort was not undertaken by official representatives of the two states in the course of deliberate policy-making, but by individual scholars and pilgrims in the pursuit of philosophical and religious interests, does not detract from the universal significance of this historical episode. On the contrary, this very circumstance would seem even to enhance the relevance of this effort to the twentieth century.[38]

B. THE PROCESS OF ADAPTING BUDDHISM TO CHINA[39]

The ancient Chinese tradition of formulating their relations with the neighboring barbarians in predominantly cultural rather than political terms was opened to a vastly broader range of regional relations in Asia when Greater China officially accepted the adaptation of Buddhism to her local needs. It is not certain when this foreign religion first appeared in the Middle Kingdom. History records something of the far-flung activities of Ashoka's missionaries and their influence is generally regarded as the first stage of the diffusion of the creed out of India.[40] Scholars consider it possible, however, that Buddhism may already have been brought into Bactria and the other provinces west of the Pamirs in the train of Alexander's expedition.[41] Subsequently, between 128 B.C. and A.D. 6, those Chinese envoys who encountered representatives of the new faith on their journeys to

[38] The remembrance of this episode in Sino-Indian relations may have contributed, in the twentieth century, to that strong sense of Asian solidarity which imbues India's foreign policy in particular.

[39] In the present limited context, which is devoted to a survey of methods of international adjustment and conciliation, the emphasis will be placed not on the religious and ethical substance of the Buddhist creed itself but on the process by means of which it was introduced into China. See Heinrich Zimmer, *Philosophies of India*, New York, 1951, pp. 464ff. on Buddhism.

[40] For a full discussion of the circumstances in which Buddhism reached China in various historical periods see P. C. Bagchi, *India and China—1000 Years of Cultural Relations*, 2nd ed., Bombay, 1950.

[41] See Goodrich, p. 58.

Afghanistan and to lands bordering the Indian Ocean are almost certain to have reported their impressions when they returned home. Furthermore, there are some early references which indicate that at least one Chinese official was orally instructed in the Buddhist *sutras* by an ambassador of the king of the Yüeh-chi, who was governing northwest India in the year 2 B.C.[42] By A.D. 65 a definitely identifiable community of Buddhist monks existed near an estuary of the Yangtze, and there enjoyed the protection of the reigning emperor's brother. And somewhat later, between A.D. 148-170, we read of a Parthian prince who abdicated his throne in favor of the new religion, and whose subsequent missionary activities in China extended from the capital to the coast.[43]

The transnational appeal not only of the Buddhist faith but also of the task of propagating it in China is evidenced by the fact that many of the first missionaries did not come from India but from Iran, Central Asia, and Kashmir. A recently published list of the scholars who served in China and assisted in the translation of Buddhist texts from the second to the eleventh centuries A.D. reveals that seventy-six came from India, Kashmir, and Ceylon; thirty from Parthia, Sogdiana, Gandhara, and other regions in Western Asia; sixteen from Khotan, Kashgaria, Kucha, and Turfan in Central Asia; and two from Java and Cambodia.[44] These intermediaries, who devoted their lives to the translation of Sanskrit manuscripts and the composition of original works in the Chinese language, left a prodigious literary inheritance. Indeed, one of the most illustrious in this brotherhood of scholars, Kumarajiva, has forty-seven volumes to his credit.[45]

As the knowledge of Buddhism spread in China, a long procession of Chinese pilgrims and learned men, daring perilous travels overland across the Gobi desert and the mountains of Central Asia, and by the sea through Indo-China, Java, and Malaya, began to establish direct and personal contact with the sacred sources of Buddhism in India. The first of these of whom there is a record was a Chinese monk who left in A.D. 259 for Khotan, where he remained until his death half a century later. Thereafter, between A.D. 259 and 790 some one hun-

[42] See Bagchi, pp. 31ff., on the role of the Kushanas in the dissemination of Buddhism and Indian culture during the first century B.C.

[43] Goodrich, pp. 58-60.

[44] *ibid.*, p. 62, quoting Professor Pelliot in "La Haute Asie," p. 10.

[45] See Bagchi, p. 33, on the biography of this fascinating Central Asian scholar. See also *Le Canon Bouddhique en Chine*, by the same author, 2 vols., Paris, 1927, for a detailed account of Kumarajiva's activities.

dred and eighty-six known individuals made such pilgrimages.[46] The two-way traffic of the learned and the pious attained its greatest intensity during the T'ang dynasty, when certain unprecedented cultural developments in China were favoring the reception of new ideas. For instance, there was Fa Hsien (fifth century A.D.) who, before his departure from China, was carefully instructed by a Buddhist scholar not to spend all of his time gathering religious knowledge while on his pilgrimage, but to study India's general life and habits, so that China might come to understand the new country as a whole. And the most famous of all, Hsüan Tsang (596-664), who crossed the Gobi desert and journeyed throughout India, found time to study at the great Nalanda University, where he discovered as many as ten thousand students and monks in residence. Hsüan Tsang returned by way of Central Asia, transporting a large number of Buddhist *sutras*; although he lost one load while crossing the Indus, he conveyed most of his sacred texts safely home, in thirty volumes of translations. Concerning his arduous and devoted life as a scholar, as well as his many adventures and observations in strange places, Hsüan Tsang wrote a fascinating book, "The Record of the Western Kingdom," which he dedicated to Buddha's "Pure Land." And besides reporting there on the popularity of Buddhism in Khorasan, Iraq, and Mosul—as far as to the frontiers of Syria—he commented on many interesting miscellaneous facts—for example, on the position of respect that Iran enjoyed among her neighbors, and on the queer little kingdom of Turfan (a crossroads of cultures coming from China, India, Persia, and the Hellenistic world) whose deities represented, in his eyes, the happiest combination of Hindu suppleness, Hellenic eloquence, and Chinese charm that he had ever seen.[47]

When Buddhism lost its hold over India, at about the time Islam came into India, the Sino-Indian exchange of scholars decreased. Dur-

[46] Goodrich, pp. 61-64.

[47] See Bagchi, pp. 58ff., on the travels, adventures, and contributions of these two illustrious scholars. See p. 75 to the effect that the record lists sixty Chinese monks as having sojourned in India during the second half of the seventh century A.D.

See Wu Ch'eng-en, *Monkey*—a famous Chinese novel of the sixteenth century— (Arthur Waley, tr., London, 1942) for a fictional account of Hsüan Tsang's adventures. See the Japanese painting of the priest Genjo Sanzo (Chinese: Hsüan Tsang) by an unknown artist of the thirteenth century (Nat. Mus. Tokio), N.Y. Met. Mus. Cat. of Exhibition of Japanese Masterworks, no. 15, 1953, which depicts the sojourning priest carrying the scriptures in a box on his back. For further records see *Chinese Accounts of India* (from the Chinese of Hiuen Tsiang), Samuel Beal, tr., 4 vols., Calcutta, 1957-1958; *The Travels of Fa-hsien* (A.D. 399-414), or Record of the Buddhistic Kingdoms, H. A. Giles, tr., London, 1956.

ing the political revolutions that began in India in the eleventh century, however, crowds of Buddhist monks trekked through Nepal and the Himalayas to Tibet bearing with them large bundles of manuscripts. There, once again the cause of intellectual understanding was advanced by a richly productive cooperation of Indian, Tibetan, and Chinese scholars. Such joint labors had already produced, in the ninth or tenth century, a Sanskrit-Tibetan-Chinese dictionary of Buddhist technical terms. A Tibetan alphabet had been designed, based on the Indian Devanagari. And so highly was the work of these men appreciated that they were regarded in some cases as Bodhisattvas. Many of the basic works of medieval Indian Buddhism survive to this day—it is interesting to note—not in the Sanskrit of the originals, but only in Tibetan or Chinese.

Most of the intellectuals whose biographies constitute the history of Sino-Indian relations during that remarkably long stretch of time were heroic adventurers, forever willing not only to brave the hazards of travel and the solitude of prolonged foreign residence but also to pit themselves against the established Hindu and Chinese traditions of cultural isolation. Through many centuries people of their kind had the intellectual courage to leave the quiet of their established local patterns of life and immerse themselves completely in the cultures of alien lands. Inevitably the question arises: why did so many undertake such journeys into the unknown? And again: what was it about the Buddhist doctrine that so deeply stirred the minds of the Chinese, not only learned Confucians, government officials, and courtiers, but also the uneducated and the lowly?[48]

The systematic pursuit of transcendental goals, to which several generations of the Chinese committed themselves from the third century onward, was in many respects a deliberate departure from the time-honored but constraining Chinese system of ethics. The ancient view that life on earth was of the highest value, and that it had to be lived in conformity with rigidly established hierarchical relationships, tended both to imprison the sophisticated Chinese intellectual and to disappoint the unsophisticated, whose initial trust in China's life-af-

[48] See Hu Shih's essay, "The Indianization of China," in *Independence, Convergence and Borrowing in Institutions, Thought and Art*, Harvard Tercentenary Conference of Arts and Sciences, 1937, p. 225, to the effect that the process probably started among the poorest in China, long before A.D. 68. But see Arthur F. Wright, "Some Reflections on the Indianization of China" (a paper read at the Annual Meeting of the Far Eastern Association, Spring, 1949) for a different treatment of the general theme.

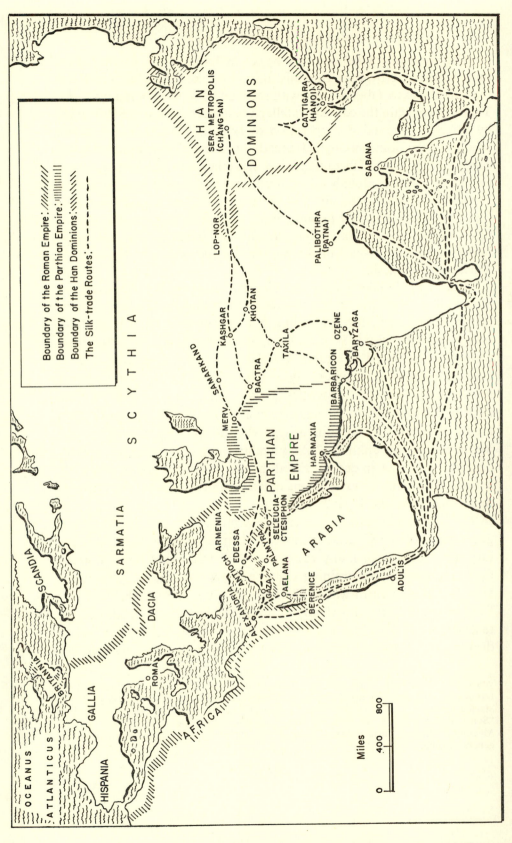

The Roman Empire and China, A.D. 200

firming institutions was not always sustained when confronted with the immutable realities of the Confucian social order. Since the Confucian philosophy, furthermore, did not compensate for its negative effects by appealing to the emotions of the less educated, it is no wonder that the Chinese, in the course of time, became somewhat tired of their native ethical religion and receptive to new ideas. Under such circumstances, the religious interest shifted, first to a revival of the teachings of Lao Tzŭ and of his great successor Chuang Tzŭ, and subsequently —or perhaps even simultaneously—to a profound involvement in the new faith from India. Activated by a general cultural upsurge of the T'ang period, the popular imagination was irresistibly attracted by the new world of rich imagery and mythology that the study of Buddhism unfolded. The Chinese individual, weary of identifying his personal life with the narrow family circle and his expectations of social justice with the conduct of a remote ruler, discovered not only that man could transcend his entire earthly environment with all of its inherited traditions, but also that heavenly bliss and enlightenment were within his reach; he had only to aspire earnestly to learn the Buddha's truth. Thousands of Chinese felt both free and eager to engage in this quest when they learned that Buddhism was a hospitable religion that respected all other creeds as stepping-stones toward the enlightenment that it intended, and permitted in China the retention of many non-Buddhist rites and images, such as the worship of ancestors and state gods, and the recognition of the emperor as mandatory of Heaven. Hence it may be said that it was to a considerable extent the very nature of Buddhism itself that best explains its establishment as China's third religion. Yet it would seem that the new faith could never have settled beside Confucianism and Taoism in the Middle Kingdom had the Chinese not possessed a peculiar capacity to accept and absorb a variety of world views without feeling compelled to synthesize them in all particulars.[49]

A careful study of Chinese needs and Buddhist doctrines[50] might provide an explanation for China's interest in the Indian way of life, yet it would not answer two further questions which for the purposes

[49] Glasenapp, Vol. I, pp. 216ff.

[50] Neither of these inquiries can here be thoroughly pursued. For an exhaustive analysis of this relationship see Arthur F. Wright, "Buddhism and Chinese Culture: Phases of Interaction," in *The Journal of Asian Studies*, Vol. XVII, no. 1, November, 1957, also the same author's essays, "The Indianization of China," 1949, and "The Chinese Language and Foreign Ideas" in *Studies in Chinese Thought*, The American Anthropologist, Arthur F. Wright, ed., Chicago, 1953.

of the present discussion are more important: just how was Buddhism made to yield such rich rewards for the entire Chinese nation? And to what, if any, extent did the acceptance of the new religion of salvation lead to a new adjustment of practical Sino-Indian socio-political relations?

The translation of innumerable texts and the compilation of a Buddhist dictionary will always bear testimony not only to the painstaking, life-consuming efforts of a multitude of extraordinarily able linguists and translators, but also to the determination of those hundreds of scholars, from India, China, and various intermediate regions, to cooperate in such an enterprise, across boundaries and centuries. On these grounds alone their labors would merit a lasting place in the annals of international history. Behind their obvious accomplishment in thoroughly mastering a foreign language and translating Sanskrit words into Chinese words, however, lies a far greater achievement. Those intellectual go-betweens, who crossed and recrossed the frontiers that separate China from India, discovered that Chinese words could not always be found for the Sanskrit words, since traditional Chinese thought simply did not include the Indian concepts. What was required of them, they realized, was not a mere translation of words but an interpretation of the images and experiences that had originally inspired the words. This meant that Buddhism had to be conveyed as a body of thoughts and realizations rather than as an assemblage of terms. It implied, that is to say, that Buddhism had to be studied, experienced, and understood for its own sake before it could be communicated.

Professor Daisetz Suzuki tells us that when the Indian scholars were trying to translate the Buddhist works into Chinese, they found whole categories of Sanskrit terms[51] that could not be satisfactorily rendered into Chinese at all. And while it was possible to keep some of them in the original Sanskrit without impairing the clarity of the general context, greater difficulties arose when the entire concept seemed to have no equivalent in the Chinese pattern of thought, however much it might have fascinated an individual Chinese scholar. The imagery of Buddhism, to give but one illustration, proved too rich for the essentially practically inclined Chinese. As Professor Suzuki puts it: "The Chinese are above all a most practical people, while the Indians are visionary and highly speculative. The Indians are subtle in analysis

---

[51] Daisetz Teitaro Suzuki, *Essays in Zen Buddhism*, London, 1927. Professor Suzuki lists in particular five such categories.

and dazzling in poetic flight; the Chinese are children of earthly life. . . . Being practical means in a sense being historical, observing the progress of time and recording its traces as they are left behind. The Chinese can very well boast of their being great recorders, such a contrast to the Indian lack of sense of time. . . . Their weakness is that they are willing to sacrifice facts for literary effects, for they are not very exact and scientific. . . . Logic is not one of their strong points. Nor are their philosophy and imagination. When Buddhism with all its characteristically Indian dialectics and imageries was first introduced into China, it must have staggered the Chinese mind. . . ."[52]

Since the Chinese "have no aptitude, like the Indians, to hide themselves in the clouds of mystery and supernaturalism,"[53] Chinese Buddhists were confronted with the task of adapting what must for them have been quite tenuous concepts to rather definite and concrete expectations. This approach to the task of interpretation explains why in China's early biographical history of Buddhism, commentators, expounders, and philosophers far outnumbered translators, properly so-called.[54] The Indian Mahayanists,[55] for instance, who make the Buddha perform all kinds of magical feats in order to illustrate through imagery something that in the very nature of things defies explanation by the ordinary logical means, soon found that they were unable to clarify the doctrine of Buddhist enlightenment to the satisfaction of their more practical minded Chinese disciples. Instead, they had to think up ways of fitting the teachings to the deeply rooted Confucian view that superior men never talk about miracles and wonders.[56] Almost every aspect of Buddhism had to undergo, in this way, some degree of domestication[57] during the following thousand years. The process affected not only the religious, moral, and philosophical teachings of Buddhism, but also their expression in music, painting, and architecture.[58]

The remarkable success that attended this adjustment was due in no small measure to the mediating influence, however, of another Chinese philosophy, Taoism. For since Lao Tzŭ's teaching had certain affinities

[52] *ibid.*, p. 94.

[53] *ibid.*, p. 98.

[54] *ibid.*, pp. 104f.

[55] See Zimmer, pp. 507ff., for a discussion of the various schools of Buddhism.

[56] Suzuki, pp. 97-102. Many tales about the Buddha's magical feats were thus omitted from the Chinese translations of the *sutras* because they could not be adequately stated for Chinese use.

[57] Hu Shih, p. 232, and Arthur Wright, "Some Reflections on the Indianization of China," 1949.

[58] See Hu Shih to the effect that Indian melodies were made vehicles for Chinese songs, also Bagchi, pp. 146ff. on the migration of Indian arts and sciences to China.

with Buddhism, his doctrines became, as it were, a bridge for the importation of the Indian faith. It was quite fashionable for a while, for example, to translate Buddhist terminology more or less verbatim into words taken from the Taoist schools. And such interpretations—whatever their shortcomings—prepared many Chinese minds for the ultimate reception of Buddhism.

Through all of her efforts to grasp the essence of Buddhism and to reconcile it with native Chinese thought, China created gradually her own version of the doctrine of enlightenment—Ch'an Buddhism, which reached the height of its development during the Sung Dynasty (960-1279). The Ch'an (Buddhist) masters succeeded in emancipating their system from the traditions of Indian metaphysics by disregarding the outward forms of presentation that had initially so disconcerted the Chinese mind, reducing the exposition of conceptual and analytical interpretations to a minimum[59] and inviting the individual's total concentration on the essence of enlightenment. This, they suggested, was to be found through personal involvement in life itself, independently of scriptural teachings or of another's help. Feeling that it was more natural to be moving about than sitting still, the Chinese Ch'an patriarchs even transformed the notion of posture that had been favored in traditional Indian thought. Whereas the Indians had been able to reach complete concentration while in a very formal sitting position, the Chinese patriarch Hui Neng found that walking was even more conducive to the attainment of an ultimate realization of the universal truth.[60]

C. THE INTERNATIONAL SIGNIFICANCE OF THE SINO-INDIAN ADJUSTMENT

The new ideology that entered Chinese thought could attract non-Indians because it was essentially a system of universally valid norms addressed to every man and all humanity. Its development in India had not been based on provincial concerns peculiar to Indian life but on

---

[59] Suzuki, pp. 1, 102 for illustrations; see also p. 52 on this subject.

[60] See Arthur F. Wright, "Fu I and the Rejection of Buddhism," in "Chinese Reactions to Imported Ideas—A Symposium," *The Journal of the History of Ideas*, Vol. XII, no. 1, Jan. 1951, pp. 33ff., and "Buddhism and Chinese Culture—Phases of Interaction" for an account of the developments that slowly undermined Buddhism's dominant position in China. The decisive factor was the revival of the native tradition of Confucianism by an important segment of the Chinese elite. From the time of the reunification onward, Wright points out, the rulers adopted more and more those measures of traditional Chinese statecraft which are usually associated with Confucianism: neither Taoism nor Buddhism had developed any such arsenal of social and political formulae. See also Wright's "Fo-t'u-teng, a Biography, *Harvard Journal of Asiatic Studies*, December 1948, Vol. II, nos. 3 and 4.

fundamental human spiritual needs. An essentially nationalist creed could hardly have survived in any identifiable form a radical transplantation to another culture sphere. Students of Asian thought have cited a variety of factors in explanation of China's acceptance of Buddhism. But it would seem that none of these factors would have been ultimately effective had it not been for this general validity of the creed itself and a consequent flexibility in the Buddhist system of forms. The history of its gradual diffusion shows clearly that had locally accumulated interpretations been regarded as essential to the doctrine, Buddhism would not have been transferable. We may say therefore that a new form will be borrowed only if it proves flexible enough not only to adapt itself to the past experiences of its new converts but also to invite the participation of their creative abilities.

It takes time, devotion, and knowledge, first to recognize the universally valid concepts of an ideology, and then to abstract these from the matrix of their original, locally valid forms and adapt them to the needs and aspirations of another people. That this was accomplished in the process of adjusting Buddhism to the civilization of China is to be attributed exclusively to a company of internationally minded saints and scholars. There was in their work no design to "Indianize" the Chinese. This literate Buddhist elite of both countries shared fundamental religious ideas, and yet they were realistic enough to appraise the environmental and historical differences that separated their worlds of experience from each other. And it was this realistic appraisal that made it possible for the nonliterate majority to follow them in the Buddhist path. One should not assume that the various phases of this process of adjustment were in any sense deliberately coordinated over the centuries. They were the consequence rather of a continuous, communicated effort to incorporate in life a discovered truth. The scholarly vanguard, which was in the end responsible for the introduction of Buddhism into China, was at first not very numerous, and its primary aim was not the quick conversion of a maximum number of people, but the painstaking instruction of truly interested disciples. For instance, it was not uncommon for a Buddhist master to devote the major part of his life to the training of a single promising interpreter of the faith. The new religion, nevertheless, did not remain the religion of an elite. There would, in fact, have been no "history of Buddhism" had it ended here. Indian Buddhism was rendered fit to become a popular Chinese religion because the scholars so transposed the doctrine that it reached the hearts of the many and not merely the minds of the select.[61] It then steadily became—despite several severe persecutions—an integral part of China's entire culture. New forms of writing appeared in Chinese literature as a result of the translation of the Buddhist texts; Chinese folklore profited richly by absorbing Indian tales; and the Sanskrit language had an immediate effect on the Chinese.[62]

It is of more than incidental importance to note that this intricate process of adjustment never was marked by any resort to force. The evolution of Buddhism in China is all the more remarkable, therefore, when contrasted with the propagation in the Far East of Zoroastrianism, Judaism, Nestorian and Roman Christianity, Manichaeanism, and Islam. Not one of these more rigid and militant creeds ever succeeded in penetrating Chinese life deeply enough to become permanently meaningful.[63] It may seem profane to some to draw an analogy between the appeal of a time-tested universal religion and that of a modern, as yet imperfectly defined, political ideology. Nevertheless, it is surely not irrelevant to study the processes by means of which a way of life can be peacefully but successfully implanted in a new environment. Many of our present, earnest efforts to propagate the cause of democracy and spread ideas about the collective security and solidarity of all humanity might greatly benefit if they were brought into some relationship with the experiences that the Buddhist chapter of Asian history records.

Whether the cultural adjustment between two such different systems as the Indian and Chinese had any directly appreciable impact on the conduct of foreign policy eludes conclusive analysis. Whereas Confucianism and most Western religions (such as Islam and the later versions of Christianity) are not only religious philosophies but also political theories, Buddhism professes to concern itself exclusively with the inner life of man, regardless of his secular environment. It might be contended, therefore, that Buddhism does not properly aspire to any alteration whatsoever of the practical world of the Arthashastra, and that Ashoka's inspired efforts to apply the Buddha's teachings to

[61] See *ibid.*, for efforts made in behalf of mass conversions.

[62] See Goodrich, pp. 63ff., to the effect that some six or seven thousand new terms found entrance into Chinese.

[63] Judaism lost the precarious foothold that it gained during the Sung Dynasty; Roman Catholicism and Nestorian Christianity withered away after 1368, partly because they had few adherents and partly because their land and sea connections with the supporting constituencies in Rome and Baghdad were cut. Islam alone had a measure of success—perhaps because its strongholds in Central Asia and on China's western frontiers were not wiped out. See Glasenapp, Vol. I, p. 175. Also Goodrich, pp. 174-181.

the domain of international relations—ill-starred as they were eventually for India's destiny—were derived from that monarch's strictly personal reading of the faith. Indeed, it may well be that the ancient Indian mythological image of the Chakravartin played a greater role in the formation of the chief policies of Ashoka than any concept derived from his comparatively late conversion to the Buddhist fold.[64] A comparative review of China's international relations as they were conducted before as well as after the introduction of Buddhism seems to support the conclusion that Buddhism did not have a decisive impact on the making of foreign policy. Not only can particular policies, such as China's approach to Korea, and particular concepts, such as that of the "satellite," be traced more logically to Confucian than to Buddhist principles,[65] but the general trend of China's actions in the field of international politics also points to the conclusion that Confucianism remained the official reference until at least the eighteenth century A.D.

In any case there is little evidence to prove that China's acceptance of India's new faith greatly displaced or altered the national interests and traditions of either of the two nations. Indian knowledge of China was slight and imperfect and seems to have remained so to this day, and Chinese histories have almost nothing to say about India.[66] Modern Indian interpretations of this phase of Sino-Indian relations, which have given prominence to the view that "Buddhism brought the two countries, China and India, together,"[67] and that India and China came to know each other through Buddhism,[68] must have been suggested by the intense awareness of an all-Asian destiny that has come to characterize Asian attitudes toward international relations in modern times rather than by a careful study of history.

It cannot be denied that China's acceptance of Buddhism constituted

[64] Sufficient authentic information is not available on Menander's policies; since Buddhism and Stoicism seem to have blended in Menander's world view, the specifically Buddhist factors are particularly difficult to isolate.

[65] The most concerted, but nevertheless abortive, effort to use Buddhism as a Chinese state ideology was that of the Sui between A.D. 581 and 604. See A. F. Wright, "The Formation of Sui Ideology," in *Chinese Thought and Institutions*, John K. Fairbank, ed., Chicago, 1957. See also by the same author "Buddhism and Chinese Culture: Phases of Interaction," pp. 31ff. Also H. G. Creel, *Chinese Thought from Confucius to Mao Tsê-tung*, Chicago, 1953, pp. 186ff. to the effect that for approximately a thousand years the Chinese mind was largely dominated by Buddhism.

[66] This conclusion was confirmed by Arthur F. Wright in an unpublished written memorandum.

[67] Bagchi, pp. 8, 194.

[68] Nehru, *The Discovery of India*, New York, 1946, p. 190.

a distinct breach in the long history of the nation's isolation, and that it helped to dispel many of the phobias that had previously encumbered China's attitudes toward foreign lands. Chinese Buddhists travelled widely throughout the entire Asian region, propagating the faith or discussing its meaning and implications with co-religionists from other areas. Indeed, in Japan, where their message was particularly well received, the Chinese cultural influence was prodigious, and a Far Eastern type of Buddhism (Chinese *Ch'an*; Japanese *Zen*), freed completely from the historical and mythological traditions that had initially been attached to the doctrine as an Indian religion, became a decisive transforming influence, touching every aspect of Japanese life.[69] But a further conclusion that a distinctly Asian *Weltanschauung* was created when "the stream of culture which originated in India, was combined with Chinese culture, and swept over the east and southeast of Asia,"[70] does not seem warranted by the realities of cultural interactions in Asia. It calls to mind Spengler's comment that historians, intent upon establishing causal series, are apt to count only the influences that are present, whereas the other side of the reckoning—those that are not—does not appear. "Two Cultures may touch between man and man," this German scholar writes, "or the man of one Culture may be confronted by the dead form-world of another as presented in its communicable relics. In both cases the agent is man himself. The closed-

[69] China's later encounter with the European world took place under circumstances that bear no resemblance whatsoever to her contacts with Buddhist India; yet it reveals incidentally certain possibilities for the complementary interaction of Eastern and Western ways of thinking. Modern European psychology and logic, for instance, have furnished new sets of terms through the use of which a number of Chinese and Japanese have been enabled to understand Buddhist concepts that their ancestors of the sixth century were not ready to grasp and transmit to China. See Hu Shih, p. 234.

[70] Masaharu Anesaki, "East and West: the meaning of their cultural relations" in Harvard Tercentenary Conference, *Independence, Convergence and Borrowing in Institutions, Thought and Art*, p. 260. This author points out that the concept of oneness, which pervades the separate Asian systems of thought, is expressed in the Hindu term *advaita* (non-duality), in its Buddhist equivalent of *ekatva* (oneness) or *sunyata* (vacuity or transcendence), and in the Taoist idea of *hsu-wu* (the void, i.e., the final reality transcending all actual distinctions). With respect to Confucianism, he adds that "Though Confucianism stood on a somewhat different plane and there was an amount of Confucian opposition to the abstract transcendence, its ideal amounted to the realization of the way of Heaven in man's life. . . . It was rather the methods and means than the ideal itself that differentiated Confucianism from the other teachings."

Cf. also F. S. C. Northrop, *The Meeting of East and West; An Inquiry Concerning World Understanding*, New York, 1949. But see Arthur F. Wright's attack on this view in "Northrop on the Traditional Culture of the Orient," *Journal of the History of Ideas*, Vol. x, 1949, pp. 143-149.

off act of A can be vivified by B only out of his own being, and *eo ipso* it becomes B's, his inward property, his work, and part of himself."[71] In Spengler's view there was thus no movement of "Buddhism" from India to China but an acceptance of part of the Indian Buddhists' store of images by Chinese of a certain spiritual tendency, who fashioned out a *new* mode of religious expression having meaning for Chinese, and only Chinese, Buddhists. "What matters in all such cases," Spengler continues, "is not the original meaning of the forms, but the forms themselves, as disclosing to the native sensibility and understanding of the observer potential modes of his own creativeness. Connotations are not transferable. . . . Even though Indians and Chinese in those days both felt as Buddhists, they were spiritually as far apart as ever. The same words, the same rites, the same symbol—but two different souls, each going its own way."[72] And the same conclusion is reached by a modern authority on Indo-Chinese relations when he explains that it was not the Buddhism of Buddha which became the religion of Eastern Asia, but a Buddhism developed and infinitely varied through centuries by men of different interests and different cultural backgrounds.[73] It is this approximation of different Asian world views rather than their total unification which makes the great moral and intellectual effort, begun by a handful of Buddhist scholars and sustained over the centuries by a steadily growing number of followers, so richly suggestive for those in the contemporary world society who are striving to improve known techniques for the attainment of understanding between cultures, in order ultimately to identify the moral goals that can be shared.

[71] Oswald Spengler, *The Decline of the West*, New York, 1930, Vol. II, "Perspectives of World History," p. 57; German ed. Vol. II, pp. 64f.

[72] *ibid.*

[73] Arthur F. Wright, "Buddhism and Chinese Culture."

CHAPTER 5

THE PLACE OF ROME IN INTERNATIONAL RELATIONS

A. The Coexistence of Rome and China in the Ancient World

CHINA AND ROME were great and independent states at the turn of the era that began A.D. 1. Each pretended to be the world's sole sovereign. Each argued its claim to omnipotence by referring to cosmic principles or the will of providence, and in each realm such claims were protected by particular philosophers and administered by appropriate policies. In actuality, the two self-styled worlds coexisted; and beyond the reaches of both was the greater part of what was already known of the actual world.

China, under the Ch'in and Han Dynasties (221 B.C.-A.D. 220),[1] had advanced south of the Yangtze River to the South China Sea, conquered the old kingdom of the Yueh and various half-savage tribes, overrun Korea, and extended her power toward the northwest into Mongolia, Kashgaria, and even beyond the Pamir watershed to Ferghana. Rome had assumed mastery over the Mediterranean world, after emerging from the second Punic war, and her imperial frontiers ran from Gibraltar in the west, northward along the coasts of the Atlantic Ocean and English Channel to the mouth of the Rhine; thence, by way of the Rhine and Danube, to the Black Sea, and from the Black Sea south to the Euphrates and the Syrian desert. In Africa, west of Egypt, the Sahara gave a natural protection to the coastlands of the Roman Mediterranean. Extensions beyond these boundaries were rare. Britain, however, was invaded by the Romans in A.D. 43 and retained until the fifth century; Dacia, the region north of the Danube in the bow of the Carpathians, was added to the Empire by Trajan, A.D. 106.

Both Han China and Imperial Rome were surrounded by rings of uncivilized tribes, and both, by the second century B.C., had succeeded in conquering and consolidating the inner rings of their respective orbits. Excluded from their domains, however, were vast regions of Africa, Oceania, Europe, and Asia, where innumerable and variously organized political societies were known to exist independently. Outside, also, was the area of Indian civilization, where ancient empires had claimed supreme world power long before Rome had come into

---

[1] *Relative Chronologies in Old World Archeology*, Robert W. Ehrich, ed., Chicago, 1954, p. 131.

being. The Indian bids had lapsed with the fall of the Maurya Empire at the beginning of the second century B.C., however, and by the second century A.D. the Indian subcontinent was divided between the powerful Kushana kings (whose sovereignty centered in Pachawar or Kabul, and was acknowledged over northwest India, Kashmir, Afghanistan, and Chinese Turkestan) and the domains of independent monarchs.

During the span of their coexistence as world powers, Rome and China showed certain striking affinities. They shared not only the great gesture of pretending to hold unique and undisputed world power, but also some of the images that buttressed both the pretension and certain institutions designed to make the images concrete. While the two empires developed their own systems of imperial rule in accordance with political requirements and religious or philosophical preferences, and while the imperial theme underwent many variations in the course of each empire's history, they shared from the first century A.D. onward the archetypal figure of the universal monarch who surveys all by reason of his divine investiture, his power, and his excellence of character. And whenever the illusion of sole grandeur was disputed by unexpected or untoward events, each took refuge in futurist dreams of a distant but resplendent time to come when a universal state would blissfully envelop all humanity from sea to sea. Also, each of these civilizations was destined to be rejuvenated through the absorption of a religion of universal appeal—China through incorporating Buddhism, Rome through accepting Christianity. Of such affinities the contemporary Chinese and Romans were, for the most part, unaware, however, as they were, likewise, of their joint indebtedness to that cradle of all political life, the ancient Near East, where generations of men before them had entertained and forfeited similarly ambitious expectations.

Meanwhile, the two world states and the great area of Indian civilization touched at their peripheries. And since each had expansive tendencies, the contacts between them were occasionally rendered emphatic by planned campaigns of conquest and exploration, or the unscheduled migrations of peoples. Imperial frontiers were forever shifting and vistas into other realms were disclosed. Within each realm, furthermore, were men who could not be constrained within either a given body of doctrine or a political system of marked geographical frontiers. The hope of gathering new wisdom or religious truth, of experiencing new pleasures, or of discovering shores yet unknown, released a small but steady flow of intellectually adventurous people from the confines of the vainglorious empires. Such groups, for example, as the Rhodian merchants and lawyers who had established themselves as experts in international maritime affairs during the last centuries of the pre-Christian era, and the Indian and Chinese scholars of Buddhism who were soon to begin their revolutionizing intellectual mission, were set free for the pursuit of transnational quests. And insofar as they succeeded, through the imaginative use of literacy, in making foreign ideas accessible to their less venturesome fellow citizens or in synthesizing formerly disconnected sets of customs and beliefs for the convenience of inhabitants from many lands, they stimulated a general awareness in the ancient world that no one empire is ever quite as self-sufficient as it pretends to be. Moreover, this awareness was deepened by the gradual advancement of literacy that attended the spread of paper in the civilized world. The new writing material which Han China had made available in the first century A.D. could be manufactured less tediously and was found to resist moisture more readily than the papyrus. And, although the Chinese mandarins lacked the incentive to share these new advantages with their underprivileged compatriots, other societies in the known world knew how to profit richly from an invention that made it possible to accelerate and intensify the communication of the written word.[2]

The exchanges of ideas and fusions of thought that were thus stimulated during the first centuries of our era, in defiance of existing boundaries, were perhaps nowhere as manifest as in the field of religion. During the eleven hundred years that separated the rise of Buddhism from the appearance of Islam all of the world's now existing great religions presented their first offerings to the soul of man. Of course, the original constituencies of these religions were rather closely identified with specific territories and races. Buddhism addressed itself to India; Confucianism to China; Zoroastrianism to Persia; Christianity as well as Judaism to Palestine; and Islam to Arabia. But between the second and the seventh centuries A.D. all of these creeds, with the exception of Confucianism, became, as it were, travelling religions. This was so because each included doctrines that appealed to salvation-seeking individuals everywhere, regardless of their race or place of

[2] Lancelot Hogben, *From Cave Painting to Comic Strip*, New York, 1949, p. 127. Paper started on its trek to the still nonexistent printing presses of Europe A.D. 750, the year in which the Arabs captured Samarkand. It was introduced to Christendom c. A.D. 1200.

domicile,[3] and because each could rely on the fervor of some of its missionaries to propagate abroad the universal truths that had been found at home.

In the communication of their messages, whether orally or in writing, the missionaries of the great religions did not (and indeed, because of the very nature of their self-set task, could not) restrict themselves to "heathen" areas, that is to say, to peoples not touched by one or more of the other gospels. They penetrated each other's original domains and the encounters resulted, as a matter of course, in interreligious disputations and competitions, which in turn often made for interreligious adjustments in the form of doctrinal borrowings and syncretisms. Thus Buddhism spread over China and Japan after absorbing significant elements of the native religions, and entered Central Asia and the Near East by blending with Zoroastrianism.[4] Through the medium of Mithraism (a cult that had originally issued from Indian and Zoroastrian sources)[5] it affected the thought of peoples in Armenia, Asia Minor, and the western part of the Roman Empire, and it may have contributed certain themes to the New Testament of the Christians.[6] Islam and Christianity expanded in a similar fashion. Both developed on the foundations of Judaism, and, like the latter, were strongly influenced by Zoroastrianism. Indeed, in the small Near Eastern world where these four great religions evolved, cross references in matters of faith were frequent. The Christian groups in Mesopotamia were so deeply impressed by the teachings of Mani (born c. A.D. 215), who had returned to Persia in A.D. 272 after long wanderings said to have taken him to India, Tibet, and China, that many were converted to his syncretic creed. The Manichaean sect recognized Zoroaster, Buddha, and Christ as divine messengers, and its appeal was so broadly persuasive that it reached Central Asia and Tibet in the east, and in the west as far as to Western Rome, including southern France.[7]

[3] Helmuth von Glasenapp, *Die Fünf Grossen Religionen*, Düsseldorf, 1952, Vol. II, p. 440, refers to Hinduism, Jainism, Buddhism, and Chinese Universalism as "Religionen des ewigen Weltgesetzes," and to Zoroastrianism, Judaism, Christianity, and Islam as "Religionen der geschichtlichen Gottesoffenbarung."

[4] Some of Kanishka's coins, for instance, bear the image and name of Buddha, whereas his general currency displays predominantly Iranian deities.

[5] On "Mithraism," see James Hastings, ed., *Encyclopaedia of Religion and Ethics*, New York, 1916, Vol. VIII, p. 752. This cult was first transplanted to the Roman world by the Silician pirates whom Pompey captured in his campaign; and it gained a firm hold over Italy in the following centuries. Its downfall began toward the end of the third century A.D. when it could no longer withstand the competitive force of Christianity.

[6] Glasenapp, Vol. II, p. 249.   [7] On "Manichaeism," see Hastings, pp. 394ff.

The Roman Empire, which had become the administrator of the rich legacy of Hellenistic cosmopolitanism, was a particularly lively meeting ground of proselytising creeds. Within and on its boundaries, Egyptian, Phrygian, Syrian, and Greek cults—to number only a few— flourished freely in an environment that favored reciprocal influences. Indeed, when the Christian missionaries invaded the Hellenistic provinces of Rome, where the tradition of free religious and philosophical speculation was deeply rooted, they found themselves under an irresistible pressure either to absorb certain elements of the local cults or to adapt their own teachings to the local beliefs. The need for such adjustments explains why the evolution of Christianity was profoundly affected, from c. A.D. 220 onward, by certain Greek philosophies and mystery religions (in particular the Dionysian, Orphic, and Neopythagorean movements) which had impressed upon their numerous disciples the assurance that communion with the divine principle was possible and that spiritual salvation and immortality were within reach. Moreover, the fluidity that characterized such religious associations facilitated the formation of separate sects whenever any of the principal religions failed to satisfy its members. The Gnostic movement, for example, which aroused considerable controversy in the first century A.D. and became prominent in the second, seems to have been largely patronized by Christians strongly attracted to Oriental cults.[8]

The imperial claims to universal sovereignty of the various great states were thus disavowed by innumerable individuals in quest of kingdoms not of this world, and men all over Asia, Europe, and Africa were migrating freely from one such spiritual kingdom to another, searching for the keys to an experience of their oneness with the universe.

But these were not the only adventurers who were breaking horizons in that rich period of intercultural exchange. The several great areas whose illusions of separate existence were being assiduously emphasized not only through governmental policy pronouncements but also through regionally oriented popular legends, were being brought into communication with each other by a large number of bold individuals in pursuit of sheerly temporal gain. When, in the course of time, the interests of these merchants from India, China, and Rome converged in regular channels of commercial intercourse, the governments began to find it advantageous to relax their rigid postures of avowed self-sufficiency. The seas between the Roman world and that

[8] On "Gnosticism," see Hastings, pp. 231ff.

of India, the vast tracts of desert and mountain blocking China from both India and Rome, then ceased to suggest separation and fear. They became, during the first and second centuries A.D., when Rome, China, and the Kushana Empire had settled to conditions of relative peace and prosperity, the highway of an ever-increasing volume of steady trade.

The Roman Empire comprised such varied regions that all the essential commodities could be produced within its confines. Since it was Rome's policy to foster freedom of trade by eliminating tolls and exactions (with insignificant exceptions), and suppressing piracy, interprovincial trade prospered. However, the economic liberalism that stimulated these commercial developments also favored the rise, in each constituent region, of a wealthy cosmopolitan class, whose rapidly developing taste for luxuries could be satisfied only by imports from abroad. And since the imperial government did not restrain such interests, but permitted trade to spill over the Roman boundaries, commercial explorations were soon being pursued on a cosmopolitan scale. Amber from Northern Europe found a ready market on the Adriatic Sea, and wealthy Romans were willing to pay any price for pearls, precious stones, textiles, and, above all, pepper from India, as well as for silk from China.

The trade between India, Iran, and the Mediterranean area was actually centuries old. But the coastal voyage from Egypt, or from Aden, to India and back had always been a tedious enterprise that required some two years and was threatened constantly by piracy, tribal anarchy, and sundry interceptions by Near Eastern middlemen, who succeeded in evading the controls of the great powers. Sometime in the reign of Tiberius (A.D. 14-37) the situation changed, however, when the sea merchants and captains mastered a technique of using the monsoons. Thenceforward the sea voyage from Italy to India and back could be made in sixteen weeks, including the landstage in Egypt, without incurring the sort of risks that still beset the overland and Persian Gulf routes from India to Syria.[9] Taking advantage of the improved trading conditions, merchants from the Mediterranean poured into the ports of the Kushana Empire, and for the next four centuries the sea route to India remained the chief vein through which Rome

[9] Geoffrey Francis Hudson, *Europe and China; A Survey of their Relations from the Earliest Times to 1800*, London, 1931, pp. 68ff.

G. H. Stevenson, "Communications and Commerce," in *The Legacy of Rome*, Cyril Bailey, ed., Oxford, 1924, p. 165, to the effect that the journey from Alexandria to India and back took approximately six to seven months.

drew on the wealth of the Far East. This route remained paramount even after China joined the circle of economic intercourse that began in this period to bring together the separate civilized realms.[10]

The conditions favoring China's expansion westward were similar to those of Rome's expansion eastward. Unity and prosperity at home released latent energies, stimulated new ambitions, and developed new tastes. Already in the second century B.C. China's door to the farther west had been opened with the epoch-making mission of Chang Ch'ien. This envoy had been dispatched to discover the whereabouts of the Yueh-chi and conclude with them an alliance against their ancient enemies, the Hiung-nu, who had been responsible for their westward trek and were still harassing the frontiers of Han China. Though unsuccessful in his principal mission, Chang Ch'ien nevertheless reached Bactria, and there his attention was drawn to the magnitude and importance of India and the numerous Central Asian states. His carefully collected information aroused the emperor's curiosity concerning the large countries beyond the Pamirs, which, apparently, abounded in rare riches. Chang Ch'ien's report also suggested new goals for China's foreign policy and new uses for the arts of diplomacy. Indeed, the Emperor Wu-Ti seems to have entertained a plan for the extension of a great web of diplomacy to the farthest west, by the opening of permanent relations with the non-Chinese societies in that region, for the triple purpose of glorifying the Han court at home, impressing as many foreign nations as possible, and gaining access to desirable but remote objects of luxury.[11] As a result of several embassies sent out to many countries (they consisted of one hundred or more members each, and often remained eight or nine years at their destination) the conduct of Chinese diplomacy began to be linked to the development of trade. Chinese silks were shipped to Bactria, Sogdiana, Parthia, and other western lands, in return, often, for such mere curiosities as jugglers and large birds' eggs.

Han China, in charting its diplomatic and commercial penetration of Central Asia, relied heavily on supporting military campaigns. During the first great imperialist period—the second century B.C.—the Emperor Wu-Ti's regime delivered smashing blows to the Hiung-nu; and in the second such interlude—the first century A.D.—the great general Pan Ch'ao conducted a series of brilliantly successful cam-

---

[10] E. H. Warmington, *The Commerce between the Roman Empire and India*, Cambridge, England, 1928; Hudson, p. 88; Hugh George Rawlinson, *Intercourse between India and the Western World*, Cambridge, 1916.

[11] Hudson, pp. 62-65ff.

paigns in Central Asia. Indeed, in this phase of her foreign policy, Han China revealed a remarkable aptitude for the synchronization of explorative diplomacy, economic infiltration, and military pressure, with the ultimate purpose of pressing through to the west. And since Rome's foreign policy was employing similarly coordinated techniques as it penetrated eastward to envelop Western Asia, the geographical distance between the two great world states was being steadily narrowed, thus foreshadowing a direct encounter for some remoter date.

Contrary to what one might expect under such circumstances, this prospect does not seem to have fanned fear or rivalry in either of the imperial camps. The indications are in fact to the contrary, namely, that their imperialistic policies moved each of these two powers toward an interest in direct, reciprocal, and friendly commercial relations. It is impossible to say whether this amicable attitude would have endured following the consummation of a direct meeting, however, for the Sino-Roman trade was destined to remain indirect. The silks that constituted 93 per cent of China's exports to Rome, as well as the cargoes of furs, iron, cinnamon, and rhubarb, passed through numerous intermediaries before they arrived in the Mediterranean markets, and similar impediments encumbered the shipments of Roman glass to its Chinese buyers.[12]

The periphery of the Roman Empire was studded with markets and fairs that had developed in seaside towns and on the frontiers of independent, often even hostile, nations. In these all kinds of persons were engaged in a regular international commerce, which included shipments ultimately destined for either Rome or China. Lyons in Europe and Cyrene in Northern Africa were two such popular cosmopolitan junctions. Dioscurias, on the eastern shore of the Black Sea, was described by chroniclers as a market for seventy-six nations of different tongues.[13] However, it appears that no single traveller ever completed the entire journey, through these ports and markets, from one end of the line to the other, and all the efforts that were made both by the Chinese and by the Romans to bring trade into orderly, direct channels completely failed.

According to a Roman road book, there was a certain Isidore, who journeyed in the first century A.D. from Syria, through Parthia, and

---

[12] See Hudson, p. 73, for a map of routes of the silk trade between China and Rome in the first and second centuries A.D.

[13] Wyndham Bewes, *The Romance of the Law Merchant*, London, 1928, pp. 3ff., 102ff., and the authorities there cited.

thence to Afghanistan, where he seems to have met with traders from China,[14] while on the Chinese side, there was an emissary sent to Syria in A.D. 97 by Pan Ch'ao, the Chinese general in charge of military operations in the region. But this man was intercepted near the coast of the Persian Gulf by the wily Parthians, who had their own good reasons for wishing to prevent any direct commercial intercourse between Rome and China. The Parthians were so successful in frightening the Chinese stranger with announcements of the horrors of the sea, the certain emotional malaise that would overtake him so far from home, and the unavoidable ultimate loss of his life, that the emissary had no physical courage left to proceed with his historic journey.[15]

The end effect of all these interferences seems to have been that no Chinese ever reached Rome by any of the overland routes and no Roman reached China. The sole direct communication between the two great powers during the Han period may have occurred in A.D. 166, after the establishment of a continuous sea route. In that year something purporting to be a Roman embassy bearing tribute from "Antun," who has been identified as Marcus Aurelius Antoninus, "the King of Ta Ch'in" (a Chinese term for the eastern part of the Roman Empire), arrived at the Chinese court. In all likelihood, however, this mission was not official, but a private commercial undertaking of either Syrian or Egyptian merchants who were trying to raise their prestige and bargaining position by pretending to official status.[16]

Rome's trade with the Orient declined from the third century onward, and during the centuries that separated the reign of Caracalla from Vasco da Gama's voyage to Calicut in 1498 there was virtually no unimpeded direct communication between Europe and the Indies.[17] One of the chief causes for this decline and the severance of whatever tentative and experimental relations may have existed between the two great states, lay in the existence and policies of second and third rate powers. There were Arabs and Abyssinians, for example, who made it their business to intercept the Red Sea commerce; Armenians, Parthians, and others who knew how to capitalize on their controlling positions along the West Asian landroutes. A heterogeneous interna-

---

[14] Hugh Last, "A Roman Citizen Surveys the World," *Harmsworth's Universal History*, Vol. III, p. 1990.

[15] Sir Percy Sykes, *A History of Persia*, Vol. I, London, 1921, p. 387.

Lionel Giles, "China's Expansion and its Westward Pressure," *Harmsworth's Universal History*, Vol. IV, ch. 75, p. 2107, quoting from the Later Han History.

[16] Hudson, pp. 89ff.; Sykes, p. 387.

[17] See Hudson, p. 104.

tional community of piracy—so to speak—had thus developed along every possible track of the silk route.

Although divided by their disparate and conflicting interests, the greater and lesser nations alike had stakes in the continuance of this far-reaching trade. All were affected—however variously—by any disturbance that blocked its course anywhere along its path. Indeed, Cicero's observation that war could not occur anywhere in the east without shaking to its foundations the money market at Rome, seems to have been substantiated time and time again. A study of correlations in the historical events of Europe and Asia during this international epoch indicates that war along the Chinese trade routes in the Tarim basin resulted, many times, in disturbances in Parthia, in Armenia, and on the borders of Syria; and that, likewise, it was interruptions of the traffic on the Black Sea that stirred the people north of the lower Danube and so led to the long train of violent disturbances that concluded in the historic collisions of the barbarians with the Roman legions along the Rhine. Even peoples in no way connected with the silk route were affected by the remoter repercussions of any serious interruption along its course between the Chinese Wall and Rome.[18]

Of the Near Eastern buffer states that had the discretionary strength to interpose themselves either as barriers or as links between the Roman West and the Chinese and Indian East, none was more important than Parthia. This semi-eastern, semi-western nation, which had entered the Near Eastern arena when pressed from the farther east by the Kushana Empire of India, succeeded for over three centuries (c. 140 B.C. to c. A.D. 226) in retaining mastery over Iran and Iraq. From this key position Parthia persistently exploited the silk route in spite of all the separate and joint efforts of the three major realms—India, China, and Rome—to disestablish her influence in that critical region.[19]

[18] Frederick J. Teggart, *Rome and China, A Study of Correlations in Historical Events*, Berkeley, 1939, pp. 120ff., 240ff.

[19] See Sykes, Vol. I, pp. 305ff. on the history of Parthia and the appearance of Rome in Asia; pp. 346-390 on the relations between Parthia and Rome; also *The Cambridge Ancient History*, Vol. IX, ch. XIV. See map of Parthian Empire of 51 B.C. on p. 613.

G. Rawlinson, *The Sixth Great Oriental Monarchy*, London, 1875, rates the Parthians not merely as the sole rival daring to stand up against Rome in the interval between 65 B.C. and A.D. 226, but very little below the great power whose glory has thrown them—in the written annals, at least—so much in the shade. In Rawlinson's opinion, Parthia maintained from first to last a freedom unknown to later Rome and excelled the Romans in toleration and liberal treatment of foreigners.

The authors of articles on "Parthia," "Persia—the Parthian Empire," in *Encyclopaedia Britannica*, N.Y., 1929 (1944), Vol. XVII, pp. 344ff., 575ff., on the other hand, explain Parthia as a state that had come into existence through fortuitous external

Parthia was a greater threat to Rome than to either China or India; for Rome's reliance on imports from Asia, which had to pass through Parthia, was far greater than Asia's need of products from the Mediterranean world, and Rome's system of military security was particularly vulnerable in the Asian sector—especially after the annexation of Syria (63 B.C.) had extended Roman interests across the Euphrates river and into the highlands of Armenia, where they clashed with those of Parthia. After Augustus had realized the futility of resolving his conflicts with Parthia through warfare,[20] Roman diplomacy aimed at a modus vivendi that would accord with the new imperial policy of consolidating the *Pax Romana* within well-defined and defensible frontiers while keeping the eastern trade routes open.[21] With these ends in view, Rome tried for a while to control Armenia through choosing its puppet king, but the international pretext had to be dropped during Nero's principate, and the attempt was abandoned. Furthermore, the Roman emperors did their best to encourage the centrifugal tendencies of Parthia's eighteen imperial provinces and of the rings of minor states generally dependent on the Parthian king. However, although some of the vassals actually did transfer their allegiance to Rome when pressure was successfully applied, most remained disposed to the Parthian Empire, whose loose organization afforded greater independence than could be enjoyed under the suzerainty of Rome.[22]

During the second century A.D. Rome was holding her own in the diplomatic game. In A.D. 165 she even succeeded in making Parthia cede northwestern Mesopotamia. But in the third century anarchy overtook the Near East. The Roman legions destroyed each other and soon were powerless not only against the Syrian rebels and Arabs, but also against the Persians, whose Sassanid Dynasty replaced the Parthian in A.D. 226 and was to reach the zenith of its glory under Shapur the Great, in the second half of the fourth century. The same critical decade witnessed the end of the Kushana Empire (A.D. 220) and the fall of the Han Dynasty in China (A.D. 220). The period of division ended in China in A.D. 265 with a new unification under the western

---

circumstances and never developed any inner strength. According to their views, Parthia, as a largely nomadic and disorganized society, would have had no chance for survival if the Roman policies under Augustus had not favored its continuance as a second great power.

[20] Ambitious military leaders, like Crassus in 54 B.C., had resorted to full-scale military operations.

[21] See Michael I. Rostovtzeff, *Caravan Cities*, Oxford, 1932, p. 31, on an agreement with Parthia regarding the caravan trade.

[22] *Encyclopaedia Britannica*, Vol. XVII, p. 577.

Chin. India's political resuscitation as a great power, however, had to wait until A.D. 320 when the newly formed Gupta Empire put a temporary end to the local disunity. In the Near East the interlude of anarchy saw the city of Palmyra attempt to unify all the lands traversed by the caravan routes into a single state—a caravan empire. But the evolution of this potential buffer state was frustrated by the revival of Roman power under Aurelian (270-275) and Diocletian (284-305).[23]

One century later, under the impact of the Germanic invasions from the northeast, Rome's power decayed and the Empire's center of gravity shifted to the east. The consequent emergence of Constantinople as the major capital of the Empire, and the transfer of residence of the emperor to that city in A.D. 330,[24] opened a new period in the history of international relations.

B. The Roman State as an International Society

The history of the union of the separate Mediterranean states under the hegemony of Rome was first written by Polybius (b. 201? B.C.), a cultured and politically experienced Greek expatriate living in Rome, who had come to regard the political supremacy of his adopted city as the world's incontestable and irreversible destiny.[25] Deeply influenced by Stoicism as taught by Panaetius of Rhodes, he addressed his life work to his contemporaries and posterity with the recommendation that men should study the world, not in its several parts, but as a whole. And yet, such was his faith in the historic mission of Rome that he was led to identify the "whole" with the Empire. When he asked: "For who is so worthless or indolent as not to wish to know by what means and under what system of polity the Romans in less than fifty-three years have succeeded in subjecting nearly the whole inhabited world to their sole government—a thing unique in history?"[26] he chose to forget that the inhabited world was far from being exclusively Roman, and that empires were not unique in the annals of mankind, since many

[23] Rostovtzeff, p. 34; Theodor Mommsen, *The History of Rome. The Provinces, from Caesar to Diocletian*, William P. Dickson, tr., London, 1886; Part II, pp. 92-112.

[24] In A.D. 324 Constantine decided upon the foundation of the new capital and in 325 the construction of the main building was begun. The dedication took place in A.D. 330. In this year Christian Constantinople was superimposed upon pagan Byzantium. See A. A. Vasiliev, *History of the Byzantine Empire, 324-1453*, Madison, 1952, p. 59.

[25] See Theodor Mommsen, *The History of Rome*, W. P. Dickson, tr., London and New York, 1921-1930, Vol. III, pp. 435-440 for an appreciation of Polybius.

[26] Polybius, *The Histories*, W. R. Paton, tr., in 6 vols., London, New York, 1922, Book I, I. (4).

had risen and fallen before he wrote. Nevertheless, even today, when almost two thousand years of history separate us from the facts then recorded, the story of Rome's evolution from a nation of intelligent peasants into a cosmopolitan society, from a city-state to an expansive republic, and finally into an empire, remains one of the most fascinating chapters in world history.

This, no doubt, is so, partly because Polybius was present to continue the great Greek tradition of historiography—a tradition such as had never developed in those Asian and African realms where the evolution of national states into international empires had proceeded without the benefit of any extensive literary commentary. Nevertheless, it is more than likely that even without the writings of the contemporary historiographers the events that constitute Roman history would never have ceased to exercise the imagination of subsequent generations in the Western world. Roman law, Roman military strategy, and Roman statesmanship continue to inspire the work of scholars and statesmen, and to influence the policies alike of despotisms and of republics. Indeed, there is hardly a nation in Europe that has not had to come to terms with the legacy of Rome, and there has been hardly a period in European history when the collective memory of its diverse nations has not been stirred by the remembrance of Rome as a unified world state. Empires and leagues have been blueprinted or created with this image in mind, and hopes for future unity and harmony continue to issue from a nostalgia for the lost unity of civilization that was Rome.[27]

It is easy to explain this inspiring image as a "mystique," formed gradually—and in spite of reality—through an accumulation of biased judgments. It would also be possible, no doubt, to demolish the factual evidence usually cited in support of the vision by pointing to those phases of Roman history that were marked by social division, human suffering, and international warfare. Neither effort could obliterate the image itself, however, for it seems to have become a historic reality by virtue of its continuous operation on the European mind. Its hold was already strong on many Greek intellectuals in the second century A.D., to whom the Roman Empire appeared as the final realization of the Hellenistic idea of the unity of the civilized world.[28] And already at

[27] This point has been well expressed by Alfred N. Whitehead in "The Place of Classics in Education": "Europe is always flying apart because of the diverse explosive character of its inheritance, and coming together because it can never shake off that impress of unity it has received from Rome. . . . The vision of Rome is the vision of the unity of civilization." *The Aims of Education and Other Essays*, New York, 1929, p. 115.

[28] e.g., Dio Chrysostom and Aelius Aristeides.

that time, the image of Roman unity was linked closely with that of a benevolent and powerful, universal father-emperor. For since Augustus had put an end to the great moral and intellectual confusion that had come to a head in the revolution of the first century B.C., he had become the symbol of all the benefits associated by the people of the Mediterranean with Roman rule. The Jewish Platonist Philo spoke for his co-religionists in Alexandria, as well as for countless others, when he claimed that the whole human race would have been exhausted by mutual slaughter had it not been for one man and leader who had put an end to the wars, both open and secret, which had been caused by the attacks of robbers; had cleared the sea of pirate craft and filled it with the ships of merchants; delivered all the cities into freedom; tamed and harmonized the wild tribes; and thus succeeded in securing peace for all.[29]

Many of the facts that inspired these eulogies have never been questioned. The empire created by the Romans in the brief span of a few generations extended over Asian and African as well as over European regions. It included, therefore, a wide diversity of races, states of various sizes and cultural complexion, tribes with differing moral codes, urban centers with strong particularist traditions, and religious communities held together by various mystical appeals. All of these component parts and groups were integrated within one broad governmental framework, which was successfully maintained for about five hundred years. By virtue of its very composition and organization, therefore, the Roman Empire was an international state. And since Roman rule was, on the whole, respectful of local autonomy, protective of individual rights, and favorable to the free communication between its various regions, it stimulated the evolution of a new spirit of cosmopolitanism and thus transformed the Mediterranean world into an international society.

Some of the institutions that supported the Roman state as an international society resembled those of other comparable empires; others, however, were unique. Like any great empire, the Roman was defended by an army; and like most imperial armies, the Roman was a melting pot of nations—and to that extent a school of internationalism. Its soldiers were recruited from every part of the Mediterranean world. Moreover, the security and unity of the Roman Empire, like that of the earlier Persian, depended on an efficient system of com-

---

[29] From *Legatio ad Gaium* as quoted in Sir Paul Vinogradoff, "The Work of Rome," in *The Evolution of World-Peace*, Francis S. Marvin, ed., London, New York, 1921, pp. 28ff.

munication. The successive Roman governments saw to it that their military and civilian personnel should be able to circulate freely and swiftly along a well planned, empire-wide network of roads.[30]

On the other hand, in their use of their legions as an administrative device, the Roman statesmen seem to have shown more discrimination than the leaders of any earlier empire. Only in the barbarous West were the military governors omnipotent. In the sophisticated East, Roman administration was closely guided by diplomacy. And there Rome could rely on a fund of diplomatic experiences accumulated during the earlier centuries of her statehood when circumstances had required the recognition of other sovereignties on a basis of reciprocity. Such relationships underwent a drastic change in the third century B.C., when Carthage became a dependent of Rome and the great monarchies of the East were obliged to accept Rome's claim to paramount sovereignty. However, by that time certain diplomatic traditions not only had entered into Roman thought and practice, but were actually being preserved in a set of quasi-legal principles, known collectively as the *ius fetiale* and administered by a college of special officials, the *fetials*, under religious sanction.

The fetials watched over the general observance of good faith in international relations and served as a living depository of archives. It was their particular task to remember conventions concluded with neighboring communities, to express authoritative opinions on alleged violations of treaty rights, and, when necessity arose, to demand restitution or to declare war.[31] Functioning in combination with other colonial institutions, they guided Rome's conduct in the attempt to maintain effective control over such areas as were officially independent kingdoms or city-states.

For it must be remembered that a large part of what was ultimately to be included in the Roman Empire was long ruled by so-called "client kings," whose nominal independence as the "friends and allies" of Rome was recognized officially by the senate, even though they were expected to render assistance in war and subordinate their foreign policy to Roman interests.[32] The Roman policy of utilizing such buffer states continued—at least in the East—long after the principate had

[30] See G. H. Stevenson, "Communications and Commerce" in Bailey, ed., pp. 141ff.

[31] Coleman Phillipson, *The International Law and Custom of Ancient Greece and Rome*, London, 1911, Vol. I, pp. 96, 303-335; Vol. II, pp. 318ff.

[32] These were the obligations of the Kings of Numidia, Mauretania (North Africa), Galatia, and Cappadocia (Asia Minor). See also *The Cambridge Ancient History*, Vol. IX, pp. 442f.

embarked on its program of rigidly centralizing the provincial system of government.[33]

In the shaping of her imperial administration, Rome interfered as little as possible with pre-existing political arrangements. This tendency was particularly marked in her relations with city-states, perhaps because here it was reinforced by Rome's remembrance of her own civic traditions. There was a small number of such communities, described as *civitates foederates*, that stood in theory outside the provincial system and were linked to Rome by sworn alliances. Such Greek cities, for example, as Athens, Rhodes, and Massilia, were bound by treaty to support Rome's friends and fight Rome's enemies, but in all other respects were left free to organize their own governments.[34] Moreover, Rome pursued a determined policy of diffusing such semi-sovereign cities over the entire empire, thus illustrating emphatically her preference for the semi-sovereign *civitas* as the chief lower unit of imperial government. Cities were built along the entire length of the far-flung frontier, where they immediately became outposts of defence as well as centers of civilization. Since each was granted extensive liberties (due provision being always made against any threat of sedition) each also functioned as a provincial school of government and citizenship. Furthermore, although the various municipal charters differed in particulars, all were replicas of the Roman constitution as far as the major organs of government were concerned. As a consequence, the city became, to a considerable extent, an internationally shared form of community life and, by virtue of this fact, an agency in the process of counteracting provincial and racial differences.

In this policy of utilizing and establishing municipal governments for the purposes of an international society the Romans cannot be counted as particularly original, however, since they were following here the example of Alexander the Great. Moreover, in the course of the development and final organization of their provincial system, they ultimately turned away from the Greco-Italian legacy of federalism, which had already failed in the period of Athens and the Achaean League, and so was too badly discredited in the ancient world to merit

---

[33] In areas outside the far eastern zone the system of protectorates came to an end as kingdoms were absorbed into the Empire. This happened preferably upon the extinction of native dynasties when the last prince of a line could be persuaded to make a proper bequest of his realm.

[34] *The Cambridge Ancient History*, Vol. IX, p. 464. See also H. Stuart Jones, "Administration," in Bailey, ed., pp. 101ff., 112, 130.

serious consideration as a pattern of international government.[35] They borrowed, instead, from the imperial models of the immediately preceding Hellenistic despotisms—perhaps particularly from Ptolemaic Egypt.[36] According to this system, the aggregate of states included in a province was placed under the rule of a provincial governor, who was supposed to carry out the will of the central sovereignty in Rome. And yet, even with this centralized organization, Rome, in dealing with her provinces (as distinguished from her client kingdoms) continued the practice of making direct arrangements with each component community rather than with the province as a whole. And in further derogation of the local governor's centralized authority, the provincials were granted a right to send embassies to Rome directly, where, during a certain time of the year, their missions, as well as those of foreign kings, had precedence over all other business in the senate. Another tradition frequently mentioned by the political commentators of the first century B.C. was that the leading citizens or families of Rome would undertake to watch over the interests of particular provinces or cities, especially in Asia.

Apparently the Romans, in promoting the unity of their world, remained most true to their classical tradition of democracy when their imperial functions required them to regulate matters of personal status. By the end of the period of the republic, the concept of the municipal citizenship of the citizens of Rome itself had been supplemented by that of the state citizenship of the inhabitants of Italy. As colonies were founded in the provinces, or provincials were admitted either to full Roman citizenship or to the intermediate right of Latinity, state citizenship became the privilege of many communities and individuals in the Empire, regardless of race or prior nationality. Furthermore, after Julius Caesar had realized how immensely significant the provinces were for the future of Rome, social distinctions began to be progressively effaced. Caesar's policy of admitting freedmen to the highest municipal offices was continued by his successors, and in the fully developed principate all governmental positions, including the highest, were open to men without regard to their legal status at birth.

Italy's privileged position in the commonwealth over which Augustus

[35] See T. R. Glover, *Democracy in the Ancient World*, Cambridge, 1927, pp. 222-227, to the effect that federalism could not possibly have served the ancient world at that time, since it had failed in Athens, in the Achaean League, and in Rome, and since it required moral standards that were wanting.

[36] H. Stuart Jones, p. 93; but cf. also *ibid.*, p. 113; and consult Sir Ernest Barker, "The Conception of Empire," in Bailey, p. 62 n. 1.

had watched so jealously was thus gradually weakened. It was abolished by Hadrian (A.D. 117-137)—himself a provincial from Spain—who regarded the Empire as one indivisible state, rather than a conglomeration of separate *civitates*, and was therefore impatient with any national or local particularism, whether expressed in Jewish uprisings in Palestine or in Roman conceit in Italy. The development culminated in A.D. 212 with Caracalla's promulgation of the *Constitutio Antonina*, under the terms of which all freeborn inhabitants of the Empire were granted Roman citizenship.

The remarkable fact that the final phase of this process of enfranchisement was the work of emperors who were firm believers in absolutist rule renders apparent the complex nature of this entire evolution, for it shows that Caracalla's Edict actually capped two parallel political processes. The emperor confirmed, by his act, on the one hand a principle of equality that had had its inception in ancient republicanism, and on the other the victory of imperial authoritarianism over local rights to self-government. Moreover, the cause of internationalization had been furthered in the Roman commonwealth of many races not only by deliberate efforts to perfect administrative devices, but also—as in earlier empires—by less coordinated policies directed toward the propagation of a basic fund of education and the allowance of the widest possible competition between the sciences, arts, and crafts that had previously been developing separately in the several provinces.[37] The Romans seem to have been more successful than their predecessors in this field of broad human relations, perhaps because they were always ready to recognize their own deficiencies and to appropriate serviceable ideas from friend and foe alike. Their increasingly close contacts with the East, furthermore, had convinced them that Hellenistic learning could not be matched anywhere; and they therefore permitted and even fostered its free development alongside their own Latin culture. Roman intellectuals were expected to know Greek, and a certain Roman governor of Asia delivered his judi-

[37] Mommsen (Everyman's edition), Vol. III, p. 399, takes a dim view of this development: "The immediate result of this complete revolution in the relations of nationality was certainly far from pleasing. Italy swarmed with Greeks, Syrians, Phoenicians, Jews, Egyptians, while the provinces swarmed with Romans; sharply defined national peculiarities everywhere came into mutual contact, and were visibly worn off; it seemed as if nothing was to be left behind but the general impress of utilitarianism. What the Latin character gained in diffusion it lost in freshness; especially in Rome itself, where the middle class disappeared the soonest and most entirely, and nothing was left but the grandees and the beggars, both in an equal measure cosmopolitan."

cial decisions according to the requirements of the case—to the con-sternation of native Greeks—sometimes in ordinary Greek, and some-times in one or another of the four dialects that had become provincial written languages.[38] The same respect for knowledge explains also why Plutarch's thesis that the Greeks could boast of men and warriors easily comparable to the heroes of Roman history met with general approval and helped to convince his contemporaries that there was a heritage outside of the narrow bounds of Roman experience in which all men could share.

In the period of the emperors, Roman education was gradually mod-ernized. The liberal arts curriculum that had been evolved in the Cice-ronian Age (the last century B.C.) was cleared of traits limited specifi-cally to the peculiarities of Roman life, so that it might be applied in the greatly various communities of the Empire,[39] and the concept of "humanity" (*humanitas*)[40] was introduced as the chief goal of intel-lectual aspiration. However, in their selection of jurisprudence as the chief means of approach to this goal of *humanitas*, the Romans were essentially uninfluenced by foreign ideas. This discipline was trans-formed under their imaginative treatment into a science of human rela-tions, and it became in due time the most effective instrument of in-ternational coordination in the Roman world.[41]

As a science of human relations, jurisprudence was held to re-gard the human being as its chief object. And the human being whose life and conduct had been the inspiration for the evolution of its scientific rules had been the citizen of early Rome. There were cer-tain qualities that this citizen had displayed in his relations with other men and in the context of his political community in general which had come to be regarded as virtues and for the cultivation of which the Roman home was held responsible as the chief educa-

[38] *ibid.*, p. 398.

[39] See Michael I. Rostovtzeff, *History of the Ancient World*, Oxford, 1926-30, Vol. II, "Rome," p. 264, to the effect that the imperial government showed little interest in popular education, leaving the subject to the attention of local municipalities.

[40] Mommsen (Everyman's edition), Vol. III, p. 417, compares Rome's new "hu-manity" to the European notion of "general culture" current when he wrote, for the two had the same "nationally cosmopolitan and socially exclusive character." These educational developments in Rome were, according to Mommsen, yet another re-flection of "the revolution which separated classes and levelled nations."

[41] Charles Norris Cochrane, *Christianity and Classical Culture*, London, New York, 1944, p. 147, summarizes his analysis of Roman education in the Augustan period with this statement: "Thus in a society constituted in the last analysis upon the basis of a common body of ideas, this education became a passport to the rights and privileges of the community."

tional institution. What these virtues were is still apparent in Cicero's discussion of ethical conduct in his *De Officiis*,[42] even though, by that time, Roman education had already become heavily encrusted with Greek concepts of pedagogy and learning. The foremost of the virtues associated with Roman character was courage, but as the society became more complex, and therefore more demanding in matters of personal and public behavior, three other qualities delineated themselves. A Roman had to comport himself, above all, with *gravitas*— he was to approach all undertakings, great and small, with a well-developed sense of responsibility and restraint. Next, he was expected to discipline his emotions, and to show to all established institutions the proper degree of submission (*pietas*). And lastly, he was not to indulge in flights of imagination beyond the boundaries of his empirical vision, but to see things clearly, as they really were (*simplicitas*).

Rome's political institutions developed on the foundations thus laid by early Roman education. The whole concept of the *pater familias* (father of the family) with his long undisputed power of life and death over the members of his immediate and extended family (the family, that is to say, as extended through adoption and the inclusion of servants, slaves, etc.) is unthinkable except as limited by the bounds of virtuous conduct publicly recognized and protected. And since all political authority, including the *imperium* of a consul or emperor, was chiefly derived from this contingent *patria potestas* (power of the father), it can be said without exaggeration that the entire constitution of the Roman world state rested, in the ultimate analysis, on a definite understanding of how people and their governments *ought* to behave. Nevertheless, in the later course of Roman history the traditional standards of ethics were frequently violated. Under the pressure of revolutionary events they were weakened, and as a consequence of contact with foreign values and customs[43] they were to some extent diluted. Furthermore, since they had been elaborated by a very special breed of people in response to very special social surroundings, they were not as readily exportable to other communities of the Empire as, for example, the Greek concepts of morality and education had been. Nevertheless, amid the welter of ethical norms that had been brought together by the intermingling of numerous nations, the Roman ideas

---

[42] This was the great orator's last contribution to literature. Written between 46-43 B.C., it reflects the influence of Stoicism as presented by Panaetius of Rhodes.

[43] Mommsen (Everyman's edition), Vol. III, p. 400, refers to the national decomposition of the Roman population as one of the repulsive aspects of cosmopolitanism.

of virtue maintained their identity and continued to supply a source of regenerative strength in periods of empire-wide reconstruction. Indeed, during the Augustan Age they inspired not only an emperor's concrete program of progressive reform, but also a poet's vision of the Empire as a world community united by ties of the spirit.[44]

There were definite limits, however, to the usefulness of the axioms of Roman ethics as props of imperial unity. The new Mediterranean society that had emerged in the Augustan Age was so diverse that it could not be made to rally around Roman theories of virtue in order to become a morally cohesive community. Nor, for that matter, could it long rely for its political stability on Rome's traditional republican institutions. The Romans, therefore, looking around for a more adequate instrument of imperial rule, hit upon the device that had already recommended itself to so many empire-conscious nations before them: they associated their world government directly with the force that was presumed to rule the universe by announcing the divinity of its human emperor.

Ruler cults of one kind or another had been common in the Near East before that area passed under the sovereignty of Rome. In fact, since many inhabitants of the eastern provinces regarded the creators of the *pax romana* as the inheritors of their own political and religious traditions, the Roman governors were in some cases deified even before the apotheosis of the emperor. Pompey, for instance, was declared to be a god by the Athenians and celebrated in certain inscriptions as a savior because he had effectively warred against the pirates and the king of Pontus. The Romans were deeply impressed by these traditions which they encountered in conquered Egypt, Syria, and Bithynia. Also, they were flattered by the widespread disposition of their subjects to accord to them divine honors. Roman officials and soldiers, therefore, who had been stationed in the East, as well as eastern slaves, merchants, and scholars who had become assimilated residents of the West, carried the idea of emperor worship into regions where it had never been known before. Roman rulers like Julius Caesar studied the example of Alexander the Great. Latin intellectuals found that they could readily connect the politically useful idea of emperor-worship with the familiar Aristotelian proposition that deference should be paid to the best, and with the accepted Stoic belief that the individual of true virtue has gained immortality. Of course, for the average Roman citizen, whose memory was still steeped in republican traditions, deifi-

[44] Virgil's *Aeneid*. Cf. Cochrane, p. 73.

cation was an obvious departure from the established political patterns of Rome. Yet he could accept it by interpreting it in terms of the familiar image of the *pater familias,* whose theoretically unlimited quasi-divine power was in actuality restrained by virtue and reason. Such an approximation of two different positions of authority was especially convincing to Roman citizens in the Augustan Age because they had many reasons to venerate Octavian-Augustus as a model ruler. It can therefore be assumed that the Greek geographer and historian Strabo was expressing the sentiments of many contemporaries in the reign of Tiberius (A.D. 14-37) when he wrote: "It is hard to administer so great an Empire save by committing it to the care of one man, as of a father: never, in fact, has it fallen to the lot of the Romans and their allies to enjoy such abundance of peace and plenty as that which Augustus bestowed on them from the day when he assumed sovereign power. . . ."[45]

Very different mental processes thus converged in the empire-wide readiness to accept emperor-worship as a legitimate or reasonable concept. But it was Augustus himself who transformed the concept into an effective imperial institution by defining both its meaning and its use. Research has made it clear that he did not follow Oriental precedents in thinking himself divine. According to his interpretation of the concept, he was the foremost citizen while exercising his imperial functions on earth, and he would become a god only after death, by virtue of his excellence. The cult, for him, was primarily a part of the government, its function being to personify the power and the peace of Rome, and to create urgently needed bonds of unity between the different races of the realm.[46]

Like many preceding and succeeding empires, the Roman had thus become a religious community. But unlike most other empires, it continued to function, nevertheless, as an essentially secular international society, until the general acceptance of Christianity necessitated a recasting of all its political forms. For the image of the Empire as a cult did not absorb, or otherwise alter, the older image of the Empire as a commonwealth of men; and the newly discovered imperial tie between God and man did not supplement the older, traditional links

[45] As quoted by H. Stuart Jones, "Administration," in Bailey, p. 119.

[46] Lily Ross Taylor, *The Divinity of the Roman Emperor,* Middleton, Conn., 1931, pp. 146, 237ff. While many later rulers were much less restrained than Augustus in their interpretation of this institution, it survived essentially unaltered up to the reign of Diocletian (A.D. 284).

of the various peoples of the Empire with the supernatural,[47] or materially weaken those bonds of shared worldly interest that had previously united citizens of differing origins and callings in the pursuit of the common good.

The Roman success in maintaining the unity of the Empire both as a conception and as a reality is a remarkable achievement in the comparative history of international societies. It followed from the fact that in a world of conflicting images, conflicting institutions, and conflicting interests, the Romans had found an ultimate coordinating measure. This measure was reason as embodied in law. The Romans had derived it from two main sources of insight and experience: their already proven capacity to think creatively in terms of law, which had yielded the civil law of Rome, and their ability to borrow intelligently from the accumulated wisdom of the philosophy of the Stoics.

C. The Influence of Natural Law on the Roman Empire

The Stoic doctrines of a universal law had reached Rome in the first century B.C., when Roman law was in a crucial stage of development. At this time the image of an empire unified for the common good was beginning to crystallize in public opinion, and Roman intellectuals were being stirred by their first contacts with the East. As formulated by Panaetius (189-109 B.C.) and Posidonius (135-51 B.C.), both of Rhodes, Stoic philosophy assumed that reason was a law for all men, not merely for the wise; that people everywhere ought to be assured of that minimum of rights without which human dignity is impossible; and that if the universe is ever to be as companionable and comfortable for the whole of humanity as reason indicates that it should be, the law must satisfy the normal requirements of justice by recognizing fully this indicated minimum of human rights.

In its earlier version Stoicism had confirmed Alexander's views of the universe and the commonwealth of man. It also had influenced decisively the administrative policies of the Hellenistic kings in Bactria and India. But never had it been brought into any direct relationship to the actual legal system of a multinational society until the Romans succeeded in adapting its tenets to their own needs and predilections as the administrators of the Mediterranean world.

In judging this Roman record we must first remember that most, if

---

[47] The imperial cult was adapted to the rites and requirements of such locally prevalent creeds as e.g., the Jewish faith.

not all, world states have sought to identify themselves with the universe by pleading a celestial law as the fundamental constitutive principle of their existence and of their several claims to universal government. In fact, as one authority has stated the position of modern jurisprudence: "Philosophical sociological jurisprudence recognizes that each particular living law culture of the world regards its particular philosophy as a natural law jurisprudence which is universal, (and suggests that all are) merely different provincial philosophies of nature and culture generalized dogmatically for the rest of the world."[48] This generalization is probably broad enough to include the natural law theories elaborated in the contexts of Indian, Chinese, and traditional Roman Catholic thought. Yet it seems somewhat inadequate as an explanation of the Stoic position in general and of its Roman version in particular. In contrast to the natural law philosophies of China, India, and the ancient Near East, where universalist ideologies were developed in close alignment with the dominant nation's or caste's political aspirations, Stoicism was not originally connected with any one people's particular imperialism, nor geared to any one system of theology or ethics. Stoicism can be distinguished also from those later Western views of a universally valid law of nature that were derived from a special moral preference as to how people ought to behave. In contrast to our later Western moralists, the Stoic philosophers rested their case on their analysis of the nature of man and the quality of reason in general. Consequently, their conclusions proved applicable to human relations on many levels of existence and in very different culture realms. They were particularly relevant in the framework of Roman history. For even before discovering Stoicism, the Romans had been accustomed to test their actions by reference to an objective body of principles; they had notions of civil law into which the Stoic theory of man's rights could be readily fitted; and they had cherished, as their political goal, the idea of an imperial commonwealth to which the Stoic conception of the universe brought support.

The chief credit for perceiving these connections between the local and the universal, as well as between the practical and the ideal, belongs to a class of educated Romans who had had the opportunity and interest to study the manifold aspects of the revolution of their time. Among these, Cicero (106-43 B.C.) in particular succeeded in communicating universally appealing ideas to the Roman public by reconciling them with provincially prevalent traditions.

---

[48] F. S. C. Northrop, "Contemporary Jurisprudence and International Law," in *The Yale Law Journal*, Vol. 61, no. 5, May 1952, p. 651.

According to Cicero's reading of Stoic philosophy, the universe constitutes one immeasurable commonwealth. Gods and mortals alike are its members, and they are united by the indissoluble bond of reason.[49] Moreover, since God has permitted men, as well as gods, to share in his divine reason, he has made it possible for man to attain to that *right* reason or law which is, in the final analysis, the power to distinguish between things just and unjust. Law, on this universal level, is, in Cicero's conception, as old as the mind of God. In other words, it antecedes human associations, societies, and states. "True law," he writes, "is right reason in agreement with nature; it is of universal application, unchanging and everlasting. . . . It is a sin to try to alter this law, nor is it allowable to attempt to repeal any part of it, and it is impossible to abolish it entirely. We cannot be freed from its obligations by senate or people, and we need not look outside ourselves for an expounder or interpreter of it. And there will not be different laws at Rome and at Athens, or different laws now and in the future, but one eternal and unchangeable law will be valid for all nations and all times. . . ."[50]

Starting with these premises, Cicero concludes that mankind is born for justice;[51] that right is based, not upon men's opinion, but upon nature; and that all human associations are formed within the great universal city in order to realize this supreme purpose of all human existence. But before distinguishing among different kinds of groupings, Cicero establishes the primacy of the entire human race as man's chief association on earth; for "it seems that we must trace back to their ultimate sources the principles of fellowship and society that nature has established among men. The first principle is that which is found in the connection subsisting between all the members of the human race, and that bond of connection is reason and speech."[52] While the knowledge itself may be endlessly diversified, he writes elsewhere, the faculty of acquiring knowledge is similar in all human minds, and that faculty of speech which is the soul's interpreter agrees in the ideas it conveys, though it may differ in the syllables that express them, since troubles, joys, desires, and fears haunt the minds of all men without distinction.[53] Thus, if man's true nature would assert its rights and

[49] Cicero, *De Legibus* (Laws), C. W. Keyes, tr., London, New York, 1928, Book I, vii.
[50] *De Re Publica*, C. W. Keyes, tr., London, New York, 1928, Book III, xxii.
[51] *De Legibus*, Book I, x.
[52] *De Officiis*, Walter Miller, tr., London, 1947, Book I, xvi.
[53] *De Legibus*, Book I, xi.

teach men the noble lesson of the poet: "I am a man, therefore no human interest can be indifferent to me," then justice would be equally observed by all.[54]

Cicero recognizes, however, that while there is a bond of fellowship which has the very widest application, uniting all men together, and each to each, this bond of union is closer between those who belong to the same nation than between those of alien minds, and more intimate still between the citizens of one city-state. Now this smaller moral community—the *res publica*, which exists within the great city of humanity—is held together by its own civil law. Indeed, it does not qualify as a state unless it has such a system of law.[55] Nevertheless, Cicero insists, all states and all particular systems of civil law remain subordinate to the precepts of that universal natural law which rules over all matters divine and human. In other words, although the civil law is not necessarily the universal law, the universal law *ought* to be also the civil law.[56]

In this world hierarchy of law and politics the Roman Empire was conceived to occupy a definite place. Along with most other contemporary Romans, Cicero thought of it not only as an administrative unity, but also as that superior human association in which all individual aspirations could find expression. Yet he never implied that Rome was the only state. On the contrary, he reaffirmed those ancient Roman traditions according to which relations between all states should be governed by the standards of reason and justice that are deemed operative within each civil society. Thus he denied the legitimacy of war (except to redress injuries or to secure peace, and then only after a formal declaration of war), denounced all forms of national aggrandizement motivated by the love of power and glory, and warned against all recourse to expediency and force.[57]

Cicero, citing Rome's destruction of Carthage in illustration of this last point, declared that nothing is ever expedient that is shameful, and that all differences between states can be settled best by employing reason and speech properly through debate and discussion. Cicero never tired of pointing out that Rome had become great because she had complied in large measure with these ethical requirements: the empire had been founded by acts of service, not of oppression; wars had been waged in the interest of Roman allies, or to safeguard Rome's

[54] *ibid.*, xii.
[55] *De Re Publica*, Book I, xxxii; a state is a partnership in law.
[56] *De Officiis*, Book III, xi, xvii. [57] *De Officiis*, Book I, xi.

187

supremacy; and the ends of wars had been marked by acts of clemency, or by no more than the necessary degree of severity. The Roman senate was a haven of refuge for kings, tribes, and nations, and the highest ambition of Roman magistrates and generals was to defend the Roman provinces and Rome's allies with justice and honor. And so, he concluded, Rome's government might be called, more accurately, a protectorate of the world than a dominion.[58] Cicero mourned, however, that all of this was changing fast in his lifetime. For under the impact of Caesar's policies the old republic had become a despotism. Inasmuch as Rome was ceasing to act as a Big Brother[59] and had begun to bully weaker peoples like a foreign tyrant, her international prestige had already declined.

Cicero's passionate involvement in the developments that marked the transition from republic to principate prevented him from realizing how deeply his own Stoicism had penetrated Roman thought. He died profoundly disillusioned. Yet the philosophy he had propagated throughout his lifetime triumphed during the two centuries that followed his death, informing the great political adjustment that characterized the Augustan and Antonine periods. It reached the throne with Marcus Aurelius, who conveyed the essence of Stoicism in his statement: "My city and country as Antoninus, is Rome; as a man the world."[60] It expressed itself in Caracalla's edict granting citizenship to all inhabitants of the Empire, and it pervaded the evolution of Roman private law. Cicero's legacy became internationally significant also because it inspired a new religious version of Stoicism. As understood by the Latin philosopher Seneca (4 B.C.-A.D. 65), the city of man was really separate from the city of God, and every man was, therefore, a member of two commonwealths: the civil state and the greater state of all rational beings to which he belonged by virtue of his humanity.[61] And since Seneca suggested that the "superior" commonwealth was a society rather than a state, and that it was held together by moral or religious, rather than by legal and political ties, the idea gained ground that political government had no divine license, being actually tainted by evil.

It was this, rather than Cicero's reading of Stoicism, that supplied the intellectual foundation for the Christian order, which replaced Rome's secular state in the fourth century A.D. And it was through

[58] *De Officiis*, Book II, viii.
[59] Cf. the use of this concept in Chinese politics.
[60] *The Communings with Himself of Marcus Aurelius Antoninus*, rev. text, C. R. Haines, tr., London, 1924, Book VI, p. 44.
[61] G. H. Sabine, *A History of Political Theory*, rev. ed., New York, 1950, pp. 174ff.

this circuit that the ancient Stoic theory of a law of nature reached the Christian fathers, on its way to becoming ultimately an integral part of Western European civilization.

Viewed in this perspective, the Roman application of Stoicism assumes immense importance. Indeed, it is difficult to say what turn the international history of political thought would have taken if the belief in natural law had not been disseminated by Rome's literary and legal elite.[62] And yet, when all this has been admitted, one cannot but wonder what might have happened had Stoicism not become linked in the following period to Christianity. From the Christian, and even from the broader, secular Western point of view, there is reason in the contention of such Christian writers as Prudentius (348-c.410) that Roman universalism was simply a prelude to the greater universalism of the new religion: "What," asks Prudentius, "is the secret of Rome's historical destiny? It is that God wills the unity of mankind, since the religion of Christ demands a social foundation of peace and international amity. . . . This is the meaning of all the victories and triumphs of the Roman Empire: The Roman peace has prepared the road for the coming of Christ. For what place was there for God, or for the acceptance of truth, in a savage world in which men's minds were at strife and there was no common basis of law?"[63] From a provincial Western point of view, such a paragraph may seem to represent the obvious line of human progress. The international historian, on the other hand, cannot but see that the potential scope of Stoic universalism was definitely contracted by this sectarian interpretation. The conceptual unity of the Stoic universe disintegrated, and the great commonwealth of man became the society of Christian believers. The dictates of right reason, which had earlier been deemed to be within the reach of every man, were transformed into the supernatural truths revealed uniquely to Christians. The state as a partnership in law was superseded by a theocracy held together by dogma.

In the perspective of this long evolution, which began with Zeno's announcement of the Stoic philosophy, the record of pre-Christian Rome is of everlasting and universal importance, for it reveals a consistent and successful rational effort to adjust national institutions to the needs of an expanding international society by incorporating internationally valid concepts into the machinery of government. And it

---

[62] Sir Henry Maine, *Ancient Law*, 3rd American ed., New York, 1879, p. 71. See also W. A. Robson, *Civilisation and the Growth of Law*, New York, 1935, pp. 212ff.
[63] Quoted in Christopher Dawson, *The Making of Europe*, New York, 1945, p. 23.

shows, above all, that this was accomplished without whittling down the universal meaning of any of the concepts so employed.

The credit for initiating this process belongs to those scholarly politicians who assimilated and reinterpreted Stoicism, notably Cicero. And yet, like all of the later Christian Stoics, many of them were moralists, so prone to argue in terms of what people "ought" to do in order to qualify as decent Romans, that they frequently failed to appreciate the practical necessities that required compromise with their announced abstractions. For the true moralist compromise is anathema. Moreover, many of these good men were so carried away by sentiment and conviction, that their philosophical theses frequently suffered from a lack of rational precision. Had it been left with them, the Stoic theory of a law of nature would hardly have yielded any substantial practical consequences. The true measure of the Roman achievement does not become evident until one turns to see what the Romans *did* with the concepts that interested their moral and political philosophers. And this aspect of the process of adjustment was the province of Roman jurisprudence.

D. The Private Law of Rome

The private law of Rome—the *ius civile*—has a recorded history of about one thousand years of practically uninterrupted progress.[64] It developed steadily from c. 450 B.C., when it was compiled in twelve tables, to A.D. 527, when it was codified by the Emperor Justinian. During this long span of time, Roman jurisprudence developed most strikingly in the final century of the republic and attained perfection in the course of the three first centuries of the Empire. It was unaffected, that is to say, by the constitutional change from republic to principate. However, in the ensuing period the growth of Roman law lost momentum, and in the sixth century A.D. it stopped. At that time the Romans defined their law in the following terms of the Institutional Treatise published under the authority of the Emperor Justinian: "Every community governed by laws and customs uses partly its own law, partly laws common to all mankind. The law which a people makes for its own government belongs exclusively to that state, and is called the civil law, as being the law of the particular state. But the law which natural reason appoints for all mankind obtains equally among all nations, and is called the law of nations, because all nations make use of

---

[64] Maine, p. 23, says in effect that Roman jurisprudence has the longest known history of any set of human institutions.

it."[65] The philosophy that had inspired this statement was unmistakably a repetition of Cicero's thought. But the precise lines of distinction between civil law and the law of nations as appointed by natural reason, which Justinian's legalists took for granted, had not been delineated by the jurists of the early republic. The creative genius of those earlier thinkers, the initiators of the entire science, had not been concerned with such subtle systematic distinctions.

The lawyers of the classical republic had constituted a very special literate elite in their society. They were neither philosophers nor narrowly oriented specialists, but educated men, familiar both with the traditions of their city and with the realities of imperial politics. Their interest in the affairs of the commonwealth was so great that they approached the study of law as an adjunct of statesmanship, and since they were men of independent means, they could engage in the practice of law as a public service rather than as an occupation for pecuniary gain. Indeed, the function of law in later Rome's multinational empire can be appreciated only if it is borne in mind that law was developed at first, not by the acts of the legislature, but by the opinions (*responsa prudentum*) of individual lawyers (*prudentes*), who were recognized as the chief legal authorities alike by private citizens and by magistrate-judges, because they were learned in the law and trusted as men. In the exercise of their authority, these *prudentes* naturally honored established principles, but in an ever more complex and extended commonwealth the principles of the past became increasingly inadequate as yardsticks for the measuring of rights and wrongs. The jurists therefore had to draw heavily on their own reason and insight in order to render socially just opinions. And this reliance on a wisdom gained outside of the statute books became even more pronounced in the subsequent stage of legal development when a new type of magistrate—the *praetor urbanus*—was instituted in 367 B.C. for the express purpose of administering equitably existing civil laws. By about 242 B.C. the increase of the foreign populations in Rome necessitated the creation of a second praetor (*praetor peregrinus*) for the decision of suits between foreigners, and between citizens and foreigners. Both classes of official— *praetor urbanus* and *praetor peregrinus*—were required to announce the rules that they would follow during their magistracies and to explain the circumstances under which they would depart from ancient

---

[65] *The Institutes of Justinian*, Thomas Collett Sandars, ed. and tr., tenth impression, London, 1900, Lib. I, Tit. II, p. 8.

or otherwise established laws in order to grant relief by the exercise of their equity.[66]

As the center of political gravity shifted from the senate to the emperor, this method of gradually improving the law was superseded by direct imperial legislation and by officially approved commentaries compiled by great court lawyers. In the middle of the third century A.D. the long succession of eminent classical jurists ceased; the growth of equity jurisprudence came to a close, and law lost its intimate organic connection with Roman life and thought to become a mere tool in the hands of authoritarian emperors. The way was thus opened to the systematic cerebrations that produced, eventually, the codifications of the Institutional Treatise of Justinian.[67]

E. The Relationship of the Civil Law and the Natural Law

There is obviously nothing very remarkable about the mere incidence of law and of a law-making process in society. Every political association—whether known as a state or as a tribe, located in the East or in the West, composed of literate or of nonliterate people—has evolved its own system of legal rules for the protection of group solidarity and the guidance of individual conduct. It must therefore be recognized, first of all, that there are as many different legal systems as political societies, and that contemporary efforts to find an internationally meaningful approach to the function of law in the world society today must proceed on the assumption that each legal system has contributed to the world heritage of legal experience by virtue of the simple fact that it has existed. After a preliminary understanding of the multifarious legal traditions that compose the international history of law has been reached, however, it becomes legitimate to single out those particular legal systems that have proved applicable beyond the confines of the particular societies in whose contexts they originally evolved. And, in the perspective of the past as well as in the world of the pres-

---

[66] See F. de Zulueta, "The Science of Law," in Bailey, pp. 173ff.; also *The Cambridge Ancient History*, Vol. IX, ch. XXI. Sir Henry Maine, see pp. 27, 42, 55 on equity; pp. 59ff. on the praetor. John H. Wigmore, *Panorama of the World's Legal Systems*, pp. 396ff., 420ff. Fritz Schulz, *History of Roman Legal Science*, London, 1946, several chapters on the jurists and their functions in different phases of Roman history. Hans Julius Wolff, *Roman Law, an Historical Introduction*, Oklahoma, 1951, ch. IV. Edward Gibbon, *The Decline and Fall of the Roman Empire*, 2 vols., New York, Vol. II, ch. 44.

[67] See Wolff, *Roman Law*, for an account of this evolution.

ent, no legal system has had such prodigious consequences for the course of human relations throughout the world as that which issued from the classical Roman method of producing laws.

This is so because Roman law was developed neither by priests, whose special interest was the protection of a local creed, nor by a supreme lawgiver, in whose view the purposes of the law would be identical with those of the political system effective at the time of his legislation. Instead it was developed by a class of lawyers who made it their special business to cleanse legal notions of all the particularisms adhering to them, and to abstract the concepts that would seem generally applicable. As a result of the efforts thus pursued systematically over the centuries, Roman private law was kept from being confounded with any particular religion, form of government, or generation of men. It emerged as an independent system of norms, for which validity could be claimed outside of religion, outside of government, outside of Rome, and even outside of any special epoch in time.

Such an acknowledgment of Roman originality in the field of jurisprudence does not imply that Rome did not borrow from the legal theories and practices elaborated in other cultures and earlier centuries. On the contrary, the genius of the Roman jurists lay precisely in their readiness to study law in all of its intricate manifestations, and to observe its operation in the varied civilizations of the Mediterranean. The Roman achievement in lawmaking can be measured best, in fact, when it is compared with the law ways of the Greeks—the only nation whose cultural superiority Rome unhesitatingly accepted in all domains of thought excepting that of jurisprudence. And Rome's discerning rejection of Greek leadership in this realm, it should be noted, has stood the test of modern research in the field of ancient legal practice.[68] For the Greeks, it has been found, were so absorbed in perfecting the state as the fulfillment of the individual's talents and aspirations that they could not conceive of any law except in association with a particular political society. Moreover, since the political society of the Greeks was synonymous by and large with the city-state, law was in their estimation just another aspect of such a political community. It was "good" or "bad" to the extent that it supported or frustrated the purposes of the state.

Now, it is certainly true that the Greeks never tired of arguing ques-

[68] Sir Henry Maine, *Ancient Law* and *The Early History of Institutions*, New York, 1888; Sir Paul Vinogradoff, *Outlines of Historical Jurisprudence*, Oxford, 1927, Vol. II, the Jurisprudence of the Greek City; Rudolph von Ihering, *Geist des Römischen Rechts auf den verschiedenen Stufen seiner Entwicklung*, 5th ed., Leipzig, 1891, Vol. I, p. 318.

tions of "good" and "bad," "right" and "wrong"; but through all of this they associated the goal of justice with the perfectibility of the city-state rather than with that of the processes of law. As Professor McIlwain puts it, they thought of law in terms of the state, rather than of the state in terms of law.[69] The great classical philosophers of Greece assumed, of course, that a universal norm of political life could be apprehended through human reason, and that various political societies could be judged by reference to this universal norm. Yet they never really suggested that this norm could be elaborated as a practical guide for the perfectibility of laws. Throughout their discourses on law and justice, the legal norm remained a purely intellectual standard, which could not be used as a yardstick for the testing of the legitimacy of any particular law. Such a view involved a failure to distinguish between the public law of the state (*ius publicum*) and the private rights of individuals (*ius privatum*).

But it was precisely in the recognition of this distinction that the Roman lawyers made their revolutionary contribution to political thought. In their differentiation of the *ius publicum* from the *ius privatum* the jurists of Rome made it perfectly clear that both were derived from the same essence—law, and that both were addressed to the same subject—the natural person. The Romans departed, however, from the more ancient traditions of law by establishing the proposition that private rights affect private citizens exclusively, whereas all individuals alike participate in the public law by virtue of the fact that they together constitute the state.[70]

This legal distinction had momentous consequences for the evolution of the modern society of nations, and may be said, indeed, to represent the fundamental legal proposition of the modern Western world, for the doctrine of the state as a bond or partnership in law as set forth by Cicero became the foundation for all our Western theories of constitutionalism. The general Roman theory that law is antecedent and thus superior to the state, made it possible to think of law as a

---

[69] Charles H. McIlwain, *Constitutionalism, Ancient and Modern*, p. 39. See also Maine, *Ancient Law*, p. 72, to the effect that Greek tribunals tended to confound law and fact. Although questions of law were constantly argued in the Greek cities, no durable system of jurisprudence could be produced. "A community which never hesitated to relax rules of written law whenever they stood in the way of an ideally perfect decision on the facts of particular cases, would only, if it bequeathed any body of judicial principles to posterity, bequeath one consisting of the ideas of right and wrong which happened to be prevalent at the time. . . ." (p. 73.)

[70] It was only after a long and bitter struggle that the dominance of the state over the individual was finally established in the later centuries of the principate.

regulating force in relations between states. And the legal disengagement of the individual from the political group led in due time to the elaboration of a category of "inalienable human rights," as well as to the general realization that it is constitutionally possible to render international relations in terms of human relations.

All of these principles of legal thought were discernible in the classical civil law (*ius civile*) even before it made its epochal contact with the Stoic theory of the natural law (*ius naturale*). For common sense and reason had moved the early Roman lawyers to give expansive interpretations to the established laws and to respect the common customs of mankind in the Mediterranean world as the chief informing principles of their law-making process. Rome's acceptance of the Stoic theory of natural law was nevertheless of inestimable importance for the further evolution and subsequent diffusion of the Roman system. It gave a theoretical consistency to the isolated legal pronouncements, directed the exercise of praetorian equity, and provided a standard for the selection and coordination of non-Roman concepts and customs. As a consequence of its adoption, a generally acceptable philosophy was gradually infused into the local legal process, and this philosophy itself then became the chief medium for the effective communication of Roman law, not only within the area of the empire but also (as subsequent history was to show) across the bounds of geography and time.

As an illustration of the interaction between the civil law process and the natural law theory, one might cite, at this point, the establishment of the Rhodian Law as the international authority on most maritime matters in the Mediterranean society. The choice was probably determined as much by Rome's well developed talent for appreciating effective practical devices, whatever their origin, as by the known Stoic orientation of the emperor Marcus Aurelius, who pronounced himself officially in favor of receiving the Rhodian Sea Law as the supreme international government of the seas. However, the relationship between the *ius civile* and the *ius naturale* was not precisely defined at that time, and we today cannot confidently retrace, therefore, the lines of distinction first drawn between these terms. The Roman jurists apparently were not prepared to abide by Cicero's doctrine that natural law is superior to civil law. They seem rather to have regarded the natural law simply as a system of norms with which the civil law ought to be made to comply whenever possible, in order to be kept from degenerating into rigidity.

The most fundamental and internationally significant legal changes that derived from this continuous alliance between Roman law and Stoic philosophy were those that affected the status of the individual. The powers of the father over the son, the master over the slave, and the husband over the wife, on which Rome's early institutions had rested in considerable measure, were slowly dissolved under the impact of the Stoic doctrine of equality.[71] A case in point, for example, is the enfranchisement of women. Roman law commenced by giving all the wife's property to the husband, because she was assumed to be, in law, his daughter. It ended by supporting the general rule that all of the wife's property is to be under her own control. And the same influences arrested the tendency to look upon the slave as property. They led, indeed, to the general realization, clearly affirmed by the jurisconsults of the Antonine era, that all arbitrary distinctions between classes of persons are untenable both philosophically and legally, that every man is to be recognized as an individual, rather than as the member of a particular family or group, and that such human activities as the acquisition and disposal of property, or the free association with other individuals, require the protection of the law, since they are the natural extensions of the free personality.

The evolution of these legal principles within the sphere of the Roman Empire revolutionized, in the end, the conduct of human relations throughout the world.

F. The Roman Law of Contract

The influence of Roman jurisprudence on international relations is illustrated best by the emergence and subsequent diffusion of the Roman concept of contract. When we speak of "contract" today we mean a voluntary agreement between persons or groups of persons that is concluded under the protection of accepted legal rules. So understood, the idea of contract figures rather prominently in contemporary human affairs. We are familiar with contracts of marriage and adoption, for example, as well as with contracts that institute partnerships, corporations, and trade unions, and we assume that such associations can, as a general rule, be formed across geographic and political boundaries. We read of "social contracts" from which states and governments are said to be evolved. We realize that international law rests on innumerable treaties between two or more states, and that these treaties are commonly interpreted on the analogy of private contracts. Now this

---

[71] Maine, *The Early History of Institutions*, p. 312; See also F. de Zulueta, in Bailey, ed., pp. 204ff.; Sabine, pp. 170ff.

idea of contract appeals more to men in Western societies than to those in Eastern societies, whose domestic legal systems leave only scant room for contractual relations. Nevertheless, in the sphere of international politics it has stimulated all nations to think of world government in terms of a contractual relationship.

A review of the early history of the idea of contract is, therefore, pertinent to the present discussion of man's emancipation by law, since it marks the emergence of a device that has released man from his dependency on local groupings and facilitated the formation of greater unions.[72]

The individual can create for himself few if any rights or responsibilities as long as he lives in a society, literate or nonliterate, in which his social position is irreversibly fixed at birth, or in which his personal activities are circumscribed by rules that emanate from forces beyond his control. Under such conditions the human will cannot disengage itself from the encumbrances of custom, and the minds of men cannot meet in voluntary agreement. In the Mediterranean world, however, where the historical records of such great trading peoples as the Phoenicians, Rhodians, and Greeks reveal quite various associational patterns, it was clear long before the Romans appeared that commerce could not be promoted by a rigid adherence to inherited social customs, or by a blind obedience to imperative commands. The pursuit of commerce required the exercise of individual discretion, and the safety and profitableness of the operations depended on men's willingness to define their particular interests and obligations in the form of mutually satisfactory agreements. We can assume, therefore, that the amply documented story of Roman contract law must be in many respects similar to, if not precisely typical of, the legal developments of various other ancient societies from which we have only the scantiest records.

---

[72] On some of the influences that have deadened and depersonalized the concept of contract see K. N. Llewelyn, "Contract," in *Encyclopaedia of the Social Sciences*, New York, 1930, Vol. iv. This scholar sees the major importance of legal contract in the fact that it provides "a framework for well-nigh every type of group organization and every type of passing or permanent relation between individuals and groups up to and including states—a framework highly adjustable, a framework which almost never accurately indicates real working relations, but which affords a rough indication around which such relations vary, an occasional guide in cases of doubt and a norm of ultimate appeal when the relations cease in fact to work. . . ." (p. 336.)

Karl Llewelyn and E. A. Hoebel, *The Cheyenne Way, Conflict and Case Law in Primitive Jurisprudence*, Norman, Oklahoma, 1941, pp. 50ff., to the effect that modern law has been moving uninterruptedly toward an expansion of group relations and group responsibility.

And yet the Roman development of the idea of "agreement" must be singled out for two principal reasons. In the first place, it would seem that the notion of contract has never emerged anywhere as clearly as in Rome, and in the second place, it is certain that only the Roman law of contract has had a lasting influence on the affairs of the world.

Rome's early history of contract is obscure, but we know for certain that from a remote date onward the Romans had a general legal form for the binding of any sort of personal engagement.[73] And like most other peoples, the Romans commenced by emphasizing the form, rather than the substance, of any given transaction. Promises to do, or to refrain from doing, certain things were wrapped in ceremony, and as long as the ceremonies were properly observed, the intentions of the parties to the bargain were deemed to be of little interest. For example, the *way* in which property was conveyed was much more important than the underlying agreement to convey *a certain thing*.

In Rome the shift of attention from the form to the substance of an agreement of this kind was gradual but steady until, in the end, all technicalities were brushed aside and the mental engagement was isolated as the sole ingredient in any contractual relationship. The essence of the idea of contract emerged when the Romans recognized the will of the parties, and attached a legal obligation to the personal "pact" or "convention" thus identified. In other words, a contract came into being when the law joined persons or groups of persons together in consequence of certain voluntary acts.[74]

In the first stage of this fascinating intellectual development external acts still retained considerable legal significance. Not only were they long regarded as indispensable guarantees of the authenticity of the promise, but also they supplied a necessary key for the classification of contractual relations. For at an early date the Romans realized that human transactions may involve an infinite variety of circumstances, but that the law, if it is to fulfill its function of regulating and protecting such human relations, has to provide broad, simple categories of obligation. A pronounced talent for coordinating differences and an inborn respect for form as the indispensable framework of order led the Roman jurists to distinguish between four main types of contract, in accordance with the external acts that were required over

[73] *The Cambridge Ancient History*, Vol. IX, p. 861.

[74] Sir Henry Maine, *Ancient Law*, pp. 304ff., 313ff. The Romans spoke of a "nude pact" as long as the law did not couple it with an obligation. "Obligation" could signify rights as well as duties, i.e., the right to have a debt paid, as well as the duty of paying it.

and above the mere agreement of the parties. The so-called Literal Contract demanded an entry into the ledger; the so-called Real Contract was consummated with the delivery of the goods; the so-called Verbal Contract issued from an exchange of certain specified words. All three of these contracts were used widely, and all three are historically significant. In the great perspective of international history, however, it was the fourth kind of contract—the Consensual Contract —that has assumed supreme importance. The legal obligation here attached itself as soon as the parties reached a consensus, and all the accompanying external acts were regarded merely as the symbols of human volition.

When the Roman magistrates had perfected the Consensual Contract as the most appropriate device for the implementation of all contracts of sale, hiring, agency, and partnership, the orderly process of emancipating the individual from the constraining customs of his local community was immeasurably furthered. For in the Roman view, such a relationship as "partnership" meant any sort of continued joint enterprise, not merely the commercial.[75] With the help, therefore, of these legal devices men were encouraged in every field of life to extend the radius of their interests and experiences, to seek new outlets for their spirit of adventure, and to invent new patterns of association beyond those of the accustomed bounds.

As we have already noted, the great expansion of human interest and energy that Roman legal history records could not have occurred without, on the one hand, the stimulus of Roman imperialism, and on the other, the influence of the Stoic doctrine of natural law. The interconnections in this development between the *ius civile* and the *ius naturale*, and between jurisprudence and international politics generally, appear clearly in the last phase of the revolution in contract law—when the praetor announced that he would grant equitable action upon pacts that had never become contracts in the strict legal sense, provided only that he could discover a valid justification (*causa*) for his policy. In isolating and defining the factors that make for mutual assent in human relations, the Roman jurists had concluded that the discernment of an intention does not necessarily hinge on the existence of written evidence. A contract of sale, for instance, could be a perfectly good contract without ever having been committed to writing.[76]

---

[75] See *The Cambridge Ancient History,* Vol. XI, ch. XXI, for a discussion of these concepts.

[76] The Roman Law also accepted oral wills as good wills.

But this was a notable departure from the practices that had been followed in the most esteemed society of the ancient world, that of Greece. There the law had required a commitment to writing of most transactions, suggesting that the Greeks did not trust each other unless their promises were recorded.[77] We cannot but assume that the contrary development in Rome must have been intimately connected with the Roman version of the law of nature, but here, as in so many other Roman situations, it is difficult to disassociate the Stoic concept from the other contributing causal influences.

When probing the intentions of the parties to a contract, the Roman jurists had to examine their "good faith." Such an approach to a human relationship was certainly in accord with the Stoic philosophy of reason, but it issued also from a deeply rooted respect for the plighted word, which had characterized the conduct of the ancient Romans long before Cicero began discussing Roman ethics in the new light of the Stoic doctrines. The evolution of contract law and its relation to the vast orbit of intense human relations within the Roman Empire can be understood, therefore, only if it is remembered that the Romans were extremely competent in discerning and coordinating the various separate sources of their strength. As in many other phases of their imperial administration, they relied in their development of the contract chiefly on the skill of their most literate and most politically conscious group of citizens—the jurists. The achievement of this class is thus of timeless significance in the comparative history of international government. It is richly suggestive also as a case study in the political uses of literacy,[78] for it illustrates clearly that ideas can become effective principles of international cohesion if they are tended responsibly by an internationally oriented and educated elite.

The lasting reputation of the Roman jurists rests, briefly speaking, on the following record. They were conversant with the world of letters as well as with the world of politics, and so were able to find meaningful relationships between philosophical truths and empirical situations—an accomplishment illustrated, for example, by their imaginative adjustment of Stoicism to the *ius civile*. Moreover, their general ability to discern universals in particular human transactions helped them to simplify and thus to master the mass of materials that were

[77] W. W. Buckland and Arnold D. McNair, *Roman Law and Common Law*, Cambridge, Eng., 1952, pp. xix, 267ff., 276ff., 280.

[78] Compare with the policies of literate elites in the ancient Near East, India, and China.

their perennial professional concern. As a consequence, they fixed the categories of juristic thought for all time. Indeed, they created, as it were, a legal alphabet, through the use of which law could become an intelligible medium of communication between peoples. Their process of definition led to the making of a clear distinction between form and substance; established the lines of difference between ethics, religion, and law; separated law from the state; and, without disrupting the political community, isolated the individual as the bearer of legal rights and responsibilities. These achievements culminated in the constitutional theory that public rights are not the rights of the state, but the interests of all the individuals who constitute the state. For reasons such as these the entire corpus of Roman Law was once described as a hymn to the value and vocation of the personality.[79]

The Roman jurists' abstraction of the idea of law and acknowledgment of the individual as the chief legal entity led them to their revolutionary exploration of the constitutive elements of "agreement." The theory of contract that emerged from their intellectual labors yielded an entirely new approach to the old problem of governing men. For if the will of the state is, in reality, the will of its citizens, then all law must be viewed as an agreement between equals—a contract by means of which the citizens commit themselves to a certain action. In its objective sense, therefore, law appears not as an authoritative order but as a collective obligation, or as the Roman legalist Papinian (died A.D. 212) succinctly put it, "a common engagement of the republic (*communis rei publicae sponsio*)"[80]—*sponsio* ("engagement") being the technical term denoting the essence of the old Roman verbal contract.

G. The Importance of the Law of Contract for the Conduct of International Relations

No such constitutional framework of contractual security as the Roman was evolved by any other people in the ancient world. Although many nations of medieval[81] and modern Europe have tried to ad-

---

[79] Ihering, Part II, p. 303: the source of the system was the idea of the personality, and the goal of the system was the creation of a situation in which the personality could unfold itself freely in public and in private life. Also Part I, p. 209.

[80] See Henry John Roby, *An Introduction to the Study of Justinian's Digest* together with a full commentary on one title. Cambridge, Eng., 1884. See ch. XVI on Papinian's life and work.

[81] See Sir Paul Vinogradoff, *Roman Law in Mediaeval Europe*, London, New York, 1909.

minister Rome's legacy of constitutionalism, it is doubtful indeed whether any has ever succeeded in formulating an equally convincing system of individual and collective security. Roman law, consequently, may perhaps be regarded as a function of the Roman style of government alone.

No later government of continental Europe can be understood, however, unless we remember that all have their roots in the Roman tradition and are unified by virtue of the simple fact that they are the joint legatees of a great estate at law. Many feudal institutions developed on the foundation of Roman contract law. The international authority of Christianity's canon law derived chiefly from concepts that had been previously clarified in Roman jurisprudence. The social philosophies of continental Europe employed consistently the language and modes of reasoning peculiar to the Roman civil law. And Europe's consciousness of this common Roman inheritance was refreshed at the opening of the present period by the conquests of Napoleon I, which diffused the rules of Roman law over the whole continent.

Moreover, in other parts of the world vast regions were opened to the Roman forms of law as a consequence of the European expansion into Asia, Africa, and America. This steady multiplication of similarly rooted legal systems through a seemingly limitless borrowing of the entire phraseology and greater part of the norms of Roman jurisprudence has been so prominent in recent times that it impressed an English jurist in the nineteenth century as one of the most important phenomena of his day.[82] According to Sir Henry Maine's estimation, Roman law was fast becoming the *lingua franca* of universal jurisprudence,[83] and English-speaking people would have to study it seriously if they were really interested in understanding the political transactions of the continent.

Apart from their timeless importance for the history of European constitutionalism, Roman theories of obligation are directly relevant also in the context of international relations. For the history of Roman institutions has illustrated clearly that the conduct of foreign affairs, or the administration of international concerns, will of necessity reflect the theories and practices that prevail in the member nations of any given international system. It is significant, therefore, that the principle of obligation, which pervaded Rome's republican constitution,

---

[82] Sir Henry Maine, "Roman Law and Legal Education," in *Village Communities in the East and West*, New York, 1880, p. 355.
[83] *ibid.*, p. 361.

found entrance also into Rome's policies toward other members of the Mediterranean society of sovereign states. The theory became prevalent, for instance, that a treaty with another state was a common engagement of the republic, like a domestic law, and should be interpreted in accordance with the same legal and ethical rules that guided the application of contracts. A Roman citizen who violated a treaty with another nation was, therefore, customarily surrendered to that other nation on the ground that he had broken an obligation that rested on him personally. Cicero narrates many historical case studies in support of the proposition that obligations of individuals do not disappear simply because the states of which they are members are at war; that good faith is a minimum universal law in the performance of any contract;[84] and that an oath made to an enemy is as binding as a treaty,[85] even if it is made under the stress of extraordinary circumstances.[86]

To Cicero's profound disappointment his countrymen did not persist in extending the principle of individual obligation to the realm of interstate relations. All efforts previously made in this direction were discontinued as a matter of course when the Mediterranean world ceased to be a system of multiple sovereignties and became instead a unified cosmopolitan empire in which Roman ethics were internationalized through recourse to different methods. Rome's imperial tradition of unity was strong enough to carry the Christian world through several centuries. When it weakened in the fourteenth century under the impact of revolutionary ideas and newly found national interests, the Western world returned to the ancient pattern of multiple sovereignties that had been predominant in the days of Babylonia, Greece, and republican Rome.

The precedent of republican Rome was the most suggestive of these three for the newly emerging European system of multiple sovereign-

---

[84] *De Officiis*, Book III, xvii.

[85] *ibid.*, xxix.

[86] *ibid.*, Book I, xiii.

Cf. *ibid.*, xi, on general attitudes toward war on the part of the state and on the part of individual fighting men; also on the violation of Roman law and ethics that is evidenced by Rome's treatment of Carthage and Corinth.

See Hugo Grotius, *The Rights of War and Peace including the Law of Nature and of Nations*, A. C. Campbell, tr., Washington, London, 1901, for numerous similar citations of Roman practices and quotations from Cicero. Cato is said to have proposed that Julius Caesar should be delivered up to the Germans for having attacked them in violation of his promise. *ibid.*, p. 59.

See Coleman Phillipson, Vol. II, p. 293, on a personal covenant (*sponsio*) between a Roman general and the enemy.

ties, not only because it had been recorded the most recently, but also because it had been crystallized in clearly defined and generally valid legal concepts. For these historic reasons, a true understanding of the modern system of national states, which developed in Western Europe from about the fourteenth century onward and was to spread subsequently over the entire world, demands a preliminary understanding of Roman jurisprudence. Furthermore, many of the basic international differences between the Western European and the other members of the contemporary society of states become clarified when it is remembered that the non-European culture areas were not impregnated with the science or phraseology of Roman law until they adopted the ways of Western constitutionalism, or were otherwise implicated in the Western states system. It is true that many of the Roman concepts lost their original meanings in the course of being interpreted by Rome's successor nations on the continent and that some even acquired a new, sham significance as convenient legal phrases. But this does not diminish the force of the Roman influence on the basic mentality of the West.

Several of the international institutions that have recently been developed reveal a particularly close connection with Roman thought. In all ages such processes as diplomacy, arbitration, and international law have facilitated international communication, but the contemporary versions of these processes betray very strongly the special influence of Rome. The prelude to this influence is to be found in the history of modern Europe, where treaties have long been drafted on the model of Roman contracts, where diplomatic and philosophical arguments concerning the rights and responsibilities of the sovereign prince or state have always drawn heavily on analogies from Roman private law, and where the evolution of arbitral and judicial procedures followed largely the ancient Roman practice of persuading disputants to accept the judgment of an impartial third party. Indeed, no one can read the table of contents of Grotius' monumental treatise, *The Rights of War and Peace*, without being struck by the recurring inspiration of ancient Rome—in the chapters, for example, on promises, contracts, and oaths; moderation in the conduct of war; and good faith between enemies.

Grotius' great secular manual on public international law was written in the first half of the seventeenth century, when Europe had lost its sense of unity and was rent by war and anarchy. The author undertook to marshall the wisdom of the ages, in order to determine "the law of nature and of nations." Among the many illustrious personages from Judaic, Greek, Roman, and early Christian history who wander through the pages, lending their authority to the newly stated rules of international behavior, no one appears more regularly or with more dignity than Cicero. For the history of international relations Grotius' treatise has been of inestimable importance. It has influenced the conduct of governments, the proceedings of such international conferences as the Congress of Westphalia in 1648, and the thought processes of all subsequent writers on the law of nations.

The international consequences of the continental respect for Roman jurisprudence have not always been adequately appreciated in English speaking societies. Sir Henry Maine noted with regret that few nineteenth century English publicists had an adequate view of the relation of Roman law to the international scheme. "If International Law be not studied historically," he wrote, "—if we fail to comprehend, first, the influence of certain theories of the Roman jurisconsults on the mind of Hugo Grotius, and, next, the influence of the great book of Grotius on International Jurisprudence,—we lose at once all chance of comprehending that body of rules which alone protects the European commonwealth from permanent anarchy, . . . we can understand neither its strength nor its weakness, nor can we separate those arrangements which can safely be modified from those which cannot be touched without shaking the whole fabric to pieces. . . ."[87]

The fabric of the modern states system was to wear precariously thin during the six-odd centuries of its existence. When men became alarmed about its marks of wear and tear, they often sought new strength and peace by envisioning greater governmental unions beyond the existing framework of international politics. But on such occasions, too, they fell back on the recorded uses of the Roman law. Federal pacts, as well as plans for perpetual peace, were cast in the moulds that the Roman lawyers prepared when they isolated the notion of subjective agreement in legally objective terms. And as the technical possibilities for international cooperation were steadily improved, articles of international partnership were formulated to unite in the pursuit of common goals nations occupying different continents.

With the establishment of the League of Nations in 1919 and the United Nations in 1945, the theme of international association was carried to the plane of political administration. And, it is significant to note, for both of these world organizations constitutionalism provided the official frame of reference, even though it did not prevail in the

[87] *Village Communities in the East and West*, p. 352.

domestic political systems of all the member nations. Moreover, collective security was acknowledged as the pivotal point in the relations between the states, and all of the governments agreed, in several important instances, to look behind the façade of the sovereign state and locate basic human rights and obligations.

H. The Internationalization of the Law of Contract and the Ius Gentium

It is customary in modern jurisprudence to distinguish public international law, or the law of nations, from private international law, or the conflict of laws, as it is called in American legal terminology. Private international law has been defined as consisting of "rules which the courts of each territorial jurisdiction follow when a dispute containing some foreign element arises between private persons."[88] In accordance with this definition its existence presupposes an international order of multiple sovereignties in which each state claims exclusive legal jurisdiction over all persons, things, and events within its territory. But since individuals have long been in the habit of communicating with each other across the boundaries of states and legal cultures, governments have not been able to disregard foreign rules of law by hiding behind the principle of the state's territorial sovereignty. On the contrary, the policy was recognized that national courts in one jurisdiction must, under certain conditions, take account of foreign law maxims even if the latter happen to be at variance with the native system of law. A special set of legal rules, known as private international law, thus developed in each state as a matter of course, for the purpose of regulating the relationship of national to foreign law. These norms were initially different under the various national jurisdictions, but the governments soon realized that their joint interest in preventing or solving conflicts of law could best be served by promoting uniformity in private international law. In the course of time this awareness led to the conclusion of numerous conventions for the adjustment of conflicting legal references.

As one retraces the evolution of private international law in the different law cultures in the West, one finds, first, that it was determined by doctrines that had found acceptance on the European continent, and second, that these continental doctrines had their inception in Roman jurisprudence. When studying the primary sources of this im-

---

[88] G. C. Cheshire, *Private International Law*, Oxford, 1935, p. 20.

portant body of modern international thought, however, one must remember that the Romans began the systematic treatment of the subject matter now covered by private international law under political circumstances that greatly differed from those attending the subsequent elaboration of international jurisprudence in the nineteenth and twentieth centuries A.D.

In the period of the early Roman Republic, as in the early stages of most political systems, the theory prevailed that law and the state existed for the exclusive benefit of the citizen. It followed that a foreigner could not, for example, be a party to a Roman contract or sue by the traditional Roman modes of litigation. This position changed, however, under the compelling force of several factors.

As one of the most important cities in the Mediterranean world, Rome had come to depend on foreign trade as the chief source of her prosperity and prestige. It was therefore in the best interest of the republic to protect as well as to police the visiting strangers by subordinating them to some regime of law. The question remained, however, as to what kind of law should be applied to the non-Romans. The *ius civile* was inappropriate, because Romans, on the one hand, were too patriotic to extend its use to non-Romans, and on the other, sufficiently observant to realize that its provisions were often meaningless to people attached to other legal traditions. The Romans, consequently, were challenged to find a special set of rules that could be applied whenever foreigners were involved in legal disputes. And thus they developed in the course of time a new branch of law—the *ius gentium*.

Like other ancient peoples, the Romans had an early custom of concluding private arrangements with non-Romans under the terms of which mutual guarantees of *hospitium* (guest friendship) were exchanged. This relationship was depersonalized toward the end of the period of the Republic, when whole cities sought and received the protection of influential Roman citizens. The relationship was permitted to evolve into a public institution when the Roman Republic itself began to act as host to those foreigners whom she invited into her protective orbit. It is significant that this and other devices for the assimilation and control of foreigners (for example, adoption) were borrowed from the domain of family life, where they had been developed originally to extend the traditionally limited radius of human relations. Ultimately proving inadequate to support Rome's expanding interests in trade, however, they were supplemented by official treaty relations, according to the terms of which Rome conferred the rights of trade (*commercium*) or intermarriage (*connubium*) on numerous foreign communities.

Rome's relations with foreign nations and her policies toward foreigners as individuals underwent considerable change when the republic became the dominant empire in the Mediterranean world. In this phase of history Roman law acquired a new function. It became the chief informing principle in the administration of a community of many races. Anyone studying the international commerce that flowed in the path that was opened by this particular development of Roman jurisprudence will observe immediately that it was not used only as a one-way street for the export of Roman concepts. The *praetor peregrinus* (who functioned from 242 B.C. onward) quickly discovered that Rome's newly acquired eastern provinces were ancient political communities with their own well-developed laws, and that the cause of order would not be served by eradicating or disturbing what had so long been settled. An inborn respect for law as such, a practical interest in the preservation of order, a lack of vanity in cultural matters, and a ceaseless quest for effective principles of imperial administration, kept the Romans from imposing their own legal system upon the conquered countries, prompting them, instead, to adjust their *ius civile* to the spiritual and material needs of each particular province. For example, in Egypt only those few Roman citizens who had come over from Italy were governed by the civil law. The national Egyptian system was permitted to remain in force between Egyptians, while Greek law continued to apply to the Greek residents of Egypt.[89]

Many legal problems, in particular those arising in connection with status, marriage, and succession, could be solved in this fashion by a simple reference to foreign law (an approach that is comparable to the process implicit in modern private international law). But there remained the vast field of commercial relations which was not susceptible to any such legal regulation, since it encompassed the far-flung and interlocking interests of Romans, provincials and foreigners alike. International agreements of sale, partnerships, or charter parties required internationally acceptable legal forms. It was this need in particular which prompted the Romans to identify and formulate the universal

[89] Erwin Seidl, "Law," in *The Legacy of Egypt*, S. R. K. Glanville, ed., Oxford, 1953, pp. 212-216.

elements shared by the positive laws of all nations[90]—a process that yielded, ultimately, the concept of the *ius gentium*.

The original connotation of the term *ius gentium* is hard to recover. According to one authority, "the law of the world" was probably, in its origin, a phrase from popular speech which the ordinary man of that age might coin to designate a felt antithesis to national law.[91] But most of the elements of this *ius gentium* were derived from Roman civil law; and Rome's early magistrates, therefore, felt justified in treating it "as an ignoble appendage of the *ius civile*,"[92] a mere concession to foreigners that had been forced upon them by political necessity. It required the great intellectual revolution set off by Rome's contact with the Stoic doctrine of natural law to reveal the *ius gentium* in a new light. Henceforth the belief began to prevail among the lawyers that the old *ius gentium* was actually the lost code of nature,[93] and that it should therefore be considered a great, though as yet imperfectly developed, model to which all law, as far as possible, ought to conform. In fact, in framing their edictal jurisprudence on the principles of the *ius gentium*, the praetors were now supposed to supersede the civil law as much as possible.[94] When the holders of this office became imbued with Stoic doctrines they grew more and more inclined to identify their equity with the dictates of the *ius naturale*, and therefore to submit the *ius civile* to the levelling influences of the *ius gentium*. The close and exceedingly complex relationship between the *ius civile*, the *ius gentium*, and the *ius naturale* that was thus promoted over the centuries, became the pivot on which the Roman process turned to accommodate different civilizations.

Despite its close and constant association with the philosophy of natural law and the customs of non-Roman nations, the *ius gentium* remained in its practical significance the product of native Roman jurisprudence, which in this particular aspect had been stimulated by the circumstances of the newly acquired empire.[95] The *ius gentium*, in

---

[90] de Zulueta, in Bailey, ed., p. 201, defines this law as: "The law common to those nations which the Romans had the means of observing, and who sent successive swarms of immigrants to Rome, i.e., the Italian tribes." See Maine, *Ancient Law*, p. 474.

[91] *The Cambridge Ancient History*, Vol. IX, p. 866.

[92] Maine, *Ancient Law*, p. 50.

[93] By the second century A.D. the terms *ius gentium* and *ius naturale* were used almost interchangeably.

[94] Maine, *Ancient Law*, pp. 50-55; *On the Commonwealth: Marcus Tullius Cicero*, George H. Sabine, Stanley B. Smith, trs. and eds., Columbus, O., 1929, pp. 35ff.

[95] *The Cambridge Ancient History*, Vol. IX, p. 868.

this practical sense, included "those rules, institutions and principles of actual Roman law which, owing to their simplicity and correspondence with the general practice of mankind, were applied to *cives* and *peregrini* indifferently."[96] In other words, the *ius gentium* covered the law of contractual relations. It included very little of family law and of the law of succession and nothing of the law of civil wrongs because these categories dealt with complex questions to which each constituent community of the Mediterranean world had found its own answer outside the context of international relations. The very opposite was true of the law of contract. For the conduct of Mediterranean commerce proceeded from a mutuality of interests and required agreement on legal forms, and it was axiomatic then as it has been ever since that agreements are easiest to come by when the underlying issues are isolated in their simplest, most widely meaningful form. Now the Roman contract law had a great international appeal throughout the Mediterranean world because the Roman lawyers had succeeded in abstracting its essence from local traditions and in adjusting its requirements to the customs generally observed in the commercial intercourse of neighboring peoples. And its applicability was further extended when the praetors internationalized the simple *bona fidei* contracts by elaborating the rules of good faith and restricting the formalism of the old civil law.[97] The *ius gentium* which was completely developed by the Augustan[98] period can for these reasons be described best as the modernized Roman law relating to contract and to the informal methods of acquiring property;[99] in other words, it was essentially commercial law.

As one reads the history of Roman contract law in the light of subsequent developments in the field of international law and organization, one is consequently inclined to agree that "contract" is indeed the root concept from which the chief political institutions of the modern states system evolved. It provides the clue for an understanding of the

---

[96] de Zulueta, in Bailey, ed., p. 202. When Gaius (a Roman legalist, A.D. 160) states that he is speaking of that kind of partnership (*societas*) which is *iuris gentium*, he implies a point of practical law, namely, that a Roman court will enforce such a partnership regardless of whether the parties are *cives* or *peregrini*.

[97] Cf. *The Cambridge Ancient History*, Vol. IX, pp. 867-868. On the modernization of the *stipulation* which became a contract *iuris gentium* because of its simple and rational form, see *ibid.* p. 871, and p. 861. The *stipulation* of classical law was a unique combination of the new and the old, being a formal *stricti iuris* contract, but except in one form (*sponsio*) *iuris gentium*: in other words, it had become applicable to *peregrini*, but its character had been fixed in the early period.

[98] *ibid.*, Vol. XI, p. 809.

[99] *ibid.*, Vol. IX, p. 867.

state, legislation, the community of nations, and much of international law.[100]

Before concluding this discussion of the international significance of Roman law, it must be emphasized that law in the Roman Empire had provided more than the technical tools for the political coordination of national and international differences. By supplying the main symbols and concepts around which men of various origins could rally, it became the chief carrier of the idea of universality, which, coming into contact with the idea of nationality, dissolved it.[101] This complicated process of unifying a world that arms and diplomacy had called into being could not have taken place without the services of Rome's legal elite. Throughout a period of more than several hundred years, the Roman lawyers made it their business to propagate the twin ideas of agreement and obligation, to adjust differing value systems, to isolate core concepts that would have universal appeal, and to make possible, by internationalizing the law of contract, those associations which would span space and time.

In a world of constantly shifting human fortunes these jurists thus supplied the kind of security that comes with clearly defined and generally applicable ideas. One can argue, of course, that human relations within the Empire *had* to be cast into secure moulds in order to compensate men for some of the ruder aspects of imperial government; and it is certainly true that imperial aggrandizement was frequently screened by the façade of Roman law. Nevertheless, the recorded relationship between Roman politics and Roman law shows convincingly that calculations of power and expediency were constantly subjected to the restraining influence of legal principle. Furthermore, if it is remembered that the Roman Empire was unified through the perfection of a system of secular norms,[102] that it included more widely divergent areas[103] and lasted longer than any other international society, and that its influence has not yet spent itself in the affairs of our contemporary world, one is entitled to regard the story of the Roman Empire as one of the most remarkable chapters in the annals of international relations. It is this record which prompted the German jurist Ihering

---

[100] Ihering, Part I, p. 224 "das ganze Voelkerrecht loest sich in Vertraege auf . . ." (the entire law of nations may be read in terms of contracts).

[101] Cf. *ibid.*, p. 314.

[102] Compare with the unifying effect of great religions.

[103] The achievement of the British Commonwealth and Empire may be comparable, but Rome had to cope with more nations culturally her equal or superior than Britain.

to begin his dissertation on the spirit of the Roman law with the following observations:

"Three times the world received its laws from Rome; three times did Rome unite the nations; the first time when the Roman people enjoyed the fullness of their strength, it shaped the oneness of the state; the second time after Rome's political fortunes had declined, it called into being the oneness of the church; the third time as Roman law was copied and received by medieval Europe, it created the oneness of the law. Unity came the first time through the power of the sword; it came the second and the third times through the power of the mind."[104]

[104] Ihering, Part I, p. 1: "Drei mal had Rom der Welt Gesetze diktiert, drei Mal die Voelker zur Einheit verbunden, das erste Mal, als das roemische Volk noch in der Fuelle seiner Kraft stand, zur Einheit des Staats, das zweite Mal, nachdem dasselbe bereits untergegangen, zur Einheit der Kirche, das dritte Mal in Folge der Reception des roemischen Rechts im Mittelalter zur Einheit des Rechts; das erste Mal mit aeusserm Zwange durch die Macht der Waffe, die beiden andern Male durch die Macht des Geistes. . . ."

PART III

CHRISTIANITY AND ISLAM

CHAPTER 6

NEW PERSPECTIVES

A. The Meaning of Time and Epochs in International History

THE GREAT HISTORIANS of the literate cultures in the ancient world have left a rich legacy of writings that illumine the times in which they lived. They wrote about the deeds of men they knew and the fortunes of nations as they observed them. They narrated the incidents of war and peace, of exploration, travel, and adventure. Indeed, the history they wrote encompassed all of life around them. And since many ancient historians were unusually gifted and sensitive thinkers to whom historiography was, above all, an extension of literature or philosophy, they were able to render accounts that have continued to retain a timeless value in the international annals of literacy and thought. However, if we read these ancient records as twentieth century students of history, we must conclude that they were strictly limited chronicles, since they registered only special events that had occurred at particular times and places. For no ancient historian—whether in the East or in the West—ever pretended that he knew all there was to know about the affairs of man on earth, or that he could gain mastery over the processes of time.

As knowledge accumulated and literacy spread, people realized, of course, that their past had greater depths and their present further extensions than had been assumed before. But such new insights by themselves did not necessarily affect man's fundamental attitude toward the great historical processes in which his personal life was so obviously caught. Nor did the realization that more had happened in more places than his ancestors had known provide an irresistible challenge to compile fuller accounts of history. Before he could undertake the business of writing history systematically, man had to be convinced that the events and dates of his life on earth were sufficiently important to merit such retention. This kind of assurance is forthcoming only when it can be clearly deduced from a general philosophical orientation.

According to the Hindus and the Buddhists, many worlds have come and gone, and many others are to follow in a timeless cycle of creation and destruction. Life on this earth is merely incidental to the cosmic order. It has moved through many ages and its end is not in sight.

Within its everlasting context, the individual soul must seek perfection, it is true, but mankind as such can never hope to be delivered to a final and unearthly state of bliss. In this perspective of the universe and time, human activities have no historical significance. If they cannot be seen as constituting one generally valid and coherent sequence of events, there is no reason to trace the main lines of the travelled route, or to remember when this or that specific fact occurred.[1]

Western theologies developed a very different approach to time. The Jews, the Christians, and the Muslims share the general belief that mankind's life on earth is one great drama, which began when God created the entire world from nothing, and will end at an appointed moment, with the destruction of the present universe, the resurrection of the dead, and the coming of a state of everlasting beatitude. In other words, all of man's activities on earth, taken singly and collectively, form one unique undertaking through which God's will is to be realized progressively. This religious conception of a dramatic historical process was the foundation on which later Western philosophers constructed their theories of history. This foundation was reinforced when nineteenth century science contributed the general thought that nature should be understood in terms of a gradual evolution on an ascending scale.[2] Under the influence of religion, science, and philosophy the Western mind was thus conditioned and instructed to regard each and every event as a unique occurrence on the path of time from creation to perfection. Indeed, "time" now weighted with many special facts, and dates, and meanings, became a rather heavy concept in the thoughts of Western men. The need was great, therefore, from the eighteenth century A.D. onward, to sift the facts, arrange the dates, and clarify the meanings, so that "history" might be made intelligible to the growing class of literate people in the civilizations of the West who were searching for certainty and knowledge.

This newly felt need for a clear and precise rendition of the historical process was not experienced with equal poignancy by the Jews, the Christians, and the Muslims—the three peoples of The Book, who had so closely shared their early readings of the cosmic process. The flowering of letters that had lent such great distinction to the early Muslim

[1] Cf. Helmuth von Glasenapp, "The Concept of Gradual Progress in Indian and Western Philosophy," in UNESCO, *Humanism and Education in East and West*, Paris, 1953, pp. 90ff.

[2] On the other hand it must be noted that many other traditional religious tenets were contradicted sharply by nineteenth century thought, as for instance by social Darwinism.

Cf. Glasenapp, pp. 96-101.

commonwealth spent itself without conducing to a spread of literacy among the nations acknowledging the Koran. Hence, when new developments in the Western world supplied the first great impetus to the organization of the records of the past, there was no public interest in dates and documents in Islam. Whereas the *concept* of world history was of interest to the Near Eastern and European nations alike, the actual systematic *writing* of world history took place only in Europe and America. The countless historical texts that were compiled and composed on the Occidental continents in the nineteenth and twentieth centuries represented, therefore, in their very nature, limited and biased accounts of man's activities on earth.

This bias showed itself chiefly in the preferential treatment of the space inhabited by the European peoples and of the times that have been of special significance to the evolution of what has come to be known as Western civilization. Moreover, since it is immensely difficult, even in this limited context, to come to terms with the general element of time and to convey that special perspective of an ascending human destiny which had been revealed by religion and confirmed by nineteenth century science, historians developed the convenient stratagem of dividing the entire past into separate but connected periods. In looking backward from the vantage point of the Europe of the nineteenth century, it became customary to distinguish between ancient, medieval, and modern history. All records that had preceded the establishment of the early Christian state and pertained to those affairs of pagan societies that could be brought into some meaningful relationship to the subsequent history of the West—in particular Babylon, Egypt, Persia, Greece, and Rome—were classified as "ancient history," a category sufficiently broad to accommodate multifarious additional data as they became available. But since no research could specify the date when history began, beyond referring vaguely to a prehistoric period when man first became conscious of his social and spiritual situation, ancient history gradually became a boundless field, incorporating chronologies from far and near.

Now history's beginning can perhaps recede to unknown depths without upsetting the modern historian's pattern of divided time, but each historic period must have a definite end before the next can be said to have begun. Where then was the end of ancient history? Where mark the start of the Middle Ages? It did not really help to say that Christ was born A.D. 1, or that a pagan Roman emperor was converted to Christianity in A.D. 312. The question was: when did times so change as to justify a differentiating nomenclature? What was the last moment in the history of the last pre-Christian society that seemed to hold the "ancient" spirit? In short, when did Rome fall and Europe's Christian culture assume a separate identity? For it was this second sector of the historical process—the Middle Ages—that carried the greatest meaning for nineteenth century historians. Here they hoped to discover the foundations upon which *modern* European history could rest securely, even though Europe's world-environment was revealing itself to be in constant flux. Here, too, they would look for the origin of the great forces and institutions that were determining the course of Europe toward world ascendancy and the course of the progress of mankind. For these and other reasons the Middle Ages assumed a cardinal importance in the European historians' view of world affairs. And yet, encompassed by two other periods, it could be neither fixed, nor opened into unpartitioned time. For where, precisely, was the threshold beyond which lay the new, the present modern era?

It was clear to the historians that two causes of modernity had greatly altered Europe's destiny and were to revolutionize the lives and future prospects of populations everywhere: the spread of literacy and the growth of science. Hence it was apparent that modern history must have begun at that moment when many Europeans turned to learning to find the chief incentives for their lives on earth. It is difficult to date the evolution of an orientation; nevertheless, the historians found that a number of critical trends tended to converge upon the fifteenth century as the great divide. And so it was that, finally, the fifteenth century came to be regarded as the close of the Middle Ages.

It was more difficult, however, to establish the earlier line that was to mark the commencement of the Middle Ages. A medieval Europe seemed to be identifiable around the year one thousand, and appeared to retain a form that could be called its own until about A.D. 1400 or 1500. But what about the irksome half millennium that had followed the "collapse" of Rome? Not only were the records scant, but everything one knew about this time indicated clearly that the collective achievements of the early Christian world did not compare too favorably with the records left by the defunct and ancient pagan civilization. In short, one could not prove through this period that history was progress. For a long time, therefore, those little known and troubled centuries were dismissed summarily as "the Dark Ages,"[3] while to

[3] The term is not as common today as it was in the nineteenth century.

medieval history proper were assigned the four or five more illuminated centuries that filled the period from A.D. 1000 to 1400 or 1500.

As the European scholars continued to clarify the antecedents of their own civilization and of those civilizations related to it, they began to correct the old approach to Europe's past and mankind's history. In fact, the whole European scheme of time, which had issued from the religious revelation that to man a fixed span of moments was allotted for his transit on this planet, seemed strangely out of focus in the context even of Europe's own development. Moreover, the arbitrary lines that had supplied a ceiling and a base to man's collective destiny were growing steadily fainter. Europeans today take it for granted, generally, that the modern period may be thought of as extending indefinitely into future time, and that the ancient period drops into an apparently bottomless past. And yet there still remains that vexing problem of the middle period, an unchanging pivot in our changing view of mankind's place on earth, which asks to be assimilated conceptually in its three-fold significance as a continuance of ancient history, a distinct European epoch, and a prelude to the European present.

If medieval European history presents a range of problems to the modern European and American student, it obviously implies even greater difficulties for those non-Europeans who have acceded to the Western view of history under the compelling force of European education and scholarship; or who are interested, for other reasons, in finding an entrance to this historical enclosure. For it must be recognized at the outset that none of our time sequences can have a direct bearing on the historical experience of, say, the Chinese or Sudanese. Non-Europeans may find a way of relating themselves, however tenuously, to the European concept of ancient history, and may discover a stake, or even membership, in Europe's organization of modern history; but where do they fit in when it comes to Europe's medieval age? It is in the greater perspective of an internationally meaningful treatment of the historical process that the centuries from 500 to 1500 present their greatest challenge.

Indeed, in the context of an international history of relations between nations, the existing boundaries through time will retain validity only if we can determine rather precisely those occurrences in medieval history that have a universal meaning. And these are found to open a retrospective view from which it may be inferred that the millennium here at issue constitutes the first great chapter of a narrative analysis of modern international relations. For not only did the outlines of the modern world become apparent as that period closed with great discoveries, but at the same time the several modern nations and their separate culture realms began to emerge. Not only do the records show, furthermore, that national destinies converged in this period more frequently and intensely than before, but they reveal also certain basic principles and patterns that have been associated ever since with conflict and cooperation in world affairs.

It can also be maintained that most of the contemporary forms of international contact received their modern shape through the usages of those Mediterranean and Western European regions that supplied the geographic stage for Europe's medieval epoch. For it was there that the modern state evolved with its attendant institutions, which soon were to be zealously emulated everywhere. Furthermore, it was in this area that that complex fabric of traditions and beliefs developed, which, while retaining its identity as Western Europe's culture, has in modern times supplied the mainsprings of human movements on all continents.

These, in brief, are the grounds that make it just to say that present international relations have their anchorage in the European region and in the millennium from A.D. 500 to 1500.

B. *The Great Powers in the Sixth and Seventh Centuries* A.D.

The known world was not united in the first half of the first millennium A.D. Its inhabitants were distributed in separate political societies and culture realms and had few means of communicating with each other across the boundaries that enclosed their particular communities. However, two of these states, Rome and China, were small worlds in themselves, covering vast expanses of land and including numerous races and civilizations. Each had been successful in building and maintaining its own cosmopolitan empire. Each had developed its own techniques of adjusting cultural and political differences by locating rallying points of regional unity. And each had created its own great power orbit, within which neighboring satellites were left to exist in nominal autonomy though subject to the controlling force of imperial diplomacy.

However, in both the Roman and the Chinese international systems divisive forces operated and there were periods in the histories of both commonwealths when the cause of unity seemed to be all but lost. Realizing in the fourth century that the Empire's center of gravity had shifted eastward and that the administrative unity of the vast and complex Mediterranean world could no longer be maintained, Rome's imperial governors decided to shift the imperial residence to Byzantium (Constantinople) and divide the state in two by drawing a line of demarcation through Illyria. Although these arrangements were not supposed to infringe upon the theory of a unified cosmopolitan state, they had, nevertheless, the practical effect of sanctioning an evolution toward dualism that had been in the making for a long time. All efforts to reverse this trend thereafter proved ineffective. The Latin West and the Hellenistic East continued to drift apart after the sixth century, until eventually they came to constitute two distinct sovereignties and culture realms. Moreover, since each was a composite of many nations, each had to find its own pattern of international organization; and since each was also a great power, each had to fashion its own system of conducting foreign relations on a constantly widening stage of world politics.

During these same centuries China, too, was torn by inner conflict. Rival houses fought bitter wars for total supremacy over the empire, lesser dynasties were locked in incessant rivalries, and subordinate kings rebelled against all higher authorities. But discord and disorder subsided with the advent of the T'ang Dynasty in A.D. 618, when a unified China could begin another "Golden Age." In the ensuing process of cultivating foreign affairs, China's influence was extended toward the Caspian Sea, and her knowledge of other nations was enriched immeasurably. Indeed, it is largely through the extant chronicles of Chinese travellers that the modern world knows anything at all about seventh century developments in that other Oriental culture realm—India.

The political character of India had undergone several changes since the fourth century A.D. The domain of the Kushana Empire had broken up when Chandragupta (to be distinguished from Chandragupta Maurya) inaugurated the Gupta Kingdom in Magadha about A.D. 320. About A.D. 480, the "White Huns" (a nomadic Asian race described as having been more akin to the Turks than to the Mongols proper) overran the Gupta Kingdom and established themselves over all of northern India during the early sixth century. But about the middle of that century their power was broken, and in the first half of the seventh a new monarchy arose in the area (excluding, however the Punjab) which established a great reputation through the piety of its Buddhist ruler Harsha[4] and the humaneness of its administration.

Politics in the Near Eastern region were dominated by a rejuvenated Parthia. This nation became known as Persia under the Sassanid Dynasty, and it reached the zenith of its power under Chosroes I who ascended the throne in A.D. 531. Under the rule of this house the state continued to capitalize on its geographic position as a link between the Oriental and the Mediterranean worlds. And since neighboring Byzantium had superseded distant Rome as the Empire's trade-minded, luxury-loving capital, Persian middlemen found themselves in a vastly improved position, profiting from the far-flung commercial transactions instigated by the Byzantine merchants. The Roman imports from China had to be shipped by caravan through Sogdiana to the Persian border, where Persian merchants possessed the exclusive right of shipping the wares to the customhouse on the Byzantine border. Or else, coming from China by sea, the imports had to be reloaded in Ceylon into Persian vessels, which carried them across the Indian Ocean and Persian Gulf, and then along the Tigris and Euphrates rivers to their ultimate destination, a Roman customhouse.[5] For the Romans, this dependence on the Persians was very irksome, especially since it affected their imports of silk, and they did their utmost during Justinian's reign to neutralize the Persian power by bolstering the competitive strength of seafaring Abyssinian merchants. Their efforts were of no avail, however. Persia's control of the silk trade was broken only when Justinian's emissaries succeeded in smuggling some silkworm eggs out of China, after which the cultivation of home-grown silk spread rapidly over all of southern Europe. This was an epoch-making coup in the history of international economics. It did not alter the fact, however, that in matters of high policy Persia was the axis around which not only the relations between the great empires of the West and East revolved, but also those between the Latin and the Greek halves of the Roman commonwealth.

Whenever Rome and Persia fought each other, Rome's communications with the Far East were severed. When Justinian in A.D. 535 en-

[4] A born Brahmin, Harsha was converted to Buddhism and is said to have emulated Ashoka's policies.

[5] An Egyptian trader and Nestorian by faith has left a fascinating account of these involved operations, "The Christian Topography," in which he describes Ceylon, then known as Taprobane, as the center of world commerce in the sixth century, servicing China on the one hand, and eastern Africa, Persia, and the Byzantine Empire on the other hand. See J. B. Bury, *History of the Later Roman Empire* (A.D. 395-565) 2 vols., London, 1931, Vol. II, pp. 316-333. See also A. A. Vasiliev, *History of the Byzantine Empire, 324-1453*, Madison, 1952, pp. 164ff.

gaged in his ambitious enterprise to regain mastery over Western Rome, Persia was able to harass his Byzantine domain. And when peace was concluded in A.D. 562, Byzantium had to pay for the return of a Black Sea port by promising Persia substantial annuities.[6] Even under the shadow of their constant belligerency, however, cultural exchanges continued without too much inhibition and led to important cross references in matters of scholarship and religion. For instance, when the college of Edessa was closed in the fifth century by the Byzantine government on account of its heretical teachings, it could reestablish itself across the frontier at Nisibis; and when Justinian chose to silence the great school of Athens, which had up to then been the chief intellectual center for pagan scholars, several homeless Neo-Platonists found a ready refuge in the Persian academies of learning.[7] But in the seventh century, these and similar contacts ceased when the Persians launched a campaign of unmitigated aggression against the Byzantine Empire. They occupied Antioch and Damascus, conquered Syria, and invaded Palestine. Their siege of Jerusalem, which began in 614, culminated in a ferocious massacre of the Christians in which the Jews participated as allies of the Persians.[8]

Eastern Rome was saved in this extremity by one of her most renowned emperors, Heraclius, whom later historians have regarded as the creator of medieval Byzantium because his concept of the state was Roman, his language and culture Greek, and his faith Christian.[9] As a result of brilliantly executed military campaigns, which anticipated the crusades in many respects, the Persians were completely routed in A.D. 627. With the elimination of her one great rival from the political scene, the restoration of Syria, Palestine, and Egypt, and the defeat of lesser enemies in the north and west, Byzantium emerged as the uncontested major power in the Mediterranean world. It is significant that this supremacy was recognized by the sovereign of India, when he sent his congratulations to Heraclius, as well as by King Dagobert of the Franks, who dispatched special ambassadors for the purpose of concluding a perpetual peace.[10] But at precisely this moment in history, when peace seemed to have descended once more upon the Near

---

[6] See Bury, Vol. II, pp. 75-124.

[7] Vasiliev, p. 138. It appears that these expatriates were overcome with homesickness; a treaty between Persia and Byzantium (A.D. 562) provided, therefore, at the insistence of Chosroes, that the scholars could resume their residence in Byzantium without incurring any recriminatory treatment.

[8] *ibid.*, p. 195.

[9] Georg Ostrogorsky, *Geschichte des byzantinischen Staates*, München, 1940, p. 96.

[10] Vasiliev, p. 199.

East, the entire Mediterranean order was shaken to its foundations by the appearance of the Arabs and the announcement of Islam. What had appeared to be settled was put in issue under the relentless impact of Arab conquest and Muslim propaganda. Boundaries were effaced and states overthrown; truths were questioned, loyalties reviewed, and institutions undermined. It became suddenly obvious that an old order had already passed away and that international affairs would henceforth move in new directions.

These new directions had been indicated by earlier developments. The frontiers of Western Rome had been fluctuating for centuries under the pressure of the Germanic tribes, and Byzantine diplomacy had been severely taxed ever since its inception by the aggressive presence of the ever mobile Slavs and Mongols. In the wake of the great migrations that had been initiated by the wanderings of Central Asian tribes, the Goths had settled in Italy and Spain and the Vandals in North Africa. The stage of Mediterranean politics had widened to include many new nations, that is to say, even before the Arabs made their dramatic entrance. Furthermore, intransigent revealed religions had been known to the ancient world long before it met the challenge of Islam, for tightly knit communities of Jews and Christians had for centuries been competing everywhere with the established creeds, and the Roman Empire itself had been transformed into an aggressive theocracy.

A just appreciation of the Arab factor in seventh century affairs must begin with the admission that even before the prophet Muhammad called upon his followers to form one ecclesiastical commonwealth, tribal nationalism, religious dogma, and theocratic government were not only known to the world but were largely accepted phenomena. Nevertheless, their restatement by the Arabs revolutionized the course of world development; for they were presented not only simultaneously but suddenly, and with extreme belligerence, as a challenge to all existing sovereignties at a time when military and moral resistance were very low. The Arabs, it must be remembered, left their primitive abodes not only because they wanted more attractive land, but also because they were imbued with a strong sense of religious mission. And being fully conscious of the superiority of their faith, they were not easily impressed by any aspect of an alien civilization. They were different in this respect from the German tribes, for example, who, although capable of reaching their military objective—the conquest of Rome—had not been sustained in their drive by any kind of religious fervor. The evidence shows, in fact, that the Germanic peoples had already outgrown their ancient pagan creeds and that an acute awareness of their cultural inferiority had quite prepared them not only to become the captives of Rome's superior civilization, but even to support the political identity of the Roman state and to accept the new monotheistic faith that had entered Rome from the East. In other words, the virile new Germanic nationalities and the dogmatic new Christian religion had come to Rome from different quarters and at different times, and this had permitted the Empire to adjust to each new element separately and gradually, within the established context of its own imperial government.

No such "domestic" adjustment was possible, however, in the Arab case. The new thrust from the eastern desert was an uncompromising move that could not be absorbed or diverted—either by Rome or Persia. For it was made at a time when the Roman Empire was divided along both secular and religious lines, when Persia was prostrate after having lost a war, and when the strength of victorious Byzantium was seriously depleted. These mid-seventh century circumstances demanded the recognition that the old Mediterranean order—long closely associated with the traditions of one great cosmopolitan empire—had passed away, and that the next great era in world affairs would be decisively influenced by the policies of three separate Mediterranean powers: Western Rome, Eastern Rome, and the Commonwealth of the Arabs.

CHAPTER 7

THE CHIEF ELEMENTS IN MEDITERRANEAN POWER POLITICS

A. Expanding and Disintegrating Empires

WESTERN AND EASTERN ROME were the principal Occidental focal points of political attraction and international organization when the new tribal peoples from the north began to press their northern frontiers. Between the fourth and the tenth centuries A.D. a number of the Germanic nations beyond the Alps were romanized, converted to Christianity, and accepted as political partners in the Latin Roman Empire. The new Roman-German state then continued its expansion northward and eastward, in the lands inhabited by the Anglo-Saxons, Celts, Scandinavians, Balts, Poles, Czechs, and Hungarians. The interests of Eastern Rome also shifted northward during this period. For not only had the Arabs moved into its southern and eastern domain, forcing it to withdraw, but the Bulgars, Slavs, Mongols, and Turks had entered the Byzantine orbit from the north, and were submitting to the superior culture. Thus, by the appearance of these various northern folk, the circle of international politics was immeasurably extended. Although the established world states were forced to recognize the movements and the interests of the barbarians by shifting the centers of gravity of their respective empires, they were, generally speaking, quite successful in integrating the newcomers into either their administrative or their diplomatic systems. Neither of these possibilities had been open, however, when the Roman world had been challenged, in the fifth century, by the Huns.

This group of Altaic pastoral tribes from Central Asia[1] surged westward at the close of the fourth century and overran most of central-eastern Europe. At that time they seem to have been interested chiefly in the subjugation of Scythia, Media, and Persia; and it was this orientation which prompted them to seek the neutralisation of Rome's power in the west. Their efforts culminated in the conclusion of a treaty between their leader, Attila (died 453), and Theodosius II (401-540),

---

[1] There is no certain ethnic or linguistic identification of the Huns. They were probably of Turanian-Turkish stock, but their physical characteristics were variable and no doubt included strains from all of Asia.

the emperor of Eastern Rome, which provided for the payment of annual subsidies as Rome's price of peace, the surrender of fugitives, the institution of free markets, and the settlement of some outstanding jurisdictional disputes regarding certain Danubian tribes.[2]

In the context of fifth century power politics this diplomatic episode, for a number of reasons, is revealing. It shows that the uncivilized Huns were not only redoubtable warriors but also, when occasion demanded, skilled diplomats; that the subject matters of Attila's diplomatic effort in no way differed from those of the diplomatic dealings between the more sophisticated representatives of the long-established civilized states; and, lastly, that Rome was vulnerable not only to the military attacks of the barbarians but also to their political maneuvers. It must be noted, however, that the power of the Huns to achieve and maintain their chosen objectives depended, ultimately, upon the wills and whims of their leaders. Any advantages gained in their campaigns were disregarded and all diplomatic skills discarded when Attila surrendered to his ambition to become the universal emperor of the world around him. He broke, then, the Western peace, and launched his armies across the greater part of Eastern Europe, the Balkan peninsula, Gaul, and into Italy as far as to Rome—announcing to the Goths that he had come to deliver them from the Romans and to the Romans that he was their savior from the Goths. But Attila's ultimate goal eluded him. Not only did the Romans and Goths combine in their resistance, but the organization of Attila's own empire proved to be too flimsy to withstand the strain of a sustained expansion. The Huns withdrew from Rome,[3] Attila died the following winter in Gaul, and with him vanished the phantom of another empire.

When the Arabs started on their road to conquest in the seventh century, on the other hand, the two Christian orbits in the Occident, as well as the Chinese and Indian power centers in the Orient, were decisively reduced. Within one hundred years after Muhammad's flight from Mecca, his successors severed Syria, Egypt, and North Africa from Byzantium, acquired the largest part of Spain from Western Rome, and conquered Persia. Later campaigns extended their supremacy to vast parts of inner Africa between the Nile and the Atlantic; and to Central Asia, where they incorporated eastern Persia,

---

[2] See the article on "Huns" in the *Encyclopaedia Britannica*.

[3] The reasons for Attila's withdrawal from his enterprise are somewhat obscure. Tradition has it that he was overawed by Pope Leo, but the view is current also that his camp was ravaged by the plague.

Afghanistan, and the Indian province of Sind before they pressed toward Turkestan and the frontiers of China, and India, where the Sultanate of Delhi was formed in 1206, and where the empire of the Great Moghuls was later (sixteenth century) to attest their continued strength. Since all of their conquests, whether in Europe, Asia, or Africa, were transmuted into effective governments, there emerged in this era another commonwealth of nations, which, in later centuries, none of the existing empires of the world could disregard.

All of the new frontiers that had been established in Europe and Asia by the various expansive, and often competitive and convergent movements of the pagan, Christian, and Muslim peoples, were challenged, in the thirteenth century, by still another great power—a Mongolian force that had arisen in the steppes and deserts of Central Asia. Composed of numerous nomadic tribes[4] and held together by the personalities of individual leaders, this huge yet mobile force became a threat to all established empires in both the Orient and the Occident, for it struck out in all directions with irresistible vigor and astonishing speed. Indeed, there was hardly an area or a nation in Asia and Eastern Europe that was not shaken to its foundation by the thrust of this new military power. Led by Jenghiz Khan (1162-1227), the Mongolian armies defeated the Kin Tartars, who were in control of north China,[5] the Persians, the Georgians, the Kipchak Turks, and a confederacy of Russian princes (1222). In later campaigns they subjugated most of north China and Russia, conquered the Bulgarians, invaded Poland and Hungary, then crushed a German army at Liegnitz and reached the Adriatic Sea. However, no sustained attempt was made by them to hold their conquests west of Russia, perhaps because the Mongols were aware of their inability to administer non-Asian regions.[6] Their mighty conquerors concentrated on Asia. The Mongolian steppe remained the nucleus of their Empire and China, at all times, the object of their chief ambition. And here their successes exceeded all historical precedents. For eventually both China and Russia were absorbed. This amazing consummation of national expansionist

---

[4] The Altaic nomads of Mongoloid stock are known variously as Mongols, Turco-Tatars, and Tungus, according to their linguistic classifications, but in their historical and cultural manifestations they appear as Mongols, Huns, Turks, Manchus, etc. The line of Jenghiz Khan, apparently, was Mongol in both senses.

[5] By 1223, the Kin Empire had virtually ceased to exist, and Jenghiz's frontiers thus became coterminous with those of the Sung Emperors who ruled the whole of central and southern China.

[6] Cf. Geoffrey Francis Hudson, *China and Europe; A Survey of their Relationship from the Earliest Times to 1800*, London, 1931, p. 140.

policies meant that the immense Asian land mass between the Black Sea and the Pacific Ocean could be united under a single sovereign power.[7]

The Mongols could not maintain the identity of the commonwealth that they had created; the interests of their ruling family demanded the partition of the Empire. There remained, as the chief Mongol power, the so-called Great Khanate, which included Mongolia and China, and during the enlightened reign of its Buddhist emperor Kublai Khan (1260-1294) was to attain great fame and influence throughout the world. Four sub-Khanates were regarded, originally, as dependent administrations; but under the leadership of ambitious rulers these developed soon into independent states, which took an active part in Central Asian and Near Eastern affairs.[8] And since each of these Mongolian successor-states was eager, above all, to maintain, or if possible to expand, its own power within the greater Mongolian realm, the Empire was soon disrupted by internecine rivalries—the separate dynasties even seeking alignment and support from the various Christian and Islamic states around them.

The relations between this expansive Mongolian power, on the one hand, and China, India, and the Christian and Islamic states, on the other, must have been extremely taxing for all of the peoples concerned. Conditions of belligerence and amity alternated brusquely at all times, but when Tamerlane, or Timur (born 1336), came to power in inner Asia, all existing interests—whether religious, political, or cultural—were thrown into complete confusion. Tamerlane was a patriotic native of Transoxiana,[9] a fervent Muslim, a distinguished scholar,[10] a military genius in the tradition of his Mongolian predecessors, and an egomaniac interested chiefly in the subjugation of the world. All of the interests and traditions so strangely merged in his personality seem to have supplied motivations for those boundless in-

---

[7] See Edward Gibbon, *The Decline and Fall of the Roman Empire*, two vols., New York, 1934, Modern Library, Vol. II, pp. 1201ff. for a description of the empire. See Hudson, p. 157, for a map of the empire and of the trade routes between Europe and China.

[8] These divisions covered the following territory: 1) Central Asia, including Dzungaria, Kashgaria, and Bokhara; 2) the area north of the Aral Sea, where the White Horde (or Eastern Kipchaks) was in command; 3) Russia and the Volga lands, where the Golden Horde (or Western Kipchaks) reigned; 4) Persia and Mesopotamia, where another Jenghizid line assumed the title of Ilkhans in 1260, after having sacked Baghdad in 1258.

[9] Either of Mongolian or of Turkish extraction. Cf. Gibbon, Vol. II, p. 1234, to the effect that he was of Turkish descent.

[10] In contrast to Jenghiz Khan who could neither read nor write. See *ibid.*, p. 1204.

roads of expansion and destruction throughout Asia which broke the fabric of many ancient governments and left innumerable nations shipwrecked. In the course of about fifty campaign-filled years, Tamerlane subdued the Mongols of the Caspian area, conquered Turkestan (eastern Tartary), Kipchak (western Tartary), Syria, Anatolia, Armenia, Georgia, and vast parts of Russia and India. He died suddenly in 1405 while he was charting the conquest of China, and his great empire fell to pieces, leaderless.

This fierce interlude of battles and migrations prepared the stage for the last chapter that was to be transacted in Byzantium's eight hundred year long history as a Christian commonwealth. For the advancing Mongols had driven the Ottoman Turks from their original home in Northern Asia, first to Bithynia, and finally to the boundaries of Europe. Encouraged by the decline of power in Byzantium and by the rapid spread of Islam among the Turkish tribes in the Danubian basin and along the Black Sea coast, the Turks had already been scheming for an attack on Eastern Rome when they were routed by Tamerlane in 1402. Fifty years later both of their adversaries, the Mongols and the Christians, had degenerated, and the Turks moved in and achieved their end. Constantinople fell in 1453. From this moment onward, the Turks became preponderant in the Muslim world.[11]

The Turkish conquest of Constantinople and the year 1453 are simple historical facts, yet they carry inexhaustible meaning when seen in the context of international history. Not only do they mark the end of much that had taken a long time to mature, but they also signal many new beginnings. Facts such as these are chief junctions, as it were, in the dense network of human movements in the world. In them are gathered the long chronologies of numerous empires, peoples, and ideologies, which began their journey into time on widely separate tracks.

The transfer of strength within the Muslim ranks was paralleled by a drastic change in the balance of power throughout the Mediterranean world. After the elimination of Christian Eastern Rome, Islam was supreme in the entire Near Eastern and Central Asian realm, and Christendom gradually became centered in the West. Boundaries were fluid in this era. Indeed, one finds upon inquiring closely into the circumstances that attended the expansion of the three Mediterranean empires, that the battle was a three-cornered affair, since Rome and Byzantium were as antagonistic toward each other as toward Islam. Furthermore, each

---

[11] In the sixteenth century the Sultan of Turkey controlled thirty kingdoms and a coastline of eight thousand miles. R. Vipper, *Ivan Grozny*, Moscow, 1947, p. 10.

of the three great domains was expansive at the cost of the lesser peoples encountered on their paths to greater power in Europe, Africa, and Asia. Some of these lesser nations were nomadic, others were settled. Some were to be included ultimately in the inner circles of the empires, while others were to remain outside, as nominally independent satellites or colonial "backward" peoples who had to be kept in tutelage. Often interlocking, the three rings of influence and power that finally emerged from the long interplay of great historical forces were vast and very complex constellations that could not long maintain themselves as single power realms. All were to experience the impact of secular and particularistic interests and forces, and all were subject to deviation and defection within their own folds. In each of the zones the center of gravity shifted steadily. It moved from Rome across the Alps into the region of the Rhine; from Damascus to Baghdad and thence to Constantinople; and from Byzantium (Constantinople) across the Black Sea to Kiev and eventually to Muscovy. As the sixteenth century approached, the ancient centers were vacated of their power, peripheral communities emerged from their apprenticeships, and many of the uncouth little nations of bygone times appeared transformed as national states possessed by great ambitions.

Moreover, the expansive policies of the Mediterranean empires were not limited to invasions of each other's territory and the envelopment of lesser border peoples. They affected also the formerly secluded realms of inner Africa and the ancient isolated empires of the Chinese and the Indians. The wide dilation of the Islamic power circle in particular was brought about by a continuous and obstinate infringement of the spheres of India and of the native African societies.

It is true that, when viewed in the context of foreign policy-making, the methods of these expanding empires were most aggressive. In the historical perspective of an evolving interdependence between nations, however, the same imperialistic programs of aggrandizement may be viewed as unifying factors also. When the continents of Asia, Africa, and Europe were drawn together, the scene of world affairs was greatly broadened and innumerable states and cultures that formerly had been ignorant of each other became aware of their coexistence.

B. Revealed Religions in International Affairs

The circumstances that attended the expansion of the great political domains in this long epoch were in many respects similar to those that history has recorded of earlier imperialistic instances. One can easily identify in them such seemingly perennial human obsessions as drives for personal power or adventure, search for security, and the fear of foreign aggression. However, the period is particularly important in the history of international relations because it added a new motive— the urge to spread a special doctrine or ideology by force.

The motives of human behavior usually have a way of coalescing, especially in the field of political action, until it is difficult in a particular instance to measure the influence or strength of any one of them. But a retrospective view of international affairs permits the inference that human relations began to move in new directions when religious proselytism became linked to the pursuit of political objectives.[12] This revolution in the relations between nations occurred when Rome, Byzantium, and the Arab caliphates began to propagate one or another of the two revealed religions as the only truth. Their uncompromising statement and defence of Christian and Islamic doctrines influenced the policies and institutions of all the peoples enjoined to choose their various sides, and the ensuing competition between the rival creeds themselves created a pattern for the ideological controversies that were to agitate the world in later centuries.

A study of this momentous precedent must begin with the accepted fact that Christian and Islamic theories had a common source in the Judaic view of world affairs. Just as it is next to impossible to render the full meaning of a faith by defining its concepts and explaining its traditions, so it is pretentious to single out certain aspects of a creed in order then to evaluate those chosen aspects in one particular context only. With the understanding that much of the religious substance is bound to get lost in the process of relating a creed to the secular activities of nations, it is possible to extract from Judaism the themes that were destined to acquire great international significance when they were restated by the Christians and the Muslims.

Official Hebrew thought departed from all previously recorded national views of the world in projecting an uncompromising faith in the future of humanity, and relaying the vision of a world at peace "when nation shall not lift up sword against nation."[13] Christian, and to a lesser extent Islamic, universalism had its inception in the prophetism that embodied these themes. However, the Jewish traditions contained

[12] When earlier societies, such as the Near Eastern city-states, fought in behalf of their gods and associated victory and defeat with the cause of their divine sponsors, they did so without specifying a body of abstract rules and insisting on their unequivocal and general acceptance as the only true set of beliefs.

[13] Isaiah 2:4.

also a fanatically nationalistic motif, for they announced that the people of Israel had been chosen above all others to maintain the purity of God's word, to spread the knowledge of God among the heathen,[14] and to lead all the peoples of the earth to God's true and only kingdom.[15] This notion that God ruled the world by delegating important functions to a special people by virtue of a special covenant came to the Christians and the Muslims, who adopted the wisdom of the Holy Book. And each of these three religious groups was convinced, thenceforth, that it, and it alone, had been set apart deliberately from all other groups of human beings and constituted, therefore, the center of the universe.

Now, the Jewish sources are ambiguous as to precisely which role the Hebrews were to play in the community of nations, and which, if any, functions they should ascribe to other peoples. There are inspiring passages in the Old Testament to the effect that the Jews should be the gentle teachers of mankind, and also that they should accept God's choice of other men for the execution of His great design on earth. But there are other savage and vindictive statements which express profound contempt for all non-Jews and strangers—indeed for all men who do not side with God's chosen people in their espousal of His Holy Cause.[16] To this ambiguous position the Christians and the Muslims acceded likewise, and their acceptance of this particular legacy had, perhaps, more far-reaching consequences on the conduct of international relations than their obeisance to any other definitely stated Biblical norm. For since the contradiction between universalism and pacifism on the one hand, and extreme nationalism and belligerence on the other hand, was not resolved officially by either of

[14] On Jewish proselytism in the Biblical period see William F. Albright, "The Biblical Period," in *The Jews, Their History, Culture, and Religion*, Louis Finkelstein, ed., 2 vols., New York, 1949, Vol. I, pp. 17, 19.

On the missionary spirit in postbiblical Judaism see Elias J. Bickerman, "The Historical Foundations of Postbiblical Judaism" in Finkelstein, Vol. I, p. 76. The idea of proselytism, which was startling for the ancient world, began with Second Isaiah and was repeated by later prophets again and again.

See also *ibid.*, pp. 90, 101, 103. Proselytism became widespread in the Hellenistic Age. On patterns of Jewish propaganda see *ibid.*, p. 104.

[15] It is important to note that the prophet Amos qualified his conception of a universal history over which the God of Israel presides as a sovereign with the thought that the "Holy One of Israel" was a transcendent God who would both use and reject the special mission of Israel in his universal designs. See Reinhold Niebuhr, *The Children of Light and The Children of Darkness*, New York, 1944, p. 156.

[16] See especially, on these contradictions, the Books of Isaiah, Ezekiel, and Daniel. Cf., for example, Isaiah 2:4 and 60:18 with Isaiah 61:5, 6. See F. Melian Stawell, *The Growth of International Thought*, London, 1929, ch. I, "Ancient Thought: Hellenic and Hebraic" for a discussion of these themes.

these religious groups, it was perpetuated in the world views of all nations that recognized the fundamental wisdom of The Book. And since the first formative period of the modern society of nations was influenced decisively by the peoples of The Book, this ambiguity was bound to be the source of much international confusion.

The inner contradictions that were implicit in this orientation to the world environment were increased by the acknowledgment that all three religions were closely tied to pagan Hellenism. To the dispersed Jews, for example, who felt at home in Alexandria and other seats of Hellenistic culture, the Jewish scriptures were not the only source of wisdom, and some of them engaged in lifelong quests to reconcile the contradictions of their separate legacies. Among the scholars who set out to find a synthesis between Judaic and Hellenic thought none showed the connection as clearly as Philo of Alexandria (born c. 20-10 B.C.). His philosophy soon became the most suggestive common source for the progressive thought of later Jewish, Christian, and Islamic students.[17] However, these were rather isolated individual efforts that did not affect materially the propagation of the official views. Their vision of supplementary or mediating principles was eclipsed when the subsequent interpreters of the three rival faiths preferred the nearest local certainty to the more distant and demanding goal of a harmonious interplay of cultures that had been sighted earlier.

Any estimate of the impact of the new religions upon international relations in this era must include the realization that the diffusion of the Hebraic themes had instilled a common view of world affairs among the millions of Europeans, Africans, and Asians who had aligned themselves with any one of the three revealed religions. For whether men adopted Judaism, Christianity, or Islam, they still agreed in acknowledging prophetic monotheism, worshipping the same God, cultivating the notion of one great *universum* as humanity's ultimate constitutional form, and maintaining the same image of history as one great process, limited in time. Moreover, in the framework of this general orientation other parallels evolved. Not only did the kindred re-

[17] See Henry Anstryn Wolfson, *Philo: Foundations of Religious Philosophy in Judaism, Christianity and Islam*, 2 vols., Cambridge, 1947; also "Hellenistic Judaism" in Edwin R. Bevan, ed., *Legacy of Israel*, Oxford, 1927, pp. 34ff. The line of Christian Hellenistic scholarship that issued from the principles that Philo had uncovered led to the Christian Stoic Origen (A.D. 185-254), who is generally regarded as the greatest scholar of the Christian world before St. Jerome and St. Augustine. See Charles Bigg, *The Christian Platonists of Alexandria*, Oxford, 1913, pp. 49ff. on Philo, 191ff. on Origen.

ligions inspire new moral codes and value systems that bore a general likeness to each other, but they also supplied analogous principles for the organization of community life. As Jews, Christians, and Muslims insisted on the primacy of their respective religious affiliations, they loosened all the other ties that had secured their common life in ancient times. Henceforward communities were formed because their members shared a faith, not because they shared a family, country, economic interest, political allegiance, or professional pursuit. One was a Jew, a Christian, or a Muslim now, and not a Greek, Roman, or Egyptian. The principle of religious communalism thus became the foremost unifying factor in the world, since it denied that there were any limits to the commonwealth of believers.

This transformation of the meaning of "community" effected revolutionary changes in the field of law and government. For where the synagogue, the church, and the mosque displaced established secular assemblies, it was inevitable that theological dogma should acquire the force of law, and that ecclesiastical principles of organization should supply the constitutional foundation for the political society. The ancient legal order of the Mediterranean world which had rested on the Roman civil law and its treatment of local legal systems was superseded now by the separate laws of the Talmud, the Koran, and the Christian church, and great theocracies emerged in realms that had previously been held together without the binding of a special dogma.

The constitutional revolutions that were brought about by the diffusion of these three like-minded desert religions had great repercussions in the field of international relations.

It is true, as we have seen, that the Mediterranean world had expanded northward and westward under the leadership of Rome; that it assumed a separate cultural identity under the consolidating force of Roman principles of law and government; and that its connections with the eastern realms had become less close in the Roman period than they had been in the Hellenistic Age. Nevertheless, it cannot be said that the pre-Christian Western culture was antagonistic to the cultures of the East, for there was nothing either in the philosophy or in the secular body of Roman public law that barred adjustments and accords with peoples used to different value systems. The doors that had been left open to such intercultural communications closed, however, when Rome's successor states began to wall their worlds with rigid ideologies and the themes of the revealed religions became the declared goals of their foreign policies. Not only was the new world image here announced geocentric and limited in time when contrasted with the religions of the East, but it differed from Hinduism and other Oriental traditions also by not permitting any assimilation of foreign symbols. In fact, since the Near Eastern world views were upheld as the only right ones, they professed to bar all communication with the world of unbelievers save in the way of conquest or conversion. The divisive lines that were thus drawn through the world deepened in the course of time until in the nineteenth century it was generally accepted that the East and the West could never meet.[18]

The different nations that composed the western sector of the world were joint inheritors of the Hebraic view of world affairs. But their agreement on the substance of the themes that were projected through the Bible could not be translated into actual attitudes of mutual understanding, since each of the inheritors insisted on his own rendition of the themes. Indeed, the record seems to indicate that the separate national groups within this area had been more ready to find a level of communication and adjustment while each had rallied around its local cult, than when all were persuaded to recognize the transcendent truth of one religious orientation. For under the terms of the new constitutional doctrine, which recognized the consolidation of church and state, a given territory had to be either all Muslim or all Christian.[19] This meant, in the domain of international relations, that the foreign policies of the contending Mediterranean states originated in the assumption of their mutual incompatibility, and that the various Mediterranean peoples expected conflict rather than coexistence when they approached each other across the territorial boundaries of their great theocracies.

The theme of conflict and disunity was present also within the camp of each theocracy. Christians disagreed in their interpretation of the Savior's teaching. But since it was self-evident that truth was one and indivisible, the followers of Christ were under the compulsion to group themselves in separate sects,[20] each claiming the exclusive right to minister the word of God. And this new centrifugal movement in the realm of faith was reinforced, in many local situations, by long existing trends toward cultural or political separatism. It is the combined force

---

[18] Cf. also Helmuth von Glasenapp, *Die Fünf Grossen Religionen*, Düsseldorf, 1952, Vol. II, pp. 232ff.

[19] Cf. also W. E. Hocking, "Living Religions and a World of Faith," in *The Asian Legacy and American Life*, Arthur Christy, ed., New York, 1945, p. 209.

[20] See Glasenapp, Vol. II, pp. 336-384 for a discussion of the separate churches and sects.

of these different divisive factors that alone explains the deepest of all splits in Christendom—the schism between the Catholic Latin Church in Rome and the Orthodox Greek Church in Byzantium, which caused grave international disturbances from the fifth century to A.D. 1054, when it was officially acknowledged as a definite break.[21]

The Muslims, too, were intransigent defenders of God's word, and, like the Christians, apt to fight each other about the issues of their faith. But a general comparison of Christian and Islamic postures points to a greater tolerance in the Muslim camp, where rather brazen heresies were often permitted to exist as long as their adherents did not engage in activities that threatened the security of the state. Indeed, historians have suggested that it was not religious enthusiasm but the overwhelming need to free themselves from the hot prison of the desert that had driven the Arabs to aggression in the seventh century, and that fanaticism and intolerance were later phenomena, alien to the Arab nation and explainable by the influence of the proselytes of Islam.[22]

In short, the impact of the revealed religions upon the course of world affairs was as ambivalent as the religious themes to which these creeds bore witness. On the one hand, both Christianity and Islam were travelling religions whose appeal transcended all established limits and thus effected greater realms of unity and understanding than had existed earlier. But on the other hand, both new cults were in various degrees divisive forces, which undermined conventional modes of co-existence and communication between nations, for both were disrespectful of the views of others. Since this approach was alien to that of the Oriental civilizations, it was conducive to the cultural isolation of the West. Furthermore, since it did not promote agreement among the religious disputants within the theocratic states themselves, it was a divisive influence even within the Western world.

[21] *ibid.*, p. 265; p. 351 for the points of agreement and disagreement in the two Christian churches.

[22] A. A. Vasiliev, *History of the Byzantine Empire, 324-1453*, Madison, 1952, p. 208.

CHAPTER 8

THE MEDIEVAL WESTERN EUROPEAN REALM

A. Ideological Foundations

WHEN the representatives of France, the United Kingdom, Belgium, Holland, and Luxembourg negotiated the treaty of Mutual Assistance and Economic Cooperation in 1948, they argued forcefully that such a Western union would link peoples who were united by common parliamentary institutions, a common striving for economic rights, and common conceptions of democracy. However, they conceived of their alliance also as a "spiritual union," a "brotherhood" whose full meaning and implications could not be reduced to the form of a rigid thesis or written directive.[1] In this spirit the signatories of the Brussels Pact agreed that they would "fortify and preserve the principles of democracy, personal freedom and political liberty, the constitutional traditions and the rule of law, which are their common heritage . . . ," and "make every effort in common to lead their peoples toward a better understanding of the principles which form the basis of their common civilization. . . ."[2] This agreement was to become the foundation for the North Atlantic Treaty, which was signed three years later by Belgium, Canada, Denmark, France, Iceland, Italy, Luxembourg, the Netherlands, Norway, Portugal, the United Kingdom of Great Britain and Northern Ireland, and the United States.[3]

Two centuries earlier, when intellectuals from all of the Western European nations were engaged in a search for universal values, Voltaire had written: "Already for a long time one could regard Christian Europe (except Russia) as a sort of great republic divided into several states, some monarchical, others of a mixed character; the former aristocratic, the latter popular, but all in harmony with each other, all having the same substratum of religion, although divided into various sects; all possessing the same principles of public and political law,

[1] Cf. speech by Foreign Secretary Ernest Bevin in the English House of Commons on January 22, 1948, *Current Readings on International Relations*, Norman J. Padelford, ed., M.I.T. Publications in International Affairs, no. 4, 1948, pp. 110-114.

[2] See the text of the Five Power Treaty (the Brussels Pact), *ibid.*, pp. 117-121, especially Article III.

[3] The treaty was signed on April 4, 1949. See *United Nations Treaty Series*, Vol. 34, 1949, no. 541. Turkey and Greece acceded to the treaty on Feb. 18, 1952.

unknown in other parts of the world. . . ."[4] For in the broad perspective of the "Heavenly City" of eighteenth century philosophers,[5] a single political system extended over the Italian and Iberian peninsulas, France, the Netherlands, Central Europe, Poland, Hungary, Scandinavia, the British Isles, and the overseas dependencies of several European states, firmly supported by common values, a well developed system of international law, and comprehensive treaty settlements.[6]

The community of European nations that had struck the imagination of a man such as Voltaire had passed through many phases in the course of about one thousand years. Between A.D. 500 and 800 the illusion was still entertained that Eastern and Western Rome were one indivisible empire, of which Byzantium was the capital and Rome a semi-independent member; that Latin and Greek Christianity were but two aspects of one community of faith; and that the unified empire and unified religion combined to form one *universitas*. In actual fact "Romania" had become a myth. Not only was Christianity divided into two churches, but it was becoming increasingly clear, in this span of centuries, that the official religious schism was merely confirming lines of cultural and political division that had long been in the making. The cleavage was deepened when Byzantium became unable to defend the Western Empire against the invading German tribes, and it was then, in the resultant vacuum of power, that the Bishop of Rome emerged as the only executive who could be trusted to cope with the spiritual and temporal crisis of the Western realm. The Byzantine Church thereafter remained subservient to the emperor in the East, but the Roman became transformed into a more or less autonomous political power. The authority of this power was tested severely from the beginning, however, by the overwhelming presence of the Teutonic tribes within, and on the periphery of, Italy, and in the eighth century it was found wanting when the Lombards invaded the land. In this moment of peril, Western Rome was shielded only by the military power of the Franks and the political wisdom of their king, Charlemagne.

The Germanic nation that made its epochal appearance in greater Italy at this time, had already unified all of old Gaul, a section of

[4] Voltaire, *The Age of Louis XIV*, Everyman's Library, London, New York, 1935, p. 5.

[5] See Carl Becker, *The Heavenly City of Eighteenth Century Philosophers*, New Haven, 1932, for the climate of opinion in the eighteenth century.

[6] Cf. Ross Hoffman, *The Great Republic*, a Historical View of the International Community and the Organization of Peace, New York, 1942, pp. 18-19.

northern Spain, part of the Low Countries, and western Germany; had integrated the neighboring tribes into one powerful state; and had shown an interest in aligning itself with the cause of the Bishop of Rome. The successful defence of Italy promoted the Carolingian Dynasty to the role of the chief defender of the Western Christian system. This meant that the papacy—having found a reliable supporter in its close vicinity—could afford to sever some of the ties that had linked it to distant Byzantium. The reorientation on the part of the papacy did not imply the cancellation of other important links between the two parts of Rome; nor did the papal transfer of titular sovereignty to Western potentates affect the legal rights of the Eastern sovereign in all those areas that were actually in the purview of his power (as, for instance, southern Italy, Thrace, Greece, and the Asian provinces).[7] Nevertheless, the lines of division between Eastern and Western Rome were now more marked than they had been before, and the Roman Church was drawn increasingly into the political and cultural orbit of the Carolingian Empire, while the latter was acceding to the tradition of unity commonly associated with the administration of the ancient Roman Empire and the Catholic Church. A new imperial order was thus evolved through a coordination of the Roman and Germanic traditions. This Christian Roman Empire of the Carolingians, later known as the Holy Roman Empire of the German Nation, may be said to have supplied the earliest antecedent for the Western European Union of the twentieth century.

The political organization of the multinational Western European commonwealth that came into existence in A.D. 800 and remained valid until the fifteenth century was not embodied in one written constitution. Its sources were varied, and they were used and interpreted differently by successive generations. But a summary and retrospective view of all its phases permits the generalization that the new international system had arisen on foundations supplied by the traditions of classical Rome, the tenets of the organized Christian church, and the interests and habits of the Germanic peoples. Each of these component elements in the constitutional set-up, as well as their actual relationship to each other, has supplied a subject of never-ending scholarly speculation.

Since Christ had told his followers that His Empire was not of this

---

[7] James Bryce, *The Holy Roman Empire*, New York, 1928, p. 323. See also Christopher Dawson, *The Making of Europe*, an Introduction to the History of European Unity, New York, 1945, pp. 214ff.

world,[8] the early Christians had felt that they were strangers on this earth, unconcerned with political affairs, waiting only for the world to end and for that true citizenship in the Kingdom of God which, they had reason to anticipate, would surely follow all their earthly sufferings. It was only when they were constrained to realize that the end of earthly life was not in sight that they began to give some serious thought to the problem of how best to organize the world. Since the Christians conceived of the human race as one single family, they began with the assumption of one ecclesiastical community, coequal with the earth. And since, in their opinion, Christians were the only defenders of the good in the unending cosmic conflict between good and evil, they naturally concluded that the unity of the race meant the unity of the Christian faith, and that only a Christian empire could prepare mankind for citizenship in the forthcoming city of God. From the application of these principles Christendom emerged as an all-embracing corporation, constituting "that Universal Realm, spiritual and temporal, which may be called the Universal Church or, with equal propriety, the Commonwealth of the Human Race."[9] And since, in the immediate memory of the Christians, the human race had been gathered in the secular empire of the Romans, the new mandate was explicitly related also to this precedent.

The constitutional dualism that is implicit in such a reading of the past was indicated already in the fourth century when Eusebius of Caesarea (died A.D. 340) wrote: "One God was proclaimed to all mankind; and at the same time one universal power, the Roman Empire, arose and flourished. The enduring and implacable hatred of nation for nation was now removed; and as the knowledge of one God and one way of religion and salvation, even the doctrine of Christ, was made known to all mankind; so at the self-same period, the entire dominion of the Roman Empire being vested in a single sovereign, profound peace reigned throughout the world. . . ."[10] This dualism was to remain the chief source of political thought for centuries to come.

Throughout the European Middle Ages[11] men on the one hand were convinced that human affairs were divided into two great categories, the spiritual and the temporal, and on the other hand were uncertain

[8] John 18:36.

[9] Otto Gierke, *Political Theories of the Middle Ages*, F. W. Maitland, tr., Beacon Hill, Boston, 1958, pp. 10; nn. pp. 103-104.

[10] Dawson, pp. 34ff.

[11] In the context of European history the terms "Middle Ages" and "Medieval History" are appropriate.

how best to reconcile the need for an earthly organization with the promise of a heavenly state to come. This great dilemma intrigued the best minds among ecclesiastics and laymen alike, but no Christian did more than St. Augustine (died A.D. 430) to clarify the problem. Augustine's great work, *De Civitate Dei*,[12] was composed when Rome's temporal power was disintegrating under the onslaught of Alaric the Goth (A.D. 410), and the representative of the Christian Church was impressing all contemporaries with his steadfast resistance. In this great crisis St. Augustine expounded the philosophy that all history is dominated by the contest of the heavenly and the earthly societies. The two cities, begotten of two loves, the love of God and the love of the self apart from God, are confused on this earth; but at the end of time they will be distinct, for then all the earthly cities will have passed away, and only the city of God will remain. Many later commentators have inferred from these symbolic analogies that St. Augustine meant to identify the city of God with the church, and the city of Man with the state. But such a literal interpretation is hardly indicated by the text, which seems to point, instead, to the *Civitas Dei* as "the spiritual association, whether here or in the hereafter, of persons whose minds and lives were directed towards God,"[13] and to the *Civitas Terrena* as the domain of all who did not accept the supremacy of the spiritual motif.

St. Augustine's vision of a Christian society greatly influenced not only the early Carolingian version of the Roman Empire, but also the various argumentations that the later popes and emperors advanced in furtherance of their respective claims. It did not, however, actually answer the questions that practically minded medieval statesmen, whether of the state or of the church, were interested in settling. In response to this uncertainty later theories advanced the doctrine of the two swords. The notion that the earthly community of the faithful had to be defended by a spiritual and a material sword had already been indicated vaguely in the *Evangelium Lucae*.[14] But it was stated more definitely by Pope Gelasius I (492-496) when he wrote to the Eastern Emperor Anastasius that there are two things by which this world is ruled, the sacred papal authority and the profane royal power.

This view, in accordance with which both authorities derived from God and each was supreme in its own sphere while dependent upon

---

[12] St. Augustine, *The City of God*, Modern Library, New York, 1950.

[13] E. F. Jacob, "Political Thought," in *The Legacy of the Middle Ages*, G. C. Crump and E. F. Jacob, eds., Oxford, 1927, p. 512.

[14] Luke 22:38. Cf. Gierke, pp. 113-114, n. 22.

the other, was maintained officially after the pope had shifted his trust from the Byzantine to the Carolingian Empire.[15] But from the ninth century onward, when the papacy became interested in winning an all-out victory in its power contest with the Empire, it was found to be ideologically inadequate. Spokesmen for the pope then proposed that both the secular and the spiritual powers were vested in the church; that every secular authority was subject to the overlordship of the pope; and that the church was free to bestow the material sword on whomsoever it regarded as worthy of its trust. This was the context in which Pope Gregory VII (in office 1073-1085) claimed the right to free the clergy from all secular controls, to excommunicate the recalcitrant emperor (Henry IV), and to absolve all subjects from their allegiance to a wicked ruler.

By the eleventh century the church had acquired the characteristics of an earthly empire: it claimed all Italy with Corsica and Sardinia as "states of the church," Spain because it supposedly belonged of old to St. Peter, Hungary as a gift from King Stephen, Saxony as a Carolingian bequest, and the entire Christian Roman Empire as a fief of Rome.[16] Toward the twelfth century the pope presented himself as the one and only head of mankind, the wielder of what is in principle an empire over the community of mortals, and the supreme judge with an unlimited right to punish all offenders. In this understanding of the doctrine of the two swords, the state—insofar as it had existed before the church, or continued to exist outside of the church—was the outcome of sin: it had to be hallowed by the authority of the church, which meant, of necessity, that the state was subservient to the ecclesiastical order. For, continues the theory, God gave both swords to Peter and through him to the popes, who are to retain the spiritual sword and deliver the temporal to servants or vassals of their choice. In the single great society, Innocent III declared, it was the Apostolic See that had taken the empire away from the Greeks and given it to the Germans in the person of Charlemagne, and the authority that had then been exercised by Pope Leo as God's representative remains vested forever in his successors, who may therefore at any time recall the gift and present it to a person or nation more worthy than its present holders.[17]

---

[15] Barker, "The Conception of the Empire," in *The Legacy of Rome*, Bailey, ed., p. 87.

[16] James Westfall Thompson, *Feudal Germany*, Chicago, 1928, pp. 108ff.

[17] Gierke, pp. 13-14ff.

This is the theory of the Translation of the Empire which was featured continuously in constitutional and philosophical controversies down to the seventeenth century. See also Bryce, p. 219.

In the face of these papal claims to omnipotence, however, the defenders of the secular empire were arguing that the empire was a commonwealth of Christian peoples, governed by the concordant and interdependent powers of the emperor and the pope. This was a position that could be maintained as long as the theory was consonant with reality. During the rule of Charlemagne, for example, it could not be questioned, since the Carolingian king had become the Roman emperor precisely because, even before his coronation, he had been the actual master of Western Christendom.[18] The power of the Carolingian was never equalled, however, by any of his successors. The frontiers of the earthly Christian commonwealth were, indeed, immeasurably extended by later emperors, until they came to include Poland, Bohemia, and Hungary; and such monarchs as Otto I (912-973) and Frederick II (1194-1250) ruled wider areas than had been included in the realm of Charlemagne. When the later monarchs were compelled to invoke the support and unifying influence of the papacy itself to resist the rising tides of local particularism within their fold, however, they greatly weakened the imperial case. Nor did any emperor ever succeed either in reuniting Byzantium and Rome[19] or in merging Germany and Italy into a single politico-ecclesiastical empire that would bend "like a mighty arch over the whole of Christendom."[20] Such imperial dreams were frequently entertained, but they were checked not only by the new ambitions of the papacy (an obstacle that had not confronted Charlemagne) but also by the growing fears of those lesser temporal rulers in the Empire who began to suspect that the imperial schemes for cosmopolitan societies were screens behind which certain German princes might prepare for their national ascendancy. For these reasons, the imperial arguments that the secular ruler derived his powers directly from God, that his functions were as divinely sanctioned as those of the ecclesiastical dignitary, and that mankind had been enjoined by Jesus, Paul, and Peter to submit to the powers that be, were simply not as persuasive as the rival arguments of the pope, whom none could accuse so easily of local or national partisanship, whatever the bent of the pontiff's individual ambitions might have been. Even after the balance of ecclesiastical and secular powers shifted to the total advantage of the church, however, the hope remained ever present

[18] H. W. Carless Davis, "Innocent III and the Mediaeval Church" in *The Evolution of World-Peace*, F. S. Marvin, ed., London, New York, 1921, pp. 48ff.

[19] Otto II (955-983) married Theophano, daughter of the Eastern emperor, in the hopes that such a matrimonial alliance would yield a true political union.

[20] Thompson, introduction, p. xv.

in medieval Europe that one day it would be possible to reconcile the two great orders locked in rivalry. It was, as Gierke has put it, about the nature of this reconciliation that the Middle Ages fought.[21]

The search for a harmonious human society was greatly stimulated in the thirteenth century when scholars recovered a knowledge of Greek philosophy and Roman law and were thus led to the realization that the state could be conceived and fashioned as a beneficial instrument in mankind's education toward the future reign of God. It was in this context that St. Thomas Aquinas (died 1274) revived the theory of the Two Coordinate Powers, with the understanding that the temporal power was inherent, not derived, and that the secular state must be recognized, instead, as part of God's plan and as rooted in man's nature. This argument was supported by the accumulated fund of one thousand years of political history, which seemed to indicate not only that God had ordained the unity and oneness of mankind under one great system of law and government, but also that the divine plan had been executed in fact through a series of universal monarchies of which the world-wide Roman dominion was the final member. Hallowed by the birth and death of Christ, this empire was transferred first to the Greeks and finally to the Germans. All peoples and kings were to be subject to the Romano-German Kaiser, as the immediate successor to the Caesars, until Judgment Day. God, they believed, had instituted the emperor as his trusted vicar in all matters temporal, charging him to supervise men in their dealings with one another so that they might be better able to pursue undisturbed the spiritual life that was the appointed goal of their existence.[22] This revised view of the doctrine of the two swords was supported by the political developments in the fourteenth and fifteenth centuries. For by this time the peoples of Europe had split up into separate and hostile nationalities, and the need was great to locate a supranational power that would restrain the factions and limit strife and warfare in the interest of Europe's general peace.

Now, there was no agency more qualified theoretically to execute the functions of a protector of the peace than the papacy, but God's spiritual representative on earth had, by this time, forfeited much of the esteem in which he had formerly been held. His constituents had come to realize that the papacy was more occupied with developing its

[21] Gierke, p. 11.
[22] Gierke, pp. 19ff.
See also Robert Maynard Hutchins, *St. Thomas and the World State*, Milwaukee, 1949, pp. 7ff.

temporal strength in Italy than with tending to its presumed obligations in the wider jurisdiction of a united Christendom.

In this crisis of suspended power, when the great debate about the true sources of all political authority seemed stalemated, the ancient images and doctrines that had inspired so many earlier generations came to momentary life again through Dante's political vision and philosophical insight. His book *De Monarchia*[23] which was composed (probably between 1310-1313) when Italy was rent by strife, restates the medieval theory that man has need of two guides for his life; "whereof one is the Supreme Pontiff, to lead mankind to eternal life, according to the things revealed to us; and the other is the Emperor, to guide mankind to happiness in the world, in accordance with the teaching of philosophy, and to direct men to blessedness."[24] But Dante denied explicitly that the papacy possessed any temporal power, arguing that such possession could not be deduced from either natural law, divine command, or universal consent. In fact, he claimed, any assumption of such powers was against the very form and essence of the model of the Church, namely, the life of Christ, who had said, "My kingdom is not of this world." Monarchy alone, thought Dante, was the true and rightful form of government, since man's principal objective on earth—the realization of his full potentialities—can best be attained during peace, and peace can be secured only under the rule of a monarch who is the servant of all, history having shown conclusively that every other form of government is invariably abused, in time, by one social class or another. And since the world had been quiet and at peace when the Roman Empire had been ruled by Augustus, Dante concluded that it was Italy, as Rome's successor, that was destined to effect the union of all the peoples.

Unfortunately, just at the moment when Dante was invoking the ideal of a powerful universal monarch as mankind's best shield of peace, Western Europe's aspirants to such leadership were rather hapless people. Some were mere tools in the employ of feudal factions, some had degenerated into docile creatures of the papacy, others were simply royal beggars wandering through the land in search of shelter. Indeed, no version of the doctrine of the two swords seemed to fit the political

---

[23] *De Monarchia*, Oxford Text, Dr. E. Moore, ed., Oxford, 1916. See Richard William Church, *Dante: An Essay to Which is Added a Translation of "De Monarchia" by F. J. Church.* London, 1879. F. Sherwood Smith, "Dante and World Empire" in *The Social and Political Ideas of Some Great Mediaeval Thinkers*, F. J. C. Hearnshaw, ed., London, 1923. Bryce, p. 280.

[24] Church edition, p. 302.

realities of the fourteenth century. Neither the emperor nor the pope could supply a positive answer to that great quest for a logical and just constitutional order which had both inspired and frustrated the medieval mind for all these centuries. And this was the actuality that impressed itself upon a certain French lawyer in Normandy who was counsellor to Philippe le Bel, Pierre Dubois (died 1312).

Dubois was convinced that any attempt to revive the past would lead to political disaster. "No sane man," he wrote in his *Recovery of the Holy Land*,[25] "could really believe that at this period of the world's history one individual could rule the whole world as a temporal monarch, with all men obeying him as their superior. If a tendency in this direction did appear, there would be wars and revolutions without end. No man could put them down because of the huge populations involved, the distance and diversity of the countries, and the natural propensity of human beings to quarrel."[26] Therefore he suggested the total abolition of papal power in temporal affairs, the recognition of national monarchies as the chief carriers of Western Europe's destiny, and the creation of a confederation of Christian sovereigns as the only meaningful representation of the principle of European unity. Differences between the Catholic powers should be submitted to the arbitration of a council of nations, and if the council could not agree, nine judges were to be selected to settle the dispute. In order to prevent any undue influence by the disputants upon the judges, three judges were to be selected by the council to represent each contestant, and three from among the ecclesiastics. The pope was to be appointed to hear any appeal from the court's decision.[27] The project also included enforcement measures. All members should be obligated to comply with the decrees of the appointed agencies by applying collective economic and diplomatic sanctions to any nation that would disobey the award or otherwise violate the constitution of the Western community.

Here, then, was Europe's first rough draft for the organization of a community of separate nations. And as one reads its varied and intricate provisions, one encounters other themes that were to be featured prominently in later European history. But just as Dante was an Italian patriot when he dreamt of a universal empire, so was Dubois an ardent

[25] Pierre Dubois, *De Recuperatione Terre Sancte: traité de politique générale*, pub. d'après le manuscrit du Vatican par Charles V. Langlois, Paris, 1891.

[26] As transl. in F. Melian Stawell, *The Growth of International Thought*, London, 1929, p. 63.

[27] See Sylvester John Hemleben, *Plans for World Peace Through Six Centuries*, Chicago, 1945, pp. 1-4, for a discussion of this plan.

Frenchman while envisioning the unity of Europe.[28] The elaborate international structure of the projected Council of Europe was designed to serve the special interests of France, and there were intricate secret proposals outlining ways in which the power of the French monarchy might be increased at the expense of Germany, Italy, the Papal Patrimony, Spain, and the Eastern Empire—the latter to be weakened if necessary by a resort to war. Since Dubois was convinced that Western Europeans in general, and Frenchmen in particular, were the best fitted, by virtue of their superior reasoning powers, to rule other people, he fully expected the Catholic confederation to manifest its supremacy in regard to all other areas of the world, especially toward the "Eastern" and "barbarian" nations. As a matter of fact, Dubois drafted an elaborate system for the colonization of the Near East. Insubordinate Western leaders were to be shipped off with their families into that region; colleges were to be opened for the teaching of medicine, surgery, and Eastern languages; and trade was to be planned in such a way that the Mediterranean Sea should be turned into a European lake.[29]

Dubois' work had no practical consequences at the time, but it is of timeless importance in the history of Western European and international organization, since it announces several motifs that were to become typical features in the subsequent evolution of the modern European states system.

B. The Relationship of Image to Reality in Western European Politics

It is evident from a comparison of prevailing approaches to the problems of peace, power, and unity, that the peoples in the Western European culture realm are more inclined to emphasize principles of constitutionalism in their regional and world-wide policies than the nations connected with other civilizations. This does not mean that despotism has been absent from the records of Western Europe's long and complex history, but rather, that its incidence is overshadowed by efforts to curb the use of power in national as well as international associations. However, a survey of recent international politics cannot but leave the impression that the Western nations are, on the whole, unsure about the proper place of power in the constitutional govern-

[28] See Eileen E. Power, "Pierre du Bois and the Domination of France" in Hearnshaw, ed.
[29] Stawell, pp. 64-67.

ment of human affairs; for they condone with an uneasy conscience its use as a shield of unity and peace.

No satisfactory relationship between peace, power, and unity—these three important values—has yet been found in the context of Western politics, perhaps because the Western Europeans have found it difficult to be faithful executors of their Christian legacy. For although Christians have no difficulty in acknowledging the images of unity and peace as morally and politically valid goals, they always face a great dilemma when trying to assimilate the idea of power in its political connotation. This elusive concept has been, therefore, the chief object of their most tortuous inquiries, and these, in turn, have often yielded such bizarre discrepancies between the Christian world of thought and the Christian world of fact, that men became increasingly discomfited in their attempts to translate morally accepted values into terms of social usefulness.

This long, intense, frustrating preoccupation with the relationship between image and reality in political organization had important consequences for the evolution not only of processes of government but also of approaches to human relations in general. Through it the business of governing people was established as an inexhaustible subject matter of thought and experimentation, and a tradition was gradually formed to the effect that power, since it could not be fully known, should never be fully trusted. Consequently, whenever there was evidence of concentrated power in a person or an institution, such power was required to explain itself. And since it could not be measured adequately in terms of its own image, it was measured instead through its relationship to other values and institutions about which men had reached a greater degree of certainty.

If one inquires closely into the origin and nature of the ultimate set of moral references accepted in the Middle Ages, one finds, first, the body of the Christian ethic, permeated with the certainty that man can identify the one truth to which all thought and action ought to be conformable and know, therefore, that certain things are right and that certain people or agencies possess rights. And one finds, second, the acknowledged legacy of Roman law, providing Christians with the forms through which they could express their notion of what is right. In this way the idea of right as embodied in law became the leading motif in Western European history between 1000-1500. Or, as Bishop Stubbs has put it in his lecture "On the Characteristic Difference between Mediaeval and Modern History,"[30] there was, in the greatest men of the period, a conscious attempt to exalt law and a willingness to abide by it, and in the inferior actors, in the worse men, a disposition to maintain their own rights within recognized limits; so that when they attacked the possessions or infringed the apparently equal rights of their opponents, they did so on the ground of legal pleas. In other words, although men did not necessarily love law, they so far respected it as to seem to wish to have it always on their side.

All power, then, was limited both by the strength of a conviction that its use should be legal and by the institutions that this conviction fostered in the course of time. And this applied also to the seemingly absolute powers that were claimed by the popes and emperors. For in their own and in the public's estimation, both were merely the agents of the one and only God, who was the supreme governor of mankind. Their respective jurisdictions were, therefore, subject always to the twofold limitation, that the individual's primary allegiance was due to the maker of all men and things, and that each human being was possessed of inalienable individual rights by virtue of Christ's sacrifice. It was the shared acceptance of this divine omnipotence which alone explains why the prestige of Henry IV was not impaired when God's spiritual representative inflicted upon him seemingly humiliating punishments, and the sanctity of the papal office not seriously affected in the European Middle Ages when an emperor or some other agency succeeded in deposing an individual pope. Furthermore, there was a general agreement in Western Christendom that the exercise of every authority was bound by the all-transcendent law of nature—an ultimate legal reference that was established indisputably when Roman law became the chief objective of studious inquiries at the great university of Bologna, and when St. Thomas defined this discovery as "nothing else than the rational creature's participation in the eternal law."[31]

The acknowledgment of divine law, natural law, and Roman law made for a general public awareness of the place in society of law. In fact, no legal or political development in medieval Western Europe is understandable unless it is remembered that the generations here in-

---

[30] William Stubbs, *Seventeen Lectures on the Study of Mediaeval and Modern History and Kindred Subjects*, Oxford, 1900, pp. 240 and 249.

[31] *Summa Theologica*, Part II, I Q. 95, article 2. See also R. W. Carlyle and A. J. Carlyle, *A History of Mediaeval Political Theory in the West*, 6 vols., Edinburgh and London, 1928-1936, Vol. II, Part I, ch. III; Part II, ch. III; Vol. III, Part II, ch. I.

Sir Frederick Pollock, *History of the Law of Nature*, Columbia Law Review, 1, 1901, pp. 11ff.

volved looked upon law as a truth to be uncovered, rather than as a command to be enforced. It was this approach to law in human relations, for instance, which stimulated people to search their history and their customs in order to locate a common law of the land that should restrain the powers of the monarch.[32]

The entire body of political and legal experience that had thus accumulated in the preceding one thousand years supplied the early Christian democrats with the argument that all government derived their just powers from the people. In the realm of church politics, for instance, the doctrine gained adherents that final sovereignty does not reside in the pope but in the great ecclesiastical community of which he was merely the corporative head. In fact, it was even maintained that the entire church consists, in the final analysis, of all the people, not only of the clergy; and that the supreme authority in the church should reside, therefore, in a general council composed of laymen and clerics, with the pope acting only as a kind of president of the Christian republic, which should be governing itself under the guidance of the emperor.[33]

In the domain of imperial politics the idea of popular sovereignty was developed even more fully, for here the Roman principle of law was well established that an emperor's authority consists in powers delegated to him by the people. Such a precedent for the curtailment of his jurisdiction was reinforced, furthermore, by strong Germanic customs, in accordance with which lordship was always limited by the incidents and requirements of fellowship (*Genossenschaft*).[34] And these relationships were fully exploited by the papacy when it became interested in restraining the emperor. Gregory VII, for instance, absolved the emperor's subjects from their temporal allegiance on the ground that Henry IV was tyrannous and had failed to live up to the terms of his kingship, which implied the duty to maintain the law, protect society, and do justice. Moreover, this stand was backed by the nobles, who claimed to be fighting for the maintenance of their rights against the superior's absolutism,[35] for the same tenets that supported

[32] See Charles H. McIlwain, *Constitutionalism Ancient and Modern*, Ithaca, New York, 1940, ch. IV; Sir Frederick Pollock and Frederic William Maitland, *The History of English Law*, 2 vols., Cambridge, 1923. See in particular ch. VII "The Age of Bracton."

[33] See Marsilius of Padua (1270-1342), whose famous book *Defensor Pacis* (written in 1324) was dedicated to Louis of Bavaria, King of the Romans. Cf. also Bryce, p. 225. Carlyle and Carlyle, Vol. V, ch. IX.

[34] See Gierke, pp. 37ff.

[35] Cf. Thompson, pp. 249ff.

the theory of ultimate popular sovereignty also inspired the derivative doctrine of popular representation. If the people could not, or did not, exercise their right—for example, of choosing a new king when necessity required such action—they were entitled (so the argument ran) to delegate their powers. As distinguished from most other European monarchies, which rested on the principle of heredity, the German monarchy had become recognized in the thirteenth century as an elective one. However, whereas the process of election had been identified in Germany's early constitutional history with the diet of all the princes, it was later associated with the special powers of several great magnates. Even in the early thirteenth century it had been generally accepted that three Rhenish Archbishops (of Mainz, Trier, and Köln) and four secular dignitaries (of the Palatinate of the Rhine, the Duchy of Saxony, the Kingdom of Bohemia, and the Markgravate of Brandenburg) should enjoy the privilege of deciding by their unanimous vote who was to occupy the German throne.[36] And since the German king was also, after his coronation by the pope, the Roman emperor,[37] the entire Holy Roman Empire, which pretended to encompass all of Western Christendom, had come thus to rest on the principle of an elected monarchy.

Some weighty questions touching the interpretation of this international constitution remained outstanding, however. Should the elected king be automatically promoted to the imperial position, or should such an ascension depend on papal action? Popes such as Boniface VIII pressed the latter viewpoint, and one of Boniface's successors excommunicated a king for assuming the imperial crown without awaiting papal assent. The theory of this papal prerogative was implicit in the argument that the pope, acting as the people's delegate, was authorized by his constituents either to create the electoral college or to elect the monarch personally.[38] But on the other hand, the electoral body claimed that it had been divinely instituted to discharge the functions that had once belonged to the senate and the people of Rome, and that it was by its election, rather than by any choice or confirmation of the pope, that the emperor acquired his rights. An important decision was reached in 1338, which favored the latter view, and it was invoked,

[36] This arrangement was confirmed by the Golden Bull in 1356, and the Electoral College continued to function, in a somewhat altered composition, until the Holy Roman Empire was officially dissolved in 1806. See Bryce, pp. 234-244 for an analysis of the election procedures.

[37] Otto I (912-973), the elected King of the Eastern Franks, was the first to take the title of "Roman Emperor of the German People." This happened in 962.

[38] Gierke, pp. 42, 149ff.

one year later, when the electors deposed King Wenzel. The German Estates, in diet assembled in 1338 and 1339, announced a similarly restrictive view of papal and imperial powers by declaring that Louis IV did not hold the empire as a fief of the Holy See but from God alone and that the sovereign, once duly chosen by the electors, needed no confirmation or approval by the pope.[39]

It is apparent that the controversy about the true seat of power was not the pastime of a few philosophers, but a general public cause. Indeed, it has been suggested that the war of investiture be regarded not only as a test of strength between the empire and the papacy[40] but also as the first great issue in medieval history that actually excited popular interest.[41] For example, the Concordat of Worms (1122), which settled the quarrel by providing that appointments to higher ecclesiastical positions should be made after consultation between the church and the imperial authorities, was not really arranged either by the emperor or by the pope, it has been suggested, but by the German feudal princes,[42] whose growing power was even then beginning to eclipse the strength of the two major contestants.

By the middle of the fourteenth century it was clear that the ancient medieval order was dissolving. The all-pervading sense of community, which had made it possible for St. Thomas Aquinas to write with conviction that ". . . between a single bishop and the Pope there are other grades of dignity corresponding to the grades of unions insofar as one congregation or community includes another one, as the community of a province includes the community of the city, and the community of the kingdom includes the community of the province, and the community of the whole world includes the community of a kingdom,"[43] grew gradually weaker as the various cities and provinces and kingdoms developed separate interests, which they knew not how to fit together convincingly into a *universitas*. The great institutions that had maintained the peace, unity, and power of Western Christendom seemed to have lost their contact with reality. The peace was frequently broken, the power proved illusory, and the unity was gone. In the ensuing period of growing insecurity and unrest, the European

[39] Bryce, pp. 225ff., 249ff.

[40] See also Carlyle and Carlyle, Vol. IV, Part II. Ernest F. Henderson, *Select Historical Documents of the Middle Ages*, London, 1925, pp. 365-410 for documents relating to the war of the investiture.

[41] Thompson, p. 249.

[42] *ibid.*, p. 158.

[43] Hutchins, p. 11, quoting from the Commentary on the Sentences.

peoples narrowed their horizons, withdrew into the safer circle of their special national and economic interests, or looked toward the local prince for power and protection. The age of nationalism was at hand, and a new international order was preparing itself as Western Europe became transformed into a plurality of national states.

C. The Reality of the Western European Community in the Middle Ages

A. THE INFLUENCE OF THE CATHOLIC CHURCH ON INTERNATIONAL GOVERNMENT AND INTERNATIONAL RELATIONS

1. *The Papacy.* The union of the Christian commonwealth of Western Europe, which has so impressed later generations of unity-seeking Europeans, originated in the shared conviction that there was one God-given truth that could be ascertained, and that man was capable, therefore, of infinite moral progress. This conviction stimulated certain unity-forming processes in the fields of religion, government, and law, which, in turn, yielded certain definite community-serving institutions. Among these institutions none was more important, between the tenth and the fourteenth centuries, than the Catholic Church.

Western Europe was much harassed in the ninth century. Raids by Norsemen, Saracens, Hungarians, and Slavs threatened all frontiers, and rivalries among the descendants of Charlemagne had brought anarchy and warfare to vast sections of the land. The papacy was so deeply involved in Roman party strife that it was incapable of exercising any leadership, while the local kings were powerless beyond the boundaries of their petty domains. At this critical moment in the affairs of Western Christendom, when the common people were frightened and helpless, a movement toward moral regeneration was launched in southern France by a group of churchmen and laymen, backed by public opinion. The movement was directed at a reform of monasticism, for it was generally believed that the establishment of law and order in the Carolingian Empire had to be predicated upon the restoration of moral strength and discipline in the monastic orders. The center of the movement was the newly founded monastery of Cluny,[44] which was ideally situated for this purpose in the very center of Western Europe, in that "middle kingdom" of Burgundy, on the edge between Germany and France, easily accessible to pilgrim routes

[44] Founded in 910 by William of Aquitaine. See Henderson, p. 329 for the foundation document.

and commercial highways that led across the Alpine passes to Italy.

The new foundation was immediately successful. Cluniac monks were requested by multifarious communities, both ecclesiastical and secular, to establish other houses, or to reform old ones, and Cluniac principles thus radiated from Burgundy, Aquitaine, and Brabant to greater Germany, Holland, Poland, Spain, south Italy, England, and western Switzerland, until the chief house ruled about two thousand separate priories.[45] Under the terms of its charter the Cluniac organization was immune from any ecclesiastical or secular jurisdiction except that of the papacy; was centrally directed by the arch abbot of Cluny whose powers included the right to choose his successor; and was bound together by one set of uniform rules, as well as by the periodical meetings of the various Abbey heads. Cluny thus came to constitute an international brotherhood which has been termed the most effective international organization of its time.[46] Under the leadership of remarkably astute abbots, it not only reached its primary objective in the area of moral reform, but was recognized generally as the chief support of the public peace, the most effective agency for the rallying of public opinion against feudal violence, a well-equipped bureau of information for the dissemination of Christian ideas, and a smoothly operating political machine that was to be ultimately responsible for the establishment of papal supremacy.[47] For the first great pope, Gregory VII, who has often been called the greatest of all popes, was himself a Cluniac.[48] And, while the exact connection between Cluniac principles and Gregorian reforms is a matter of dispute,[49] there is no doubt

[45] Thompson, p. 80.

[46] David Jayne Hill, *A History of Diplomacy in the International Development of Europe*, 2 vols., London, 1921, Vol. I, p. 203. But see L. M. Smith, *Cluny in the Eleventh and Twelfth Centuries*, London, 1930, pp. 114-120, to the effect that Abbot Hugh was unsuccessful in his attempt to consolidate the Cluniac power in France, Germany, Italy, Spain, England, and Jerusalem.

[47] August C. Krey, "The International State of the Middle Ages: Some Reasons for its Failure," *American Historical Review*, Vol. xxviii, no. 1 (October, 1922), p. 3.

[48] Gregory VII (Hildebrand) himself, though probably not a monk of Cluny, had been a monk of a Cluniac monastery in Rome.

[49] See Thompson, p. 107, to the effect that "The century of Gregory VII might with much better reason be called the age of Cluny. For it was only because he was the greatest of the Cluniacs that Gregory became the greatest of the popes." *ibid.*, p. 87, to the effect that it was the Italian national party which saw political advantages in the Cluny reform and began to agitate against lay investiture as a means of emancipating Italy from Germany, and that Cluny began, there and then, to spearhead the movement against the German monarchy. But see Smith for the view that the influence of Cluny upon the evolution of papal strength and prestige was indirect, since there is no evidence of any close connection between the Cluniacs and the Gregorian reforms.

that the latter were strongly influenced by the former, and that Cluny was vitally interested in freeing the church from all secular controls.[50]

What Cluny was in 910, the papacy was two centuries later.[51] Under Innocent III the church had become an international state. It had the power to set large armies in motion, to create and destroy coalitions, to control the mighty and the meek, to raise funds by direct taxation, and to bring offenders to justice. It controlled education, propaganda, social welfare, and the courts, and it wielded the awesome power of eternal life and death.[52] However, when one inquires into the circumstances in which these great prerogatives were exercised, one finds that the Cluniac spirit was no persistent influence, since the church was really more interested in its own secular supremacy than in the moral salvation of its vast constituency.[53]

It was this overriding interest that moved Innocent to reduce a multitude of kings and princes to complete subservience.[54] He laid an interdict upon France and withheld all rites of the church from the lands that were subject to France, until King Philip Augustus agreed to take back a Danish wife whom, in the pope's opinion, he had repudiated unjustly. He gave the empire to Otto of Brunswick and forced him to renounce his chief imperial claims in Italy (1201). A few years later (1211) he deposed Otto for perjury and placed Frederick II of Hohenstauffen upon the imperial throne. And by sentence of interdict, excommunication, and deposition he forced King John of England to surrender his crown in order to receive it as a vassal of the pope. In none of these dealings did Innocent show much respect for established secular rights. He felt free, for example, to ignore the privileges of the German electorate and to cancel the charter of liberties that the English barons had won from their king.

Thus, within the church-state as it existed until around 1300, the pope was the ultimate source of power. And this power had been secured and was maintained by the wisdom and statesmanship of the individual popes. For most of the holders of this great office were not

---

[50] Cluny's exemption from local authorities made a strong papacy essential to its undisturbed existence. But in the conflict between papacy and empire, Cluny tried to preserve a cautious neutrality. See *The Cambridge Medieval History*, Vol. v, p. 658.

[51] Krey, p. 5.   [52] *ibid.*, p. 7. Davis, in Marvin, ed., p. 56.

[53] See also Hill, Vol. I, p. 319 for Innocent's view of the papal power as comparable to the greater of the two luminaries, which presides over the day, while the royal authority is comparable to the lesser, which illuminates the night.

[54] But see John Eppstein, *The Catholic Tradition of the Law of Nations*, Washington, 1935, pp. 189, 197ff. for the view that Innocent, as all other popes, was interested above all in peace and in the exercise of his supreme right to settle disputes.

only strongly imbued with a sense of mission and confident of their cause, but also highly trained in theology, philosophy, law, and diplomacy. As efficient politicians, they knew how to accumulate the material power that was necessary for the conduct of their policies. Furthermore, the popes established themselves as the recognized temporal rulers of valuable territories, received money and other tributes from numerous sources, and extended their patronage steadily over hundreds of wealthy churches and monasteries.

In establishing this power, the papacy had learned from the Cluniac organization that an adequate promotion of its cause would depend on an effective information and intelligence service. So we find Gregory VII showering all of Germany and Italy and parts of France with pamphlet literature through the intermediary of monks, travelling priests, pilgrims, and even itinerant merchants.[55] In close connection with these services, the papacy maintained elaborate records for the use of its archivists, lawyers, and diplomats. This well-equipped treasury of legal chicanery[56] could provide its legates with all the necessary arguments when they were sent on trouble-shooting missions. Moreover, the latter constituted such an important liaison service between the papal office and the Christian constituency that they were closely supervised. In fact, when the occasion warranted a more direct and incisive approach, the popes were even ready to do their own field work. For instance, during his bitter contest with the emperor, Leo IX (1049-1054) travelled personally from country to country, checking upon the bishops, preaching to the people in their own languages, presiding over the synods, proclaiming everywhere the teachings of Cluny, and asserting vigorously the preeminence of the church.[57]

The organization of the church as Christendom's supreme government was streamlined in the eleventh century, when the ancient right of electing the Bishop of Rome was taken from the people and clergy of Rome and transferred to the college of cardinals with the legal proviso that the cardinals were to act as representatives of the people, and when the sovereignty of the papacy was extended to include the oecumenical councils. In contrast, the early synods of the fourth century[58] had been creatures of the imperial power; for it then had been the emperor who decided who should be summoned and what topics were to

---

[55] Thompson, p. 256.   [56] Stubbs, p. 248.   [57] Thompson, pp. 98ff.

[58] Councils were held from the second half of the second century A.D. onward, but it is not clear whether they were of apostolic origin or the inevitable outcome of the need of the leaders of the churches to take counsel together. They were modelled, perhaps, on secular provincial assemblies. See *Encyclopaedia Britannica,* "Councils."

be discussed. In fact, in that period synods were used as the chief instruments for the imperial supervision of the church. Their functions changed drastically, however, after the success of the Cluniac reform established the church's power and prestige. The rights which the pope as bishop of the Roman Church had exercised over its synods, were extended, from 1059 onward, over the oecumenical councils. Indeed, the papal control in this area of politics was soon much broader and stricter than the imperial control had ever been in the earlier centuries.

Under the guidance of strong popes such as Innocent III, the synodical jurisdiction was reduced to the ratification of papal policies, while the resolutions of the assembly were formulated as papal edicts, and it was in pursuance of this relationship that the Lateran Council of 1215 ratified the following papal acts: Raymond of Toulouse was disinherited and the conquests made at his expense by the crusaders were confirmed; Frederick II was acknowledged as the lawful emperor; the barons of England were excommunicated for denying the pope's right to cancel the Magna Charta; a new crusade for the recovery of the Holy Land was proclaimed, and a suspension of all wars in the West for the ensuing years was agreed upon in order to secure the success of this crusade.[59] Somewhat later, however, in the fourteenth century, when a power vacuum resulted from the rivalry of several popes for sole authority, and when the great schism of 1378 showed a divided church, the idea gained wide currency that supreme sovereignty resided not in any pope, but in the oecumenical council as the representative body of the entire Christian community.[60] And this so-called conciliar theory expressed itself in the proceedings of a meeting at Constance (1414), when the council disposed of all three rival popes and proceeded to elect a new one (1417). But the influence of this idea was arrested in the later fifteenth century when the papacy recovered some of the ground it had lost.

2. *The Canon Law and its Relation to a Law of Nations: The Problem of Peace.* The records of medieval history establish the pope as Western Europe's most trusted executive. He, the hierarchy of persons under him, and the idea of his personal stewardship most convincingly symbolized the cause of Western Christendom in the public opinion. In the long range perspective of history, on the other hand, this system of

[59] Davis, *loc.cit.*

[60] Amleto G. Cicognani, *Canon Law*, 2nd rev. ed., Philadelphia, 1935, p. 51, refers to the councils as a medieval League of Nations.

symbols pales when contrasted with the body of legal rules and forms that slowly and undramatically—indeed almost imperceptibly—evolved as receptacles of the Christian faith. These institutions of the canon law, which translated the Christian images into everyday reality and conveyed the reality of the Christian community not only beyond the Middle Ages, but also beyond the original geographical limits within which it had been developed, had arisen from rich and varied sources.

The canon law consists of the Holy Scriptures and the Apostolic tradition; the statements of the fathers of the church, notably St. Augustine; papal and conciliar decrees;[61] and those constitutions of the Christian emperors that determined the temporal position of the church. In this body of law the Roman law occupied a special place, since, when the church began its legislative history, it was generally regarded as the common law of mankind. Practical considerations prompted the church to adopt already existing legal axioms as long as they were consonant with Christian ethics.[62] The same reasoning moved the Christian lawmakers to deal respectfully with accepted local customs. As a matter of fact, no attempt was ever made, least of all during the early centuries, to draw up a uniform system of legislation for the whole of the ecclesiastical community, so that the separate churches, such as those of Africa or Rome, were left free to govern themselves in accordance with their own traditions or improvisations.

As time went on, however, it was the Roman collection of canons as it existed when Pope Hadrian submitted it to Charlemagne at the Council of Aix-La-Chapelle in 802 which became the code of canon law for almost the whole of Western Christendom.[63] In the ninth century this collection was enriched by several famous forgeries, and throughout the early period the popes were left free to elaborate and interpret the numerous rules which had gradually merged to form one great legal context, by using their right to give "dispensation" and "privilege" when they felt that an injustice would result in an individual case from the literal application of existing norms.

The trend toward centralizing the canon law, which began with the alliance between the Carolingians and the papacy, was continued with

---

[61] The history of the canon law passed through the same stages as that of the church. During the conciliar phase the canons are the work of the councils, and during the papal phase the canons are for the most part the product of the legislative power gradually acquired by the popes. However, much of the ancient canon law constitutes a collection of canons from local councils or individual bishops. "Roman Law and Canon Law in the Middle Ages," in *The Cambridge Medieval History*, Vol. v, p. 706.

[62] Cicognani, p. 47.

[63] *The Cambridge Medieval History*, Vol. v, p. 709.

the result that there appeared, during the period from the end of the ninth to the middle of the twelfth century, about forty systematic collections of varying value and circulation. However, just when the canon law had reached the stage of completion and perfection, the church began to decline as an international state.[64]

Up to the period of this decline the jurisdiction of the canon law had been practically boundless. As the sum of the laws framed by the ecclesiastical bodies for their own regulation, it had concerned itself with the constitution of the church, and with the relations between the church and all other bodies, whether religious or civil. Laity and clergymen, nations and cities, kings and peasants were subject to its jurisdiction, and its provisions applied to all matters that could be related to the salvation or damnation of the soul, whether these involved heresy, sacrilege, and oaths; birth, marriage, death and burial; or wills, contracts, and conveyances of property.

All of these legal facts and transactions were liable to have effects beyond the physical confines of the Christian community, and they did, indeed, have such effects—especially after the twelfth century, when the revival of trade began to lead to more intense international relations. For the canon law of contract,[65] which frowned upon formalities and emphasized the observance of good faith, exerted a considerable influence on the law merchant, even though St. Thomas Aquinas had stated that the practice of usury surely implied the prospect of damnation, and that commerce in general should be viewed as a danger to the soul.[66] Furthermore, although nothing very precise or definite can be said about the influence of church law upon maritime law, it is an established fact that the church took a determined stand against the so-called "right of wreck," under the terms of which the goods of shipwrecked merchants and mariners were forfeited and their persons often sold into slavery. The church's stand against this legal policy was embodied in a decree of the Lateran Council of 1179.[67] Related maritime matters were taken up in a thirteenth century Bull, which provided

[64] See Gabriel Le Bras, "Canon Law," in Crump and Jacob, p. 356.

[65] See Le Bras, pp. 352-357 for the evolution of the canonist theories of contract and obligation.

[66] Bewes, *The Romance of the Law Merchant*, London, 1923, p. 9. W. F. Oakeshott, *Commerce and Society, a short history of trade and its effects on civilization,* Oxford, 1936, pp. 38ff., 72ff.

[67] Such secular medieval collections of maritime customs as the rules of Oleron stated the same or similar principles. See also Sir Travers Twiss, *The Black Book of the Admiralty*, as quoted by R. F. Wright, *Medieval Internationalism, the Contribution of the Medieval Church to International Law and Peace*, London, 1930, p. 207.

for the excommunication and anathematization of pirates, corsairs, and maritime freebooters, and of all those who seize the goods of ship-wrecked people, impose new tolls without the pope's license, or supply the Saracens and Turks with arms and aid.[68]

The Catholic legal system of shared values, which helped to trans-form Western Europe into one law culture, was administered uniformly by supranational ecclesiastical tribunals, functioning in each diocese but closely fitted together as one great legal pyramid over which the pope towered as the ultimate decision making power. The procedural rules[69] that were formulated in these courts have influenced all of the later secular courts in Europe. The entire legal structure has evoked the admiration of lawyers everywhere as a wonderful system in which the whole of Western Europe was subject to the jurisdiction of one tribunal of last resort, to which appeals were encouraged by all manner of means[70]—the Roman curia.

In their enforcement of the law that had thus been evolved in the ecclesiastical realm, the authorities could count on a general public readiness to comply with directives emanating from God's appointed agencies. For the same values that had originally inspired the substan-tive legal norms conditioned people to regard the procedural devices of the church as mandatory. This explains why the oath was recognized as the chief sanction for the performance of contracts, and why people dreaded the possibility of being either expelled from the community of the faithful through a decree of excommunication or excluded from the Kingdom of Heaven through death without proper sacrament. If men were found guilty of violating a canonized obligation, they were, on the whole, ready to assume the burden of their punishment. The rich would part with their possessions, and kings would do penance under circumstances that strike us today as ignominious. Nevertheless, the church was too circumspect to rely exclusively upon its own meth-ods of law enforcement. The secular princes, therefore, were enjoined to guarantee the reign of law and justice in their lands, and their sub-jects were admonished to obey all of those secular powers that the church supported or condoned.

In the general frame of legal reference that enclosed the Western world in the Middle Ages, the ecclesiastical institutions came to occupy

[68] See Wright, p. 32.

[69] The canon law courts were modelled closely on the courts of ancient Rome. Cesare Foligno, "The Transmission of the Legacy" in Bailey, ed., p. 13. However, the church also borrowed procedural elements from the Germanic systems of law.

[70] Pollock and Maitland, Vol. I, p. 114.

a preferred position. Not only was it assumed that the agencies of the church had a more obvious connection with the dictates of the divine lawmaker than justice-dispensing lords of the manor, but multifarious experiences with litigation had made it clear to the average man that the canon law courts were more inclined to seek equity and promote justice than their secular competitors. Such empirical conclusions were fully supported, furthermore, by the logic of the Christian system, which required the canon law to attach the same importance to the individual that was expressed so persuasively in Christian theology. Any ecclesiastical judge who wanted to comply with this moral and legal directive in an actual case would inquire into the state of mind of the person who was before him. He would be concerned with the intention that motivated a questionable action, check on the presence or absence of good faith in any given dealing, and try to find out whether a contract could really be performed before insisting on its execution.

The church showed its concern for the individual also by vindicating the rights of women and by mitigating many of the hardships attending the condition of slavery. As a matter of fact, there is reason to believe that it was in the area of human servitude that the ecclesiastical authorities reached a particularly high degree of consistency in coordinating Christian ethics and Christian law. Papal and conciliar decrees prohibiting the mistreatment of slaves and the enslavement and sale of human beings, encouraging manumission, and insisting on the duty of ransoming captives, multiplied between the fourth and the fourteenth centuries. And although these regulations were formulated for the express purpose of protecting fellow Christians who were, or might be, captured and enslaved by the enemies of Christendom, they were presently to acquire great significance as statements of the fundamental Christian position on issues affecting the general human right to liberty when the later Christian thinkers and reformers challenged the enslavement of the pagan natives of the New World and propagated instead the Christian image of the brotherhood of man.[71]

By way of summary it may be said, therefore, that the ecclesiastical institutions inspired the public with confidence for many centuries and were effective, on the whole, both in maintaining the common faith and in cultivating the shared values around which Western Europe had rallied. The public trust was weakened, however, and the effectiveness of the religious authorities impaired when men began to question the

[71] See Eppstein, ch. xv and documents on "The Rights of Backward Races."

fundamental values and when religious institutions, bent on their own survival, lost contact with the minds of their constituents. The resultant discord between image and reality was already clearly evident in the pontificate of Boniface VIII (1294-1303), whom Dante called the "Prince of the new Pharisees" (Inferno, XXVII, 85). This pope, consumed by secular ambitions at a time when the very foundations of the papal throne were cracking, could exclaim: "Am I not the Sovereign Pontiff? Is not this the throne of St. Peter? Am I not able to safeguard the throne of the Empire? It is I, it is I, who am Emperor."[72] His subsequent arrest at the instigation of the king of France and various Italian princes was the prelude to the long captivity of the papacy (1305-1378), during which Christ's vicar on earth was constrained to recognize that new forces and new institutions had made an effective bid for the reorganization of Western Europe. Not only did emboldened monarchs extend their jurisdiction, but local groups of citizens took issue with the authority of both kings and priests and began to stake out new claims to political representation in such assemblies as the English Model Parliament of 1295 and the French Estates General of 1302.

The church had not ignored the early symptoms of the rise of nations and national monarchs. Indeed, in its great contest with the Roman emperor the Holy See had often done its best to conjure up the separatist interests most likely to undermine the authorities of its rivals. Nevertheless, up to the fourteenth century the church could claim, with a good deal of justification, that its religious, legal, and political institutions were supplying the sheltering roof for all of Western Europe's separate governments. For, in the early centuries of religious fervor or acquiescence, the papacy was able to exert itself forcefully as Western Europe's supreme legislative, executive, and judicial organ, and the canon law provided an all-European system of norms, which bound each monarch both personally and in his relations with other monarchs, just as it bound all Christians both personally and in their relations with each other. In the later centuries, when the pope's moral superiority began to wane, he could fall back upon his power as a temporal prince. Moreover, since he was usually better qualified and equipped than other princes to make the utmost use of his material power, he was able to play the game of politics successfully enough to retain his transnational authority.

But in this latter phase of his relations with the other European powers, the uses of the canon law as a law regulating relations between

[72] Hill, Vol. I, p. 353.

political sovereigns contracted noticeably. The law of treaties provides an illustration. The church had been accustomed to deal with treaties as it dealt with contracts: they were regarded as personal engagements between sovereigns whose oaths attested to the validity and guaranteed the performance of any agreement. As in the case of contracts, so here, too, performance was excused only if the obligation was found to be improper or impossible of execution—or if the pope for some reason chose to exercise his right of granting a dispensation from the oath. The latter type of papal interference soon became objectionable, however, to the princes, and they therefore invented a treaty stipulation under the terms of which they could obligate themselves, under oath, never to apply for any pontifical dispensation.[73]

The international character of the canon law, which had been apparent in the law's double function as a general European system of public and private law applicable with equal force to each separate region and to each individual and as a set of norms guiding the relations between the separate Christian governments, derived, in the last analysis, from the recognition that the individual Christian, regardless of his residence or status, was the chief subject of the law's concern. As long, then, as the papacy could treat monarchs as individual Christians, the canon law could influence the relations between the kingdoms represented by the monarchs. But when the Christian kings became conscious of the unchristian sources of their own power, the papacy was left to fight its political battles without the aid and comfort of objective norms, and the canon law lost its character as a regulatory force in the relations between governments.

This may be termed the opening phase of modern Western Europe's international relations. In that transition period, when cosmopolitanism in politics had first been weakened by the impact of nationalism, there were no generally proven and accepted international institutions to offset or mitigate the steady growth of national ambitions. The long supremacy of effective ecclesiastical organs of international government had either retarded or completely prevented the evolution of purely secular peace-supporting agencies. It is true that the canonist writers had never tired of presenting lengthy expositions of "that law of nations which nearly all the nations use."[74] However, not only did such references always remain inseparably connected with the canon

---

[73] The first such bargain was struck in 1477, between Louis XI of France and Charles the Bold of Burgundy. Wright, p. 110. Arthur Nussbaum, *A Concise History of the Law of Nations*, New York, 1947, p. 24.

[74] See Cicognani, p. 35.

law proper, but they also remained, in every sense of the word, *legal*. And since these particular legal references were the outgrowth of a religious view of the world that distinguished sharply between good and evil, they issued from the assumption that somebody had to be wrong if somebody else was acknowledged to be right.

As long as right and wrong, or guilt and innocence, were associated with the individual representatives of states, international conflicts could perhaps be solved and the European peace maintained by taking an absolutist stand. But after the distinction between good and evil had been transferred from the plane of individual relations between monarchs to that of relations between nations, disputes proved to be not easily susceptible to settlement by the mere application of legal principles and apportionment of guilt. And here the close student of the history of international affairs cannot but discover that the medieval Christian authorities, who had been in charge of elaborating adequate institutions for the preservation of peace in the community of Western Europe, failed to tap the most profound source of Christian thought concerning the relations between peoples. For by and large they ignored, or realized obliquely only, the fact that the principles of charity and conciliation which pervade the New Testament and some of the early Christian writings might have been made to yield a more effective and enduring system of international pacification than the principles of law and righteousness upon which the international institutions of the church had been eventually built.

The great potential strength that inhered in this neglected set of concepts was demonstrated only sporadically, and then only by a few saintly and intellectually superior Christian leaders whose moral courage to transcend officially established tenets had brought them to the personal awareness that efforts to understand and conciliate different sorts of men and their conflicting views were more likely to establish peace than attempts to bend an existing human relationship or a troublesome agreement into conformity with a set of absolute standards of justice.

The spell that Bernard of Clairvaux (1090-1153) exercised over Europe as a peacemaker did not derive from his fanatical adherence to the official cause of Christendom. He was asked to mediate between disunited Italian bishops, to pacify the Lombard cities, to compose the differences that divided the Milanese, and to advise both the pope and the emperor because it was generally known that he could penetrate to the heart of an issue and that he was interested in serving the cause of peace rather than the cause of power. A similar position of trust was held by the Grand Master of the Teutonic Order, Hermann von Salza, whose capacity to conciliate people became proverbial, and by St. Louis of France, the canonized arbitrator of the Middle Ages about whom his chronicler, Sire de Joinville, writes that he was always ready to show, by his own example, that charity must override the laws of strict justice if concord between people is to prevail. To the dismay of his advisers, Louis held to the view that this principle of Christianity was also politically the wisest directive. In his opinion, therefore, a ruler should feel free to cede territory even though he had a just claim to it, and reconcile feuding foreign kings, even though their mutual bloodletting would secure his own dominion, if he felt that such actions would promote the general good will.[75] These isolated individual affirmations of the ethics of conciliation as the guiding principle in the organization of peace were geographically limited, in that they were addressed only to relations within the Christian world. In the sixteenth century, however, the theme was to be taken up in an extended frame of reference, when several influential Christian leaders, notably Bartolomé de Las Casas, reviewed the sordid record of Spain's dealings with the native population in the new world of America in the light of the newly discovered but ancient Christian principle of charity and understanding.

During the Middle Ages the official line of Christian politics continued to stress only man's primary obligation to abide by the principles of law and morality as fixed by the recognized ecclesiastical authorities of the day. One looks in vain for any explicit statement to the effect that it is the duty of a Christian to seek a pacific settlement of outstanding issues. This does not mean that the church did not favor the peaceful settlement of disputes. Neither does it mean that issues were not, in fact, often settled peacefully. But it does mean that the principle of composing disputes peaceably was not regarded as a substantive principle of ethics but only as a procedural device, which the authorities could—but need not—use in implementing their moral and legal certainties. Such an approach to the problem was quite logical in the context of the Christian religion, as it had become set in the Middle Ages. For, if a peacemaker starts with the major premise that the church knows what is right and wrong, and that he is the delegate of the church, he must begin by judging, not by conciliating, the parties.

[75] Cf. Eppstein, p. 161; James J. Walsh, *The Thirteenth, Greatest of Centuries*, New York, 1929, pp. 289-299.

As one follows the evolution of this Western attitude toward the adjustment of disputes it must be borne in mind also that the supreme right to compose differences between peoples was exercised at that time by the individual who happened to occupy the papal throne. This right was tied up inextricably with the material interests of that great prince,[76] even though all his interventions were carefully explained as papal translations of the moral law.[77] The same was true of so-called papal arbitrations, which are officially distinguished from the "pacific interventions" on the ground that they are effected at the request of the disputants, or offered spontaneously by the pontiff.[78] Both forms of conciliation bear witness to Innocent III's claim that the pope is the sovereign mediator upon earth,[79] and both support the conclusion that the pacific settlement of disputes was understood only as a corollary of the duty of Christian princes to respect the right of the Holy See to mediate, arbitrate, and impose truces.[80]

As the European princes became less docile, papal interventions decreased in number, and the nature of the obligation to submit disputes to peaceful forms of settlement began to be discussed from other angles. The following procedure was suggested, for example, by John Lupus (1450-1496): "If he on whom one wishes to declare war is disposed to conform to the right as it may be defined by a decision either of arbitrators or of learned men, one must not, even if one has justice on one's side, go to war; for war can only be justified by necessity."[81] Such was the direction that many European scholars and statesmen followed from the sixteenth century onward, when they began to develop a law of nations and system of diplomacy that would serve the cause of world peace.[82] Both sets of institutions, however, that of the law of nations and that of the techniques of diplomacy, as they have since been understood and practiced in the Western European culture realm, bear to this day the marks of medieval Europe's predilection for moral absolutes and legal phrases.

[76] Eppstein, p. 188, to the effect that power is the keynote of papal interventions regarding peace in the first great period of the church's rule in Europe, from the age of Hildebrand to the fourteenth century.

[77] See *ibid.*, pp. 463ff., Appendix I for a list of "pacific interventions."

[78] See the list of arbitrations before 1500 in Eppstein, pp. 464-468; also Wright, p. 85.

[79] Eppstein, p. 464.

[80] Cf. *ibid.*, p. 162.

[81] Quoted in *ibid.*, p. 163.

[82] See James Brown Scott, *The Spanish Origin of International Law*, Oxford, 1934, on the work of Francisco de Vitoria and Francisco Suarez.

B. THE CHRISTIAN COMMUNITY OF WESTERN EUROPE
AND THE PROBLEM OF WAR

1. *The Distinction between Private and Public War.* The Christian attitude toward peace and conciliation in the relations between governments was no doubt influenced by the types of warfare with which it had to take issue. The early pacifism and nonresistance to violence which Christians displayed rather consistently up to the fourth century were modified after Christianity became the official religion of the Roman Empire. The necessity to sustain the commonwealth against the pressures of barbarians and other potential enemies, and the need, in later centuries, to come to terms with institutionalized fighting as it existed among the Germanic tribes, prompted Christian theorists and statesmen to revise the traditional approach to war.

The new official theory dealt with war in the context of the established legal system by distinguishing just wars from unjust wars. War was regarded as an act of vindictive justice when it was undertaken in the proper circumstances and by the proper authorities. As such it was to be waged not for conquest but only for defence, the restoration of peace, the punishment of evil doers, the avenging of unredeemed injuries, and the prevention of injustice; and in all these instances it was to be undertaken only if no adequate peaceful means for accomplishing these ends could be found.[83]

The church took notice of the fact that wars were fought in either of two contexts: there was, first, the variety called "private" warfare, which had developed within the Western European community between separate Christian rulers as an incident to the feudal system, and there were, second, "public" wars, which ranged the Western community against foreign enemies. Subject to the approval of the papacy as Christendom's court of last resort, public wars were usually recognized as "just" wars, whereas private wars were relegated to the category of "unjust" wars. However, these lines of distinction tended to become blurred, since the church was not only the international arbiter of Western Europe's internal and external affairs, but also a separate political power which had to defend its claim to absolute superiority against foes within as well as outside of Western Europe. If its own interests required it, the papacy was not restrained by any theory from instigating or supporting "just" wars against such Christian enemies as

[83] See Le Bras, p. 342; Quincy Wright, Vol. I, p. 158.

Byzantium, the Roman emperor, recalcitrant princes, and heretical sects.

While private warfare was condemned in ordinary circumstances as a crime against the social order, the ecclesiastical and secular authorities were rather lenient in their execution of this directive. For they were fully aware of the fact that this type of feuding was an ancient institution which public opinion accepted variously as a pleasurable pastime, a social duty, or an approved way of adjusting disputes.[84] It was only when the belligerent spirit broke all bonds of law, caused widespread insecurity, threatened church property, weakened the defensive and offensive strength of Western Christendom, or revealed the inconsistency between Christian theory and Christian practice in too glaring a light, that the church intervened with force.

The efforts of the ecclesiastical authorities to mitigate the incidence of fighting led to two internationally significant institutions—the Truce of God and the Peace of God. It should be said at the outset that there is nothing very original about these Christian arrangements, for various literate as well as nonliterate peoples had realized centuries earlier that it was prudent to secure a respite from belligerency by arranging a limited peace for special occasions, or by exempting certain places and certain people from the hazards of warfare. Also, long before the church initiated its policy of pacification in medieval Europe, the Germans seem to have accepted the principle that it was the duty of the king to maintain the public peace.[85] In the early Middle Ages, however, the royal authority had collapsed in France, with the result that private warfare had become a scourge; and it was here in southern France— where the Cluniac movement had released strong forces of moral regeneration—that the first Truce of God was declared in the eleventh century. The original provision of this enactment, that all fighting was to cease between Saturday and Monday, was amplified by later amendments which extended the truce from Thursday to Monday, to all holidays, and sometimes over several months.[86] The truce was supported by the enactment of the Peace of God, under the terms of which the following were declared to be immune from all warfare: churches, other ecclesiastical buildings, orchards and highways; cattle, seeds, and

---

[84] See Stubbs, pp. 248-253, to the effect that medieval wars were, as a rule, wars of right, and that they were viewed as ordeals to which men resorted when all inferior tribunals had failed to satisfy the litigants.

[85] Thompson, p. 315.

[86] Krey, p. 4, indicates that only one quarter of the year was left for the unabated practice of feudal warfare. Cicognani, p. 160, writes that one half of the year was so exempted.

farm implements; women, clerics, peasants, and merchants. Both institutions were effectively propagated by the Cluniac monks and by many interested parties (such as the groups of declared noncombatants), and as a result of such support, the Peace of God was diffused over many European regions, enacted by universal councils, and proclaimed by the pope as general law.

The place of these arrangements in the history of Western Europe's political organization cannot be appreciated properly unless it is remembered that special peaces of this kind were sponsored also by secular authorities. A German emperor such as Henry III was so sensitive of his own royal prerogative, as against the prerogatives of the church, that he insisted on declaring and supporting his special *Landfrieden* in the various imperial regions;[87] and Frederick Barbarossa went even further by proclaiming one general land peace in place of the temporal enactments of former rulers,[88] thus setting a precedent that was to be followed regularly by his successors. When the latter was ineffectual in enforcing these measures for the maintenance of the peace, some of the stronger local rulers took it upon themselves, separately and collectively, to restore a kind of order by means of local *Landfrieden*, sworn usually for a period of years.[89] Furthermore, since cities and communities of merchants often declared their own particular "peace" also, and since all of these truces and peaces had the same general objective, medieval Western Europe was gradually being induced to develop a common approach to the general problem of peace.

The complicated process of Europeanizing the idea of an instituted peace, which was set in motion under these various auspices, was supervised in the last resort by the church, which could muster more power and persuasion when projecting the image of the peace than any of the separate local sponsors. The paramountcy of the church in this situation was due also to the fact that Europe's secular society did not possess an adequate machinery for the enforcement of its pacific institutions, whereas the church had succeeded in sublimating and internationalizing the ancient oath of fealty as the chief sanction for their due observance. Not only were princes and nobles required to swear that they would uphold the Peace of God in the knowledge that noncompliance was punishable by excommunication, but each candidate

[87] Thompson, pp. 315-317.

[88] See Henderson, pp. 208-211 on the Truce of God and pp. 211-215 on Barbarossa's *Landfrieden*. Also William Seagle, *The Quest for Law*, New York, 1941, pp. 78ff.

[89] See *The Cambridge Medieval History*, Vol. IV, p. 125 for some illustrations.

for knighthood was asked in his initiation ceremonies to make the same commitment. This early connection between chivalry and the Peace of God had an internationally significant corollary, inasmuch as it helped to foster the evolution and diffusion of a special ethic of behavior, the code of chivalry, which bound knights throughout Christendom into something like an international brotherhood. And since the laws and ideas that guided the conduct of knights in Western Europe were not anchored solely in religious faith, but derived from sources, and served purposes, that lay beyond Christianity,[90] they retained a great unifying force even in the thirteenth and fourteenth centuries, when religious fervor was gradually ceasing to support Europe's institutions.

The idea that one man, whether pope or emperor, could institute the general peace began to lose its promise as a principle of Western European unity toward the end of the twelfth century. But the notion that a public peace should—and could—be legislated for the entire continent retained its validity in subsequent centuries, after the pope had forfeited many of his original political privileges, after the emperor had lost all semblance of power as the secular head of the Roman Empire of the German Nation, and after both the larger Western commonwealth and the narrower German realm had been transformed into aggregates of separate national sovereignties. For in the last decade of the fifteenth century, when continental Western Europe was in great political turmoil and every aspect of human life was changing rapidly, the German Federal Diet proclaimed the Edict of Eternal Pacification, which purported to abolish private warfare for all time (1495). This measure was of limited importance in the actual context of Germany's troubled constitutional history, since it could not be enforced. But it may be regarded as an interesting early precedent for the twentieth century effort of securing peace by "outlawing" war. By means of the Briand-Kellogg Pact of Paris (1928-1929) more than sixty sovereign nations in the modern world proclaimed "that they condemn recourse to war for the solution of international controversies and renounce it as an instrument of national policy in their relations with one another."[91] The solemn international contract did not ensure the peace of the world, as the ensuing decades were to demonstrate; nevertheless, the idea enclosed in this and similar agreements was carried forward into many other constitutions for the better organization of world peace, of which the United Nations Charter is the latest.

[90] See *The Cambridge Medieval History*, Vol. VI, pp. 799ff.
[91] Art. I. See International Law Association, *Briand-Kellogg Pact of Paris*, London, 1934, p. 9.

The influence of the special peace of medieval Europe upon the conduct of international relations in the twentieth century is tenuous and indirect, however, as compared with the effects of that same medieval institution upon the organization of law and order within the several national states. For it was the national state and not the international society of states which first organized itself as the ultimate source of sovereignty when the international authorities of the medieval European commonwealth faded from their jurisdictions. From that time forward local rulers assumed the guardianship of the public peace, and acts of lawless violence within each jurisdiction became punishable as criminal offences against the peace of the particular realm. In brief, the concept of the local peace suggested the fundamental principles of national criminal law.[92]

The localization of the concepts of war and peace, which was implicit in the slow but steady shift of power from the international authorities to the national state, helped to reduce the total incidence of fighting that had disturbed the Western European world. But it effected also an internationally momentous transformation of the very meanings of peace and war. Henceforth, and for a long time to come, it was to be the exclusive privilege of each national sovereign to define the conditions of peace and to decide whether wars were private or public, just or unjust.

2. *The Crusades as an Instrument of Foreign Policy.* When one inquires into the problem of why Western Europeans were, on the whole, satisfied with the new treatment of the problem of belligerency, one finds an answer in the failure of the old system of collective security, for by the thirteenth century most people were disillusioned by the papacy's use of its broad powers to administer the realm of war. It had become clear, in particular, that the pacification of Western Europe was not really an end in itself, but very largely a means to further the cause of the church in its relation with Islam.[93]

The policy of the church toward the non-Christian world, as it emerged in the eleventh century from long considerations of doctrine and interest, issued from the basic view that all non-Christians were enemies if they were not ready to accept the Christian faith, and that the church was there to propagate the right faith and defend Christendom against the enemies of Christ. A spirit of belligerency was there-

[92] Pollock and Maitland, Vol. I, p. 44; Vol. II, pp. 453, 463 for the connection between the King's peace and criminal law in England.
[93] Cf. Eppstein, p. 156.

fore implicit in Western Europe's official attitude toward other culture realms, and this spirit was activated in the Mediterranean area by the military and ideological aggressiveness of Islam.

As Christianity's high command, the papacy had to meet the situation by providing whatever offensive or defensive action it might deem requisite, and the limitation of private warfare in Europe thus became a necessity if the public warfare in behalf of the cross were to be conducted successfully. Conversely, however, it was realized also that a common Christian cause against a declared enemy of all the Christians would deter fraternal bloodshed in Western Europe more effectively than any specially instituted Truce or Peace of God. In other words, the church thought of the crusades as wars to end war among the Christians. And this connection between the two varieties of conflict was emphasized when the same laws of chivalry that were supposed to mitigate the inequities of private warfare were invoked for the purpose of sublimating the fight against the infidel—a just war waged in the name of the Redeemer for the defence of Christendom, the safety of the empire, the liberation of the patrimony of the Crucified, and the freedom of Christian brethren in the Near East. And it should be mentioned, furthermore, that these declared purposes were linked, in the thinking of many ecclesiastical statesmen, with the unadvertised purpose of restoring schismatic Byzantium to the bosom of the church.[94]

All of these were causes and ideas for which the church could elicit rather ready support in all of Western Europe. But the power to determine the legitimacy of an issue and to engage all Christendom in its behalf was used also for the military implementation of papal policies within the Christian world itself, and here the doctrinal issues became rather confused. For it was through the agency of a holy war that heretical sects, such as the Albigensian and the Hussite, were exterminated and the rival Christian empire of Byzantium was overthrown; and it was through the use of all his powers in connection with the crusades that the pontiff sought to control his chief antagonist, the Holy Roman Emperor. For the papal diplomats soon discovered that a monarch could be removed to the Holy Land if he was inconvenient on the European scene, that he could be threatened with the prospect of a crusade if he did not want to comply with the papal terms of a settlement, and that he could be incriminated in the eyes of the public with charges of having been dilatory as a crusader, or of having other-

---

[94] A. A. Vasiliev, *History of the Byzantine Empire 324-1453*, Madison, 1952, pp. 396ff.

wise violated his sacred obligations, if his popularity or his success was threatening the prestige of the Holy Sea. Indeed, Pope Gregory IX was so consumed by hatred and jealousy of Frederick II of Hohenstauffen that he was willing to wreck the crusade that he had proclaimed himself, to excommunicate all who entertained the thought of joining it, and to forfeit the Holy Land, rather than see the emperor victorious.[95]

But the church was not the only interested party imbued with mixed ambitions when it professed to follow the single track of its religious duty. The emperors, too, were motivated variously. For example, no Hohenstauffen thought of a crusade without dreaming, simultaneously, of a world empire. Although Frederick Barbarossa (1123-1190) was a devout Christian and faithful crusader, he was captivated also by the Roman conception of empire as supported by the Roman system of law. And it was the merger of all these images that nourished his hope of reestablishing the great Mediterranean realm as it had existed before Constantine. This vision was passed as a legacy to his descendants. But his grandson, Frederick II, did not even pretend that a crusade was a war of religion.[96] He regarded it purely as an affair of state from which the church should, if at all possible, be excluded. Furthermore, no Roman-German leader of the Christian host, regardless of the degree of his religious fervor, was ever quite able to elude the strong attraction that the Orient exercised upon his imagination. The statement of a twelfth century writer that "God has poured the West into the East, we have forgotten our native soil and become Easterners,"[97] held particularly true of many Christian monarchs. In this respect, all of the imperial followers of Christ were also inheritors of Alexander the Great.

The crusades, then, were inextricably connected with the secular policies and personal ambitions of the various high authorities under whose auspices they were organized. But they retained their character as pure religious wars for the majority of the common folk who composed the crusading armies. It must be remembered that the people of Western Europe lived in an atmosphere of intense religious revivalism between 1096 and 1291. Their thoughts and actions were therefore

[95] Ernst Kantorowicz, *Frederick the Second, 1194-1250*, New York, 1931, pp. 179ff., 556ff., for incidents of this relationship. See also Hill, Vol. I, pp. 370ff., on the crusades as sources of papal revenue, and on the extension of papal jurisdiction in Europe, which resulted from the provision that all crusaders, their families, and their property were automatically in the custody of the church.

[96] See Kantorowicz, p. 191, on this subject.

[97] Fulcher of Chartres, as quoted in *The Cambridge Medieval History*, Vol. V, p. 305.

sustained by an all-pervading spirit of other-worldliness, rather than by an awareness of processes of foreign policy-making and diplomatic intrigue. In their eager search for new paths to Heaven they can have entertained few doubts about the justice of this pilgrims' progress, all the more so as their participation counted for full and complete penance. And yet, here again, one cannot find one simple, general explanation for the several million individual crusading commitments that were made in the course of two centuries.[98] It is hardly likely that all the members of the motley crowds that heeded the call to arms were equally interested in eternal reward. Many thought of a crusade as an emigration that would carry them away from famine or pestilence at home; others followed their instinct for wandering or adventure or their interest in the acquisition of land and wealth; countless "younger sons" had found life poor and dull in a feudal society governed by the strict laws of primogeniture, and they joined the swarm in search of new careers. Then, of course, there were the innumerable bankrupts, fugitives, tramps, and other footloose human beings, for whom the journey seemed to offer the one last chance of life. In short, the Christian cause against the infidel seemed desirable from many points of view.[99]

Whether the crusades were the only, or best, means of attaining the desired objective could not be answered conclusively at the time. Medieval Christian writers disagreed about the function of war in the implementation of a just cause, but the representatives of the church were in accord throughout this period, that for the defence of Christendom in Europe and the advancement of its cause in Asia, war was not only just, but necessary. It seems, indeed, indisputable that Europe was threatened by a Muslim conquest from A.D. 622 onward; and while the crusades did not check the actual growth of Muslim power,

[98] Steven Runciman, *A History of the Crusades*, 3 vols., Cambridge, Eng., 1952-53, Vol. I, p. 336, Appendix II on the numerical strength of the crusaders. See also Hill, Vol. I, p. 271.

[99] Obviously, the crusades are an inexhaustible subject of discussion and controversy, and historians have advanced different theories about their causes, their purposes, and their effects. See, among others, W. B. Stephenson, *The Crusaders in the East*, 1907. A. Ruville, *Die Kreuzzuege*, Bonn, 1920. Runciman, Vol. I, "The First Crusade and the Foundation of Jerusalem"; Vol. II, "The Kingdom of Jerusalem and the Frankish East." Edward Gibbon, *The Decline and Fall of the Roman Empire*, 2 vols., the Modern Library, New York, 1934, Vol. II, ch. LIIIff., and Sir Ernest Barker's essay on the "Crusades" in the *Encyclopaedia Britannica*. Commentators on the Catholic tradition of the law of nations disagree as to whether crusades were defensible on grounds either of ethics or of expediency. See Eppstein, pp. 94ff., for a brief review of different theories and pp. 65-96, on the Augustinian doctrine of war.

they may have helped, during the period from 1096 to 1291, to restrain, blunt, or delay a force that was to be thrust at Eastern Europe eventually in the seventeenth century.[100] With respect to any advancement of the Christian position, however, the crusades may be written down as a failure. They began with the Seljuk Turks planted at Nicaea and ended with the Ottoman Turks entrenched by the Danube. In the thirteenth century Christianity was still strongly represented in Asia Minor, and indeed in Central Asia. From then onward, however, its influence declined, and in the fifteenth century the crescent was victorious over the cross, both in Asia and in Europe.

The more limited, but nevertheless obstinate, Christian ambition to recover the Holy Land was frustrated also at the close of the crusading effort, after having provided an interesting test case for the respective efficacy of war and diplomacy as alternate methods of reaching the coveted end. For the loss of Jerusalem to Saladin in 1187 had been recouped, not by any military victory, but only by the negotiating skills of the excommunicated Emperor Frederick II, whose so-called Sixth crusade,[101] upon which he embarked in 1227, was unique in the annals of all crusades, since it was not only cursed rather than blessed by the pope, but also conducted without a single act of hostility against Islam. The explanation for the astounding success of this paradoxical mission must be sought in the complex personality of the richly gifted Holy Roman Emperor himself. As a life-long student of non-Western, especially Arabic, culture forms, the personal friend of innumerable Muslim savants and potentates, and a successful administrator of the multinational kingdom of Sicily, Frederick was thoroughly familiar with the laws, customs, and languages of his official enemy in Palestine. Relying on the store of knowledge that he had personally acquired, and cultivating direct and friendly relations with the Muslim leaders, the banned emperor succeeded where all other agencies— ecclesiastical and secular—had failed. He freed the city of Jerusalem.[102]

The peace of 1229 is an interesting document not only because it registered gains for Western Europe. It also announced certain political themes and put into practice several formulae of international paci-

[100] Toward the end of the century the Turks besieged Vienna.

[101] While it has become customary to distinguish between first, second, etc., crusades, the crusades were, in actuality, one continuous process. Crusades seem to have been "dignified by numbers when they followed some crushing disaster—the loss of Edessa in 1144, or the fall of Jerusalem in 1187—and were led by kings and emperors. . . ." *Encyclopaedia Britannica*, "Crusades," p. 782.

[102] See Kantorowicz, pp. 186ff., for the circumstances in which the negotiations were conducted. The negotiations and the treaty were denounced by the pope.

fication that were to re-emerge in twentieth century politics, when national and religious upheavals in the Jewish, Christian, and Muslim realms again focussed the attention of the world on that narrow strip of territory long called the Holy Land. Frederick, under the terms of the treaty, received Jerusalem (with the exception of the sacred enclosure upon which stood the Mosque of Umar), Bethlehem, Nazareth, the strip of land running from Jerusalem to the coast, Sidon, Caesarea, Jaffa, Acre, and several other places. However, in the interests of the peace of the region, he agreed to two important limitations of his sovereignty over the area: in order to limit the possibilities of renewed conflict, the kingdom of Jerusalem was not to be militarized even though the newly ceded cities might be fortified; and in order to increase the chances of the peaceful coexistence of the two religious groups, and to give each access to those places that it considered sacred to its own tradition, the treaty permitted the Christians to hold religious services in the Jerusalem area of the Mosque of Umar, and the Muslims to recite their prayers in Bethlehem.[103]

It is interesting to note that similar provisions were elaborated under the auspices of the United Nations in 1948-50, when the status of Jerusalem was put in issue by the creation of the new state of Israel and the resulting conflict between the Jews and Arabs. In implementation of a resolution of the General Assembly that the city was to be distinct from the Arab and Jewish states, as a *corpus separatum* established under a special international regime to be administered by the United Nations, the Trusteeship Council submitted a draft statute which provided, among other things, for the demilitarization and neutrality of Jerusalem, the uninhibited right to worship, free access to the city for all foreign pilgrims without distinction as to nationality and faith, the protection of all holy places and religious sites, and the international settlement of all disputes between different religious groups within the area.[104]

Frederick's peaceful acquisition of the Holy Land is, perhaps, too

[103] See *ibid.*, also Hill, Vol. I, pp. 332ff. The eighteenth century German dramatist, G. E. Lessing, wrote a fable, *Nathan der Weise*, about the problem of religious toleration, and he chose as his stage the Kingdom of Jerusalem, in which Muslims, Jews, and Christians coexisted.

[104] See *Draft Statute for the City of Jerusalem,* T/118 (Jan. 26, 1948) with revisions of March 5, 9, 1948, and *Question of an International Regime for the Jerusalem Area and Protection of the Holy Places,* Special Report of the Trusteeship Council, General Assembly, Supplement No. 9 (A/1286) Annex II "Statute for the City of Jerusalem," approved by the Trusteeship Council at its 81st Meeting held on April 4, 1950. Articles 7, 9, 30, 38.

singular an instance to prove or disprove the case for diplomacy as the more effective of the two procedures available to Western sovereigns wishing to establish rights in the East. Furthermore, the inconclusiveness of the case is apparent when it is remembered that Jerusalem was held for only fifteen years after the terms of settlement had been agreed upon. But a general review of the entire Western record of war and peace in the region in which this episode came to pass, makes it possible to conclude that neither war nor diplomacy, as then practiced by the West, was effective in maintaining what either war or diplomacy had achieved.

And here one comes, perhaps, upon the real cause of the Western losses and withdrawals from the East. Instead of finding formulae for inner unity, whether by diplomacy or by other means, the Christian forces in the Holy Land split into innumerable warring factions that hated each other more than they feared the Muslims. The final loss of Jerusalem in 1244 has to be explained as the natural corollary of Christian dissensions. And a comparable conclusion becomes inevitable when one reviews the whole grandiose adventure that brought the West to its encounter with the East. Indeed, one is constrained to say in this connection that the military crusades were ineffective in the long run, not so much because they were morally unjust or practically inexpedient, but simply because they were not undertaken with the unity of purpose that is at all times the foremost requisite when allied and related nations meet a hostile culture realm, whether in battle or in negotiation.

The sum total of medieval Europe's failures and achievements in the Near East can be analysed in a variety of ways. But as one looks at this record from the vantage point of the twentieth century, one is struck in particular by the constant recurrence of a curious, rather paradoxical dual motif: the Western Europeans showed, on the one hand, a great ingenuity in finding the proper organizational forms for many new and complex ventures. In this primary phase of their foreign operations, different individuals, agencies, and nationalities usually displayed a remarkable degree of cooperation. But when the moment came for sustaining what had just been created, the requisite abilities were missing. In this secondary phase of their task the Western European allies showed little, if any, understanding of the problems implicit in any cooperative undertaking. It seems, in fact, almost as if each great creative and concerted effort invariably exhausted the last reserves of the collective spirit that had been permitted to accumulate.

This two-faced pattern appears in the organization and subsequent decomposition of each great cosmopolitan crusade. It is evident also in the histories of the military orders and of the Latin states in Asia Minor.

The Order of the Knights of the Hospital of St. John (established in the eleventh century) and the Order of the Knights Templar (established in 1118) came into existence for the purpose of fighting just wars in behalf of Christendom and defending the civil rights of pilgrims to the Holy Land. In the pursuit of these objectives they functioned as cosmopolitan Christian brotherhoods, whose far-flung membership linked the remotest sections of Western and Northern Europe to the most distant outposts in the Near East. In their prime, these orders served the causes that had inspired their inception. But as time went on they amassed great wealth and influence in Europe and Asia; their members became increasingly avaricious, arrogant, and lawless; and their leaders behaved as practically independent sovereigns, bent on furthering their own power rather than the collective interests of the Christian cause.[105] Feared by the pope, the emperor, and all other Christian communities, especially the Kingdom of Jerusalem, yet unwilling to amalgamate their separate forces, each order soon exceeded the margin of its fortune. When the loss of Saint Jean-d'Acre (1291) discredited the Templars the tables were turned and the fourteenth century opened with another melancholy chapter of Christian disunity. The king of France and the pope decided, each on grounds of separate interest, to break the Order of the Templars. In order to suppress this rival Christian power, accede to its accumulated wealth, and find a scapegoat for losses suffered in the Holy Land,[106] an elaborate legal process which featured rather flimsy charges of heresy, immorality, treasonable dealings with the Saracens, and so on, was set in motion against the association and its individual members.

The Christian allies had been successful in extending their political system to Asia Minor.[107] *Outremer*—the European realm beyond the sea—consisted of the Kingdom of Jerusalem (established 1100), which became the chief religious, political, and commercial center in

---

[105] *The Cambridge Medieval History*, Vol. v, p. 306; see also Krey, p. 9.

[106] See George Lizerand, *Le Dossier de l'Affaire des Templiers*, Paris, 1923, for the documents of this proceeding.

[107] The early success of the crusaders was due more to divisions among the enemies than to Christian strength. See *The Cambridge Medieval History*, Vol. v, p. 306. See Quincy Wright, Vol. I, p. 587, Appendix xv, on the estimated cost of the Crusades; Runciman, Vol. I, Appendix II.

Latin Syria; the three principalities of Edessa, Tripoli, and Antioch, which were most of the time under Jerusalem's influence; the Kingdom of Cyprus (established 1195), which was to survive as an independent monarchy until 1489, when it was acquired by Venice;[108] and numerous other lesser communities, which represented European interests without being territorially delimited.[109] Where the two great hostile culture realms met, far from their home base, on enclaves surrounded by Muslim states, the oddly assorted crusaders organized a cosmopolitan community life by putting into practice the feudal theories of the age in their purest form. The jurisconsults of Cyprus drew up the Assizes of Jerusalem in accordance with the image that they entertained of the ideal feudal state; the legal administration provided separate tribunals for maritime affairs, feudal business, and the problems of the native Syrians; and the system of law that was to govern the diverse relations in this multinational area was composed from preliminary inquiries about the usages by which the different groups of crusaders had lived in their various European homes.[110] But at the capture of Jerusalem the code that resulted from these labors perished without having been put into operation.

This abortive destiny may be said to symbolize the whole story of the rise and fall of the great crusading adventure. The loss of Jerusalem and of its code, as well as the subsequent gradual decline of the Christian establishment in Asia Minor, was due mainly to the fact that the different groups whose joint labors had produced the new society were torn from the collective purpose by the pursuit of selfish interests. Not only was the European leadership disunited in its ranks, but a steadily growing cleavage separated the newcomers arriving with unslaked ambitions (whether zealous idealists or crude materialists) from the "native" European settlers who had ceased to be crusaders, had learnt the advantages of collaborating with the Muslims, and were now intent on protecting, at all costs, their vested interests. Furthermore, on the local level, too, each Christian group was busy with its own scheme to outwit the rest. Antioch feuded with Edessa; Jerusalem clashed with the military orders; and the two military orders fought

---

[108] Among the new states that were created in this epoch one may include also the Latin Empire of Constantinople.

[109] On the Kingdom of Jerusalem see Runciman, Vol. I, pp. 315ff., Vol. II, Book I.

[110] *The Cambridge Medieval History*, Vol. v, p. 302.

The technical process of building the state of Jerusalem invites a comparison with the process by means of which culturally diverse groups of Jews organized the state of Israel in approximately the same area, in the twentieth century.

each other. Then there were the representative forces of the great commercial cities—Venice, Genoa, Pisa, and Constantinople, whose separate cupidity knew no bounds. When the whole Christian cause was tottering under the onslaught of the Muslims, Pisa and Genoa were locked in open warfare (1249), and Venice had no scruples in aiding and abetting the sordid spoliation of the Eastern Christian Empire in order to become "the administrator and beneficiary of the broken fortunes of Byzantium,"[111] to capture the monopoly of the eastern trade and to transform the city-state into a colonial empire.[112] By the end of the thirteenth century, Europe's Asian establishment had become so demoralized that it lacked even the semblance of a common purpose. And in the ensuing military engagements with the Muslims the Christians were ousted from all their strongholds, except Acre.

This city then became the stage of the last act in what had begun as a noble drama and was to end here as a sordid farce. Into Acre crowded the remnants of all the special interest groups that had created and destroyed the Christian project: the legate of the pope; the bailiffs of the kings of England, France, and Cyprus; the native lords of the land; the military orders; and the traders of the Italian towns. All were gathered there together, and each group was busy mapping out the limits of its special sovereignty and fortifying the towers in its precinct —not against the common foe, but against its Christian rivals. Meanwhile, singleminded hordes of Saracens assembled outside the city walls, and beyond the Saracens rose a unified Mongolian empire. Within the walls there were seventeen separate and feuding jurisdictions when Acre fell in 1291.[113]

D. The Political Effect of the Crusades upon the Christian Community

The crusades had momentous and multifarious consequences for the course of international relations. They established contacts and exchanges between hitherto rather isolated civilizations that were to make it possible, in the course of the ensuing centuries, to formulate the concept of a world community. Within the Christian culture realm itself, on the other hand, the crusades had the immediate effect of accentuating the lines of cultural, religious, and political division that separated the Eastern from the Western commonwealth and prevented

---

[111] Hill, Vol. I, p. 325.
[112] Vasiliev, pp. 451ff.
[113] See *The Cambridge Medieval History*, Vol. v, chapter VIII.

the different Western factions from coalescing into one international empire.

All of the labors of the Byzantine emperors and Roman popes to stay the religious schism that had divided Christendom since 1054 had been fruitless, and all of the policies to rejoin the two parts of ancient Rome into a unified political empire had failed, whether shaped by Greek caesars hoping to regain mastery of the West, or by Roman popes and emperors eager to extend their power over the East.[114] The short-lived Latin Empire, which was called into being after Byzantium had been "confiscated" and partitioned by the Western Christians in 1204, was an object lesson in that it disclosed that the Greek orthodox faith and Byzantine culture forms were too deeply rooted to permit of latinization either by propaganda or by force and perfidy. Henceforth, no theological or legal pretence could hide the fact that the two Christian empires were alien powers, each faced with its own problems of international organization and foreign policy-making. Nothing emphasized this difference quite as strongly as their respective attitudes toward Islam in general and the crusades in particular.

Centuries of coexistence in the Near Eastern region had fostered certain cultural affinities between Byzantium and the Arab world which cushioned the impact of their religious rivalries and military clashes and made for many areas of mutual understanding and respect.[115] By contrast, the Frankish friends appeared upon the local scene as a culturally alien and inferior people, and this impression was deepened, naturally, when they began to loot and plunder the newly entered land. In the eyes of the Greeks, most of the Western crusaders were barbarians, and since they encroached rather freely on the Byzantine territory and possessions, actual enemies of a sort.

Much of the Eastern Empire's early power and glamor had already waned when the crusading epoch opened: social upheavals, internal treachery, governmental ineptitude, and royal excesses had combined to demoralize and impoverish the Byzantine society. And two centuries later, in the middle of the fourteenth century, a general pessimism was to seize the population when the Black Death swept over the Empire from the east and decimated its inhabitants. The lingering state of crisis and anxiety, meanwhile, was being aggravated by the

---

[114] *The Cambridge Medieval History,* Vol. IV, pp. 510ff.

[115] See on this topic A. A. Vasiliev, *Byzance et les Arabes,* Vol. I, "La Dynastie d'Amorium" (820-867), Brussels, 1935, Vol. II, "La Dynastie Macedonienne" (867-957), Brussels, 1950, Vol. III, "Die Ostgrenze des Byzantinischen Reiches" (363-1071), Brussels, 1935.

relentless pressure of the Turks, who knew how to take advantage of Byzantium's troubles. In the eleventh century they inflicted a heavy military defeat on the Byzantine army, detaching the Empire's eastern-most provinces.[116] Byzantium's foreign policy-makers, consequently, were interested primarily in weakening the Turks, not in special exertions for the recovery of the Holy Land, which struck them as an unrealistic undertaking. The crusades of this period appear, therefore, as an essentially Western project.[117] And yet the Eastern Christians never ceased, in their relations with the Latins, to claim full legal title to any Western conquests of their lost Syrian provinces.

The leadership of Byzantium was not adverse to military offensives and defensives, but in this period of its history seemed to lay more stress on diplomacy than on war. And since the Empire had existed for centuries on the threshold of many culture realms, its diplomacy was not affected by any racial or religious prejudices. During the crusading era diplomatic understandings were sought and consummated, as occasion demanded, either in the Muslim or in the Christian camp. It is true that the diplomatic dealings of the Western factions were characterized by similar considerations of expediency—especially when schemes to subdue Byzantium took priority over programs to recover the Holy Land.[118] But whereas Byzantium's hostility to Rome was on the whole tempered by its centrally directed, long-range statesmanship, the West's antagonism to its Christian rival was, by comparison, frequently irrational—particularly since each small faction claimed the right to formulate its own objectives and vent its own vindictiveness. In the absence of any over-all evaluation of the Western stake in Asia, Western statesmen did not recognize the fact that Byzantium, despite its many weaknesses, was yet the strongest, indeed the indispensable, bastion of the entire Christian culture realm in its relations with the Asian world. And in this state of contracted vision they organized a Holy War against Constantinople.[119]

The records indicate that the Turkish westward movement had what

---

[116] Vasiliev, *The History of the Byzantine Empire*, ch. IX, "The Fall of Byzantium." See *ibid.*, pp. 356ff., to the effect that there was no longer a Byzantine army after 1071 to resist the Turks.

[117] Cf. Vasiliev, *History of the Byzantine Empire*, pp. 403ff.

[118] Frederick Barbarossa showed no qualms of any kind when he tried to induce a Muslim prince to invade Byzantium. See *ibid.*, p. 425.

[119] See *ibid.*, pp. 451-463 and the authorities there reviewed on the question whether (and if so for what reasons) the attack on Constantinople was premeditated, or whether it can be ascribed rather to a combination of accidental circumstances that were helped along by irresponsible forces in Christendom.

may be called an irresistible momentum, and that Byzantium's military strength had been greatly weakened before the thirteenth century.[120] Nevertheless, and be this as it may, had it not been for the West's perverted action of aggression in the thirteenth century, which sapped Byzantium's remaining strength in a most crucial period of medieval Europe's great struggle with the Asian powers, and for the failure of the West to respond with concerted action to Constantinople's entreaties in the fourteenth and fifteenth centuries in favor of a united front against the growing threat of Turkish forces,[121] the Greeks might have maintained a more solid defence against the fifteenth century invasions that brought the Asian Ottomans to Eastern Europe.[122]

Within the international framework of the Western union itself the crusades had far-reaching consequences. They left a lasting impact on the Western ways of conducting relations with other, and especially non-Western, peoples; effected a westward shift of the center of political gravity; and influenced greatly the gradual transformation of the international ecclesiastical state into that system of secular national states which was to be diffused, eventually, over the entire world.

The practical importance of the crusades as an instrument of foreign policy declined from the thirteenth century onward. When the Lateran Council acting in execution of a papal directive, issued a summons for yet another crusade, no single prince obeyed, nor did anyone make the slightest effort to secure that general four-year truce which was to have served the foreign enterprise.[123] And when some delegates from Eastern Europe arrived before the Kings of France and England in 1240, asking for aid from the approaching Mongols, their mission was ignored. The West was wary of foreign campaigns and preoccupied with inter-European problems and dissensions. The crusades simply ceased, as Sir Ernest Barker has put it, because they were no longer in joint with the times.[124] And yet the hands-off attitude to actual expeditions into far-off places did not affect the original concept that had inspired the earlier exertions. Although the reality had lost its meaning, the

[120] See Runciman, Vol. I, p. 64, to the effect that the Greek defeat at Manzikert in 1071 provided the justification for many interventions on the part of Western authorities which were interested in staving off the progressive penetration of the East.

[121] The West, on the contrary, was plotting the destruction of the Empire. See Vasiliev, *History of the Byzantine Empire*, p. 603.

[122] *The Cambridge Medieval History*, Vol. IV, pp. 415ff.; also Vasiliev, *History of the Byzantine Empire*, ch. IX, "The Fall of Byzantium," esp. 645-654, and see the maps that illustrate the decline of the Byzantine Empire in the fourteenth and fifteenth centuries.

[123] Davis, p. 56.

[124] *Encyclopaedia Britannica*, p. 792.

image of the crusade continued to excite the imagination of European generations, from the fourteenth century to the present.

In the period of the immediate aftermath of the Near Eastern wars, the crusade theme was kept alive by a number of intellectuals who had concluded from their post-mortem examinations of the past that, although many mistakes had been committed, the crusade might be rendered useful as an instrument of foreign policy by certain practical improvements. A blockade of Egypt by an international fleet, the merger of the two military orders, and an alliance with the Mongols, were three proposals frequently made.[125] But these efforts to recall a mood long past were signal failures, for the original offensive crusading spirit, as it had existed among the early knights who had despised diplomatic shortcuts to the victory of the cross, was represented only by a handful of romantic and adventurous princes. It is true that concerted military actions were organized in the fourteenth century to stem the tide of the advancing Ottoman Turks, but these were in the nature of defensive coalitions rather than crusades, and they were failures too. Europe's brief respite from the Turkish peril (1402-1422) was not earned by any military program of preparedness; it simply happened as an incidental result of Tamerlane's victorious sweep through Asia. In the end the Turks were able to defy both their Eastern and their Western adversaries because the potential pincer movement of the Western European and the Mongolian forces, which might have closed upon the mutual Turkish enemy, was never activated. Why? We do not know. Perhaps, however, because the Western diplomats were involved so deeply in local squabbles and Biblical lore that they were unable to recognize the elementary pattern of political geography that had taken shape so clearly before their very eyes. At any rate, neither the Mongols nor the Europeans were able to prevent the capture of Constantinople in 1453.

At an earlier moment, when the West was still imbued with expectations of victory in the Near East, and when the Far East did not seem to be so far away, St. Louis (Louis IX of France) had entertained the dim notion that an alliance with the Mongols might accomplish what the exclusively Western offensive against the Saracens had sought to effect. However, the king was above all a saintly man. Not only was the cause of Christianity closer to his heart than any political advantage, but he seemed unable to conceive of diplomatic dealings outside the Christian context. This would explain why his emissaries to the

[125] See *ibid.*

court of the great Khan were supplied with Bibles rather than more suitable presents, and why they were instructed, primarily, to teach Christianity, seek the conversion of the Khan and his subjects, and chide the authorities for the devastations that the Mongol armies had wrought on Christian lands. A duly converted Khan, St. Louis hoped, might then descend upon the Turks, join in the fight for the recovery of Palestine, and give aid and comfort to the common Christian weal.[126]

Father William of Rubruck, who headed St. Louis' delegation to the Mongol Empire, returned in 1255, after a long and arduous journey, bringing detailed information about the geography of Asia, the customs, laws, and manners of the native peoples whom he had encountered, and the state of the Nestorian and other Christian communities in Asia. But he had not accomplished his objective. Mangu Khan, despite his interest in the Christian faith, did not oblige with any conversion and suggested, instead, that St. Louis and the pope might do well to become the subjects of the only representative of the one great God.[127] And then, after this perhaps perfunctory reference to his own religious dignity, Mangu Khan, in his letter to St. Louis, issued a frank invitation to exchange not only ambassadors but also mutual assurances to the effect that peace should reign between the two great realms.[128] Father William was obviously impressed with the Mongol ruler's sincerity and with the prospects of friendly relations between Western Europe and the Empire of the East; for he concluded his fascinating journal with the following bit of advice to his European principals: "It seems useless to me that another religious man like myself be sent or friar preachers go to the land of the Tartars; but if the Pope, who is at the head of all Christians, wished to send a bishop in fit manner, and answered all the letters that the Khan had three times addressed to the Franks . . . he would be able to tell the Khan all he wished to and execute all that is contained in his letters. The Khan listens willingly to all an ambassador says and always asks if

[126] See *Contemporaries of Marco Polo*, Manuel Komroff, ed., New York, 1928. See the editor's introduction and the Journal of Friar William of Rubruck, 1253-1255, pp. 53ff.

[127] *ibid.*, p. XIX.

Innocent IV had sent an earlier mission to the Mongol Empire (1245) under the leadership of Friar John Carpini, inviting Kuyuk Khan and other Mongolian princes to become Christians. After a two year journey across Persia, Tibet, and China, Carpini returned with a remarkable letter from the Khan which asked "the great Pope, with the kings" to come to render homage and learn their orders. *ibid.*, p. xvi, and the Journal of Friar John Carpini, pp. 39ff. Compare this correspondence with the letters sent by the Emperor of China to the King of England, *supra*, pp. 145ff.

[128] See Komroff, pp. 188-190, for the text of this message.

there is anything he wished to add; but it is important that he have a good interpreter, even several, and money for traveling, etc."[129]

Mongolian interest in the Christian faith and in an entente with Western Europe was demonstrated again during the rule of Kublai Khan in 1274, when sixteen Mongol delegates appeared at the Council of Lyons and reported that their king was ready to unite forces against the enemy of Christ and for the recovery of Jerusalem. There is no evidence that the council took any notice of this proposal.[130] A request for the dispatch of one hundred learned men, which Kublai Khan is said to have addressed to the pope, seems also to have been ignored.[131] Indeed, there is reason to assume that the official representatives of Western Christendom were somewhat suspicious of all Asia as a result of their military encounters with Islam, and that they were therefore reluctant to enter into any foreign relations that might lead to further entanglements in that continent.

But, if, in the aftermath of the crusades, there was a certain disenchantment in Europe with respect to involvement in the Orient, this did not affect the vitality of "the crusade" as an idea. On the contrary, the image, divorced from its original political context, was to begin a clandestine evolution of its own in Western political thought. It safely crossed the critical threshold from Europe's medieval to Europe's modern period by remaining imbedded firmly in the minds of the great explorers. Vasco da Gama, Christopher Columbus, Albuquerque, and many others, when they embarked upon their voyages to the Farther West, "dreamed, and not insincerely, that they were labouring for the deliverance of the Holy Land, and they bore the Cross on their breasts."[132] Moreover, since the medieval Christian idea of right and wrong had been absorbed in the modern secular notion of justice and injustice between both individuals and nations, the image of "the crusade" survived in the context of constitutionalism, liberalism, and socialism, in both America and Europe. Statesmen, diplomats, reformers, and propagandists discovered that men of good will throughout the Western culture realm, and regardless of their political or ideological allegiance, would warm readily to all campaigns associated with a concept of "crusading." Innumerable situations arose, therefore, in which the medieval symbol was invoked to inspire and hallow a variety

[129] *ibid.*, p. 209.

[130] See Vasiliev, *History of the Byzantine Empire*, p. 531 on other contacts between Western Europe and the Mongol Empire in the thirteenth century.

[131] Komroff, p. 209.

[132] *Encyclopaedia Britannica*, p. 793.

of collective drives against vice, poverty, or tyranny, or for freedom, peace, and democracy. Indeed, the leaders have felt free to announce their special crusades, or to summon people to undertake crusades, without explaining the precise nature of the evils to be fought; for since the very word "crusade" has come to connote, in the public opinion, a legitimate aggressive movement against iniquitous and pernicious forces, there would seem to be no need for any further contextual analysis. Under such circumstances the entire concept has become gradually emaciated. Used with increasing frequency as a political convention to cover up, or rationalize, any particularly daring course of action, or as a mere rhetorical phrase to captivate the emotions of the public, it has become a trite cliché.

The degeneration of this symbol has had a particularly adverse effect upon the conduct of modern international relations. The two world wars of the twentieth century, for example, were advertised widely and fought by many people in the Western European culture realm as crusades against despotism or as "just wars to end all wars." These were convictions, to be sure, honestly held. Yet—as we know today—they oversimplified the nature of both conflicts and obscured the very different practical war aims that were motivating the various belligerents. Entire generations in the Western democracies have been conditioned by these oversimplifications to view the great issues of war and peace—in fact the entire complex of foreign policy-making—in terms of an image surviving from the Middle Ages that can be connected only very vaguely with the actual political motives of our twentieth century environment.

The intellectual confusion attending this unsound relationship between image and reality has increased during the acrimonious war of nerves that has characterized the relations between the Western democracies and Eastern dictatorships since the close of the Second World War. For not only do many of the Western leaders still speak of "crusades" against totalitarianism and communism and for the liberation of imprisoned nations, without informing their constituents adequately of the full substance of the policies that they have in mind, but their chief enemies in the cold war, the Russian communists, now also are claiming a part of the Christian European legacy, which formerly they had disowned, and are invoking the medieval symbols of the crusade in support of their "just" campaigns against the imperialistic warmongering capitalists of the West and for the freedom of the enslaved peoples of the world.

The last great medieval crusade was fought in the thirteenth century. Its incidents make fascinating and instructive reading. But during seven hundred years of indiscriminate post-mortem use, the image of "the crusade" has been despoiled and tarnished, and therefore the time has perhaps come to lay its ghost.

E. New Departures in Intercultural Relations

The limitations of the crusade as an instrument of the church's foreign policy were recognized clearly from the thirteenth century onward, when some of Christendom's greatest leaders concluded, by virtue of their own spiritual experience, that the Christian truth should —and could—be disseminated by persuasion rather than by force.

This realization led to the organization of the Franciscan (1210) and Dominican (1214) orders; it brought St. Francis of Assisi to Egypt where he preached before the Sultan of Egypt (1219); prompted the missions of Friars Carpini and Rubruck to the Mongolian Empire; and caused the Catalan author and mystic Raymond Lull (1235-1315) to learn Arabic before engaging in mission work in Spain and North Africa, as well as to sponsor, as his chief project, the establishment of European colleges of Oriental languages for the training of linguistically competent emissaries of Christ.

The extensive missionary movement that had its inception in this new orientation supported the Christian cause effectively in pagan Eastern Europe, but its progress in Asia, the Middle East, and North Africa was arrested, slowly but surely, by the more successful religious counter diplomacy of Islam. It cannot be said, therefore, that the Christian policy of persuasion had any spectacular consequences for Western Europe's relations with the ancient societies of the East. However, after the discovery of America it led to a revolutionary reappraisal of the Western attitudes toward alien culture areas. For the Spanish conquest of America and despotic treatment of the pagan Indians stirred up great controversies in the scholarly theological circles of sixteenth century Spain.

Among the representatives of the church who felt impelled to question all established theories that condoned the enslavement of native pagans[133] and to oppose, by concrete measures, the secular policies of the *conquistadores*, which had reduced the Indian population to a state of abject misery, none was more active and influential in his time, and

[133] See Eppstein, p. 405 for a review of Christian and classical theories that supported slavery.

none deserves greater fame today, than Bartolomé de Las Casas. The bold new principles in whose service this Dominican friar and bookman placed all his physical and intellectual energies, not only redeemed much of Europe's early brutal record in the Western hemisphere, but came to constitute a philosophy of intercultural relations that is richly suggestive even today.

Our appreciation of Las Casas' work in the context of intercultural history has to begin with the statement that this reformer was a Catholic Christian who never questioned either the absolute supremacy of the Christian truth or its particular validity for the Indians of America. It has to be mentioned also that before he began to doubt any aspect of the existing order Las Casas lived in America for a period of fourteen years (first as a layman, then as a priest) during which time he was as interested in the pursuit of his own materialist ambitions as most of the other Spaniards in the new world. One day, however, in 1514, while he was preparing a sermon, it dawned on him, he reports, "that everything done to the Indians thus far was unjust and tyrannical."[134] And this revelation led him to a painstaking quest for enlightenment and truth through an exploration of all the records that had accumulated in the realms of philosophy, theology, history, and law. "For forty-eight years," he was to write later in his life, "I have engaged in studying and inquiring into the law. I believe, if I am not mistaken, I have penetrated into the heart of this subject, until I have arrived at the fundamental principles involved."[135] In other words, Las Casas the scholar, like the earlier jurists in classical and Christian times, read law not only as a collection of treatises and rules, but as a practical guide for the improvement of human relations.

The fundamental verity that Las Casas discovered in this fashion was the fact that war is wrong as a method of spreading the faith.[136] This general conclusion led him to inquire into the actual circumstances that attended Spain's dominion in America, in particular the relations between the *conquistadores* and the pagan Indians. In this phase of his search for truth he became, as it were, an anthropologist; for he both scrutinized the behavior of the Spaniards and observed the folkways of the native pagans. And these empirical investigations convinced him that the conquerors had shockingly abused their papal

---

[134] Lewis Hanke, *Bartolomé de Las Casas, Bookman, Scholar and Propagandist*, Philadelphia, 1952, p. 39.

[135] *ibid.*, p. 15.

[136] *ibid.*, p. 13.

authorization to spread the gospel among the Indians;[137] moreover, that their policies should be condemned outright because they were detrimental to the welfare of the Indians, unreasonable and unwise, against the interests of the Spanish crown, against the accepted tenets of the canon and the civil law, and against the teachings of philosophy and theology.[138]

It took great moral and physical courage, in the early sixteenth century, to draft such a blunt indictment against the controlling political forces. But Las Casas went still further. His elaborate readings, as well as his active involvement in American affairs, had persuaded him that "all peoples of the world are men," and therefore rational beings; and that "no nation exists today, or could exist, no matter how barbarous, fierce, or depraved its customs, which may not be attracted and converted to all political virtues and to all the humanity of domestic, political, and rational men."[139] Nor did he think that Spain, or for that matter any other Christian Western nation, had a monopoly on political virtue or humanity. On the contrary, he found, after his long association with the Indians and their culture, that his pagan wards in the new world were in many respects much superior to his countrymen.[140]

After Las Casas had identified the right and wrong of Spain's relations with the Indians, he devoted his remaining long life (from 1514 to 1566) to the double task of improving the lot of the Indians and establishing more harmonious communications between the two separate culture worlds that the Spanish conquest of America had joined. This, then, was his life mission, and he undertook it in order to serve the highest purpose he knew, the cause of Christendom.

In the mind of Las Casas the preservation of the Indians was connected inseparably with their conversion to Christianity. But the insights gained in the process of executing his mission had clarified his thoughts about the real nature not only of conversion but of any intellectual communication between men. He knew beforehand that Christianity could not be conveyed by force, but he found out in addition that it could not be transmitted by any stereotyped *peaceful* formula of the kind that had become customary in missionary circles. It was clear to him that an idea had to be understood before it could have a chance of being accepted; that understanding was, essentially, a matter of individual experience rather than of collective rite; and that the entire process of understanding could be induced only by teachers

---

[137] Eppstein, Appendixes A, B, of ch. xv.
[138] *ibid.*, p. 429.   [139] Hanke, pp. 96-97.   [140] *ibid.*, p. 9.

who were thoroughly familiar with the traditions, needs, and expectations of the people to whom the new ideas were presented.[141] By perfecting these insights through analysis and experimentation, Las Casas vindicated the new ecclesiastical technique of peaceful persuasion as the most promising approach to the problem of disseminating Christian values.

The Spaniards had dispossessed, impoverished, and enslaved the Indians. Las Casas insisted that Spain owed the Indians not only a living but a reparation of the damage that had been done to their lives, liberty, and possessions. In fact, he pleaded ardently and ceaselessly that Spain, as the dominating power, should assume the full moral and economic responsibility for the present well-being and future destinies of these colonial peoples.[142] This part of his political testament was largely disregarded by the victorious empire-conscious elements of the Spanish nation, and it was forgotten when other Western European peoples followed the path to empire that had brought the Spaniards so much grief and grandeur. But today—five hundred years after it was first made evident—Las Casas' work in intercultural relations should receive full credit as an inspiring source of reference and wisdom for all who are concerned with a redefinition of the relations between non-self-governing peoples and their administering powers.

The ideas for which Las Casas had engaged himself as a fighting priest, diplomat, scholar, and publicist[143] may not have had a lasting influence upon Spain's governmental circles, but they continued to permeate Spain's intellectual elites. Indeed, the records of few nations are as complex and contradictory as those of sixteenth century Spain. For the country that sent forth, and continued to support, a horde of conquering adventurers, produced simultaneously a group of most imaginative, fearless men of letters who never ceased to criticize the conduct of their compatriots. It may have been this striking, thought-provoking ambiguity in the character of early imperialist Spain which moved one of the greatest intellectuals of imperialist England in the eighteenth century to remark: "I love the University of Salamanca; for when the Spaniards were in doubt as to the lawfulness of their conquering

[141] Cf. with the process of diffusing Buddhism from India to China.

[142] Hanke, p. 40; see also Eppstein.

[143] See Hanke, on Las Casas as a bookman. Las Casas wrote innumerable memorials to the King of Spain and to various agencies that were concerned with the government of the Indies. After his return to Spain in 1547, and until his death two decades later, he served as attorney-at-large for the Indians, and in this period produced and published his most important works. *ibid.*, pp. 2, 44ff.

America, the University of Salamanca gave it as their opinion that it was not lawful."[144]

One of the most illustrious sixteenth century teachers at this University of Salamanca was Francisco de Vitoria (born probably 1483), who is generally regarded today as one of the founders of the modern law of nations. Vitoria's title to international fame rests on a series of original contributions to moral, political, and legal philosophy that are so complex and multifarious that they cannot here receive adequate treatment.[145] However, several aspects of his life work are so closely relevant to the problems raised in the preceding chapters, that it seems fitting and appropriate to conclude the present discussion with a few brief selected references to his thought.

When Vitoria began his intellectual explorations, the Western European world had ceased to possess even the vestiges of an international state. Europe appeared to Vitoria—much as it was to appear to Voltaire two centuries later—as an international community of separate and equal states. But the vision of the sixteenth century *prima* professor of theology, who seldom moved from his study in Salamanca, extended far beyond the frontiers of the Western concert. For in his time, two revolutionary events had occurred which necessitated, in his opinion, a total reassessment of all existing political issues: the discovery by Columbus that there was another world beyond the Atlantic and the discovery by Vitoria's fellow Dominican, Las Casas,[146] that the pagan inhabitants of this new world were rational human beings.

Vitoria's own effort to re-evaluate the present in terms of past developments and future prospects was practically completed within less than forty years after the discovery of America, for in 1532 he was able to present his fundamental propositions in the form of readings on "The Indians Recently Discovered" (*De Indis Noviter Inventis*). Vitoria was as troubled as Las Casas had been when he reviewed Spain's record in America. As a humanist, moralist, and jurist, he was interested in locating the truth, righting wrongs that had been committed, and drawing philosophically and legally valid conclusions from

---

[144] In James Boswell, *Boswell's Life of Johnson*, London, New York, Toronto, 1953, p. 321.

[145] See Scott, pp. 68ff. for an analysis of Vitoria's work. Also Nussbaum, pp. 58-67. Nussbaum stresses the moral and theological character of Vitoria's work but finds many of his analyses unacceptable on juridical grounds.

[146] On the Dominican Order as a source of liberal thought see Ernest Barker, *The Dominican Order and Convocation. A study in the Growth of Representation in the Church during the Thirteenth Century*, Oxford, 1913. This author concludes that the order was the highest expression of the development of the representative principle in the thirteenth century church (p. 75).

the facts of the case before him. Furthermore, as a Christian who had devoted his life and learning to the cause of his religion, he was interested in restoring and strengthening the prestige of Christendom. For these reasons he devoted many dense chapters in his works to an exhaustive analysis of all the arguments that had been advanced in justification of Spain's right to control America and dispossess the Indians,[147] and of Christendom's right to assume a mandate for the education and advancement of the natives.[148] While he did not find conclusive answers to all of the questions that had prompted his great quest, he made it unequivocally clear that diversity of religion in general, and the desire to propagate Christianity in particular, could not be regarded as lawful causes for war; and that the domination of the Indians over American land could not be cancelled by charging them with mortal sin, unbelief, or unsoundness of mind.[149] Since the Indians are human beings, he concluded, they can suffer wrongs; and since they are capable of suffering wrongs, surely they must be presumed to be capable of having rights.[150]

Much of Vitoria's reasoning in these and other titles can be understood only in the context of the sixteenth century, when all Europeans, whether enlightened or not, were confronted with a rather novel situation that severely strained their legal and moral value system. Nevertheless, the major doubts and certainties that Vitoria developed on the subject of relations between Christian and pagan, civilized and uncivilized, literate and nonliterate peoples, will continue to hold interest as long as there are unsolved problems in this field of world affairs. Vitoria concluded from his study of the Indians that all the peoples of the world are governed by the same fundamental laws.[151] Therefore he treated the "Indian barbarians" not only as individuals whose rights were equal to those of Spaniards or Frenchmen, but as individuals constituting a state; and the state of the Indians, he continued, must be identified with the same kind of rights that were enjoyed by such states as Spain or France. This meant that the European image of an exclusively European community of states was out-of-date. Since the discoveries had joined America and Europe, the community of nations was extended by natural necessity to include the "American

---

[147] See Scott, pp. 116-137, for a treatment of this topic.

[148] *ibid.*, p. 157.

[149] *ibid.*, ch. IV, especially pp. 107-115ff.

[150] *ibid.*, p. 112. Vitoria's arguments on all these points are intricate and numerous, and cannot be rendered in full in this survey.

[151] Scott, p. 63.

Principalities" on a basis of equality.[152] That is, Vitoria suggested that an Atlantic community had come into being in 1492.

Vitoria's conceptual discoveries in the realm of international relations did not end, however, with this reference. He perceived the outlines of an even broader society, composed of all states, without reference to geography, race, or religion, and was sure that the time had come when the European Christian world would have to recognize the fact that their community was already replaced, or enveloped, by a world community. This greater union, Vitoria explained, was not a superstate, imposed upon existing states and unions. It did not rest on any special pact or constitution, and was not held together by any special creed around which its various parts could rally. It represented, rather, the common humanity behind the states, and was governed by the collective will of the sum total of all states. This will or law of nations, Vitoria maintained, was naturally superior to the law of any member nation, since the whole is always more important than any of its parts.

Vitoria identified the collective will of mankind in three chief sources: the law of nature,[153] custom, and the consent of the majority of mankind ("the consensus of the greater part of the whole world, especially in behalf of the common good of all"),[154] and he described the law derived from this will in the following terms: "That international law has not only the force of a pact and agreement among men but also the force of a law; for the world as a whole being in a way one single state, has the power to create laws that are just and fitting for all persons, as are the rules of international law. Consequently, it is clear that they who violate these international rules, whether in peace or war, commit a mortal sin; moreover, in the gravest matters, such as the inviolability of ambassadors, it is not permissible for one country to refuse to be bound by international law, the latter having been established by the whole world."[155]

[152] *ibid.*, p. 282.　　　　　　　　[153] *ibid.*, p. 146.

[154] *ibid.*, p. 146, Appendix A, p. xxxviii. Vitoria illustrates the majority principle in the following passage from *De Indis*: "For if after the early days of the creation of the world or its recovery from the flood, the majority of mankind decided that ambassadors should everywhere be reckoned inviolable and that the sea should be common and that prisoners of war should be made slaves" (instead of being put to death, as in former times), "and if this, namely, that strangers should not be driven out, were deemed a desirable principle, it would certainly have the force of law, even though the rest of mankind objected thereto." Original text, p. 146, n.3.

[155] From *De Potestate Civile*, see *ibid.*, p. 172 and Appendix C, p. xc. Vitoria's law of nations is found chiefly in *De Indis* and in *De Jure Belli* (On the Law of War). For passages from these and other works see Scott.

The modern society of nations and the modern law of nations continue to rest on these conceptual foundations, which Vitoria laid more than four hundred years ago. Indeed, the visionary intelligence of this Christian theologian, which reached to continents that he had not seen, religions that he had not experienced, and times that were not his own, has remained the source of new directions for the further evolution of the present international system. In this connection, the reminder is perhaps appropriate, furthermore, that Vitoria's zeal and logic in the elaboration of morally just and legally coherent international norms were matched, at all times, by his acute sense for what was practical and possible.

As a realist, fully aware of the limitations under which any sixteenth-century political order had to labor, Vitoria was too wise to think in terms of a paramount international authority that would supervise the due formulation and observance of the law of nations. Such a "superior" did not, in fact could not, exist at the time. Furthermore, Vitoria, the priest, knew very well that the modern order was a secular order, in which the national state was the exclusive conductor through which the law of nations could reach the individual and affect relations between states, and thus interpenetrate the world.[156] He realized also that it was the national sovereign in each state who was most widely trusted as the chief support of peace and order. It is this view of the world situation that explains Vitoria's suggestion that all law —whether divine or human, international or national—should be ascertained, in advance, by learned counsels, in order then to be applied to disputes between individuals by a technically qualified judge in national courts, and to disputes between nations by the sovereign prince.[157]

Vitoria did not overlook the fact that war was—and would remain —the ultimate means of adjusting disputes between states as long as there was no "court of the superior" to which the conflicts could be submitted. He tried, therefore, to establish war as the ultimate *legal* process for the assertion and rendition of justice between nations, when all their other efforts to gain a peaceful settlement had failed. In the pursuit of this end he made it clear, however, that the medieval categories of private and public warfare were insufficient analytical devices, since modern wars were contests between national states and could no more be fully understood either as incidents to the feudal system, or as expressions of the collective will of Christendom. And

[156] Scott, p. 283.
[157] *ibid.*, p. 238.

while the distinction between just and unjust wars remained crucial to his entire international system, Vitoria thought it necessary, nevertheless, to reexamine and restate the elements of justice and injustice as they affected the causes and the objectives of a "modern" war, suggesting, among other things, that situations might arise in which *both* warring states had justice on their side.[158]

[158] *ibid.*, p. 151.

CHAPTER 9

THE BYZANTINE REALM

A. The International Significance of
Byzantium's History

THE EUROPEAN and Asian areas around the Black and Aegean Seas do not constitute a politically and culturally homogeneous region. Today they belong to such different states as the Soviet Union, Greece, and Turkey, and throughout the last two centuries they were the objects of endless rivalries between the great powers of Western Europe, Russia, and the Ottoman Empire, as well as the meeting place of various competitive religions and civilizations. These exposures of the region in recent times have attracted the interest of all students of international relations. An inquiry into the remoter past of the area, however, yields still further perspectives of international significance.

There was a time when Asia Minor, the Black Sea littorals, most of the Balkan peninsula, and many Aegean islands were included in one great cosmopolitan society, the Byzantine Empire, which maintained its political and cultural identity from the sixth to the fifteenth century A.D.[1] Any inquiry into the tested principles of international government should therefore—if for this reason alone—concern itself with the records of Byzantium. But the fact that this empire was a Christian commonwealth adds to the international significance of the case study. For it is a commonplace of our historical studies to associate Christianity exclusively with the patterns of government and foreign relations that were developed in Western Europe, forgetting that Christianity was the mainspring also of the altogether different set of political principles that supported the Byzantine Empire for close to one thousand years.

Before the end of the nineteenth century Western scholars did not show any sustained interest in the annals of the ancient Eastern Em-

---

[1] *Social and Political Thought in Byzantium, from Justinian to the last Palaeologus,* Ernest Barker, ed., Oxford, 1957, p. 27, says that the origin of the Byzantine Empire should be dated from A.D. 324 when Constantinople was founded. N. H. Baynes, *Byzantine Studies and Other Essays,* London, 1955, writes on p. 78 that Byzantine history begins with the reign of Heraclius, but records a change of view, n. 3, to the effect that this history should be dated from Constantine the Great.

pire.[2] A few works on Byzantine history were published in the sixteenth century, in Germany, Holland, and Italy, and the Byzantine period was studied in a truly scientific manner in seventeenth century France under the patronage of Louis XIII and Louis XIV, but all interest was dissipated during the Age of Reason. Since European historians became the chief chroniclers of world affairs, Byzantine history has long been one of the least appreciated chapters in the history of the world.

For the neglectful treatment several reasons can be cited. After all, the Byzantine Empire had vanished when Western Europe began that phenomenal rise in international affairs which was to reach its peak in the nineteenth century. The first great historians of the modern period were concerned more with uncovering the direct antecedents of their own victorious society than with reconstructing the records of a defunct state that had once been the rival of the West. They showed, that is, a rather natural bias in favor of their own environment. However, this apology cannot be taken to excuse the outbursts of disparagement and disdain that one encounters in the writings of many esteemed historians of the eighteenth and nineteenth centuries. Voltaire, for instance, dismissed Byzantine history as "a worthless repertory of declamations and miracles disgraceful to the human mind."[3] Gibbon described it as "a tedious, uniform tale of weakness, and misery"[4] and Lecky stigmatized the Empire as "one of the least noble forms that civilization has yet assumed . . . destitute of all the elements of greatness."[5] Indeed, this latter author seems actually relieved when he can conclude his account of "this monotonous story of the intrigues of priests, eunuchs, and women" with the statement that "at last the Mahommedan invasion terminated the long decrepitude of the Eastern Empire. Constantinople sank beneath the Crescent. . . ."[6]

Such sweeping condemnations cannot be ascribed to ignorance of the facts in issue, for at that time the records had been assembled with

---

[2] See A. A. Vasiliev, *History of the Byzantine Empire, 324-1453*, Madison, 1952, ch. 1, and Georg Ostrogorsky, *Geschichte des byzantischen Staates*, München, 1940, pp. 1-21, for a review of scholarship in Byzantine history. (English version, *History of the Byzantine State*, Joan Hussey, tr., New Brunswick, 1957, pp. 1-20.) See also Peter Charanis, "Bibliographical Note" in Charles Diehl, *Byzantium: Greatness and Decline*, New Brunswick, N.J., 1957, pp. 301-357.

[3] As quoted in Frederic Harrison, *Byzantine History in the Early Middle Ages*, London, 1900, p. 46, n.5.

[4] Edward Gibbon, *Decline and Fall of the Roman Empire*, 2 vols., New York, Vol. ii, p. 520.

[5] William E. H. Lecky, *History of European Morals*, London, 1946, ii, p. 6.

[6] *ibid.*

prodigious skill. It must be concluded, therefore, that this European anti-Byzantinism was due to the interpretations that the eminent historians chose to place upon the facts with which they dealt. These interpretations were influenced, no doubt, by the frustrating experience of having to treat of a society that was ostensibly closely related to their own and yet proved to be utterly alien upon close investigation. But a reading of the disparaging chapters and passages leaves the impression also that the learned protagonists of the West were rather pleased to have an opportunity of demolishing the very memory of a society that had inconvenienced their forefathers through the Middle Ages.

Later generations of European scholars have reviewed the judgments of the anti-Byzantinists and as a result of their painstaking efforts the position of Byzantium in world history has been rehabilitated.[7] Since due amends have thus been made for whatever injustices may have been committed, it might be thought possible to dismiss the previous acrimonious treatment of these historical matters as an unfortunate interlude in the evolution of the concept of international history. However, it so happens that it is that earlier version of the past of Byzantium that has had the decisive and long-term influence upon the actual relations between the Western world and the orbit of Byzantium's former influence. It must be remembered that Gibbon, Lecky, and their numerous colleagues wrote in a crucial period of modern history, when all peoples in Europe and Western Asia were in the process of developing a new awareness of their national character and cultural heritage, and when the established states of Western Europe were being challenged to formulate new policies toward the Slavic and other Near Eastern nations then beginning to participate actively in the modern European states system. An objective evaluation of the Byzantine traditions would have aided this policy-making process immeasurably, for it would have yielded a much needed key to an understanding of the civilizations of the Russians, Serbs, Bulgars, Greeks, and Turks, which had arisen in close association with the history of Byzantium.

The Western neglect of Byzantine affairs is not completely explained, however, by simply pointing to the bias of a few generations of modern historians. It is doubtful whether their anti-Byzantinism could have swayed the minds of so many Europeans, had it not been deeply rooted in the collective unconscious of the West. The actual experiences that produced such a pronounced resentment against a particular culture

---

[7] See Ostrogorsky, Charanis, and Vasiliev for a review of Byzantine studies.

and its various offshoots accumulated between the sixth and the fifteenth centuries as incidents to the political and cultural relations between Western and Eastern Rome.

The backdrop for the history of these relations was the theory of the essential unity of Christendom to which both realms were committed. This meant that each was bound to seek a union of the parts. When both Rome and Constantinople came to realize that such a union could not be brought about either by agreement or by force, each alleged itself to be the *universitas*, and neither was willing thereafter to tolerate the claim of the other to be the sole heir of the original Roman Empire and the supreme sovereign, therefore, over all Christians. In short, supremacy rather than unity became the primary goal of each of the two empires, and a spirit of enmity began to pervade both the official and the unofficial relations of the rival claimants to temporal and ecclesiastical omnipotence.[8]

It seems clear from the records that the battle for superiority was fought more bitterly by the West than by the East, for in the West it enlisted the aspirations to absolute sovereignty not only of the pope but also of the emperor. Since these two contenders were taking every possible opportunity to outbid each other's claims to rights and power in order to carry their case in Western Europe, they could not relax their rigid postures of supremacy when it came to dealing with Byzantium. In other words, the dualism that characterized the Holy Roman Empire influenced the evolution of its attitude toward its Eastern rival.

Conditions in the East were very different from those prevailing in the West. The church was a department of the state. The imperial functionaries had full control over all domestic and foreign policies, and tradition had settled at an early time that matters of theological dogma should be subordinated to considerations of political expediency. The opposition of Constantinople to the West was therefore usually restrained by calculations of statesmanship and strategy. By contrast the animosity of Western Europe showed overtones of great emotionalism. This difference in the quality of a historic enmity was accentuated by certain factors that might be termed pathological. For instance, the emperor of the West was never quite as sure of his title to the legacy of Rome as he professed to be. His real power, at home and abroad, was at no time commensurate to the pretensions of omnip-

---

[8] It should be noted that popular legend continued to feature the two emperors as friends. See Henry Adams, *Mont St. Michel and Chartres*, Boston and New York, 1913, pp. 32ff.

otence commonly associated with his office. Similar discrepancies between theory and practice detracted from the assumed power of the papacy. It followed that the representatives of the West were frequently unsure of themselves in their controversies with the East, where the emperor never seemed troubled about the validity of his title or the reality of his power, and that they were inclined to overstate their claim to supremacy in order thus to compensate for the appearance of their inferiority.

No one can read Bishop Liutprandt's account of his mission to Constantinople, upon which he had engaged in 968 as the envoy of Otto the Great for the purpose of negotiating a marriage between Otto's son and the Byzantine princess Theophano,[9] without being acutely aware of the emotional problems that anyone from Western Europe was bound to face when he visited the Eastern court. For here he was presented not only with an awe-inspiring and resplendent spectacle designed to dazzle impressionable foreigners hailing from humbler quarters, but also with a solid imperial establishment manifesting to all who came that they had entered a world fuller, richer, and more civilized than their own. And the spell of Eastern Rome persisted in the two ensuing centuries. It was cast over Louis VII and his crusading host when they paused in Constantinople as the guests of Manuel Comnenus, and it completely enveloped the young French queen, Eleanor of Aquitaine. Eleanor was known all over Europe as an exquisitely educated woman, and her own entourage was famed for the quality of the intellects that it included. Yet after sojourning in the Eastern capital, she was convinced that Paris was not, as she had been led to believe, the highest of all high places in Christendom. Byzantium, she came to realize, was not only incredibly vaster, but infinitely more refined.[10]

The queen of France could admit the cultural superiority of the East without inhibition or rancor because she was a cosmopolitan by inclination and upbringing. But the majority of Europeans from England, Scandinavia, France, or Germany, were less broadly oriented and therefore more self-conscious about their cultural inferiority to the East. Though they may have dreamt about the wonders of the distant fairyland, they did not feel free to express their interest or admiration openly. Instead, they often affected to despise Byzantine cul-

[9] See Ernest F. Henderson, *Select Historical Documents of the Middle Ages*, London, 1925, Appendix, pp. 441ff.

[10] Amy Kelly, *Eleanor of Aquitaine and the Four Kings*, Cambridge, Mass., 1950, pp. 42ff.

ture as a display of sodden luxury. In short, the cultural relations between the two Christian societies were psychologically much more complex than the military and diplomatic contacts between the two governments. For a military or diplomatic defeat was an obvious fact with which statesmen could take issue, but a defeat in cultural relations could not be as readily dated or defined, and since it was absorbed by innumerable individuals in a great variety of ways, its impact upon public opinion was not susceptible to governmental regulation. The cultural aspect of the duel for supremacy was, therefore, more perturbing to the Western mind than any other, and it had, of necessity, a particularly unbalancing effect upon the West's official representative in Byzantium. Such an envoy was apt to be ill at ease also because he was bound to realize through his daily experiences that his adversaries were past masters in the art of studiously exploiting the inferiority complex of any visiting stranger.

A chronic psychological tension developed under these circumstances in the relations between Latin Rome and Greek Rome, which was relieved occasionally by violent outbursts of mutual vilification. In these verbal battles the West was more aggressive than the East, because it was the more frustrated of the two parties. Bishop Liutprandt of Cremona, for example, was so humiliated by the public insults to which he was subjected that he poured his wounded feelings into the writing of his official report. And since he was a witty man, his account has remained one of the most entertaining, as well as revealing, documents in diplomatic history.

As seen through Liutprandt's eyes there was no aspect of Byzantine life that did not merit the most scathing indictment. The meals he got were foul and disgusting. The wine was mixed with pitch, resin, and plaster. The soldiers whom he saw were mere images of men, bold of tongue and frigid in war. The people in the street were poor and barefoot. The tunics of the nobles were too large and torn through age. And all of Constantinople was described as half-starved, perjured, lying, wily, greedy, rapacious, avaricious, and vainglorious.[11] But the choicest epithets of the Bishop were reserved for the august Nicephoras Phocas himself. Liutprandt described the Emperor as "a monstrosity of a man, a pygmy, fat-headed and like a mole; . . . disgusting with his short, broad, thick, and half hoary beard; . . . very bristly through the length and thickness of his hair; in colour an Ethiopian; one whom

[11] Cf. Liutprandt's report in Henderson, pp. 442, 446, 471.

it would not be pleasant to meet in the middle of the night; . . . clad in a garment costly but too old and foul-smelling and faded through age; . . . bold of tongue, a fox by nature, in perjury and lying a Ulysses. . . ."[12]

This particular grudge against the Byzantine emperor had its special causes. In the first place, Nicephoras Phocas was an absolute ruler and therefore he had to be held directly responsible not only for the many inconveniences and outrages which the Bishop had been obliged to suffer personally, but also for an incessant flow of contemptuous diatribes against that paragon of true majesty and virtue, the one and only Holy Roman Emperor in Germany. On the subject of the proposed marriage, for instance, the Byzantines insisted on treating Otto the Great as an obscure princeling, whose son was quite unworthy to be considered as a bridegroom for a princess born in the purple of an emperor who, himself, had been born in the purple.[13]

The exchange between the Western representative and the Eastern court revealed another area of great sensitivity: it appears that Nicephoras Phocas succeeded in shaking Liutprandt's conviction that his imperial principal actually represented the cause of ancient Rome. He ridiculed those Romans who had remained in Rome after Constantine had transferred the classical heritage, with all its appurtenances, to the "new" Rome as "vile minions—fishers, namely, pedlars, bird catchers, bastards, plebeians, slaves."[14] And since he made it a point also to lump together all Westerners, whether they were Latins or Teutons, as uncouth Lombards or Franks, whose "beliefs are too young and have not yet been able to reach us,"[15] Liutprandt, in his turn, felt compelled to disassociate the Latins and the Teutons from that "band of insolvent debtors, fugitive slaves and homicides,"[16] who had been said to form the Roman race. All the proud Lombards, Saxons, Franks, Lotharingians, Bavarians, Swabians, and Burgundians, whose honor he now felt called upon to defend, despised the Romans, he declared. "When angry," he continued, "we can call our enemies nothing more scornful than Roman—comprehending in this one thing, that is in the name of the Romans, whatever there is of contemptibility,

[12] *ibid.*, p. 443.
[13] *ibid.*, p. 449. In actuality the Eastern government was fully aware of the fact that Otto had transformed the Western Empire into a power that could no longer be ignored. And this appraisal of the international situation was confirmed by the ultimate consummation of the union between Otto II and Theophano.
[14] Liutprandt's report, Henderson, p. 467.
[15] *ibid.*, p. 452.
[16] *ibid.*, p. 448.

of timidity, of avarice, of luxury, of lying: in a word, of viciousness."[17] Thus the schism between the East and the West which had so far been seen in its religious, political, and cultural connotations, was here rendered also in terms of race relations.

The alienation between the rival churches, empires, cultures, and races grew in the ensuing centuries until it seemed to nullify the fact that both societies continued to acknowledge Christianity as the primary source of their existence. It is true that the Greeks lent their altars to itinerant Frankish crusaders, but they purged them afterward, as if they had been profaned.[18] And when Louis VII and Manuel Comnenus exchanged the kiss of peace in their first interview, each was guarded carefully against the possible treachery of the other. The two Christian monarchs appeared as brothers, we are told, but actually they conversed through an interpreter in the idiom of diplomacy.[19] Indeed, as one reads the record of this fascinating relationship between the Western and the Eastern Christians, one is led to question the full validity of the theory that ideological affinities are necessarily an aid in the promotion of understanding between nations.

The mutual antagonism was clearly evident in all of its perspectives when Frederick Barbarossa and his army passed through the Eastern realm on the way to the Holy Land. The contemporary German chronicler reports that the roads through Bulgaria were blocked by "puny, little double-dealing Greeks";[20] and that the German envoys who were sent to negotiate the progress of the crusaders were arrested as hostages. The Patriarch of Constantinople is said to have proclaimed publicly that "any Greek who killed one hundred pilgrims, even if he were charged with murdering ten Greeks, would receive a pardon,"[21] and pictures showing Greeks astride the necks of pilgrims are reported to have been displayed publicly. These insulting and frightening incidents so enraged the Germans, we are told, that they set churches and other buildings on fire, devastated the whole land and took huge amounts of booty.[22]

[17] *ibid.*, p. 448. Liutprandt's report has been discussed by E. N. Johnson in his article "American Mediaevalists and Today," *Speculum*, Vol. XXVIII, no. 4, October 1953. But in quoting from the report as translated by Henderson, Johnson substituted "Greek" where Henderson uses "Roman": "We call our enemies nothing more scornful than Greek."

[18] Kelly, p. 40.   [19] *ibid.*, p. 42.

[20] The report of the official chronicler of Barbarossa's march, the so-called Ansbert, is discussed in Johnson, pp. 850ff. Johnson used the translation of C. E. Wilcox (typescript in University of Nebraska Library).

[21] *ibid.*   [22] *ibid.*

Controversies about precedence, titles, and rank, which had figured prominently during Liutprandt's mission, gained in acerbity in the twelfth century. For instance, Frederick Barbarossa threatened that unless the Greek emperor "salutes me with due respect by the name of Roman Emperor, let him know that I . . . will unhesitatingly cut my way through with the sword." And he duly ordered his regent at home to make plans to have Genoa, Venice, Ancona, and Pisa "supply a squadron of galleys and smaller vessels in order that, meeting us at Constantinople around the middle of March, they may besiege the city by sea and we by land." "Do not neglect," Frederick wrote in his letter, "to write the Lord Pope to send monks to the various provinces to exhort the people of God against the enemies of the Cross, and especially against the Greeks."[23]

The peculiarly stereotyped form of hostility toward all things Byzantine that had been generated in the West from about the fifth century onward as a result of jealousy, ignorance, and misinformation was channelled into open aggressiveness when the military and political power of the West increased, and the fortunes of the East declined. This led, eventually, to the fourth crusade and contributed materially to the downfall of Byzantium in 1453.

These, then, were the circumstances that created a predisposition among the subsequent generations of Western Europeans to see the entire orbit that once was Byzantine in a jaundiced way. It is a matter of common knowledge that the contacts between the Germans and the Latins on the one hand, and the Eastern European, especially Slavic, nations on the other, have been marked by much tension, misunderstanding, and conflict; and while there are many reasons for this state of affairs, the supposition is unavoidable that these and other antagonisms in the area are a sequence also of the traditional enmity between Western and Eastern Rome. Any study of contemporary foreign affairs stands to profit therefore from further explorations of the medieval history of the nations involved. Indeed, this point is demonstrated persuasively in E. N. Johnson's article, where the reader is invited to read Liutprandt's report about his visit to Byzantium while bearing in mind Soviet-American relations: ". . . We can substitute vodka for the 'Greek wine, mixed with pitch, resin, and plaster,' and the Russian equivalent for a 'fat goat . . . stuffed with garlic, onions, and leeks, and steeped in fish sauce,' and all served 'Without a tablecloth.' In spite of the difference in the centuries, many of us are easily convinced about the 'barefoot (Russian) multitude . . . clad in tunics . . . too

[23] *ibid.*, p. 851.

large and torn through too great age'; and understand well the remark concerning German nobles who are much better dressed. What Liutprandt calls the 'Attic eloquence' of Byzantine chief chamberlains, marshals, state secretaries, and masters of the wardrobe, we call the boring loquacity of Mr. Vishinsky. We would use other words to describe eunuch generals, capon Greek bishops, and the caresses of 'soft, effeminate, longsleeved' party functionaries. Our American would easily find a substitute for an emperor described as 'bold of tongue, a fox by nature, as perjuring and lying as Ulysses.' It need not be Santa Sophia where the crowd called out 'Long life to the ruler!' 'Adore him, ye people, cherish him, bend the neck to (and write your book and compose your symphony for) him alone.' There would be a lusty American profanity for 'Come, thou burnt-out coal, thou fool, old woman in thy walk, wood devil in thy look; thou peasant, thou frequenter of foul places, thou goat foot, thou horn-head, thou double-limbed one, bristly, unruly, countrified, barbarian, harsh, hairy, and a rebel.' "[24]

It is important to note, by way of further comment on the relations between Western and Eastern civilizations, that Byzantine history was not given an autonomous place in the historical studies of the nineteenth century even after it had once been rediscovered. Some scholars treated it as an appendix to the history of ancient Rome; others, as a prelude to the history of modern Greece. Some found that a knowledge of Byzantine civilization was indispensable as an introduction to the non-Christian culture of Islam; others realized that Byzantium was important because it had administered the cultural legacies of ancient Greece and Rome until the West was ready to reclaim what it considered to be its own particular birthright. In short, modern Europe long tended to misrepresent the history of Byzantium much as medieval Europe had misunderstood and misrepresented the actual Empire. It required the devoted labors of such scholars as J. B. Bury and others before the perspectives cleared and Byzantium could be seen as an entirety.[25] When this point was reached in the reconstruction of the records it became evident, first, that the cultural autonomy, if not supremacy, of Byzantium had been acknowledged by many generations

---

[24] pp. 849-850.

[25] Bury saw the history of Rome as an undivided sequence of events from the first to the fifteenth century. See the introductory chapters in Ostrogorsky, also Vasiliev, for an evaluation of his work and a review of modern scholarship in this field. It should be noted that historians have not agreed on a nomenclature when they deal with Byzantine history. Some speak of the history of Eastern Rome, others of the history of the Later Roman Empire; still others of Byzantine history.

of the medieval Occident and, second, that its civilization had never really ceased to infiltrate the rival Christian realm. For not only did Byzantium transmit to the West its knowledge of the ancient Greeks and Romans, but it also rendered a rich variety of original contributions in the fields of architecture, the ornamental arts, military science, administrative law, government, and foreign relations, from which the people of the West borrowed freely, even if unconsciously.

Since Western Europe harbored many aspirants to princely power and prestige, it is not surprising that the chief object of emulation should have been the imperial Byzantine administration itself. The Occidental rulers, whether powerful or petty, tried to imitate the monetary and fiscal system, the code of diplomacy, the scientific body of civil law, the military and naval establishment, the bureaucracy of the civil service, and the complex hierarchy of courtly dignities, upon which the domestic and foreign reputation of the Byzantine emperor seemed to rest. But their efforts to transplant the substance of Eastern government to the Occidental environment proved unsuccessful in the long run simply because the existing political theories and practices of the West so greatly differed from those of the Byzantine realm. No difficulties of the kind seem to have obstructed, however, the process of borrowing the forms and symbols of Byzantine power. As a matter of fact, it is doubtful whether it was the actual power of the Empire that impressed the Western emulators so much as the appearance of power enveloping the person of the Eastern monarch.

Now the Byzantines were masters of the art of evolving forms—whether in architecture, liturgy, legal codes, diplomacy, or court etiquette, and they had a highly developed sense for the value of images and symbols in the administration of human relations—whether in the foreign or in the domestic context. As employed by the Eastern Empire, symbolism became, as it were, an international political language through which the government could convey the power and the unity of the empire to its multifarious component groups, whether literate or nonliterate. These aspects of the political artistry of Byzantium seem to have made a lasting impression upon the West. At any rate we find that practically all European monarchies and aristocracies adopted with alacrity such external paraphernalia of the Eastern Roman Empire as its crowns, sceptres, vestments, coins, titles, and rules of etiquette.[26]

[26] See Frederic Harrison, *Byzantine History in the Early Middle Ages*, London, 1900, p. 16, to the effect that Byzantium's colossal bureaucracy was ridiculed by

The migration of one such symbol holds particular interest for a study of international relations. When the emperor received the low and high from East and West, he was shrouded in a magnificent imperial robe covered with emblems attesting to the universal validity of his power. This ritual garment was, indeed, a cosmic robe. Studded with stars and other celestial formations, it seemed to have descended upon the emperor from heaven itself. Since it showed also the hemispheres and the continents of Asia, Europe, and Africa, it reflected the immense terrestrial jurisdiction of the bearer, thus informing the onlooker that he was in fact in the presence of a unique and holy prince. This symbolic robe appeared in the West in the early eleventh century, we are told,[27] when the Duke of Apulia presented such a garment to Henry II of Saxony at whose court he had found refuge after Byzantium had dispossessed him of his dukedom. And it was from this German court that the use of the symbolic vestment was diffused subsequently to the other European kingdoms.

The major monarchies of Christendom in the East and West thus came to share an important symbol of imperial government, however disparate their cultural traditions and political interests may have been. Since the garment included many insignia that can be traced to the royal ritual of ancient Egypt and the Talmudic mysteries of Judea, besides being analogous to representational motifs found on the sacrificial robe of the Emperor of China,[28] one may regard the symbol also as a time- and space-transcending link between the great organized societies of Asia, Africa, and Europe. In the perspective of international history, then, the cosmic robe appears as a symbolic manifestation of the continuity and connectedness of the great recorded efforts to govern mankind. Since Byzantium was the central junction of these efforts, both geographically and chronologically, it can be described indeed as "the surest witness to the unity of history."[29]

---

many Western commentators, but copied closely by every bureaucratic absolutism in modern Europe. "The *chinovnik* of Russia, the *Beamten* of Prussia, the *Administration* of France trace their offices and even their titles to the types of the Byzantine official hierarchy." For Byzantine influences on the ruling institutions, especially the bureaucracy, of the Ottoman Empire, see H. A. R. Gibb and Harold Bowen, *Islamic Society and the West*, Oxford, 1951, Vol. I, pp. 39ff.

[27] Robert Eisler, *Weltenmantel und Himmelszelt*, Religionsgeschichtliche Untersuchungen zur Urgeschichte des Antiken Weltbildes. Two vols., München, 1910, Vol. I, pp. 21ff.

[28] *ibid.*, p. 21.

[29] Freeman, *Historical Essays*, Third Series, 1879, p. 241 as quoted in Harrison, p. 5.

B. The Foundations of the Byzantine State

A. THE POSITION OF BYZANTIUM IN THE MIDDLE AGES

Byzantium was a great power in terms of international relations throughout its history, even though its boundaries were to recede steadily from the seventh century onward. But any inquiry into the policies and institutions that secured the Empire its remarkable place in world affairs must begin with the reflection that its very existence represented a victory over adverse circumstances. For the government at Constantinople had to administer and defend vast areas in Europe, Africa, and Asia, which were not enclosed by natural geographical frontiers. And within this far-flung domain it had to deal with a host of nationalities widely separated from each other by racial, linguistic, or cultural differences.[30] It must be remembered, furthermore, that Byzantium was a "middle kingdom," as it were. Beyond its periphery lived a great variety of lesser nations, some settled, others nomadic, which gravitated toward Constantinople as a result of complex centrifugal or centripetal forces. How should the Empire treat such restless and aggressive northern folk as the Avars, Bulgars, Petchenegs, Russians, and Seljuk Turks, who transgressed its boundaries, laid waste its provinces and threatened its capital? Defensive military actions were usually successful in checking intrusions after they had occurred. But the experience of these encounters made it clear that the interest of the Empire required not only military vigilance but also long-range policies that would control the population movements on the periphery and if necessary, accommodate those foreign elements that seemed intent upon settling in the close vicinity of the imperial state. Byzantium responded to these conditions by creating gradually an intricate system of political controls in which secondary and culturally inferior states came to exist in various degrees of tutelage and dependence.

Beyond this circle of lesser states was a broader circle of aggressive and expansive great powers—Western Rome, Persia, and from the seventh century onward, the Islamic califates. Byzantium's strength in relation to these competitors varied in the course of their mutual relations. But there was no moment when Constantinople was not the junction as well as the target of rival imperialisms. And since the Empire's own destiny was expansion also, its statesmen were forever con-

[30] Charles Diehl, *History of the Byzantine Empire*, George B. Ives., tr., Princeton and London, 1925, pp. 87f., also Steven Runciman, *Byzantine Civilisation*, London, 1948, pp. 277ff.

fronted with the necessity of warding off assaults, loosening the noose around the imperial heartland, and taking due advantage of any opening that would permit a more direct initiatory action on behalf of its own security and greatness. Here, as in the case of the lesser neighboring states and tribes, Byzantium could not rely solely on its military and naval forces as an adequate shield against its foes. Aggressive moves on the part of one or several foreign nations had to be anticipated, forestalled, or weakened whenever possible if the Eastern Christian Empire were to gain mastery over the adverse elements of its geographic and political position. Byzantine statesmanship always implied the mandate, therefore, to exploit the rivalries of the Empire's enemies, to transform the ring of satellites into a system of protection and defence, and generally to cultivate policies short of war which would assure some possibility of coexistence with one or the other of the empires in the outer ring of encirclement.

It must be noted, however, that the Eastern Empire's orientation toward its environment was not only a product of political and strategic consideration, but also a manifestation of certain involuntary communications that had long linked the middle empire to the adjoining orbits. After all, Byzantium occupied an area that had been the crossroads, for more than a millennium, of diverse cultural forces emanating from all directions. By virtue of its geographical associations alone it was thus particularly receptive to influences from Persia, Egypt, the Arab regions, and the great Oriental realms lying beyond the circle of Central Asian and Middle Eastern civilizations. In short, Byzantium could not insulate itself from the outside world. On the contrary, it was conditioned by its very situation and cultural heritage to develop an acute awareness of other nations, religions, and value systems. This situation compelled the Empire's governing elite to distinguish beneficial or innocuous forces from those threatening the integrity or stability of the state and to regulate the impact of all cultural influences from abroad by developing for each case appropriate policies.

Now the due dispatch of these complex functions required very special human skills and faculties, and it is clear from a survey of the history of Byzantium that the policy-makers of the Empire were not all equally qualified for the execution of this trust. Furthermore, while the foreign policies of the Empire had to be flexible, to match an ever-changing environment, it is clear from the records that the range of fluctuation tended to become excessively wide when strong-willed, opinionated, and unrestrained emperors chose to impose their personal whims and predilections upon the policy-making processes of the state. For example, Justinian's passionate concern for the ecclesiastical unity of the Empire had made him so fearful of the divisive effects of unorthodox beliefs that he was resolved throughout his reign to close the roads that might lead to error.[31] And since he had concluded that most of these roads originated in the East, he proceeded to exterminate every separatist religion and intellectual movement that he could identify in that region. Leo III the Isaurian (A.D. 680-740), on the other hand, followed a radically different course. His analysis of Byzantium's position between East and West led him to the view that the Eastern sects had to be respected and conciliated even at the cost of antagonizing Christian authorities in the West. Indeed, the Isaurian chiefs seem to have been fully aware of the fact that the Asiatic portion of their Empire was ready at that time to accept some form of Islam.[32] And this consideration no doubt influenced their policy of support for the bold efforts of the Asian Christians to free the European Christians from the fetichism and image worship with which, the Asians felt, their common faith had gradually been encumbered.[33]

Historians disagree in their estimates of the respective merits of these religious policies as they disagree in interpreting many other phases of Byzantine politics. However, the most negative version of the Empire's record between the fifth and the fifteenth centuries cannot ignore the fact that this state managed to retain its identity as a great power, a cosmopolitan society, and a distinct culture realm to the very end of its appointed time, even though its very survival was an issue in each successive century.

An inquiry into the intellectual sources of the vitality of Byzantium reveals first the conviction, firmly held throughout the centuries, that the Eastern Empire was the sole successor of Rome, the only legitimate conveyor of the Roman idea of the *universitas* and therefore the greatest ruling power on earth. When the exclusiveness of this position was refuted in the domain of international relations by the rise of Islam

[31] See J. B. Bury, *History of the Later Roman Empire, from the death of Theodosius I to the death of Justinian A.D. 395-565*, 2 vols., London, 1931, Vol. II, pp. 361-372, 518ff.

[32] Harrison, p. 38, and Ostrogorsky, p. 107, to the effect that the imperial attitude toward image worship was moulded decisively by influences emanating from the Arabian culture realm.

[33] Leo III himself was nicknamed by his opponents as one "imbued with the temperament of an Arab." Harrison, p. 38.

In his *Byzantine Studies and Other Essays*, Baynes takes issue with all historians, notably Diehl, who stress the impact of Asian influences upon the Empire.

and the Western Empire, and within the Byzantine orbit proper by the evolution of vigorous barbarian nations, the Byzantines entrenched themselves firmly and proudly behind the residuary argument that their cultural superiority was incontestable and absolute. This certainty was re-enforced by the relationship that the governing elite assumed toward Hellenism. For whether of Greek origin or not, they never ceased to cultivate the notion that they were the sole custodians of the Hellenic and Hellenistic heritage. Indeed, Byzantium's identification with Hellenism seems to have become so complete in the course of time that it eclipsed, eventually, the Empire's association with Romanism.

Another striking evidence of the Byzantine propensity to utilize a body of established transcendent ideas as the ultimate frame of reference for the inner integration and outer representation of a multinational and multicultural populace is supplied by the Empire's reading of Christianity. In estimating the place of religion in Byzantine politics, we must bear in mind first, that this Christian state occupied a median position between Western Christendom and the non-Christian societies of the East, and second, that it assumed the characteristics of a separate theocratic state at a time when the political organization of the great culture realms to the east of Constantinople—Sassanian Persia, India, China, and somewhat later the caliphates of Damascus and Baghdad—was being subjected also to the impact of strong religious forces. As a consequence of these geographical and historical circumstances the Eastern Christian state was destined to reflect the influences that had emanated for many centuries from the neighboring Asian orbits, particularly the Persian and Arab domains. Indeed, most Byzantine statesmen and theologians took full account of these connections when they planned the Empire's policies. The voluntary and involuntary processes of borrowing and restating foreign forms, which ensued from the encounter with these multifarious influences, were so intricate in their various phases that they cannot be reconstructed here. However, a cursory survey of the impact of the foreign cults on Byzantine thought and politics permits the inference that the Empire was attracted chiefly by the element of mysticism that was strongly prevalent in all of the entering creeds.

The ready reception of these converging mystical traditions had its social and political causes. The intellectual elite was drawn to the rich symbolism which seemed to offer the greatest possible latitude for religious and metaphysical speculations. The unsophisticated many, on the other hand, who needed emotional security in a world that their untrained intellects could not comprehend, accepted the same body of religious forms because it was made manifest to them on the level of direct, immediate, and sensuous experience. In other words, here was a ready focus of existence, accessible and meaningful alike to the literate and to the nonliterate, to the Greek and the barbarian, the European, the Asian, and the African. Small wonder, therefore, that certain forms of religious mysticism assumed great political importance as carriers of the idea of imperial unity. For while the educated man could accede to the common fund of Byzantine culture by following the mystical philosophy of the Greek fathers, and the uneducated had no difficulty in identifying himself with the many-colored imagery of religious art and legend, both could find a common ground in the liturgy and dogma of the Greek Orthodox Church.[34]

The empire-conscious statesmen of Byzantium showed a keen awareness of the political advantages inherent in this situation. It was clear to most of the emperors, beginning with Justinian, that the power and unity of the realm would best be served if the state and the church were blended into a single organism,[35] and that their cherished conception of the state as a divinely instituted autocratic monarchy could be propagated most effectively if it were presented to the people in a garb of generally accepted mystical rites. In other words, one could best assure the secular territorial jurisdiction of the autocratic ruler if the state were made to appear as the church. These seem to have been the premises upon which Justinian built his empire in the East. However, if the state was to derive its strength from the religious unification of its residents, and if the jurisdiction of the state was to be coterminous with that of the church, then it followed that the state should not acknowledge any religious divisions within its confines. The maintenance of the unity of the established church, consequently, was Justinian's leading political consideration.[36] This conception of the church-state was not easily reconcilable, however, with the Byzantine ambition to regain control of Italy and reconstitute the whole *universitas*; for it conflicted with the prevalent constitutional theories of the West. Any serious effort to substantiate the Byzantine pretensions would have necessitated a close alignment with the Church of Rome as the chief

[34] Cf. Christopher Dawson, *The Making of Europe*, New York, 1945, pp. 110, 121.

[35] Cf. Bury, Vol. II, p. 360. See also a letter from the Patriarch Antonius to Vassilii I, Grand Prince of Russia, on the Unity of the Empire and the Church and the Universality of the Empire (c. A.D. 1395) in Barker, ed., *Social and Political Thought in Byzantium*, pp. 194ff.

[36] Bury, Vol. II, p. 367; Dawson, p. 111.

carrier of universalism in that part of the Christian world, rather than with the local ecclesiastical establishment in Constantinople. It was only after Byzantium recognized that it was futile to compete with the Holy Roman Empire in the West and that the Greek Orthodox Church had gained an unrivalled ascendancy among the Slavic nations to the north and east of Constantinople, thus opening up entirely new possibilities for political expansion and control, that the local church was recognized unequivocally as the appropriate agent of imperial ambitions abroad.[37]

Byzantine ecclesiastical diplomacy proved eventually to be so successful in penetrating the neighboring belt of barbarian nations and in conditioning the political habits of many Slavic and other peoples that it is properly regarded today as one of the most interesting case studies in the comparative history of diplomatic and cultural relations. This particular manifestation of the church-state in international affairs should not be permitted to obliterate the rest of the record, however; for it was Justinian's ruthless insistence on religious uniformity that cost Byzantium the loss of its most civilized provinces. In Egypt and Asia Minor, where the Monophysites, Nestorians, and other Christian sects had long been the nuclei of community life, people were driven to separatism and disloyalty by the central government's ideological despotism. And since they had little, if anything, to lose by a change of masters, they were not prepared to offer any strenuous resistance in the defence of the cause of Constantinople when the Islamic armies invaded their realm. The historic shift of power from the Christians to the Muslims was thus consummated in the Mediterranean world largely as a result of Byzantine religious intransigence.[38] The expatriated sects found a great following, on the other hand, beyond the Eastern Empire's boundaries, where they established independent Christian churches.[39] And so—quite ironically, when regarded in the context of the Byzantine imperialist theocracy—Christianity's greatest expansion in Africa and Asia was brought about by its persecuted members rather than by the established Eastern church, and the Empire's most fateful contraction was caused by policies initially designed to ensure its stability and growth.

[37] See Ostrogorsky, p. 235, pp. 315-333 for the negotiations between Vatatzes and the Pope in Rome.

[38] See Alfred Guillaume, *Islam*, Penguin Book, 1954, p. 79.

[39] By the sixth century the Nestorians had reached Central Asia and Ceylon and in the following century they penetrated as far as China. Monophysitism became the religion of the Abyssinians, Nubians, and other desert tribes. See Glasenapp, Vol. II, pp. 347ff., Dawson, pp. 132ff.

B. BYZANTINE INSTITUTIONS

The Byzantine government acquired certain definite characteristics in its formative period which were to survive all subsequent modifications of the regime and set the Eastern Christian Empire apart from other contemporary great powers, especially the Christian society of the West. Some of these characteristics devolved from the Byzantine solution of the conflict between politics and religion. The fiat against the autonomous evolution of any theological traditions, which was imposed at an early time, lent strong support to the view that the official doctrines of the church should be determined by considerations of political expediency. After the revolutionary movement of the Iconoclasts had failed to emancipate religion from the state, this orientation hardened until it was taken for granted in the later history of the Empire that the church was there to serve the needs of the state, and that the chief ecclesiastical dignitary derived his authority from the imperial establishment.[40] In other words, the emperor was the head of the church, and his jurisdiction did not depend, either in theory or in practice, upon his coronation by the patriarch.

As a priest-king, sustained by God alone, the monarch was absolutely sovereign in temporal as well as in ecclesiastical affairs. This conception of autocracy, which seems to have been a synthesis of Roman, Persian, and Hellenistic traditions, was the focal point of the Eastern Empire's government. Theoretically then, there was no human authority that could call the ruler to account, but practically there existed several institutions that had a restraining effect upon the actual exercise of his unlimited powers. The church, paradoxically enough, was one of these influential agencies. Removed from the scene of power

[40] The place of Iconoclasm in Byzantine history is a controversial subject among Byzantinists. Baynes, *Byzantine Studies and Other Essays*, p. 128, regards the Iconoclast controversy as the decisive moment in Byzantine history. But he disputes the view held, among others, by Louis Bréhier that Iconoclasm was but an outgrowth and indeed the climax of the caesaro-papistic theory and practice of the state as represented by some of the most successful Byzantine emperors, finding, instead, that the movement was primarily religious in inspiration. See p. 239. "It is possible," Baynes writes on p. 53, "that in the heat of controversy an Iconoclast emperor may have exclaimed: 'I am priest as well as emperor,' but he spoke in haste," for the change came only in the days of the Empire's weakness, Baynes insists. Then, on the fall of Latin rule after the Greeks had returned to Constantinople, the person of the emperor becomes increasingly exalted. Some support for Diehl's view that the Byzantine emperor was a priest can be found in the writings of late Greek canonists, Baynes admits on p. 51, but the basic and most significant theory is the one that establishes the patriarch and the emperor as allies, not as rivals (p. 53). But see Diehl, *Byzantium: Greatness and Decline.*

politics and sheltered by the government from all attacks upon its established identity within the state, it could use all its energies for the purpose of solidifying its position within the Byzantine society. By accommodating the religious needs of the literate and nonliterate classes it gained great prestige among the people; and by artfully administering the mythos of the Basileus, it established itself securely as an indispensable agent of the imperial cause. Since the church was thus fitted "to be the soul and life of the Empire, to maintain the Imperial unity, and to give form and direction to every manifestation of national vigour,"[41] it could not possibly be ignored by any emperor.[42]

In the general context of the Greco-Christian tradition it was generally assumed furthermore that the monarch would always honor the moral dictates of *philanthropia*—an unwritten moral obligation that required him to serve his subjects in a humane way.[43] And what deference to *philanthropia* did not accomplish, fear of the populace oftentimes did. Each ruler knew that the people were quite ready to resort to riots, assassinations, and other violent gestures calculated to embarrass the existing regime, if they felt the emperor had flagrantly offended the popular will. Each monarch knew also, since he was the heir of a long line of Near Eastern potentates, that a successful revolution was usually not regarded as a usurpation of power, but rather as a divinely instituted process of establishing the right sovereign. As a rule, therefore, emperors were careful not to provoke the temper of their subjects. Confronted with the need to assuage popular feelings, they developed instead the art of leadership.[44]

The question whether the Eastern emperor was subject to a rule of law can receive only an ambiguous answer. It has been maintained that he was not above the law, but held himself bound by the accumulated traditions of the Roman inheritance and his own imperial edicts.[45] But there is scant if any evidence that imperial policies or actions were ever influenced decisively by the emperor's deference to legal prin-

[41] Sir William Ramsay as quoted by Norman H. Baynes, *The Byzantine Empire*, London, New York, 1925, p. 98.

[42] For the powers that a patriarch could exercise in an emergency even in opposition to an emperor, see Ernest Barker, p. 96.

[43] See Baynes, *The Byzantine Empire*, p. 70. Cf. the classical Roman theory that government is an obligation, not a privilege.

[44] Baynes, *The Byzantine Empire*, p. 68 says that "it is indeed their capacity as leaders of men which is the outstanding feature of the long line of East-Roman sovereigns."

[45] Dennet, "Pirenne and Muhammad," *Speculum*, XXIII, April, 1948, pp. 165-190, infers that the emperor was not a despot.

ciples. In other words, it is hardly possible to identify in Byzantium a body of constitutional law in the sense in which one could be found in the domain of the Western Christian Empire. This does not mean that law had no place in the Byzantine frame of government. On the contrary, the mere fact that the history of Roman law, from Justinian's codification onward, was essentially a Byzantine development[46] indicates already that law had indeed a recognized function in the scheme even of the most despotic rulers. For since the emperors were vitally interested in authenticating Constantinople as the second Rome, they were committed, as it were, to the maintenance of the Roman conception of law. And since they realized also that a vast empire could not be governed effectively by the exertion of mere personal power, they favored the further cultivation and adaptation of legal methods of administration that had proven their worth in Rome's earliest incarnation. But contrary to the doctrine prevailing in the West, law (as, for that matter, every other institution) was definitely regarded as subject to the state. Byzantine law served secular and practical ends, and was applied by secular officers under the surveillance of the absolute ruler of the state. Under these auspices there developed in Byzantium a special class of civil servants who emulated the intellectual traditions set by the Roman jurists of an earlier age.[47]

At a time, then, when Western Christendom was being ruled either by ecclesiastics or by unlettered soldiers, the Eastern Empire was being administered (at least until the sixth century) by an official class of scholarly politicians, much after the manner of the Chinese.[48] And since the ranks of this group were open to talent from all national contingents of the state[49] there came into being a kind of international secretariat imbued by an esprit de corps and professional standards of its own. This political and intellectual elite was the nucleus of Byzantium's famed bureaucracy.

The influence of this bureaucracy upon medieval Byzantine affairs can be understood best if it is remembered that the Byzantine Empire comprised a vast area subjected to an elaborate territorial organization

[46] See Barker, p. 31, for the view that the Byzantines were extremely active and successful in digesting and indexing law, but not in reflecting and speculating about matters of jurisprudence.

[47] Dawson, p. 106, suggests that the civilian bureaucracy was not, like the theocratic ideal of royalty and the court ceremonial, a result of new oriental influences, but was essentially an inheritance from the imperial service of the Antonine age and from the bureaucratic organization of the Hellenistic monarchies.

[48] *ibid.*

[49] *The Cambridge Medieval History*, Vol. IV, p. 736.

into prefectures, dioceses, provinces, and the like. Each of the units was ruled by a particular class of officers, and each set of bureaucrats constituted a check upon the jurisdiction of the others. Moreover, this civilian administration was paralleled for many centuries by a military organization of equal complexity. The task of governing the Eastern Empire had thus been delegated to a vast and well-coordinated service of trained administrators, whose advice the emperor could not afford to ignore. For they were the people who had found the ways and means of making the central government generally respected within the orbit of imperial power, who assured the stability of the nation's social life by maintaining the rule of law, and who protected the mystique of the imperial establishment by controlling an elaborate court ceremonial.

The Byzantine civil service was responsible for the organization of a financial system that elevated Byzantium above the vicissitudes of the feudal economies of all the other states of the Middle Ages. By methodically developing direct and indirect taxation as the state's chief sources of revenue, they succeeded in creating a permanent fisc. And it was this financial machine and its apparently inexhaustible capacity to make payments that supplied the essential foundation for the Eastern Empire's longevity and prestige.[50] As one authority explains it: "In the period of eight hundred years from Diocletian to Alexius Comnenus the Roman government never found itself compelled to declare bankruptcy, or stop payments. Neither the ancient nor the modern world can offer a complete parallel to this phenomenon. This prodigious stability of Roman financial policy secured the 'byzant' its universal currency. On account of its full weight it passed with all the neighbouring nations as a valid medium of exchange. By her money Byzantium controlled both the civilized and the barbarian worlds."[51]

This successful establishment of a money economy influenced in a vital way Byzantium's conduct of international relations. Since the emperor had a gold treasury at his disposal he could not only maintain a standing army and fleet, but could also keep these establishments subservient to his central power. Contrary to the feudal traditions prevalent in the West, he did not have to remunerate his vassals for their military aid by granting them land and thus diminish the scope of his own territorial jurisdiction. Instead he could pay salaries. Nor

[50] Cf. Ostrogorsky, p. 18.
[51] M. Gelzer, *Studien zur Byzantinischen Verwaltung Egyptens*, Leipzig, 1909, as quoted in Baynes, *The Byzantine Empire*, pp. 130-131.

was he as easily tempted as the Western princes to confiscate the land of a vassal, or to invade the domain of a rival state, simply to replenish the sources of his own material power.

Moreover, in the framework of an economy in which the army was viewed as a permanent manifestation of the state, war itself acquired a new meaning and was assigned new functions. Since the Western statesmen were compelled to raise armed forces for each particular campaign, they could not develop any long range military policies.[52] This meant that they were stopped, as it were, from thinking of war as a normal function of the organized society. Byzantium, on the other hand, was conditioned to regard war as an ever-present possibility and the standing army as the chief instrument for the preservation of the state. This orientation did not imply that every opportunity should be seized to test the strength of the state on the battlefield. On the contrary, it meant that the highly prized military instrument was to be handled with utmost care and precision and in close coordination with all the other services of the government in times of peace as well as of war. And it was probably this integral treatment of civilian and military institutions, indeed of the very concepts of peace and war, which best accounts for the fact that Byzantium was able to assert itself continuously rather than spasmodically in the field of international relations. In the complex hierarchy of interlocking governmental agencies the army thus came to occupy a key position. As one emperor put it: "The army is to the State what the head is to the body. If great care be not taken thereof the very existence of the Empire will be endangered."[53] This admonition seems to have been heeded by most of the Byzantine monarchs.

The place of the military in Byzantine affairs is seen in yet another perspective when one remembers that it functioned also as a proving ground for citizenship in a multinational commonwealth.[54] Just as the civil service included officials who were Italians, Bulgarians, Arabs, and Turks, so did the army employ generals of Armenian, Persian, and Slavic origin and hold its ranks open to aliens without much regard to their original provenance.[55] One of the regiments of the em-

---

[52] Cf. Baynes, *The Byzantine Empire*, pp. 129-130.

[53] *The Cambridge Medieval History*, Vol. IV, p. 737.

[54] Cf. the army's role in ancient Rome; *supra*, ch. 5.

[55] After the sixth century foreign mercenaries tend to disappear and the army is raised mostly from within the Empire, especially in Armenia. It was again opened wide to foreigners in the twelfth century, when Byzantium was hard pressed by the Seljuk Turks. See Baynes, *The Byzantine Empire*, pp. 138ff. for the causes of the army's eventual decline.

peror's bodyguard, for instance, was composed almost exclusively of Russians, Scandinavians, and Chozars. And the Varangian guard, originally formed of Russians, was successively recruited from among Russians, Scandinavians, Northmen of Norway and Iceland, and Anglo-Saxons. In the tenth century Armenian contingents were numerous and highly esteemed, while in the twelfth century the Latin troops were regarded as the best.[56]

In view of the extensive services which Byzantium demanded from its military establishment it is interesting to note that the army was deliberately kept small, the theory being that its real strength did not lie so much in its numbers[57] as in the intelligence with which it faced the Empire's enemies. It was the business of military administrators to learn each opponent's particular method of warfare and to assemble a whole arsenal of stratagems and tricks that could be employed to demoralize, weaken, or outmaneuver possible antagonists. Only when the enemy's defences had been thoroughly undermined would Byzantium employ its fighting forces.[58] And the army then would be guided by elaborate instructions outlining techniques for the feigning of flights, staging of night attacks and ambushes, and the conduct of truce negotiations for the purpose of winning time. Similar principles guided the operations of the navy until the eleventh century, when the Byzantine naval strength was permitted to decline.[59] Through such an interpretation of the uses and limitations of warfare the Byzantines discovered on numerous occasions that a smaller force could defeat a larger and that the state could hold its own against the odds even of a permanent encirclement. In other words, Constantinople's military policy reflected the same artful management of human relations as was reflected in many phases of its ecclesiastical and administrative policies.

The further question as to why the Byzantines were capable of evolving such systematic quasi-scientific methods of administering war and peace finds an answer in the general intellectual orientation of the Eastern Empire. As a Near Eastern society Byzantium had suc-

[56] *The Cambridge Medieval History*, Vol. IV, p. 738.
[57] The total strength of the army has been estimated at 120,000 in the ninth century, and at 150,000 in Justinian's time. See Baynes, *The Byzantine Empire*, p. 136.
[58] See Runciman, p. 144; Stanley Casson, *Progress and Catastrophe*, New York, London, 1937, pp. 225ff.
[59] Baynes, *The Byzantine Empire*, p. 148, suggests that the fourth crusade might have been directed against Egypt and not against Constantinople had the Eastern Empire maintained a fleet in being. See A. R. Lewis, *Naval Power and Trade in the Mediterranean*: A.D. *500-1100*, Princeton, 1951, p. 103 to the effect that Byzantium neglected the navy from A.D. 800 onward.

ceeded to the immense fund of learning that had accumulated in this area in the course of the preceding thousand years; and as the chief inheritor of the Hellenistic civilization in particular it had accepted the idea, cultivated consistently by all Greek-speaking peoples in the Mediterranean region,[60] that the preservation and pursuit of knowledge were noble human enterprises. The political elite charged with tending the Empire's far-flung political commitments thus operated in a social climate of intense intellectual activities. Indeed, the influence of this environment upon the minds of the administrators was so strong that the business of government itself assumed many aspects of a scholarly calling. This perhaps somewhat intangible connection between government and learning becomes quite obvious and concrete when seen in the context of the dominant Byzantine political theory. Since the state was generally regarded as the paramount expression of society it was taken for granted that all human activities and values were to be brought into a direct relationship to it. This meant that knowledge was not to be pursued for its own sake alone but also as a service to the state. It meant, in fact, that learning had an official political value, just as faith did. Any holder of a political office, whether civilian or military, was thus obligated, as it were, to use his intellectual capacity to the utmost in order to explore all available information likely to promote the due execution of his official functions and thus ensure the survival of the state.

Such approaches to learning were totally at variance with the intellectual traditions of medieval Western Europe. This incongruity explains why the Western critics were always ready to deprecate Byzantine learning as barren, stilted, and above all, remote from the great quest for the discovery of the divine truth which they felt to be man's foremost mission while on earth, and also why they failed to understand the political uses to which knowledge was being put in the rival Christian empire. Whereas the Western Europeans were concerned chiefly with creating institutions that should ensure the rights and obligations of all individuals and groups in their society, the Byzantines were absorbed in the task of securing the foundations for one great political organism: the state. Hence, East and West had developed fundamentally different concepts of society. A comparison of the records led Bryce to the view that Byzantine government was a pure

[60] All efforts to Latinize the Greek Empire proved to be in vain.

despotism, devoid of any constitutional history;[61] a crude reality, drawing neither strength nor beauty from any theory. The Holy Roman Empire, on the other hand, was seen as a dream of the unity of mankind, a sublime conception, half poetry and half theology.[62] With this comparison one may readily agree. But the further comment of the distinguished historian that the imperial agents of Byzantium were motivated by mere considerations of survival rather than by any respect for ethical or constitutional principles, overstates the case for historical comparisons as the true measure of the worth of a particular society. After all, survival is no mean accomplishment under any circumstance, and in the case of the Byzantine Empire it can properly be viewed as a great political victory over extraordinarily adverse circumstances regardless of the cost at which it was achieved.

If one reads Byzantine history on its own merits, one may conclude that the search for the means of survival as a great power was properly regarded by the imperial administrators as their foremost task. Such an interpretation of the functions of government may strike Western critics as narrow or unethical, but it conditioned the Byzantines at an early period to accept the state as the chief instrument for the preservation of society.[63] And the fact that the agency of the centralized state was used for the preservation of an ethnically and linguistically heterogeneous, rather than homogeneous, society would seem to enhance the historical significance of the political record.

No such community of thought for the preservation of a politically united society existed at that time in Western Europe. The Holy Roman Empire was an association of many different self-governing units, not a centrally governed state. It was concerned not so much with maintaining its identity as a power in international relations, as with developing principles of law and justice for the regulation of personal and governmental relations within its boundaries. As we have already noted, it is precisely this orientation which accounts for the influence of Western European constitutionalism upon the organization of the modern world. By contrast, the records of Byzantium contain few if any suggestions for the ordering of the world along legal and constitutional principles. But they, too, are of general interest for the student of international administration, because they reveal a variety of methods and institutions carefully designed to assure the longevity of one

[61] James Bryce, *The Holy Roman Empire*, New York, 1928, p. 331.
[62] *ibid.*, p. 347.
[63] Cf. Dennet, p. 184.

of the greatest multinational societies of all times. Moreover, since the Byzantine system exercised an immense influence on the political development of several Eastern European peoples, notably the Russians, its records will hold a special interest for anyone wishing to uncover the antecedents of the modern societies in this critical area.[64]

C. Byzantine Diplomacy

A. BYZANTINE DIPLOMACY IN MODERN HISTORY

Webster's New International Dictionary (Second Edition, Unabridged, 1949) defines diplomacy as "the art and practice of conducting negotiations between nations, as in arranging treaties, including the methods and forms usually employed; the business or art of conducting international intercourse." And the history of diplomacy as recorded in the modern European states system in the last centuries shows that this definition is an adequate rendition of the attributes commonly ascribed to this institution. Indeed, one may assume from a general survey of available historical material that this definition is an apt description also of similar practices that have facilitated dealings between peoples in earlier ages and under the auspices of different international systems. However, the word which is here defined does not have merely a generic and technical meaning. It also carries a rich substantive content, which cannot be conveyed in a single phrase, for we are dealing here with one of the most complex of all institutions that man has devised for the purpose of establishing contacts with other men. In approaching this subject one must remember that each society is moved by the circumstances of its existence to develop its own approach to foreign relations. This means that diplomacy, as for that matter every other social institution, is bound to incorporate the traditions and values peculiar to the civilization in which it is practiced.

When modern diplomacy was officially defined in dictionaries, international relations throughout most of the accessible world were managed by a concert of European and American nations that had come to agree on the basic meaning of diplomacy. And since the style of diplomacy that had thus been established in the Atlantic Community was diffused through imposition or imitation to all continents, the

[64] Russian scholars of the nineteenth and twentieth centuries—whether Western or Slavophile, Tsarist or Communist—fully acknowledge these affinities between the two empires.

impression prevailed, especially in the diplomatic circles of the Atlantic region, that the world's peoples were in genuine accord on all the substantive elements of diplomacy. The full complexities implicit in this institution began to become apparent after the First World War, however, when the supremacy of the Western European nations was contested both politically and culturally by the rise of new nations, the spread of revolutionary ideologies, and the resurrection of ancient civilizations.[65]

Of the various regions that were activated by one or the other of these challenging movements none underwent greater and swifter change and none had a greater impact upon the existing international order than the new Russia. For the processes of change which were here initiated by the communist revolution resulted, during the course of three decades, in the transformation of Russian society; the creation, in a vast Eurasian space, of a monolithic multinational empire; the diffusion of communism over most of the other parts of the world; and the extension, on an unprecedented scale, of Russian influence over all phases of political life everywhere. These developments had a very unsettling, indeed a revolutionary, effect upon established theories and techniques of conducting international relations. They threatened to vitiate the premises that had supported the European states system, and therefore they severely strained the resources of the diplomacy that had been practiced in the nineteenth century. Western statesmen came to realize in the course of their encounters with the representatives of communist Russia, that the foreign policies of the Soviet Union issued from a view of the world alien to their own traditions, and that the diplomatic methods there employed for the furtherance of foreign policies were disconcertingly different from those that had been evolved in the context of Western civilization.

An exploration of the sources of Soviet Russian conduct led Western scholars to a reappraisal of the various ideologies, notably those of Western Marxism, that had ignited the revolutionary explosion in the East, and to a study of the particular historical experiences that might be presumed to have led to the modern Russian use of these revolutionary doctrines in the domain of foreign affairs. It was this second set of inquiries that led to the recognition of Byzantine diplomacy as a major determinant of the behavior of the Soviet Union. But the same historical investigations, it is interesting to note, led also to the

[65] The misunderstanding between China and the two English-speaking nations about China's diplomacy in Korea may be taken as an early evidence of conflicting assumptions.

rediscovery of close connections between the ancient Byzantine and the later Western European methods of diplomacy. For the influence of the powerful Orthodox Empire had after all not been confined to the northern Slavs. It had been experienced also, either directly or indirectly, by many other impressionable peoples drawn into close contact with Constantinople while in the decisive stages of their political evolution. This was true particularly of the Venetians.

When the great trading city of Venice first became associated with the Eastern Empire, it was not only an autonomous republic with strong political traditions of its own but also an integral part of the Western European civilization. This civilization, as previous chapters have shown, had given rise to a political system markedly different from the one prevailing in the rival Christian domain. Venice thus became one of the most important junctions[66] between the Eastern and Western worlds as they were distinguished from each other in the Middle Ages. But since its citizens recognized the East as the chief source of all that was new, exciting, and desirable in their times, the traffic was westbound in the main, and Venice became a gateway, as it were, through which goods and ideas readily could pass, ultimately to reach the most western bounds of the Western commonwealth.

This was the process that brought the Byzantine diplomatic tradition to Renaissance Italy. For the Venetians, in the course of their close commercial and political dealings with Constantinople, which was first their ally and later their foe, became convinced that the much-envied worldly success of Byzantium was due principally to diplomatic prowess, and that the fortunes of their own city stood to benefit immeasurably from an equally skillful application of the science of managing other states. As the fabric of the Holy Roman Empire grew weaker under the impact of secular and particularist interests, the Byzantine art and practice came to exercise, through Venice, an increasing influence on European politics, until, when the Florentine and papal courts followed the Venetian suit in the fifteenth century, they were transformed into the Italian method of diplomacy. This so-called Italian method then set the pattern, first for the rising nation states of Spain and France, and eventually all of Europe.[67]

In the course of the following centuries the peoples of the West were to find new political directions in the field of international relations which would be more in line with the trends of their own political and

[66] Others were Sicily and Spain.
[67] Cf. Harold Nicolson, *Diplomacy*, London, New York, 1950, p. 43.

economic development, as well as with the legacy of political thought that originally distinguished the Christian West from the Christian East. The evolution of this separate Western European method of diplomacy would naturally imply a growing divergence, not only from the classical Byzantine model, but also from the variant of the Byzantine style developing in Russia, so that by the middle of the twentieth century it would be clear to all observers of the international scene that the problems of diplomacy were being approached differently by the Soviet Union and the member nations of the Atlantic community. But any real effort to understand this aspect of our present crisis would seem to require a preliminary reading of the history of Byzantine diplomacy. These records not only contain the mainsprings of Russian diplomatic practices, but also inform the student that the international history of diplomacy is indivisible.

B. THE BYZANTINE THEORY AND PRACTICE OF DIPLOMACY

Like the diplomacy of any other state, that of Byzantium reflected the inner structure of the society in which it was evolved. The pivotal point in this structure was the concept of the centralized state, and this concept was realized by many separate but interlocking institutions of government. Each of these institutions had its own frame of reference because it was designed to serve a particular aspect of the state. But all, including those concerned with ecclesiastical affairs, proceeded from the premise that the ultimate success of all government is dependent upon the proper management of human susceptibilities rather than upon the faithful obeisance to preconceived theories and images. The external policies of the Empire were meant to further the same paramount purpose that pervaded all of the domestic institutions: the power and prestige of the state. And since the imperial statesmen were usually aware of the limitations of the state's material power and the disadvantages of its geographical position, they pursued this supreme goal in the domain of international relations by relying heavily on the same methods of influencing the behavior and expectations of human beings that had proved their worth in the area of domestic administration. This was the context in which Byzantium developed diplomacy as the art of managing foreign peoples to its own advantage.[68]

The geographic range of Byzantine diplomacy was immense. It extended from China and India to the Atlantic Ocean, and from inner

---

[68] The Byzantines were not the first to develop this kind of diplomacy systematically. For a similar approach see Kautilya's *Arthashastra*.

Africa to the steppes of Northern Europe. It encompassed great powers and ancient civilizations as well as small nations and culturally undeveloped societies. Within this jurisdiction Byzantine diplomacy pursued a variety of goals. Apart from addressing itself to the general and constant aim of ensuring the Empire's security and prestige, it assumed many specific functions, particularly in that inner ring of lesser nations which separated the state from the other great powers of the world. Here the Byzantine diplomats had the mandate of maintaining the Empire's existing spheres of influence, and of coping with the steady pressure of the barbarian tribes by drawing the new arrivals into the circle of hedge-guarding imperial client states that was meant to serve as an outer line of defense.[69] The great design of the Empire's foreign policy was translated into fact by the establishment of a whole constituency of vassals which included at one time or another the Arabs of Syria and Yemen, Berbers of North Africa, Lazi and Tsani in the farthest confines of Armenia; Heruli, Gepidae, Lombards, and Huns on the Danube. Other satellites in the north and east were the Caucasians, Albanians, Croats, Serbs, Bulgars, and Russians. In the western Mediterranean the Byzantine protectorate was long accepted by the republics of Venice, Naples, Gaeta, Amalfi, and by the princes of Salerno, Capua, and Beneventum.[70]

Within the fluctuating boundaries of this great orbit, Byzantine diplomacy was required to ascertain the degree of control that could be exercised over each separate community and to supervise the evolution of each particular relationship. Also it had to counter whatever competitive appeals rival great powers might address to these lesser states or tribes, to keep abreast of native movements toward independence, and in extreme cases to modify, and if need be to discard, outworn terms of suzerainty. These were the general terms of reference, but the particular diplomatic objectives varied from region to region. The chief problem in the north was to secure the imperial frontier against invasion; in the Caucasian area Byzantium had to contend against the influence of Persia; and in the Red Sea district the objectives were largely commercial.[71] A summary view of the entire diplomatic record shows that the Byzantines were able to execute most of these complex assignments in a spirited manner. Indeed, in many instances they dis-

[69] Cf. this political arrangement with the organization of China's imperial orbit.
[70] See Diehl, *History of the Byzantine Empire*, pp. 27, 87ff.; also *Byzantium: Greatness and Decline*, 1957, pp. 53ff., 176ff.
[71] See J. B. Bury, *History of the Later Roman Empire*, 2 vols., London, 1931, Vol. II, pp. 292ff. See also Runciman, pp. 290ff.

played such an ingenuity in finding patterns of accord between their own sophisticated and powerful society on the one hand, and culturally inferior and politically weaker nations on the other, that one is justified in defining their type of diplomacy as the science of managing the barbarians.[72]

The people who were called upon to perfect and apply this science were expected to possess many talents and skills. Their qualifications were first enumerated in the fifth century, during the reign of Theodoric (died 526), the Ostrogothic king of Rome, who had been imbued with Byzantinism while a hostage at the imperial court in Constantinople. At that time Theodoric's chief of the civil service, Cassiodorus, wrote his master the following advice: "If, indeed, every embassy requires a wise man, to whom the conservation of the interests of the state may be intrusted, the most sagacious of all should be chosen, who will be able to argue against the most crafty, and to speak in the council of the wise in such a manner that even so great a number of learned men will not be able to gain a victory in the business with which he is charged."[73]

Byzantine political theory assumed that the emperors themselves were the best diplomats, since all power and wisdom were supposed to emanate from them. And this presumption was borne out in many cases.[74] But even the most proficient emperors needed assistants if Byzantine foreign policy was to be systematically transacted. This service was rendered by a special department of external affairs and an elaborately organized body of foreign service personnel, whose status and prestige in the society were fixed in all details.[75] The trained envoys and negotiators who were recruited in this fashion had to pass rigid examinations and receive detailed instructions before they could be entrusted with foreign missions.[76] While on duty at a foreign court the envoy was supposed not only to represent his sovereign but also to collect as much information as possible about the domestic affairs

[72] See J. B. Bury, "Roman Empire, Later" in *Encyclopaedia Britannica*, 1944, p. 444.

[73] David J. Hill, *A History of European Diplomacy*, London, 1921, Vol. I, p. 39, and see pp. 35-40 for a general account of Theodoric's diplomacy.

[74] Justinian laid the groundwork for Byzantine diplomacy. Bury, Vol. II, ch. xx. See Vasiliev on the diplomacy of other emperors.

[75] See the "Ceremonies" drawn up by the emperor Constantine VII Porphyrogenitus in the tenth century which prescribe the appropriate dress and deportment for the various classes of state functionaries, including the diplomats. These rules of etiquette and ceremonial were widely copied by the courts of Western Europe, the Slavonic states including Russia, and the Ottoman Empire. See Vasiliev, p. 363.

[76] Hill, Vol. I, pp. 206ff. Also Nicolson, pp. 25, 26. It must be noted that Byzantium did not maintain permanent embassies abroad.

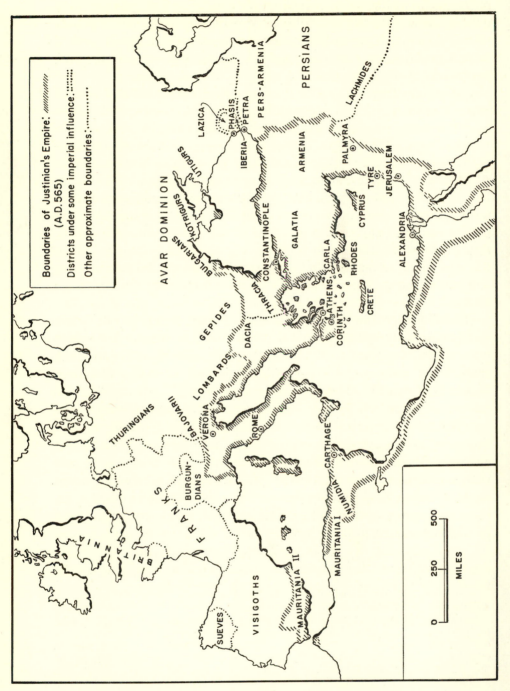

The Byzantine Empire in the sixth century A.D.

Legend:

Boundaries of Justinian's Empire: (A.D. 565)

Districts under some imperial influence:

Other approximate boundaries:

Labels on map:

BRITANNIA

THURINGIANS

FRANKS

BURGUN-DIANS

BAJOVARII

VERONA

ROME

SUEVES

VISIGOTHS

MAURITANIA II

MAURITANIA I

NUMIDIA

CARTHAGE

LOMBARDS

GEPIDES

DACIA

THRACIA

CONSTANTINOPLE

GALATIA

AVAR DOMINION

BULGARIANS

KOTRIGURS

UTIGURS

LAZICA

IBERIA

PHASIS

PETRA

PERS-ARMENIA

ARMENIA

PERSIANS

LACHMIDES

PALMYRA

TYRE

JERUSALEM

CARIA

ATHENS

CORINTH

RHODES

CYPRUS

CRETE

ALEXANDRIA

MILES

0 250 500

of the host country, for he would be obliged, upon his return, to give a full account of his findings. The envoys to barbarian courts had particularly complex assignments. They were supposed to study the habits, morals, and institutions of all tribes in the vicinity, ascertain their military strength and weaknesses, follow the flow of commerce and the trends of intertribal and regional relationships, watch for and investigate internecine quarrels, and identify existing and prospective leaders in the district. An effective diplomatic agent was expected to be a good observer of human nature, for he had to analyse the personalities of the barbarian chiefs in order to find out whether they would be susceptible to flattery or threat, to women or wealth.[77]

The professional services that these trained civil servants rendered the state were supplemented by the activities of other citizens who had special opportunities of contacting and influencing foreign peoples. Being an empire with far-flung commercial connections, Byzantium could rely on its merchants, particularly those who lived abroad or in frontier towns, as competent collectors of information and exponents of its cause. Such cities as Cherson and Bosporus on the Black Sea, for example, were not only centers of trade and focal points of Greek civilization, they were also valuable outposts of observation where numerous agents were stationed. Being a proselytizing theocracy, the empire was well served also by those missionaries, monks, and other members of the ecclesiastical hierarchy, whose lives were dedicated to the dissemination of the Byzantine creed and culture. However, the imperial administration expected more than professional proficiency from the various groups and individuals who represented its cause among the barbarians. As loyal subjects of the state all diplomats and pseudo-diplomats, whatever their special fields of interest or competence, were supposed to be familiar also with the forces and institutions that were traditionally regarded as the Empire's greatest sources of internal and external strength. It was thus taken for granted that the diplomats would capitalize on the appeals of Hellenism and orthodoxy, as well as on the mystique of the capital and its imperial establishment. It was assumed, furthermore, that the conduct of diplomacy would be coordinated at all times with the work of all the other agencies of government, notably the military, ecclesiastical, and fiscal authorities.[78]

---

[77] See S. Bakhrouchine, A. Ephimov, E. Kosminski, A. Narotchnitski, V. Serguiev, S. Skazkine, V. Khvostov et E. Tarlé, *Histoire de la Diplomatie*, 3 vols., tome premier, publié sous la direction de M. Potiemkine, Paris, 1947, pp. 86ff.; hereafter cited as Tarlé, *Histoire*.

[78] Diehl, *History of the Byzantine Empire*, p. 28.

Before the foreign agents of Byzantium could make an appropriate use of their own skills and their country's intellectual and material resources, they had to acquire a knowledge of the local conditions they were meant to influence, define the role that each particular community was best suited to play in the great Byzantine design, and evolve the synthesis of imperial and native interests that would best promote the objectives of the Empire without unnecessarily antagonizing the native populations. The responses to these and the other assignments that fell to them varied with the circumstances, but certain general policies can be discerned in the total record of the Byzantine effort to manage barbarian peoples and lesser states.

The imperial government was exceedingly economical in its use of actual force. Vanquished nations were treated with calculated mildness. In conquered Bulgaria, for instance, an imperial directive (issued by Basil II) called for the widest possible respect of local customs. The people were permitted to pay taxes in kind, this having been their earlier custom; retain their native officials, but subject now to the authority of a Byzantine high commissioner; and maintain an independent church under the direction of a Bulgarian prelate. Similarly, in southern Italy, the members of the native aristocracy were allowed to participate in the provincial government.[79] Except for extreme cases, where the defeated proved to be entirely intractable and were therefore removed to other districts, making room for more amenable populations,[80] the government ruled by indirect and devious means, skillfully exploiting such human foibles as ambition, pride, cupidity, and jealousy. New tribes invading the domain were appeased by grants of territory or of political status, while the settled nations were often kept from rebellion and aggression simply by annually paid subsidies, or by fixed remunerations in return for some useful political function that they had been induced to undertake. For example, Justinian subsidized the Utigurs as long as they kept the Huns from attacking Cherson and Bosporus.[81] Nor were such arrangements restricted to the so-called barbarians. In the tenth century Byzantium paid Venice for policing the Adriatic, Syria for protecting the eastern frontiers, and various Armenian states for replenishing the ranks of the imperial

[79] *The Cambridge Medieval History*, Vol. IV, ch. XXIII.
[80] *ibid.*
[81] See Bury, Vol. II, pp. 310ff. Much of the gold that was thus paid out to the satellites and other nations returned to Constantinople in the form of trade. See Lewis, pp. 37ff., who compares these Byzantine policies to those of Great Britain in the 18th and 19th centuries.

army.[82] This particular method of utilizing lesser nations proved profitable also when Byzantium had to cope with great powers that could be neither bought nor defeated. When Justinian wished to divert Persia's attention from the imperial boundaries, he found ways of persuading the Huns and Arabs of the desert to harass this enemy. Indeed, the Byzantines discovered in the course of their international dealings that most people could be induced to quarrel with their neighbors, and they concluded from this observation that immunity from aggression could be gained with comparative ease by playing one foreign nation against the other. This inexpensive diplomatic tactic proved particularly effective among the undeveloped, unsophisticated barbarians whose predatory designs the imperial government had reason to fear. The Byzantine diplomats were therefore continuously engaged in sowing seeds of jealousy, suspicion, and discord among the lesser nations in the immediate vicinity.

However, the general diplomatic record shows that the imperial government did not cater only to man's grosser instincts and material interests. Its agents were acutely conscious also of the intellectual and cultural vacuum that existed in most border regions. And since they represented a monolithic state in which the spiritual and material spheres were closely integrated, they were committed to the task of filling this void by organized campaigns of cultural infiltration. This political circumstance added great momentum to the proselytizing drive that issued from the Eastern Christian church and penetrated the deep interior of all surrounding lands. In reviewing these ecclesiastical enterprises abroad, one finds, as in the case of secular diplomacy, that native institutions were respected and native needs well understood.

The missionaries seem to have known as well as the diplomats that the leadership principle was the pivotal point in the political organization of most barbarian nations. Proselytizing campaigns were therefore usually initiated by efforts to convert the native chief and his entourage. If those dignitaries appeared to need additional schooling or pressure, a visit to Constantinople was arranged. Here the pagan candidates were exposed to a variety of compelling experiences, carefully planned for the religious and political exigencies of each case. Thus we find a sixth century king of the Huns receiving baptism in the capital with the emperor himself acting as his sponsor.[83] Other monarchs who entered the Byzantine religious fold were Tsar Boris of Bulgaria (864), Tsarina

[82] Diehl, *History of the Byzantine Empire*, p. 87.
[83] Bury, Vol. II, p. 311.

Olga of Kiev (957), who was converted fifty years after she had been a guest at the imperial court, and Vladimir of Kiev, who received baptism after his capture of Cherson (988). Indeed, the conversion of the Russian prince Vladimir, which was followed by his marriage to the Byzantine princess Anna and the collective baptism of his pagan subjects, must be regarded as one of the most important events in the history of the political and cultural relations of Byzantium. Kiev not only became an orthodox Christian state with a metropolitan appointed by the patriarch of Constantinople and with its dogma, constitution, and laws modelled on the Byzantine pattern, but also a political ally and disciple of the Empire. Moreover, since Kiev was destined to become Russia, and since Russia was destined to become the successor of the Second Rome, it would even be justifiable to treat Vladimir's conversion as one of the chief events in world history.[84]

These were dramatic triumphs of the Byzantine church-state. But most carriers of the orthodox faith did not confine their efforts to the titled and illustrious. Being devout and humble Christians uninterested in reward and fame, they were ready to risk their lives in return for a chance to lead the unknown simple folk of the barbarians into the protective orbit of the Christian God. This devotion to the cause of orthodoxy was best illustrated by two ninth century missionaries, the so-called apostles of the Slavs, who invented an alphabet for the natives, translated the Holy Scriptures for their use, preached in Slavic, celebrated offices with a Slavic liturgy, and tried to create a Slavic clergy. Their great program of evangelisation was eminently successful in many Slavic countries where it provided a lasting foundation for all religious life.[85]

The religious alignment between Byzantium and its satellites that the exertions of these theologians brought about had far-reaching cultural implications, for in propagating the orthodox faith the ecclesiastical emissaries also propagated the cause of education and learning. Countless Slavic peoples received their own alphabet and literary language in the process of imbibing the alien creed and were thus stimu-

---

[84] Cf. Runciman, pp. 279-290; Baynes, *The Byzantine Empire*, pp. 233ff.

[85] The early successes of the two apostles were reversed in Hungary and Croatia. Byzantium's religious missions failed also among the Chozars. This people was caught between the contending forces of Christianity and Islam but obstinately refused to accept either of these faiths. In the end the Chozars chose Judaism. See Runciman, pp. 279-290. Also Diehl, *History of the Byzantine Empire*, p. 69. J. B. Bury, *A History of the Eastern Roman Empire from the fall of Irene to the accession of Basil I* (A.D. *802-867*), London, 1912, ch. XII, pp. 375ff. on the conversion of Slavs and Bulgarians; ch. XIII, pp. 402ff. on the Chozars (Khazars).

lated to explore the further areas of knowledge that their Byzantine mentors had placed within their reach. The widespread diffusion of Byzantine theology, jurisprudence, literature, and art that followed in the wake of these educational efforts was tantamount to the creation of a more or less ideologically unified orbit. And, of course, the Byzantine foreign service favored this development since it greatly facilitated their task of managing the barbarians.

Apart from supporting such general trends toward acculturation, the government conducted special orientation programs for kings and other leaders. Under the terms of this policy, which was initiated by Justinian, young chiefs arrived at the imperial court either as guests or as hostages; others, exiled from their home country, were granted asylum, while still others were kept in storage, as it were, being pretenders to native thrones. All were befriended, protected, educated, entertained and indoctrinated during these sojourns, in the hope that they would in time become pliable tools in the arsenal of Byzantine diplomacy.

Of the many enticements employed to lure the visiting apprentices into the Byzantine fold, none was more effective than that of the imperial establishment. There was Constantinople itself, with its breathtaking wealth and splendor, whose spell no uncouth stranger could escape. In this greatest of all cities was the abode of the one and only King, representing God on earth. The visitor, overwhelmed by the court's magnificence and intimidated by its mystical rites and forms, became convinced, before he had a chance to think, that all power, grace, and honor must surely emanate from this throne, and that he was greatly privileged to kneel before it. The mood has been recaptured by Norman H. Baynes in the following imaginative passage: "Picture for a moment the arrival of a barbarian chieftain from steppe or desert in this Byzantine Court. He has been royally entertained, under the vigilant care of imperial officials he has seen the wonders of the capital, and today he is to have audience with the Emperor. Through a dazzling maze of marble corridors, through chambers rich with mosaic and cloth of gold, through long lines of palace guards in white uniforms, amidst patricians, bishops, generals and senators, to the music of organs and church choirs he passes, supported by eunuchs, until at last oppressed with interminable splendour he falls prostrate in the presence of the silent, motionless, hieratic figure of the Lord of New Rome, the heir of Constantine, seated on the throne of the Caesars: before he can rise, Emperor and throne have been caught aloft, and with vestments changed since last he gazed the sovereign looks down upon him,

335

surely as God regarding mortal men. Who is he, as he hears the roar of the golden lions that surround the throne or the song of the birds on the trees, who is he that he should decline the Emperor's behests? He stays not to think of the mechanism which causes the lions to roar or the birds to sing: he can scarce answer the questions of the logothete speaking for his imperial master: his allegiance is won: he will fight for the Roman Christ and his Empire."[86]

An analysis of the various factors that combined to produce this posture of awe, humility, and submission shows that the Byzantines were very clever in manipulating two images that were sufficiently transcendental to appeal to many peoples. The first conveyed the thought that Constantinople was the Second Rome and thus the nearest earthly approximation to that divine city which was the fatherland of all races. The second embodied the notion that the emperor was the divinely appointed father of all men. With the aid of these images the Byzantine Empire was made to appear as a magnificent family held together by a benign but forceful and resplendent paternal power. The psychologically astute politicians of Byzantium realized also, however, that the family and father symbols required a more explicit, positive, and practical implementation if they were to inspire the subalterns to serve the central powers. For it could hardly be expected that meek and awestruck tribal chiefs would have the spirit or incentive to execute some of the highly complex functions which were to be assigned them in the great strategic scheme. The vanquished had to regain some kind of self-respect; those dispossessed of dignity and status had to be honored, albeit in terms of the imperial value scale, if they were to identify themselves with the Byzantine cause. In brief, the second phase of the program of political education called for a proper measure of rehabilitation, to be accomplished largely by dispensing flattery in the context of the Empire's courtly ceremonies and rites.[87] The emissaries of the satellites were often ostentatiously preferred to those sent by the governments of the great;[88] they were decorated and titled, they were given crowns and sceptres,[89] and, if their services were deemed espe-

---

[86] Baynes, *The Byzantine Empire*, pp. 72-73.

[87] *ibid.*, p. 71; Charles Diehl, *Les Grands Problèmes de l'Histoire Byzantine*, Paris, 1943, p. 129.

It is interesting to compare these aspects of Byzantine imperialism with ancient China's imperial order.

[88] This was one of Bishop Liutprandt's complaints.

[89] In order to conciliate the Bulgarians when they were particularly threatening, the Tsar was even permitted to call himself "Basileus." Diehl, *Les Grands Problèmes de l'Histoire Byzantine*, pp. 126ff.

cially desirable, they were even given Byzantine princesses in marriage. By these and other means each of the many princelings was made to feel that he had a definite, recognized, and honored place in the greatest imperial establishment of all time, while all were made vaguely conscious of the fact that the authoritarian empire was actually a co-prosperity zone beneficial to the high and to the low.[90]

When the imperial authorities treated with the representatives of powers outside their special orbit, they adopted many of the diplomatic devices they had used with the barbarian chiefs. Here too, in order to captivate the senses and anesthetize or dull the mental fortitude of the alien emissary, the diplomatic atmosphere was deliberately charged with ostentation, mystery, and magnificence.[91] However, the ultimate purposes pursued in the realm of the satellites on the one hand, and that of the great powers on the other, were sufficiently different to require some rather significant variations in the diplomatic method.

In the context of its paternalistic policies of guiding and conciliating the inferior barbarians, Byzantium could afford to humor the susceptibilities of visiting chiefs without fear of losing prestige. But in the area of great power politics, in which every foreign nation was presumed to be a foe, and in which Byzantium was keenly aware of the limitations of its power, it was found necessary to overwhelm the visitor with impressions of Byzantine strength and invincibility. Since an envoy from one of the great countries was regarded as an enemy, and therefore as a spy, he was kept under close surveillance. An "honor" guard, staffed by members of the secret police, received him at the boundary and conducted him on circuitous routes, past formidable fortifications, often of an entirely spurious kind, to the majestic and impregnable city of all cities. Here he was surrounded by luxury and refinement;[92] here also he was liable to undergo great trials and tribulations. From Bishop Liutprandt's diary,[93] for example, we learn that this emissary from Western Europe was held in virtual captivity. Confined to his lodgings, supervised by the police, unable to communicate with his friends, unsure of the chances of his mission, humiliated, lonely, sick and often

---

[90] In many instances Byzantine diplomacy fell short of the aims that it pursued.

[91] A special office was in charge of arranging the reception of foreign ambassadors. See Nicolson, *The Evolution of Diplomatic Method*, London, 1954, pp. 25ff. See also Tarlé, *Histoire*, pp. 90ff. The reports and analyses contained in this volume are of special interest today because they invite reflections upon the relationship between modern Russian and Byzantine practices of diplomacy.

[92] Cf. Eleanor of Aquitaine's visit, mentioned earlier in this chapter.

[93] The bishop's account, while no doubt exaggerated, presents a creditable account of Byzantine practices.

starving, he was kept waiting many weeks before permission arrived for him to present his case at court. On this momentous occasion he was suddenly lifted out of his misery and translated to a scene of pomp and splendor. Such a sequence of personal experiences, similar in many respects to the one usually arranged for the political education of the satellites, was evidently designed to unstring the foreign emissary and thus prejudice his cause in the ensuing negotiations. For it was expected that the stranger would emerge from the confinement less confident of the purpose of his mission, more fearful of the Eastern Empire, and quite determined to make whatever concessions would be necessary to enable him to conclude the negotiations and leave the dreaded place.[94]

It has been on the strength of evidence of this kind that Byzantine diplomacy has been indicted[95] as an immoral method of conducting international relations. But before concurring in this judgment, we must evaluate the method in the context of the system in which it evolved.

The ruling circles of Byzantium regarded the state as the highest value in society. They did not admit that the actions of the state were subject either to law or to morality. Nor could they attribute any political validity to such concepts as "humanity" or "the unity of mankind," since they saw the world around them in terms of disconnected and conflicting parts. In the tradition of Byzantine statesmanship no moral opprobrium attached to war and no intrinsic value inhered in peace. Both had their time and place in accordance with the interests of the state. As the paramount manifestation of the Byzantine state in the realm of competitive power politics, diplomacy was as amoral as the state itself. Its chief purpose was to protect the state, ensure its survival, and promote its power by any method that promised success. Diplomacy, then, did not issue from a moral preference for conciliation and peace, but from considerations of expediency. This implied that neighboring nations were to be either appeased or infuriated, and that their rivalries were to be either adjusted or fanned deliberately, as the occasion demanded it.

Byzantine diplomacy must therefore be regarded primarily as an organic part of the entire political structure of the empire. But since

---

[94] A prolonged detention was sometimes supposed to delay the suspected imminence of aggression or of some other decisive move on the part of the court that sent the envoy. See Tarlé, *Histoire*, pp. 90ff., for a discussion of this diplomatic device.

[95] See Dawson, also Nicolson.

the state was an expression of the general civilization, Byzantine diplomacy must be viewed also in this larger context. Byzantine culture has been much disparaged. Yet few will deny that it reveals an astute and all-pervading sense of the value of stylised forms as ordering principles of thought and action. A symbolic vestment represented the imperial principle in all its complexity, a religious liturgy set the pattern for a coordinated expression of multifarious religious ideas, and a legal code provided the general moulds for all the variants of human behavior in society. Diplomacy was an integral part of this great system of symbolic forms. And since it was supposed to draw upon all the other structured organisms in the state, one may say indeed that it gave the Empire its "Gestalt" in foreign eyes.

This was especially so in the orbit of the satellites to which diplomacy addressed itself in a special way, and it is therefore in this field of foreign operations that the merits and deficiencies of the method are most apparent. Diplomacy may be credited here with the following achievements. It controlled the political development of numerous barbaric nations, contributed materially to the consolidation of urban life and the rise of commerce, and promoted the diffusion of religion, learning,[96] and the arts. Reviewing these accomplishments retrospectively, one may be disposed to conclude that diplomacy must have been the chief instrument by means of which isolated barbaric peoples were drawn, in that period, into the society of civilized nations. Such, however, was neither the intended nor the immediate effect of the diplomatic exertions of Byzantium. The chief purpose of the Byzantine policy in this sphere was the attainment of influence, and it was in the pursuit of this objective that the diplomats of the Eastern Empire made their most original contribution to the art of international politics. They created a form of tutelage and control over less developed nations that has retained great significance for the causes both of imperialism and of international administration.

Byzantine diplomacy had several characteristics, on the other hand, that inevitably became liabilities in times of stress. Since it was by nature an expensive undertaking, it contributed greatly to the depletion of the treasury and the impoverishment of the Empire, and since it was designed to play upon the cupidity of the subaltern peoples, it tended to promote greater greeds than could be satisfied and more rebellion

[96] Doubt has been expressed as to whether Byzantium really promoted learning among the barbarians. Dawson, pp. 184ff., suggests that the Slavonic peoples inherited only the religious and artistic elements of Byzantium's civilization.

and unrest than could be safely contained. Another element conducive to decay was the close relationship of the diplomatic art to warfare. In the Byzantine view, as we have already noted, diplomacy was always meant to operate as an auxiliary to the military establishment and was expected to incorporate the tactics of warfare. These affinities were not to be exhibited openly. However, when both the financial and the military powers of the Empire waned and diplomacy was the only mainstay of the country's faltering fortunes, it was deprived of the means to mask its action, and its kinship with the military art could no longer be denied. Ruses, frauds, and tricks were then often the only ammunition that the diplomats had left.

These negative manifestations of Byzantine diplomacy brought to light several fundamental conceptual limitations. In retrospect it is evident that the excessive concern of the Empire for self-gratification was too limited an objective to sustain an institution that depended in actuality, if not in intent, upon the support of many different peoples. It may be argued in this connection, furthermore, that this diplomacy was bound to be an inexact and unreliable instrument for the control of human behavior, since it issued from a very partial view of human nature and operated, by and large, within the narrow range of human weakness. If one reflects upon these limitations, however, one finds, ironically, that they stem from the same fundamental premise that assured the success of the Byzantine technique in the period of its prime, namely, an unswaying regard for the circumstances that would best support the unrivalled power of the Empire in an orbit of culturally and politically inferior satellites. It was this conceptually rather rigid relationship between the institution and its environment which severely handicapped the operations of diplomacy when the circumstances changed and the power of the Empire began to decay. One may conclude that Byzantine diplomacy lost its force when the uncivilized grew civilized and the weak gained strength. Then it became apparent that the art of managing barbarians could not be practiced where there were no more barbarians.

D. The Continuance of the Byzantine Tradition in Diplomacy: The Russian Realm

A. THE BYZANTINE IMPACT UPON THE RUSSIAN NATION

The Byzantine Empire of the Paleologi (1261-1453) was a Byzantium greatly reduced in size and power. It comprised in mid-thirteenth century the northwestern corner of Asia Minor, the major part of

Thrace and Macedonia, Thessalonica, several islands in the northern part of the Aegean Sea, and three formerly Frankish fortresses in the Peloponnesus. The vast, formerly multinational empire had shrunk to a small essentially Greek state, and this truncated realm was threatened on all sides by nations whom it had formerly been able to control. It faced the Turks in Asia Minor, the Serbs and Bulgars in the north, the Venetians on neighboring islands, the Genoese on the Black Sea coast, and Latin knights on the Peloponnesus and in middle Greece.[97] Each of the new nations had emerged from the shadow of the ancient Empire and was to have a political destiny of its own; but since all had entered the field of international relations as disciples of Byzantium, they were all conditioned to see the world through Byzantine lenses. Their conceptions of foreign policy reflected their experiences in the imperial orbit, and their diplomatic practices were modelled closely on the imperial techniques to which they had so long been exposed. Among these rising nations the Russians and the Venetians deserve the special attention of students of international history. Through their agency the diplomatic tradition of the Second Roman Empire became an integral part of the modern states system.

Byzantine opinion regarded the Russians as an inferior barbarian nation, from the ninth century, when they made their appearance in the Black Sea region,[98] to the thirteenth, when they were subjugated by the Mongols.[99] In the fourteenth and fifteenth centuries the Russians succeeded in throwing off the Tartar yoke and established an independent state. But the governmental structure and orientation toward foreign affairs of the new tsardom were influenced decisively by the two great empires with which earlier Russian societies had been affiliated. The nature and extent of these influences upon Russia's political organization have been and continue to be matters of opinion among specialists in Russian history. A Soviet study of the Muscovite state[100] extols the merits of the Mongolian example and relegates Byzantinism to a secondary place in the evolution of Russia toward independence and uniqueness, suggesting that the founders of the modern

[97] See Vasiliev, p. 610, for maps showing the expansion of 1) the Serbs and Bulgars; 2) the Turks; 3) the Venetians and Genoese—all in the fourteenth century.

[98] See V. O. Kluchevsky, *A History of Russia*, C. J. Hogarth, tr., three vols., London, New York, 1911-1912, Vol. I, pp. 28-76, for the beginnings of the Russian nation.

[99] Russia's official relationship to Byzantium was a matter of doubt at the time and has continued to be a controversial issue among historians. See A. A. Vasiliev, "Was Old Russia a Vassal State of Byzantium?" in *Speculum*, Vol. VII, July, 1932, no. 31, pp. 350ff.

[100] R. Vipper, *Ivan Grozny*, Moscow, 1947.

Russian state were inspired chiefly by the Mongolian ideal of a centralized military monarchy in which all social forces were organized effectively for war, and that the political value of this pattern of government was simply enhanced when the Muscovite scholars of Byzantine history assured the Tsar that similar principles and practices obtained also in the ancient Eastern Empire.[101] As a rule, however, when Russian politics are studied in the full context of the country's social and cultural history, the Byzantine influences are regarded as paramount.[102] A full exposition of this point of view may be found in the writings of Nicolas Berdyaev.[103]

According to Berdyaev, no inquiry into the origins of Russian despotism can ignore the fact that Russia developed in the shadow of one of the greatest and most effective of all centralized monarchies. Byzantine principles of administration impressed themselves indelibly upon the minds of the Slavic leaders who came into contact with the Empire, and the spirit of Byzantine orthodoxy impregnated the common Slavic folk. The tutelage of the Orthodox Church fostered, as the chief qualities of the Russian character, dogmatism, asceticism, the ability to endure suffering and to make sacrifices, and the need to profess some orthodox faith. And this essentially religious orientation was favorable to the acceptance and further elaboration of the Byzantine theory of the church-state. Not only were government and religion inexorably linked in the consciousness of the Russian people, but it was generally assumed that the ruling authorities had a dual mandate: to govern and to save souls. Berdyaev concludes that Russian governments have therefore always been in a position to evoke and direct the latent religious spirit of the masses in behalf of purposes that may be said to have a religious or quasi-religious appeal.[104]

Other Russian historians have disassociated themselves from some of the implications of Berdyaev's thesis,[105] but few have denied that the Byzantine influences must be taken into account if Russian history is to be understood. This point is stressed by a Soviet historian in the following passage: "Russia received christianity from Byzantium. Along

---

[101] *ibid.*, pp. 32, 167. See George Vernadsky and Michael Karpovich, *A History of Russia*, three vols., New Haven, 1943-1953, Vol. III on the Mongolian period.

[102] Vasiliev, *History of the Byzantine Empire*, pp. 32ff. for a review of Russian historical opinion.

[103] *The Origin of Russian Communism*, London, 1937, and *The Russian Idea*, New York, 1948.

[104] See the opening chapters in *The Origin of Russian Communism*.

[105] See Vernadsky and Karpovich, Vol. II, "Kievan Russia," p. 15.

with christianity the Slavs received writing and some elements of higher Byzantine culture. It is clear that the working masses of our country are right in becoming interested in the history of the Byzantine empire and the Soviet historian must satisfy this interest and give a scholarly history of Byzantium erected on the foundation of the Marxist Leninist methodology."[106]

Since Byzantinism pervaded Russian life it must be regarded as one of the mainsprings of Russian diplomacy. Theory and practice in the conduct of international relations reflect not simply the form of government of a country but the entire culture. In Vipper's study of Ivan Grozny's epoch we find the following acknowledgment of this relationship: "Although owing to the difficulties of communication with western Europe, the Moscow state lagged behind the latter in technical inventions, it far excelled it in its harmonious and mighty military administrative organization and skillful carefully thought-out and consistent diplomacy. This was the effect of the peculiar culture of the Great Russian people, which, as comrade J. V. Stalin expressed it, was disciplined 'by the requirements of self defense,' and was fostered by the traditions of Byzantine scholarship which was zealously studied in Moscow."[107]

That the Russians of this era were skilled practitioners of the Byzantine art of influencing people becomes evident when one reads the story of Moscow's gradual emancipation from the Tartars. It seems that the Muscovite princes never dreamt of openly resisting the Mongolian overlord, since they knew very well that the Horde could be dealt with more easily by "peaceful cunning"—i.e., by complaisance and money —than by force of arms. Therefore they paid assiduous court to the Khan and made sure never to arrive empty-handed at an audience. According to V. O. Kluchevsky,[108] liberation was achieved because the Muscovites managed to use the Mongolian himself as the instrument of their schemes.

The ready reception by Russia of the diplomatic tradition of Byzantium was facilitated by several special circumstances. In the first place, the Kievans, who were to form the first Russian state, lived from the ninth to the eleventh century in the Byzantine power orbit. During this period they had many opportunities, as an inferior barbarian nation, to find out at first hand how the imperial diplomats built and

[106] M. V. Levchenko, *History of Byzantium*, Moscow and Leningrad, 1940, p. 4.
[107] See Vipper, p. 169. See also Tarlé, *Histoire*, pp. 100ff.
[108] *A History of Russia*, C. J. Hogarth, tr., 3 vols., London and New York, 1911-12, Vol. I, p. 285.

wielded power and camouflaged weakness. In the course of this apprenticeship they learned also how to appreciate and bargain for commercial privileges, monetary compensations, and dynastic marriages. Byzantine diplomacy thus was a major and ever-present phenomenon in Russia's earliest society.

But apart from the broad significance that it had for Kievan life, Byzantine diplomacy assumed a special meaning in the sphere of Russo-Byzantine relations, since it supplied the most direct and immediate contact of the inferior with a superior civilization. It was through the preliminary experience of diplomacy that opportunities for further experiences opened to the Russians. In this sense Byzantine diplomacy became, as it were, a master-key that gave the Kievans access to many fields of interest and advantage that might otherwise have remained closed. Of the areas thus unlocked none proved more attractive to the Russians than those of commerce and religion. Hence it was here that the Byzantine influence was most effective in shaping Russia's orientation to the outside world.

B. THE RELATIONS BETWEEN KIEV AND BYZANTIUM

Trade with Constantinople was the first manifestation of the existence of a Russian nation of which we have any record. Its inception may be found in the irresistible drive with which many communities of pagan Slavs sought an outlet for their products in the cities on the Black Sea coast. From the middle of the eighth century onward, we are told,[109] when the Russians were still tributaries of the mighty Chozar Empire,[110] merchants trekked in this direction, paid the Byzantine emperor a tenth of all the merchandise that they carried, and then frequently pressed farther eastward; for Baghdad, too, was a point of great allure. Among the trading towns that arose along the river routes as a result of these commercial activities were many that became, in time, centers of provincial life, and some of these were transformed into fortified political capitals when the power of the Chozars collapsed. The most important was Kiev. As a junction of the chief trade routes and the final link in a chain of trading towns connecting the Baltic

---

[109] *ibid.*, p. 52.

[110] The Chozars were a nomad race of Turkish origin which eventually adapted Judaism as its faith. They were a nation of traders and built a great commercial empire. In their cities, Christians, Jews, Muslims, and pagans are known to have mingled freely. See *ibid.*, pp. 50ff. See also D. M. Dunlop, *The History of the Jewish Khazars*, Princeton, 1954.

with the Black Sea, it was destined, by virtue of its geographic location alone, to become the arbiter of Russian trade relations.[111]

Kiev was in this position in the first half of the ninth century when companies of armed Varangian merchant princes, followed by their retinues, began appearing on the Russian scene. Since the Varangians, like everyone else, were being drawn by commercial ambitions toward the promise of the Greco-Roman markets, they converged in great numbers upon Kiev and soon succeeded in gaining full control. When their military support was then accepted by other communities and provinces, whose livelihood depended on the security of commercial relations with Constantinople, a process of amalgamation began which culminated in the formation of the Kievan state. Since Kievan Russia is the root from which the modern Russian Empire grew, one may regard the securing of these trade relations with Byzantium as the first enterprise in the establishment of the Russian state.

In accordance with the interests that had determined the evolution of Kiev, the principality was committed to the pursuit of two primary objectives: it had to acquire markets in the Roman Empire, and it had to open and protect the lines of communication leading to those markets. This orientation toward trade implied that Constantinople should be the focus of Kievan policies, and that Russo-Byzantine relations were to become the determining factor in the entire economic life of the young Russian nation.[112] Each winter the Kievan government was busy collecting export merchandise throughout the land. The bulk of this intake was tribute in kind, which the people paid the governing prince and his retinue, and which the members of the retinue then used as trading matter when they acted in their capacity as the nation's leading merchants.

The Varangians organized an official convoy for the shipment of produce southward. This was an elaborate annual undertaking, and since the convoys were exceedingly well protected they attracted large numbers of private traders and vessels. A great flotilla was made ready each spring to descend the Dnieper and proceed to Constantinople, where its cargo of furs, honey, wax, and slaves would be bartered for

[111] Kluchevsky, Vol. I, p. 69.

[112] The Byzantine intelligence service seems to have followed these developments in Russia very closely. We find at any rate that the emperor Constantine Porphyrogenitus was able to compose two chronicles in the middle of the tenth century that contained detailed information about the administration of Kiev and the organization of the annual commercial expeditions. These accounts are treated as essential sources in Russian historiography. See Kluchevsky's notes on Russian Chronography, *ibid.*, p. 3.

silk, spices, wines, fruits, and other luxuries from the east. The journey was long and hazardous, but the attraction of the terminal point was such that the Russians were prepared to brave the cataracts of the river as well as the hostile interventions of savage tribes. In fact, the martially minded merchants were so determined to consummate the aims by which their lives were guided that they did not hesitate to defy the imperial government itself and force their entrance into Constantinople. And here we come to one of the most interesting aspects of the relations of the Russians with Byzantium.

Between 860 and 1043 the Kievans are known to have staged six military expeditions against the city of their desires, and some of these aggressions had devastating effects upon Constantinople and the adjoining provinces.[113] But an exploration of the motives that underlay these actions and of the agreements that concluded the incidents reveals what other international relationships in their archaic stages have also shown: that war and trade were closely related pursuits, and that military force was often used as a short-term measure designed to secure the long-range benefits of peaceful intercourse. For it appears that the Kievans resorted to piracy and plunder only when their trading connections with the Empire were obstructed. The Byzantines, on the other hand, were usually willing to find new bases of accord, for they were familiar with the pattern of behavior in uncivilized nations and were capable of appraising their own calamities realistically. In one instance the imperial diplomats succeeded in averting an intended assault upon Constantinople by making appropriate peace overtures and presenting the Kievans with rich gifts. On other occasions they were able to win the invaders as allies. A Byzantine campaign against the eastern and Cretan Arabs in 910 included a sizable Russian contingent;[114] the Russo-Byzantine peace treaty of 911 contained a special clause permitting all Russians desirous of honoring the Emperor to join his armed services at any time; and a subsequent agreement (945) committed the Kievans to protect the Empire's interests in the Crimea against the aggressions of the Black Bulgars. These provisions indicate the range and general character of the complex relationship; but they were definitely subsidiary to the commercial understandings reached in the tenth century as a result of the belligerent insistence of Kiev upon a share in the Empire's trade.

[113] See A. A. Vasiliev, *The Russian Attack on Constantinople in 860*, Cambridge, Mass., 1946.
[114] *ibid.*, p. 231.

The treaties of the years 907, 911, and 945, the ones about which historians know the most, had a dual content. They defined the system of annual trading that was to prevail between the two governments, and they regulated the private relations that were to be observed between the visiting Russian merchants on the one hand and the mercantile community in Constantinople on the other. Under the terms of these agreements the imperial government invited the Great Prince of Rus and his boyars to send to the Great Greek Emperor each year as many ships as the Prince might desire, together with the commissioners and guests of the Prince, i.e., official government traders and private merchants. The foreigners were to be allowed to spend six months in Constantinople. During this time the Byzantine government would provide them with free board and "baths," equip their boats with provisions for the homeward journey, exonerate them from customs duties, and pay all the other incidental expenses of the sojourn. The official trading commissioners of the Prince of Kiev would be entitled, furthermore, to allowances in accordance with their rank, while the private merchants were to receive monthly stipends in accordance with the relative seniority of the towns from which they came.[115]

The grant of these rights and privileges reflects the strong bargaining position of Kiev as well as the rich resources of the moneyed diplomacy of Byzantium. But the treaties contained other provisions which make it clear that the host country never ceased to suspect the intentions of its trading partner. The Russians had to give the contractual assurance that "all do come in peace" and the Byzantine government insisted on an elaborate system of inspection and control, so that no entering Russian might create a mischief. The first prerequisite was a document, duly signed by the Kievan prince, specifying the number of vessels dispatched and the names and descriptions of all official representatives and private merchants on board. Other control measures provided that the visitors should be unarmed and that they should enter the city through a specified gate in parties of not more than fifty at a time. Each contingent was to be accompanied by an imperial official and escorted to special living quarters in the city where their private lives and trading activities would be kept under constant surveillance.[116]

The unilateral sternness of these measures was offset by the amity

[115] See Kluchevsky, Vol. I, p. 82, for a description of the trading conditions.
[116] Kluchevsky, Vol. I, pp. 78-83.

and mutuality with which the two nations approached certain other problems. The coexistence of Byzantine and Kievan merchants in Constantinople was bound to give rise to private friction and public disorder. Any such nuisances had to be settled in a way acceptable to all parties concerned if trading was to yield advantages. Under the stress of these conditions, Byzantine and Kievan jurists collaborated on legal definitions that would be meaningful in both systems of law. Their cooperation was reflected in the treaty of 911, which contains detailed legal provisions for the treatment of civil and criminal offences involving the nationals of both countries as well as a clause binding each contracting party to aid the shipwrecked merchants of the other.[117] This process of jural accommodation, which paralleled the commercial adjustment of the two nations, was in some respects tantamount to a Byzantine tutelage over the evolution of Kievan law; for the Kievans recognized the preeminence of the Byzantine system and were ready to accept many of its norms and precepts.[118]

The new legal directives received by the Russians in the course of their contacts with the Empire undoubtedly influenced the formation of their attitudes toward trade in general, but they were after all only one aspect of the total commercial experience of Kiev. The most important of their realizations were assimilated without being committed —as the legal directives were—to writing. Thus it is unlikely that any Russian in this epoch could ignore the fact that the first national Russian state was founded on trade, that the success of this trading state was due to the leadership of a strong governing elite, and that the foreign trade sought by Kiev in Constantinople was under strict governmental control also. In short, the Russians must have been left with the overwhelming impression that commerce is essentially an affair of state. And this view was later confirmed by the theories and practices of government and trade that came to prevail in Muscovy under the auspices of the Mongols. Generations of Russians thus were conditioned by impressions accumulated over the centuries to see commerce in a certain relationship to the state.

In view of these facts it is not surprising that the Soviet Russian scholars emphasize this fund of historical experience when they write about the foundations of the modern Russian empire. Vipper's study of the Muscovite tsardom is a case in point. Western European mer-

---

[117] Vernadsky and Karpovich, Vol. II, p. 26.

[118] See Kluchevsky's comments on the extraordinary cultural significance of this legal development, Vol. I, p. 84.

chants, he claims,[119] were never able to understand the mainsprings of commercial life in the Eastern European state, since they were products of a civilization in which trade was piracy, having emerged from the rivalries of individual merchants, whereas the Muscovites adhered to a tradition cultivated steadfastly by the Roman Empire and the Arabian caliphates,[120] according to which commerce was the business of the state, with the government functioning as the creditor, customer, and director of all commercial affairs. Moreover, since the government was instituted for the primary purpose of preparing for the eventuality of war, it had the unquestioned right, indeed the obligation, to mobilize and organize all the wealth and talent in the country that would support this supreme cause, and merchants in such a political framework were properly regarded as servants of the state, liable to be drafted for any activity likely to enhance the governmental program. Unlike the European merchant, Vipper continues, the Muscovite enjoyed no independence and could not form companies or guilds. In brief, when the Western Europeans and the Eastern Europeans entered into trade relations they proceeded from entirely different premises. In sum, according to this twentieth century exposition, there can be no doubt that the Byzantine tradition, as amplified by the practices of the early tsardoms and illumined by the science of Marxism-Leninism-Stalinism, has been at all times superior to the tradition represented by the West.

Non-Russians or non-Marxists may well differ with the arguments and conclusions advanced in this treatment of the question. Nevertheless, since few Russians, either in the tenth or in the twentieth centuries, have admitted their country's political vassalage to the Second Roman Empire, such unequivocal present-day acknowledgments of the supremacy of Byzantium are remarkable additional evidence of the strength of the Empire's institutions and the efficiency of its art of influencing foreign peoples. And these impressions of the long-range effectiveness of Byzantine influences upon Russian attitudes toward foreign affairs are strengthened when one passes from the area of commercial to that of ecclesiastical politics.

For it is clear in retrospect that the place of modern Russia in the world was determined largely by the medieval Russian acceptance of the Greek Orthodox faith and the response of the Russians to the ecclesiastical symbols and institutions that were relayed to them in the process of conversion. The general circumstances that made the im-

[119] *ibid.*, pp. 117ff.
[120] This reference is not elucidated.

perial ideology attractive and in the end irresistible in Russia were the same as those that had facilitated its spread in the other culturally un-developed Slavic nations. In the context, however, of Russo-Byzantine relations in general and the well-integrated Byzantine system of di-plomacy in particular, it is interesting to note that the introduction of Christianity was closely related both chronologically and organically to the commercial contacts that had first linked the pagan people of Rus with the civilization of the Empire. For it was this early bilateral system of trading that had provided the opening wedge for the opera-tions of the religious missions.[121]

The ecclesiastical attachment of Kiev to Constantinople was secured by certain formal principles that must be noted if Russia's subsequent reactions to the imperial theocracy are to be appreciated properly. The fact that the Kievan church was a branch of the Byzantine church im-plied, at least in theory, that the Kievan people acknowledged not only the supremacy of the Patriarch of Constantinople, but also the suze-rainty of the Emperor; for in the conception and administration of the imperial church-state it was the Emperor who was the ultimate author-ity in both secular and religious matters.[122] The Princes of Rus seem to have been quite aware of these political corollaries. At any rate they went so far as to risk military conflict in order to establish the inde-pendence of the Russian church and thus extricate themselves from a relationship that fettered their political status.

But the Byzantine diplomats were able to counteract these efforts and preserve the claim of the Empire to supremacy by resorting to their usual stratagems. A Byzantine princess was married to a Rus-sian prince and a trade agreement was negotiated that contained terms favorable to the Russians. From the imperial point of view the Russians were vassals both in theory and in fact, and the issue was definitely settled, as far as Byzantine prestige was concerned, when Jaroslav the Wise accepted a metropolitan from Constantinople in 1037. The funda-mental thesis of the suzerainty of the Empire over Rus was taken for granted by an early Byzantine historian who referred to a war with Russia as "a revolt of the Russians."[123] It was to gain support again when later historians compiled records showing that all but two of the Kiev metropolitans during the pre-Mongol period were Greeks; that a metropolitan was sent from Constantinople even during the Mon-

---

[121] Kluchevsky, Vol. I, p. 83, says in effect that Russia's conversion to Christianity was the most important long-range consequence of Russo-Byzantine trade.

[122] Cf. Vernadsky, Vol. II, p. 348. See also Tarlé, *Histoire*, pp. 109ff.

[123] Vernadsky, *loc.cit.*

golian occupation;[124] that about half of the bishops and most of the secretaries attached to the ecclesiastical missions were Greek; and that each bishopric contained a substantial number of Byzantine intellectuals.[125]

The purposes of the present study are not served by an exploration of the official character of the early affiliation of Russia with the Second Roman Empire. A knowledge of the historical incidents that provoked the controversy about the political status of early Russia is relevant to this inquiry, however, because it contributes greatly to an understanding of the social and political climate in which later generations of Russians were to accept the Byzantine heritage, consciously and unconsciously, as the cornerstone of the new political structure that was to enclose their achievements and support their aspirations for centuries to come. The evidence is incontrovertible that the Russians continued to recognize the absolute authority of Byzantinism in its varied political manifestations long after they had ceased to respect the ancient Empire's actual power.

Indeed it was the fall of Constantinople that gave the legacy of Byzantium its full significance in Russian eyes. The extinction of the Second Roman Empire occurred at a time when Muscovy had become the leading state in Russia, and when the Tsars of Muscovy had great designs to extend the boundaries of their domain, further the cause of their personal rule, project the grandeur of their undertaking to their subjects, and establish the power and prestige of the Russian state in the international society of other potentates and nations. The Russians knew through experience and memory that the Greek Orthodox Empire had been eminently successful in the realization of ambitions similarly vast. They had learnt, moreover, in the long course of their contacts with Constantinople, that political designs of this kind cannot be promoted exclusively by material means. Indeed, no aspect of the Empire had been as impressive and hard to refute as the strength of certain spiritual principles that had supported the entire political edifice. Two of these principles in particular appealed to the Russians in their quest for an empire on the Byzantine model: the idea of the church-state and the idea of the unity of the orthodox world. Both ideas could be used to justify and sublimate the territorial and personal aspirations of the tsars.

As one follows Moscow's efforts to establish an authentic and im-

[124] Vasiliev, "Was Old Russia a Vassal State of Byzantium?" p. 352.
[125] Vernadsky, Vol. II, p. 350.

mediate linkage with the fallen Empire, one discovers that the Russian people had become deeply susceptible to the myths, symbols, rites, and ceremonies associated with the principles and policies of Byzantium, and that the Russian leaders were adept practitioners of the art of manipulating these phenomena in behalf of their own ambitions. As a matter of fact, it was the Byzantine system of forms that lent to the new state the semblance of dignity and power when it actually had none, and suggested goals and standards of political achievement that were bound to stimulate the aspirations of the later tsars.[126] However, it would be erroneous to conclude that such forms and symbols had an official or assigned place in early Russian politics. Rather is it true to say that they pervaded Russian life and thought, as they pervaded the life and thought also of other regions that had been exposed to the impact of the culture of the Eastern Empire and the specific methods that this great literate civilization had employed persistently in order to communicate its values to the largely nonliterate barbarians. In fact, one may conclude from the history of this entire epoch that most men everywhere were thinking less in theories than in forms, symbols, rites, and legends.

This, then, is the context in which one has to understand the myths and legends—some with an authentic popular ring, others obviously spurious fabrications—that relate the Russian destiny to the origins of Christian orthodoxy and of worldly power. There is one legend, for instance, which bolsters the claim of Russia to a unique position among all Christian nations by affirming that the Apostle Andrew himself once visited Russia, blessed the site of Kiev, and foretold the people's greatness as the leader of the new faith.[127] But there is another ancient tale which conveys a sense of anxiety and fear lest the Russians should lose the true faith that they received and abandon themselves to the rule of the antichrist. When such uneasiness invades the land, the legend declares, the people must go forth and seek the mystical city of Kitezh, which lies hidden beneath a lake, in order to find solace and redemption.[128]

The most widely current legends, however, were those that connected the rulers of Muscovy with real or fabled Roman emperors; here one is inclined to agree with Kluchevsky's thesis that most of these stories were concocted by politicians in order to support the preten-

---

[126] Cf. Kluchevsky, Vol. II, p. 17.
[127] Kluchevsky, Vol. II, p. 21.
[128] Berdyaev, *Origin of Russian Communism*, p. 7.

sions of the tsars.[129] This kind of imaginative documentation was inspired by a dual vision of Ivan III, in which it had been revealed that the Tsar of Moscow was destined to be the national autocratic ruler of the whole of Russia as well as the secular and ecclesiastical successor of the Byzantine emperors; and the success of the legends was made possible by two events of great political importance. The first was the emancipation of Moscow from the Mongols, which inaugurated the principle of an independent national Russian state under the leadership of the Muscovites, and the second was Ivan III's marriage to Sophia Paleologina, a niece of the last Byzantine emperor.

This matrimonial union, which established an actual connection between the Muscovite and the Byzantine dynasties, became the point of anchorage for the subsequent elaboration of the Russian claim to the Byzantine succession. It was significant primarily as a political demonstration to all the world that the new tsarina had transferred the supreme rights of the Byzantine house to Moscow[130] and that the capital of the Russian state had become the new city of Constantine.[131] And the impact of this demonstration was accentuated greatly by the simultaneous transfer of that complex and impressive system of ceremonies, rites, and titles which had been designed in Constantinople for the purpose of substantiating the imperial prerogative in the public consciousness. Transferred to now holy Moscow, the highest of all available honors and titles in the new ceremonious environment were carefully retailored, in order to convey the idea that the tsar was at once independent and orthodox, the sole remaining ruler in the world who approximated the type of the Byzantine emperor and was at the same time supreme over the Rus, which hitherto had been owned by the Tartar Khans.[132] When these claims seemed securely fastened both in fiction and in fact, the Muscovites felt free to borrow still another vital symbol of the ancient Empire, namely, its crest. From the close of the fifteenth century onward we find the double-headed eagle upon all the seals affixed by the tsars to documents of state.

Success stimulated the tsar and his boyars to employ their sense for imagery in behalf of even more extensive claims to greatness, and the result of their endeavors was the legend of the emperor's cap. The historical background of this remarkable story was the biography of Vladimir Monomakh of Kiev, who was the grandson of the Byzantine

129 Vol. III, ch. II.
130 Kluchevsky, Vol. II, p. 19.
131 Vasiliev, *History of Byzantium*, p. 590.
132 Kluchevsky, Vol. II, p. 20.

emperor Constantine Monomakh, having had the emperor's daughter as his mother. Actually the Byzantine emperor died some fifty years before the grandson ascended his local Russian throne; but a document prepared by the boyars made the claim that Vladimir plotted to overthrow his grandfather, and that the emperor, getting wind of the conspiracy, was so alarmed that he sent the Greek metropolitan to his grandson, bearing a crucifix and his own imperial cap with its golden brim and crown of carnelians, for the purpose of effecting a reconciliation, so that all Orthodox Christians should continue to dwell in harmony "under the common power of our Empire and of thy Grand Autocracy of Great Rus."[133] The cap, according to the boyars, was subsequently used by Vladimir at his coronation, and from that moment onward the tsar has called himself Monomakh, or the divinely crowned Tsar of Great Rus.

Moscow became dissatisfied with its historical status as the successor, or even equal, of Byzantium as it grew more powerful and ambitious. Beyond Constantinople, the tsarist advisers discovered, lay the primary and ultimate source of all world power, imperial classical Rome herself. A new family tree was clearly needed, therefore, if Moscow was to occupy its rightful position in the world. Early in the sixteenth century, Kluchevsky writes,[134] a story was invented that Augustus Caesar had divided the world among his kinsmen, and that he had appointed his brother Prus the ruler of the region later known as Prussia. "From Prus" the legend concludes, "the fourteenth generation was the great lord Rurik." By thus tracing their descent to the legendary brother of Augustus, the Soviet historian Vipper explains,[135] the tsars exalted the name and prestige of the Moscow Tsar over the rest of the European kings and rulers.

The curious interplay of reality and myth that is made manifest by these and other episodes in early Russian history supplied the foundations on which Muscovy could claim to be the leading orthodox state and the carrier of a unique mission on earth. These claims were announced in a doctrinal form in the early part of the sixteenth century when the orthodox monk Philoteus proclaimed that Moscow was the third Rome, charged with the sacred mission of saving mankind—a mission in which the Western Rome on the Tiber and the Eastern Rome on the Bosporus had failed. He wrote the following dissertation to the Grand Prince Vassilii III:

"Of the third Rome: . . . Of all the kingdoms in the world, it is in

[133] *ibid.*, p. 22.　　　　[134] *ibid.*　　　　[135] *ibid.*, p. 18.

thy royal domain that the holy Apostolic Church shines more brightly than the sun. And let thy Majesty take note, O religious and gracious Tsar, that all kingdoms of the Orthodox Christian Faith are merged into thy kingdom. Thou alone, in all that is under heaven, art a Christian Tsar. And take note, O religious and gracious Tsar, that all Christian kingdoms are merged into thine alone, that two Romes have fallen, but the third stands and there will be no fourth. Thy Christian kingdom shall not fall to the lot of another."[136]

This grandiloquent statement of the messianic idea that had been deduced from the factual and fancied records of Russia's relations with the Romano-Byzantine Empire announced the dual theme of Russia's religious and political superiority. It was accepted in Russia as the doctrine of the Third Rome and became the principal consolidating force in the early Russian state as well as one of the chief determinants of the Russian orientation toward other states and peoples. Its great political significance in international history, furthermore, was no doubt due to the fact that it was a composite of religious orthodoxy and secular imperialism. For if Russia was the first land of Christianity, and if orthodox Christianity was the only true Christianity, then Russia was obviously in a class by itself, at least in the society of Christian nations, as the lone protagonist of what is right.[137] This exalted version of the Russian mission was linked from the beginning of the country's history with the power of the national state and the ambitions of its autocratic rulers. And the fusion of these elements brought forth the messianic kind of imperialism that has characterized the conduct of Russian foreign relations in several historical epochs.[138]

[136] Berdyaev, *The Origin of Russian Communism*, pp. 4-5. See also Kluchevsky, Vol. II, p. 23, who comments on this theme in the following way: ". . . a monk of one of the old monasteries of Pskov is found almost at a loss to express his delight as he writes to Vassilii III that the Christian States are now centered in the person of Vassilii alone, and that henceforth, in all the world, he is the one Orthodox Emperor, and Moscow the third and final Rome."

Anatole G. Mazour, *Russia, Past and Present*, New York, 1951, pp. 51-52, gives the following translation of this passage: "The first Rome collapsed owing to its heresies, the second Rome fell victim to the Turks, but a new and third Rome has sprung up in the north, illuminating the whole universe like a sun. . . . The first and second Rome have fallen, but the third will stand till the end of history, for it is the last Rome. Moscow has no successor; a fourth Rome is inconceivable."

[137] Berdyaev, *The Origin of Russian Communism*, p. 6, writes thus: "If the orthodox faith was the Russian faith, what was not the Russian faith was not the orthodox faith."

[138] Berdyaev, *The Russian Idea*, p. 9, develops this idea in the following passage: "The spiritual pit into which the idea of Moscow the Third Rome falls, is due precisely to the fact that the Third Rome presented itself . . . as a manifestation of sovereign power, as the might of the State. It was taken as expressed by the Tsardom of Moscow, and then in the Empire and in the end as the Third International."

The evolution of Russia toward statehood and empire was influenced decisively, as we have seen, by the Byzantine traditions of diplomacy that had infiltrated Russian politics through various channels from the ninth century onward. The Russians, like the Byzantines, accepted orthodoxy and governmental absolutism as the chief principles of political organization, and professed the supremacy of their own state in the society of nations. Russian diplomacy was thus developed in the same general moulds of thought that had contained the diplomatic theories and practices of the ancient empire. But with this the analogies end.

For the actual historical foundations of the Third Rome had been very different from those of the Second Rome, and the uses to which Russian diplomacy was put were very different, therefore, from those that had been characteristic of the diplomatic history of the earlier empire. Byzantium, when it developed the art of managing adjoining nations, was a powerful multinational state interested primarily in its own survival. Russia, on the other hand, was a relatively small national state interested in aggrandizement when it borrowed the diplomatic techniques from the great society that it tried to emulate. In other words, diplomacy in Russia was not the established method for assuring an existing power and controlling an existing orbit, but was a means of realizing the promises implicit in the doctrine of the Third Rome—a weapon valuable chiefly for the advancement of the predatory aims of an expansive national government.

The subsequent success of Russia in transforming the state of Muscovy into a multinational empire approximating the Byzantine model, and in administering the orbit thus called into being, may attest in no small measure to the intrinsic merits of the Byzantine art of influencing peoples. But the long sequence of events that might justify such a speculation forms a complex chapter in modern world history and lies outside the scope of the present retrospective inquiry.

CHAPTER 10

THE MUSLIM REALM

A. Connections between Past and Present

THE BYZANTINE EMPIRE and the Western European common-wealth had evolved certain well-defined methods and institu-tions of organizing political life in their multinational orbits which gave stability and continuity to the development of their civilizations and supplied successive generations in each culture with directives for the establishment of government and the conduct of in-ternational affairs. The medieval Islamic Empire did not develop com-parable patterns of organization, and later generations of Muslims were consequently left without the guidance of historically tested political traditions. The dangers implicit in this situation were evident already as early as the ninth Christian century when the great Islamic realm disintegrated into numerous separate units in a dramatic reversal of political fortunes. For a century and a half, under the leadership of Muhammad and his immediate successors, the Islamized peoples of the Near East had been expanding their religious and political domains with a rapidity unmatched in either of the two Christian realms. With incredible ease, they had succeeded in creating an empire vaster and more varied in its racial composition than any in the history of the world.[1] Having taken into their fold a large variety of races inhabiting vastly differing realms, they had faced problems of assimilation con-siderably greater than those resolved by the Christians in the Western European and Byzantine orbits. But the new political system which the Arab leadership had announced in the Mediterranean region when it created the new imperial domain proved inadequate, and the Empire passed quickly from power to impotence. The record of historical ex-periences which is the intellectual property of the Islamic, and espe-cially the Arabic, peoples is thus more ambivalent and less conclusive than that of either Western Europe or Byzantium. This aspect of the Islamic past must be borne in mind as one approaches the study of contemporary politics in the Muslim world. For the partial fulfillment, yet ultimate frustration, of seemingly limitless political possibilities has left in the traditions of Islam a residue of poignant but highly ambigu-ous memories which have never ceased to influence the conscious and

---

[1] Consult Harry W. Hazard, *Atlas of Islamic History*, Princeton, 1952.

unconscious political attitudes of all subsequent generations. These connections between past and present have become particularly evident in the twentieth century. When the Arabs allied themselves with the Western European powers during the First World War in order to defeat the Muslim Empire of the Ottoman Turks to which they had belonged for several centuries, they initiated a new epoch in the affairs of the Islamic peoples. For the cause of national independence which the Arabs espoused at that time under the influence of Western political thought was also adopted in subsequent decades by all other Muslim nations that had experienced the impact of the European idea of national sovereignty. The successful promotion of this cause contributed greatly to the gradual disintegration of the long-established multinational empires of the French, British, and Dutch, and to the collapse of the short-lived Asian empire of the Japanese. Eleven new states with predominantly Muslim populations were created in Asia and Africa between 1919 and 1956 through the instrumentality of international and civil wars and bilateral and multilateral negotiations, thus bringing the total number of separate Islamic sovereignties to sixteen.[2] Two others are scheduled to gain their independence in the very near future.[3] These states represent different racial and linguistic

[2] See United Nations, *Demographic Yearbook 1955*, New York, 1955, to the following effect:

Countries	Total population in millions:	(1954 as mid-year unless marked otherwise)
Egypt	22.7	
Morocco	8.3 plus 1.0	
Tunisia	3.7	
Sudan	8.9	
Libya	1.1	
Afghanistan	12.0 (in 1951)	
Indonesia	81.1	
Iran	20.7	
Iraq	4.9	
Jordan	1.4	
Pakistan	80.2	
Saudi Arabia	7.0 (in 1952)	
Syria	3.7	
Turkey	22.9	
Yemen	4.5 (in 1949)	
Albania	1.3	

[3] The Federation of Nigeria expects recognition in 1960. Of a total population of 30.3, the predominantly Muslim Northern Region claims 16.5. Italian Somaliland with 1.3 is to become independent in 1960.

Comparable political developments have not occurred in the Muslim communities of the Soviet Union. These communities and their populations are listed as follows

groups, exist in widely separate geographic regions, are of greatly varying size, and have had separate political histories in the last millennium.
But most of them have issued directly or indirectly from the original
Muslim Empire and continue to affirm their common heritage in one
form or another. What is the nature of the heritage to which the Muslims refer? In which respects does it differ from the legacies left by the
civilizations of Western Europe, Byzantium, India, or China? Does
the concept of Muslim unity actually provide the successor nations
with a unifying political framework, and if so, just what is the nature
of this framework?

Further questions of equal if not superior importance arise from the
encounter, in the twentieth century, between the Islamic and the Western systems. For it is a paradoxical yet obvious fact that the new Muslim nations are more nearly in accord today in claiming the political
legacy of Western Europe than in demanding a resuscitation of the
political traditions of Islam. Occidental ideals of the state have inspired
their national movements of independence, and the Western vocabulary
of constitutionalism is generally employed today in most Muslim societies. This was as true of the constitutions of Syria, which were
drafted in 1930 and 1950,[4] as it is of the constitution of Libya, which
was written after an exhaustive study of the constitutional charters of
seventeen other states, notably that of the United States.[5]

This convergence of Islamic aspirations in political symbols denoting
Western institutions is a very interesting development in the history
of intercultural relations. But the actual extent and nature of this agreement upon words and forms cannot be ascertained until one examines
the ancient political traditions that are now enveloped by the new
terminology. For example, Muslim peoples have long been accustomed

---

in *The National Economy of the U.S.S.R.*, Statistical Summary, Statistical Publishing
House, Moscow, 1956:

	1956
Uzbekian	7.3
Kazakh	8.5
Azerbedjian	3.4
Kirghiz	1.9
Tadjik	1.8
Turkmen	1.4

[4] See Majid Khadduri, "Constitutional Development in Syria with emphasis on
the Constitution of 1950" in *The Middle East Journal*, Vol. v, no. 2, April 1951.

[5] Henry Serrano Villard, *Libya, The New Arab Kingdom of North Africa*, Ithaca,
N.Y., 1956, p. 52.

to view the community in religious and transnational terms,[6] and this image continues to control the thinking of some contemporary theorists.[7] The modern Western state, on the other hand, was conceived as a secular nation-state. How will the old framework accommodate the new ideal? What type of synthesis is possible in an Islamic state between religion and nationalism, or religion and secularism? The new Muslim states have not given uniform answers to these questions. Some, notably Turkey, have renounced Islam as a political ideology in order to establish the nation on unequivocally secular foundations. Others are officially committed to policies of secularization but have to contend with a strong Islamic opposition in their citizenry.[8] States like Saudi Arabia and Yemen, on the other hand, continue to regard the ancient religious traditions as their primary political frame of reference. Here, as in most other Arab states, Islam is not only a religious faith and a way of life. It is also the principal aspect of Arabism, since

[6] See H. A. R. Gibb, "Social Reform: Factor X; The Search for an Islamic Democracy" in *Atlantic*, October 1956, pp. 137ff., for a succinct analysis of the complex factors that have brought about the disintegration of the ancient forms of social cohesion.

[7] One of the most influential among them, the Indian Muslim poet and philosopher, Sir Muhammad Iqbal (d.1938), went so far as to write: "Believe me, Europe today is the greatest hindrance in the way of man's ethical achievement. The Muslim, on the other hand, is in possession of these ultimate ideas on the basis of a revelation, which, speaking from the inmost depths of life, internalizes its own apparent externality. With him the spiritual basis of life is a matter of conviction for which even the least enlightened man among us can easily lay down his life; and in view of the basic idea of Islam that there can be no further revelation binding on man, we ought to be spiritually one of the most emancipated peoples on earth. . . . Let the Muslim today appreciate his position, reconstruct his social life in the light of ultimate principles, and evolve, out of the hitherto partially revealed purpose of Islam, that spiritual democracy which is the ultimate aim of Islam."

See Arthur J. Arberry in the preface to his translation of Iqbal's *The Mysteries of Selflessness*, London, 1953, p. xv. This philosophical poem and several lectures evoke the Islamic concept of a community unbounded in time and space, and (in the sixth lecture) suggest the establishment of a Muslim league of nations which would do justice both to the national aspirations of each Muslim country and to Islam. Before the collapse of the Ottoman Empire and the creation of independent Arab states, Iqbal had been thinking most intently of the possibility of a revived caliphate, bringing together in a single theocracy all Muslims of the world. See F. Rahman, "Internal Religious Developments in the Present Century Islam" in *Cahiers d'Histoire Mondiale*, Vol. II, no. 4, 1955, p. 878.

[8] Edwin M. Wright illustrates the great complexity of the conflict between nationalism and Islam by referring to the following episode: "In Indonesia, certain Dutch adventurers became Muslim during World War II and led bands of mountaineer guerrillas against the Japanese. They operated under the title of units of the Dar al-Islam. When an Independent Indonesia was established, these same Dutch leaders with their Muslim fighters continued the struggle against a Westernized Indonesian state in the name of establishing an Islamic society." "Conflicting Political Forces and Emerging Patterns" in Proceedings of the Academy of Political Science, Vol. XXIV, January 1952, no. 4, *International Tensions in the Middle East*, pp. 69f.

it is indissolubly connected with the most glorious chapters in the political history of all Arabs. The conflict between political nationalism and religious universalism is thus not as acute and obvious here as it is in the non-Arab communities. However, within the Arab world conflicts of another kind have appeared, for the Arabs today are not sure whether they do or do not constitute one nation. The political leaders of Iraq, Syria, Jordan, Saudi Arabia, and Yemen have answered this question in the negative when they organized separate nation-states. But their separatism is offset by a strong loyalty to the Pan-Arab cause, which springs from the remembrance of the past and finds expression in schemes of a greater unity to come. The ambivalence implicit in contemporary Arab approaches to politics is illustrated by the Syrian constitution that preceded the union of Syria and Egypt in 1958. This document states that Syria is an indivisible political unity, but it also contains the following preamble: "We further declare that our people who constitute a part of the Arab nation in their history, their present and their future, look forward to the day when our Arab nation is united in one state and will tirelessly work for realizing this sacred aspiration while maintaining their independence and liberty."[9] Projects for the creation of a "Greater Syria" and "Fertile Crescent Unity" were actually drafted in the last decades, but none was translated into reality. However, the latent sense of solidarity was activated toward the close of the Second World War, when the Arab and Egyptian[10] nations concluded an alliance, known as the Arab League, probably in order to forestall a postwar disposal of Arab territories, and after 1947, when a concerted front was created in opposition to the new non-Arab state of Israel.[11] These attempts at coalescence were of limited political effectiveness, but the causes that had inspired them became the mainspring of Egypt's foreign policy when the leaders of this nation began to entertain dreams of an empire that would one day extend from the Indian to the Atlantic Ocean.[12]

It is evident from the foregoing references that contemporary Muslim approaches to the conduct of international relations and to political

[9] See *ibid.*, p. 69; Khadduri, p. 152.

[10] It should be noted that the Egyptians ethnically are not an Arab nation.

[11] See Ezzeldin Foda, *The Projected Arab Court of Justice* (with specific reference to the Muslim Law of Nations), The Hague, 1957, pp. 3ff., 68ff. for discussions of various plans of Arab unity, and p. 5, n. 5 on the impetus to the creation of the Arab League that was given by policy statements made by Mr. Anthony Eden in behalf of the United Kingdom on May 29, 1941 and February 24, 1943.

[12] Consult in particular Gamal Abdul Nasser, *The Egyptian Revolution*, New York, 1955.

institutions on the national and international levels are anchored in the history of the medieval Muslim Empire. Efforts to understand this section of the present society of nations have to begin, therefore, with an analytical scrutiny of the early records of the Dar al-Islam as an international community.

B. The Theory of the Unity of Islam

In the first place, it has to be noted that the Islamic idea of unity was not political in its primary connotations but religious and social. Its vision of a community composed of those who held to the right faith and the right way of life existed outside the bounds of time and space and transcended the divisions of humanity into classes, races, and nations. The religious ideal of individual salvation and the social idea of fraternity, which were evoked jointly in this view of the unity of mankind, required no precise elaboration in terms either of principles or of institutions in order to become theoretically acceptable and practically operative. Indeed, these were unifying concepts precisely because they were unencumbered by autocratic meanings and were thus hospitable to all human aspirations attuned to similar ends, whether institutionally explicit or simply innate in the mind. This being the case, it is perhaps justifiable to assume that the very attempt of Islam to circumscribe the scope and nature of these universal ideals would have detracted from its magnetic appeal as an egalitarian creed, and thus contributed to arrest the expansion of the Islamic orbit, particularly in the nonliterate areas of the world.

The transcendental community of all believers was conceived as a theocracy. This has been true also of the two Christian societies. Through their Roman heritage, however, the Christians were committed to maintain and further not only the cause of a community of God, but also that of a specific, historically grounded, secular and territorial union. In their domain, the religious idea was soon clothed in concepts and institutions that had been developed in the classical Roman Empire for the perfection of life on this earth. At an early date, the Levantine religious concept of the consensus of all believers,[13] which inspired early Christendom no less than Islam, was adjusted to the old and well-established secular ideals of the *polis* and the *civitas*. In the Islamic community, on the other hand, no such practical invest-

---

[13] This concept was common also to the Jews and Persians. See Oswald Spengler, *The Decline of the West*, New York, 1930, Vol. II, "Perspectives of World History," pp. 73ff.; German ed., Vol. II, pp. 86ff., for a discussion of its significance.

ment of the transcendental principle was ever allowed. There, in fact, no one dared to distinguish conceptually between secular and ecclesiastical affairs, since it was considered axiomatic that in all matters, whether pertaining to this life or to the next, the community was ruled by God alone. And this absolutely ideal proposition furnished the basis of the whole Islamic approach to law.

The Muslim commonwealth, like the two Christian empires, acknowledged the supreme importance of law in human affairs, but the actual place that it assigned to law in its regulation of society differed no less from that of Byzantium than from that of Rome. In the two Christian realms, where the influence of Roman jurisprudence proved to be stronger than that of the religious norms, two varieties of secular public law developed.[14] In the Muslim realm, on the other hand, no tradition of public constitutional law could evolve, since it was generally understood that "the Law, which is the constitution of the Community, cannot be other than the Will of God, revealed through the Prophet."[15] This is to say that, in the opinion of the Muslim legists, law and religion formed one composite concept. For since God alone had the knowledge of the perfect law, He was presumed to be the only lawgiver, and the law that emanated from His divine wisdom was regarded as the ideal and only rational system of law in the world. Defined by medieval Muslims as "the knowledge of the rights and duties whereby man is enabled to observe right conduct in the world and prepare himself for the future life,"[16] law was thus an essentially religious science.[17]

[14] This public law effectively limited the power of the state in the Western European commonwealth. The relationship between law and the state was interpreted differently in Byzantium.

[15] H. A. R. Gibb, *Mohammedanism*, London, 1950, p. 89. See Carleton S. Coon, *Caravan: The Story of the Middle East*, New York, 1947, p. 102 on the place of civil law in Islam: "Among the Arabs as among the ancient Children of Israel and other Semitic-speaking peoples, no clear distinction was made between religious and civil law. What was offensive to the community was offensive to God, their symbol of the mutual relationships of its members. Only what we call torts, or offences to the individual rather than to the community, fell into a secular category, and these usually were nothing more than quarrels over physical property, such as when A's cow ate B's millet or when a man broke a twig from another's tree. In the tightly intimate familial communities in which Semitic-speaking peoples lived, few offences which affected an individual failed to disturb the group as a whole."

[16] David de Santillana, "Law and Society," in *The Legacy of Islam*, Sir Thomas Arnold and Alfred Guillaume, eds., Oxford, 1947, p. 294. See also M. Khadduri, "Nature and Sources of Islamic Law," in *The George Washington Law Review*, Vol. 22, October 1953, pp. 6-9, and Gustave E. Von Grunebaum, *Medieval Islam*, A Study in Cultural Orientation, Chicago, 1946, pp. 144ff. The Shi'ite concept of law is different from the Sunni concept. See Khadduri, p. 22; Joseph Schacht, *The Origins of Muhammadan Jurisprudence*, Oxford, 1950, pp. 262ff.

[17] According to Schacht, pp. 190ff. Islamic law came into existence through the

Such a notion may seem negative to people conditioned by long tradition to an association of jurisprudence with political theory. It is a positive notion, however, for those who do not favor such an association, but, instead, identify law with nonpolitical purposes. To the Muslims the Dar al-Islam is primarily an ideological community. It is taken for granted, therefore, that law should have as its primary function that of serving the cause of ideological unity. And this goal certainly has been attained, as history shows. Indeed, the conclusion is permissible that the *shari'ah* (the sacred law) was the most effective unifying agent in the Islamic world, and that in spite of the political instability of that vast and various domain, it was, in a cultural sense, the most closely integrated international society of its epoch. Had Islamic law been severed from religion and invested with secular meanings and political functions, this remarkable spiritual solidarity might never have been achieved.

The unifying qualities of the *shari'ah* derive from its character as a code of individual and social ethics. In this character it was so unequivocal, simple, and inoffensive to local traditions that men in widely differing regions and civilizations could readily accept it in all sincerity as the ultimate measure of their rights and wrongs as human beings.[18] The law thus became instrumental in creating and maintaining a broad area of agreement on fundamental religious and ethical values, and this accord, in turn, led to that striking convergence of nontheological human interests and activities that is the distinguishing mark of the great Islamic community of nations. Later developments seemed to justify the emphasis placed upon the ideological and cultural, rather than political, aspects of the idea of unity; for even when the military and political foundations of the commonwealth crumbled during the tenth and eleventh centuries,[19] the unifying social fabric that theology and the law had produced did not give way. In fact, Islamic history shows, on the contrary, that the widest possible measure of religious, social, and cultural unity was attained only after the political unity of Islam had been disrupted, partially recreated, and then disrupted again.[20]

---

application of Islamic jurisprudence to the raw material supplied by the administrative practices of the Umayyads. See pp. 283ff. for the Islamizing policies of the ancient jurists, which eventually effected the establishment of the law.

[18] See Gibb, *Mohammedanism*, p. 10, to the effect that Islamic law reached deeper than Roman law.

[19] Cf. *ibid.*, p. 11.

[20] Gibb, "An Interpretation of Islamic History" in *Cahiers d'Histoire Mondiale*, Vol. I, Juillet, 1953, p. 40.

In view of these connections and developments one may conclude that the Islamic ideas of unity and law were organically related. As long as the former was viewed as a religious and cultural constant, the latter could not be developed pragmatically and was bound to remain, as a political principle, ineffectual and amorphous. We do not know whether the legalists of medieval Islam faced consciously the implications of their position. And whether it was wise or right of them to prefer the widest possible degree of cultural unity to any kind of political cohesion will remain a matter of opinion. However, what appears to be incontrovertible—and for the purpose of the present discussion most important—is that Islamic dogma never condoned the view that unity and government could be regarded as secular political ideals. Social unity was to be a derivative of the ideological concept of the Dar al-Islam and government to be subordinate to religion. Both conceptions were encased so firmly in the broad ideal of a dynamic community of socially and ethically like-minded peoples that it would have been difficult to extricate them for purposes of definition without damage to what was generally recognized as the superior unifying structure. Ironically, therefore, the very principle that chiefly supported the homogeneity of Islam in the social and religious spheres signified chaos in the legal and political. For, whereas the absence of clearly defined principles conduced in large measure to the solidity of the concept of the brotherhood of all believers, the ambiguity was fatal to the cause of territorial empire and political organization.

Still another ambiguity appears in the search for principles of political unity and organization the moment one shifts one's regard from the realm of theory to that of fact, from the clear geometry of Muslim thought to the ever-spreading domain in which the Dar al-Islam was actually functioning as an empire. It is no doubt true that the early unity of this Empire owed much not only to the practical effectiveness of religious and fraternal ideals but also to the successful application of military power. These factors by themselves cannot have been the decisive ones, however, since they continued to be present, in varying degrees, long after the unity of Islam had ceased to be a political reality. It has been suggested, also, that the Dar al-Islam was galvanized into an empire only by the personal genius of Muhammad, and that it was consequently destined to disintegrate the moment its leadership lost the qualities that had been displayed so singularly by the Prophet. There can be no doubt, of course, that the Prophet was a particularly talented political leader; or that brilliant leadership was an important political factor, not only in the affairs of the pre-Muslim and Muslim Arabs, but also in those of many other Islamized tribes and nations. But an explanation that would treat the special organizing skill of one man as the keystone of the entire political union would have the effect of invalidating the intrinsic vitality of the Muslim cause, and such an inference is certainly not justified.

When one reads attentively the historical records it becomes clear that the Dar al-Islam had a political dynamic of its own, which was not identical with personal leadership, military force, religious zeal, or social egalitarianism. Its specific political dynamic was movement; for the Dar al-Islam was cohesive as an empire only when in a state of continuous forward motion. As a result of its orientation toward space, it had no fixed territorial contours. Any boundary once reached was due to be transcended by another forward thrust, if not immediately, then in the very near future.[21]

The Dar al-Islam was an empire-in-motion. For most people movement is an attractive state of being because it signifies activity, alerts the imagination, and promises human experiences beyond the realm of expectation in a life confined within geographically established limits. In the Muslim context, these general appeals received an immense and unique increase of momentum; for as there interpreted, the commitment to expansion had the added effect of activating simultaneously the fervor of religion and the spirit of fraternalism—the deepest and the most provocative and effective internationalizing principles of the Islamic ideology. Nations adhering to this empire-in-motion joined in effect the greatest of all caravans, for they were assured here of moving forward not only in unison but in behalf of the right cause.

Now this great caravan, like all other caravans, was moving toward an appointed end. The end was meaningful because it was the factor that hallowed, or otherwise justified, participation in the journey. Yet it did not really affect the fundamental nature of the undertaking. For not only was the ultimate objective distant, but it was destined in its turn to become the beginning of another journey. What informed the whole enterprise under these circumstances, then, was the quest of the end rather than the end itself, the moving rather than the arriving. Indeed, this kind of journey would in all probability have lost both its allure and its unity of purpose—and therefore also its political mo-

---

[21] It should be remarked that the Muslim empire-in-motion was different from the steppe empires of Central Asia, where the principle of movement had many additional connotations.

mentum—could all of its incidents have been anticipated and defined and had its end seemed less remote.

Since the political dynamic of the Muslim Empire was not arrested by processes of definition and clarification, it is more difficult to fathom than that of the Byzantine and the Western Roman Empires of pre-Christian and Christian times. Whereas the life force of the latter was stored, as it were, in well-defined principles and institutions from which it was released whenever necessary, that of the Islamic Empire was left fluid, unformed, and therefore not susceptible to direction or control. For these reasons it did not manifest itself either in clear understanding of the character of the political union or in the development of enduring forms of international government.

C. The Theory of the Caliphate

The inadequacy of the political principles at the disposal of the Muslim leadership became fully apparent only after the Prophet's death, when a brief but vivid period of expansion had transformed the Dar al-Islam into a territorial empire of immense proportions. Under what political forms was this union of disparate peoples and widely separated regions to express and maintain itself? To what political institutions were people supposed to look for guidance and protection? Where, moreover, was the seat of supreme temporal power? The answers to these questions could not be found either in the Koran or in the *sunnah* of the Prophet,[22] nor were they discoverable in the sacred law. Compelling historical precedents of the kind that had influenced the ultimate organization of the Byzantine and Holy Roman Empires were also missing, for the areas comprised in this Empire had not been administered in pre-Islamic times as one great union.

In this vacuum of principles and practices the community of believers took the step, upon Muhammad's death, of electing a leader or *imam*,[23] with the designation of successor (caliph) of the Prophet of God. And after this functionary had been installed, a theory was developed by Muslim jurists and theologians that God had set the imam or caliph over the community as governor so that he might maintain the sacred law. This doctrine of the caliphate, which seems to have

---

[22] These are the usages set by Muhammad either in the form of definite prescriptions or prohibitions. They were handed down in the form of short narratives told by one of the Companions. The whole corpus of the *sunnah*, as recorded and transmitted, is generally called the *hadith*. See Gibb, *Mohammedanism*, pp. 73-75.

[23] Gibb, "Constitutional Organization," in *Law in the Middle East*, Khadduri and Liebesny, eds., 1955, p. 4.

been initiated under rather obscure circumstances,[24] was thus not basic to the Islamic ideology. Being an expedient that lacked the sanction of the fundamental sacred law, it could be interpreted in different ways. Indeed, its very legitimacy was open to question. This explains why the institution of the caliphate became the object of acrimonious controversies in the ranks of the learned as soon as it was established. And since the authoritative interpreters of the Islamic ideology were unable to agree on a definition of the government that purported to be the pivot of the Empire, the community of believers could not develop a sense of its own political identity.

In its ideal version the caliphate seems to have been regarded as the highest type of political organization on earth. According to this view, the caliphs could do no wrong, for they were presumed to embody the whole sense both of the faith and of the sacred law. It followed that all of the faithful were obliged to render them total obedience.[25] But such a broad understanding of the nature of imperial rule could not allay the doubts implicit in the doctrine. Was the caliph meant to function as the spiritual as well as secular leader of the community? If so, then what was his relationship to the theological elite? Or, on the other hand, if the correct view was that he was only a secular ruler, while the *'ulama'* (the learned) were to have full jurisdiction over all spiritual matters, then how was one to reconcile such a theory with the generally accepted principle that temporal and spiritual matters formed an indivisible whole subject exclusively to the sacred law? And even if an agreement could be reached on a formula justifying the caliph's supremacy in temporal affairs, just how could such a formula be applied, practically, in the face of the doctrine that God alone is the legislator in both the temporal and the ecclesiastical fields?[26]

Controversies bearing on these and related issues rent the community of believers from the first Muslim century onward and undermined the actual imperial establishment that had been called into being by the Umayyad and early Abbasid caliphs. But the most far-reaching of these critical assaults upon the intellectual and political position of

---

[24] Sir Thomas Arnold, *The Caliphate*, Oxford, 1924, p. 11.

[25] Gibb, "Constitutional Organization," p. 14.

[26] By the time the Abbasids had come to power, the *'ulama'* had made good their claim to be the only authoritative exponents of the law. In other words, it was henceforth impossible to regard the caliphs as legislators. See Arnold, p. 54.

Gibb, *Mohammedanism*, p. 123, suggests that the caliph was the political and religious leader of the community, but that he was not entitled to define dogma. Arnold, p. 17, writes that he is a political functionary who is only occasionally called upon to exercise certain religious functions.

the existing Islamic government emanated, in the tenth century, from the *Shi'ah*. The members of this sect, which had begun as a political movement among Arabs contesting the legitimacy of the past rulers,[27] recognized as legitimate imams only Ali, the Prophet's son-in-law, who, as the fourth caliph, had been murdered, and his descendants, who had been deprived of their throne. All of the caliphs and princes who had been publicly recognized in Islam since the death of Ali were, in the eyes of the Shi'ites, mere usurpers and tyrants. Their true imam, on the other hand, was the indispensable, infallible, and exalted ruler, teacher, and guide, since he alone was the medium through which divine guidance became manifest in the world.[28]

This revolutionary, tenth-century doctrine of the quasi-divine imam had been evolved under the influence of ancient God-King memories and Asian traditions as well as Platonic ideas of government, and received in the course of its development various strands of esoteric thought. It found wide acceptance in the Dar al-Islam, especially in the strategically important eastern provinces of the realm. And even though the community of the Shi'ah was soon weakened by fragmentation into numerous sects, they retained the necessary strength to persist in their intransigent opposition to the Sunni majority of Islam. Moreover, since its antagonism was not confined to the sphere of intellectual disputations but expressed itself also in violent political animosity, it contributed greatly to the disintegration of the Empire. Indeed, in the thirteenth century its pernicious effects became catastrophically evident when influential Shi'ites showed themselves ready to receive the pagan Mongols as liberators from the Sunni yoke. We are told[29] that it was a Shi'ite vizier (of the Sunni caliph) who suggested the conquest of Baghdad to the Mongol prince Hulagu, and another Shi'ite dignitary who, following the fall of Baghdad, persuaded the alien conqueror to kill the captured caliph.

The intellectual difficulties that complicated and ultimately obstructed the quest for a politically effective form of imperial government in Islam were aggravated by the physical and cultural conditions under which the quest was pursued. Already in the ninth century it had been clear that the Abbasid Empire was geographically too vast and culturally too diverse to be held together by any central government patterned on inadequately developed Arab ideals. Under such a

---

[27] Gibb, *Mohammedanism*, p. 120.
[28] Von Grunebaum, pp. 186ff. Gibb, *Mohammedanism*, pp. 120-124.
[29] Von Grunebaum, p. 189.

system various non-Arab traditions of government would be bound to assert themselves, and in the course of time this is what actually happened. The most influential of the alien traditions that came into the field were three: the Persian, the Turkish, and the Byzantine. The first, that of Persian (Sassanian) ideas and practices, gained its position of strength when the Abbasid dynasty was brought into power with the aid of the Islamized Persian nobility of Khurasan[30] and then became totally dependent upon the services of Persians and Persianized Turks. The second alien tradition, that of the Turkish (Central Asian) manner of government, was channelled into the Islamic world by successive waves of Turks and Mongols. And finally, suggestions of the Byzantine, or third alien tradition, were present constantly in the world of Islam, since they emanated both from the great neighboring empire of their origin, which had produced the most impressive imperial establishment of the time, and from the Islamic provinces that had formerly been ruled by Constantinople and were still permeated with Byzantine culture.

All three of these alien traditions, different though they were from each other, nevertheless agreed in one important way: they all developed the common theme of monolithic secular power. But this theme was fundamentally alien to the value system of the Muslim Arabs. Its introduction, therefore, was bound to give rise to a serious cultural dissonance in the Dar al-Islam. Nevertheless, it continued to sound and even became in time the leading political motive; for the old Islamic value system was so rigidly unpolitical in character that it allowed neither for the evolution of autonomous Islamic principles of political organization nor for the qualified acceptance of foreign principles. A qualified acceptance being impossible, total acceptance was inevitable. In the end, therefore, the cultural dissonance between the Arab and the non-Arab systems of value was resolved by the unqualified adoption of the principle of the secular despot. And the most striking external evidence of this evolution is to be found in the court life that came to prevail at Baghdad and in the rules of statecraft and diplomacy to which the caliphs of that capital subscribed. That these rules were modelled closely upon the ancient Persian and Byzantine traditions and owed little if anything to Arab and Islamic sources, becomes quite apparent as one reads the "Book of Government," written in the eleventh cen-

[30] See Gibb, "An Interpretation of Islamic History," pp. 45ff.

tury by the renowned political scientist and vizier Nizam al-Mulk and used by all the later generations of Persian and Turkish rulers as their leading text in the Muslim art of government.[31]

D. The Position of the Jurists

The caliphate as the jurists imagined it has never existed in fact, and the theory of the caliphate must therefore be regarded as a fiction.[32] But such a conclusion, however well supported by history or logic, does not dispose of the theory. For it was the fiction, rather than the reality, of the caliphate that was accepted by successive generations of believers as the immutable symbol of the ideal state presumed to exist above and beyond the caliphate of the day. This ambivalent orientation toward the political scene, which has never ceased to pervade Muslim thought, was developed under the auspices of the same learned class that had called the fiction into being.

Contrary to the practice of the intellectual elites of certain other societies known to history, who chose to interpose themselves as mediators between the real and the ideal, the Muslim scholars had committed themselves to the doctrine that the real and the ideal should be identical: any political organization gaining their approval would have to coincide with the ideological concept of the Dar al-Islam that they themselves had formulated. This meant that they had excluded themselves from the possibility of seeking to reconcile the obvious conflicts between the actual political and their own normative systems. For since these men of learning were fundamentally opposed to the principles of secularization and centralization upon which the caliphate

[31] Nizam al-Mulk (le Vizir), Siasset Nameh. *Traité de Gouvernement composé pour le Sultan Melik Chah*, trad. par Ch. Schefer, 1894 (Publ. de l'Ecole des langues orientales vivantes, 7).

See Haroon Khan Sherwani, *Studies in Muslim Political Thought and Administration*, Lahore, 1945, pp. 129-143. Cf. Gibb, "Constitutional Organization," pp. 20ff.

See Gaston Wiet, "L'Empire Neo-Byzantin des Omayyades et l'Empire Neo-Sassanide des Abbasides" in *Cahiers d'Histoire Mondiale*, Vol. I, no. 1, Juillet 1953, pp. 63ff. on the influences exerted by Byzantine statecraft on the Umayyads, and of Persian statecraft on the Abbasids.

The absence of indigenous political principles of government and the consequent readiness of the Islamic elites to borrow foreign ideals and forms of government is evident also in the twentieth century.

[32] Cf. de Santillana, p. 301. The theory regained life and vigor with the installation of the caliphate by the Turks. But this version had few if any conceptual connections with early Islamic thought on the subject. See p. 302 to the effect that the caliphate has actually been extinct since 1543 if not since 1258. It may also be maintained that the caliphate ended in 1517 when the Turks took Cairo.

had finally come to rest, and since they could not tolerate the thought of allowing their sacred norms to become contaminated with anything like a pragmatic convention, they had no choice intellectually but to extricate Islam as a religious institution from all the nefarious political connections of its history and to disavow completely the actual imperial establishment. This approach to the problem was followed with such success that the theory, having been salvaged in its purity, became the beacon light that led believers away from the frustrating reality of the Empire and toward the ideal commonwealth that the jurists had conjured up in the name of righteous living.

The radiant realm of the jurists, however, was not as secure and well-ordered as it pretended to be. Everyone agreed, it is true, that their ideal Islam was subject exclusively to the sacred law; but this law itself proved disconcertingly ambiguous whenever an attempt was made to define it precisely enough for application to the domain of public or constitutional affairs. There was a general agreement, of course, that the law was to be interpreted by the learned, since they had been recognized in the Tradition as the inheritors of the Prophet. But how were the learned to exercise their function? That is, how were they to establish an effective rule of law absolutely in accord with the Prophet's revelations and traditions?[33]

The search for an answer to this question led the Sunni jurists in the eighth century to probe the legal properties of the concept of the *ijma'* or consensus.[34] This idea of the community of Islam devolves from Muhammad's directive that his spiritual prerogatives would be inherited not by his successors (the caliphs) but by the community as a whole. The special grace bestowed upon all believers by this word of the Prophet has been defined as follows: "When the Muslim community agrees to a religious practice or rule of faith, it is, in a certain manner, directed and inspired by God, preserved from error, and infallibly led toward the Truth. . . ."[35] The consensus, then, is the divinely prescribed manifestation of the community of believers, and as such it underlies the entire structure of Islam. For the assertion that truth comes from agreement and error from divergence was in Islam more than a theological dogma. It supplied the community with the first

[33] Khadduri, "Nature and Sources of Islamic Law," pp. 14, 16, for a discussion of some of the problems here involved.

[34] The Sunni theories on this subject were rejected by the Shi'ah.

[35] De Santillana, *Instituzioni di diritto musulmano malichita*, Vol. I, p. 32 as quoted in Gibb, *Mohammedanism*, pp. 96f. Gibb here refers to the *ijma'* as a third channel of revelation.

principle of a social and political philosophy, and imbued all Muslims with a distinct if somewhat mystical sense of their corporate identity in the world.[36] In fact the *ijmaʿ* may be said to have provided the trans-territorial and hence invisible commonwealth with a definite, permanent, and yet highly flexible *Gestalt*. For while it projects clearly and convincingly the image of a togetherness across time and space, it reserves the realization of that image to the community of the day.

Now it is in the latter context that the consensus becomes particularly important as a source of law; through its agreement the community can accept an innovation that was at first regarded as heretical, and as a result of such acceptance, the new principle is incorporated in the *sunnah*.[37] The records of Islamic thought leave no doubt that this concept of the consensus, which is in perfect accordance with the Prophet's injunction that that is lawful or unlawful which the community so considers, is richly suggestive as a theological, legal, political,[38] and social principle. But they reveal equally clearly that the concept was an extremely puzzling one. For just what was its relationship to the other sources of the sacred law? And precisely how was it to be applied in practice? When could the community be presumed to agree, and through what procedure could its agreement be established? These questions exercised the minds of all the leading scholars, particularly in the early creative period of Islamic jurisprudence, when the main patterns of legal thought were being set. The ancient law schools tended to identify the consensus with the traditional, albeit ideal, usages (*sunnah*) of the community.[39] But to Shafiʿi (died 820), who exercised a revolutionary influence on the development of Islamic legal thought, the term *sunnah* referred only to the traditions of the Prophet which he considered to be the highest of all legal authorities. The consensus of the community, in Shafiʿi's opinion, was a valid source of law only when the community was unanimous in its opinion on fundamental matters. However, neither this illustrious lawyer nor any of his successors was able to say with any degree of defi-

[36] See Spengler, Vol. II, pp. 73ff., 210, 242, 315-317, 320; German ed., Vol. II, pp. 80, 86, 208ff., 286-297, for some interesting reflections on the consensus in Persian, Jewish, early Christian, and Islamic thought.

[37] See Schacht, pp. 82-95; Gibb, *Mohammedanism*, pp. 96ff.; Von Grunebaum, p. 149.

[38] The early caliphate is in effect a manifestation of the *ijmaʿ* of the community. See Gibb, *Mohammedanism*, p. 99.

[39] Schacht, p. 2.

niteness just how a unanimous opinion of the believers was to be attained; or, if attained, how ascertained.[40]

The failure of the learned to clarify the full meaning of the concept of the *ijma'* or consensus may have marred the logic of the individual systems of thought of which the concept was supposed to be an integral part but it did not impair the influence of the concept in the community as a general and autonomous principle of orientation. On the contrary, it is even probable that the *ijma'* retained its magic potentiality as a fundamental ideological norm precisely because it was never fettered by an explicit definition. The inability of the jurists to come to terms with it, however, had another, decidedly negative result. For the *'ulama'* had consistently regarded themselves as the guardians of the Koran and Traditions, and as their authority grew they came to be recognized in public opinion as the representatives of the community in all matters relating to faith and law. This communal mandate was held by them collectively, and its exercise itself was supposed to be governed by the rule of the *ijma'* or consensus; that is to say, the learned were expected to agree in their readings of the fundamental law, which included the *ijma'* of the community.[41] As the main mechanism for the ascertainment of the perfect law, this *ijma'* was the pivotal institution in the ideal order that the jurists had fathomed, and as such it should have been defined as unequivocally as possible. The scholars were quite aware of this necessity, as the record of their cerebrations on the subject shows.[42] However they were unable to produce a generally acceptable definition and to clarify the terms of reference for the use of the institution because they could not agree in their answers to such questions as the following: Who are the scholars whose opinions must be included in the consensus? What are the qualifications of an eligible scholar? Is the consensus to be understood as implying the unanimous

[40] Cf. Khadduri, "Nature and Sources of Islamic Law," p. 14.

[41] The circumstances in which the theory of the consensus was evolved are somewhat obscure and have been interpreted differently by modern authorities. This topic is discussed under various headings in Schacht. Gibb, *Mohammedanism*, p. 96, states the relationship between the Ulamā and the community, and between the two forms of *ijma'*, in the following way: "At an early date, probably some time in the second century, the principle was secured that 'consensus of the community' (which in practice meant that of the Ulamā), had binding force. *Ijmā'* was thus brought into the armoury of the theologians and jurists to fill up all the remaining gaps in their system. As the Tradition was the integration of the Koran, so the consensus of scholars became the integration of the Tradition."

Von Grunebaum, p. 150, writes: "Gradually the *ijmâ'* came to be interpreted as the agreement of those competent to judge in religious matters; it became the agreement of the learned."

[42] Schacht, pp. 42, 68, 81-97, 135f.

or the majority view of the learned? Must the consensus continue through time, or does it summarize opinion in a certain period of time? What procedures should be employed in order to collect the views of the select? How in particular is the *ijma'* secured when jurists are scattered throughout the land? Who determines eventually whether a consensus exists? As the law schools in different geographic sections of the land and the separate factions within each law school endeavored to settle these issues in accordance with their own predilections, violent intellectual conflicts ensued. The most influential theory, propagated by the legal centers of Medina and Iraq,[43] was that the consensus formed itself separately in each region when the views of the lawyers, who were regarded as authorities by their contemporaries, coalesced in a majority opinion. But this version of the consensus was subjected to sharp criticism by Shafi'i because it violated the paramount principle of unanimity and left the decision to the most recent generation in each particular region. Indeed, the great legist was so disenchanted with the consensus of the learned, as a result of his studies, that he became increasingly doubtful about its true place in Islamic law,[44] and the ultimate failure of his attempts to lower the prestige value of the consensus as a source of law and to resurrect instead the Traditions of the Prophet as the highest legal authority, led him in the end to the utter rejection of this disturbing concept. The later, so-called classical, theory, on the other hand, was that a return should be made to the principles advocated by the ancient schools.[45] But since no precise definition of the *ijma'* had been given by those schools, none was forthcoming now.[46] The whole theory of the consensus of the learned became logically tenable only when there was appended to it the doctrine that divergence of opinion is admissible on secondary points.[47]

The ideal commonwealth, which the jurists had created in their imagination and in which the faithful were supposed to find a lasting

[43] On the differences between these two schools see Schacht, pp. 83-87.

[44] Schacht, pp. 88ff. on the changes in Shafi'i's theory. He started out by distinguishing between the consensus of all Muslims on essentials and the consensus of the scholars on points of detail.

[45] In the classical doctrine the consensus was regarded as the ultimate mainstay of legal theory and of positive law in their final form. It was presumed to cover every detail of the law, including the recognized differences of the several schools. Whatever the consensus sanctioned was right and could not be invalidated by reference to other principles. Schacht, p. 2 and authorities there cited.

[46] Khadduri, "Nature and Sources of Islamic Law," p. 16.

See Gibb, *Mohammedanism*, p. 97 and Von Grunebaum, p. 150, on the limitations of the *ijma'* of the learned as a source of law in later centuries.

[47] Von Grunebaum, p. 152.

home, thus reveals the same basic imperfections that had made the worldly empire objectionable in the eyes of the learned. For it, too, was a divided house in which the rule of law was understood but incompletely.

The ambiguous nature of Islamic law and the unresolved relationship between law and political organization in the Islamic realm are subjects that have interested many Muslim and non-Muslim scholars. A stimulating essay by David de Santillana[48] suggests that "What was lacking in Muslim law is what has been wanting in every respect, viz. a more synthetic spirit. A tendency to anarchy, and a fundamental incapacity for organization and discipline, the causes of the political incapacity of the Arabs, have been intellectually a source of weakness within their legal system." This statement seems to imply that the weakness of the Islamic legal system, which was created by a highly literate multinational elite, was due to the fundamental political incapacity of the Arabs, who were largely nonliterate, as were also the other national contingents of the empire. Santillana's view that the Arabs show a tendency to anarchy and an incapacity for organization and discipline is well supported by the records of the medieval caliphate and the modern nation-states that Arab and other Islamized peoples were called upon to create in the twentieth century. But the medieval annals of Islamic history indicate strongly that the political incapacity of the peoples comprised in the Dar al-Islam was the result, rather than the cause, of the intellectual weakness of the medieval literate elite who had constructed the legal system and assumed the tutelage over the great mass of nonliterate believers. According to the Prophet's instruction, this tutelage involved the task of leading the largely nomadic Arabs into settled ways of life. Now the information we have received from historians, anthropologists, and travellers does not indicate that the Arabs of the desert were undisciplined or incapable of organization. On the contrary, they seem to have been able to develop very effective forms of communal life.[49] But settled life requires a kind of discipline and political organization that is not called for in tribal nomadic life, and this meant that the Islamic community had to be helped to develop new political capacities. However, the 'ulama' were not competent to assume this pedagogical role. In the critical formative

48 "Law and Society," p. 309.

49 See Charles M. Doughty, *Travels in Arabia Deserta*, one vol. ed., New York, Random House; H. R. P. Dickson, *The Arab of the Desert*, London, 1951; the writings of St. John Philby, and numerous other works on the subject.

376

period of the caliphate they had withdrawn from the entire scene of actuality in order to construct the right ideology and build the perfect state. Their brilliant expositions of legal concepts and lucid drafts for a model state were written in the ivory towers to which they had removed themselves.[50] Few of their works were addressed to the real political issues that begged for settlement or clarification, and most of them were composed with an entire disregard for the facts of history.[51] At a time when the entire Islamic world had actually acquiesced for more than a hundred years in the existence of multiple caliphates, a thesis gained prominence that only one imam can exist on earth and that the election of other imams is to be considered illegal and invalid.[52]

Since the jurists had never related themselves to the actual community, they were unable to provide their nonliterate coreligionists with an orientation to political matters. It is true that they succeeded in imbuing every Muslim with the firm conviction that he was a citizen of the ideal state,[53] but it did not, and in the context of their thinking could not, occur to them to develop a doctrine of civic rights and duties that could be considered relevant to the actual situation.[54] The concept of the consensus of the community, which students of Western political thought may be inclined to regard as an expression, or potential source, of democracy, remained politically sterile under these circumstances. However, in estimating the possible political uses to which this idea might have been put, one must bear in mind that the consensus of all believers reflects a collective personality, not the sum total of individual personalities. In other words, the concept does not lend itself to the evolution of a theory of individual value judgments. And in the absence of such a theory, political democracy as understood in the West is inconceivable.

The conclusion seems inescapable, therefore, that the Islamic and Western European traditions of government are fundamentally incongruous, at least as they have been interpreted thus far. This incongruity has proved to be a source of considerable intellectual confusion for

[50] These intellectual activities were supported by the secular government. It was Nizam al-Mulk, for example, who created the great university of Baghdad which contained four separate law schools, one for each of the orthodox sects of the Sunni. See Alfred Guillaume, "Philosophy and Theology" in *Legacy of Islam*, p. 24.

[51] Arnold, p. 70. See Sherwani, also Schacht, for a record of some of these theories.

[52] Von Grunebaum, p. 157, referring to Mawardi's (died 1058) Statutes of Rulership.

[53] Arnold, p. 182.

[54] See Gibb, "Constitutional Organization," p. 15, to the effect that the 'ulama' failed to build a doctrine of civic duty on the basis of the community's loyalty to the shari'ah.

those Muslim scholars in the twentieth century who have tried to assimilate modern Occidental forms of the state and government without impairing their own native heritage. A recent study of the relationship between Islam and communism[55] illustrates the point. Here we find such passages as the following: "The spirit of Islam contains the essentials of democracy in a manner not equalled by any other system of social existence . . . with respect to democracy, Islam has nothing to learn either from the U.S. or from the U.S.S.S.," for "Islam started as a theistic socialist republic with liberty, fraternity and equality."[56] The study continues with the admission that the modern Muslim world is technically backward but advances the thesis that this condition is in no way a consequence of political thought or organization. It is due exclusively, we read, to the fact that the Dar al-Islam has been "bypassed owing to unfortunate historical conditions by the scientific and industrial development of the last two centuries."[57] Moreover, "since technical progress is not difficult to achieve,"[58] in the author's opinion, no more searching of the sources of this current malaise is needed. Other influential Muslim writers have returned to the rigid conservative doctrine of Islam as the exclusive and ultimate source of political regeneration. To the Pakistanian Abu al-'Ala' Maududi, for example, Western democratic forms of government are satanic devices through which men satisfy their whims and evil desires. Islam, on the other hand, is a monolithic system in which Allah alone legislates. The only acceptable agent of Islamic rule is therefore a caliph who is chosen by the people in order to rule according to the divine law.[59]

These views, which are widely shared by Muslim intellectuals, are a significant commentary on the long range influence that the medieval elite has exercised on the formation of political attitudes in the Muslim world. Whereas the performances of Western democracy and communism are to be tested on the basis of their present records and without regard to the ideals that inspired them, Islam is to be evaluated exclusively in terms of the ideal that Muhammad proclaimed fourteen hundred years ago. The actual medieval records of Islam show, however, that the 'ulama' established a pattern of life and thought that left the community without either a political constitution or political rights. Neither state nor government was brought into any relationship to "man," either as an individual or as a member of the community at

---

[55] Khalifa Abdul Hakim, *Islam and Communism*, Lahore, 1953.
[56] *ibid.*, pp. 123, 157, 162.   [57] *ibid.*, p. 160.   [58] *ibid.*
[59] F. Rahman, p. 878. See also Iqbal's views on the subject.

large.[60] Indeed, the concept of the state was not defined at all and the power of government was unlimited by any system of practically effective norms.[61] Public opinion thus became dulled and insensitive to abuses of power, all the more so since no principle was recognized in accordance with which an evil-doing imam could be deposed without provoking civil war. Instructed by their legal mentors that all governments other than the ideal caliphate were tainted by usurpation, violence, and corruption,[62] the believers were conditioned at an early time to obey him who holds power. For "which is to be preferred," the great Ghazali (died 1111) asked, "anarchy and the stoppage of social life for lack of a properly constituted authority, or acknowledgement of the existing power, whatever it be? Of these two alternatives the jurist cannot but choose the latter."[63] And the same idea was impressed upon the faithful two centuries later by the *qadi* Ibn Jama'ah of Damascus: "The sovereign has a right to govern until another and stronger one shall oust him from power and rule in his State. The latter will rule by the same title and will have to be acknowledged on the same grounds; for a government, however objectionable, is better than none at all; and between two evils we must choose the lesser."[64]

The jurist-theologians in medieval Islam were members of one of the most remarkable intellectual elites in history. For at a time when the cause of learning was eliciting but scant interest in the rest of the Mediterranean world, it was being furthered immeasurably within the protective orbit of the Muslim Empire, where Islamic, Christian, and

---

[60] Cf. Gibb, "Constitutional Organization," p. 12: "Islamic theory gives the citizen as such no place or function, and no scope for moral development." Compare this theory with the Greek view according to which the state exists in order to improve man.

[61] See Gibb, "Social Reform: Factor X, the Search for an Islamic Democracy," p. 138, for the comment that the Islamic state should be only the public exponent of Islamic ideology, ensuring the security and well-being of the Muslim peoples, and enforcing the Law of Islam but itself subject to that Law; and that the authority of the state derives wholly from the degree to which the state is considered to do so. See also Khadduri, "Nature and Sources of Islamic Law," pp. 7-9 on the relationship of the believer to the state and government on the one hand, and to the community on the other.

[62] Gibb, "Social Reform . . . ," p. 138.

[63] De Santillana, "Law and Society," p. 302.

[64] *ibid.*, pp. 302-303. See H. A. R. Gibb and Harold Bowen, *Islamic Society and the West*, Oxford, 1951, Vol. I, pp. 204ff. for the effect which this concept of government had left upon Arab Asia in the eighteenth century, when the region was part of the Ottoman Empire. At that time, we are told (p. 205), the conception of authority implied in the minds of the subjects themselves an assertion of power accompanied by a certain measure of harshness and violence. Compassionate administrators were despised, local chroniclers report.

Jewish scholars were tirelessly at work as translators and philologists, chemists and physicians, mathematicians and astronomers, geographers and historians.[65] And since the knowledge here acquired by several generations of scholars was being circulated widely within and beyond the Dar al-Islam by libraries and universities, as well as by correspondence and travel,[66] one is in effect justified in regarding these intellectuals as the designers of that international concert of scholars which functioned successfully throughout the Middle Ages while states and governments were either ignorant of each other or locked in war and strife.

Now in this literate elite the jurists had a unique position, for law is an intellectual discipline with direct and immediate social consequences. It has been pointed out earlier that law contributed particularly significant concepts to the political ideologies of the Christian and Muslim societies. Legal scholarship was therefore by definition tainted with political considerations, and legalists could not be as oblivious to actual problems in human affairs as, for example, astronomers. The work of the Islamic jurists must thus be evaluated in two contexts. As theorists they contributed considerably to the total intellectual achievement that has earned Muslim learning its great repute in the international history of ideas. But as administrators of the official ideology and as educators of their nonliterate coreligionists they fell far short of the expectations that would seem to have been implicit in their assumption of this dual position. By preserving the simple and internationally appealing forms into which the Prophet had cast his truth, they made possible the extension of the Empire's ideological frontiers, it is true. But their failure to relate the ideology to the conduct of government and the actual lives of the people made a consolidation of this empire impossible.

The Byzantine and Western European approaches to law and the state—different as they were from each other—were anchored in the legal system that the jurists of classical Rome had created. But the jurists in the two Christian empires did not form as distinct an elite group in their respective societies as the one that had supplied them with their conceptual tools. The Muslim approach to the relationship between law and government had little in common with the one that Rome had passed on to its successors, and yet the position of the Mus-

[65] Consult specialized works on the record of these intellectual activities.
[66] See the itinerary which Ibn Battuta followed in the course of twenty-five years of travelling. Ibn Battuta, *Travels in Asia and Africa*; (1325-54), H. A. R. Gibb, tr., London, 1929.

lim jurists was, paradoxically enough, somewhat analogous to that of the legal elite in ancient Rome. In fact, it has been suggested that the *ijma'* of the *'ulama'* corresponds to the *opinio prudentum* of Roman law, and that the idea underlying the *ijma'* was transmitted to the Arabs by Roman schools of rhetoric.[67] However, this convergence in form and status cloaks a profound divergence in matters of substance. In fact, it is the divergence that supplies the principal explanation for the political success of the Roman and failure of the Muslim Empire. For the Roman lawyers were statesmen, not theologians. Roman jurisprudence was a science of human relations, not a scholarly exercise upon religious themes. Roman law was thus the product of human intelligence and experience, not the distillation of revealed truth. An *'ulama'* and a jurisconsult, a *qadi* and a praetor may be comparable figures in a sociological study, but they represent totally different principles of thought. The principles to which Roman law and Roman lawyers subscribed were used to mediate between image and reality, and therefore they made the law-state possible. The principles to which the *'ulama'* subscribed perpetuated the cleavage between the real and the ideal and thus led to the separation of law and state, of people and government. Unrestrained by any practically applicable principle of law or human rights, the caliphate was bound to become a despotism. And unsupported by any practically applicable theory of unity, the Dar al-Islam was bound to disintegrate as an international state.

E. The Disintegration of the Muslim Empire

The Abbasid Empire reached the apogee of its fortunes around the year A.D. 800, when it reflected the powerful personality of the caliph Harun al-Rashid. But already in the ninth century it was reduced to a mere kingdom,[68] and by the tenth century it had broken down completely as a political organization.[69]

The circumstances that determined this rapid passage from glory to decay were varied and complex. But after due allowance has been made for the physical unwieldiness of the imperial domain, which confronted the government with staggering administrative problems, one is justified in concluding that the Empire failed because it had been unable to produce realizable ideas of political unity and government.

[67] Schacht, pp. 83, 99. See also Von Grunebaum, p. 152, n. 23.

[68] This was the view which Ibn Khaldun took in the fourteenth century. See Arnold, pp. 107ff.

[69] See *ibid.*, p. 57, and Gibb, "An Interpretation of Islamic History," p. 55.

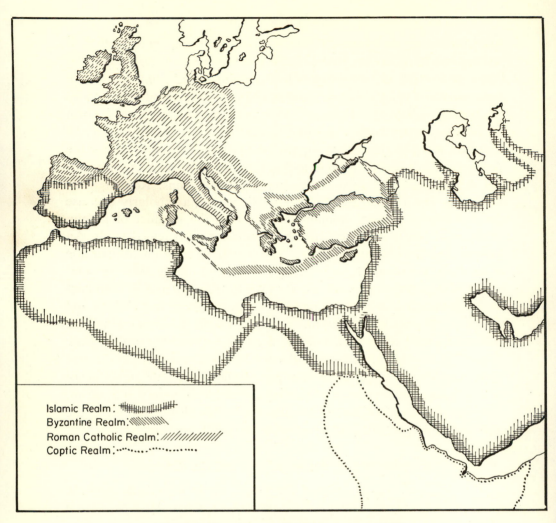

The Mediterranean World, c. A.D. 800

The political talent of a strong sovereign could at times compensate for the absence of generally accepted objective principles of cohesion. But strong and talented caliphs could not be expected as a matter of course. Moreover, their incidence and their effectiveness were bound to diminish as the vestiges of moral and material authority departed from the supreme imperial institution. Unsupported by impersonal institutions, the Empire was subjected, from the ninth century onward, to the anarchical play of rival human ambitions.

The geographic and intellectual factors that were primarily responsible for the political and moral corrosion of the caliphate thus had the corollary effect of encouraging political disunity and disorder. And the process of disintegration became relentless as the caliphs were compelled by their weakness to delegate authority to strong men in their entourage and to acquiesce in the usurpation of lands, titles, and prerogatives to which regionally prominent princes and commanders felt free to resort.

Islamic theory taught, it will be remembered, that there could be but one supreme ruler. But Muslim Spain became a separate kingdom as early as A.D. 756, and a caliphate in A.D. 928. North Africa left the imperial fold in the same period under the leadership of the Fatimid Dynasty, and similar processes of emancipation occurred in varying degrees of completeness in all Islamic regions in the world. In the end the title of caliph had passed from the supreme authority, who used to nominate sultans, to any sultan who cared to assume a designation once held to be unique.[70] Already in the eleventh century there were eight Muslim potentates who called themselves caliph.[71] The thirteenth century opened with the creation of an independent sultanate in New Delhi (1206), and this event was followed by the establishment of other separate sovereignties in Bengal, Bihar, Gujarat, and the Dekhan. Indeed, the curve that marked the disintegration of the Islamic Empire reached its nadir in this century. For not only was the North African region split into fragments which attacked each other ceaselessly, and Spain, with the exception of the kingdom of Granada, already lost to Islam, but all the eastern lands were being ravaged by waves of Mongol invaders. The vast area from the Oxus frontier to the Halys and the Euphrates was subjugated by these barbarians, and the great cities of Damascus and Baghdad fell.[72] The process of dismemberment continued in the fourteenth century when Persia and Mesopotamia were incorporated in Tamerlane's immense personal empire. In the fifteenth and sixteenth centuries these aggressions were followed by the onslaughts of the Ottoman Turks, who succeeded in consolidating their conquests of Byzantine and Islamic possessions by creating the vast Ottoman Empire.[73]

Whatever actual political identity the Islamic commonwealth may once have possessed had thus been effaced by incessant internecine wars and foreign conquests. And the strong sense of cultural homo-

[70] Arnold, p. 129.

[71] The Abbasid in Baghdad, the Fatimid in Cairo, and six princes of less importance in Spain.

[72] Consult Hazard, pp. 12-20 for developments between the tenth and fourteenth centuries.

[73] See *ibid.*, pp. 24-34 for maps depicting the rise and contraction of this realm.

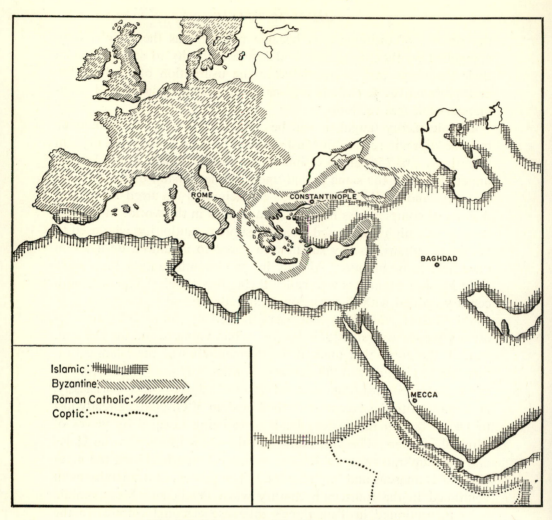

The Mediterranean World, c. A.D. 1200

geneity, which had pervaded the Dar al-Islam, was weakened immeasurably by the utter disregard shown by the Mongols for the civilization of this area, and by the forcible union with culturally alien nations from the steppes of inner Asia, which followed in the wake of the successful invasions. But these recessive developments did not call into question the religious identity of the Muslim community.[74] On the contrary, the frontiers of Islam were greatly advanced even as those of the ancient Empire vanished.[75] For not only did Islam gain numerous

[74] However, it should be noted that the Safavids forcibly converted Persia to Shi'ism in 1500. This meant that Transoxania and Afghanistan were cut off from the rest of Sunni Islam.

[75] Only in the West was its domain contracted, where all of Spain was lost with the fall of Granada in 1492.

converts in Africa and Asia but it captivated also the minds of those whose swords had brought ruin to its territorial domains.

On the basis of the medieval records one must conclude that the Muslims were more successful than their Christian rivals in winning the allegiance of men, especially in nonliterate regions. The chief sources of strength in furthering their religious cause were the Koran, which relayed the divinely revealed truth in understandable terms acceptable to people in all walks of life, and a system of time-consuming but simple religious rituals and procedures which served to break down cultural and racial barriers[76] and to equalize human behavior in widely separated areas. However, the remarkable success of the Dar al-Islam as an international association of coreligionists was offset by its equally remarkable failure as a political commonwealth.

Contrary to the Byzantines, the Muslims did not transform their religious union into an effective empire. And contrary to the Western European Christians, they had not been stimulated by their intellectual elites to strive for a politically harmonious union of nations and to develop regional and international organizations in restraint of separatism and anarchy. The only pattern of political coalescence on the international level that Islamic history suggested was that of the unconsolidated empire-in-motion. It is not surprising to find, therefore, that expansion became the principal international policy of each separate Islamic sovereignty after the unified Empire had ceased to be a reality.[77]

The legacy left by the early Empire also determined the evolution of political organization on the local or national level. For each political division and subdivision inherited the ambiguities and contradictions that had beset the development of the caliphate. Each sultanate, emirate, and lesser caliphate was as deprived of the protection of a fundamental public law as the original union had been, and each dynasty and government was subject to the same ever-present threat of violent displacement that had jeopardized the chances of the imperial regime. In other words,

---

[76] Coon, p. 128.

[77] This was evident already during the early phases of the contest with Byzantium, when the Muslims were unable to maintain or organize the control over the Mediterranean Sea that they had wrested from Constantinople. Each of three separate Islamic naval centers insisted upon using its strength for its own purposes rather than join in common action against the Christian foe. The Fatimids who held the Mediterranean center thus began in the early tenth century to direct their naval strength against the eastern and western representatives of Islamic naval power. See A. R. Lewis, *Naval Power and Trade in the Mediterranean: A.D. 500-1100*, Princeton, 1951, pp. 162ff.

the political destiny of each separate region was determined in the final analysis by the same factors that had proved decisive in the early Empire—the personality and power of the ruling prince.[78]

[78] At their best, Islamic governments were benign and progressive despotisms which furthered the welfare of their subjects and promoted cultural and commercial activities. See Carl Brockelmann, *History of the Islamic Peoples*, Joel Carmichael and Moshe Perlmann, trs., New York, 1947, pp. 196ff., for the records of certain caliphs in Spain. At their worst they were ruthless tyrannies such as those which existed in India before the establishment in 1526 of the Mogul dynasty. The principle of unlimited personal power was mitigated only in those areas in which Islamic rule was superimposed upon strong native traditions of government that did not accommodate despotism easily, as for example in certain parts of West Africa. See Leo Frobenius, *Und Afrika Sprach* . . . , Berlin, 1912, ch. 16, "Die Brille des Islam," for an exhaustive and stimulating discussion of the political effect exercised by Islam on the ancient nations of the Sudan.

PART IV

INTERNATIONAL HISTORY AND THE WORLD
SOCIETY TODAY: A RECONSIDERATION
OF REALITY AND MYTH

CHAPTER 11

PATTERNS OF INTERNATIONAL AND INTERCULTURAL RELATIONS AT THE OPENING OF THE MODERN AGE

A. The Image of the World

THE MEANING OF HISTORY is determined by the time and place in which men think of the past. What once was actual and real often loses its poignancy for later generations, and what is only dimly discernible in the present may assume clear contours sometime in the future. Facts and dates that were important in the eighth century, for example, may signify little in the fifteenth or twentieth centuries, and memories that control the thinking of the Arabs may not suggest significant recollections to the Chinese or the French. Each nation, then, has a different image of the past, and each generation a different perspective over the passage of time. Every individual effort to order the multifarious records of international history as they have accumulated in a given moment is therefore a somewhat arbitrary undertaking.

When Luiz de Camões reviewed the world before he died in A.D. 1580, he saw all history converging upon Christian Portugal. From here, he felt, had sallied forth a race of heroes, the Lusiads,[1] destined by Providence to join the oceans and the continents in the service of all humanity and for the greater glory of Christianity and Western Europe. He wrote,

> "This is the hostel of humanity,
>   Who, not content in overweening pride
>   Only to bear the hard ground's injury,
>   The perils of the unstable deeps have tried."[2]

And among the few to whom the many were to owe so much, none was greater in the poet's estimation than Vasco da Gama (born 1460, died 1524). This was the man who epitomized for Camões the spirit of the future. For it was Vasco da Gama above all other Portuguese who braved "the nameless perils in the world that be, Shipwrecks and

---

[1] The sons of Lusus, companion of Bacchus and mythical first settler in Portugal.

[2] *The Lusiads of Luiz de Camões*, Leonard Bacon, tr., New York, 1950, Book x, 91, p. 371. See Roy Campbell, "The Poetry of Luiz de Camões," in *The London Magazine*, August 1957, Vol. 4, no. 8, pp. 23ff. for a perceptive appreciation of this poem.

sharks and the great deeps of the sea,"[3] and thus beheld the world in its exciting newness as he made his double journey, in the last years of the fifteenth century, outward by the coasts of the African mainland, Abyssinia, Arabia, Persia, India, Burma, Malaya, China, and then back again by way of many islands, Japan, the Moluccas, Borneo, Timor, Java, Sumatra, Ceylon, the Maldives, Socotra, and Madagascar.[4] The memory of these great exploits, the experiences of his own adventurous travels, and the vision of Europe's forthcoming mastery over Africa, Asia, and America entranced Camões even as he lamented the decline of his own beloved nation, "Sunken in harsh, depraved and gross distress."[5] And it was in this mood that he called upon his knowledge and imagination in order to join reality and myth in an epic poem, "The Lusiads."

The final book in this exalted celebration of the deeds and dreams of men is the legend of da Gama's vision of the world and of his country's destiny. On a guarded mount the hero beholds, suspended in the air, a globe of great transparency, a supernatural artifice without beginning or end, in all things uniform, perfect, and self-sustained like God its maker. This miraculous thing, a pagan Goddess explains, is a representation in miniature of the marvellous universe. Its center is the abode of mankind, where, separated by the same tempestuous seas, the various regions lie, inhabited by different nations under different rulers, with different ways of life and different religions: Africa, still grasping after the things of this world; the three Arabias, where swarthy nomads dwell; India with its graceful rivers flowing from heights nearby; Siam and Malacca, soon to be the great emporium for the wealth and merchandise of luscious isles and lands; the mighty China, boasting greater territories and riches than it knows of yet; and vast expanses of the earth, dotted with names of a thousand nations, still hidden from the wondrous gaze of the discoverer. These are the countries of the East, the prophetess declares, which Portugal is adding to the modern world as its explorers brave the mighty oceans. And as she unfolds the universal panorama of vast space and time in which "fair and exalted" Europe "shall strike chill dread into the whole mighty hothouse of the East," she finds it fitting, too, that da Gama should cast at least a glance westward to America, where Portuguese Brazil shall

---

[3] *ibid.*, Bk. x, p. 147.

[4] See *Luiz Vaz de Camoens The Lusiads*, Wm. C. Atkinson, tr., Harmondsworth, Middlesex (Eng.), 1953, pp. 7-28.

[5] Bacon, Bk. x, p. 145.

rise, and where another of his race will blaze a trail that none had ever thought of.[6]

Columbus discovered America in 1492, and this year—which witnessed also the death of Lorenzo the Magnificent and the fall of Muslim Granada to Christian Spain—has been remembered ever since as a glorious date in international history. But to men in the sixteenth century 1498 was an even greater year, for it was then, on May 20th, that Vasco da Gama dropped anchor off Calicut in India, the first European to have crossed the Indian Ocean.

Europe and Asia were now in direct contact with each other. The eastern nations that had controlled Eurasian relations in the Middle Ages had been bypassed, and in the wake of these developments came momentous shifts of influence and power, which have been summarized succinctly by a twentieth century historian in the following juxtaposition of dates and events: "In 1498 the Ottoman advance-guards reached Vicenza, but Vasco de Gama landed at Calicut. In 1503 the Turks scored great victories over the Venetians, but six years later Francisco d'Almeida . . . obtained mastery of the Indian Ocean. In 1522 Rhodes fell to Suleiman the Magnificent, but before five years were out, the Portuguese dispersed the Muslim fleet at Gujerat. In the later sixteenth century, the Turks were able to ravage Austria, but could not dislodge Joao da Castro from India. . . ."[7]

B. Western Europe and Eastern Asia

International relations in the twentieth century have been marked by many cultural and political discords between the nations of the Atlantic community, on the one hand, and those bordering the Pacific and Indian Oceans, on the other. The source of most of these misunderstandings is conventionally found in the imperialist policies of the various European powers that entered the Orient after Portugal had shown the way. Now it is undoubtedly true that European governments and trading companies have been insensitive to the indigenous civilizations that they encountered after the turn of the sixteenth century, but the records of history make it clear also that Oriental and Occidental ways of life were too different to permit harmonious interaction and adjustment.

This becomes particularly apparent when one compares the political

[6] Bk. (Canto) x.
[7] Grousset, "Europe et l'Asie" as rendered by Joseph Needham, *Science and Civilisation in China*, 3 vols., Cambridge, Eng., 1954-59, Vol. I, p. 225.

and ideological legacy left by China with that of Western Europe, and when one remembers that each of these realms had studiously nurtured an all-pervading sense of its own supremacy on earth. The evolution of intercultural affinities was impeded, furthermore, by the immense physical distances that separated the great societies of the East from those in the West, and by the deliberate obstruction of any intercourse between these two poles of the known world that was interposed first by Parthia and subsequently by the Arabian and Islamized nations of the Middle East.

The total estrangement between Europe and China which had thus taken place in the course of centuries was somewhat eased by the policies of the Mongols[8] and the exploratory overtures of a few Venetians. But even the Pax Tartarica was not auspicious for the creation of Eurasian understanding. An interesting episode in the intercontinental affairs of the thirteenth century will illustrate this point.

The Mongolian Khanates and the Western European courts were greatly alarmed by the expansive tendencies emanating from the Mamelukian regime in Egypt. Each of the parties attempted to contact the other in order to meet the threat by joint action, and various diplomatic missions were dispatched from West to East, and from East to West to consummate the great design of encircling the mutual enemy.[9] However, nothing came of this scheme. In fact, the records contain no proof that its European and Asian protagonists ever succeeded in overcoming the technical and intellectual difficulties that inhibited a rapprochement at that time. The transcontinental journeys that their emissaries had to undertake in order to convey points of view from one center of government to the other were extremely lengthy and hazardous. None of the governments here involved had at its disposal a regularized diplomatic system capable of spanning time and space such as the one maintained by Venice. Each sovereign was therefore totally unfamiliar with the conditions obtaining in the country of the other, and each entrusted the task of carrying and collecting information to individuals who were chosen more or less at random without regard to their professional suitability for the task. Every diplomatic mission was thus conceived and executed as an independent transaction, destined to terminate with the return of the envoy and quite devoid of

[8] See L. Carrington Goodrich, *A Short History of the Chinese People*, New York, 1943, pp. 174ff. for China's place in the Mongol Empire.

[9] It is interesting to note that Byzantium had anticipated this approach in the seventh century A.D.

any consequence if either of the sovereigns or any of their agents happened to be overtaken by death or some other untoward event.

One explanation for the absence of significant cultural and political understandings between Western Europe and Eastern Asia can thus be found in the purely technical aspects of all Eurasian relations. But the recorded contacts, sparse as they were in the thirteenth century, reveal also that the two realms could not communicate with each other intellectually. This point is made forcefully by Joseph Needham.[10] Observations, ideas, and theories, whether pertaining to philosophy or to science, did not—and in Mr. Needham's estimation could not—circulate in this era, for not only had China and Europe developed entirely different modes of thought, but both systems of thinking had become so fixed by the tenth century A.D. that neither could accommodate concepts emanating from the other. Traffic between China and Europe—mostly Europe-bound during the first thirteen centuries of the Christian era[11]—was limited therefore to concrete objects such as textiles, plants, and crops, and technological inventions, such as musical instruments, medical secrets, and mechanical skills.[12] In view of this general sterility of Sino-European contacts it is not surprising to find then that Christian sovereigns and emissaries, whether they represented secular or ecclesiastical interests, were unable for the most part to exclude purely religious motives from their diplomatic approaches to the Mongols, and that Mongol rulers and functionaries, accustomed to the monolithic order of their society, were usually incapable of understanding the legal and moral norms with which their potential allies were constrained to comply. The dialogue between Orient and Occident which had ensued from the dim recognition of a mutual enemy was thus essentially a "dialogue des sourds."[13]

[10] Vol. I, pp. 239ff., 150ff., 223.

[11] The current was to flow the other way in subsequent centuries. *ibid.*, pp. 150, 239.

[12] *ibid.*, p. 242, for lists of exchanges. See also L. Carrington Goodrich, pp. 174ff. The rigidity of these early exchanges was greatly eased from the seventeenth century on, when the Jesuits succeeded in familiarizing the Chinese with Occidental philosophy and science, and in relaying Chinese thought to Europe. On Leibniz as a bridge builder between Oriental and Occidental thought, see Needham, Vol. II, pp. 497ff.

[13] Denis Sinor, "Les Relations entre les Mongols et l'Europe jusqu'à la Mort d'Arghoun et de Bela IV" in *Cahiers d'Histoire Mondiale*, Vol. III, 1956, no. 1, p. 61. The best discussions of international relations in this period are found in: V. Minorsky, "The Middle East in Western Politics in the 13th, 14th and 15th centuries" in *Journal of the Royal Central Asian Society* (publ. by the Royal Central Asian Society), Vol. XXVII, 1940, pp. 427ff., especially pp. 433ff.; R. Grousset, *Bilan de l'Histoire*, Paris, 1946, especially the chapter "Europe et Asie"; same author, *L'Em-*

C. The Middle East and the Far East

The Muslim governments that had evoked the abortive diplomatic maneuvers of the Christian and Mongolian courts used consummate skill in establishing themselves as brokers between East and West. Not only did they take full advantage of the distances and differences that separated their enemies, but they were able also to exploit the divisions that rent the camp of the Christians. For the cause of Euro-Mongolian friendship, which had been advanced by sovereigns in the West and upheld by the Christian kingdoms of Georgia and Armenia in the East, was refuted by the Syrian Franks who chose instead to side with the Islamic regime of Egypt in order to repulse Mongol invasions of the Near East. But when the Sultans had attained this objective, they turned against their Christian allies. And when the last Frankish strongholds in the Holy Land fell in 1291, the Mamluks emerged as the undisputed rulers of the Middle East and as comptrollers of all Middle-Eastern lines of communications, attuned alike to Orient and to Occident.

The median position in the traffic of intercultural and international relations, which the Arabized nations occupied until the end of the fifteenth century, can no doubt be viewed as a corollary of favorable geographic circumstances and successful campaigns of conquest and conversion. But the actual evolution of cultural and commercial accords between the Middle Eastern nations on the one hand, and their Eastern and Western neighbors on the other, was not due so much to propitious external conditions as to the deliberate activities of generations of intellectually mobile individuals who preferred travel, exploration, and adventure to the quiet of settled life. This orientation to the world, already implicit in the folkways of the Persians and Arabs,[14] was made explicit in the Prophet's admonition that the faithful should seek learning, "Though it be as far away as China,"[15] and in al-Man-

---

pire des Steppes, Paris, 1939; Paul Pelliot, "Les Mongols et la Papauté," *Revue de l'Orient Chrétien*, Vol. XXIII, 1922, pp. 3-30; XXIV, 1924, pp. 225-335; XXVIII, 1931, pp. 3-84; Denis Sinor, pp. 39ff.; also Geoffrey Francis Hudson, *Europe and China; A Survey of their Relations from the Earliest Times to 1800*, London, 1931, p. 135.

[14] See S. A. Huzayyin, *Arabia and the Far East, their commercial and cultural relations in Graeco-Roman and Irano-Arabian times*, Cairo, 1912, and G. F. Hourani, *Arab Seafaring in the Indian Ocean in Ancient and Early Medieval Times*, Princeton, 1951.

[15] See Needham, Vol. I, p. 216 for a discussion of this directive. The pronouncements of prominent Muslim jurists to the effect that the believers were not supposed to trade with the world of war, do not seem to have had a deterrent effect. See Khadduri, *Law of Peace and War in Islam*, p. 114.

sur's bold exposition of the fact that "we have the Tigris to put us in touch with lands as far as China, and bring us all that the seas yield as well as the foods of Mesopotamia and Armenia," and ". . . the Euphrates to carry us all that Syria and adjacent lands have to offer."[16] Sind and Chinese Tartary were after all part of the empire of the Ummayad caliphs, as Payne points out in his explanatory notes to *The Book of the Thousand Nights and One Night*.[17] After the conquest of Turkestan in the first century of the Hegira, regular commercial communication was established with China by the overland route from Aleppo through Samarkand. Diplomatic relations, also, were early established between the successors of Muhammad and the sovereigns of Cathay, and the Caliph al-Mansur (second of the Abbasid dynasty) was on such terms of alliance with the T'ang Emperor as to dispatch four thousand Arab troops to his aid against a rebel. The troops afterwards settled in China, where their descendants are, it is said, still to be traced.

To follow the lure of the East was thus an officially sanctioned directive, and many a Sinbad was encouraged, therefore, to set sail with his merchandise in order to pass bartering from island to island, and from town to town, experiencing the terrors and the wonders of the unknown. Reliable sea lanes to the Orient were charted in this fashion, among them the route from the Persian Gulf to Canton, which was the longest known to mankind until the Portuguese struck across the oceans. The ports of China, India, and Malaya became accessible, and a steady stream of voyagers went forth promoting their commercial, diplomatic, and scholarly interests.[18] It was this motley crowd of footloose cosmopolitan individuals that linked the civilizations of the world between the seventh and fourteenth centuries; for the knowledge that they carried from the Far East to the Near East was also relayed westward to the great centers of Mediterranean life and thought.

The fabric of the universe that unfolded itself to a sophisticated Muslim in this epoch was thus immensely intricate and colorful. It has been preserved for us in the scholarly accounts of cosmographers, geographers, and historians; in the mythical interpretations of poets and bards, and above all perhaps, in that rich collection of lore and legend—the Arabian Nights. For the tales that Shaharazad tells in the *Thousand Nights and One Night* reach into the recesses of time as it was remembered in the Middle Eastern capitals in the thirteenth century; incorporate all the regions and nations with which the Persians,

---

[16] *ibid.* [17] London, 1882, 9 vols., Vol. IX, p. 296, n. 1.
[18] See Needham, Vol. I, pp. 214ff. on Chinese-Arabian contacts.

Arabs, and Egyptians were in contact; and recall the whole range of physical and metaphysical vicissitudes that confronted the faithful and the infidels, the rich and the poor, sages and conjurers, merchants and thieves, fishermen and lazy-good-for-nothings, princesses and slave girls. Most of the stories are rooted in the predominantly Persian humanistic movement that pervaded Islam after the fall of the Arabian Ummayad Caliphate and the founding of Baghdad by the Persian-supported Abbasids. But many themes derive from Greece, pre-Muslim Arabia, Western Europe, India, China, and Japan, while others (i.e., the saint and hermit legends) are directly referable to Christian, Jewish, Brahmin, and Buddhist sources.[19] The entire compilation can thus indeed be viewed as "a universe of story, or rather the universe as story."[20]

D. The Middle East and Western Europe

One of the strongest impressions left by a reading of the Arabian Nights is that of a manifold intercourse between Muslims and Christians. Christian kings are found allied with Muslim sultans; Muslim merchants sail for the cities of the Franks; Syrian physicians minister to the infirmities of Western monarchs; Greek maidens become favorite concubines in the harems of Baghdad, and Frankish princesses gain renown in the Orient for their fluency in Arabic and their wit and ardor in the affairs of love. Characters from all Mediterranean lands are encountered here as they mingle in palaces and bazaars, on ships and open roads, in monasteries and on the battlefields, their separate destinies caught in one great web of commercial, military, diplomatic, erotic, and accidental relations. The comédie humaine thus unfolds itself in these pages as a fascinating intercultural spectacle. The reader learns through stories, myths, and allegories that individual Muslims and Christians were moved by similar impulses, aspirations, and traditions, and that the great Mediterranean civilizations had converged upon many values and institutions, however divergent the causes that the governments of the times espoused.

[19] See *The Portable Arabian Nights*, Joseph Campbell, ed., New York, 1952, editor's introduction, pp. 1-35.

Richard F. Burton, *The Book of the Thousand Nights and a Night*, 6 vols. New York, 1954, writes in the "Terminal Essay," p. 3673, that the framework of the book is purely Persian, perfunctorily Arabized; that the oldest tales may date from the reign of al-Mansur; that the latest are as late as the sixteenth century; and that the work assumed its present form in the thirteenth century.

[20] Joseph Campbell, ed., p. 1.

The medieval tales that suggest the existence of these transcultural linkages and accords originated in the imagination of the Persians and Arabs, it is true, but the validity of the images implicit in this lore is corroborated by the romantic literature of medieval Western Europe, which shows similar strands of phantasy,[21] by the episodes that contemporary chroniclers such as Joinville and Froissart narrate in their journals, and by the conclusions that modern scholars have reached after studying the history of the period. In fact, no aspect of this compilation is quite as fascinating to students, whether of history, literature, sociology, religion, or psychology, as the steady interplay of fact and fiction through its stories.[22]

Baghdad was the dream capital of "The Nights," as it was also the seat of supreme Muslim power during the centuries preceding the crusades. Aix-la-Chapelle was far away, but the Franks are given the same prominence in the stories that they enjoyed in the reality of Mediterranean politics. Western European as well as Middle Eastern[23] legend presented Harun al-Rashid and Charlemagne as personal friends, and diplomatic history has registered the same relationship between the monarchs of Eastern Islam and Western Christendom. For Charlemagne's predecessor already had solicited the friendship of Baghdad in order to cope with his two chief enemies—the Christian Byzantines and the Muslim Ummayads in Spain—and the Abbasids in turn had been receptive to these overtures because they shared the Western monarch's hostility toward both these realms. This alignment was solidified by Harun al-Rashid and Charlemagne. Elaborate diplomatic missions circulated between the two courts, and costly personal gifts, which included the famous elephant Abul-Abbas, were exchanged by the monarchs in token of their friendship.[24] These dealings in behalf of a common political cause may not have had a long-term effect upon Mediterranean power politics, but they have convinced a twentieth century historian that the ties between the two rulers were much closer than had been assumed previously. For Muslim constitutional theory,

---

[21] See the twelfth century cantefable of Aucassin's love for a Saracen slave girl.

[22] See Joseph Campbell, ed., Introduction, for an illuminating discussion of these connections.

[23] See "Ali Noureddin and the Frank's daughter" in Campbell, ed., p. 594. Here the king of the Franks appeals personally to Harun al-Rashid in behalf of a Frankish girl who has been abducted by a merchant's son from Cairo, offering the caliph in return half of the city of Rome as an appropriate site for the building of mosques.

[24] See F. W. Buckler, *Harunu'l-Rashid and Charles the Great*, Cambridge, Mass., 1931, pp. 6ff. and Appendix III for a record of these transactions. Brockelmann, p. 181, on one of Charlemagne's interventions in Spain.

we are told, treated the Frankish rulers as vassal emirs of the Abbasid caliph, charging them with the specific task of administering the interests of Baghdad in Spain.[25]

The reality of international relations during the crusades was particularly auspicious for the evolution of intercultural myths, and the stories that refer to this period are replete, therefore, not only with amorous intrigues between Christians and Muslims but with all kinds of political matter. "The Man of Upper Egypt and His Frank Wife"[26] tells of truces and prisoner exchanges between the warring nations, and "King Omar and His Sons"[27] makes elaborate references to diplomatic alliances that cut across religious lines. The stage in all tales is make-believe, the plot imaginary, the heroes quite fictitious, but it does not take the student of history long to realize that the adventurous French heroine in the novel "King Omar" bears a close resemblance to Eleanor of Aquitaine—the spirited European queen whose romantic life inspired fables also in her native France. For Frenchmen in the twelfth century seem to have delighted in the rumor that she had carried on relations of the most improper kind not only with a Saracen slave of great beauty but with the noble Saladin himself.

These and other royal figures captured the public imagination when it fastened upon international affairs because they symbolized the transcultural connections of the age. However, kings and caliphs were not the real architects of that superstructure of common values which accommodated the separate Mediterranean societies. It is true that most of them were cosmopolitans by virtue of their offices and functions, and that they were able, like heads of state in other historical periods, to find levels of communication and cooperation with each other from which the great majority of their subjects were excluded. But the most meaningful patterns of accord which medieval literature and history mirror were fashioned by less exalted men in less publicized circumstances. These people, anonymous for the most part, belonged to the knightly, commercial, and scholarly elites that had evolved simultaneously and in similar manner in each of the contending states. The equivalence of their social roles and interests made for a wide measure of respect and understanding among the members of each vocationally unified group, and the interaction between like-minded elites that ensued from this community of individual interests promoted the growth of shared ideals, institutions, and forms of behavior.

[25] Buckler, pp. 24-40. For a denial of this view see Khadduri, p. 114.
[26] Joseph Campbell, ed., p. 602.
[27] *ibid.*, pp. 147-213.

CHAPTER 12

THE MEDITERRANEAN ELITES AND THE FURTHERANCE
OF CULTURAL AFFINITIES

A. The Knights

THE TIMES that witnessed this remarkable evolution of trans-cultural correspondences were an aristocratic and a martial age, and the hero figure of this age was everywhere the knight, who placed his arms in the service of his God, his lord, and his beloved. The Western European feudal baron, upon whom was incumbent the duty of defending the peace, had his counterpart in the warrior type that had developed among the Byzantines and Persians, and the aristocratic standards of chivalry and courtly love that were observed throughout Christendom obtained also in the Middle East and North Africa. Whether these ideals and institutions arose independently in each of these realms, or whether they were diffused after having made their appearance first in one society, cannot be said with any degree of certainty. The epic of Firdausi and other poems indicate that the norms of chivalry developed somewhat earlier in Persia than elsewhere, and twentieth century scholars have traced the beginnings of courtly love to Bengal, which was famed for its courts of love already in the seventh and eighth centuries A.D.—three or four centuries before similar social customs were cultivated in France.[1] Tantric texts embodying the "new" concept of mystic love reached Persia first, we learn from another source,[2] and there they were translated into Pehlevi by a medical man at the court of Chosroes I. Recast in Syrian, Arabic, Latin, and Spanish renditions, the idea is then supposed to have spread throughout Europe. The assumption is thus at least possible that courtly love, as understood in Europe in the twelfth century, did not originate in southern France (as European scholarship has long maintained) but was, rather, a synthetic concept incorporating the influences of several Mediterranean civilizations. A study of troubadour literature[3] in Christendom and Islam has revealed that Christian as well as

[1] Mircea Eliade, "Note sur l'érotique mystique indienne," in *La Table Ronde*, no. 97, Janvier 1956, pp. 28ff.

[2] Denis de Rougemont, "Tableau du phénomène courtois," in *La Table Ronde*, no. 97, Janvier 1956, p. 26.

[3] Andreas Capellanus, *The Art of Courtly Love*, with introduction, translation, and notes by John Jay Parry, New York, 1941, pp. 3-13. See also H. A. R. Gibb, "Literature" in *The Legacy of Islam*, Sir Thomas Arnold and Alfred Guillaume, eds.,

Muslim concepts of love were influenced decisively by Plato and Ovid, that certain literary interpretations, long considered peculiarly French, had actually appeared a century earlier in the poetry of Muslim Spain, and that wandering court poets were familiar figures in Spain before they were encountered in France.[4]

Whatever the date or place of their origin, chivalry and courtly love were two institutions upon which twelfth century knightly life converged in the Mediterranean world. They were the cornerstones, as it were, of an international system of aristocratic attitudes that incorporated all Mediterranean warriors in one great knightly fellowship. For the demands and rewards of warfare, whether in the context of crusade or jihad, were essentially alike, however different the religious and social norms that governed knightly life in times of peace. Whether men were Greeks or Berbers, Franks or Arabs, they showed analogous qualities of mind and inclinations of the heart. And this equivalence of human tendencies made, in turn, for a correspondence of human responses to the great challenges of life and death that warriors encountered throughout these centuries. In these circumstances it became natural that knights should test each other by the same standards, whether in military battle or in moral behavior. For martial valor elicited respect, whether it was manifest in friend or in foe; and the predicaments of love called forth sympathy whatever the nationality or religion of the afflicted individual. Many vivid episodes in history and literature illustrate this remarkable concord of sentiments and dis-

---

Oxford, 1947, pp. 185ff. and 199ff. Carleton Coon, *Caravan: The Story of the Middle East*, New York, 1947, pp. 151ff.

[4] After the fall of Cordoba, Spain was divided into numerous petty states—some of them Christian—whose sovereigns vied with each other as protectors of the arts. Each Spanish court had its court poet, as did practically every town and village. Before the advent of the fanatical Almoravids in 1086, these poets enjoyed considerable liberties of thought and movement. In fact, their peripatetic functions were greatly favored by the princes, who found it profitable to employ the bards as diplomatic spokesmen on missions to rival courts. See Capellanus; Carl Brockelmann, *History of the Islamic Peoples*, Joel Carmichael and Moshe Perlman, trs., New York, 1947, p. 184, for the dispatch of a court poet to a Norman leader who had his residence on one of the Danish islands. The purpose of this mission was the negotiation of a truce.

Another literary form that developed more or less concurrently in the Mediterranean area was the *Chanson de Geste*, which made its appearance wherever there were border struggles between civilizations. Sir Ernest Barker refers in this connection to the Byzantine *Chanson de Geste* which was brought forth by conflicts between the Greeks and Turks, and to the Song of Roland and the Legend of Cid, which were stimulated by the battles of Christians and Muslims in Spain. However, he notes that similar poetry was not composed by the Arabs. ("The Crusades," Encyclopaedia Britannica.)

positions. During an expedition to Africa, Froissart records,[5] the French observed in the ranks of the Saracens a young Moorish knight who rode a fresh and prancing steed. All of his accoutrements apart from his white turban were black, and he generally carried three feathered, pointed javelins which he handled with skill. The Christians, we are told, concluded that his deeds of prowess were inspired by his love for a lady of his nation, the daughter of the king of Tunis—a most beautiful lady, according to the report of some Genoese merchants who had seen her in the town of Tunis. During the siege, the chronicler adds, the French knights took great pleasure in beholding the deeds he performed for the love of his lady, and they often tried to capture him, but the young Moor was too well mounted to allow himself to be taken.

The same transcendent spirit of chivalry, which made it possible for Frenchmen to identify themselves so closely with an unknown Muslim in Africa, is strongly reflected also in the epic poetry of the West, which represented the Saracen knight as conspicuously noble and distinguished. "Think only of Feirefiss, Parzival's black and white brother," Kantorowicz reminds us, "of Ortnit's helper, of the wise heathen Zacharias, or Ariosto's Medor, and, above all, of Saladin, the pearl of oriental chivalry, to whom Dante accorded a place in Elysium, . . . though it was he who had taken Jerusalem from the Christians."[6]

B. The Merchants

The international communities of interest that involved the medieval merchants and scholars of the Mediterranean region may not have stirred the imagination of contemporaries as much as the fellowship of knights, but they are perhaps of greater significance today. For knights have left the scene of history without leaving direct heirs. Merchants and scholars on the other hand belong to less time-bound professions. They had formed professional groups in periods preceding the medieval epoch, and they continue to function cooperatively today. All of the vocabularies of shared values that they have evolved are therefore invested with a permanent interest for those who seek to perfect the international traffic of goods and ideas.

[5] See the discussion of this incident in F. S. Shears, "Chivalry of France," in *Chivalry*, Edgar Prestage, ed., New York, 1928, p. 67.

[6] Ernst Kantorowicz, *Frederick the Second, 1194-1250*, New York, 1931, p. 189. He also refers to the fact, evidently not entirely verifiable, that Frederick II had knighted the Amir Fakhru'd Din and had permitted him to wear the imperial eagle on his shield.

If medieval commercial documents, almanacs, and manuals[7] are read in the light of what is known today about the economic history of the Mediterranean peoples, they will be found to refer to the same type of merchant whether written by Arabs, Hebrews, Greeks, Normans, Berbers, Catalans, or Pisans. This Mediterranean character might be a Jew, a Muslim, or a Christian; he might have his permanent residence in the Byzantine Empire, the Middle East, North Africa, Spain, southern France, or Italy; but the human traits and dispositions that made him what he professed to be were his by virtue of his vocation rather than of his religious or political allegiance.[8]

The Mediterranean merchant, as he appears in the records, was interested in the acquisition of wealth and cultivation of thrift. He relied upon his own intelligence, but was careful to enlist the support of superior authorities. He was respectful of legal regulations and yet determined to evade them whenever necessary. He was enterprising and adventurous but also cautious and conservative. He invoked the protection of his deity for each of his transactions, but was bent upon pursuing predominantly worldly purposes. He was loyal to his native country but itinerant in his thoughts and actions, always seeking to expand his field of operations. And while he was ever ready to outwit his competitors from abroad, he was yet acutely conscious of the fact that a certain degree of international cooperation was indispensable for the success of most of his ventures. In other words, the members of the multinational merchant class whom we encounter in this period were not only similarly endowed and oriented but showed themselves to be also similarly ambivalent in their efforts to reconcile their personal predilections with the normative systems prevailing in their respective communities. For since the latter were in their basic premises alike, as we have seen, they presented merchants with the same type of contradiction between freedom and authority, will and law, and autonomy and cooperation. This coincidence explains, in turn, why Mediterranean traders discovered in their several nations similar synthetic formulae for the satisfaction of conflicting motivations. For example, the religious prescriptions against usury[9] were generally circumvented

[7] Robert S. Lopez and Irving W. Raymond, *Medieval Trade in the Mediterranean World*, Illustrative Documents Translated with Introductive Notes, New York, 1955.
[8] See Lopez and Raymond, pp. 409ff. for bibliographical references.
[9] The Muslim law adhered to the Mosaic principle which forbade the charging of interest for loans to coreligionists but permitted it in business transactions involving foreigners. The Christian canon law as applied in the West followed the same general principle without this distinction. The official Byzantine attitude toward the problem was permissive and relaxed. See Lopez and Raymond, pp. 157ff., 163ff., and Wyndham Bewes, *The Romance of the Law Merchant*, London, 1923, p. 59, also p. 77.

by disguising interest in one way or another, or by not mentioning it at all in writing; and governmental penalties against smuggling and piracy were evaded by dissimulating the nature of the particular transaction and the identity of the persons involved.[10]

This broad agreement in modes of mercantile thought and behavior was a corollary of lively trade relations between all Mediterranean peoples.[11] It did not manifest itself before the turn of the eleventh century because the earlier Mediterranean commerce, while involving Jews, Byzantines, Arabs, Berbers, and Venetians, had bypassed the great majority of Western Europeans. The latter lived in essentially rural conditions during the eighth and ninth centuries, far removed from the highways and market places of international trade. Being inhabitants of what we today would call an underdeveloped area, they were unable for intellectual as well as economic reasons to participate in the intricate commercial activities that were having a unifying influence among the citizens of the economically more advanced societies.

The chief credit for narrowing this gap between the Eastern and Western peoples belongs to the Jews. For the trading members of this widely dispersed nation were the first emissaries of the economically sophisticated Mediterranean world to penetrate Carolingian Europe.[12] Adventurous, multilingual, well-organized professionally, and at home in different cultural environments, they were in fact the foremost advocates of that new spirit which was destined to integrate all trading classes. By drawing Western Christendom into the orbit of their operations, they greatly expanded the radius of international commerce, and by diffusing the goods and ideas that denoted the superiority of the Orient, they were instrumental in awakening the dormant and backward nations of the northwest to the exigencies and promises of a new way of life.[13]

Among the many intricate developments that contributed to the subsequent resurgence of economic life in the West and to the gradual effacement of the disparities between Latin Christendom on the one

[10] Piracy was a common economic enterprise in those days, and merchants alternated rather regularly between privateering and ordinary trade. See Lopez and Raymond, p. 221.

[11] The commercial intercourse between the Christian and Muslim worlds was only briefly interrupted during the first period of the crusades. J. H. Kramers, "Geography and Commerce," in *Legacy of Islam*, p. 103; Lopez and Raymond, p. 50.

[12] See Kramers, p. 102 and Lopez and Raymond, pp. 29ff.

[13] The crusades mark the decline of the Jewish preponderance in international trade and the ascendancy of the maritime towns of Italy as intermediaries between the two parts of the Mediterranean. Jewish interests were henceforth focussed upon money lending.

hand, and the Byzantine and Muslim realms on the other,[14] none was as effective in promoting a feeling of solidarity between the merchant classes of East and West as the movement toward urbanization. In the Middle Eastern and North African societies most literate merchants were also townsmen, for their rise to social eminence had been paralleled by the ascendancy of cities as the nuclei of life. The qualities and interests that marked men as merchants were thus derived from a dual set of social references. The Western European regions could not produce professional elites with equivalent characteristics until they, too, had brought forth strong municipalities. When such centers arose in the areas adjoining the Mediterranean Sea, the nations of the West could move toward parity with those of the East. And when Genoa, Pisa, and Marseille had become the equals of Byzantium, Cairo, and Fez,[15] all Mediterranean economies were interlocked through their participation in one vast network of similarly organized urban communities. The necessary conditions for a synchronistic evolution of interests and institutions among all mercantile elites were thus ensured.

The coordinate development of commercial usages presupposed an agreement on basic commercial concepts and a mutual understanding of the words that conveyed these concepts in different languages. These conditions were approximated when the Europeans adopted certain basic trade terms that the Arabs and other Oriental nations had fashioned in earlier centuries,[16] and when all Mediterranean merchant communities converged in respecting the fundamental customs that had been the rallying point of trading folk long before the medieval cultures had arisen. These processes were not initiated deliberately, but their effectiveness was fostered greatly through the purposeful application of literate skills. For instance, the dictionaries of the time rendered the meanings of most shared concepts in a variety of Eastern and Western tongues, and manuals about "practical philology," "practical geography," and "practical arithmetic" purported to cover every subject that was likely to interest a Mediterranean trader.[17]

The concurrence of commercial terminologies and the widespread dissemination of economically important information enabled merchants from different parts of the Mediterranean to cooperate in the production, propagation, and use of more intricate intellectual tools of

---

[14] A consideration of these developments is not within the scope of this discussion.

[15] See Coon, pp. 234ff. for a stimulating description of this city.

[16] The commercial vocabularies of the European languages are still full of words of Arabic origin.

[17] Lopez and Raymond, pp. 342ff.

trade. Sales, loans, currency exchanges, and insurances became regionally valid commercial conceptions. And as the documentary forms of these transactions became standardized, new fields opened for joint and far-flung operations. A special kind of partnership agreement, which made it possible to undertake costly maritime ventures by spreading risks and pooling capital, illustrates the unifying impact that written instruments of this kind had upon the separate destinies of merchants. This contract appeared in the western Mediterranean in the tenth century. It had different names in different legal systems, but it provided a stable framework for international ventures because its essence was virtually the same in all local versions.[18]

The multinational merchant classes of the western Mediterranean that were responsible for the evolution of this commercial device were singularly successful in registering their concordant interests and ideas. This was due to geographical and political reasons as well as to rather special human talents. In terms of geography the Maghreb (the North African territories of the Berbers and Arabs), Spain, southern France, Italy, and Sicily formed a regional unit distinct from the adjoining eastern area.[19] Their inhabitants, whether Africans or Europeans, Muslims, Christians, or Jews, were thus stimulated by the mere fact of their physical proximity to develop patterns of coexistence. In terms of

[18] See *ibid.*, pp. 174ff.; Kramers, pp. 103, 105; Bewes, pp. 7ff., also 20.

[19] The medieval history of the relations between the Maghreb and southwestern Europe, notably France, is of special interest today, because it provides a backdrop for two distinct yet similar projects aiming at the constitution of greater political and economic unions between the presently separate sovereignties of this region.

The nationalist leaders of newly independent Tunisia and Morocco envision the day when their lands, Algeria, and Libya will be joined in what they call a "Greater Maghreb," while the representatives of France have published plans for a future economic federation between metropolitan France and its former North African protectorates, colonies, and departments, including the vast region of the Sahara. These two projects are competitive if they are viewed in terms of the traditional conflict between Western imperialism and African nationalism, but they are closely related if they are considered in terms of the great economic and political controversies that currently divide the West from those eastern parts of the world veering toward the communist orbit. For both are responses not only to the economic needs of the western parts of Europe and Africa but also—perhaps even principally—to the challenge of Egyptian imperialism and Russian communism. This orientation, which is implicit in the French project, permeates the North African scheme as well. For the Tunisian spokesmen have made it clear, in explaining the rationale of their dream, that a greater Maghreb would gather the Muslim forces of northwest Africa, thus offsetting the dynamic forces emanating from northeast Africa, and that such a western Mediterranean coalition would remain part of the larger Western Community of Atlantic and Mediterranean nations.

Compare this African effort to resurrect the past with the influence that the memory of the mythical Ghana empire had upon the formation, in 1957, of the new state of Ghana, farther south in West Africa.

politics the area was not unified at all. In fact, nowhere had the disintegration of the early medieval empires had more marked consequences than in North Africa, Spain, Italy, and Sicily.

Now this system of plural sovereignties made for political conflict and competition, it is true, but since it implied the existence of multiple centers of industry and trade, it was very favorable to the development of lively commercial interchanges. Indeed, the regional records of this period concur in leaving the impression that the merchants of Tunis, Tripoli, Oran, and Ceuta; of Valencia, Barcelona, Majorca, and Marseille; of Sicily, Pisa, Florence, Genoa, and Venice were not greatly inhibited in their transnational activities, either by the feuds that divided their respective governments, or by those shifts in regional supremacy which vested maritime control first in the Arabs and Berbers, then in the Normans, and finally in the Italian city-states. Majorca, Sicily, and certain provinces in North Africa changed sovereigns in rapid succession; Muslim Tunis paid tribute to Sicily when it was governed by the Christian Normans; the Iberian peninsula accommodated Islamic and Christian dynasties, and its cities were hospitable to men of all faiths. It is small wonder that in these circumstances the merchants of Pisa felt as much at home in Tunis as those of North Africa did in Norman Sicily, and that Christians found it possible to prosper in Morocco while Muslims and Jews made the most of liberal trading facilities in Christian Majorca. However, the spirit of reciprocity and mutual respect[20] that marked economic transactions at that time, and the intricate forms of cooperative action through which international commerce was channelled in this area, were not merely the concomitants of geographical and political factors. They were the fruit equally of the energy and ingenuity displayed by the merchants themselves.[21]

The mingling of cultures which attended the historical developments in the western Mediterranean makes it difficult to identify the particular contributions that each component nation made to the progress of international commerce. But a comparison of the traditional Muslim and Christian attitudes toward the aliens settled in their midst sup-

[20] W. Cunningham notes the "curious" (quotations mine) fact that there was little difference between the trading provisions laid down for the Christians in Morocco and those which were necessary for the pursuit of ordinary trade within Christendom, or even between the towns in any one of the Christian realms. *An Essay on Western Civilization in its Economic Aspects*, 2 vols., Cambridge, Eng., 1913, Vol. II, p. 122.

[21] Cf. with Henri Pirenne's tribute to the merchants of medieval Europe. *Economic and Social History of Medieval Europe*, New York, 1937, p. 158.

ports the view that the roots of cosmopolitanism were deeper in the communities of the former than in those of the latter.[22] Local conditions in cities under Arab or Berber control were thus particularly auspicious for the evolution of transnational understandings. The Christian nations, on the other hand, being the heirs of the Latin tradition, excelled in the art of finding proper legal forms for a clear expression of mutual aspirations and agreements, and of inferring generally applicable principles from a maze of particular transactions. And these latent dispositions were activated by a driving ambition to penetrate the flourishing settlements of the Muslims. Most of the numerous bilateral treaties that linked the European and North African shores between the eleventh and fourteenth centuries thus seem to have been initiated by the Europeans, who had a special interest in gaining official recognition of their mercantile establishments in African ports, in defining the jurisdiction of their consuls, and in obtaining assurances for the protection of the lives and property rights of their citizens.[23] And the same reasons make it plausible to assume that most of the normative clauses aiming at the stabilization of maritime intercourse in general—the proscription of piracy, the protection of the shipwrecked, the abolition of the right of wreckage, and the limitation of the right to reprisals—were inserted at the instigation of Christian negotiators.[24] However, the point bears repeating that no agreement would have been possible had there not been a meeting of Muslim and Christian minds. Merchants and officials of both creeds were at one whenever they realized the desirability of pacifying the ocean space between them.

It goes without saying that the aims which the treaties purported to further were not always attained. The execution of these instruments was often obstructed either by misunderstandings between the signatories or—and this was the case more frequently—by contrary

[22] The Muslims were cruel and intolerant when engaged in military operations, but their aggressiveness gave way to tolerance after they had incorporated an area containing alien elements.

[23] See Jacques Marie Joseph Louis de Mas Latrie, *Traités de paix et Documents Divers concernant Les Relations des Chrétiens avec les Arabes de l'Afrique Septentrionale au moyen age*, Paris, 1866, for illustrations of and comments upon the matters here discussed: p. 275 on the form of these treaties; p. 86 on the rights of Christian consuls in Muslim towns and on the nature of Christian "Foudouks" (settlements); p. 186 on the Arab functionaries who supervised Christian trade relations; pp. 209-224 for a list of the merchandise that was the subject of the trade relations.

[24] The European initiative revealed itself clearly after the Italian towns had gained absolute maritime supremacy in the Mediterranean. See *ibid.*; Lopez and Raymond, p. 304; also E. W. Bovill, *Caravans of the Old Sahara*, 1933, pp. 118ff.

actions on the part of individual merchants, Christian as well as Muslim. In fact, some of the violations of mutually accepted covenants are as illustrative of the shared interests of the mercantile classes as the legally justifiable objectives upon which agreement had been reached. This was true particularly in the case of piracy. For the records abound with instances in which Christian and Muslim traders combined as corsairs in order to prey on other such combinations,[25] or in which their respective authorities were agreed in finding it convenient to overlook such contraventions of the law. But the overriding interest of all concerned, as it emerges from the documents, was the creation of a stable maritime and mercantile order, and this long term quest is delineated most convincingly in the continuous efforts to establish an internationally binding law of the seas.

The maritime customs of the Mediterranean Sea have a very long history, as an earlier discussion of the Rhodian Sea Law has already shown. This history began in the East, where commercial activities had absorbed the energies of nations long before the dawn of Western cultures, and it was carried forward between the seventh and tenth centuries by the Persians, Arabs, Byzantines, and Venetians. But a summary written statement of maritime customs as they were being observed in the medieval Mediterranean world was not formulated until the cities of the western Mediterranean, especially those of Italy and Spain, had assimilated the knowledge left by their eastern neighbors. Most of them delegated the task of supervising international trade and navigation to judges, consuls, and specially appointed committees of merchants,[26] who were enjoined to pass sentences and make decisions in conformity with the customs of the sea. International relations on the open sea, over which no single government could claim jurisdiction, were thus regulated by locally distinct but functionally interlocking *consulados*, and these succeeded, in the course of time, in bringing forth different, yet essentially concordant, collections of the customs of the sea. Some authorities assign the earliest known compilation to Amalfi (tenth century), whose primary commercial contacts were with the Levant, others to Trani, also in southern Italy (eleventh century). Some ascribe great importance to the *Constitutum Usus* of the city of Pisa, which was committed to writing in 1156 and published in 1160, and the Assizes of Jerusalem (1100-1187), while others are inclined

<hr/>

[25] Bovill, p. 121.

[26] On the differentiation of these offices see *The Black Book of the Admiralty*, Sir Travers Twiss, ed., 4 vols., London, 1871-76, Introduction to Vol. II.

to minimize the significance of these two collections on the ground that they were not accepted unequivocally as law by other prominent seafaring nations.[27] But practically all scholars agree in regarding the *Consulato del Mare* of Barcelona as the most influential of all the medieval collections.[28] Probably compiled in the thirteenth century, published in Catalan in 1494, and translated into several European languages, it became a model for numerous other medieval communities in Europe and a fundamental source of reference for modern maritime law.

The second part of the Barcelona Consulato begins with the announcement that "These are the good constitutions and good customs in matters of the sea, which the wise men who have navigated the world have handed down to our ancestors, and which make up the books of the science of good customs."[29] The claim put forth in this document is justified by the records which leave no doubt that the Consulato was anchored in immemorial customs, and that its draftsmen were fully conscious of their role as the inheritors of the wise men of all ages and cultures and as the spokesmen for maritime and mercantile elites everywhere. However, the facts remain that the compilation was made by Western European Christians, that it had been influenced particularly by earlier similar efforts also made by Western European Christians, and that it addressed itself primarily to the needs of seafarers from Western Europe. Indeed, the very date of its publication may be said to convey the essentially European character of this entire enterprise. For the Barcelona Consulato was published in 1494—two years after Columbus had discovered America and four years before Vasco da Gama had reached India. In other words, it belongs chronologically and conceptually to that momentous decade in the history of international relations which Camões celebrated in *The Lusiads*. The legend that Vasco da Gama had been led to India by an Arab pilot conveyed a great historical truth, for European merchants and mariners had indeed been guided in all their undertakings by their more experienced Mediterranean neighbors. But the Mediterranean ceased to be "the Central Sea," as the Arabs had liked to call it, and the Islamic nations forfeited their superiority in matters maritime. More-

[27] See Sir Travers Twiss; W. Ashburner, *The Rhodian Sea Law*, Oxford, 1909; Pardessus, *Collection des Lois Maritimes antérieure au XVIIIe siècle*, 6 vols., 1828-1845; W. S. Lindsay, *The History of Merchant Shipping and Ancient Commerce*, London, 1874-1876, for accounts of the evolution of maritime law.

[28] For a contrary view see Ashburner, cxxi.

[29] For the complete text see Twiss in an appendix to Vol. III.

over, Christians and Muslims lost touch with each other and withdrew into the folds of their own civilizations when the water space between them ceased to be a unifying factor in their cultural relations. Not having to make mutual adjustments in multifarious local encounters, they ceased to cultivate the ideas and institutions around which they had rallied in previous centuries and, instead, began to confine their attentions to their local traditions.

The European method of delegating judicial and legislative powers to professional groups of merchants and lawyers and of spelling out in writing what had thus far been tacitly understood, had been instrumental in establishing a legal and commercial order, which the non-Europeans of the time do not seem to have found objectionable. A retrospective view of these crucial centuries reveals, however, that significant cultural divergencies were accumulating behind the façade of acquiescence and agreement. Thus, while we know that the rules of maritime intercourse were respected, by and large, by mariners of all Mediterranean nations, we have reason to surmise that they were being obeyed because they had behind them the authority of immemorial usage rather than because they had been written down by the Italians and Spaniards. For example, the records supply no evidence to the effect that the European methodology implicit in the Consulato was culturally congenial to the trading communities in the Muslim caliphates and sultanates.[30] All Western European nations, on the other hand, were most receptive to the Consulato with its various conceptual and practical connotations. For the great movement toward legal consolidation which pervaded the western Mediterranean was operative simultaneously in Atlantic Europe, where the Rolls of Oleron (compiled in the twelfth century)[31] found acceptance in Brittany, Normandy,

[30] Particular laws were widely diffused, however. For instance, the law governing the conditions in which goods could be cast overboard in order to save the ship (the right to jettison) appeared in a sea code which the first Malayan sultan promulgated in the thirteenth century. See John H. Wigmore, *A Panorama of the World's Legal Systems*, St. Paul, 1928, Vol. III, p. 904.

[31] A learned seventeenth century advocate in the Parlement of Bordeaux credits Queen Eleanor of Aquitaine with the inception of this code. The story as rendered by Sir Travers Twiss is that the Queen, having observed during her visit to the Holy Land that consulates of the sea were held in high esteem, directed on her return that a record be made of the judgments rendered by the marine court of Oleron, in order that they might serve as law amongst the seafarers of the Western Sea. This court was so highly esteemed for the quality of its sentences that mariners of other countries preferred, whenever possible, to submit their disputes to its judges. See Twiss, introduction to Vol. II and article on "Sea Laws" in Encyclopaedia Britannica.

Flanders, and England, and in Northern Europe, where the laws of Wisby and of the Hanseatic League were regarded as supreme.

In composing new patterns of maritime order in the Mediterranean and other international waters, the Europeans may be regarded as the successors of the Rhodians who had approached the problems of international commerce in analogous ways. However, the Rhodians had functioned only in a society of Mediterranean nations, and this society had been culturally unified in Hellenistic and Roman times. The European elite, on the other hand, assumed its supervisory powers in the Middle Ages, when the area of international trade included realms beyond the Mediterranean sea, and when the nuclear Mediterranean nations had developed separate civilizations within the framework of rival theological and political systems. The task of finding legal and commercial formulae that would fit each culture and yet serve the common interests of all was therefore infinitely more demanding in the Middle Ages than it had been in the preceding period. And it was made even more difficult by the fact that non-European civilizations had alienated themselves from the tradition of Roman law to which the Rhodian heritage had attached itself, whereas the European civilization had kept its roots in Latin institutions of law. The process of establishing principles outside the local context that had distinguished the methods employed by the Rhodian elite was thus Europeanized between the eleventh and fifteenth centuries. And the momentum of this process was accelerated and intensified by the peculiar economic and social conditions in which maritime and terrestrial trade was being carried on by the mercantile elites of transalpine Europe.

The wandering merchants who plied their trade in underdeveloped rural Europe displayed the same federative instinct as their counterparts in Africa and Asia. Coming from distant localities, they, too, banded together in caravan fashion in order to protect themselves against the countless perils of long journeys overland. They, too, secured the sense of mutuality upon which the success of their cosmopolitan undertaking depended by developing their own rules for the regulation of all human relations. The places of exchange to which they trekked were similar to those found in the plains of Africa[32] and Asia; for they, too, were protected by a specially instituted peace designed to cover the market ground as well as the merchants and their transactions. And here, as elsewhere, commerce was being carried forward by the movement toward urbanization. But the great fairs to which the mer-

[32] See Bovill for a description of African trading customs.

chants of the different European nationalities flocked between the eleventh and thirteenth centuries were more highly organized as centers of international or regional commerce than the trading places outside of Europe. The Peace of the Fair of Champagne, for example, was circumscribed and assured in more definite terms than that of Timbuktu. The piepowder courts in England dispensed justice more speedily and objectively than their analogues in the Levantine bazaars. The "law merchant" which governed trading all over Europe was more autonomous in its structure and more neatly defined as a special international law, outside and above civil statutes and local commercial usages, than the collections of usages in other continents. The European towns were more insistent in their demands for independence from local sovereigns and more successful in securing municipal constitutions embodying the special peace and law of the city than the urban communities outside this region. And the European merchant class was more conscious of its social and political leadership in urban life and more prepared to take the initiative in finding new answers to new problems, than the merchant classes in other cultures. The old international order of the Mediterranean, which had been marked by the confluence of commercial traditions and the cultivation of affinities between mercantile elites from different cultures, was thus gradually being eclipsed by a new system of economic attitudes and institutions, which had its anchorage in the culturally unified world of Western Christendom, but was destined to project its influence on many lands beyond.[33]

C. The Scholars and the Propagation of Literate Knowledge

The range of intercultural relations is bound to be limited severely as long as intellectual communications depend only upon the spoken word. The great literate civilizations of the ancient Near and Far East developed the power of the written word, but its use was the jealously guarded prerogative of a very small minority. Within the framework of the Greek and Latin societies the written word became available on an unprecedented scale, but even here there were very few who read much or read often, and among those who could read, there were few who could also write.[34] Between A.D. 700 and 1500 two events oc-

---

[33] The topics to which this chapter has alluded briefly are fully discussed by numerous authorities on the history of medieval Europe.

[34] Lancelot Hogben, *From Cave Painting to Comic Strip*, New York, 1949, p. 124.

curred that revolutionized the relationship between men and knowledge: the invention of paper, which provided those who wanted to write with a thin, smooth, and flexible surface; and the invention of printing from movable type, which made it possible to circulate the written word among all who cared to read. The formula for the production of paper originated in China in the first century A.D.; but since the Mandarin elite did not elect to propagate the advantages of this discovery among their compatriots, it lay dormant, as it were, devoid of significant international consequence, until the Arabs found it on their eastern route of conquest during the eighth century and brought it westward, where it was diffused rapidly from the thirteenth century onward.[35] The ideal material for the easy impress of the written word was thus available when the Western Europeans developed the art of printing from movable type about fifty years before Columbus discovered America. In other words, the two great inventions that were to promote literacy throughout the world from the end of the nineteenth century onward were tested and perfected by the intellectual elites of the Mediterranean nations in the epoch that began in the eighth, and ended in the fifteenth, century.

However, the singular contribution to the intellectual history of mankind that Muslim, Jewish, and Christian scholars made in the time span separating these two inventions was not determined by the existence of paper and printing presses. For the manufacture of paper and the establishment of a press are obviously idle processes unless put to use by men who have something to say. Now, the literate classes in the medieval Mediterranean world had very much to say, as the voluminous extant records of their intellectual labors testify. Indeed, a survey of their lives and writings indicates that they never tired of exploring the nature of the world around them. Science and alchemy, history and demonology, philosophy and theology, geography and cosmology attracted their inquisitive minds. This seemingly boundless urge to discover and record the categories of facts and ideas that might contribute to an identification of life manifested itself first among the literate classes in the Islamic orbit, which included, at least in the early period, professional intellectuals as well as kings, courtiers, merchants, and other men of action. The tremendous expanse and diversity of the domain in which Arabic was spoken, the strong stimulus to travel that was implicit in the Muslim systems of religious, economic, and political

---

[35] *ibid.*, p. 127. Paper mills existed in Germany by A.D. 1336.

existence, and the general atmosphere of tolerance that came to prevail in the various provinces after their subjugation had been effected, made for an easy communion among all who were interested in the pursuit of learning, whether Jews, Nestorian Christians, Muslims or pagans. The vigor of intellectual life within the Islamic world abated with the advent of orthodoxy, but the scholarly elites of the various Mediterranean nations had become so closely attuned to each other under the early tutelage of the Muslims that they continued to cooperate in advancing the frontiers of knowledge when the Western European Christians emerged as the most dedicated proponents of literacy and learning.

Among the many fields of knowledge that exemplify the confluence of Jewish, Christian, and Muslim interests none has greater relevance for a historical study of intercultural relations than have geography and history. These two subjects fascinated the Mediterranean nations, not only as ends in themselves, but as avenues to an understanding of all other realms of thought. Generations of seafarers, geographers, astronomers, and cartographers were insistent in their curiosity to know about the earthly scene. They travelled east and west, determined to locate countries and nations, oceans and mountains, animals and plants, and they returned with elaborate, often quite fanciful, descriptions of the things they had found. The most renowned traveller of Islam, Ibn Batutta, spent 24 years of his life journeying approximately 75,000 miles in the pursuit of knowledge of all kind. The whole littoral from Spain to Syria was covered in the thirteenth century by a single savant, Ibn al-Baytar (died 1248), who collected 1400 plants and drugs and then proceeded to analyse their properties in one of the most outstanding early books on botany. A large geographical dictionary, listing all of the known geographical names in alphabetical order, was composed by another in the same century.[36] Manuscripts bearing such titles as "The Book of Countries" and "The Book of Roads and Kingdoms" had appeared as early as the ninth.[37] Encyclopaedias filled with cosmographical data were composed and large world maps constructed, usually at the request of empire-conscious rulers.[38]

[36] See Kramers, "Geography and Commerce," in *The Legacy of Islam*, Arnold and Guillaume, eds.

[37] *ibid.*, p. 85.

[38] The Abbasid Caliph al-Ma'mun (813-833) had ordered 70 scholars to design an image of the earth, and Roger II, the Norman ruler of Sicily, had commissioned al-Idrisi, the most brilliant author of geographical texts in his time, to compose a synopsis of the known world.

Most of the cosmographical works were authored by geographers and astronomers under the spell of religious traditions and ideological myths, and the images of the earth that they conveyed fell far short, therefore, of the reality that scientists were to ascertain in later centuries. But some of these medieval versions, incorrect as they proved to be, had a direct bearing upon the subsequent evolution of the scene of world affairs because they sparked the imagination of those who initiated the modern period of geographical exploration. The discovery of America might not have occurred as early as it did if Christian scholars at the University of Toledo, long the Islamic center of scientific studies, had not held fast to the Muslim doctrine of the sphericity of the earth, and if Columbus had not accepted the theory that the earth was shaped in the form of a pear. This notion originated in the view, which the Arabs had borrowed from the Indians, that the known world had a center, or "world summit," situated at an equal distance from east, west, north, and south. Cultivated in the twelfth century by Adelard of Bath and Gerard of Cremona, and in the thirteenth by Roger Bacon, it was incorporated by Cardinal Peter of Ailly in his *Imago Mundi* (published in 1410), from which Columbus derived many of his inspirations.[39] The same theory is said to have induced Dante to place the *purgatorio* in the southern hemisphere. In fact, it deeply affected the general world view of the medieval Christians, for it seemed to complement the ancient Christian doctrine that the terrestrial paradise was in the East.

The Occidental image of the East as the geographical home of utopian bliss developed in conjunction with the Christian conviction that all history was moving from East to West, and that mankind would meet its final doom when this movement had reached the uttermost limits set by Providence in the West.[40] As early as the fourth century A.D. Severian of Gabala had explained that "God looked into the future and set the first man in that place (i.e., Paradise, in the East) in order to cause him to understand that, just as the light of heaven moves toward the West, so the human race hastens toward death." The theme was restated in the twelfth century by Hugh of St. Victor, who declared that "the course of events has gradually been moving westward, until now it has reached the end of the earth and we must face the fact that

[39] Kramers, pp. 93ff.
[40] See Gustave E. Von Grunebaum, *Medieval Islam*, Chicago, 1946, pp. 59-63 for a succinct rendition of this relationship between East and West.

we are approaching the end of the ages,"[41] and by Otto of Freising (died 1158) and Alexander Neckam (died 1217), who traced the procession of learning from Egypt and Babylon to Greece and Rome, and finally to the western Mediterranean, namely, Italy, Gaul, and Spain.

The dismal dogma about mankind's relentless progression toward dissolution which is conveyed by these and other Christian writers, was being disestablished gradually as the Western Europeans discovered new realities in time and space. By A.D. 1500 it was clear that the end of man was not in sight, that the eastern centers of culture had been vacated of their strength, and that civilization was in fact moving westward rapidly.[42]

The Western attitude toward history was a corollary of the world view upon which Judaism, Christianity, and Islam converged, for it originated in the Bible, which was a sacred text to all "Peoples of the Book." From this shared source of reference the truth had been deduced that life was to be understood in terms of its progression from Creation to Judgment Day, and that the stage of this progression required remembrance. This common outlook on history, which set the nations of the Mediterranean apart from those of the Orient, imbued the work of the medieval literate elites. For while it suggested different emphases and perspectives to Jews, Christians, and Muslims, it fostered among all of them an indomitable spirit of inquiry and a determined will to trace and record the evolution of all that had come to be in the realms of corporeal and incorporeal existence. Individuals, dynasties, and nations as well as sciences, philosophies, and ideas thus became subjects of historical research.

The men who conducted these explorations were certainly prejudiced in favor of their own epoch and civilization, as many of the histories and maps that they composed reveal. But in their persistent endeavors to identify the entire range of life and to ascertain all sources of metaphysical, scientific, and other wisdom, they functioned in effect as the first international historians; for they realized what other literate elites before them had not realized, namely, that the history of medicine—to take but one example—transcended the history of a particular culture or period. A new view of time and space was thus being propagated gradually, between the eighth and fifteenth centuries, as history-

[41] See *ibid.*, p. 62 for both quotations.

[42] The myth of the superiority of the East, so assiduously propagated in this period, has lingered on in Western thought until comparatively recent times.

minded scientists, theologians, and philosophers revived the past of many nations. As some of the sociological complexities of life south of the Mediterranean coast were noted by shrewd Muslim observers, the nonliterate civilizations of Africa began to yield their secrets;[43] and as Middle Eastern scholars became aware of the immense significance for their own time of Chinese science and technology and of India's numberlore, the literate societies of the Far East were made accessible to intellectual investigation. But in all the realms of thought and experience that were thus opened up in this formative period of modern thought none proved as fascinating and rewarding to Muslims, Jews, and Christians as the Hellenic and Hellenistic culture worlds. Here was a common heritage, the scholars realized, that permeated the very ground on which they stood. What Plato, Aristotle, Euclid, and Galen had recorded proved meaningful to literate men in Bactria as well as in Spain.

The geographical distance between Spain and the Central Asian lands long known as Bactria has not changed in the past millenniums, but no one today would think of these two regions as in any way related to each other culturally. In the public consciousness Spain, however different from France or Italy, is a part of the Latin Occident, whereas Afghanistan, Turkestan, and Khorasan are far beyond the line that separates what is conventionally called the West from what is conventionally called the East. Such a division between East and West was not recognized in Hellenistic times, when Bactria, while certainly an eastern outpost, was yet an integral part of the Greek culture realm. Nor was it assumed in medieval times, when that ancient kingdom became the center of the revival of Hellenistic thought.[44] In terms of cultural history, the "East," then, began east of Bactria, as Needham points out when he writes that "the science of Asia has a dividing line running north and south through Bactria and the opening of the Persian Gulf . . ." and "that the science and scientific thought of Arabic civilisation forms in a very real sense a unity with European science. . . ."[45] And within the Eurasian expanse that accommodated the cul-

[43] Ibn Khaldun (born 1332 in Tunis) in his *Muqaddimah* presented for the first time a theory of historical development which recognized the physical facts of climate and geography as well as significant moral and spiritual forces. See Ibn Khaldun, *The Muqaddimah, an Introduction to History*. Transl. from the Arabic by Franz Rosenthal, 3 vols., Bollingen Series, XLIII, New York, 1959.

[44] Christopher Dawson, *The Making of Europe*, New York, 1945, p. 163, especially his reference to the Bactrian origin of some of the most illustrious medieval scholars.

[45] *Science and Civilisation in China*, Cambridge, Eng., 1954-1959, Vol. I, p. 220.

tures of Persia, Byzantium, Latin Christendom, and Arabic Islam, no lines between East and West could be drawn at all. Western Europeans and Americans, as well as Persians and Arabs, of the twentieth century may be impressed with the Asian character of the Near and Middle East, but no one could have identified Christendom with the West and Islam with the East in the tenth century A.D., when the most civilized region of Western Europe was the province of what today is regarded as an alien culture, whereas Asia Minor was then still a predominantly Christian region.

The context that favored the mingling of peoples and traditions had devolved from the political expansion of Islam, but the actual development of close understandings between the various civilizations was due to that examination of the Hellenic substratum of shared historical experience which West Asian scholars of all religions conducted with such singular success. A discussion of the scope and content of the Hellenistic legacy and of its effect upon the intellectual histories of the separate Mediterranean societies is obviously outside the bounds of these commentaries upon the interlocking activities of the literate medieval elites. But a few references to some medieval developments in theology and philosophy may illustrate the circumstances in which the transmission of this legacy effected the evolution of concordant patterns of thought.

In the course of daily intellectual encounters Jewish, Christian, and Islamic theologians came to realize that Hellenistic mysticism could be meaningful to any individual willing to transcend the official dogma of his faith in order to experience the Divine directly in his personal consciousness. Their multifarious exchanges have not been preserved in written records, but the homogeneity of their thoughts is registered in the fact, to which R. A. Nicholson has drawn attention,[46] that the ideas, methods, and systems produced by the mystics in this period bear the stamp of one and the same spiritual genius. And similar lines of convergence upon Hellenic ideas were found by students of philosophy—in those days inseparably connected with theology. The view has been expressed frequently that the philosophies of the Jews, Christians, and Muslims are culturally and nationally distinct, and that one must have preceded the other. For example, some modern Arab and Western writers regard Arab philosophy as the parent system of Occidental philosophy, while others maintain that the Arabic-speaking peoples

[46] "Mysticism" in *Legacy of Islam*, pp. 211ff.

cannot be credited with any originality in philosophical matters, since they merely took over the Greek philosophy that was current among the Syrian Christians and cultured pagans of Harran.[47] That Platonic ideas had permeated early Christian thought long before it came into contact with Islam is beyond dispute, and that Greek philosophy predominated in the speculations of early Muslim thinkers is equally clear, as a ninth century scholar from Basra admits when he says: "Did we not possess the books of the ancients in which their wonderful wisdom is immortalized and in which the manifold lessons of history are so dealt with that the past lives before our eyes, did we not have access to the riches of their experience, which would otherwise have been barred to us, our share in Wisdom would be immeasurably smaller and our means of attaining a true perspective most meagre."[48] Indeed, even after this impregnation had taken place and Arab philosophy had come into its own, it was apparently taken for granted that all philosophers should follow the Aristotelian path, save in a few details borrowed from Plato and the earlier Greek thinkers.[49]

The Muslim indebtedness to non-Muslim thought is certainly great, but a retrospective view of cultural cross-references in this age leaves the paramount impression, nevertheless, that it was the Arabic zeal to incorporate Hellenic learning which fostered similar interests among the Jews[50] and the Western European Christians, and that it was the Arabic talent for synthetic thinking which was instrumental in circulating the wisdom of the Greeks throughout the Mediterranean.

The close intellectual alignment between Muslim and Christian thinkers that evolved from this continuous interaction became strikingly evident in the independent but parallel systems of thought of Averroes (1126-1198) and St. Thomas Aquinas. Summarizing a lucid discussion of the numerous resemblances and coincidences that the theories of these two great exponents of medieval philosophy reveal, Guillaume concludes that "East and West (in the Mediterranean region) were intellectually much more closely aligned in the thirteenth century than they have ever been since."[51]

[47] Alfred Guillaume, "Philosophy and Theology," in *ibid.*, p. 239, for a discussion of these theories.

[48] *ibid.*   [49] *ibid.*, p. 254.

[50] Early Hebrew thinkers were profoundly influenced by Arabic renditions of Aristotle since they had none of their own. See Guillaume, p. 267. But see Guillaume, "Influence of Judaism on Islam" in *Legacy of Israel.* Charles and Dorothea Singer, "The Jewish Factor in Medieval Thought" in *Legacy of Israel*, Edward R. Bevan, ed., Oxford, 1928, p. 184, emphasize that Jewish and Muslim philosophical thought were inseparably linked.

[51] *Legacy of Islam*, p. 282.

The process of transmitting Greek thought that culminated in such far-reaching cultural accords was complex and continuous, but it is possible, nevertheless, to distinguish two principal phases. The first was initiated by Syriac-speaking Nestorian Christians and by Jews, who set Greek ideas into circulation in the Middle East. For example, Nestorians (whose activities are recorded as early as the fifth century A.D.), Monophysites, and pagans alike carried Greek medical knowledge from Harran (Mesopotamia) to southwest Persia, where the texts of Galen and Hippocrates were studied in conjunction with research in Indian medicine. Between the seventh and ninth centuries most scientific works were composed by Christian and Jewish physicians bearing Arabic names, who knew Greek, Syriac, Arabic, and often also Persian, and travelled far and wide in search of Greek manuscripts. The great age of translating medical as well as astronomical, physical, mathematical, and philosophical source material climaxed in the reign of the Abbasid Caliph al-Ma'mun, who established a library and translation bureau in Baghdad.[52] In this so-called "House of Wisdom" all of Galen and much of Hippocrates was translated by the Nestorian physician Hunayn and his disciples, and from here medical textbooks were diffused to all Middle Eastern centers of learning. By about A.D. 900, Muslim physicians and scientists had absorbed Greek science, as complemented by Persian and Indian thought. This is evidenced by an enormous comprehensive manual of more than twenty volumes in which its Persian author Rhazes is able to document each proposition by the citation of all available Greek, Syrian, Arabic, Persian, and Indian authorities.[53] And the trend toward scholarly coordination continued in the tenth century, when the most illustrious representative of Arabic medicine, Avicenna from Bokhara (best known as a philosopher), brought out his *Canon*, a magnificent attempt at integrating the medical doctrines of Hippocrates and Galen with the biological concepts of Aristotle.[54]

The second phase in the diffusion of Greek thought is characterized by a pronounced westward shift of intellectual energy. Some Greek

[52] Brockelmann, pp. 124ff.; Arturo Castiglione, *A History of Medicine*, E. S. Krumbhaar, tr., New York, 1941, p. 258; Cyril Elgood, *A Medical History of Persia and the Eastern Caliphate*, Cambridge, 1951; Max Meyerhoff, "Science and Medicine," *Legacy of Islam*, pp. 313ff.

[53] Meyerhoff, p. 322, regards this work as perhaps the most extensive ever written by a medical man.

[54] Castiglione, p. 258.

texts reached Latin Christendom directly from Byzantium,[55] but the great bulk of accumulated learning was channelled from Baghdad by Jewish and Muslim intermediaries to Spain and Sicily, and from these areas of contact between Islam and Christendom it was forwarded by wandering Christian scholars[56] to the universities farther north.

All of these complex movements disseminating thought, which were to culminate eventually in the internationalization of learning, had been made possible, as the preceding references indicate, through translations of texts. The rendition of knowledge from one language to another is generally regarded in the twentieth century as a technical process that individuals can master with relative ease if they are familiar with the cultural context of which the foreign language is a part. In the Middle Ages "translation" must have implied something rather different; for the decision to enter the realm of a foreign language was then tantamount, in most cases, to entrance into a totally alien culture world. A few men, endowed with superior intuitive and intellectual powers and privileged by circumstance with many opportunities to penetrate the minds of those employing the foreign tongue, were richly rewarded for their courageous undertaking. This was true, for example, of the Catalan Raymond Lull,[57] the greatest Christian missionary to Islam, who had a deeper understanding of the Muslim mind than any other medieval Latin, and who was instrumental, eventually, in promoting the establishment of five colleges in Rome, Bologna, Paris, Oxford, and Salamanca for the express purpose of teaching Hebrew, Arabic, and Chaldean.[58] The great majority of Christian students, however, were less gifted, and less fortunate, consequently, in the realization of their wish to penetrate a foreign language realm—as the following passage suggests:

"We are at the beginning of the twelfth century. An eccentric and restless European student, dissatisfied with the teaching of the schools of his native land, is attracted by floating stories of the wonders of Arabian learning and wisdom and power. He determines to try his fortune in Spain. After many adventures he arrives at Toledo, which

[55] Guillaume, "Philosophy and Theology," *Legacy of Islam*, p. 246. The earliest but incomplete version of Aristotle's *Metaphysics* reached Paris in c.1200 from Byzantium. The *Nicomachean Ethics* arrived first from Greek sources, then from Arabic, and lastly in its entirety, translated direct from Greek, about 1250.

[56] See Helen Waddell, *The Wandering Scholars*, London, 1927. See p. 67 on Gerbert, the most famous wandering scholar in the tenth century, who went to Toledo to study magic.

[57] Stoned to death in 1316.

[58] Von Grunebaum, pp. 49-52.

passed to Christendom in 1085. The country is in disorder and fighting between Moslems and Christians is still going on in outlying districts. He has crossed the frontier from the Spanish march, having evaded or bribed the sentries. He brings with him a letter, from a patron in his own land, to an official of the native Church. Such officials are all in a state of nervous apprehension, for the Moslem rule is a recent memory. Our student seeks to establish his credentials. His host can converse with him in Latin, but only with difficulty for their pronunciations differ greatly.

"Even when our student is accepted for what he is, his troubles have but begun. The very last thing he is likely to get from his clerical friend is any help with the accursed science of the Infidel. For one thing the poor man knows nothing of it. It stands to him for all that is abominable; it is 'black magic,' accursed, unclean. Moreover, the language of these Mozarabs, or native Christians, is a non-literary patois, of mixed Arabic and Latin origin, and quite useless for the investigation of Arabian philosophy. It is the patois, not the literary tongue, which our student picks up while looking round him for more efficient aid. At last he sees where help may be found.

"The Spanish Jews of that age had entered with far greater spirit than the Spanish Christians into the philosophical and scientific heritage of Islam. While ignorant of Latin, with which they have not the same spiritual link as their Christian fellows, many speak and write good literary Arabic. Our student, now with some command of the vernacular, makes the acquaintance of a Jew of this type, and arranges a series of secret meetings in some back attic of the Jewish quarter. He soon finds, however, that the vernacular patois, with which he has still but an imperfect acquaintance, is an inadequate means for scientific discussion. Help from another source must be invoked. A none too reputable native Christian with a knowledge of Latin is asked to join the pair. He is of the 'Vicar Bray' type, a man who was a Muslim before the land had been re-won by the Christians. Meetings are arranged at even more secluded lodgings, for none of the three is anxious for the matter to become known to his own people.

"Now they can get to work, but all kinds of difficulties arise. The Mozarab convert reads Arabic with difficulty for he was never an enthusiastic Muslim. He knows the patois, however, and he has acquired a smattering of Latin since his conversion. The Jew reads Arabic fluently. He is no great philosopher and hardly understands the matter, but he can eke out his knowledge from his Hebrew studies. He, too, is well acquainted with the patois. Of Latin he knows only a few words. The European member of the conspiracy is by far the most intelligent of the three. He knows no science nor any philosophy save logic, but he is eager to learn and has a turn for languages. In the absence of a grammar, however, the classical Arabic is too hard for him, and he can make little of the constant discussion that goes on in the patois between the Mozarab and the Jew.

"The work is very laborious. The Mozarab and the Jew painfully turn the Arabic text sentence by sentence into the patois. The three then beat out the meaning between them, and get it into some kind of Latin. What kind of Latin those accustomed to read medieval translation know only too well!"[59]

Most pioneering scholars faced the predicaments here discussed in regard to translations. Some faltered on their self-set course, having only the faintest notion as to what the knowledge was that they were seeking so assiduously, where it could be found, and how it could be absorbed; others were so eminently successful in their pursuits that they have been regarded ever since as authorities on the subjects that they undertook to study.[60] But all were lonely men in their native societies; for they had chosen to forfeit the intellectual security that comes from compliance with established modes of thought, and to rely primarily upon their own spirit of initiative and perseverance. Many found congenial conditions for the pursuit of their interests by associating with like-minded coreligionists or compatriots. This had been true at an early time of the Nestorian Christians in Asia Minor, of the Islamic Sufis (esoteric students of the Koran), who had created a network of affiliated colleges spanning villages, tribes, and cities for the concerted exploration of Hellenic mysticism, and of the Fatimid Isma'ili (organized toward the end of the third century A.H.) who pursued their aim of integrating Islam with Hellenism by maintaining centers of systematic instruction throughout the Muslim world.[61] But countless other scholars of all denominations, too individualistic to fit into such organizational schemes, were moved by their overriding zeal for learning to seek companionship among men in other cultures. In all of the Mediterranean centers of learning, then, there were Jews, Christians, Muslims, and pagans, who were eager to share the tribulations and rewards

---

[59] Charles and Dorothea Singer, pp. 204-206.

[60] *ibid.*, and the essays in *Legacy of Islam*, for biographical references.

[61] See Gibb, "An Interpretation of Islamic History," *Cahiers d'Histoire Mondiale*, Vol. I, Juillet 1953, pp. 52-59.

of their endeavors in order to explore the full meaning of one text or to cull one great thought from the records of the past.

These tendencies and aspirations found strong support among the Mediterranean sovereigns. Most of these, if not all, were despots in the exercise of their political functions and cosmopolitans in their approach to intercultural relations. As despots they may have felt affinities with the scholars, for both types of men relied primarily upon their own talent in the pursuit of their professional callings and thus formed what Burckhardt, commenting upon their relationship in Renaissance Italy, has termed a "natural alliance";[62] while as cosmopolitans, fully aware of the place that learning occupied in their age, they naturally committed themselves voluntarily to the scholars' cause. Most rulers, then, whether Muslim or Christian, followed the example that eastern caliphs like al-Ma'mun had set, by patronizing individual scholars and establishing universities, libraries, translation bureaus, observatories, hospitals, or medical schools, for the collective advancement of research.

The contacts between the various scholarly elites in the Mediterranean area and the affiliations between scholars and monarchs were nowhere so close, continuous, and fruitful in producing intercultural understandings, however, as in Spain and Sicily. These two regions had already had a long history as the crossroads of Mediterranean races and cultures when their urban centers became the principal way stations in the medieval traffic of peoples and ideas. Cordoba's book market and library of approximately 400,000 books attracted streams of students; Toledo was the principal meeting ground of translators from all language realms;[63] Salerno's secular medical school, which legend ascribes to the founding act of four physicians—a Greek, a Latin, a Jew, and a Saracen[64]—was recognized from the tenth century onward as the terminal point of all great currents of medical thought; and Palermo, the Sicilian capital of successive Christian and Muslim dynasties, was a cosmopolis in which cultured men from all shores seemed to feel at home.

The evolution of these cities had been favored greatly by geographical and historical factors, but their actual functioning as reception centers of wisdom variously gathered was due primarily to the remarkable

[62] Jacob Burckhardt, *The Civilization of the Renaissance in Italy*, New York, 1954, p. 162.
[63] Hogben, p. 132; Haskins, *Studies in the History of Mediaeval Science*, Cambridge, 1927, pp. 3-19.
[64] Castiglione, p. 300.

talents of despots who were also scholars. Alfonso the Wise, known as a benefactor of Toledo's scholars, was acclaimed also as the greatest apostle of Islamic learning, the compiler of astronomical (the Alphonsine) tables, an authority on chess and other games, and the author of numerous literary, historical, and scientific works. Roger of Sicily assembled illustrious scientists at his court but never ceased to pursue his own deep interests in geography, while his grandson, Frederick II, was so erudite and intellectually adventurous that he was *stupor mundi* to his own age and is a marvel still to ours, as Haskins concludes.[65] Just as the court of this "second baptized sultan on the Sicilian throne"[66] attracted sages representing various schools of thought, so did Frederick's mind absorb the knowledge accumulated in the civilizations both of his own time and of the past. But the paramount impression left upon modern authorities by a study of the emperor's famous treatise on falconry is that of "a first-rate mind, open, inquiring, realistic; trying to see things as they are without *parti pris*, and working throughout on the basis of systematized experience."[67] In other words, this medieval emperor was not a medieval scholar. For the rationalism that characterized his numerous original experiments in the natural sciences and the elaborate questionnaires that he addressed to fellow scholars in India, Egypt, Syria, Iraq, Yemen, and Morocco pervaded his entire approach to theology, philosophy, logic, mathematics, law, and literature. Indeed, by openly raising such questions as: Just where are heaven and hell and purgatory? Exactly how far is one heaven or one abyss from another? In which heaven is God to be found? Where are the souls of the departed? he cut to the heart of all medieval cosmologies and projected a new image of man's place in the universe.

D. The Intellectual Ascendancy
of Western Europe

Literate elites had been effective mediating agencies between different civilizations before the rise of the medieval Mediterranean societies, but in no preceding period had their intercultural exchanges neutralized as many ideological differences, linked as many separate political societies, and encompassed as many different fields of thought, as in the centuries here reviewed.[68] These circumstances make memo-

[65] *ibid.*, p. 269.
[66] *ibid.*, p. 243.
[67] *ibid.*, p. 264.
[68] The Hellenistic period was characterized by lively intellectual activities, but intercultural relations were not exacerbated by profound ideological differences.

rable the achievement that Jews, Christians, and Muslims of varied ethnic extraction and political allegiance have recorded in the annals of international history. They may also make it instructive today. For the voluntary and involuntary intellectual encounters that produced synthetic concepts and correspondent values during the Middle Ages occurred in a world environment not unlike the present one. International society was divided then, as it is now, into separate sovereignties and ideologically hostile camps, and individuals interested in truth and learning pursued their quests then, as they do today, in an uneasy state of "no-peace, no-war." Indeed, the very term "cold war," commonly applied today to the chronic tension between communists and liberals, was used first in medieval Spain in order to denote the conflict between Muslims and Christians.[69]

However, the situation confronting intellectuals in contemporary intercultural relations is nevertheless sufficiently different from its medieval analogue to suggest that the achievement of the Mediterranean elites cannot be approximated today. The present conflict between communism and liberalism is infinitely more pervasive in its scope and effects and more susceptible to deliberate manipulation than the medieval war of nerves. The latter had intense psychological repercussions only in those crossroads of culture in which the two faiths were in daily competition for the loyalty of men, whereas the former envelops the world. And most importantly, perhaps, the modern cold war occurs at a time when the peoples of the earth are rallied in mass democracies or classless societies that do not favor the emergence of intellectually autonomous elites. The medieval period was, by contrast, an aristocratic age in which the contending civilizations were represented by elites that had a clear sense of their identity within, as well as without, the political systems in which they had evolved. And since the governments of the day, despotic as many of them were, were in principle neither interested in, nor technically capable of, exercising total control over the thought processes and activities of their citizens, men were generally free, both mentally and physically, to engage in transcultural dialogues.

These dialogues grew fainter after the thirteenth century, as we have seen. They ceased to have appreciable consequences after the turn of

[69] A thirteenth century Spanish writer, Don Juan Manuel, applied the term "guerra fria" to the situation that prevailed in his native land during the coexistence of Islam and Christendom. See Luis Garcia Arias, *El concepto de guerra y la denominada "guerra fria"* (1956) reviewed in Annuaire Français de Droit International, 1956, p. 925.

the sixteenth century, and by the eighteenth century their very incidence seems to have been forgotten, by and large, as the historical writings of that age reveal. The nineteenth and early twentieth centuries
witnessed the political and economic predominance of Western Europe
in world affairs, and it became common to think of intercultural relations almost exclusively in terms of imperialism, colonialism, the expansion of Europe, or the Western impact on the non-Western world.
The actual circumstances that favored this mode of interpretation
have been drastically revised in the last decades, but the memory of this
particular chapter in intercultural history continues to control Western
and non-Western minds. For most current speculations about the causes
of discords and antagonisms between cultures center on the negative
effects that Western policies have had upon the destinies of Africans
and Asians, and ignore the fact that the great cultures of the world
were estranged from each other long before the era of imperialism
dawned. Today, when national legacies of pre-colonial times are being
resurrected in the non-Western world, it is important also to reconstruct the international scene in which the great cultures came to a
parting of the ways.

The Byzantine and Islamic civilizations, which had been primarily
responsible for the early cultural exchanges between all Mediterranean
nations, ceased to contribute to the cause of learning after the age of
transmission had come to an end. Both had brought forth ideological
and political systems that proved to be inhospitable to the development
of creative thought. Apart from being internally corroded by political
absolutism and intellectual quietism, both were embattled by foes from
without. The Mongols had devastated the Islamic domain in the east
(Baghdad was destroyed in 1258); the Western Christians had sapped
the roots of Islam in the west (Cordoba fell in 1236); and the Turks
undermined the foundations on which both Islam and Byzantium had
rested for centuries when they reorganized the entire Near Eastern
region as a self-contained empire, essentially aloof from the new societies that had formed themselves in the west. These developments
hastened the intellectual decline in the Arab realm. They spelled the
end of Byzantinism as a living intellectual force. Dislodged from its
century-old seat of authority, cut off from its traditional associations
with the Mediterranean peoples, Byzantine culture was reduced to the
status of a provincial heritage. Associated henceforth with the destinies
of Slavic peoples who had not participated in the cultural exchanges

between East and West, it was used and abused as a frame of reference for the evolution of locally relevant wisdom only.

As Islam found its principal orientation in the east and Greek Christianity moved to the north, Latin Christendom consolidated its position north of Sicily and Spain. These shifts, gradual as they were, suggested a possible extension of the radius of contacts between nations, it is true, but they had the actual negative effect of inactivating the Mediterranean as a synthesizing factor in intercultural relations and thus lengthening the physical distances between the traditional intellectual centers of the three civilizations. The establishment of reliable and meaningful communications between the literate elites of the time would therefore have been difficult even for purely geographical reasons. However, the principal explanation for the growing alienation between Byzantium, Islam, and Western Christendom must be sought in the disparate internal developments within each of these realms.

The Byzantine and Islamic systems differed from each other in many significant respects, as previous discussions have shown; but they converged, nevertheless, upon certain broad lines of agreement. Both had conditioned the peoples under their tutelage to view life on two separate planes: that of the real, which was subject to the unrestrained power of temporal authorities; and that of the ideal, which was seen as the reserve of religious and philosophical speculations, uncontaminated by references to the political and social actualities of the day. Each of these two spheres was conceived and organized along authoritarian lines by separating the elect from the nonelect. Just as the conduct of government was the monopoly of the few who happened to have actual power, so was the pursuit of knowledge the privilege of those in whom tradition had vested the right to indulge in thought. No significant communion could take place between these two elites, for each insisted upon the absolute validity of its own particular context. The men of action thus furthered the cause of worldly power and success, heedless of any suggestions that might originate in the ivory towers of the learned, while the men of thought persisted in cultivating dreams about a perfect human order, unmindful of the problems that men confronted in their daily existence. Being far removed from life, knowledge thus became increasingly sterile in the commonwealths of Byzantium and Islam.

These intellectual developments made for a striking realignment of cultures in the world. Indeed, they may be held responsible, in the final analysis, for that great rift which is commonly known as the conflict between East and West. For the general decline of creative learning in the Near East contrasted so markedly with the steady upsurge of intellectual explorations in the West that a cultural estrangement between these formerly closely allied civilizations became inevitable. It accorded so well, on the other hand, with the patterns of culture that had become established in the Farther Orient, that it was possible after A.D. 1500 to think in rather undifferentiating terms of the East as beginning east of Greece, and this alignment is supported by such reflections as the following.

The compartmentalization of life and thought into distinct provinces, some reserved for the pursuit of power and pleasure, others for that of virtue and salvation, distinguished modes of existence in India as it did in the Near East. To be sure, it was not as marked in China, where the traditional Confucian ethic aspired to encompass man's entire condition. But in China and India, as well as in the Near East, we find all thought strongly allied with custom and authority. Acknowledged as the prerogative of small literate elites, it was meant to sanction, rather than to question, the reality that had come to be.

This reality included governments that were either totally immune to reformist philosophical thought, as in Islam, or privileged to special philosophies giving broad license to the exercise of power, as in India, where the *artha* had no relation to the *dharma*; and as in China, where the ethic of politics as defined by Confucius had little connection with the standards of behavior enjoined upon men in other human relationships. Against the power of established conventions, whether political, social, or religious, men were in general helpless. The educated among them, whether Hindu, Buddhist, or Muslim, were instructed by their culture to disengage themselves from the calamities and frustrations of life and to seek, instead, that inner peace which could be theirs through communion with the absolute. The great mass of the unsophisticated, on the other hand, were taught that they could escape suffering only by trusting religion, ritual, and tradition, as interpreted by the sages. All societies east of the Mediterranean thus became oblivious to the possibilities of progress and improvement. They were in essence static societies in which the chosen few held fast to their established social and political prerogatives, while the many viewed life on earth in ignorance, apathy, and resignation.[70]

The evolution of culture west of Greece proceeded along signifi-

[70] For a stimulating discussion of these issues see Joseph W. Cohen, "The Role of Philosophy in Culture" in *Philosophy East and West*, Vol. v, no. 2, July 1955.

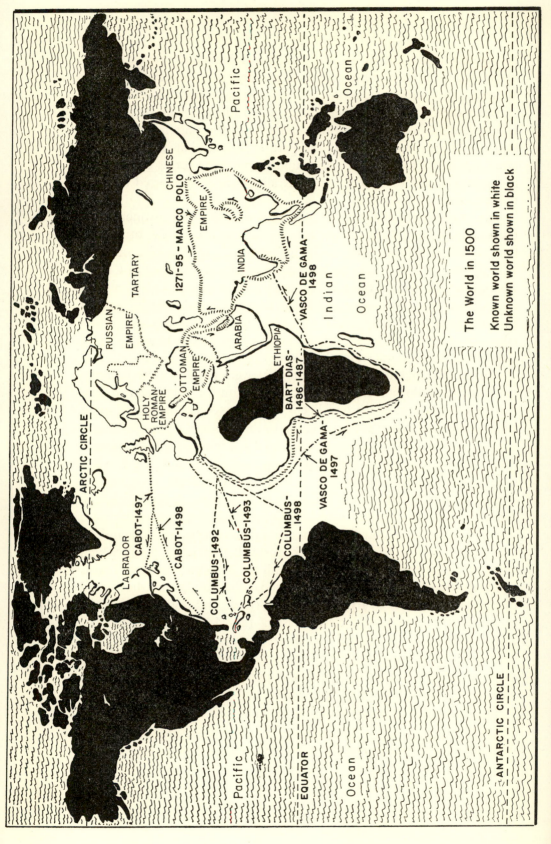

The World in 1500

Known world shown in white
Unknown world shown in black

ARCTIC CIRCLE

RUSSIAN EMPIRE

TARTARY

CHINESE EMPIRE

1271-95 – MARCO POLO

HOLY ROMAN EMPIRE

OTTOMAN EMPIRE

ARABIA

INDIA

ETHIOPIA

BART DIAS – 1486-1487

VASCO DE GAMA – 1498

Indian Ocean

Pacific Ocean

LABRADOR

CABOT-1497

CABOT-1498

COLUMBUS-1492

COLUMBUS-1493

COLUMBUS- 1498

VASCO DE GAMA 1497

Pacific Ocean

EQUATOR

ANTARCTIC CIRCLE

The World in A.D. 1500

cantly different lines. In fact, the great civilizations of the East and West developed in diametrically opposite directions. The distance between the literate minorities of the two poles of the Eurasian realm was consequently not only a physical but also an intellectual phenomenon; and in this latter context it was bound to deepen after A.D. 1500, when the Europeans acquired a sense of their superiority over the Oriental societies that their ancestors had held in awe.

The new approaches to knowledge with which the West became identified in the period known as the Renaissance were destined to revolutionize man's view of the universe and his conception of himself. They were in essence those that Frederick II had announced as early as the thirteenth century and that Paracelsus urged upon his students when he counselled them to abandon Galen and Avicenna and to think for themselves after consulting nature. The point of departure here was the critical mind of the individual, not established conventions and beliefs; and the road to truth was sought by observation and experiment, rather than by unquestioning reliance upon authorities of the past. This new spirit became the life force, as it were, of Western Europe. It gave scientists and artists the intellectual courage to rethink the world, and it provided the less gifted aspirants to knowledge with a strong incentive to seek emancipation by perfecting their capacities for thought. A profusion of ideas, inventions, and discoveries was generated in this manner, especially after printing became an established art in the second half of the fifteenth century and literacy an aptitude accessible to many.

The new attitude toward knowledge imparted a dynamic to life that had been missing in the cultures of the Orient and Occident since the days of ancient Greece. Its immediate effect was to set Europe apart not only from Asia but also from its own most recent past. For it prompted the modern men of learning to review the truths by which their predecessors had abided. This great process of revisionist exploration led to the discarding of many theories and beliefs that had dominated the medieval scene. But it was conducive also to the resuscitation of ideas that had long been encased in the neglected records of pre-Christian Europe. Indeed, the rediscovery of the life-style of the pagan Greeks and Romans, which fortified the Europeans of the Renaissance in their search for self-realization, has had a continuously stimulating effect upon all later generations, even though—or perhaps precisely because—it put in issue some of the most fundamental tenets with which the Europeans had been identified as Christians.

The same spirit that instructed the European mind to arbitrate between the past and the present, and to integrate divergent traditions in rationally tenable systems of thought, was operative also in regulating the relationship between the real and the ideal. For the classical and Christian traditions agreed, albeit on different grounds, not only that the realms of thought and action were complementary aspects of the unity of life, but also that each was perfectible in terms of the other. This interplay between the "ought" and the "is," between the normative and the actual, pervades all categories of European history. But nowhere, perhaps, is it as strikingly manifest as in the realm of politics. To be sure, pagans and Christians, Germans and Latins, asked different questions and found different answers when they considered political problems on the national or international level. But the accumulated records of their political institutions and philosophies reflect a general Western European consensus that knowledge should encompass all of life and consequently that the realities of government are proper subjects of scholarly investigation and reformist thought. This Occidental commitment to an integral and synthetic view of the human condition found its most enduring expression in the medieval universities.

E. The Medieval Universities
of Western Europe and their Contributions
to the Modern Society of Nations

The idea of a place that should enclose the universe of knowledge and accommodate generations of teachers and students in a joint and continuous enterprise probably arose independently in Islam and Christendom as a natural response to intellectual challenges that were virtually the same wherever scholars conglomerated. The great Islamic universities in Baghdad, Nishapur, Damascus, Jerusalem, Cairo, and Alexandria in the Near East, and the great Christian universities of Bologna, Paris, Montpellier, and Oxford, were in this sense members of one transcultural fraternity, for they had issued from similar premises and aspired to analogous goals.[71] But within the context of this

---

[71] The earliest Muslim universities arose in the eleventh century and were thus a century older than the earliest Christian places of learning. This fact has stimulated the speculation that the latter were modelled upon the former. However, no evidence has been adduced in support of this view. See Alfred Guillaume, "Philosophy and Theology," pp. 244ff. In connection with this issue it is pertinent to remember that numerous Islamic universities had been established on sites that had been famous as intellectual centers in pre-Islamic times and that several of the great Arabian libraries and hospitals have been patterned upon the Greek schools of Alexandria and the Christian schools of Syria. Castiglione, p. 286.

broad agreement as to the meaning of their existence, they were bound to develop along significantly different lines. The Near Eastern universities (about whose organization much less is known, unfortunately, than is known about their counterparts in the West) have had no significant impact upon the actual order of their societies, for they were as remote from the social and political scene as the learned men who were their denizens. The Occidental universities, on the other hand, became the laboratories of socially and politically significant thought. As such they had a prodigious influence upon the course of events that transformed the political organisms of medieval Europe into institutions that were deemed, in later centuries, to have world-wide applicability. The secular state, to which most people of the earth subscribe today as their ultimate frame of reference, rests on foundations that were defined and solidified in medieval law schools, such as that of Bologna, and the contemporary system of conducting relations between states derives many of its guiding principles from the same academic enclaves. For the formulation of a secular law of nations in the seventeenth century was made possible by the renaissance of Roman law in the Italian law faculties; and the congressional method of diplomacy, which has been a cardinal feature of the modern European states system since the Congress of Constance (1417-1421), emanated from constitutional devices that had been adopted first by the University of Paris.

These linkages between the medieval history of the Western universities and the modern history of the society of nations may at first seem surprising. They become comprehensible, however, when it is remembered that the European universities were themselves members of a kind of European concert. Bologna happened to be in Italy, and Paris in France, but the Europeans did not regard the Italian school as an Italian affair or the French school as a French affair.[72] Both were cosmopolitan centers of learning to which students flocked from all over Europe, where masters taught whose learning had won an international reputation,[73] and from which ideas were migrating into all corners of Western Europe.

[72] See Etienne Gilson, "Medieval Universalism and its Present Value" in Harvard Tercentenary Conference of Arts and Sciences, *Interdependence, Convergence and Borrowing in Institutions, Thought and Art*, Cambridge, Mass., 1937, p. 202, for the comment that the slightest pretension, on the part of any nation, to be the independent source of a merely local truth would have made life unbearable to that crowd of Englishmen, Germans, Italians, Belgians, Spaniards, Danes, Swedes, etc. who were teaching and working together.

[73] The first professor of international repute at the University of Paris was Alexan-

The same inter-European spirit pervaded each great academic center. A university in medieval Europe was a *universitas* in the authentic sense of the word. It was a whole; it promoted the quest for the whole rather than for any partial truth, and it was committed to maintain its integrity and identity as a whole against all possible encroachments from without and within.

The constitutional provisions that were designed to secure these purposes differed from university to university, but all reflected the same great movement toward association that was manifesting itself throughout medieval Europe in the form of merchant guilds and craft guilds, religious brotherhoods and knightly orders, leagues of cities and federations of cantons. In fact, the university itself was, in its scholastic sense, a particular kind of trade guild.[74] At Bologna it was organized in order to protect students against the political authority of the city and to help them to extract civic rights and favorable living conditions.[75] And this pattern was followed by most universities in Italy and southern France. In Paris, on the other hand, the university was, in essence, a guild of masters, even though the latter cooperated closely with the students in order to defend their joint interests against the outside world. In the end, this organizational scheme was copied by most of the universities of Northern Europe.

However, the concept of the guild was found to be inadequate when it came to the problem of governing the *universitas* as a whole; for the collective will of a heterogeneous community composed of an enormous, cosmopolitan student body, as well as of the various resident masters, could not be determined reliably through congregations of the entire membership. The solution of the problem was suggested by the fact that the university—whether conceived as a guild of scholars or as a guild of masters—sheltered smaller groups of special interest. These were permitted to evolve their own forms of self-government, so that they should be represented properly in meetings of the central administrative body. Masters sharing a field of study joined in separate faculties, and scholars coming from the same region grouped them-

---

der of Hales, an Englishman; he was succeeded by Albertus Magnus, a German; Bonaventura, an Italian; and Duns Scotus, a Scotchman. *ibid.*, pp. 198-203.

[74] *The Cambridge Medieval History*, Vol. VI, p. 561.

[75] In later years the students used their power of combination and collective bargaining also in order to reduce their masters to a condition of quasi-servitude. All students, whether native or foreign-born, lived in houses that enjoyed special municipal protection, were exempt from many taxes, could not be expelled before the end of the term, and were granted all rights of citizenship under the terms of a statute of 1284.

selves in separate nations. And the early recognition of this latter sub-division led to results that hold a special interest for the student of international organizations. For not only did the universities here announce a political principle of community life that was to shape decisively the modern system of states, but their way of putting the principle to use was imitated in the fifteenth century by the international assembly of Constance.

The identification of nations at a university was determined by the numerical preponderance within it of the particular national groups. Bologna, for example, distinguished between the Roman, Tuscan, and Campanian nations, which were again subdivided into smaller bodies of those coming from the same locality. The Faculty of Arts at the University of Paris, on the other hand, recognized France, Normandy, Picardy, and England.[76] The principle of nationality, as understood by the universities, was thus primarily a functional device, intended to serve the international corporation, and this may explain why it was interpreted somewhat broadly. The members of nations not officially recognized therefore found themselves allotted rather arbitrarily to one or another of those enjoying official status. For instance, at the University of Paris, all of Southern Europe was assigned to France while Germany was included in England. But, when the numerical strength of the English masters declined and that of the Germans increased, a reversal occurred and the English nation was simply restyled the German nation.[77]

The organic connection between the self-governing faculties and nations on the one hand, and between these bodies and the central organization of the university on the other, was secured by a complex system of discussion and voting. This arrangement, too, deserves particular notice when the medieval university is being viewed in the context of international constitutionalism, for the techniques employed at

[76] The University of Paris was a federal corporation by the middle of the thirteenth century, composed of three superior faculties, namely, theology, canon law, and medicine, and the inferior faculty of arts. Only the latter acknowledged the existence of nations.

[77] See *The Cambridge Medieval History*, Vol. vi, pp. 561, 567ff. A single English master was at one time endowed with a voting power equivalent to that of the whole body of French masters.

In view of the early rise of political nationalism in England it is interesting to note that the University of Oxford, which had grown in close alignment to the University of Paris, resolved solemnly in 1274 not to recognize separate nations. See *ibid.*, p. 589. For further information on the nations see Pearl Kibre, *The Nations in the Medieval Universities*, Medieval Academy of America, 1948, and C. H. Haskins, *The Rise of Universities*, New York, 1923.

the University of Paris to determine the collective will of its various component groups were taken over by the Council of Constance for the organization of its meetings.

The ultimate source of these techniques was a strong loyalty to the ideal of unity. In consonance with this ideal it was assumed that the decision of any group—whether large or small—should mirror the agreement of *all* its members. In other words, here, as in most other medieval assemblies, unanimity was supposed to be the voting norm. However, since the university was conceived as a place in which each individual scholar was expected to pursue the quest for truth in his own way, the problem arose of reconciling the principle of unity with that of individuality. The scholars found their answer to the dilemma by interposing the twin devices of discussion and conciliation. These affirmed full respect for individual opinion while providing ways of dissolving conflicting views. And since it was realized that discussions in small groups of like-minded people would yield agreement more easily than discussions in a single group of very different participants, it was established at the University of Paris that each item on the agenda of the general congregation should be discussed and voted upon in the separate meetings of the several faculties and nations. Furthermore, in view of Western Europe's present-day preference for majority rule, it is interesting to note that it required a long evolution of constitutional practices before the University of Paris was ready to accept decisions reached by a majority of its faculties, and before the Paris Faculty of Arts considered itself bound by a majority of its component nations.[78]

The universities derived great strength and stability from the forms of government that they had devised. Secure in their inner structure, they were able to exert considerable influence upon the world around them; and this was true particularly of the northern universities, whose corporate identity commanded the unqualified respect of both church and state.[79] Among these none was as powerful in inter-European affairs as the University of Paris. Cosmopolitan in its composition, closely allied with all other centers of learning, abreast of secular and ecclesiastical developments, yet immune from outside interference, it became a great organ of informed public opinion and the principal agency for the cultural integration of Western Europe.

[78] See *The Cambridge Medieval History*, Vol. VI, pp. 567ff., 589ff.
[79] The Italian universities manifested their influence largely through the activities of individual masters.

As a workshop of political science, the university elaborated new principles and modes of administration that were to prove their practical worth beyond the confines of academic life. And as an independent, internationally trusted corporation, it assumed the political leadership of the European community by directing the settlement of several vexing issues that beset the continent during the centuries of the University's preeminence. The antiquated theology of the Western church was reformed by the introduction of secular, anti-monastic, anti-curialist principles that the Paris faculties had defined with consummate care. The Great Schism was repaired when the University, aided by the emperor and other secular princes, succeeded in imposing a settlement upon the rival claimants to the papacy. And a totally new method of coping with outstanding European problems was established, when the Council of Constance was convened and organized under the auspices of the same academicians.

The accomplishments of this French institution made a great impression on medieval society. In fact, they persuaded contemporary writers that the University of Paris was the third of the great European powers or "virtues" preceded in importance only by the papacy and the empire.[80] This medieval testimony deserves the attention of modern students of international affairs since it explains much of the European approach to international unity. For each of the three great powers—significantly also acknowledged as "virtues"—was an inter-European or transnational agency whose "power" was not grounded in an actual occupation of territory. Each derived its real strength from spiritual or intellectual, rather than from material, resources, and all three rested on premises that had been carefully defined in terms of law. The power of this triad of organizations was to become eclipsed in subsequent centuries as "power" became associated with the national secular state, but the remembrance of its various manifestations has continued to influence the European mind whenever it has engaged in the search for greater unions. In the perspective of the past, therefore, it has been no accident that all great designs for transnational order and security have emanated from countries belonging to the Western European culture realm.[81]

[80] See *The Cambridge Medieval History*, Vol. vi, p. 598.
[81] See Haskins; Lynn Thorndike, *University Records and Life in the Middle Ages*, New York, 1944; Hastings Rashdall, *The Universities in the Middle Ages* (new ed. by Powicke and Emden), Oxford, 1936; *The Cambridge Medieval History*, Vol. vi, pp. 560ff.

CHAPTER 13

THE POLITICAL ASCENDANCY
OF WESTERN EUROPE AND THE ESTABLISHMENT OF
THE MODERN STATES SYSTEM

A. Residual Political Themes in
the Non-Western World

THE LITERATE and nonliterate civilizations that coexisted in the world before the nineteenth century had no system of shared political references. Forms of unity, security, and peace had been recorded at all times and in all parts of the world. Most of these had had a consolidating effect upon the societies within which they had arisen. Some had even proved attractive to peoples outside the region and beyond the age for which they had been fashioned. This had been true, for example, of the values propagated by the Greeks under Alexander the Great and his successors, the Romans, the Byzantines, and the Muslims. Each of the systems brought forth in the course of history contained some particular suggestion or set of suggestions for the integration or coordination of separate cultures and nations. However, a comparison of the schemes as they have been presented in the present study points to the conclusion that few could qualify as integrating systems of political reference for a world of many interconnected cultures. It is self-evident that the complex of references developed by nonliterate civilizations was inapplicable to literate peoples. But it becomes clear upon reflection that the residual, or basic, values manifest in the literate societies of the Far East could not gain currency as transcultural references either. For since each of the great Oriental schemes was an integral part of a particular imperial design, it was incapable of spanning other cultures. Since each was linked inextricably to a religious or quasi-religious orientation,[1] it could not incorporate the secular realities that have controlled life since the fifteenth century. And since each was anchored in the assumption that the majority of human beings would always be illiterates, it could not adjust to an age of growing literacy.

The principal political systems that had arisen in the Mediterranean region were different from those developed in China and India, for all of them had been responsive to the traditions of other civilizations,

[1] The Mongolian empire of the steppes was an exception.

since the area had always been the scene of lively international relations. The nations that had commingled in the medieval societies of Byzantium, Western Christendom, and Islam thus shared a rather solid substratum of affinities when they organized themselves as multinational theocracies. However, the three commonwealths had deduced different values from their joint inheritance, and three totally different political systems had emerged within the contours of broadly similar structures. These systems were put to the same test from about the thirteenth century onward. For at that time it was realized throughout the Mediterranean region that theocratic designs were outdated, since human interests were shifting to secular concerns, and that multinational societies were unable to maintain themselves as effective international governments, since the loyalties of people were being attracted to local or national centers of power. In brief, it had become evident that traditional approaches to government and the conduct of foreign relations would have to be revised if they were to encompass the realities of the ascending age.

A comparison of the responses that this crisis elicited from the various Mediterranean powers shows great disparities. Indeed, it suggests that the reactions to the challenge were as dissimilar as the values that had come to characterize each of the three societies. The medieval Muslim authorities had succeeded in creating what Oswald Spengler has called a magical community of nations, but they had failed to suggest a political framework within which believers, let alone unbelievers, could find political security in their domestic and foreign relations. And this dual motif had been retained by the separate principalities upon which the legacy of Islam had descended, for each of them evoked the spirit of unity without being able to give it political form. The Byzantines, on the other hand, had concentrated upon the establishment of political order within their orbit, but their political symbols and institutions, not unlike those found in the Oriental monarchies, had been geared exclusively to the maintenance of their own intricately fathomed power structure. Valid everywhere as sources of inspiration for individual aspirants to monolithic power, they were void as patterns for the organization of international relations between coordinate cultures and states.

Over most of the area that had been comprised in the medieval theocracies of the Byzantines and Muslims the Ottoman Turks exercised control from the middle of the fifteenth to the end of the nineteenth century. And their administrative system, strongly impregnated by Persian and Byzantine principles of statecraft, was effective in providing a long period of relative tranquillity after the turmoil associated with preceding regimes. However, the new Asian governors failed to break the bondage in which Islamic traditions had held the thoughts of the faithful throughout the preceding centuries. Hostility to intellectual initiative and social change thus continued to characterize life in the Asian provinces, as Gibb observes in the following passage:

"We shall never know whether some Arab Jacquard devised an improved loom or some Turkish Watt discovered the power of steam, but we can confidently assert that, if any such invention had occurred, it would have been entirely without result. The whole social organism, in fact, was one characteristic of, and only possible in, a stationary or retrograde civilization, and herein lay its essential weakness. It is not an exaggeration to say that after so many centuries of immobility the processes of agriculture, industry, exchange, and learning had become little more than automatic, and had resulted in a species of atrophy that rendered those engaged in them all but incapable of changing their methods or outlook in the slightest degree.

"It was this incapacity, rather than unwillingness, to learn that above all characterized Asiatic Moslem society in the seventeenth and eighteenth centuries. Its sterilized brain could not effectually conceive any idea that lay outside the narrow range of its experience and tradition, nor could it meet any situation which deviated from the path traced by routine."[2]

These comments were elicited by a study of the Ottoman Empire, but the intellectual climate to which they refer obtained also in far Eastern Europe, Africa, and other parts of Asia, as preceding chapters have shown. Life in all these regions was generally held immune to change and had in effect been stationary and retrograde for many centuries when it was subjected to the impact of the West from about the eighteenth century onward. And nowhere was this intellectual atrophy quite as evident as in the field of politics. It was in this domain, therefore, that Occidental thought was bound to have its most unsettling effects. For since the non-Western nations had not been able to develop new ideas about the relationship between government and society, or to suggest new images of the world society and new norms for the conduct of international relations, they were constrained, ultimately, to adjust to a political order and to adopt a vocabulary of

[2] H. A. R. Gibb and Harold Bowen, *Islamic Society and the West*, Oxford, 1950, Vol. I, Part I, pp. 215-216.

political ideas that had been devised in the context of Western Europe's history, and had no organic connection with the patterns of accommodation to which they had been accustomed for centuries, in some cases for millenniums.

The first generations of post-Renaissance Europeans, on the other hand, were intellectually ill-prepared[3] to mitigate the impact of their ideas upon the ancient orders from which their own civilization had become alienated in the course of time. In the initial phases of this renewed encounter with non-Western systems they were unfamiliar with the histories of Asian and African societies and had not yet developed the sciences of archaeology, ethnology, and anthropology that were to facilitate intercultural accords from the nineteenth century onward. Already accustomed to change and attuned to a life style favoring intellectual and physical adventure, they were more conscious of the present and its promises than of the past and its traditions. Indeed, it may be surmised that few Europeans were at that time vitally concerned with the historical aspects of their own civilization. In other words, they were not conscious of the fact that an intricate morphology lay behind each of the truths to which they held and behind each of the institutions that they propagated.

B. European Approaches to Political
Myths and Realities

The medieval Roman Catholic realm from which modern Western Europe issued had also been conceived as a multinational theocracy, and the Western Europeans had been haunted by the same double image of a unified and powerful realm that had controlled the evolution of the two rival Mediterranean societies. But the design here had never been realized unequivocally, having been challenged from its inception by a great variety of secular interests and traditions as well as by constantly operative, speculative, and corrective thought. The Western realm was thus unlike the Islamic caliphates, since it had at no time been immune to reformist opinion; and it was unlike Byzantium, since it had not become a monolithic international government in which the powers of state and church were fused harmoniously. As the conglomerate of several principles that balanced each other precariously, the Western Empire has, in fact, always been difficult to define. At one time it had been visualized in terms of the theory of the

---

[3] With the exception of the Jesuits.

two swords, which assumed that the unified ecclesiastical administration had its secular counterpart in a unified international government. But in attempting to measure the reach of its actual power in the period between the tenth and thirteenth centuries, one finds oneself on quicksand, as it were. For where precisely was the Empire? And what were the powers of its representative agents? One reads that the Holy Roman Empire of the German Nation possessed sovereignty over Germany, Italy, the Low Countries, and the Two Burgundies; that it exercised suzerainty over Bohemia, Poland, and Hungary; and that it claimed a theoretical lordship over France, England, Spain, Denmark, and Scandinavia.[4] But the actual territorial outlines of the Empire were always hazy at best, for sovereignty, suzerainty, and lordship were fluid concepts, changing their meanings from one administration to the next. It should be noted, moreover, that the continuity of the imperial government was not assured by firmly established institutions,[5] that the imperial representative did not possess the prerogatives associated by other international governments with the office of a supreme executive, and that the material power of the Empire was seldom superior to that of less exalted and nominally subordinate Western European sovereignties, such as the kingdoms of France and England. Formless, powerless, its substance indefinable and its nomenclature meaningless—for what reality could be attached to the words "Holy," "Roman," "Empire," and "German"?—the Holy Roman Empire of the German Nation definitely lacked the attributes commonly found in an international administration. It is not surprising, then, that this Empire has been dismissed by most later commentators as a mere figment of the medieval imagination.

This negative evidence, overwhelming as it may seem to modern minds, was not accepted at face value by contemporaries. The European commonwealth may have been an artifice even in medieval terms

---

[4] O. H. Gierke, *Political Theories of the Middle Ages*, tr. Maitland, Beacon Paperback, 1958, pp. 126-127, n. 56, on the universal extent of the empire. James Bryce, *The Holy Roman Empire*, New York, 1928, p. 180 for a map of the empire in the twelfth century, also pp. 182ff., 193 for a description of imperial titles and pretensions.

[5] There is some reason to regard the Electoral College as a permanent agency of the imperial government, for in addition to electing the emperor and functioning as part of the imperial diet, it constituted also the electoral union—an independent political organization which was supposed to meet annually under the provisions of the Golden Bull for the purpose of deliberating about "the safety of the empire and the world." Most attempts to execute this last named function were abortive. It should be mentioned also that the emperor succeeded, for some time, in maintaining his own general court of interstate justice, which became known in 1495 as the "Reichskammergericht." However, no imperial agency had any real power of enforcing its decisions.

but it was real nevertheless. For the lines separating reality from myth were not drawn as harshly then as they are today. Visions and dreams were part of everyday life, and men responded to them as if they were true. Impressed above all by the logic of a conceptual design, contemporaries were apt to overlook the weaknesses of the actual institutions that had been set up to realize the design. Peace and unity were the controlling political myths in medieval Europe. They were accepted as the supreme norms by which life ought to be governed, however great the turmoil in actual inter-European affairs. The Empire was real because it symbolized these values. Since it stood for peace, its imperial agent was regarded as the peacemaker, expounder of justice, and chief legislator, even though he lacked the power to uphold peace and law. And since it had been conceived as a continuation of Rome's unified cosmopolitan society, the emperor was viewed as a "Roman," and therefore as an impartial, international executive, even though his office was, for practical purposes, coequal with the German throne.[6]

Analogous relationships between reality and myth existed also in the Chinese, Byzantine, and Islamic realms and in numerous non-literate societies. Indeed, this theme of life and thought seems to have been one upon which most cultures converged before, roughly, A.D. 1500. But the visions brought forth in the non-Western civilizations were captured in early phases of their evolution. Compressed in rigid social and political institutions they became, in fact, indistinguishable from the reality of organized life. This development enhanced the solidarity of the societies in which it occurred, but it arrested reformist thought by stopping the mainsprings of the human imagination. Western Europe, on the other hand, did not resolve the ambivalence between reality and dream, and the tension between the "is" and the "ought," between fiction and fact, became the principal theme of its constitutional history. Unable to find the perfect harmony that their firmly held visions suggested as the necessary goal of political endeavor, the Western Europeans exerted themselves strenuously and continuously in finding approximations of this elusive ideal.

The speculations and activities that issued from the felt inadequacy of the actual situation were frequently idle, haphazard, disjointed, or ill-fated at the time of their undertaking. Seen in retrospect, however, they may be said to have had the cumulative effect of transforming medieval Europe into a dynamic civilization, capable of adjusting to change and of expanding in new directions. For since the Europeans

---

[6] Bryce, p. 267.

were unrestrained, at least in comparison with the denizens of other civilizations, by an effective superior power, or, for that matter, by a fixed territorial or constitutional frame of reference, they were freer than their contemporaries in Africa and Asia to transcend the actual scene of time and space by which their lives seemed bounded. Thus they were able to recall the past in the hope of finding new wisdom rather than in awe of its immutable commands; they could think of the future as a time of promise rather than of certainty; and they could use the present as an opportunity for the exercise of choices rather than for compliance with preordained patterns of life.

These time perspectives suggested new conceptions of unity, security, and peace. Since the Empire did not have fixed territorial frontiers, the Europeans began to think of unity in nonterritorial terms. Having to dispense with the notion of geographic contiguity as a prerequisite of union, they developed, instead, intangible criteria to unite heterogeneous political organisms. And being unable to rally around a central seat of transnational power, they proceeded to formulate principles of voluntary association and cooperation. In other words, they solved the medieval paradox of myth and reality as it appeared in European politics by evolving a totally new order of political references. Some of these references had been tested in the orbits of the Catholic Church and the University of Paris, as previous discussions have shown. Many had been set forth, at least as basic conceptions, by the private and public law of ancient Rome. These precedents and traditions taught the Europeans that peace and unity were essentially moral concepts, dependent on the strength of individual convictions and positing requirements for cooperation between individuals and groups. They converged also on the recognition that ideals of this kind were best expressed in terms of law and best realized in terms of constitutions.

The conclusion that law was the most effective carrier of political values received further emphasis from the experience, also recorded in Roman and Christian traditions, that law had been a tested arbiter between conflicting interests. A normative legal order thus appealed to all who felt the need for peace and security and the lack of an integral system of secular government, capable of enforcing compliance with centrally established principles of conduct. A plurality of legal systems, each designed to guarantee the integrity of a special group or region, was thus brought into being as like-minded people rallied in cities, provinces, and states, or in guilds, universities, and other voluntary associations. The Holy Roman Empire, itself defunct as a collective security organization, became a maze of conflicting jurisdictions during the first phase of this development. However, several remarkable movements toward legal concurrence had the gradual effect of lessening the divisions and furthering the cause of Western European concord. Feudal courts throughout the continent showed a growing inclination to accept each other's decisions as generally valid statements of the law in point.[7] An apt compilation of maritime law became the model for many seafaring communities; the constitution of an established university was emulated freely by new institutions of learning; and a municipal franchise or a set of provincial customs commended itself frequently, because of its excellence, to other localities.[8]

These voluntary and involuntary movements toward the Europeanization of disparate legal customs were quickened under the influence of three normative law systems that were transnational and transterritorial in their very inception: the canon law, the law merchant, and the Roman law. The latter in particular had a continuously pervasive effect after the twelfth century, when the jurists in the law schools of Bologna and Ravenna had assimilated and reformulated the secular principles of jurisprudence found in the Digest of Justinian and other ancient legal texts. As feudal and ecclesiastical influences decayed, it spread northward rapidly, penetrating the entire commonwealth,[9] until its supremacy was acknowledged openly by secular practitioners and judges who had been trained in the law faculties of the universities and proceeded, as a matter of course, to Romanize the substance of the local law that they were supposed to administer.[10] After the establishment of the Reichskammergericht in 1495 the Roman law entered the highest imperial court of justice, and by the first half of the sixteenth century it had become decisive in the practice of the courts.[11] "With much less noise but more effect than the Holy Roman Empire," Edouard Meynial writes,[12] "Roman law in the Middle Ages filled the part of an

---

[7] For instance, decisions rendered in Lombardy were cited practically everywhere. See Munroe Smith, *A General View of European Legal History*, New York, 1927, pp. 270ff.

[8] Charters devised in Argonne were copied again and again in hundreds of communities, and the customs of Breteuil, a medium-sized town on the confines of Normandy, inspired charters of liberties in a number of towns in England, Wales, and Ireland. See Sir Paul Vinogradoff, "Customary Law," in *The Legacy of the Middle Ages*, G. C. Crump and E. F. Jacob, eds., Oxford, 1927, p. 313.

[9] The diffusion of Roman Law in England was arrested by the early development of the Inns of Court.

[10] *The Cambridge Medieval History*, Vol. v, pp. 728-762.

[11] Bryce, p. 365.

[12] "Roman Law" in Crump and Jacob, p. 387.

international unifying agent, appealing to and ensuring a willing acceptance of the same ideas of equity and social justice, of discipline and administrative order." In this context, then, it could be said that Roman law stood in the place of what was later called international law; for it was generally assumed by German lawyers that the relations of the commonwealth, whether inside or outside of the Empire, ought to be regulated by the pure law of Rome, whether they were actually susceptible to such regulations or not. And these developments in the field of secular jurisprudence were paralleled by the findings of generations of ecclesiastical lawyers, as previous chapters have shown.

Before the actual establishment of the modern states system the Europeans had thus become convinced that it was necessary and possible to institute peace and unity in local and inter-European affairs; that these goals were best attained by the creation of normative principles of individual conduct; and that these normative principles, having been susceptible to objective definition in each phase of their evolution, could be channelled into the life stream of nations by propagating their meanings through appropriate forms of legal symbolism. By the time that Western Europe had become intellectually and politically dominant in world affairs these conclusions, accumulated slowly in the course of Western European history, had hardened into the firm assumption that power should not be condoned unless its use was lawful and right; that peace and unity were not acceptable unless they were anchored in a just and logical constitutional order; that there were legal concepts for which universal validity could be claimed; and that it was possible, by the employment of legal procedures, to create extraterritorial concerts in behalf of collective security and international peace. Endeavors to execute the mandates implicit in these references were fraught with ambiguities, but they produced a consensus to the effect that law, rightly understood, was the only proper and reliable measure of political life whether on the local or on the international level, and that the individual was the chief subject of the law's concern.

These pivotal values survived the disintegration of the medieval commonwealth and could accommodate new and different truths because they had become independent of the particular political framework within which they had originated. Objectively defined in a variety of legal systems and constitutional forms of government, they had become extraterritorial, as it were. And deeply imbedded in the minds of successive generations, they had generated a particular disposition to question all appearances, whether in the realm of image or reality, to identify the universals in any field of human experience, and to express conclusions in abstract legal terms. This fund of accumulated traditions and aptitudes sustained the momentum of Europe's intellectual ascendancy in intercultural relations. It also generated the powers of political renewal and regeneration that enabled Western nations to evolve new sets of political references on the local and international levels.

C. The Modern State

A. SICILY: A PROLOGUE

An attempt to mark the beginning of the modern state is as arbitrary as an attempt to date the beginning of the modern era. For political, as all other, life is in constant flux, and the moulds that contain it are being cast and recast imperceptibly in the course of time. Each institution, however clear its identity in a given moment, has its antecedents in some other form, and the line that separates the emergent from the defunct cannot be drawn exactly.

If the continuous metamorphosis of political forms is viewed retrospectively in the context of the twentieth century system of sovereign, independent, and equal states, as it has been recognized in the Charter of the United Nations, it is possible to find the beginnings of the modern state in the decaying framework of the medieval European commonwealth, and to suggest, in particular, that the formal attributes and operative ideals commonly associated today with the nation-state were established gradually, between the thirteenth and twentieth centuries, by the nations of Western Europe, notably England and France. However, the story of this archetypal organization which has become the pivotal political reference for all peoples in the world, has a prologue that was composed in the western Mediterranean between the eleventh and thirteenth centuries in response to suggestive influences emanating not only from the Occidental, but also from different Oriental, civilizations. For the outlines of the sovereign secular law state were drawn by European dynasties in southern Italy when this small area was a universe of cultures, and the principles that were to yield the modern diplomatic method were formulated first by the Venetians after they had absorbed the lessons that Byzantium had taught them.[18]

---

[18] The transcultural auspices under which political forms developed in the western Mediterranean existed also in Spain. European, particularly Spanish, historians treat Spain as an integral part of Occidental civilization and pay scant attention to the

It will be recalled that Sicily, Apulia, and Calabria had been the crossroads of all Mediterranean cultures since the dawn of history when the Normans arrived on the scene in A.D. 1060, intent upon consolidating this multinational region as a base for further conquests in Africa and the eastern Mediterranean. As conquerors the Normans were as insatiable in their desire for power as their Muslim and Byzantine predecessors; but as political organizers they revealed talents and skills that no previous dynasty in the area had possessed. Widely travelled, at home in many parts of Eastern and Western Europe, and astute in recognizing regional realities in their full complexity, they were able, in the course of a few decades, to weld the former provinces of Byzantine, Islamic, and Italian rulers into a political society that had most of the characteristics of the modern state. Unified under a powerful central government, secular in its orientation, and independent of the great theocracies of the day, the Norman establishment was also studiously cosmopolitan in the conduct of domestic and foreign affairs. Political institutions that had proved their worth in the history of other civilizations and seemed adaptable to the Norman scheme were borrowed and integrated freely; local customs, languages, and religions that did not inhibit the exercise of central power were respected; and men known to be competent and knowledgeable were employed regardless of their religious or ethnic affiliation.

This fusion of cultures, which was fostered deliberately in the interests of the state, explains the following political arrangements. Royal power was anchored in Norman ideas of kingship, but the symbols denoting the authority and functions of the sovereign were taken from all civilizations to which the Mediterranean peoples had been attuned in the past. For example, the king appeared in a royal robe that integrated in its design Byzantine, Western, and Muslim motifs of leadership, and he was attended by two bodyguards, one composed of European knights, the other of African Negroes. French remained the language of the court, but Greek, Latin, and Arabic were used freely in oral and written communications. Norman laws, amplified by borrowings from various legal systems, especially the Byzantine, were binding on Arabs, Greeks, and Lombards, but they were applied ". . . without prejudice to the habits, customs, and laws of the peoples sub-

---

long-range influences that Islam has exerted on Spanish attitudes toward government. Franco's twentieth century dictatorship is thus customarily reviewed as a mere variety of European fascism, whereas it shows, in actuality, many of the hallmarks of a typical Islamic caliphate.

ject to our authority, each in its own sphere. . . ."[14] A *curia regis* of councillors was the principal advisory body, but Saracen emirs and Byzantine logothetes worked side by side with Norman justiciars, while local subordinates, representing the various ethnic groups, were permitted to retain their old Greek, Lombard, and Arab titles. Indeed, in the field of administration the merger of civilizations was so complete that scholars today are not certain whether so fundamental a department of the Sicilian state as that of finance was modelled upon the *diwan* of the caliphs, the *fiscus* of the Roman emperors, or the exchequer of the Anglo-Norman kings.[15]

The profile of the centralized, secular, multinational state that the Normans had delineated so boldly became even more distinct when southern Italy was administered by Frederick II of Hohenstauffen, heir of the Norman kings through his mother. Renowned for his experimental approach to knowledge and international politics, yet unsuccessful in his attempts to reorganize the Holy Roman Empire, the German emperor transferred his attention to this royal patrimony, determined to realize here the image of a politically effective and progressive society that he had come to entertain as a result of insights variously gathered.

As a workshop for the testing of new administrative principles and policies, Sicily-Apulia projected clearly the personality of its royal governor. Since Frederick loved wealth and power, his kingdom was to become a thriving, independent, political community which would take dictation from no authority except its sovereign. In the imperial vision this state was to be an end in itself. Since Frederick aspired to encompass the wisdom of all ages and cultures, Sicily was to become the center of all learning. And just as Frederick's mind had been moulded by influences from classical and Christian, Roman and Byzantine, Islamic and Indian sources, so was the government of his state to be shaped to perfection by methods that had proved their superiority in mankind's collected experiences of the art of government. The records of the Greek tyrannies in Sicily, the ancient Oriental empires, the Roman and Byzantine principates, the Muslim caliphates, and the Catholic papacy were thus explored assiduously by a cosmopolitan elite of scholars under Frederick's direction until they yielded the ideas, symbols, and institutions best suited to buttress the imperial conception

[14] Preamble of the Assizes of Ariano, A.D. 1140, see *The Cambridge Medieval History*, Vol. v, p. 204.

[15] Charles H. Haskins, *Studies in the History of Medieval Science*, 1927, 2d ed., Cambridge, Mass., pp. 155-156.

of a secular despotism. This borrowing process had some ironic implications. For the new secular state incorporated many constitutional aspects of the Byzantine theocracy which had been the implacable enemy of the Normans, and of the Roman Church, whose representatives opposed Frederick II with relentless enmity throughout his life. Indeed, the systems of reference that these two ecclesiastical establishments had evolved in order to capture and retain the loyalties of their multinational flocks provided, paradoxically, the protective framework within which ambitious policies of secularization were being carried out in southern Italy.

The ultimate aim of Frederick's policies was the same as that which the Normans had pursued, namely, the maintenance of unlimited sovereignty. Although the emperor found it politically advisable to govern Sicily as a nominally Christian state, he held to the theory that his kingdom was the political equal even of the Catholic Church, and that its interests should be reflected in its laws.[16] This commitment to law as the principal guardian of sovereignty reveals the impact that Western European, especially Roman, traditions had upon the emperor's thinking. But the purposes that law was designed to serve and the administrative methods by which it was applied were borrowed from the East. The codes that Frederick's lawyers composed after thoroughly exploring numerous jurisprudential systems were thus as unmindful of the liberties of citizens as was their imperial sponsor. However, they accomplished the single purpose for which they had been drafted: the establishment of southern Italy as a secular, imperial law-state.

The experiment in state-making in which the Normans and the Hohenstauffen engaged reflected the medieval spirit in its reliance upon theocratic principles as well as in its evocation of the universalist norms that had distinguished life in the Mediterranean region for many centuries. It projected a new order of political organization, however, in its espousal of secularism and political independence. By cultivating a close relationship between learning and statesmanship[17] the two dynasties contrived an artful, though in many instances spurious, alliance between the residual values found in international history and the emergent values discerned in the ascending age. And in the context of this synthesis they succeeded in realizing the political principle of territorial sovereignty without impairing the vast transterritorial con-

[16] See Ernst Kantorowicz, *Frederick the Second, 1194-1250*, New York, 1931, pp. 222-245.

[17] Similar relationships had been cultivated in earlier periods of Mediterranean history by, e.g., the Roman lawyers and the Rhodian merchants.

nections with other cultures from which the Sicilian society had developed originally.

The state of southern Italy was less successful in reconciling Eastern and Western concepts of government. Indeed, its failure to resolve the contradiction between Oriental forms of administration on the one hand and Occidental ideas of law on the other, may well account for the ephemeral existence of each of the two successive regimes. It is hardly likely that men less imperious than the Norman and Hohenstauffen monarchs could have built this particular state. But the excessive emphasis placed upon despotism, as it had shown itself in the Eastern empires, and the utter disregard of constitutionalism, as it had manifested itself in the traditions of Greece, Rome, and medieval Western Europe, had the effect, eventually, of demoralizing the royal establishment and paralysing the life force of the state that these two talented European dynasties had generated with such singular foresight and acumen.

The Sicilian state is certainly far removed from the political ideals and experiences with which the majority of Western Europeans like to associate themselves today. But the records of its evolution and existence merit continuous study not only because they constitute the first chapter in the international history of the sovereign secular law state, but also, and perhaps principally, because they present the first systematic endeavor on the part of the West to relate the image of the sovereign state to the realities of a local culture. The twentieth century has brought forth many designs of this kind, as the constitutional histories of such new states as Ghana, Libya, the Sudan, and Jordan indicate. But it remains to be seen whether the accomplishments of the modern experts in state-making will equal that registered by the Normans.

B. THE MODERN STATE IN ITS WESTERN EUROPEAN SETTING

The Western Europeans north of the Alps and the Pyrenees had developed their civilization far from the Mediterranean scene of intense intercultural relations. In the crucial period of their coalescence into separate local sovereignties they were therefore hardly aware of the non-Western cultures that had contributed so markedly to the shaping of the Sicilian state. Culturally isolated and introspective, they found their new identities as politically independent communities by relying exclusively upon European traditions. And since each group of European peoples had brought forth its own variant of generally current European themes, each new state was built upon locally prevalent customs and institutions. The contrast with Mediterranean Europe was therefore great. For Sicily became a state precisely because it had not been either wholly Lombard, Norman, Greek, or Arab,[18] while England, France, and Denmark—to name only three of the new constellations—became states because their inhabitants had come to be English, French, and Danish.[19]

However, all European states, whether they enclosed cosmopolitan or national communities, and whether they developed in the north or in the south, were constituted in accordance with legal principles that were essentially analogous wherever they were being applied. For not only had these basic principles been deduced from the great integral law systems that had conditioned European life before the rise of the modern state, but they were being revised, during the rise of the modern state, by transnational law schools whose authority was accepted throughout the European continent. These circumstances explain why most early states of the thirteenth and fourteenth centuries were the work of law-minded kings and citizens, and why their legislative histories show so many concordant themes. St. Louis, Simon Montfort, Edward I, Philip August, and Frederick II were entirely different characters, pursuing different political interests, but each thought of himself as a lawgiver and reformer, and all approached their administrative tasks in much the same way. The cortes, states-general, diets, and parliaments that arose between the twelfth and fourteenth centuries reflected different local customs, it is true, but all were representative assemblies, devised to comply with patterns of constitutionalism that antedated their existence and had always distinguished the political system of Europe from that of other societies. Further parallels present themselves when one surveys the relationship between the principle of despotic rule on the one hand and that of representative government on the other. For the interplay between these contradictory conceptions, which had been a basic theme in the histories of the ancient and medieval European commonwealths, continued to characterize political life in each of the modern European states. Indeed, it

[18] This statement must be qualified by the observation that Sicily became "Sicilian" in the last decades of Hohenstauffen rule; for not only did the influence of the Arabs decline but the government went out of its way to cultivate the language and literature of the "native" Sicilians.

[19] The most notable exception is Switzerland which was multinational and multilingual from the beginning of its statehood.

provides the indispensable context for an understanding of the rise and functioning of the modern Western state.

Local kings and representative assemblies coexisted in Europe's pluralistic society. But the great revolt against the governing international establishments of this society occurred in most instances when autocratic monarchs repudiated all rival authorities, whether secular or religious, in order to assert the absolute independence and secular character of their states. During the sixteenth and seventeenth centuries Europe was thus being transformed into a galaxy of separate sovereignties, and its new identity was recognized officially in the multinational treaties of Westphalia (1648), which stipulated that states, not governments, were members of the society of nations; that states were secular political organisms; and that all states were sovereign, independent, and equal.

The propositions here recorded retained validity in international relations, but the internal structure of the Western state was modified in subsequent centuries as absolutism gave way to constitutionalism. This development manifested itself at different times and in different ways in the various European nations, but it stemmed everywhere from the realization that the state was an expression of the nation, rather than an extension of the ruler's personality and interests, and that the concept of the nation was meaningless unless it was understood as signifying a conglomeration of individual human beings who had political rights and obligations.

The conclusion that the individual was the primary carrier of the idea of the modern state was a corollary of complex intellectual movements that had been confined to the European and American scenes. The early intellectual revolt against the authority of traditional beliefs had emphasized the creative and critical mind of the individual as the ultimate determinant of all myth and reality. And the pattern thus set was followed in subsequent centuries in all European countries. For the primary reference of the great religious reform movements was the conscience of the individual; the focus of the scientific and industrial revolutions was the individual genius and the individual's ability to think in secular terms; and the center of the social revolution was the new urbanized, commerce-minded middle class which advertised, by its very existence, the merits of individual initiative.

The investigation and validation of the individual's claim to political representation proceeded in the context of these new realities. But the new realities were in essence modern responses to truths to which many earlier generations of Europeans had also attached paramount importance, as preceding chapters have shown. It is not surprising to find therefore that these residual values were reactivated during the eighteenth and nineteenth centuries,[20] when the nations of Western Europe and North America identified the modern democratic state in terms of the supremacy of law and the inalienable rights of man. And a similar logic in the history of the West explains why the "new" theories and practices of constitutionalism gave rise to many "new" forms of federalism. For political experience as accumulated in this civilization had registered the fact that a system of objectively defined norms was persuasive extraterritorially, and that it could, therefore, accommodate voluntary political unions of separate areas or groups of peoples.

The modern democratic state as it had been developed by the Atlantic nations was thus in effect an archetypal organization. Not only could it be transplanted into other regions, but it could be expanded, conceptually and practically, to world dimensions. The twentieth century society of nations bears the unmistakable imprint of both manifestations.

C. THE MODERN EUROPEAN STATE AND NON-WESTERN SOCIETIES

The vocabulary of political terms that is at present in use throughout the world was composed during the histories of the Western European and North American nations. Words such as self-determination, self-government, democracy, independence, and nationalism acquired the meanings they convey today only slowly in that intricate process of defining the particular ideals and historical experiences that had produced the concept of the modern European state. Most of the new states that have arisen in the last decades in Asia and Africa have been formed in the image of this Western model.[21] Some nations voluntarily selected this model when they had occasion to revise their political identities. Others were guided in their choice either by the colonial administrations of the Western powers whose dependents they had been in the preceding century, or by the United Nations after this organization had assumed responsibility for the future of the non-self-governing territories in the world. Some may have responded to the Occi-

---

[20] The process of redefining the realm of politics had begun much earlier in Switzerland, the United Provinces, and England.

[21] The obvious exceptions are the communist states. However, even they have adopted the political vocabulary of the Western democracies.

dental system because they were convinced of the intrinsic merits of constitutionalism, others because they associated it with material wealth and power. But all agreed in regarding the Western state as the supreme expression of nationalism and independence.

This positive response to the political terminology of the West led to a widespread assumption that the peoples in the world were in genuine accord upon the fundamental goals of their political existence. But behind the façade of a broad agreement on words and forms, disagreements on content and substance have become apparent. For words and forms change their meanings, it has been recognized, when they are used in cultural and political contexts for which they had not been originally intended. Terms like "self-government," "human rights," and "democracy," have been implemented differently in the various regions of Western Europe and America,[22] it is true; but since they originated in a shared preference for legal abstractions and denoted shared traditions of constitutionalism, they have continued to carry the same basic meanings to the citizens of all Occidental democracies. The histories of the non-Western societies into which these concepts have been recently transplanted, have never favored the emergence either of a public sentiment for individual rights and self-government, or of general human aptitudes for abstract legal thought. The new symbolism of written constitutions and declarations of rights is thus hardly in accord with native political traditions, and this incongruity is especially great in the nonliterate civilizations.

The most elusive words in the political dictionary of the West are "independence" and "nationalism." These concepts are the least susceptible to objective abstraction and have never been defined unequivocally. Nor can any general rule be deduced from the histories of the Occidental states as to the precise circumstances in which national independence should be within the reach of a people. However, the records of these nations, including those that were independent before they became democratic in the modern sense of that term, suggest that the inhabitants of each country had a strong and identifiable will to constitute an independent nation,[23] and that this will was closely related to their interest in securing individual liberties. In other words, independence and nationalism on the one hand, and self-government and democracy on the other, had become kindred or cognate concepts in

[22] It should be noted that this discussion is confined to the Western democracies, since they are the object of emulation in the non-Western societies.

[23] But see E. H. Carr, *Nationalism and After*, London, 1945, on the relationship between democracy and integral nationalism.

an early phase of the history of the modern democratic state. And it was in this combination that they were projected into the non-Western regions of the world.[24] For not only was it taken for granted in Western as well as non-Western circles that the desire for independence is innate in nations and therefore unassailable on economic, historical, or other grounds, but it was also widely assumed that the attainment of independence would be tantamount to the establishment of democracy. Indeed, in the absence of any objective, minimal requirements—such as the demonstrable capacity to maintain the prospective state as a politically stable and economically viable community—the acceptance of democratic institutions was often viewed as the only necessary prerequisite to independence. Independence was thus usually installed by means of declaratory legal documents. An exception to this has occurred in certain formerly colonial areas in which the administrative authorities could allow for a gradual evolution, first to self-government and then to independence, and provide for a careful adjustment of modern democratic institutions to native traditions.

The cultural realities of the non-Western regions did not warrant the assumption that words would continue to carry the meanings with which they had been associated in the history of the West. Most of the nonliterate and literate civilizations of Asia and Africa accepted the concept of the political community in one form or another, but they did not recognize the individual as the carrier of inalienable political rights. Modern aspirations toward statehood have therefore been fastened not to the ideals of constitutionalism, but to those of independence and nationalism, which refer to the interests of groups of individuals rather than individuals. And this difference in emphasis has not been annulled by the habit—logically indefensible—of including the community's interest in national self-determination and independence in the category of the individual's inalienable rights. On the contrary, it was bound to become more marked as the non-Western societies became engulfed in nationalism.

Some of the complexities implicit in the process of transplanting the modern Western state into non-Western areas are illustrated by the creation of the independent state of Libya. The charter that proclaimed the federation of Fezzan, Tripolitania, and Cyrenaica in the form of a representative, democratic, constitutional monarchy was drawn up with infinite care. Modelled on the constitutions of seventeen different

---

[24] Cf. the impact of these concepts upon the reorganization of Eastern Europe in the last half of the nineteenth and early part of the twentieth centuries.

nations, among which that of the United States was considered most suggestive,[25] it represents in effect the quintessence of wisdom and experience that literate peoples in the Occidental world have collected in the course of their existence as modern states. However, it is doubtful whether this constitution can supersede or integrate the traditional political norms by which various groups of the population have lived for centuries and thus sustain Libya's existence in the society of nations as an independent democratic state. For its draftsmen had no compelling evidence before them that the nonliterate, largely nomadic inhabitants of these desert regions really wanted to coalesce in this, or any other, type of state. Indeed, to many of the experts complete independence seems to have been only a last resort, an expedient, an experiment to which they could subscribe without qualms[26] presumably because it conformed to the generally accepted ideal form of political organization.

The methodology of state-making employed in this case was thus strikingly different from that applied to Sicily. The twelfth century Norman despots had not been morally committed to one particular civilization and were unconvinced of the absolute superiority of one system of government. In their efforts to create institutions that would secure Sicily's independence and stability, they had been free, therefore, to borrow from the records of any society, literate or nonliterate, Oriental or Occidental, that they deemed pertinent to their task. The twentieth century experts in constitutionalism, on the other hand, were committed, if not by individual choice at least by world opinion, to uphold the ideal of the democratic state. In the measure of their commitment to this image they were closed not only to any wisdom that might be found in non-Western systems, but also to the cultural and geographic realities of Libya itself.

D. European Patterns of Diplomacy

A. THE PLACE OF VENICE IN INTERNATIONAL RELATIONS

The history of modern diplomacy parallels the history of the modern state of which it is an integral part. Since the prototype of the modern Western state was developed in Italy, where the decay of the unifying medieval structure became apparent earlier than elsewhere, it was also in Italy that the new forms of conducting relations between states were first elaborated and tested. Among these, none was destined to achieve

---

[25] See Henry Serrano Villard, *Libya, The New Arab Kingdom of North Africa,* Ithaca, N.Y., 1956, for an account of the evolution of this state.

[26] Villard, p. 33.

greater importance in subsequent centuries than that of diplomacy.

The Italian mode of conducting diplomacy, which set the pattern for all other Western European states, originated in Venice. A proper understanding of the place that diplomacy has come to occupy in the modern European states system requires, therefore, a preliminary inquiry into the diplomatic theories and practices of the Venetians. Such an inquiry must begin with the statement of two rather paradoxical facts. At the peak of its diplomatic success Venice was neither a typical Italian city-state, i.e., small and dependent upon alliances with other Italian states, nor a component part of the Western European community. Venice, it is true, was Italian and Catholic, but these geographic and religious affiliations were not the primary determinants of its destiny. An examination of Venetian history shows, on the contrary, that the state was for centuries a great power, independent, for the most part, of the pattern of alignments that had imposed itself upon all other Italian states, and that its history was tightly linked with the fortunes and misfortunes of the Eastern Christian Empire rather than with those of the West.

For Venice, it must be noted, began its meteoric rise as a satellite of Byzantium and thus learnt about diplomacy under conditions of tutelage similar to those that had attended the early development of Kievan Russia. In terms of history one can maintain, therefore, that the diplomatic systems of modern Russia and of the contemporary Western world are variations on the same original theme. In terms of current international politics, however, one finds between the Russian and the Western techniques of diplomacy few if any such similarities as would reveal their common origin. Indeed, the view is widespread today that all the existing international tensions in the world are exacerbated by the fact that diplomacy occupies a different place in the political thinking on the one hand of the Russians and on the other of the Western Europeans and Americans.

Unless one is ready to explain the difference solely in terms of the influence that Marxist-Leninist theories have exercised upon modern Russia, it is imperative to follow the transformations that the Byzantine motif underwent in each of the two societies. This will reveal another measure of divergence between the rival diplomatic systems. For the transformations of the Byzantine pattern were less marked in Russian than in Venetian diplomacy. Whereas the former continued to develop in the relatively homogeneous context of Russian national history from Kievan to Soviet days, the latter was denaturalized and internationalized, as it were, in a process of gradual diffusion first over Italy and subsequently throughout Western Europe. The evolution of modern Western diplomacy is thus a particularly complex story, and this story begins with the diplomatic history of Venice.

The Venetian state was founded when Italy belonged to Byzantium, and, though a Catholic community, it remained in the political and cultural orbit of the orthodox Empire after the rest of the peninsula had been reorganized by conquering Germanic nations. The small island republic in the northern Adriatic thus existed midway between the Western and Eastern Christian empires. It was able to overcome the precariousness of its military and economic situation, transcend its religious and territorial affiliations, and profit from the ambivalence of its geographic and historical origins by developing a close relationship to the sea. The Venetians built a fleet and became a mobile adventurous nation, making contact with ports and peoples throughout the Mediterranean. However, within the vast radius of the commercial connections that linked this small nation with distant countries and civilizations, Venice was tied to Byzantium in a very special way.

Not only did Byzantine influences pervade the Venetian way of life, but it was the Byzantine protectorate that permitted Venice to engage in its far-flung naval and economic operations. The Eastern Empire was interested in the city both because its harbor was the most important in Italy and had to be controlled if the imperial Mediterranean trading system was to function smoothly, and because the Venetian fleet was an indispensable auxiliary of the Byzantine navy. These interests were accentuated, furthermore, after the empire lost to the Muslims its provinces in Asia Minor. Up to that period—in fact up to the beginning of the eighth century—Syrians, Egyptians, Greeks, and Jews had functioned as the chief Byzantine agents in the East-West trade. But when the momentous shift of power in the eastern Mediterranean area made necessary a choice of new middlemen, Venice was already there to fill the vacancy. The city-state, shrewdly utilizing its new opportunities, succeeded in greatly advancing the cause of its independence.

The autonomy of Venice had been recognized since 742, yet the city had remained under Byzantine control, occupying a position analogous, perhaps, to that of a British dominion in the first quarter of the twentieth century.[27] This relationship with the Eastern Empire was

[27] A. R. Lewis, *Naval Power and Trade in the Mediterranean*: A.D. *500-1100*, Princeton, 1950, p. 119.

deliberately affirmed by the Venetians when they helped to thwart the attempts of the Western Empire to win control over all of northern Italy and break the Byzantine monopoly of the eastern trade. But even while the Venetians were continuing to enjoy the trading privileges that Constantinople granted to those who acknowledged its overlordship, they were managing to circumvent the Byzantine trading system whenever their own interests would be served by such a course of action. Moreover, since the Venetian statesmen were little affected by religious considerations when called upon to serve the national interest,[28] they succeeded also in exploiting the rivalries that rent the Christian and the Muslim realms, and extracted favorable trading terms alike from Christian and Muslim sovereigns.[29] After the ninth century we thus find the Venetians circulating freely between the ports of the three great theocracies, penetrating lands beyond the Mediterranean shores, and seeking commercial profits wherever they were offered.

The policies that yielded these advantages were formulated in the interests of the national cause of Venice, but had momentous effects, nevertheless, on the entire course of international relations in the Mediterranean region. For at a time when the unity of the Mediterranean world had given way to the interplay of competitive and expansive forces,[30] and long before the crusades were to establish official lines of communication with the Orient, the Venetians were there acting as middlemen between rival cultures and feuding governments, and finding channels of trade with the East through which new goods and ideas were being steadily relayed to the farthest western limits.[31]

[28] Henri Pirenne, *Medieval Cities; their Origins and the Revival of Trade*, Princeton, 1939, p. 86 says that the Venetian religion was a religion of businessmen. But see W. Carew Hazlitt, *The Venetian Republic; its rise, its growth and its fall*, A.D. *409-1797*, two vols., London, 1915, Vol. II, pp. 4-5 to the effect that Venice showed a strongly Catholic instinct, at least after the fifteenth century.

[29] See Pirenne, p. 86. Also François L. Ganshof, *Le Moyen Age* in Pierre Renouvin, *Histoire des Relations Internationales*, Paris, 1953, pp. 132ff. for illustrative evidence.

[30] Pirenne, pp. 24ff., has advanced the thesis that "the familiar and almost 'family' sea which once united all the parts of this (Mediterranean) commonwealth was to become a barrier between them," when it was transformed into a Muslim lake. From then onward, the author suggests, the tie that was still binding the Byzantine Empire to the German Kingdoms of the West was broken. In taking issue with this thesis, Lewis, pp. 86, 97ff., charges that Pirenne picked the wrong villain. Not the Arabs but the Byzantines had destroyed the ancient unity of the Mediterranean, because they had engaged in a war to the death with the Umayyads between 715-752. It was Byzantium's economic blockade, Lewis claims, which brought ruin to many western provinces and eventually shattered the unity of the Mediterranean area.

[31] Sir Ernest Barker, "The Crusades," in *Encyclopaedia Britannica*, Vol. VI, pp. 771ff. *The Cambridge Medieval History*, Vol. V, pp. 330ff. Ganshof, pp. 160ff.

By the end of the eleventh century the Italian fleets had triumphed over the sea powers of both Islam and Byzantium.[32] Venice was expanding rapidly and the Eastern Christian Empire was retreating on its borders. A new phase had opened in the complex relationship between the imperial monarchy and its former satellite, and this had been announced in the Golden Bull of 1082. Under the terms of this contract with the Second Rome Venice promised to relieve the Norman pressure on Constantinople in return for a virtual monopoly on Byzantine commerce.[33] The Venetian merchants would henceforth have the right to buy and sell throughout the Empire without being subject to the jurisdiction of the Byzantine customs officials; they would occupy spacious quarters in the capital and they would have access to three landing spaces where their vessels would load and unload freely. As a result of these arrangements Venice ruled the trade route to the Holy Land without rival, and, after participating in the first three crusades, gained commercial supremacy in the Levant.

The time had now come, in the opinion of the Venetian government, to contest the Eastern Empire openly, despoil it of its wealth, and succeed to its position in the world. The fourth crusade was organized by the Venetians for the consummation of these purposes, and when the Empire was partitioned, Venice claimed and received "a half and a quarter of the Roman Empire": the Cyclades, the Sporades, the islands and eastern shores of the Adriatic, the shores of the Propontis and the Euxine, and the littoral of Thessaly. After the purchase of Crete Venice was a naval empire, sovereign over an area that included vast water spaces in the Mediterranean, the Adriatic, the Sea of Marmora, and the Black Sea, and in full command of the trade routes that linked the Black Sea region and Asia Minor with Western Europe.

The Venetians solidified their newly gained position in the Near East by concluding special agreements with several local governments. Under the terms of the so-called capitulations of the thirteenth century, Venetian residents in Egypt were permitted a vast measure of personal freedom; their property was regarded as inviolate, and all complaints against them, whether preferred by Christians or by Muslims, had to be filed, not in Egyptian courts, but in the courts of the Venetian consul. At the beginning of the fifteenth century the influence of the republic in this region was extended further when Egypt permitted the establishment of a Venetian consulate in Jerusalem and this agency

[32] Lewis, pp. 226ff.
[33] The ports of Cyprus and Crete were excluded from this grant.

then was empowered to assume jurisdiction over all Western European pilgrims to the Holy Land.[34] Such legal arrangements are important not only because they illustrate the extent of Venetian influence and the skill of Venetian diplomacy, but also because in the general history of intercultural contacts, they show that Christians and Muslims could ignore their ideological differences to accommodate their commercial and political interests.

The intercontinental routes and sea lanes that were established and policed by the Venetians in order to secure their various outposts carried a continuous stream of travellers from the Adriatic republic. These men were interested in knowledge, commerce, and adventure, and they succeeded in penetrating many lands that lay beyond the known periphery of the Empire's maritime domain. Foremost among these were the Polo brothers, who crossed the Pamirs and traversed regions that were later closed to travellers from the West and remained so until the nineteenth century brought a renewal of exploratory activities in this area of the world. Marco Polo was the first to trace a route across the whole latitude of Asia, and the first to tell of China, Tibet, Burma, Japan, and India. We also owe to him the first distinct account of Abyssinia. A direct bridge was established between the Far East and the Western European nations by these and other means, and Venice held this bridge, at times precariously it is true, even after the Mongolian Empire had disintegrated and the Turks had interposed a barrier between the societies of the Orient and the Occident.[35]

Since Venice had thus come to occupy a key position in world affairs, it was generally recognized by its contemporaries as a great power. The Venetians themselves, however, were never content with their political fortunes. To them security meant absolute supremacy in all the areas that had any bearing on the pursuit of their commercial activities. Several wars waged in this interest against Genoa ended in 1380 with the complete rout of the Genoese fleet and elimination of this competitor from the Mediterranean scene. A series of aggressive maneuvers on the Italian mainland, furthermore, led to the creation of a land empire designed to hedge the approaches to the city and as-

[34] Herbert J. Liebesny, "The Development of Western Judicial Privileges" in *Law in the Middle East*, Majid Khadduri and Herbert J. Liebesny, eds., Washington, 1955, Vol. I, pp. 312ff.

In later centuries, when European powers gained ascendancy in the East, the capitulary system was imposed on many weakened native governments.

[35] Cf. Ganshof, p. 241, to the effect that Turkish control over trade with Asia would have been complete had it not been for Venice.

sure its control over the land routes to and from northern Europe. These two great victories, however, marked the zenith of the Venetian destiny. The subsequent history of the remarkable state was one of a gradual but steady decline.

The retrogression of the commercial empire of Venice was precipitated by three major developments. The unbridled passion for power and supremacy that characterized the Venetian policies of the fourteenth century had been a challenge to which the other rising states in Italy and Western Europe had responded with belligerence. Hence a league for the dismemberment of Venice was formed in Cambrai in 1508 and this proved eventually effective in containing Venetian expansion. The Turks in the East, furthermore, had become increasingly resentful of the preferred position occupied by the republic in what they regarded as their exclusive sphere of influence. Venice was willing to pay tribute for its trading rights in the Turkish area, but the new masters of Constantinople were unprepared to continue the commercial privileges that their predecessors had granted the Venetians for so many centuries. Venice was forced, several times in the fifteenth century, to give battle to this new eastern power at a steadily mounting cost to its own strength.[36] However, the principal event in the spelling of the doom of Venetian greatness occurred when navigators from another West European land (Diaz in 1488, Vasco da Gama in 1497) discovered a new way to the Indies around the Cape of Good Hope. Although the Venetians had been strangely unprepared for these revolutionary maritime developments, they realized with striking lucidity, when they heard of Diaz' exploit, that the world trade route had passed from the Mediterranean to the Atlantic Ocean, and that they would henceforth be excluded from its course.[37] The great age of the Venetian Empire ended, therefore, when that of the modern European states system began. Yet in this new order Venice continued to exist as an independent sovereign European state, never recognizing any secular Western authority within its boundaries save its own,[38] until its statehood was extinguished in 1797 by the French.

As one reflects upon the long and chequered history of this ancient state one finds that Venice holds a curious place in international his-

[36] The Turkish wars continued until 1716.

[37] On the organization of Venetian business and shipping enterprises and the interest of the state in navigation, see F. C. Lane, "Family Partnerships and Joint Ventures in the Venetian Republic" in *Journal of Economic History*, 1944, IV, pp. 178-196; also *Andrea Barbarigo, Merchant of Venice*, 1944, and *Venetian Ships and Shipbuilders of the Renaissance*, 1934.

[38] Bryce, p. 191.

tory. For although it pursued its course to power and distinction outside the framework of the medieval Western commonwealth and in
close alignment with the Eastern Christian empire, it established a pattern of political behavior that all Western governments, great and
small, were to emulate studiously when the pursuit of national interests
began to take precedence over other political values. The new nationalistic style of conducting international relations thus projected
upon Western Europe by the westernmost Byzantine dominion revolved around the theory and practice of diplomacy.

B. VENETIAN DIPLOMACY

The cumulative record of the policies that the Venetians charted in
the course of one millennium in their efforts to secure, first independence, then supremacy, and ultimately survival as a sovereign state,
shows that the Venetian success was due primarily to the continuous
and methodical study of foreign affairs. This study was directed by the
Venetian oligarchy at home, but it was made possible by a host of
well-trained diplomats who were sent to all parts of the world in order
to represent the interests of the state abroad and to collect information
that would serve the purposes of the government. The steady cultivation of these approaches to foreign affairs led to the establishment of
the first systematized diplomatic service known in history.

We know from contemporary sources that Venetian statesmanship
was the object of unqualified admiration among all political observers,
whether friendly or hostile to the island state. Generally known as "the
school and touchstone of ambassadors,"[39] or as the "promised land
of the ambassadors,"[40] Venice struck the envoy of Louis XI, King of
France in the fifteenth century, as "the most triumphant city," as he
phrased it, "that I have ever seen; the city that bestows the greatest
honour on ambassadors and strangers; the city that is most wonderfully
governed. . . ."[41] Venetian diplomacy still retained its high prestige in
the middle of the sixteenth century, when Venetian power was being
gradually eclipsed by the rising monarchies of continental Europe. In
a decree of the Emperor Charles V we read that the high title of ambassador was applicable only to the representatives of crowned heads
and of the republic of Venice.[42] Even much later, in the eighteenth

[39] David J. Hill, *A History of European Diplomacy*, London, 1921, Vol. I, pp.
296, 359.
[40] M. de Maulde-La-Clavière, *Histoire de Louis XII*, Deuxième Partie, *La Diplomatie au temps de Machiavel*, 3 vols., Paris, 1893, Vol. II, p. 270.
[41] *The Cambridge Modern History*, Vol. I, p. 282.
[42] Hill, Vol. I, p. 359, n.1.

century, when the demise of the state was imminent, Venetian diplomats were still reputed to be the best informed men in any capital; a traveller was admonished to court their company if he was truly interested in keeping abreast of the news.[43]

The diplomatic genius of the Venetians developed in response to complex factors. It should be observed, first, that diplomacy is not a socially autonomous institution but an outgrowth of the society in which it is practiced. As such, it is bound to reflect and incorporate the political conventions by which the given state exists. Venice had borrowed many fundamental political ideas from Byzantium, and Venetian diplomacy was therefore cast, at the beginning, in essentially Byzantine moulds. But an examination of the mature Venetian system shows that it was no mere replica of the Byzantine precedent[44] but a unique political organism. In seeking the measure of Venetian originality in this field one must bear in mind that the Venetians were never "barbarians" for whom Constantinople was the only place of inspiration, even though they began their political existence as satellites of the Eastern Empire. As a nation of travellers and seafarers they always had access to many sources of political wisdom beyond the radius of Byzantine interest and experience. As a people who had made trade their calling they were challenged by a great variety of encounters with foreign nations to elaborate their own techniques of observation and bargaining, and as a Catholic Italian city-state they had absorbed political traditions peculiar to the Western Christian Empire and absent in the East. All of these factors influenced the Venetian approach to foreign relations. But the ultimate integration of these factors in the form of a system was brought about by deliberate planning on the part of the Venetians themselves. Indeed, nothing is more striking in the history of Venetian diplomacy than the talent displayed by this people in finding, utilizing, and organizing the most varied kinds of intelligence in the interests of their national cause. This talent manifested itself first in the realm of commerce and finance.

As a community of merchants whose livelihood depended on the careful execution of bold programs of action, the Venetians were called upon daily to take exact stock of their environment, however new and complex it might be; to report the facts as they were found; to appraise their opportunities objectively, and to calculate realistically all risks.

[43] Lord Chesterfield's advice to his son, see *ibid.*, p. 297.

[44] See Harold Nicolson, *Diplomacy*, p. 44 and *Evolution of Diplomatic Method*, p. 27, for a contrary view.

In the course of their financial and commercial activities they revolutionized the existing methods of calculations and classification. At a time when the northern towns, including those of the Hanse, continued to rely on the simple commercial balance sheet for the measuring and recording of their transactions, Venice became the birthplace of statistical science.[45]

The spirit of objectivity that was generated in the Venetians by the cultivation of their commercial and financial arts and abilities was bound to pervade their attitude toward foreign lands and peoples. It is probably no coincidence, therefore, that it was a Venetian who showed the Europeans how to observe and write about alien realms and folk. Men like St. Louis and Joinville, the Christian missionaries and the papal diplomats, had journeyed much in distant regions, but had actually seen little, since they had not been able to disengage themselves from the moorings left behind. Marco Polo, the Venetian, on the other hand, could see and understand the Orient on its own terms, for his intellect had been conditioned to perceive things as they were. It was this quality of mind that won him great renown at the cosmopolitan Mongolian court of Peking and prompted Kublai Khan to employ him on a series of difficult administrative missions.[46]

The Venetian character impressed contemporaries in other ways also. A Venetian was generally reputed to have more common sense at thirty than men elsewhere at fifty. He was considered to be more broadly educated and better mannered than the citizens of other countries.[47] And finally, no aspect of his character evoked more comments, both grudging and admiring, than the deep loyalty and devotion to the republic which seemed to envelop all of his other interests and attachments.

Now this feeling of patriotism and national solidarity, which was evident in Venetian politics as early as the seventh and eighth centuries, was, to say the least, exceptional in medieval Europe. To understand its incidence in Venice one must remember that the island state had grown in greatness by defying the historical links that tied it to its neighbors and by strengthening every bond apt to unite its citizenry into

---

[45] Jacob Burckhardt, *The Civilization of the Renaissance in Italy*, New York, 1954, p. 57.

[46] See Sir Percy Sykes, *The Quest for Cathay*, London, 1936, pp. 127-200 and Eileen Power, "The Opening of Land Routes to Cathay" in *Travels and Travellers of the Middle Ages*, A. P. Newton ed., New York, 1926. Journal of the Peking Oriental Society, Vol. III, No. 2, Peking, 1892, W. S. Ament, "Marco Polo in Cambaluc: a comparison of foreign and native accounts."

[47] de Maulde, Vol. I, pp. 335-344.

a cohesive political union. All Venetians, whatever their social status or profession, were conscious of their primary attachment to the state. This orientation was of great moment for the official conduct of foreign affairs, for it meant in fact that any citizen abroad was a natural agent of the republican government, ready at all times to place the interest of the state above all other considerations.[48]

This supposition is supported by much historical evidence. Venetian merchants, bankers, ship captains, and travellers were in the habit of collecting and forwarding information that might be useful to the state while they were engaged in private business.[49] Venetian physicians whose services were loaned to foreign sovereigns are known to have composed detailed reports about political and commercial matters that they had reason to believe would be of interest to the government at home.[50] Even Venetian cardinals were nationalists first and foremost; for we read that they could be persuaded easily to transmit confidential intelligence to which they had access in their capacity as servants of the Catholic Church at Rome.[51] And this propensity of every Venetian to act as a spy for his government, amply documented in the annals of Venetian diplomacy, was accentuated after the fifteenth century when most European courts had expunged morality from the conduct of political affairs and the Venetian government felt constrained, under the relentless pressure of many enemies, to make increasing use of bribery and subversion.[52]

However, the fame of the Venetian system of diplomacy does not rest either on the unofficial and *ad hoc* functions of Venetian citizens abroad, or on the *sub rosa* and often unsavory activities of secret agents and native informers, but rather on the official operations of a specially qualified diplomatic personnel and the systematic supervision of all foreign missions by the home government. The records of this integral system of conducting foreign relations are preserved in a unique set of documents described by one author as the richest and most varied storehouse of diplomatic history in the world.[53] Indeed, no single aspect or phase of Venetian diplomacy is as impressive as the very conception of these archives and the sum total of their contents. For the entire scheme here presented shows convincingly that the Venetians did in fact regard the national interest as a continuous cause, transcending the particular concerns of each generation, and that they

---

[48] Cf. Burckhardt, p. 55.
[49] de Maulde, Vol. I, p. 385. Also Ganshof, p. 267.
[50] de Maulde, Vol. I, p. 450.   [51] *ibid.*, Vol. II, p. 382.
[52] *ibid.*, Vol. I, pp. 449-455.   [53] Hill, Vol. I, p. 297.

viewed the conduct of foreign affairs as a pursuit susceptible of objective treatment.

The practice of collecting all information and registering all transactions and experiences of a nature to illumine international relations was initiated in the ninth, and continued to the end of the eighteenth century. The earliest collections of these documents are now lost, but the extant materials tell us much about the people who engaged in the business of diplomacy, the matters of state with which they dealt, and the methods of operation that they devised. These documents conjure up also the entire atmosphere in which foreign policy was carried on in the island empire. Thus we learn from them that in Venice, just as in Byzantium, diplomacy was staged in the manner of a grand spectacle, impressing all foreign envoys and their retinue with its dignity, munificence, and decorum. But these aspects of the diplomatic art, which were later emulated with great zeal by most European courts, had only peripheral value in Venetian eyes. They were considered important because they set the political scene, as it were, and enhanced the prestige of diplomacy as a public institution. The great diplomatic effort that secured the continuance of Venetian history for nearly a millennium was marked, on the other hand, by discipline, even by austerity.

The diplomatic service of the Venetian state was organized for the primary purpose of collecting and relaying the kind of information that the government would require in order to know what its contemporaries in other lands, remote and near, were doing or planning. As time went on and relations with the foreign courts became both more regular and more complex, however, the diplomats added to their functions all those other ways of representing their state abroad that are now customarily associated with the existence of foreign embassies. To the execution of these various tasks, diplomats were expected to bring a selfless devotion to the cause of the state. A succinct and eloquent reminder of the primacy of this orientation toward life is contained in the essay *De officio legati* which was written toward the end of the fifteenth century by the Venetian humanist, nobleman, and diplomat, Ermolao Barbaro. "The first duty of an ambassador," Barbaro says, "is exactly the same as that of any other servant of government, that is to do, say, advise and think whatever may best serve the preservation and aggrandizement of his own state."[54] The officers to

[54] See Garrett Mattingly, *Renaissance Diplomacy*, Boston, 1955, p. 109, for a discussion of Barbaro's thoughts. Mr. Mattingly's analysis of the issues implicit in Barbaro's writings stems from a view of diplomatic history that is somewhat at variance with the one expressed in the present study.

whom these tasks were entrusted were selected with the utmost care. Candidates not only had to be experienced, educated, gifted, and politically reliable, but also were expected to be keen observers, fluent linguists, and adroit statesmen.[55] It was taken for granted that they would follow orders, but it was assumed also that they would be capable of initiating courses of action when their instructions were not adequate in a given situation. If it was found that the stakes of diplomacy at a particular court were exceptionally high, two ambassadors would be dispatched in order to secure two different opinions for the guidance of the government at home.[56] The duration of a mission was limited to three or four months in the thirteenth century and to two years in the fifteenth. Permanent resident embassies were established toward the end of this historical period. During his prescribed period of service an envoy was not permitted a single day's absence from his post. His private life was governed by rigorous provisions. As a rule he had to dispense with the company of his wife, the supposition being that she would divert her husband's attention from his official duties, that she would be apt to gossip, and that she might thus divulge important secrets of state. A personal cook, on the other hand, had to be included in the envoy's entourage in order to guard against the ever-present danger of enemies at court trying to poison the ambassador. Fear that the envoy might be subverted or become expatriated prompted the government to impose other rules of a stringent nature. An agent was usually not sent to a country in which he held property or had other personal interests. He could not receive the smallest gift from the sovereign to whom he was accredited without consigning it to the signory pending his return home. Under the terms of a fifteenth century act a diplomat was also forbidden, under pain of severe punishment, to discuss public affairs with people who were not official members of the governmental circle in which he had been placed.

The sternness of these security regulations discouraged many candidates from seeking a diplomatic career. If it is remembered, furthermore, that the financial remuneration of an ambassador was negligible when compared with the rewards offered by other professions in the state, that all journeys were extremely perilous, and that living condition abroad did not include the comforts and amenities that were the birthright of a Venetian, it is easy to see why the government was hard pressed in later centuries to find qualified men willing to serve the state on diplomatic missions. In this calamity the government resorted to

[55] Hazlitt, Vol. II, pp. 499-507; Hill, Vol. I, p. 297.
[56] Hazlitt, Vol. II, p. 537.

rather coercive recruiting practices. Thus we find that only severe sickness was accepted as an excuse for delaying the assumption of a diplomatic post, and that penalties such as fines, deprivation of public office, and loss of emolument were imposed upon those who refused to embark upon a mission.

The fact that harsh measures of this kind were necessary in order to secure the due functioning of the diplomatic service may raise doubts in the minds of modern students of diplomacy as to whether the Venetian state was really supported by the unswerving loyalty of its citizenry. But if the methods of supervising diplomats are viewed in the contexts of the times and places in which they were applied, they will not be found to invalidate the generally held opinion that the Venetian government was more free from the effects of favoritism and jobbery, and more faithfully and intelligently served by its agents, than any other contemporary government.[57] In any case, it was the recognized worth of its actual performance that made the Venetian diplomatic service the model for all other diplomatic establishments in Europe, and the Venetian ambassadors the foremost teachers of the diplomatic arts.

After a Venetian ambassador had assumed his post, he was expected to remain in close touch with the home government. Indeed, the success of Venetian diplomacy was due in the final analysis to the methodical way in which the work of the foreign missions on the one hand, and of the senate and signory on the other, was coordinated from week to week throughout the centuries. The pattern of integration that emerges from the archives revolved around the use of certain standardized forms of reporting. The usual documents in the twelfth century were the following: commissions to the ambassadors setting forth the purpose of their mission, instructions prepared by the state, advices (*avvisi*) or newsletters designed to keep the envoy in touch with affairs at home, dispatches from the diplomatic agents to their government on the progress of the particular mission, and advices from the ambassadors transmitting[58] current news—a category that included significant rumors and scandals.

The final and most important documents of the series were the relations (*relazioni*). These were comprehensive accounts that each ambassador had to render to the college of the signory and the senate

[57] Hill, Vol. I, p. 297.

[58] Many reports were relayed in coded ciphers, the Venetians being masters of cryptography. See Ganshof, p. 277.

immediately upon his return to Venice. Each was drawn up carefully for the use of the executive and delivered in great style, for it was expected to convey a complete picture of the political, social, and economic constitution of the foreign country to which the envoy had been assigned.[59] Since Venetian agents were sent to practically all parts of the known world, they returned with a great variety of such individual pictures. Each of the relations was analysed on its own merits in order then to be indexed and filed in the archives, but all were viewed together as one great mirror reflecting the entire world at a given moment.

It was this systematized respect for reality in its most varied manifestations which enabled the Venetians to see the national interest in its total international setting as a continuous cause and to support this national cause by foreign policies relatively unencumbered with sentiment, bias, and illusion. This diplomatic method had no counterpart in western and northern Europe before the fifteenth century, and it is therefore impossible to evaluate it in terms of comparable institutions in that region of the world. A comparison with Byzantine and early Russian diplomacy, however, is not only possible but necessary if the differences between these historically closely associated systems are to be understood.

The process by means of which the principles of Byzantine diplomacy were received and elaborated in Russia has been analysed in an earlier chapter, in which the conclusion is drawn that a direct line of descent may indeed be traced from Byzantine to Muscovite diplomacy. The lineage between Byzantine and Venetian diplomacy cannot be traced so clearly. The Byzantine Empire and the Venetian Republic were both sovereign states and both developed diplomacy as the principal shield of national interest. But here the analogies seem to end, for the mainsprings of social and political life, which are what determine the character of such representative institutions as diplomacy, were quite dissimilar in these two societies.

Byzantinism implied the view that the life of the individual and the life of the state were two entirely different considerations requiring different normative systems. According to this theory moral and legal maxims were quite irrelevant to the actions of the state in the realm of international affairs, even though they might provide a pertinent measure of individual behavior within the state. This meant that By-

---

[59] de Maulde, Vol. III, p. 386; Hazlitt, Vol. II, p. 498. See also Willy Andreas, *Staatskunst und Diplomatie der Venezianer im Spiegel ihrer Gesandtenberichte,* Leipzig, 1943, pp. 73ff., 198ff., 211ff.

zantine diplomacy could have no generic relation either to law or to ethics. For being a derivative of the concept of the monolithic state, it was itself an essentially monolithic institution. This type of diplomacy proved highly flexible in operational terms, but it was bound to remain static in conceptual terms, as the preceding chapters have tried to show, since it could not be thought of outside of a fixed context.

Venice, on the other hand, was not a monolithic state either in inception or in operation. While long a Byzantine satellite, it had not accepted either the governmental or the religious system from which Byzantine diplomacy had received its meaning and direction. The Adriatic republic had an oligarchic and often despotic government, it is true, but its statehood had none of the mystical quasi-religious aspects that had been cultivated deliberately in the East. Its diplomacy was therefore neither designed to support the image of a universal, omnipotent, divine-right monarchy, nor meant to function in conjunction with religious proselytism. A comparison of the two societies and their diplomatic systems reveals another fundamental difference. Although Venice had endorsed the Byzantine proposition that individual action and state action occur on different planes and are hence subject to different maxims of human conduct, it did not implement this principle in the Byzantine way, for its citizenry, while intensely loyal to the state, was also fiercely individualist in thought and action. This meant that Venetian diplomacy was informed by two somewhat contradictory sets of principles. As a manifestation of the sovereign national state it incorporated the Byzantine notion that affairs of state were not subject to considerations of law or morality. But as an institution representing multiple individual interests and aspirations it was open to the ever-present influence of privately preferred values which presumably comprised legal and ethical concepts. The dualism implicit in this approach to diplomacy was not conducive to political weakness, as the history of Venice makes abundantly clear. On the contrary, the records lend support to the conclusion that it was the deliberate and skillful management of this ambivalence which marked the superiority of the Venetian method over the Byzantine. This becomes apparent when one views the Venetian deviation from the Byzantine pattern in terms of the influence that commerce exerted on the evolution of the two systems. Foreign trade in the Eastern Empire was highly developed, but it was at all times only one of many facets of the state and only one of many fields of human activity. Thus it afforded relatively few citizens the chance to unfold and promote those qualities of the mind that a person must possess if he is to take full advantage intellectually of a new situation. The low ceiling under which foreign trade was conducted in Byzantium also constrained the evolution of cosmopolitanism in the nation at large; for knowledge of other peoples and their customs was actually confined to that select elite in the political hierarchy who were charged officially with the task of implementing the foreign economic policies of the state. Byzantine methods of seeking commercial agreements with other countries were in these circumstances essentially the manifestation of the will of the state rather than of the sum total of individual inclinations.

In Venice, on the other hand, foreign trade was a national as well as a popular cause. It supplied the chief motive power for the state, but was also the principal stimulant of individual thought and enterprise; for it presented men with a continuous challenge to explore the not-yet-known. Apart from helping to free the human spirit from the bondage of conventional certainties, commerce as conducted in Venice was instrumental also in fostering the growth of cosmopolitanism within the entire nation, since it provided the Venetians with constant opportunities to meet and mingle with people from other lands and civilizations. The entire field of operations that the pursuit of trade and travel opened up for the Venetians thus became a proving ground for the development of diplomatic skills among the rank and file of the citizenry. Each foreign transaction required the individual participants to discover those terms of minimal accord with their opposite numbers abroad which would permit the actual consummation of the projected foreign transaction.

An important point that has to be made, then, by way of differentiating Venetian diplomacy from Byzantine is that Venice was a nation of cosmopolitan citizens to whom diplomacy was, as it were, a natural pursuit. A further aspect distinguishing the Venetian method is closely related to the first.

The substance of Venetian life was commerce. Commerce expressed itself in facts and figures. These facts and figures had to be appraised if life was to retain its substance. The record shows plainly that the Venetians were more successful than the Byzantines in relating their individual lives to these objective realities. It can be maintained that the Venetians were forced to give these matters great thought because they felt the pressures of the realities around them more keenly than the Byzantines. But this argument, while certainly pertinent, is yet insufficient because it does not account for the Venetian accomplishment in actually finding and utilizing their own intellectual resources. It becomes adequate as an explanation of the Venetian superiority only when one remembers that writing and related literate skills were more widely disseminated in the republic than in the Empire, and that a great many people could therefore proceed to gain mastery over the intellectual crafts of analysis and calculation that were regarded in Byzantium, and in the other contemporary societies, as the privileged wisdom of the few.[60] The perfection of these methods of reasoning and abstraction led to the development of statistics, and the aptitude of the Venetians in applying statistics to the field of foreign affairs was responsible eventually for the transformation of diplomacy into a political science closely akin to statistics. For in the eyes of the Venetians the entire world was a complex of ascertainable facts, which had to be understood separately and collectively if the national venture was to succeed. Fleets and armies, treaty rights and trading prospects, power and influence, were therefore regarded as factors that had to be isolated and evaluated in terms of national assets and liabilities if they were to be used as reliable determinants of policy. The archives became the business ledgers of the state, and the entire republic one great joint stock company for the scientific exploration of the eastern trade.[61]

The Byzantine government, too, had prided itself on discovering a fruitful relationship between science and diplomacy. However, this juxtaposition was of a more limited nature than the one found in Venetian politics. The rulers of Constantinople could rightfully claim that they knew how to manage their barbarian satellites scientifically, but their interest in the political usefulness of science was confined to that rather narrow field of psychology which offered insights into the mentality of dependent and culturally immature peoples and could supply suggestions for the influencing and controlling of the behavior of such peoples.

The record shows that the Venetians had learnt much from the precedent that their former masters had set in this area of scientific politics, but it also supports the view that their knowledge of the science of man surpassed that of their imperial tutors. For the Venetians proved, in the course of their history, that they were adept also in managing the infinitely more complex problems presented by their relations with politically independent and culturally advanced nations. Moreover, contrary to the somewhat amorphous approach that characterized the Byzantine conduct of international relations, that of the

---

[60] Cf. Pirenne, *Medieval Cities*, pp. 109-111.
[61] Cf. Burckhardt, p. 58.

Venetians enabled them to devise a diplomatic establishment functioning so precisely and systematically in a variety of circumstances
that it could be imitated readily by many later generations of European
statesmen.

In the context of the foregoing presentation it is thus difficult to
accept in its entirety the thesis that Sir Harold Nicolson has submitted
in the following terms: "When, in the later (Byzantine) empire, pow-
er-policy declined, there came under the Byzantine system a recrudescence of diplomacy in its most unconstructive form. Diplomacy
became the stimulant rather than the antidote to the greed and folly
of mankind. Instead of co-operation, you had disintegration; instead
of unity, disruption; instead of reason, you had astuteness; in the place
of moral principles, you had ingenuity. The Byzantine conception of
diplomacy was directly transmitted to Venice, and, from those foetid
lagoons, throughout the Italian peninsula. Diplomacy in the Middle
Ages had a predominantly Italian, and indeed Byzantine flavour. It is
to this heredity that it owes, in modern Europe, so much of its disrepute."[62]

The view that finds expression throughout the monograph of which
this excerpt forms a part, clouds, and in some respects distorts, the
historical perspectives of international diplomacy. For by oversimpli-
fying the affinities between Byzantine and Venetian diplomacy and ignoring totally those between Byzantine and Russian, it fails to provide
the necessary historical clue for an accurate understanding of the differences that exist today between the diplomatic systems of the Western world and those of the Soviet Union.

What makes this thesis even more misleading is its implicit assumption that there was an organized and effective system of diplomacy in
medieval Western Europe based firmly on reason, good will, and
morality, which served the cause of unity and cooperation, until it was
contaminated by the spirit that emanated from the foetid lagoons. This
hypothesis is unfounded. There was no organized system of diplomacy
in medieval Western Europe before the Venetian was transplanted to
the Italian and European courts.[63] Indeed, there was no room for such
a system in the old European order because its operating principles
would have been antithetical to those that gave the medieval political

---

[62] *Diplomacy*, p. 43. See also the author's later volume, *The Evolution of Diplomatic
Method.*

[63] The thesis upheld by R. B. Mowat, *Diplomacy and Peace*, New York, 1936, that
diplomacy was wholly disorganized in the first period of the history of diplomacy,
i.e., from 476-1475, is acceptable in terms of Western Europe.

structure its life and effectiveness. For diplomacy, as understood in Byzantium, then in Italy, and lastly in Western Europe, was organically associated with the sovereign state, and the sovereign state was not recognized, either *de jure* or *de facto*, in the medieval European system. The most that can be said in this regard is that there were many popes, emperors, kings, city governments, universities, and other associate members of the Christian commonwealth that possessed and employed some of the skills habitually regarded today as the attributes of diplomacy. But in this context diplomacy appears more as a series of rather haphazard manifestations of political thinking on the part of individuals than as a well-defined political institution.

The further implication in the above-quoted passage that medieval Western diplomacy was imbued with moral certainties and made to serve noble ends whereas the Byzantine and Venetian style of diplomacy was marred by duplicity and ingenuity is obviously not tenable if one agrees that there was no diplomatic system in medieval Western Europe. It is even too sweeping as a generalization if one interprets medieval diplomacy as a craft exercised by certain understanding individuals. For, while one may acclaim the diplomacy of men like Innocent III, Frederick Barbarossa, and Frederick II on many grounds, one will hardly be able to find it altogether free of the stains with which Byzantine diplomacy was allegedly afflicted. It is undoubtedly true that the medieval Western commonwealth was built on loftier moral foundations than the Byzantine Empire, that its history was geared to the attainment of unity, and that it evolved some remarkable methods of intercommunal cooperation. But the images and values that inspired the great society of medieval Western Europe were not actualized through the agency of diplomacy. They became realities as a result of having been transposed into terms of jurisprudence and political philosophy. The Western European nations did not begin to recognize diplomacy as a distinct ordering principle of international relations until the Holy Roman Empire had become politically obsolete as a framework of society. And it was precisely then that the Venetian pattern of conducting foreign affairs began to impress itself upon the consciousness of European politicians. A comparison between pre-Renaissance diplomacy as understood in Byzantium and Venice on the one hand, and in the rest of Western Europe on the other, is thus historically and chronologically out of focus. What one suspects in reading such evaluations is that modern Western historians are actually comparing the old Byzantine and Venetian methods of diplomacy with the methods that were developed in the West during the eighteenth and nineteenth centuries under the impact of liberalism and constitutionalism. In other words, it appears that Venetian diplomacy is being measured here in terms of its compliance or noncompliance with the standards of political behavior that have come to prevail in the diplomatic circles of the modern Western society of states.

The pride with which many Western Europeans point to these standards is certainly justified. What is not justifiable in the context of an international history of diplomacy is the method of assessing the factors that support this pride. As one reflects upon the causes that may have induced historians to confuse epochs and civilizations, and out of this confusion to condemn the Venetian diplomatic method before concluding in favor of the modern Western system of diplomacy, one cannot avoid the impression that this process of assessment is a latter-day manifestation of the disrepute in which things Byzantine and pseudo-Byzantine have so long been held in the West.

C. THE FLORENTINE RESTATEMENT OF THE VENETIAN DIPLOMATIC METHOD

In order to understand the diplomatic theories and practices that were to gain currency in the Western world between the fifteenth and twentieth centuries it is necessary to follow the processes through which the Venetian method was diffused and transformed.

The political scene in Renaissance Italy to which this method was transplanted in the fifteenth century was very different from that in which it had been operating during the preceding five hundred years. It was characterized by a plurality of city-states among which Milan, Florence, Naples, the Papacy, and Venice[64] were the strongest.[65] Each of these five claimed to be sovereign, yet none could muster the necessary strength to realize its particular aspirations independently. Hence the principles of statecraft that Venice had developed in the period of its might to give full effect to the real power it then possessed appealed to these later governments only as offering ways and means to compensate for an actual lack of such power. For if a ruler could detect the intentions of his neighbor, defeat his hostile designs, form alliances with his enemies, steal away his friends and, above all, prevent his union with others,[66] he could hope to maintain at least the appearance

[64] The latter is viewed here as an Italian city-state rather than as a Mediterranean power.

[65] See Mattingly for an analysis of power relations in this epoch.

[66] Hill, Vol. I, p. 359. Cf. this situation with the one in ancient India as analysed in Kautilya's *Arthashastra*.

of indomitable strength and thus mask or mitigate that frustrating dissonance between illusion and reality with which his regime seemed permanently encumbered.

Diplomacy as it had been understood by the Venetians would obviously be inapplicable in a situation where power, determined by the uncertain interplay of innumerable imponderables in a variety of states, was an entirely relative and fluid phenomenon, and where foreign policies could be conceived only as short term measures. In its Italian metamorphosis, diplomacy was therefore required to assume new and different aspects. Geared to the elusive spectre of power in its most subtle manifestations, it became increasingly mercurial in its operations, until eventually it gave rise to a pattern of political relations in which plot and counterplot emerged as central themes.

The shifting and conspiratorial character that diplomacy assumed in the process of mediating between illusion and reality in the field of interstate relations was enhanced by the conflict between avowed strength and actual weakness with which all of these regimes were faced within their boundaries. Each Italian state was as committed to the principle of a centralized and strong government as Venice had been, but unlike Venice, all had to cope incessantly with the rival claims of competitive local factions. The ensuing domestic struggles and their effect upon international relations in general and diplomacy in particular can be understood only if one remembers that the Italians evolved their theory of the state during the Renaissance, when the medieval heritage of communally held values was being shaken off, and the strong individual was being given free rein to follow his ambitions and set his own standards of political behavior. In this context the state was regarded in effect as the patrimony of the man of genius and power, and foreign policies were consequently interpreted as the expression of the strong ruler's will.

In image and in fact, therefore, the Italian city-state was very different from the Venetian republic, where a fixed idea of the state had effectively spanned centuries of varied cultural and political experience, and where the national interest had been recognized as definitely superior to all individual ambitions. Since individual aspirants to power were not restrained in Italy by such political traditions and conventions as those that had inhibited the execution of personal ambitions in the Adriatic Republic, all were free, in the logic of the circumstances, to contest the power of existing regimes. The actual record of their rivalries shows, however, that aspiring factions were usually just as devoid of real power and just as much interested in soliciting outside aid as the governments that they opposed. The struggle for supremacy within the state was therefore seldom confined to the local scene. For since the Italian cities were closely related to each other both physically and culturally, aspirants to power were always tempted to seek the supplementary strength they needed by conspiring with governments or factions in neighboring communities. The area of diplomatic activities, already disturbed as a result of the uneasy distribution of power in the Italian region as a whole, was thus still further confused by the espionage, intrigues, and betrayals in which conspiring partisans engaged incessantly across the boundaries of their native states.

The affirmation of this kind of individualism in the domain of international relations had a dual effect upon the evolution of diplomacy. Its most obvious result was the promotion of instability, even anarchy, in foreign relations. But its long-range and less evident consequence was the isolation of new principles of international order. For the discovery in the annals of Venetian and Byzantine history of new principles of political behavior and the general rebellion against established political tenets that was implicit in the great movements of the Renaissance had the effect of activating the imagination of political theorists and practitioners and of causing them to sift the wreckage of their time for new political directions. Indeed, the very turmoil of Renaissance diplomacy has in retrospect the appearance of a great ordering process in which existing theories and practices of political intercourse were slowly reassessed and restated in forms that could contain the aspirations of the age that had begun to dawn in Western Europe.

The process of adapting Venetian principles of diplomacy to peninsular needs was determined by the same factors that had made the unreformed method inapplicable to the Italian states system. The focal area of external activities for each city-state was not the entire known world, as it had been for Venice, but the Italian peninsula. This physical condition fostered conflict and anarchy, as we have seen, but it also had the effect of making people acutely aware of the adversities implicit in unmitigated strife and instability. This awareness did not originate in human sympathy or in considerations of an ethical nature; nor did it express itself in peace movements and moral exhortations against war. The rulers, being sovereign, were free to choose between peaceful and belligerent techniques for implementing the goals they had in mind. But they could not exercise this freedom to their own best advantage unless they knew all that could be known about the conditions prevailing in neighboring domains. Such information would remain unavailable, however, as long as interstate contacts were subject to relentless disturbance and arbitrary interference. In the course of time, therefore, the Italian sovereigns agreed that if the cause of national independence was ever to be effectively maintained, the jungle of their political relations would have to be traversed by certain open and reliable lines of communication. This joint quest for security and survival led to an imitation of the Venetian system of collecting foreign intelligence.

The actual emergence of an Italian agreement to develop diplomacy as a peninsular institution was favored greatly by the same set of conditions that were responsible also for such manifestations of regional disorder as the interstate conspiracies in which aspirants to power were apt to engage. For all of the diplomatic accords reached in this epoch, whether destined to serve the cause of war or that of peace, whether conducive to stability or to chaos, bear witness to the irrefutable fact, already mentioned, that the peoples of Italy spoke the same language (in more than the literal meaning of the phrase) even when expressing divergent interests. This language, whether spoken in Rome, Mantua, or Florence, was the vehicle of shared world views concerning the present, shared expectations for the future, and shared remembrances of a long and glorious past.[67] Whereas the Venetian method, having been designed by an independent state in the course of contacts with many culturally and geographically remote countries, was essentially a national agency whose functioning did not depend upon the simultaneous operation of similar institutions in other states, Italian diplomacy, having been sponsored collectively by many weak and interdependent states, was an international institution by virtue of its very inception.[68]

If one compares the two methods on the level of their actual operation, one finds that the purpose of diplomacy as it appeared in Italy

[67] The ambivalence between competition and cooperation, and between independence and interdependence, which characterized the political scene, is apparent also in the field of economics. Commercial life in Renaissance Italy was rent by acrimonious trade wars between the cities, but it also gave rise to such institutionalized corporate accords as the sleeping partnership, the commercial company, and other associational designs for which secure foundations could be found in the shared heritage of Roman law. See *The Cambridge Medieval History*, Vol. VI, p. 488.

[68] Although one may distinguish the particular diplomatic objectives of Milan from those of Mantua, to give but one example, one cannot find that the Milanese and Mantuan methods differed from each other in conceptual and operational terms. Nor does the fact that diplomacy was developed somewhat earlier in some states than in others detract from the view that this evolution was essentially an all-Italian process.

had undergone a subtle but nonetheless significant change and that this change was determined by the same circumstances that had fostered a conceptual accord on the place of diplomacy in international politics. For since the need for alliances and counter-alliances was taken for granted throughout Italy, diplomacy was naturally expected to focus upon intergovernmental negotiations as the sole avenue to this goal. The Venetians, and the Byzantines before them, had likewise been masters of the art of bargaining; but as we have seen, they did not regard the exercise of this art as their primary diplomatic assignment. Furthermore, when they engaged in negotiations they always did so on the basis of premises that were quite different from those recognized in Renaissance Italy. For the Eastern Empire and the Adriatic Republic were not small states devoid of intrinsic strength. They were great powers that did not require allies in order to survive. Their negotiations with other states therefore issued, as a rule, from positions of unquestioned strength, and were aimed at the attainment of an unqualified advantage. In other words, the Byzantines and the Venetians had not been conditioned by their environment to view agreement as the principal objective of the bargaining process between nations. The states of Renaissance Italy, on the other hand, were forced by political necessity to seek mutually acceptable terms of concert and accord, albeit for the most part on a temporary basis. And such accords could usually be reached, when required, because the negotiators could communicate with each other in conditions of physical and cultural proximity, and because they could rely upon the shared legacy of Roman law, which conveyed to all of them both a strong tradition in favor of agreement and time-tested forms for the incorporation of contractual accords. The network of alliances and counter alliances that was produced in this period under the influence of political, cultural, and geographical factors thus attests not only to the insecurity of each government and to the general confusion of Italian politics, but also to a widespread predisposition in favor of negotiation and compromise as the chief purposes of diplomacy—purposes that had been absent in earlier systems.

The new emphasis upon negotiation as the core of the diplomatic art made new demands upon the professional diplomats. Apart from being observers and analysts of the foreign scene, envoys were now generally regarded as indispensable go-betweens, and, as such, they were expected to maintain communications between the governments they served, represent the interests of their sovereigns, and negotiate treaties and other understandings between their respective courts.[69] The growing realization that these were complex assignments requiring the continuous attention of highly qualified men, led eventually to the institution of permanent resident missions. Initiated by the Dukes of Mantua and Milan between 1341 and 1379,[70] this practice was diffused in the succeeding decades until it became commonplace first in Italy[71] and subsequently throughout the rest of Europe.

Other corollaries suggested by the new view of diplomacy concerned the legal and social status of the diplomatic profession. Since all of the Italian sovereigns were at one in regarding their ambassadors as very important people who should be safeguarded from the hazards besetting the average traveller and sojourner in foreign places, they became the joint sponsors of a rudimentary system of diplomatic immunities; since all, furthermore, acknowledged external magnificence to be the proper measure of prestige, all were disposed to emulate Byzantium and Venice in the development of rites and ceremonies as the most persuasive manifestations of their political dignity; and since all were of one mind also in regarding their envoys as the carriers of the power that they claimed for themselves, they were jointly responsible for fostering a continuous battle for precedence among their representatives at court, which was to resolve itself ultimately in the establishment of a complex hierarchical order of diplomatic ranks.[72]

Within the unifying framework of such shared preferences and practices diplomacy assumed certain international aspects that it had not possessed in the Venetian context. For it appeared, now, not only as the foreign arm of each separate government, but also as the nucleus of the collective system of Italian states. This dual character of the institution communicated itself, as a matter of course, to the diplomatic profession. Envoys were the agents of the sovereigns who employed

[69] The importance of these ambassadorial functions was stressed particularly by those who, like the French diplomat Philippe de Comines, were convinced that two great princes should never meet each other face to face if they wished to establish good personal relations, but instead ought to communicate through good and wise ambassadors. de Baulde, Vol. I, pp. 265ff.

[70] Mattingly, p. 71.

[71] *ibid.*, p. 89. Mattingly suggests that the republics of Venice and Florence were slower in establishing resident embassies than the princely sovereigns because they were faced with considerable constitutional and legal difficulties, whereas despots could send personal agents anywhere any time without having to justify such missions publicly. *ibid.*, pp. 73, 81. See de Maulde, Vol. I, pp. 306-322 on permanent missions, circular embassies which passed from one court to another, and cumulative embassies which consisted of envoys from various courts.

[72] See Nicolson, *Evolution of Diplomatic Method*, p. 43 for some amusing illustrations of this competition. Also Ganshof, p. 278.

them, to be sure, and, as such, regarded the interest of their native governments as the highest cause, but in the exercise of this function they were actually administering a peninsular society of nations outside of which no sovereign could survive. In this extended framework they formed a corps of cosmopolitan officers who had the same calling, represented governments of a similar type, spoke the same language, cultivated the same skills, subscribed to the same standards of behavior, expected the same rewards, and faced the same perils. In these circumstances it is not surprising to find that competence rather than nationality was often the preferred criterion for the selection of an envoy.

Among the many highly qualified Italian diplomats of the thirteenth and fourteenth centuries none enjoyed greater renown than the Florentines, for whom, as their contemporaries said, "in respect of zeal and acumen, (any) equal in negotiation could hardly be found."[73] At the first church jubilee, in 1300, ambassadors of Florentine origin "served in the quality of public negotiators not only their own country, but the kings of France, England, Bohemia, Naples, Sicily, besides Russia and the Khan of the Tartars."[74] And this fact so impressed itself upon Pope Boniface VIII that he referred to the diplomats of this state as the Fifth Element.

The Florentine method of political representation, which had thus amazed political circles in Renaissance Italy, may be viewed, in retrospect, as having initiated a new phase in the evolution of diplomacy, even though it was modelled closely upon that which the Venetians had developed. Florence followed Venice in taking it for granted that the field of international relations had to be scrutinized closely and dispassionately before any political action could wisely be undertaken. This implied that the Florentine envoys, like those of the Adriatic Republic, were expected to appraise the general distribution of power in Europe, study the people in whose midst they resided, and evaluate their various findings realistically for the benefit of the home government. In the record of these routine assignments the student of international diplomacy will find little that he has not already encountered in the practices of the Venetians. The newness of the Florentine approach to foreign relations is discovered only when one examines the uses to which political experience was put by the intellectual elite. For to Machiavelli (1469-1527) and his predecessors in the foreign service a

[73] Hill, Vol. I, p. 397.
[74] Reumont, *Della Diplomazia Italiana dal secolo XIII al XVI*, Florence, 1861, p. 11, as quoted in *ibid*.

post abroad was more than a service to the state. It was an invaluable opportunity to gain a kind of knowledge about the fundamentals of human behavior in the realm of politics that would permit the establishment of a science of politics valid beyond the time and place in which the envoy happened to be serving his government.

This was a dimension of political speculation to which the Venetians had not aspired. Being nationalists first and foremost, they had been interested primarily in establishing their own policies—rather than political thought in general—upon a solid basis of scientifically ascertainable facts. But the Florentines were constantly stimulated by their intensive contacts with culturally related nations to look for themes of political life that were common to the Western European region and susceptible of an objective definition. And the two concurrent intellectual engagements were executed brilliantly because the city's political elite knew, on the one hand, how to extract generally valid propositions from their observations of concrete political facts, and on the other, how to apply the wisdom gained through scholarship to the practical conduct of diplomacy. By thus cultivating a continuous corrective interplay between the particular and the general, and the subjective and the objective, the Florentines were successful, on the whole, in holding their political practices within the contours of tested thought, and in keeping their theories free not only from illusions but also from strictly local prejudices. The rich legacy of original definitions, abstractions, and theories which accumulated as a result of this methodical preoccupation with political matters, has established Florence, in Jacob Burckhardt's phrasing, as "the home of political doctrines and theories, . . . like Venice, the home of statistical science, and alone and above all other states in the world, the home of historical representation in the modern sense of the phrase."[75] When the Venetian diplomatic method was transposed into this intellectual climate, it was moulded as a matter of course by that wondrous Florentine spirit which Burckhardt describes as "at once keenly critical and artistically creative."[76]

The restatement of diplomacy that emerged from the political workshop of the Florentines not only incorporated the Venetian view that diplomacy was the chief shield of the national interest, but also suggested new reasons in support of this conclusion. Whereas the Venetians had found the measure of diplomacy by a careful calculation of their own self-interest, the Florentines were impelled both by choice

[75] p. 61.   [76] ibid.

and by circumstance to base their institution upon universally applicable principles. The great significance of their revision lies in the fact that it made possible a separation of diplomacy from the political apparatus of the sovereign state and a regard for it as the shared concern of all governments. This idea proved extremely suggestive in the limited context of peninsular policies, as we have seen; the opportunity to test its effectiveness in a larger and more complex area, however, did not arise until the Western European nations succeeded in organizing themselves along the lines charted in this Italy of the Renaissance. For after the passage of its formative period, Western Europe began only slowly to become conscious again of the essential unity that enveloped its diversities. When its scholars then were ready to view the continent as one great republic, and its statesmen to act as the spokesmen of a Concert of Europe, diplomacy became in effect the cornerstone of a vast international system. It is clear in retrospect that Florence occupies a key position in the intricate international history of this European institution; for it was through Florentine thought that the Venetian experience was transformed into an objective reality that all the European courts could apprehend.

D. THE BALANCE OF POWER IN RENAISSANCE ITALY

Several distinct qualities of thought enabled the citizens of the small Florentine state to become the agents, as it were, of a large international community. The talent to isolate the universal principle in the particular case has already been noted in the treatment of diplomacy. Other aptitudes that impress the student of international relations include a remarkable ability to see phenomena in their mutual relationships rather than as isolated occurrences, and to communicate the vision of such associational patterns in terms intelligible to a broad public.[77] The combined impact of these qualities explains why, in this historical epoch, diplomacy was not considered as an autonomous art but as an integral part of the total system of relations that encompassed men, ideas, and things, and why the Florentine rendition of this total system was to gain such wide currency beyond the time and place in which it had been conceived.

One of the pivotal notions that seemed in Florentine opinion to lend unity to life and thought in Renaissance Italy was the idea that the component parts of a whole ought to exist in a state of balance. This

---

[77] Compare these qualities with those displayed by the ancient Romans in the development of the notion of contract.

idea is the source of the balance of power principle, which has had a decisive effect upon the course of history in the last half millennium. It has been noted in a stimulating essay on the growth of this concept[78] that the balance appeared in Italy first in various nonpolitical connotations. For example, it was recognized as the regulating principle in music, where harmony was determined by counterpoint. Also, it was recognized in double entry bookkeeping, where debit and credit entries were supposed to balance each other on opposite pages.[79] The principle had a definite place in physics and astrology, and even entered the thinking of certain medical theorists who concerned themselves with the balance of humors in the harmonic man.

Several reasons may explain the delayed affirmation of the balance concept in foreign affairs. It has been pointed out[80] that political ideas are usually produced in fields other than politics because they seem to require outside authority before they can be considered acceptable in political life, and that the language that is necessary for the formulation and conveyance of a politically significant idea is formed only gradually by the confluence of terms from those other nonpolitical areas which an idea has penetrated first. A further explanation for the time lag in the genesis of the balance as a political concept may be provided by the fact that foreign affairs in Renaissance Italy (as, for that matter, also in other epochs and places) were the concern of a small elite, which could promote its interests without the aid of such symbols as are necessary in other spheres of public activity. In the words of a Venetian, Renaissance politicians did not have to incur "the unnecessary expense of an ideology,"[81] as long as traditional images were accepted by the public as adequate renditions of the political realities of the day.

By the mid-fifteenth century it was clear to all statesmen that Italy was in actuality a society of separate but interdependent states, which could exist only so long as the representatives of the pentarchy employed diplomacy for the maintenance of a continuous, if precarious, balance between their respective governments.[82] The principle of the balance of power thus appears in the arena of interstate relations as the concomitant of diplomacy as practiced by the strongest Italian

[78] Alfred Vagts, "The Balance of Power: Growth of an Idea" in *World Politics*, October 1948, Vol. I, no. I, pp. 82ff.

[79] In earlier methods of accounting, items were entered one below the other. It is pertinent to note here that the field of banking and finance was dominated by Florence between A.D. 1250 and 1350. See *The Cambridge Medieval History*, Vol. VI, p. 487.

[80] Vagts, pp. 87ff.   [81] *ibid.*, p. 94.   [82] Cf. Mattingly, pp. 79-83.

governments. It assumed certain aspects of a political ideology when the obsolescence of the medieval symbols of unity and harmony was recognized publicly, and when the reality of competitive power politics was explained by the diplomatic elites in terms of an imagery that could be related directly to the notion of the balance. This was accomplished, consciously or unconsciously, without completely invalidating the set of symbols with which men had so long identified their collective existence. For the new idea of balanced powers was brought into a subtle, if somewhat ambiguous, relationship with the time-honored ideals of harmony and justice. This elaboration, which included the borrowing from astrology of the symbol of the scales, is important because it made it possible in later centuries to identify the balance of power not only with the cause of national expediency but also with that of a justly measured international order.

These complex connections between old and new images, and between images and political actualities, were seen with particular clarity in Florence, and it is not surprising, therefore, that the principle of the balance of power was first formulated by the scholars of that city.

The immediate stimulus for a close examination of the political scene was the reign of Lorenzo Medici (born 1449; ruled from 1469-1492).[83] This was so for several reasons. The realm of politics was generally regarded in Renaissance Italy as an extension of the ruling sovereign's will, and such an interpretation was particularly convincing when a ruler appeared who seemed to epitomize all that could possibly be expected of a prince. In the estimation of his subjects in Florence and his peers in Italy Lorenzo was such a man. Indeed, his very personality evoked references to the balance concept, being described in diplomatic circles as "the balance of sense and wisdom."[84]

Lorenzo's great international prestige as a princely character derived essentially from the qualities of statesmanship that he displayed at a time when Italian politics were in a state of general disarray, and when Florence was threatened by numerous enemies. These qualities manifested themselves from about 1480 onward in a foreign policy that impressed contemporary intellectuals as a radical departure from the customary Italian pattern and the announcement of an entirely new approach to international relations. Some of the Florentines who acclaimed or eulogized Lorenzo's record in this fashion may well have done so for reasons of patriotism or personal ambition. But the most

[83] See Ferdinand Schevill, *History of Florence from the Founding of the City through the Renaissance*, New York, 1936, pp. 371-416, for a discussion of this period.
[84] See Vagts, p. 95, for this reference.

renowned among them were eminently qualified to engage in such a review, for they were not only highly trained theoreticians in the fields of history, law, political science, or philosophy, but also widely experienced and famed civil servants and diplomats, who desired nothing quite as much as that their view of the course of events should have as wide and deep a practical effect as possible.[85] In these circumstances the record of Lorenzo's foreign policy became the subject matter of an intensive scholarly analysis from the early part of the sixteenth century onward, and it is this analysis that has placed the balance of power principle in its modern political setting. For the gist of Lorenzo's political design, as revealed by the commentaries then composed, was the recognition that continued strife among the Italian states was bound to endanger the security of each and all, since it would doubtlessly encourage the expansionist ambitions of the Venetians and the French; and that it was, consequently, in the best interest of Florence to preserve peace among the Italian sovereignties by maintaining a judicious equilibrium between the states composing the pentarchy.

These themes were expounded with admirable lucidity by the great historian and statesman, Francesco Guicciardini (died 1540),[86] in his monumental *Storia d'Italia*,[87] a work that has been variously described as "a masterpiece of scientific history"; "the greatest historical work that had appeared since the beginning of the modern era"; "the most solid monument of Italian reason in the sixteenth century"; "the final triumph of that school of philosophical historians which included Machiavelli, Sagni, Pitti, Nardi, Varchi, Vettori, and Gianotti";[88] "the first realistic history of modern times"; and "the first clear exposition of the European political system as it emerged in Guicciardini's time and has continued without a break to the present day."[89]

The first phase in the intricate intellectual history of the balance principle in foreign affairs may be said to end with the formulation of the concept as it expressed itself in the Laurentian system; the second phase is marked by the diffusion of the concept in Western Europe. This latter process begins with an interesting convergence of Florentine and Venetian views on diplomacy, which Alfred Vagts has noted in its full historical significance.[90] For when the Venetians were

---

[85] Burckhardt, p. 181.

[86] See *Encyclopaedia Britannica* for a sketch of his remarkable career.

[87] Rosini's ed., 10 vols., Pisa, 1819.

[88] *Encyclopaedia Britannica*, "Guicciardini, Francesco."

[89] Schevill, p. 503. See *The Portable Renaissance Reader*, New York, 1953, pp. 279-284 for an excerpt of Guicciardini's treatment of the balance of power.

[90] p. 99.

compelled to realize, in the first half of the sixteenth century, that the days of empire were definitely over, they, too, began to strive for *bilancia* in foreign affairs. And since their diplomatic apparatus had remained unequalled in the world, one may say in effect that it was the superb medium of Venetian diplomacy which brought the Florentine rendition of the balance of power into general European circulation.

E. DIPLOMACY IN THE MODERN EUROPEAN STATES SYSTEM[91]

As long as the principal European sovereignties were represented by absolute monarchs who purported to be oblivious to any interest not exclusively their own, diplomacy was as predatory in its design and anarchic in its effects as it had been in its Mediterranean proving grounds. However, this general appearance of anarchy concealed the fact that Western European diplomacy was already being moulded in the first phase of its evolution by political traditions and interests that diverged significantly from the Eastern patterns.

In the Byzantine system lawlessness had been the logical consequence of a commitment to doctrinal premises that were considered permanently valid. In Italy, on the other hand, it had been the outgrowth of subjective individual dispositions that had devolved from a new realization of the potentialities implicit in an outstanding personality. Renaissance diplomacy as it manifested itself in Italy had thus emanated from small communities whose identity was coequal with that of strong-willed individual princes rather than with a historically continuous, corporate entity as in Byzantium and Venice. As such it reflected the personal interests of the man who happened to dominate the scene rather than the national interest of the state.

The absolute monarchs of Western Europe were politically and culturally the kin of the Italian princes, and their diplomatic methods, developed in the same general climate of opinion, demonstrated, therefore, the same appearances and screened the same underlying realities. In other words, anarchy did in fact mark the European system of multiple states during and after the period of the Renaissance, but it was neither irremediable nor indispensable to the continuance of the diplomatic system. For since the Western Europeans were emphasiz-

[91] The history of modern European diplomacy and diplomatic relations has been exposed and discussed in numerous authoritative texts and no attempt will be made here to reiterate the findings that are on record, or to compare the conclusions that different authors have drawn from their respective studies of the historical materials. See Nicolson and Mattingly for two different accounts of the Europeanization of the diplomatic method.

ing individual preference rather than political doctrine as the chief source of political behavior, they were free in principle to change their orientation. In this cultural context, then, lawlessness was not bound to remain the ally of diplomacy.

The search for political order and stability which issued from a further exploration of the reaches of individualism, brought the post-Renaissance generations gradually to an espousal of constitutionalism as the proper basis of the state; and this transformation of the concept of the state had as its concomitant a similar transformation of the diplomatic method. That is to say, just as government was being subjected to moral and legal restraints, so was the government's method of conducting foreign relations. Neither of these changes occurred abruptly. In fact, each had been announced in the preceding period. For the rise of the king to preeminence in the political affairs of the state had been paralleled by the emergence of representative institutions and the ascendancy of a politically alert intellectual elite. And neither of these two factors had ever been completely ignored by the autocratic monarchs who administered the foreign relations of the major European states between 1492-1559.[92] However, their impact upon the concept and conduct of diplomacy became decisive when the state was identified with the nation rather than a dynasty, and when constitutionalism was recognized as the governing principle in domestic affairs. For the commitment to processes of orderly parliamentary deliberation and the recognition of the need for a consensus, both implicit in the acceptance of democratic principles of government, became an integral part of the entire normative system by which national life and thought was being regulated in Western Europe. As such it instructed the new spokesmen of the nation-states to believe that governments should and could resolve their disputes and reach accords by resorting to the same methods of discussion and negotiation that they respected in their internal jurisdictions. In this context, then, diplomacy became the ally of law.

The truths to which the parliamentary experience pointed were corroborated by the conclusions that the new and politically influential European middle class had drawn from its involvement in commercial activities. The merchants and townsmen had become convinced that international trade was most profitable when it was being conducted as a peaceful calling in an atmosphere of mutual trust. And since they

[92] See E. Fueter, *Geschichte des Europäischen Staatensystems von 1492 bis 1559*, München, Berlin, 1919, for an exhaustive analysis of this period.

were inclined, by virtue of their professional interests, to reduce all international relations to commercial terms, they, too, became ardent proponents of the view that diplomacy was the auxiliary of peaceful exchanges between states, and that it should aim at compromise and conciliation rather than at victory.[93]

The themes of peace, law, and agreement upon which these new European approaches to diplomacy converged had pervaded the cultural and political history of Western Europe before the advent of the modern states system. They had gained wide currency through the writings of political theorists, and had become concretely manifest in numerous political institutions and systems of public law. Diplomacy had not been an original part of this fund of interlocking political references. Indeed, its tenets as they had been defined in Byzantium and Venice were not only alien, but in many respects antithetical, to the values that were emphasized in the Occidental heritage. This dilemma did not disturb the divine right monarchs and enlightened despots, as we have seen, for they were quite ready—although not always equally able—to discard the baggage of their medieval past in order to follow the example set by Eastern courts. Diplomacy to them was above all an adjunct to the *raison d'état* and their divinely inspired mission, and their diplomats were admonished to heed the advice of Barbaro that ambassadors must devote themselves exclusively to the preservation and aggrandizement of their own state.

The real problems implicit in the westernization of the diplomatic method were faced by those who held fast to the traditions of the West. For these traditions informed them that politics were subject to ethics, that peace and law were essentially moral issues, and that statesmen must comply with the same integral standards of behavior that law had enjoined upon all men. An early definition of the relationship between these principles on the one hand, and the theory and practice of diplomacy on the other, was supplied in the fifteenth century by Bernard du Rosier, provost and later archbishop of Toulouse, who insisted in his "Short Treatise About Ambassadors" (1436) that the business of an ambassador is peace; that ambassadors must labor for the common good, and that they should never be sent to stir up wars or internal dissensions.[94]

[93] See Nicolson's succinct comparison between the "warrior or heroic" theory that regards diplomacy as "war by other means," and the "mercantile or shopkeeper" theory, that regards diplomacy as an aid to peaceful commerce. *Diplomacy*, pp. 51-54.

[94] Mattingly, pp. 48ff.

The juxtaposition, in the fifteenth century, of Barbaro's and Rosier's views on the function of diplomacy epitomizes the conflict that the Europeans faced when they were called upon to accommodate this new political institution. Both versions were composed by Europeans: one by a Venetian, schooled in the Venetian system of foreign affairs; the other by a Frenchman, deeply committed to the legacy of his past. Each was logical in the context in which it had been elaborated. Each has had its dedicated adherents in every epoch of Western European history, including the present. However, neither was ever accepted unequivocally as the ruling norm in the conduct of foreign relations. Barbaro's unabashed admission of the absolute supremacy of the national interest could not be accommodated by a system of political references that had assigned strong moral connotations to all political concepts. And Rosier's thesis proved too idealistic even for those practitioners of diplomacy who identified themselves most closely with the notion of a morally unified commonwealth of nations. Indeed, the complex records of diplomacy as they have accumulated during the last five hundred years in Western Europe and North America show that the Occidental approach to diplomacy has always been ambivalent. Statesmen as well as publicists have veered between the two polar positions in a continuous search for some convincing synthesis between the realities of the national interest on the one hand and the image of a harmonious international society on the other. Some found it by including concern for law and morality in their definition of the national interest, others by cloaking the *raison d'état* in the garb of moral and legal principles. All were induced to pursue foreign policies that were moralistic and legalistic in tone and content. And this was to become particularly evident after the eighteenth century, when constitutionalism had been accepted as the ideal political norm and the governments realized that diplomacy had to have a definite relation to the public's understanding as to what was lawful and proper in human affairs. Since peace and agreement had become generally preferred values, diplomacy was geared to the attainment of international accords. And since accords were reached best by the exchange of opinion, negotiation became the preferred diplomatic technique.

This general European agreement upon the aims and methods of diplomacy as it had issued from a common understanding of the past and a joint response to the principles inherent in modern democracy and trade was supported by several other factors. Unlike Byzantium and Venice, but much like Renaissance Italy, Western Europe was a pluralistic society of coordinate states. Here the status of each sovereignty was recognized only as a corollary of the generally valid principle that all states were sovereign and equal. That is to say, the European states were legally as well as territorially interdependent, and the realization of this interdependence became a natural source of unified views on the subject of diplomacy. Moreover, it should be noted in this connection that Europe and North America were the principal theatres of diplomatic operations before the middle of the twentieth century. For during the formative period of European diplomacy international relations had in fact been for the most part inter-European relations.[95] And this identification could be maintained in subsequent centuries, even though the field of foreign affairs had actually become coextensive with the entire world, because the European and North American nations were politically and culturally dominant. In other words, the basic premises upon which all Occidental policies rested—however different or antagonistic the particular political interests—had been immune to serious questioning, since the Europeans had not had politically significant encounters with civilizations that had developed different diplomatic methods.

The same factors that determined the westernization of the diplomatic method were responsible also for the gradual Europeanization of the concept of the balance of power. This idea which had been the nucleus of the Laurentian system of coordinate city-states proved eminently attractive to the Europeans north of the Alps after they, too, had become committed to the principle of multiple sovereignties. As a measure of realistic diplomacy it appealed to all statesmen who were interested in maintaining the independence of their states by preventing the rise of an imperial power. As a statement of political ideology it was intellectually and emotionally satisfying to the politically conscious public which could not identify easily with power politics in its crass and materialistic sense, since it had been conditioned by its traditions to think of politics in terms of morally defensible propositions. Innately suspicious of unrestrained power, the Europeans responded to the image implicit in the balance of power because it provided a formula for the resolution of the ambiguities that beset their thinking. For "balance" suggested harmony, and when it was conveyed through the symbol of the scales it seemed to merge with the familiar ideals of justice and law.[96] As the linkage between residual values and contem-

[95] Relations with the Ottoman Empire were a notable exception.
[96] See Vagts, p. 88, on the felt need to provide the system of alliances with an ideology.

porary interests was being established, it became customary to assume that the balance of power denoted a just equilibrium; that diplomacy was conducted best when it strove to realize this image; and that both the image and the method of realizing the image were part of the unifying system of public international law.

These implications were generally subsumed in inter-European relations during the eighteenth and nineteenth centuries. For, by and large, governments and citizens appear to have agreed with Voltaire that Christian Europe (except Russia) was "a sort of great republic divided into several states, some monarchical, others of a mixed character; . . . but all in harmony with each other . . . ; all possessing the same principles of public and political law, unknown in other parts of the world. . . . And above all, . . . at one in the wise policy of maintaining among themselves as far as possible an equal balance of power."[97] Indeed, many Europeans went much farther and agreed with David Hume that the maxim of the balance of power was as old as history, being founded on common sense and obvious reasoning; the supposition being that "enormous monarchies are, probably, destructive to human nature; in their progress, in their continuance, and even in their downfall, which never can be very distant from their establishment,"[98] and that states are always ready, unless they have been dilatory in noting the ascendancy of a pretender to imperial might, to combine in order to banish the dreaded spectre of an omnipotent power. These arguments appeared wholly justified during the nineteenth century when the major European powers, led by Britain, united in upholding the doctrine as the most reliable arbiter of their separate interests in Europe and the rest of the world.

When the era of intense intercultural relations opened toward the end of the nineteenth century under the hegemony of the modern Western states, it was thus generally taken for granted that the European methods of conducting foreign relations were valid objectively. Neither the breakdown of the diplomatic method in the inter-European war of 1914, nor the recrudescence of jungle diplomacy that attended the rise of totalitarian states within continental Europe, seems to have shaken this widespread trust in the intrinsic merits of the Occidental diplomatic system. In the light of later developments it appears that both manifestations of the unrefined Barbaro thesis were dismissed by the leading European democracies as unfortunate, but temporary, deviations from the norm. The United States, it is true, recoiled from the

---

[97] *The Age of Louis XIV*, London, New York, 1935, ch. II, p. 5.
[98] "Of the Balance of Power," in *Essays, Literary, Moral, and Political*, London, 1752, p. 203.

entire system as it had become manifest in the twentieth century. Indicting the balance of power as a nefarious principle, incompatible with democratic ideals, it retreated to the Rosier thesis. Indeed, not only did it reinstate the ideal of a morally unified Occidental commonwealth of nations in which diplomacy should be conducted openly and honestly for the common good of all, but it extended this context to include all nations of the world. In short, all Western nations held fast, in one way or another, to the truths that their own civilization had imparted to them in the domain of international relations. And this posture seemed eminently justified since the European vocabulary of diplomacy had in fact gained world-wide currency. It thus appeared in mid-twentieth century as if nations were in full and genuine agreement upon the particular rendition of "the art and practice of conducting negotiations between nations" that the Occidental democracies had evolved in the process of their complex histories.

The preceding parts of this book have dealt in some detail with the principal political systems with which the non-Western peoples had identified before they were drawn into the Western scheme. It will be recalled, therefore, that the European complex of symbols, concepts, and methods to which Asians and Africans have recently subscribed, had few if any analogues in the traditional non-Western civilizations. All of these ancient systems acknowledged power as the ultimate measure of foreign affairs, whether they were designed for imperial orbits or coexisting sovereignties. The idea of a balance of powers could not have been entertained in Persia or China, because it was utterly incompatible with the dominant images that sustained the absolute supremacy of the Shah of Shahs and the sole ruler of the one and only Middle Kingdom. Nor could it have been accommodated in ancient India, even though the territorial organization of the realm into numerous separate kingdoms is comparable to that of Renaissance Italy and modern Western Europe. For this pluralistic political order did not suggest the conclusion upon which the Western Europeans were to agree eventually, namely, that it would be unethical or unwise to persist in bids for absolute power, and that the national interest would be served by maintaining an equilibrium in interstate relations. On the contrary, it gave rise to a science of politics that instructed each sovereign how to pursue his imperialist purposes to best advantage by consulting the Mandala chart of concentric rings of natural enemies and friends. And similar views on the function of power in international relations were developed, albeit pragmatically rather than scientifically, in the Muslim realm. For rival caliphates and sultanates were not restrained in the conduct of their foreign relations either by the reality of their coexistence or by any theory of interdependence. The norms of behavior that Nizam ul-Mulk had set out in the eleventh century, when he counselled his sultan that he must always have ten times as much as all the other princes taken together, whether in offensive or defensive weapons, in qualities of the heart, or firmness of judgment[99] if he wanted to retain his reputation as the great Master of the World, were not modified in later centuries. Indeed, the spell that Persian and Byzantine conceptions of monolithic power had cast on Nizam ul-Mulk and his predecessors continued to pervade Muslim statecraft in subsequent centuries, even though it was applied to political conditions that bore a greater resemblance to the remote Occidental than to the neighboring Oriental scene.[100] In governing its satellites, the Byzantine Empire made some allowance for the principle that rival forces should be kept in a state of equipoise, it is true; but this particular version of the balance of power did not impair the primacy of the imperial idea, since it was merely a stratagem for the ordering of relations among inferior sovereignties. And the same approach commended itself to Byzantium's Russian and Turkish successors. In short, the entire East was impregnated with the notion that sovereigns should have absolute power. Immunized against any conflict between power and law or other contradictory references such as had been faced continuously in the West, the East was in no way stimulated to produce images such as the balance of power, theories of international law, or systems of international politics in which all states were regarded as sovereign, independent, and equal.

Since foreign relations were power relations, subject only to what is known in the *Arthashastra* as the law of the fishes, diplomacy was not encumbered with ideals of peace, unity, or the common good. In Persia, India, Byzantium, the Arab domain, and Russia it was conceived as a quasi-military activity. In this context negotiation was a strategic device, designed to lead to victory rather than to compromise or mutual understanding. That is to say, it was dissimilar to the type of negotiation that the Western Europeans had cultivated in the nineteenth century.[101]

[99] Nizam al-Mulk, *Traité de Gouvernement composé pour le Sultan Melik Chah*, Ch. Schefer, tr., 1894.

[100] Parthia, ancient Persia's successor, may be said to have applied the balance of power idea to its relations with China and Rome.

[101] Harold Nicolson's analysis of the Byzantine approach to negotiation seems to apply to the Oriental approach in general:

Neither the Oriental nor the Occidental nations were fully aware of these discrepancies in the first decades of the twentieth century. The non-Western peoples were much more vitally concerned with the future than the past when they aligned themselves with the cause of the independent democratic nation-state as it had been realized in the West between the eighteenth and twentieth centuries. Unfamiliar with the history of ideas that had produced the complex modern system and inclined, in the fervor of their newly found identification, to reinterpret their own histories in the light of modern European and American histories,[102] they were emotionally and politically not disposed to remember their ancient political systems, let alone to make allowances for any cultural disparities between the old and new frames of reference. The Western nations, on the other hand, had been isolated from the Orient when they laid the groundwork for the modern political system; the non-Western traditions that they rediscovered in the centuries following their own renaissance were, in their opinion, antiquities worthy of scholarly examination, but utterly unrelated to the political realities of the modern world. In these circumstances they had no inhibitions, either on the level of conscious planning or on that of unconscious attitudes, in projecting a system that had proved its worth in their own complex realm onto a scene of world affairs that patently lacked principles of order.

The auspices under which the modern diplomatic method was developed and internationalized were thus entirely different from those that had determined the evolution and Europeanization of the original Venetian method. For the Italian republic had deduced its political

---

". . . Diplomacy is regarded as an unremitting activity directed toward ultimate triumph. The strategy of negotiation thus becomes an endeavour to out-flank your opponent, to occupy strategical positions which are at once consolidated before any further advance is made; to weaken the enemy by all manner of attacks behind the lines; to seek for every occasion to drive a wedge between your main enemy and his allies; and to hold your opponents on one position while planning an attack elsewhere. The actual tactics employed by these negotiators are also military in character. You have the surprise, and often the night, attack; . . . you have the strategical retreat at moments, and the stealthy occupation of key positions; you have intimidation, ruthlessness and force; and you have elaborate containing actions while your main forces are being massed in some other direction.

"It is obvious that under such a system conciliation, confidence and fair-dealing are not very apparent. A concession made, a treaty concluded, is apt to be regarded, not as the final settlement of an isolated dispute, but as evidence of weakness and retreat, as an advantage which must immediately be exploited in preparation for further triumphs." (*Diplomacy*, pp. 51-52.)

[102] It is significant, for example, that most revolutions in Africa and Asia, regardless of their real causes and purposes, have been likened to the American revolution.

wisdom in foreign affairs from continuous and extensive relations with foreign cultures whose peoples did not share the private values to which its citizenry subscribed. Since it would have been illusory, in these conditions, to hope for international accords on the plane of ethics, law, or other locally held values, the national interest was divested deliberately of any moral elements it may have possessed before it was conveyed to other nations by means of diplomacy.

The world that confronted the West after the war of 1939-1945 was much like the one in which the Venetians had found themselves when they perfected diplomacy as a scientific method of coping with the realities of a multicultural scene. For the political emancipation of the non-Western nations and the resurrection of their native civilizations—both processes that had been instigated by the diffusion of Western values—had the effect, eventually, of evoking and activating long-dormant memories of earlier approaches to foreign affairs. The fact that these earlier approaches had been conducive to anarchy in international relations did not register itself upon the minds of people who were more vitally concerned with adapting the Western model of the state to their local requirements than with cultivating that other Western ideal, the harmonious society of nations.

The Western response to the emergence of competitive diplomatic systems was the reverse of that to which the non-Western nations inclined. Rather than contract their definition of the national interest in the manner of the Venetians, they expanded their conception of a society of coordinate sovereignties so as to include the new political communities in Africa and Asia. Observing that all governments were now conversing with each other in the idiom of Western political thought and trusting that all nations were in agreement upon the meaning of the words they used, the West thus revitalized its traditions of unity, peace, and law as they had been realized in transterritorial unions and constitutional procedures, in order to construct an international organization that would mediate between the different national interests and supervise the conduct of international diplomacy. Now this orientation was as alien to the non-Western civilizations as it had been to the Venetians,[103] but it was an integral part of the cultural and political history of the West, as the two following case studies illustrate.

[103] The contexts in which these orientations were evolved were quite different, as preceding chapters have shown.

E. European Patterns of Transterritorial
and Transnational Organization

A. THE COUNCIL OF CONSTANCE: THE BEGINNINGS
OF CONGRESSIONAL DIPLOMACY

At the opening of the fifteenth century it was clear to thoughtful Europeans that their society was in a grave crisis. The vestiges of secular imperial power had been effaced by the impact of centrifugal forces, and the prestige of the ecclesiastical establishment had been greatly reduced as a result of the protracted schism in the church, the degenerate behavior of the last occupants of the pontifical throne, and the announcement of new religious creeds by Wycliffe and Huss. Deprived of its traditional rallying points of moral and political unity, the Western commonwealth was drifting into dissolution. To arrest this process John Gerson, the chancellor of the University of Paris and head of the reformist party in the church, conceived the plan of resurrecting the original premises on which Christian Europe had acted as a unified community.[104] He identified these premises with the great ecclesiastical assemblies, especially the oecumenical Council of Nicaea, in which the whole Christian world had participated through duly chosen representatives in order to deliberate on matters of common concern. Therefore he prevailed upon the emperor as the titular secular executive of Western Christendom to convoke an assembly of the kind that his predecessors had called in earlier centuries.[105]

The Council of Constance, convened in these circumstances, was in session from 1414 to 1418. It was attended by the emperor and his retinue; by princes, dukes, and nobles; by a crowd of prelates, monks, and simple clerks (about 18,000 ecclesiastics are said to have been present); by merchants, learned doctors, ambassadors, and a flock of sightseers, estimated to have numbered between 50,000 and 100,000.[106] Even the Greek emperor appeared toward the end of the congress, accompanied by nineteen bishops of the Orthodox Church. By virtue of the tumultuous, multifarious life that it enclosed for three and a half years, Constance became the cynosure of all Europe. By the number and weight of its civil and ecclesiastical participants it was, in Gibbon's phrasing "the States-General of Europe, for the Republic of

---

[104] Cf. with the reformist movement that had emanated from Cluny.
[105] See Bryce, p. 352.
[106] *The Catholic Encyclopaedia*, Vol. IV, "The Council of Constance."

Europe, with the Emperor and Pope at its head, had never been represented with more dignity than in Constance."[107]

That the Council of Constance was not just another synod but an entirely new kind of congress was probably evident already to contemporaries as they noted the identity of the delegates and their interests, the nature of the agenda and the procedures followed in the discussions. It is certainly established today, for a retrospective view of international politics as it has developed since 1414 leads to the conclusion that certain concepts of international organization, nowadays regarded as basic, were announced first by the Council of Constance.

The principal point before this assembly and one that elicited widespread secular concern, was the future administration of the Church. The delegates succeeded in restoring a semblance of religious unity by disposing of the schism, renewing the condemnation of Wycliffe, and decreeing the execution of John Huss and Jerome of Prague. But the currents of thought that moved the different secular and religious strata of Western Europe's society were too diverse to permit a general agreement on the question whether the Church should continue as a quasi-monarchical establishment or whether it should be transformed into a parliamentary democracy. Unable to resolve this momentous problem in terms of the principles that it implied, the delegates concentrated upon the task of devising a procedure for the election of the new pope that would reflect the secular realities of the day without doing undue violence to the images and other time-honored understandings that were commonly associated with the Church as the major representative organ of the European community. The Council's deliberations on this theme issued from an acceptance of the fact that the College of Cardinals was as discredited as the papacy of which it was an integral part, and that it alone could therefore no longer be entrusted with the function of selecting the representative of God on earth. They were inspired, furthermore, by the recognition that fifteenth century Europe was a composite of secular and ecclesiastical interests, territorial and extraterritorial associations, and national and international powers, and that the papacy could not presume to be a representative institution unless it had the approval of the principal segments in the commonwealth. And among the latter none seemed as important as the so-called nations. Indeed, even the pope and the cardinals were

[107] *The Decline and Fall of the Roman Empire*, New York, Vol. II, pp. 1427-1428.

no longer identified by their contemporaries as international servants but as Italians, primarily interested in the assertion of local and individual interests. The preponderance of their influence in ecclesiastical councils was therefore resented by the representatives of other European regions, notably England, France, and Germany. The Council's awareness of these factors explains why it was decided, ultimately, that six deputies of each of the five nations should join the college of twenty-three cardinals for the purpose of electing the pope, and why it was found imperative to depart from the voting procedures that the early synods—of which the Constance assembly was supposed to be a replica—had established.

The dilemma with which the Council was faced before it abandoned the traditional individual vote in its public sessions has been vividly described by the eighteenth century historian Jacques Lenfant. After stating the ancient custom that the votes of all members were always taken in the synods, this chronicler writes: "But the Council of Constance had very good reasons to depart from the common practice. As the points in dispute were two Capital Articles in which the Pope, the cardinals, and the prelates were extremely concerned, it were to be feared that they would bear down the Council by their multitude. There were a greater number of Italian prelates at Constance than of all the other Nations together, and most of them were poor and ready to starve; John XXIII had created no less than fifty Chamberlains whom he might depend on as so many creatures devoted to his interests . . . so that there had been no shadow of liberty at the Council, if they had told noses in it, as had been the practice to then."[108]

The solution to the dilemma was suggested by the University of Paris. For the Council adopted the formula of voting by nations that the University had evolved when it was faced with the problem of finding a new administrative pattern for the accommodation of its expanding cosmopolitan population. These affinities between the organization of the first great European congress on the one hand, and the organization of the most esteemed European university on the other, become clear when one follows Lenfant's discussion:

"Therefore it was resolved in spite of the Pope and his adherents that in the public sessions they should vote for the future by Nations; and for as much as the Spaniards were not yet come to the Council, they divided into four nations, viz., Italy, Germany, France and England. . . ."

[108] *The History of the Council of Constance*, London, 1728, new ed., Vol. I, p. 111.

"The order which these Nations observed in their deliberations was this: They nominated a certain number of Deputees of each Nation, men of weight and learning, as well Clergy as Laity, together with Proctors and Notaries. The deputees had at their head a president who was changed every month. Each nation had a particular assembly to consider of matters to be laid before the Council, and in those assemblies every member had the liberty of proposing *viva voce*, or in writing, what he thought necessary for the welfare of the Church. They communicated their resolutions to each other, in order to confer about them together and to remove the objections which anyone might raise against the opinions of another. When they had agreed upon some article, an Assembly or General Congregation of the Four Nations was held, and when the said article was unanimously resolved, it was carried ready, signed and sealed, to the next session in order to be approved by the Council. So that according to this plan, the Council assembled in public session, did but add the weight of his authority to the regulations of the Four Nations of which it was composed."[109]

The momentous conclusion that the nation was the primary unit of representation in the European community was reached after intricate processes of reasoning and bargaining had had their course, and sundry controversies and conspiracies had been resolved. Two questions in particular had been in issue: what is a "nation"? and which nations should be granted recognition at the Council? Both were answered in accordance with the precedents set by the University of Paris. Indeed, as Arnold Toynbee aptly remarks,[110] if an educated medieval Westerner had been asked what was the first association of ideas that the word "nation" called up in his mind, he would undoubtedly have answered, not a "concert of Europe," or a "balance of power," but the constitution of a university. For the word lacked the political overtones that it was to acquire in modern European history, when it would con-

---

[109] *ibid.*, Vol. I, p. 112. Later commentaries on the voting rules observed at the Council and the separate assemblies do not agree. Contrary to Lenfant who writes in the English as well as in the French edition (*Histoire du Conseil de Constance*, Amsterdam, 1727, Nouvelle édition, p. 108) that unanimity was the rule, *The Catholic Encyclopaedia* (*loc.cit.*) states that decisions were reached by a majority vote in the separate assemblies of the nations; that they were then communicated to the general congregation of all four nations, in which the vote of the majority was decisive; and that the decisions of the general congregation were presented to the public sessions of the Council where they were promulgated unanimously as conciliar decrees. See *The Encyclopaedia Britannica*, "Constance, Council of," to the effect that the successful papal candidate should be required to poll two-thirds of the suffrage, not only in the Sacred College, but in each of the five groups.

[110] *The World After the Peace Conference*, London, 1926, p. 5.

note instead a common country, language, tradition, or some combination of these three elements.

The first four nations to win recognition at Constance were Italy, Germany, France, and England. Spain was counted as the fifth when her delegates arrived in 1416.[111] However, since the principle of nationhood was not understood as an ethnic or moral concept, but as an administrative device for the conduct of congressional diplomacy, the five nations were not equated with the five most powerful states of the time to the exclusion of other sovereignties, as was to become the custom in international assemblies of the nineteenth century, such as the Congress of Vienna. Just as the few Poles, Hungarians, and Scandinavians were included in the German nation, so also did the other "great" nations include several kingdoms, peoples, and language groups. The superior principle of a Comity of Nations, or a Republic of Europe, was thus preserved by virtue of the fact that the five nations together were regarded as the whole of Western Society. That this understanding was more than a mere fiction is made evident by Lenfant's description of the constitutional methods followed within each national assembly as well as in the congregation of all nations. And the cause of cooperative diplomacy seems to have been furthered also by a joint or "steering" committee that the nations appointed for the purpose of preparing the agenda of discussion for each of the nations and of coordinating the relations between the different national assemblies.[112]

These agreements were not recorded until a controversy about the status of England had been settled.[113] The French contended that the force of Christendom was distributed among four great nations and votes—Italy, Germany, France, and Spain—and that the lesser kingdoms such as England, Denmark, and Portugal were included in one of these divisions. The English, on the other hand, were adamant in their contention that the British Islands, of which they were the head, should be considered as a fifth and coordinate nation, endowed with an equal vote. In support of their claim they adduced every conceivable argument and fable that might exalt the dignity of their country. However, their main thesis seems to have been that England was in fact a commonwealth of nations since she contained nine kingdoms and four

---

[111] Lenfant, p. 112, to the effect that this was also the order in which the nations ranked.
[112] *The Catholic Encyclopaedia, loc.cit.*
[113] Cf. with the controversy at the University of Paris.

or five different language groups.[114] The British won their case and were thus recognized for the first time as a separate nation.[115] Their victory was tantamount to a defeat for Italy, which had offered strenuous resistance to the proposal to vote by nations. The small English nation, consisting of twenty deputies and three bishops, had now become the equal, in the conciliar system of representation, to the entire Italian delegation, which accounted for half of the deputies at Constance.

The establishment of the supremacy of the nations in inter-European affairs was paralleled by the elimination of the Roman Church as a separate entity, for the resolution to vote by nations had as its counterpart the decision to withdraw from the cardinals their traditional right to vote apart.[116] The gist of the conciliar proceedings thus was that the choice of the future pope would depend not only on the vote of the cardinals, thus safeguarding tradition, but also on the unanimous consent of the various nations, by which the adhesion of the whole Catholic world to the election would be secured. This was the context in which the new pope was elected in 1417.

The syntheses between the new realities and the old myths that were embodied in the Council's record of proceedings and conclusions, furnished the premises in which the Western Europeans could proceed to reorganize their mutual relations without severing their connections with the past. However, they did not conceal the weakness of some traditional ideas and the power of certain new ones. For the papacy had been morally vanquished at Constance,[117] and the imperial institution had revealed itself a pale image of the once ideal office, as different nations began to unfold their strength. The transterritorial principle, implicit in the existence of the Church, the Empire, and the University of Paris, had been carried over into the organizational scheme of the Council of Constance, it is true, but it had been challenged effectively by the rival principle of territorially anchored sovereignty. Under the compelling influence of these developments, which converged with those registered earlier in the small arena of Italian politics, Europe gradually acquired its new identity as an aggregate of nation-states.

---

[114] See Gibbon, Vol. II, p. 1428, n.76, for a specification of this claim; also Toynbee, p. 5ff., n.2, to the effect that a British publicist writing in 1925 would have regarded the English as a commonwealth.

[115] *Encyclopaedia Britannica, loc.cit.* Gibbon, n.76, suggests that Henry V's military victories lent great support to the diplomatic maneuvers at Constance.

[116] *The Catholic Encyclopaedia, loc.cit.* The author of the article doubts the legality of the resolution and maintains that it had the effect of replacing the divine constitution of the Church by the will of the multitude.

[117] *ibid.*

B. THE HANSEATIC LEAGUE:

A TRANSTERRITORIAL UNION

The objective and subjective factors that had distinguished the Western European approach to peace and unity in religious, political, and intellectual matters, and had given rise, in consequence, to the permanent establishment of the three great concerts or "virtues" of the Church, the Empire, and the University of Paris, and the *ad hoc* assembling of all European interests at Constance were operative also in the field of Europe's economic life where they called forth a remarkable movement toward federalism among the rising groups of townsmen and merchants.

This impulse toward corporate unity was particularly strong north of the Alps, where the absence of a protective secular international order was felt more keenly than in Italy. Here, in the midst of political confusion, where travelling merchants had long been in the habit of carrying their special merchant law with them, and where cities had evolved their own law in protection of their special peace, certain German towns recorded what may well be the most suggestive chapter in the annals of inter-European constitutionalism when they formed the transterritorial League of Hanseatic cities.

In a discussion of European approaches to international unity it is important to note that the League of Hanseatic cities had its inception in fellowships of commerce-minded individuals. The conditions that evoked the voluntary formation of such companies were much the same as those that had precipitated cooperative trading ventures in the Mediterranean. The North European scene in which the German merchants operated before the twelfth century, however, presented greater hazards and greater opportunities for adventurous action than the southern region. East of the river Elbe spread the vast territorial expanse of rural, pagan Slavdom. Here the pioneering merchants are known to have conducted a border trade as early as the ninth century A.D. This penetration, later supported by organized campaigns of colonization and Christianization, brought the entering Germans into contact with local rulers under whose protection they proceeded to found and build numerous towns. Lübeck, renowned in later centuries as the leader of the Hanseatic League, was the first of these settlements that pointed, chainlike, toward the magnetic market of Novgorod. From the eastern ports of the "new" Germany the companies pushed to the farthest Baltic coast, gained economic control over the Baltic

Sea, and established a direct route between these northern waters and the Black Sea by travelling on the Oder or the Vistula to Cracow, and thence on the Pruth or Dniester to their southern points of destination.

As the dominant commercial power in the East and, consequently, as arbiters of all trade relations between England and Flanders on the one hand, and Baltic and Russian communities on the other, the fellowships of merchants were able to wring great concessions from the towns and countries whom they served. These privileges were consolidated gradually in a special status, and this status, in turn, gave rise to the term "hanse." For German traders in England or Flanders were organized into guilds; and those among them who made commercial voyages in common were said to constitute a "hanse" of their guild. Merchants from Cologne were the first group to win legal recognition as a "hanse." They were followed by natives from Hamburg and Lübeck, and, toward the end of the thirteenth century, all German merchants in England participated collectively in a uniform legal status as the *mercatores de hansa alemanie*. In this capacity they had common rights and duties and a joint establishment at London called the Guildhall (later Steelyard). In the following century another collective term, *mercatores de hansa theutonicorum* came into use to designate not merely the Germans in England but all German merchants trading outside of Germany, whether in England, Flanders, Scandinavia, the Baltic region, or northwest Russia.[118]

The recognition granted the Germans abroad coincided with the constitutional status that the trading companies had evolved for themselves, for all Germans who were natives of the Holy Roman Empire of the German Nation were actually organized at this time as a *universitas communium mercatorium*. This first all-German *universitas*,[119] the predecessor of the Hanseatic League, united the merchants of over thirty towns, from Cologne and Utrecht in the west to Reval in the east, and had its headquarters on the island of Gotland, then known as the axis and most celebrated market of Europe.[120]

The unifying factors that made this organized cooperation between individuals from widely separated communities possible were essentially of two kinds. As merchants interested in freedom as the indis-

[118] See Fritz Rörig, "Hanseatic League," *Encyclopaedia of the Social Sciences*, Vol. VII, p. 262. Cf. the status of these Germans with that of the Genoans in Byzantium.
[119] Note the ambivalence implicit in the assumption that the German merchants were a *universitas* because they belonged to the Roman, i.e., universal, Empire.
[120] See Alexander Justice, *A General Treatise of the Dominion and Laws of the Sea*, London, 1705.

pensable condition for the pursuit of their calling, the Germans realized the advantages implicit in a joint defense against piracy and other forms of lawlessness and a collective representation of their claims in foreign lands. As townsmen hailing from cities that were governed by analogous customs and laws, they were conditioned to organize their lives abroad—whether settled or itinerant—in essentially similar ways. This convergence of personal inclinations and social traditions explains why the members of the *universitas* had no difficulties in agreeing to the Wisby Sea Laws as the standard code of maritime behavior in Northern Europe; in accepting the laws promulgated by the Gotland Association for the regulation of common interests—even when they stipulated such penalties of non-compliance as expulsion from the association; and in maintaining joint trading posts in foreign towns.

These so-called counters (komtors) are a particularly interesting manifestation of the cooperative spirit with which individual merchants were imbued. Their constitutions, modelled on those of their German parent municipalities, provided for an intricate representational system, under the terms of which the principal officials in charge of administering justice and negotiating with the host country and other foreign governments were chosen from different towns and confederacies in the Holy Roman Empire. For example, the aldermen of the Novgorod branch were selected from merchants of the Gotland Association and the towns of Lübeck, Soest, and Dortmund;[121] in the London counter, which claimed jurisdiction over lesser English factories, Cologne retained the controlling interest until 1476; in the Bergen settlement Lübeck steadily asserted its ascendancy; while in Bruges, where East German merchants had succeeded in displacing the West Germans, four or five out of six aldermen were chosen from towns east of the Elbe.

Representation in the governments of the counters was thus weighted in accordance with the interests and functions that were associated with particular German municipalities. This system seems to have worked well; for each of the principal foreign settlements attained autonomy and power as a corporate entity while being able to further the individual interests of its component merchant groups. The record

---

[121] This form of government changed when representatives from Lübeck and Wisby visited Novgorod in 1361 to recodify the bylaws of the counter and to admonish its administrative officers that new statutes required the consent of Lübeck, Wisby, Riga, Dorpat, and Reval. See E. F. Gay, "The Hanseatic League" in *Encyclopaedia Britannica*, 1944, Vol. XI, p. 163; also Helen Zimmern, *The Hansa Towns*, London, 1889, 3rd ed., pp. 137-201, for a discussion of the organization of the various counters.

of their foreign relations shows, moreover, that the administrators of the counters were skillful diplomats, capable of accommodating the interests of their respective groups to those of the host town,[122] of extracting far-reaching privileges in England, Flanders, Scandinavia, the Baltic, and Russia, and, above all perhaps, of supporting in all their dealings the general cause of all Hanseatic merchants. Indeed, whenever possible, they seem to have projected their respective union in deliberately cosmopolitan terms. For example, the first treaty privileges granted by Bruges in 1252 refer to two men, of Lübeck and Hamburg respectively, as heading "the Merchants of the Roman Empire." Commenting on the services that the Bruges counter in particular rendered to the cause of the *universitas*, E. F. Gay concludes as follows: "Not merely because of its central commercial position, but because of its width of view, its political insight and its constant insistence on the necessity of union, this counter played a leading part in Hanseatic policy. It was more Hanse than the Hanse towns."[123]

The Gotland association of merchants lost its paramount position toward the end of the thirteenth century as it came under the control of a union of German towns. After Wisby had been sacked by the Danes in mid-fourteenth century this new municipal constellation became known officially as the Hanseatic League.

The unifying influences that stimulated the growth of the confederation derived from the shared conviction that the cities must retain the sovereignty they had achieved by taking advantage of the weakness of the Holy Roman Empire, resist all intervention on the part of territorial lords and imperial agencies, support the *Landfrieden*, protect their citizens abroad, expand their markets, and guard the area of their jurisdiction against inroads by foreign governments, Denmark in particular. The undisputed leader of the cities was Lübeck, whose council had repelled a Danish attack in 1227 with the aid of allied towns and displayed extraordinary diplomatic sagacity in representing German interests in all contacts with the northern monarchy. Renewed aggressions on the part of the famous King Valdemar were met, in 1367, by the formation of a special political alliance. This so-called Cologne Confederation negotiated a highly advantageous treaty under the terms of which Denmark was obliged to extend trading privileges to the German towns, relinquish to the allied cities two-thirds of the important tolls on the Sound for a period of fifteen years, guarantee this indemnity

---

[122] Bruges and Novgorod in particular owed much of their greatness to the policies of the Germans.

[123] *loc.cit.*

by the cession of strong castles on the Sound, and give the cities a veto power in the choice of Valdemar's successor.[124] These developments contributed greatly to the evolution of the League as a collective security organization. Indeed, the commitment of the towns to the cause of unity was understood so unequivocally as to prompt a Lübeck official to declare in 1380 that "Whatever touches one town touches All."[125] In mid-fourteenth century the League was an economic-political association, not a political and military alliance. It had no territorial boundaries but spanned immense spaces of land and water. No complete list of its members was ever drawn up, but the rule was fixed that only towns with Germanic populations could join. While it is customary to speak of seventy-seven participants, the number of cities actually enjoying Hanseatic privileges at one time or another is supposed to have been much greater. This network of municipalities stretched from Thorn and Cracow in the east to communities on the Zuider Zee in the west, from Wisby and Reval in the north to Göttingen in the south.[126] Grouped about Lübeck were Wismar, Rostock, Stralsund, Kiel, Hamburg, and Lüneburg; Danzig, Thorn, Elbing, and Königsberg were the most important towns in Prussia; Riga, Reval, Dorpat, and Pernau were the focal points in the Baltic region; and Cologne functioned as the leader in the division of western cities. Other members were located inland in Lower Saxony, Brandenburg, and Westphalia. The fact that some member cities were nominally subject to feudal lords, while others stood directly under the emperor, was considered immaterial to the issue of membership. However, only a town that had obtained for its citizens the right to enjoy commercial privileges abroad was considered eligible. This meant, in effect, that the identity of a Hanse town was determined by the foreign relations of its individual citizens.[127]

The principal organ of the League was the diet or *Hansetag* which met usually once a year in Lübeck in order to regulate intermunicipal and foreign relations. According to the minutes, known as "recesses," of which many have been preserved, the business before each conference was heavy and varied; for the diet decided on peace and war, sent dispatches to foreign monarchs, supervised roads and sealanes, fixed tolls and prices, evaluated the quality of merchandise, discussed

---

[124] See Rörig, *loc.cit.*   [125] Gay, *loc.cit.*

[126] Associations with southern cities like Munich and Augsburg were also formed, but none of these trade centers actually joined the League as a full-fledged member.

[127] In 1447 it was stipulated that admission to the League could be granted only by the unanimous consent of existing members.

the treatment of Hanseatic merchants abroad, passed on applications for membership, threatened and warned those who had failed to fulfill treaty obligations, settled disputes between towns that neighboring municipalities had been unable to solve, and heard private quarrels between merchants in appeal. When a weighty problem seemed insoluble at the time it arose, the assembly would carefully register in its books: "Of this matter let those think who come after us."[128]

Delegates to the session were bound by instructions from their towns, but it was understood, theoretically at least, that "Every town shall consider the benefit of the others, so far as is in accordance with right and honour."[129] The diet made its decisions "in the name of all the cities" and communicated its missives under a seal that was meant to symbolize the corporate will. However, the League had not been conceived as a democracy but as an intermunicipal oligarchy, and the Hansetag was designed to reflect the oligarchic pattern to which most legislative assemblies in the member towns conformed. All cities were supposed to send delegates, it is true, and the diet was severe in scrutinizing the excuses of those who failed to be represented and in punishing unwarranted defaults. But in actuality the League was controlled by its most powerful members. Many cities were constrained to forfeit any influence they might have exerted upon the League's policies because they could not afford the heavy expense that attendance at the *Hansetag* implied. These municipalities confined themselves to participation in regional assemblies, such as the Prussian town diets, at which local as well as Hanseatic affairs were discussed, and entrusted the representation of their interests in the Lübeck session to some larger and wealthier town in their territory.[130] Another factor that made acceptance of the principle of big-city supremacy mandatory was the absence of a permanent source of League revenues and of a standing administrative organization. All member towns thus realized that the very existence of the League was made possible by the financial contributions and administrative services of those among them who had a predominant stake in the policies and ventures of the union. And since Lübeck surpassed all municipalities in influence and prestige, they authorized this city to act as spokesman for the Hanse when the diet was not in session.

The moral unity of the League was thus in a considerable measure

[128] Helen Zimmern, p. 202.
[129] *ibid.*
[130] Cf. these constitutional understandings with those adopted by the medieval universities in respect of membership in "nations."

the corollary of the policies that Lübeck conducted while she was an effective and trusted executive of the corporate interest. By way of further comment upon the solidarity of this union it should be noted, however, that the pursuit of the corporate interests was circumscribed by the law merchant and other regulations with which the League identified itself as a whole and in respect of which all its members were equals. The general readiness of member towns to comply with such a stringent decree as the "*Verhansung*," or exclusion of a recalcitrant town from the benefits of the League's trading privileges, can only be understood in this context, for the union did not have a federal judiciary and had not developed juridical measures for the enforcement of its decisions. That the *Verhansung* was an effective device is illustrated by two interesting cases. The great city of Bremen was expelled in 1356 when she declined to discipline a refractory merchant who had violated the League's embargo on trade with Flanders. Totally cut off from the advantages of the union, she was impoverished for thirty years. The city of Brunswick found itself in such a plight after having suffered the same penalty that her representatives were ready to humiliate themselves openly in order to gain readmission to the League, as the following account shows: ". . . two of her burgomasters and eight of her chief citizens walked bareheaded and barefooted, carrying candles, from the Church of Our Lady in Lübeck to the town hall, where the Council of the League was assembled. There before a great audience they confessed upon their knees their enormous error, and implored the Council to pardon them for the love of God and the honour of the Virgin Mary."[131]

Sanctions of the kind devised by the Hanse were an outgrowth of the prevailing value system. They ceased to be effective when people ceased to feel the need to obey established social and moral norms. The disestablishing of the norms that had held the Hanseatic towns together proceeded slowly but surely under the impact of intellectual and material forces that have been discussed in earlier chapters. Within the context of the League it had become increasingly evident that the cooperative spirit, so strikingly manifest in the early fellowships of merchants, was being undermined by the pursuit of separatist policies on the part of privileged towns. By holding fast to the principle of profit and privilege and neglecting the principle of mutuality the League gradually forfeited its inner unity as well as its external prestige. Smaller towns resented the dominant role played by the great ones;

---

[131] H. Gordon Selfridge, *The Romance of Commerce*, New York, 1923, p. 103.

inland towns were reluctant to support the drive for sea power that emanated from coastal communities; and conflicts between the merchants and councils, on the one hand, and the craftsmen protesting against what they considered an unjust distribution of the tax burden, on the other, paralysed the political vigor of many member cities.[132] Outside of Germany, the League evoked resentment as an all-German association and as a monopoly determined to suppress the competition of outsiders. And this antagonism grew as a matter of course when merchant communities in England, Holland, and Scandinavia were ready to challenge the commercial supremacy of the Hanse.

Of all developments that affected the League adversely, however, none was as important as the rise of nationalism and the evolution of the sovereign state. Behind the Dutch, the English, the Danish, and the Russian merchants emerged strong governments, each keenly aware of the advantages implicit in a union with its own commerce-minded bourgeoisie, and each intent upon asserting the principle of territorial supremacy. The German merchants, on the other hand, could not withdraw into the protective order of a powerful German monarch; for the Holy Roman Empire, long the prey of centrifugal rather than centripetal forces, was dissolving fast into numerous petty principalities, each eager to enlarge its limited domain by subordinating the self-governing towns within its jurisdiction. The decline of the Hanseatic League was thus inevitable and can be explained entirely by references to developments within Europe.[133] However, it was camouflaged for several centuries by the diplomacy of the Hanseatic government which continued to arouse awe, as Rörig explains, because it continued to be successful: "After every solid economic support of the league had decayed, it (the diplomatic leadership) enabled the Hanseatic merchants to reap the fruits of the achievements of their daring ancestors. The catastrophe was postponed until the sixteenth century, when the Scandinavian countries, soon followed by England, officially abolished the Hanseatic privileges."[134]

The new European society no longer required the Hanse merchants, but it continued to reflect their influences in a great variety of ways. The successful struggle that the merchants had conducted against piracy, slave-trading, and other manifestations of lawlessness had brought peace and law to vast parts of Northern and Eastern Europe.

[132] See Rörig, *loc.cit.*

[133] See *ibid.* to the effect that the League's power was broken before the discovery of American territory and of the sea route to India began to manifest their effects.

[134] *ibid.*, p. 266.

The diffusion of urban ways of life with their various attendant institutions and artistic styles[135] had been instrumental in drawing formerly secluded and culturally backward rural areas into the realm of Europe's civilization. The strenuous and ceaseless opposition with which the merchants and townsmen had countered the tyrannous claims of princes and nobles had the ultimate effect of advancing the cause of individual liberty and contributing to the political foundations upon which later generations were able to build genuinely democratic institutions. And the ingenious application of the principle of federalism to the organization of far-flung trade relations set a precedent of economic cooperation between individuals and governments that carries significance far beyond the time and place of its enactment.

F. Conclusion: International Constitutionalism
and the World Society Today

The records of the Hanseatic League and the Council of Constance have a place in international history because they are early commentaries on certain Occidental approaches to peace, unity, and security that have no analogues in the histories of other civilizations but have found world-wide applicability in this century. The two organizations to which they refer were called into existence for entirely different purposes, as the preceding pages have shown, but they had the following common characteristics. Both were voluntary, transterritorial associations of separate sovereignties. Both succeeded in reconciling the particular interests of their members with the general interests shared by all participants. Both incorporated the principal residual values that had sustained the medieval European commonwealth while announcing entirely new motifs for the conduct of inter-European affairs. And both relied upon legal concepts and procedures with which all Europeans were familiar in order to transpose these various syntheses into working institutions.

The principles exemplified in these two case studies were eclipsed temporarily by the rise of the nation-state, but they have never been dislodged from the European mind. Between 1500 and 1800 they were cultivated and elaborated by numerous political writers who composed blueprints for the unification of nations in protest against the separatist trends of their age, in nostalgic remembrance of a unity lost, or in sanguine anticipation of a greater unity to come. A library of recorded

---

[135] The same architectural style can still be found in the churches and municipal buildings of the former Hanse towns in Western and Eastern Europe.

visions, extended in each century by comments of all kinds, has thus always been at the disposal of those who had the incentive and the opportunity to revise the existing European order.[136]

The proposals that accumulated in this fashion present a great variety of thoughts on the subject of organized unity. They ranged in character from utterly utopian schemes to shrewd approximations of what governments might have been capable of achieving in reality. They also differed greatly in terms of the geographic area to which they addressed themselves. Some confined themselves to the integration of Western Europe only; others contemplated the union of all Europe, or of all Christendom;[137] several aimed at the constitution of a trans-Atlantic community; and a few aspired to the institution of a world government that would include all races and religions.[138] However, all assumed that it was possible and desirable to institute transnational or extra-territorial unions; and all made explicit or implicit references to some previous manifestation of European unity.[139] Most of the plans were presented as treaties or constitutions; provided for elaborate representative institutions, whether in the form of periodical conferences,[140] annual parliaments,[141] perpetual congresses,[142] world assemblies,[143] or

[136] The bibliography on this subject is voluminous and will not be listed here.

[137] The majority of writers accepted the political boundaries that had come to exist, but a few proposed radical revisions of the map. For example, "The Great Design," (1620-1635), composed in all probability by the Duke de Sully, chief minister of Henri IV of France, suggested that Europe should be divided equally among a certain number of powers so that none would be tempted to covet the territory of another. And a similar idea commended itself to John Bellers, "Some Reasons for An European State," (1710), who parcelled Europe into one hundred equal provinces, each unit to be held responsible for its quota of military or financial support.

[138] The most ambitious project in this category is Emeric Crucé's "The New Cyneas or Discourse of the Occasions and Means to Establish a General Peace, and the Liberty of Commerce throughout the World" (1623). The pivotal institution here is an international assembly, composed of the representatives of the Pope, Emperor of the Turks, Holy Roman Emperor, King of France, King of Spain, with a sixth seat to be contested between the Kings of Persia and China, Prester John, the Precop of Tatary, and the Grand Duke of Muscovy. Included also were the Kings of Great Britain, Poland, Denmark, Sweden, Japan, and Morocco, and several potentates from India and Africa. All sovereigns were to maintain permanent resident missions at the seat of the assembly. See Sylvester John Hemleben, *Plans for World Peace through Six Centuries*, Chicago, 1943, pp. 22-31.

[139] The Greek amphictyonies were the model for the European Council in Sully's Great Design; the *pax romana* was recalled by Dante in *De Monarchia*; the Holy Roman Empire was the principal source of inspiration in the fourteenth century for Marsiglio of Padua (*Defensor pacis*) and in the eighteenth century for Leibniz; and the representative system used by the Council of Constance was copied by King Podebrad of Bohemia in the project for a federation of Christian princes and the institution of an international parliament that he presented to other monarchs in 1461.

[140] Hugo Grotius, *De jure belli ac pacis*, 1625.

[141] William Penn, "An Essay towards the Present and Future Peace of Europe," 1693; also John Bellers.

world courts;[144] and paid considerable attention to the regulation of voting rights.[145] All agreed that peace was the primary purpose of unity,[146] and that it was the principal function of the international government to find peaceful ways of settling disputes among member states and to develop and maintain a European or international law. These obligations were supplemented in some projects by the advice that the international and national authorities must do their utmost to overcome particularism, combat nationalism, and promote trade and economic interdependence among nations, if the spectres of disunity and war were to be effectively allayed.[147]

The formative period of the modern states system, during which these designs were composed, did not favor the establishment of international unions. But trends toward an integration of Europe's separate sovereignties were discernible even in the centuries that witnessed the revolt against the medieval conceptions of organized unity and peace and the rise of the absolute state. For example, the idea of federalism was never disavowed after it had been implemented successfully in some regions north of the Alps, notably in Switzerland;[148] the notion that territorial sovereignty should be limited in certain circumstances in the interests of regional peace and security by the institution of international servitudes was translated into practice even in

---

[142] Abbé de Saint-Pierre, "A Project for Settling an Everlasting Peace in Europe," 1712-14.

[143] Crucé.

[144] J. Bentham, "A Project for Perpetual Peace," 1760.

[145] The principles that governed representation and voting at these councils were understood and stated in rather different terms. King Podebrad of Bohemia subscribed to the rule established at Constance that nations were equal and gave each member nation one vote in his projected assembly. William Penn, on the other hand, argued for inequality of representation, with wealth determining a nation's voting strength. Most authors did not concern themselves explicitly with the internal constitutions of the member states. But Crucé and Kant were emphatic in linking the solidarity of the union to the stability of each local government, the former by upholding the thesis that the union must be a union of sovereign princes, and the latter by insisting that perpetual peace could be instituted only by republican governments. See Immanuel Kant, "Perpetual Peace," 1795.

[146] However, peace was linked by Pierre Dubois, *De recuperatione terre sancte*, 1305-1307, with a project to recover the Holy Land; by King Podebrad of Bohemia with expeditions against the infidels, and by Henri IV and the Duke de Sully with possible wars against the Muscovites and Turks and with definite plans for the weakening of the House of Habsburg and the establishment of French hegemony in Europe.

[147] See particularly "The New Cyneas."

[148] This remark must be qualified by the observation that federalism as it manifested itself in Switzerland, North America, and Germany was also an expression of nationalism, for in these instances it had been evoked in opposition to the powers of transnational empires.

periods marked by the pursuit of predatory foreign policies;[149] the movement to subordinate the behavior of states to a system of international law and to curb belligerent reactions to political conflicts by resort to arbitration was furthered assiduously by successive generations of politically astute theorists and received widespread support among the governments of the day; and the pattern set by the Council of Constance when it assembled the representatives of all European powers for a joint deliberation of issues affecting the peace of Europe as a whole, was followed by a series of conferences that ranged from the inconclusive Congress of Loutsk, convoked in 1429 in order to intercept the advance of the Turks and compose the rivalry between the Slavs and Germans, to the effectual congresses of Westphalia (1648) and Utrecht (1713), which met after major wars in order to restore the peace and public law of Europe.

These approaches were solidified in the nineteenth century when the political ideals of nations and purposes of government were related to constitutionalism as the common Western European frame of reference. Beginning with the Congress of Vienna, *ad hoc* conferences were called as a matter of course whenever the great powers found that the peace of Europe was endangered or a controversial issue required collective settlement. As these occasions multiplied in response to the growing political interdependence of all European peoples, congressional diplomacy, organized along parliamentary lines, with which all participants were familiar, became established as the most appropriate and effective mode of coordinating conflicting policies and ascertaining the general interest of Europe. Indeed, by cultivating the art of identifying common objectives and mutually agreeable methods of serving these objectives, the Western governments succeeded in transmuting the balance of power into the Concert of Europe.

This new image of unity, which had been formulated rather arbitrarily when the major powers assumed joint responsibility for the direction of Europe's affairs, was a much reduced version of the medieval conception of a transterritorial commonwealth. It was a suggestive image, nevertheless, for not only did it symbolize the general striving for peace and security that pervaded the European scene after the

---

[149] For instance, the customs-free zones of Gex and Upper Savoy had been integral parts of the European order long before they were recognized officially at the Congress of Vienna. In fact, these international arrangements had outlasted the fortunes of many nations in Southwestern Europe before they were terminated in the twentieth century. See Adda Bruemmer Bozeman, *Regional Conflicts Around Geneva*, Stanford, 1949, for an analysis of these international servitudes.

Napoleonic Wars, but it also provided the auspices for a progressive development of cooperative institutions on all levels of international relations. Constitutional governments for the joint administration of international rivers, postal services, and other transcontinental and transoceanic systems of communication, and for the promotion of public health, sanitation, and related concerns were called into being by intergovernmental charters of agreement. Voluntary contractual accords for the judicial settlement of disputes, and multilateral treaties embodying legal customs, establishing new codes of international law, regulating commerce and finance, and controlling the slave trade —to mention only some of the matters that elicited concerted action —were concluded with relative ease in this century. And parallel associational movements marked the vast realm of nongovernmental international relations; for businessmen, workers, scholars, and philanthropists were also participating in periodical international congresses and coalescing into unions in order to promote the common interests of their respective groups. When the twentieth century opened, the modern European states system was thus enveloped by a network of international organizations. Each of the unions, tribunals, commissions, and bureaus was the nucleus of a concert of nations, however limited its functions, and all together projected an entirely new transterritorial sphere of international constitutionalism.

Three distinct, yet interlocking and chronologically concurrent, movements to extend the sphere of international constitutionalism and promote the cause of organized unity among nations were sponsored by the Western nations in the first half of the twentieth century. One aimed at the political and economic integration of Western Europe and North America; one at the conversion of colonial empires into transoceanic unions of nations belonging to different civilizations; the third at the establishment of a world organization for the maintenance of global peace and security.

The development of the Concert of Europe had been arrested in the first decades of this century by the growth of integral nationalism and allied creeds; but it was resumed after the Second World War, when the Western Europeans, faced with the disintegration of their civilization and the forfeiture of their material power, united in a vigorous search for new sources of strength. The immediate objectives of this quest were suggested by the realization, in which all Occidental governments concurred, that the recovery of Europe's economy was the indispensable condition not only for the political rehabilitation of Europe but for the resurrection of Western culture in general. Only passing reference can be made in this general discussion of historically significant approaches to peace and unity to the various concerted measures that have been taken in the last fifteen years in order to attain these aims. But the records of the European Recovery Program, the European Payments Union, the European Coal and Steel Community, the European Common Market, the Council of Europe, the European Court of Human Rights, the North Atlantic Treaty Organization, and their various subsidiaries support the conclusion that the American and Western European nations have succeeded in creating an effective trans-Atlantic commonwealth, and that this commonwealth continues the traditions with which Western approaches to unity and peace have been identified since medieval times. For all of these mutual undertakings were conceived as voluntary, transterritorial associations; all were realized in the context of contractual relations and derive their character as corporate entities from elaborate charters and articles of agreement in which the purposes and functions of the joint enterprise, as well as the rights and obligations of the individual member states, are clearly defined; and all have their own governments, organized in accordance with principles of representation that obtain also in the constitutional systems of the participating nations.

Contemporaries who are acutely conscious of the unresolved problems of the present are apt to view these inter-European and trans-Atlantic organizations somewhat disparagingly, either as indispensable implements of realistic national foreign policies, or as the minimal approximations of some far loftier ideal of European unity and peace. But historians interested in the long-range significance of phenomena and familiar with the records of many civilizations have cause to note the tenacity with which the ideals of peace and cooperation have been cultivated in the West; the ingenuity with which constitutionalism has been used as a leverage in that intricate process of fusing the concepts of the sovereign state, diplomacy, and international law, from which the very idea of international organization was eventually deduced; and the determination with which this entirely new image of a community of nations has been diffused in the world.

Ideas of greater unions had also been entertained by non-Western peoples, as preceding parts of this book have shown. Indeed, some of these may have been more poetic and magical in their appeal, while others had a more incisive impact upon regional politics[150] than those

---

[150] E.g., the Byzantine and Chinese concepts of union.

projected by the West. But none of these images stimulated the formation of effective transterritorial or transcultural unions, either because they were permitted to remain as mere legendary or mythical references, symbolic of a general yearning for peace and unity but not susceptible to definition and realization, or because they were guarded deliberately by ethnocentric imperial administrations.[151]

The Occidental record in the field of transnational government was sullied by several generations of Europeans who promoted the expansion of their respective nations by despoiling other lands and cultures. Indeed, most of the histories of European empire compiled and analysed in recent times have stressed the theme of ruthlessness and exploitation. And this opprobrious evaluation is certainly justified if the imperialistic policies of the seventeenth and eighteenth centuries are to be viewed in the context of Western political thought as developed in the nineteenth and twentieth centuries. However, in the wider perspective of international history additional measures of judgment are appropriate. For a comparison of the Occidental empires with those created earlier by Far Eastern, Middle Eastern, African, and South American nations does not convince the student of international relations that the latter were more benign and humane than the former.[152] It shows, above all, that the non-Western empires remained empires, in conception as well as administration, from their initiation to their dissolution. No precedent can be found in these records for the progressive relaxation of imperial controls and the corresponding elaboration, in one form or another, of theories of trusteeship; or for the careful integration of separate colonies into regional self-governing federations and the methodical transformation of empires into commonwealths or unions of nations, such as have characterized the histories of most Western empires.

The Occidental movements toward the establishment of continental and transcontinental communities of states were paralleled by deliberate efforts to institute a world-wide organization for the maintenance of international peace and the promotion of collective security. Indeed, the experiences in constitutional thought and practice that had accumulated in the history of every Western nation, the projects and ideals of organized international peace and unity, the collection of in-

---

[151] It may be noted also in this connection that the literate non-Western civilizations have not brought forth any extensive projects to institute peace and unity in the world.

[152] Islamic rule in India—to take but one manifestation of non-Western imperialism —was certainly harsher and more destructive of native civilizations than British rule.

ternational laws and customs, and the records of congressional diplomacy and international administration, were joined, as it were, first in the Covenant of the League of Nations (1919) and most recently in the charters that established the United Nations and its various affiliated agencies.

The complex framework of international organizations that spans the world today may thus be viewed as the logical culmination of the political history of the West. As a nonterritorial power structure, embodying ideas of unity and peace for which generations have contended with varying success, it recalls the traditions set by the great medieval concerts. As an international extension of the modern democratic state it incorporates the values that have governed European and American societies in recent centuries. And as the outgrowth of a highly literate civilization it projects the preference for verbal imagery and legal abstractions that have distinguished the communication of political ideas in this civilization since the days of Rome.

By the time that this international system was instituted in 1945 as the ultimate frame of reference in the conduct of international relations, most non-Western nations had adopted the cause of the modern state. And since all had been affected, in one way or another, by the war that had just been fought, they also rallied to the new image of world unity and order that had emerged from the common political experience. It was thus generally assumed in Western and non-Western circles that the peoples of all continents were united not only in an acceptance, but also in an understanding, of the international contracts to which they had affixed their signatures. However, this assumption was not supported by the realities of history. For the written texts embodied political ideas and carried meanings and expectations that had not been developed by the non-Western civilizations. Unable to identify with the complex substantive values that were projected by the language of agreement, the non-Western peoples fastened upon the terminological and procedural aspects of the international charter as the focal points of their attachment to the new world order. And the ease with which the technical apparatus was employed by their representatives in succeeding years lent further support to the impression that all nations were in accord with the fundamental purposes of their collective undertaking. Indeed, even when discords upon substantive issues multiplied in the post-war period, the belief retained wide currency in all parts of the world that the appointed methods for the dissolution of international disputes were no longer to be associated exclusively with the constitutionalism of the West, but had actually superseded all local traditions for approximating politically desirable ends to become genuinely preferred international ways for the avoidance of conflicts and the realization of adjustments.

This trust in methods had arisen rather naturally in the process of diffusing the political heritage of the West, which had preceded the formation of the United Nations system. The Occidental nations had been schooled by their constitutional history to think of such preferred values as liberty, equality, peace, and unity in conjunction with the methods that had been designed for their defence and propagation. In other words, not only had ends and means, or substance and procedure, developed simultaneously in Western politics, but they were regarded as inextricably intertwined.[153] When the Western system was relayed to non-Western societies, however, this organic connection between ideas and the methods of implementing ideas was relaxed.

It may be observed in general that methods are more tangible than ideas. For example, such implements of democracy as the right to vote or to participate in representative assemblies can be described, defined, and installed more easily than the values they are supposed to serve. Western methods of identifying the will of the majority or drafting bills of rights could thus be received in many regions in which the Western concept of individual freedom could not take root. In fact, a retrospective view of these borrowings as they affected local and regional politics permits the inference not only that methods often assumed a quasi-autonomous existence, but that they were frequently mistaken for the ends that did not lend themselves to easy use and understanding. When the time came to implement the values of peace and unity by instituting democratic contractual relationships in international politics, the conviction was thus widespread that an acceptance of the technical apparatus of international democracy was tantamount to the incorporation of the values implicit in constitutionalism. Only when nations were found deadlocked in conflict over the interpretation of a value, or in the pursuit of mutually antagonistic goals was it realized that the subscription to internationally approved objectives and methods of attaining these objectives had not cancelled long-standing local value systems and traditional methods of coping with political disputes. Indeed, as governments grew frustrated by unresolved conflicts and individuals became disenchanted with the myth

---

[153] Cf. the relationship between "writ" and "right" in English constitutional history.

of world unity that had so recently captured their imagination, non-Western peoples everywhere began to seek security by retreating into the folds of their own ethnocentric traditions, resurrecting patterns of political thought and organization that had been commonly regarded as defunct, or at least inadequate for the conduct of modern international relations, and, objectively considered, hardly compatible with the principles to which all nations had agreed in 1945.

These unforeseen ironical consequences of the Occidental commitment to the cause of international unity and peace are emotionally disconcerting for contemporaries in the West, but they also present new and forceful challenges. As the authors of the modern system of political references, the Western nations are more deeply affected by the present disharmony between the global value scales and the various local value scales than any other people. But unlike the non-Western nations, they cannot extricate themselves from the dilemma by retreating into their own culture, for the international scale of values is also, for each, the national scale of values. Indeed, they may not even contest the paradoxical effects that have ensued from the rehabilitation of the non-Western traditions; for they themselves had supplied the initial motive power for the resurrection of the ancient orders. The particular moment in which we find ourselves today may not permit either a definitive assessment of the Western impact upon the collective fortunes of mankind, or a clear projection of new perspectives in the conduct of international relations. However, it invites the thoughtful to reconsider the realities and myths in international history that have called forth the present world society, and to resume the creative quest for intercultural accords upon which so many of their predecessors have engaged.

BIBLIOGRAPHY OF SOURCES CITED IN TEXT

Adams, Henry. *Mont-Saint-Michel and Chartres*. Boston and New York, 1922.

Ament, W. S. "Marco Polo in Cambaluc: A Comparison of Foreign and Native Accounts," *Journal of the Peking Oriental Society*, III (No. 2, 1892).

Andreas, Willy. *Staatskunst und Diplomatie der Venezianer im Spiegel ihrer Gesandtenberichte*. Leipzig, 1943.

Anesaki, Masaharu. "East and West: the Meaning of Their Cultural Relations," in *Independence, Convergence and Borrowing in Institutions, Thought and Art* (Harvard Tercentenary Conference of Arts and Sciences). Cambridge, Mass., 1937.

Arabian Nights. *The Book of the Thousand Nights and a Night*, tr. Richard F. Burton. 6 vols. New York, 1954.

———. *The Book of the Thousand Nights and One Night*, tr. John Payne. 9 vols. London, 1882.

———. *The Portable Arabian Nights*, ed. Joseph Campbell. New York, 1952.

Arberry, A. J., ed. *The Legacy of Persia*. Oxford, 1953.

Arnold, Sir Thomas. *The Caliphate*. Oxford, 1924.

———, and Alfred Guillaume, eds. *The Legacy of Islam*. Oxford, 1947.

Arrian. *The Life of Alexander the Great*, tr. Aubrey de Sélincourt. (Penguin Book.) Harmondsworth, 1958.

Ashburner, Walter, ed. *Rhodian Sea Law*. Oxford, 1909.

Augustine, Saint. *The City of God*. (Modern Library) New York, 1950.

Bagchi, P. C. *Le Canon Bouddhique en Chine*. 2 vols. Paris, 1927.

———. *India and China—1000 Years of Cultural Relations*. 2d ed. Bombay, 1950.

Bailey, Cyril, ed. *The Legacy of Rome*. Oxford, 1924.

Barker, Sir Ernest. *The Dominican Order and Convocation, a Study in the Growth of Representation in the Church During the Thirteenth Century*. Oxford, 1913.

———. *Greek Political Theory*. London, 1918.

———. ed. *Social and Political Thought in Byzantium, from Justinian to the Last Palaeologus*. Oxford, 1957.

———. "Crusades," in *Encyclopaedia Britannica* (14th ed.), Vol. VI.

Basham, A. L. *The Wonder That Was India*. London, 1954.

Baynes, Norman H. *The Byzantine Empire*. London, 1925.

———. *Byzantine Studies and Other Essays*. London, 1955.

Beales, A. C. F. *The History of Peace*. New York, 1931.

Becker, Carl. *The Heavenly City of the Eighteenth Century Philosophers*. New Haven, 1932.

Berdyaev, Nicolas. *The Origin of Russian Communism*. London, 1937.

———. *The Russian Idea*. New York, 1948.

Bevan, A. A. "Manichaeism," in *Encyclopaedia of Religion and Ethics*, ed. James Hastings, Vol. VIII.

Bevan, E. R., ed. *The Legacy of Israel*. Oxford, 1927.

Bewes, Wyndham. *The Romance of the Law Merchant*. London, 1923.

Bible. Authorized (King James) Version.

Bickerman, Elias J. "The Greek Experience of War and Peace," in *Approaches to World Peace*, ed. Lyman Bryson. New York, 1944.

Bigg, Charles. *The Christian Platonists of Alexandria*. Oxford, 1913.

Boehm, Max H. "Cosmopolitanism," in *Encyclopaedia of the Social Sciences*, Vol. IV.

Boswell, James. *Boswell's Life of Johnson*. London, New York, Toronto, 1953.

Botsford, G. W., and Charles A. Robinson, Jr. *Hellenic History*. New York, 1946.

Bovill, E. W. *Caravans of the Old Sahara*. Oxford, 1933. (New and rev. ed., under title, *The Golden Trade of the Moors*, Oxford, 1958.)

Brockelmann, Carl. *History of the Islamic Peoples*, tr. Joel Carmichael and Moshe Perlmann. New York, 1947.

Brown, D. Mackenzie. *The White Umbrella: Indian Political Thought from Manu to Gandhi*. Berkeley, 1958.

Bryce, James. *The Holy Roman Empire*. New York, 1928.

Buckland, W. W., and Arnold D. McNair. *Roman Law and Common Law*. Cambridge, 1952.

Buckler, F. W. *Harunu'l-Rashid and Charles the Great*. Cambridge, Mass., 1931.

Burckhardt, Jacob. *The Civilization of the Renaissance in Italy*. (Modern Library) New York, 1954.

Bury, J. B. *A History of the Eastern Roman Empire from the Fall of Irene to the Accession of Basil I* (A.D. *802-867*). London, 1912.

————. *History of the Later Roman Empire, from the Death of Theodosius I to the Death of Justinian*, A.D. *395-565*. 2 vols. London, 1931.

Buss, Kenneth Caron. "Persia: The Parthian Empire, 2nd Century B.C.—3rd Century A.D.," in *Encyclopaedia Britannica* (14th ed.), Vol. XVII.

Calhoun, George M. *Introduction to Greek Legal Science*. Oxford, 1944.

Calvo, Charles. *Le Droit International Théorique et Pratique*. 4 vols. Paris, 1880.

Cambridge Ancient History. 12 vols. Cambridge, 1923-29.

    Vol. I. *Egypt and Babylonia to 1580* B.C.

    Vol. II. *The Egyptian and Hittite Empires to c. 1000* B.C.

        Chap. III. "The Foundation and Expansion of the Egyptian Empire," by J. H. Breasted.

        Chap. IV. "The Reign of Thutmose III," by J. H. Breasted.

        Chap. V. "The Zenith of Egyptian Power and the Reign of Amenhotep III," by J. H. Breasted.

        Chap. VI. "Ikhnaton, the Religious Revolutionary," by J. H. Breasted.

        Chap. VII. "The Age of Ramses II," by J. H. Breasted.

        Chap. VIII. "The Decline and Fall of the Egyptian Empire," by J. H. Breasted.

    Vol. III. *The Assyrian Empire*.

        Chap. I. "The Foundation of the Assyrian Empire," by Sidney Smith.

        Chap. II. "The Supremacy of Assyria," by Sidney Smith.

Chap. III. "Sennacherib and Eoarhaddon," by Sidney Smith.

Chap. IV. "The Age of Ashurbanipal," by Sidney Smith.

Chap. V. "Ashurbanipal and the Fall of Assyria," by Sidney Smith.

Chap. VI. "The Hittites of Syria," by D. C. Hogarth.

Chap. VII. "Hittite Civilization," by D. C. Hogarth.

Vol. IV. *The Persian Empire and the West.*

Chap. I. "The Foundation and Extension of the Persian Empire," by G. Buchanan Gray.

Chap. V. "Coinage from Its Origin to the Persian Wars," by G. F. Hill.

Chap. VII. "The Reign of Darius," by G. Buchanan Gray and M. Cary.

Chap. IX. "Xerxes' Invasion of Greece," by J. A. R. Munro.

Vol. VII. *The Hellenistic Monarchies and the Rise of Rome.*

Chap. III. "The New Hellenistic Kingdoms," by W. W. Tarn.

Chap. XXIII. "The Greek Leagues and Macedonia," by W. W. Tarn.

Vol. VIII. *Rome and the Mediterranean, 218-133 B.C.*

Chap. IX. "Rome and the Hellenistic States," by P. V. M. Benecke.

Chap. XIX. "Pergamum," by M. Rostovtzeff.

Chap. XX. "Rhodes, Delos and Hellenistic Commerce," by M. Rostovtzeff.

Vol. IX. *The Roman Republic, 133-44 B.C.*

Chap. X. "The Provinces and Their Government," by G. H. Stevenson.

Chap. XIV. "Parthia," by W. W. Tarn.

Chap. XXI. "The Development of Law under the Republic," by F. de Zulueta.

Vol. X. *The Augustan Empire, 44 B.C.-A.D. 70.*

Chap. VI. "Senatus Populusque Romanus," by Sir Henry Stuart Jones.

Chap. VII. "The Imperial Administration," by G. H. Stevenson.

Vol. XI. *The Imperial Peace, A.D. 70-192.*

Chap. XI. "Rome and the Empire," by Hugh Last.

Chap. XXI. "Classical Roman Law," by W. W. Buckland.

Cambridge History of India, Vol. I, *Ancient India*, ed. E. J. Rapson. Cambridge, 1922.

Cambridge Medieval History. 8 vols. Cambridge, 1913-36.

Vol. IV. *The Eastern Roman Empire (717-1453).*

"Introduction," by J. B. Bury.

Chap. V, A. "The Struggle with the Saracens, 717-867," by E. W. Brooks.

Chap. XIII. "Venice," by Horatio F. Brown.

Chap. XIV. "The Fourth Crusade and the Latin Empire," by Charles Diehl.

Chap. XVI. "The Empire of Nicaea and the Recovery of Constantinople," by William Miller.

Chap. XIX. "Attempts at Reunion of the Greek and Latin Churches," by Louis Bréhier.

Chap. XX. "The Mongols," by Herbert M. J. Loewe.

Chap. XXII. "Byzantine Legislation from the Death of Justinian (565) to 1453," by Paul Collinet.

Chap. XXIII. "The Government and Administration of the Byzantine Empire," by Charles Diehl.

Chap. XXIV. "Byzantine Civilisation," by Charles Diehl.

Vol. V. *Contest of Empire and Papacy.*

Chap. IV, A. "The Conquest of South Italy and Sicily by the Normans," by Ferdinand Chalandon.

Chap. IV, B. "The Norman Kingdom of Sicily," by Ferdinand Chalandon.

Chap. VIII. "The Kingdom of Jerusalem, 1099-1291," by Charles Lethbridge Kingsford.

Chap. IX. "The Effects of the Crusades upon Western Europe," by E. J. Passant.

Chap. XX. "The Monastic Orders," by Alexander Hamilton Thompson.

Chap. XXI. "Roman and Canon Law in the Middle Ages," by Harold Dexter Hazeltine.

Vol. VI. *Victory of the Papacy.*

Chap. V. "Italy and Sicily under Frederick II," by Michelangelo Schipa.

Chap. XIV. "Commerce and Industry in the Middle Ages," by John Harold Clapham.

Chap. XVII. "The Medieval Universities," by Hastings Rashdall.

Chap. XXIV. "Chivalry," by A. Abram.

Vol. VII. *Decline of Empire and Papacy.*

Chap. VIII. "The Hansa," by A. Weiner.

Chap. XXII. "The Jews in the Middle Ages," by Cecil Roth.

Cambridge Modern History. 13 vols. New York, 1907-25.

Vol. I. *The Renaissance.*

Chap. VIII. "Venice," by Horatio Brown.

Camões, Luiz de. *The Lusiads*, tr. Leonard Bacon. New York, 1950.

Camoens, Luis Vaz de. William C. Atkinson, tr. (Penguin Book) Harmondsworth, 1952.

Capellanus, Andreas. *The Art of Courtly Love*, with intro., trans. and notes by John Jay Perry. New York, 1941.

Carlyle, R. W., and A. J. Carlyle. *A History of Mediaeval Political Theory in the West.* 6 vols. Edinburgh and London, 1928-36.

Carnoy, A. J. "Zoroastrianism," in *Encyclopaedia of Religion and Ethics*, ed. James Hastings, Vol. XII.

Carr, E. H. *Nationalism and After.* London, 1945.

Casson, Stanley. *Progress and Catastrophe: an Anatomy of Human Adventure.* New York and London, 1937.

Castiglione, Arturo. *A History of Medicine*, tr. E. S. Krumbhaer. New York, 1941.

Castle, Wilfrid T. F. *Syrian Pageant, the History of Syria and Palestine, 1000 B.C. to A.D. 1945.* London and New York, 1948.

Chapple, E. D., and C. S. Coon. *Principles of Anthropology.* New York, 1942.

Cheshire, G. C. *Private International Law.* Oxford, 1935.

Childe, Gordon. *What Happened in History*. (Penguin Book) New York, 1946.

Christy, Arthur, ed. *The Asian Legacy and American Life*. New York, 1945.

Church, Richard William. *Dante: an Essay* (with tr. of "De Monarchia" by F. J. Church). London, 1879.

Cicero, Marcus Tullius. *De Legibus*, with English tr. by C. W. Keyes. London and New York, 1928.

————. *De Officiis*, with English tr. by Walter Miller. London, 1947.

————. *De Re Publica*, with English tr. by C. W. Keyes. London and New York, 1928.

————. *On the Commonwealth*, tr. with notes and intro. by George H. Sabine and Stanley B. Smith. Columbus, Ohio, 1929.

Cicognani, Amleto G. *Canon Law*. 2d rev. ed. Philadelphia, 1935.

Cochrane, Charles Norris. *Christianity and Classical Culture: a Study of Thought and Action from Augustus to Augustine*. Oxford, 1940.

Cohen, Joseph W. "The Role of Philosophy in Culture," *Philosophy East and West*, v (No. 2, July, 1955).

Condliffe, J. B. *The Commerce of Nations*. New York, 1950.

Confucius. *Confucius, The Unwobbling Pivot and The Great Digest*, tr. Ezra Pound. New York, 1947.

Coon, Carleton S. *Caravan: the Story of the Middle East*. New York, 1951.

Cornford, Frances M. *Before and After Socrates*. Cambridge, 1951.

Creel, H. G. *Chinese Thought, from Confucius to Mao Tsê-tung*. Chicago, 1953.

Crump, G. C., and E. F. Jacob, eds. *The Legacy of the Middle Ages*. Oxford, 1926.

Cunningham, W. *An Essay on Western Civilisation in Its Economic Aspects*. 2 vols. Cambridge, 1913.

Dante Alighieri. *De Monarchia* (the Oxford text), ed. E. Moore. Oxford, 1916.

Dawson, Christopher. *The Making of Europe, an Introduction to the History of European Unity*. New York, 1945.

Dennett, David C. "Pirenne and Muhammad," *Speculum*, xxiii (April, 1948).

Dickson, H. R. P. *The Arab of the Desert*. London, 1951.

Diehl, Charles. *Byzantium: Greatness and Decline*. New Brunswick, N.J., 1957.

————. *History of the Byzantine Empire*. Princeton, 1925.

————. *Les Grands Problèmes de l'Histoire Byzantine*. Paris, 1943.

Dodds, Eric R. *The Greeks and the Irrational*. Berkeley, 1951.

Doughty, Charles M. *Travels in Arabia Deserta*. New York, n.d.

Dubois, Pierre. *De recuperatione Terre Sancte: traité de politique générale*, ed. from the Vatican manuscript by Charles V. Langlois. Paris, 1891.

Dubs, Homer. "The Concept of Unity in China," in *The Quest for Political Unity in World History*, ed. Stanley Pargellis. Washington, 1944.

Dunlop, D. M. *The History of the Jewish Khazars*. Princeton, 1954.

Duyvendak, J. J. L. *China's Discovery of Africa.* London, 1949.

Ehrich, Robert W., ed. *Relative Chronologies in Old World Archaeology.* Chicago, 1954.

Eisler, Robert. *Weltenmantel und Himmelszelt, Religionsgeschichtliche Untersuchungen zur Urgeschichte des Antiken Weltbildes.* 2 vols. Munich, 1910.

Elgood, Cyril. *A Medical History of Persia and the Eastern Caliphate.* Cambridge, 1951.

Eliade, Mircea. "Note sur l'érotique mystique indienne," *La Table Ronde* (No. 97, January, 1956).

Eliot, Sir Charles Norton Edgcumbe, and A. Neville J. Whyment. "Huns," in *Encyclopaedia Britannica* (14th ed.), Vol. XI.

Eppstein, John. *The Catholic Tradition of the Law of Nations.* Washington, 1935.

Escarra, Jean. *Le Droit Chinois.* Peiping and Paris, 1936.

Fă-hien. *The Travels of Fa-hsien (399-414* A.D.*), or, Record of the Buddhistic Kingdoms,* tr. H. A. Giles. London, 1956.

Fairbank, John K., ed. *Chinese Thought and Institutions.* Chicago, 1957.

Finkelstein, Louis, ed. *The Jews, Their History, Culture, and Religion.* 2 vols. New York, 1949.

Foda, Ezzeldin. *The Projected Arab Court of Justice (with Specific Reference to the Muslim Law of Nations).* The Hague, 1957.

Frank, J. N. *Courts on Trial: Myth and Reality in American Justice.* Princeton, 1949.

Frankfort, Henri, ed. *The Intellectual Adventure of Mankind.* Chicago, 1946.

Freeman, E. H. *History of Federal Government in Greece and Italy.* London and New York, 1893.

Fritz, Kurt von. *The Theory of the Mixed Constitution in Antiquity, a Critical Analysis of Polybius' Political Ideas.* New York, 1954.

Frobenius, Leo. *Und Afrika Sprach.* Berlin, 1912.

Fueter, E. *Geschichte des Europäischen Staatensystems von 1492 bis 1559.* Munich and Berlin, 1919.

Fung, Yu-lan. *A History of Chinese Philosophy,* tr. Derk Bodde. Peiping, 1937.

Fustel de Coulanges, Numa Denis. *La Cité Antique.* Paris, 1888.

Ganshof, François L. "Le Moyen Age," in Pierre Renouvin, *Histoire des Relations Internationales.* Paris, 1953.

Gay, E. F. "Hanseatic League," in *Encyclopaedia Britannica* (14th ed.), Vol. XI.

Gelder, H. van. *Geschichte der Alten Rhodier.* The Hague, 1900.

Gelzer, M. *Studien zur Byzantinischen Verwaltung Egyptens.* Leipzig, 1909.

Gibb, H. A. R. "Constitutional Organization," in *Law in the Middle East,* Vol. I, *Origin and Development of Islamic Law,* ed. Majid Khadduri and Herbert J. Liebesny. Washington, 1955.

———. "An Interpretation of Islamic History," *Cahiers d'Histoire Mondiale,* I (No. 1, July, 1953).

———. *Mohammedanism.* London, 1950.

————. "Social Reform: Factor x. The Search for an Islamic Democracy," *The Atlantic Monthly*, October, 1956.

————, and Harold Bowen. *Islamic Society and the West*, Vol. I, parts 1 and 2. London and New York, 1950-57.

Gibbon, Edward. *The History of the Decline and Fall of the Roman Empire*. 2 vols. (Modern Library) New York, n.d.

Gierke, Otto. *Political Theories of the Middle Ages*, tr. F. W. Maitland. Beacon Paperback, Boston, 1958.

Gilson, Etienne. "Medieval Universalism and Its Present Value," in Harvard Tercentenary Conference of Arts and Sciences, *Independence, Convergence and Borrowing in Institutions, Thought and Art*. Cambridge, Mass., 1937.

Glanville, S. R. K., ed. *The Legacy of Egypt*. Oxford, 1953.

Glasenapp, Helmuth von. *Die Fünf Grossen Religionen*. 2 vols. Düsseldorf, 1952.

Glover, T. R. *Democracy in the Ancient World*. Cambridge, 1927.

Gokhale, B. G. *The Making of the Indian Nation*. Bombay, 1958.

Goodrich, L. Carrington. *A Short History of the Chinese People*. Rev. ed. New York, 1951.

Goodspeed, George Stephen. *History of the Babylonians and Assyrians*. New York, 1902.

Grotius, Hugo. *The Rights of War and Peace, Including the Law of Nature and of Nations*, tr. A. C. Campbell. Washington and London, 1901.

Grousset, E. *Bilan de l'Histoire*. Paris, 1946.

————. *L'Empire des Steppes*. Paris, 1939.

Guillaume, Alfred. *Islam*. (Penguin Book) Harmondsworth, 1954.

Gurney, O. R. *The Hittites*. London, 1952.

Haas, William S. *Iran*. New York, 1946.

Hadas, Moses. "Federalism in Antiquity," in *Approaches to World Peace*, ed. Lyman Bryson. New York, 1944.

————. *Hellenistic Culture: Fusion and Diffusion*. New York, 1959.

Hakim, Khalifa Abdul. *Islam and Communism*. Lahore, 1953.

Hanke, Lewis. *Bartolomé de las Casas, Bookman, Scholar and Propagandist*. Philadelphia, 1952.

Harrison, Frederic. *Byzantine History in the Early Middle Ages*. London, 1900.

Haskins, Charles H. *The Rise of Universities*. New York, 1923.

————. *Studies in the History of Medieval Science*. Cambridge, 1927.

Hazard, Harry W. *Atlas of Islamic History*. Princeton, 1952.

Hazlitt, W. Carew. *The Venetian Republic*. London, 1915.

Hearnshaw, F. J. C., ed. *The Social and Political Ideas of Some Great Medieval Thinkers*. London, 1923.

Hemleben, Sylvester John. *Plans for World Peace Through Six Centuries*. Chicago, 1945.

Henderson, Ernest F. *Select Historical Documents of the Middle Ages*. London, 1925.

Herodotus. *The History of Herodotus*, tr. George Rawlinson, ed. Manuel Komroff. New York, 1928.

Hill, David Jayne. *A History of Diplomacy in the International Development of Europe.* 2 vols. London, 1921.

Hitti, Philip K. *History of the Arabs.* London, 1946.

Hoffman, Ross. *The Great Republic, a Historical View of the International Community and the Organization of Peace.* New York, 1942.

Hogben, Lancelot. *From Cave Painting to Comic Strip.* New York, 1949.

Hourani, G. F. *Arab Seafaring in the Indian Ocean in Ancient and Early Medieval Times.* Princeton, 1951.

Hsüan-tsang. *Chinese Accounts of India,* tr. Samuel Beal. 3 vols. Calcutta, 1957-58.

Hsüntze. *The Works of Hsüntze,* tr. H. H. Dubs. London, 1928.

Hu Shih. "The Indianization of China," in Harvard Tercentenary Conference of Arts and Sciences, *Independence, Convergence and Borrowing in Institutions, Thought and Art.* Cambridge, Mass., 1937.

Hudson, Geoffrey Francis. *Europe and China: a Survey of Their Relations from the Earliest Times to 1800.* London, 1931.

Hume, David. "Of the Balance of Power," in his *Essays, Literary, Moral and Political.* London, 1752.

Hutchins, Robert Maynard. *St. Thomas and the World State.* Milwaukee, 1949.

Hutton, J. H. *Caste in India.* Cambridge, 1951.

Huzayyin, S. A. *Arabia and the Far East, Their Commercial and Cultural Relations in Graeco-Roman and Irano-Arabian Times.* Cairo, 1912.

Ibn Khaldûn. *The Muqaddimah, an Introduction to History,* tr. Franz Rosenthal. 3 vols. (Bollingen series, XLIII.) New York, 1959.

Ihering, Rudolph von. *Geist des Roemischen Rechts auf den verschiedenen Stufen seiner Entwicklung.* 5th ed. Leipzig, 1891.

International Law Association. *Briand-Kellogg Pact of Paris.* London, 1934.

Iqbal, Sir Muhammad. *The Mysteries of Selflessness,* tr. Arthur J. Arberry. London, 1953.

Jackh, E., ed. *Background of the Middle East.* New York, 1952.

Johnson, E. N. "American Mediaevalists and Today," *Speculum,* XXVIII (No. 4, October, 1953).

Jones, H. Stuart. "Mithraism," in *Encyclopaedia of Religion and Ethics,* ed. James Hastings, Vol. VIII.

Justice, Alexander. *A General Treatise of the Dominion and Laws of the Sea.* London, 1705.

Justinian. *The Institutes of Justinian,* with English intro., tr., and notes by Thomas Collett Sanders. London, 1900.

Kantorowicz, Ernst. *Frederick the Second, 1194-1250.* New York, 1931.

Kautilya (Chanakya). *Kautilya's Arthasāstra,* tr. R. Shamasastry. Bangalore, 1915.

Kelly, Amy. *Eleanor of Aquitaine and the Four Kings.* Cambridge, Mass., 1950.

Khadduri, Majid. "Constitutional Development in Syria, with Emphasis on the Constitution of 1950," *The Middle East Journal,* v (No. 2, April, 1951).

————. *The Law of War and Peace: a Study in Muslim International Law*. London, 1940.

————. "Nature and Sources of Islamic Law," *The George Washington Law Review*, XXII (October, 1953).

————, and Herbert J. Liebesny, eds. *Law in the Middle East*, Vol. I, *Origin and Development of Islamic Law*. Washington, 1955.

Kibre, Pearl. *The Nations in the Medieval Universities*. Cambridge, Mass., 1948.

Kluchevsky, V. O. *A History of Russia,* tr. C. J. Hogarth. 3 vols. London and New York, 1911-12.

Komroff, Manuel, ed. *Contemporaries of Marco Polo*. New York, 1928.

Koran. *The Meaning of the Glorious Koran,* tr. Marmaduke Pickthall. (Mentor Book) New York, 1956.

Krey, August C. "The International State of the Middle Ages: Some Reasons for Its Failure," *American Historical Review*, XXVIII (No. 1, October, 1922).

Lane, F. C. *Andres Barbarigo, Merchant of Venice*. Baltimore, 1944.

————. "Family Partnerships and Joint Ventures in the Venetian Republic," *Journal of Economic History*, IV (1944).

————. *Venetian Ships and Shipbuilders of the Renaissance*. Baltimore, 1934.

Larsen, J. A. O. *Representative Government in Greek and Roman History*. Berkeley, 1955.

Lecky, W. E. H. *History of European Morals*. London, 1946.

Le Fur, Louis, and Georges Chklaver. *Recueil de Textes de Droit International Public*. Paris, 1928.

Legge, James, tr. *The Sacred Books of China: The Texts of Confucianism*. Oxford, 1885.

Lenfant, Jacques. *The History of the Council of Constance*. New ed. 2 vols. London, 1728.

Levchenko, M. V. *History of Byzantium*. Moscow and Leningrad, 1940.

Lewis, A. R. *Naval Power and Trade in the Mediterranean:* A.D. *500-1100*. Princeton, 1951.

Lin Yutang. *The Wisdom of Confucius*. New York, 1943.

Lindsay, W. S. *The History of Merchant Shipping and Ancient Commerce*. 4 vols. London, 1874-76.

Livingstone, R. W., ed. *The Legacy of Greece*. Oxford, 1921.

Lizerand, George. *Le Dossier de l'Affaire des Templiers*. Paris, 1923.

Llewellyn, Karl, and E. A. Hoebel. *The Cheyenne Way: Conflict and Case Law in Primitive Jurisprudence*. Norman, Okla., 1941.

Lopez, Robert S., and Irving W. Raymond, eds. and trs. *Medieval Trade in the Mediterranean World: Illustrative Documents*. New York, 1955.

Machiavelli, Nicolo. *History of Florence and of the Affairs of Italy, from the Earliest Times to the Death of Lorenzo the Magnificent*. London, 1901.

————. *The Prince, and The Discourses*. (Modern Library) New York, 1950.

MacLeod, W. O. *The Origin and History of Politics*. New York, 1931.

Maine, Sir Henry. *Ancient Law*. 3d American ed. New York, 1879.

———. *The Early History of Institutions*. New York, 1888.

———. *Village Communities in the East and West, and Other Lectures*. New York, 1880.

Marcus Aurelius. *The Communings with Himself of Antoninus*. Rev. text and tr. C. R. Haines. London, 1924.

Marvin, F. S., ed. *The Evolution of World Peace*. London and New York, 1921.

Mas Latrie, Jacques Marie Joseph Louis de. *Traités de Paix et Documents Divers Concernant les Relations des Chrétiens avec les Arabes de l'Afrique Septentrionale au Moyen Age*. Paris, 1866.

Mattingly, Garrett. *Renaissance Diplomacy*. Boston, 1955.

Maulde-La-Clavière, M. de. *Histoire de Louis XII*, Part 2, *La Diplomatie au Temps de Machiavel*. 3 vols. Paris, 1893.

Mazour, Anatole G. *Russia, Past and Present*. New York, 1951.

McIlwain, Charles Howard. *Constitutionalism Ancient and Modern*. Ithaca, N.Y., 1940.

Meyer, Eduard. "Parthia," in *Encyclopaedia Britannica* (14th ed.), Vol. XVII.

Miller, Walter. *Greece and the Greeks*. New York, 1941.

Minorsky, V. "The Middle East in Western Politics in the 13th, 14th and 15th Centuries," *Journal of the Royal Central Asian Society*, XXVII (1940).

Mommsen, Theodor. *The History of Rome,* tr. W. P. Dickson. 4 vols. (Everyman's Library) New York, 1911.

———. *The Provinces of the Roman Empire from Caesar to Diocletian*. 2 vols. London, 1909.

Motse. *The Ethical and Political Works of Motse*, tr. Y. P. Mei. London, 1929.

Mowat, R. B. *Diplomacy and Peace*. New York, 1936.

Muhammad ibn 'Abd Allāh (Ibn Batūtah). *Travels in Asia and Africa, 1325-54*, tr. and sel. H. A. R. Gibb. London, 1929.

Nasser, Gamal Abdul. *The Egyptian Revolution*. New York, 1955.

Needham, Joseph. *Science and Civilisation in China*. 3 vols. Cambridge, 1954-59.

Nehru, Jawaharlal. *The Discovery of India*. New York, 1946.

Nelson, M. Frederic. *Korea and the Old Orders in Eastern Asia*. Baton Rouge, La., 1945.

Newton, A. P., ed. *Travels and Travellers of the Middle Ages*. New York, 1926.

Nicolson, Harold. *Diplomacy*. London and New York, 1950.

———. *The Evolution of Diplomatic Method*. London, 1954.

Niebuhr, Reinhold. *The Children of Light and the Children of Darkness*. New York, 1944.

Nietzsche, Friedrich. "Unzeitgemässe Betrachtungen, aus dem Nachlass 1873-75," in Nietzsches Werke (Taschen Ausgabe, Band II). Stuttgart, 1921. (*The Use and Abuse of History*, New York, 1957.)

Nizam al-Mulk, Abu 'Ali Hasan. *Siasset Namèh, Traité de Gouvernement composé pour le Sultan Melik-Chah,* tr. C. Schefer. (Publ. de l'Ecole des langues orientales vivantes.) 2 vols. Paris, 1891-93.

Northrop, F. S. C. "Contemporary Jurisprudence and International Law," *The Yale Law Journal,* LXI (No. 5, May, 1952).

——. *The Meeting of East and West: an Inquiry Concerning World Understanding.* New York, 1949.

——. *The Taming of the Nations.* New York, 1952.

Nussbaum, Arthur. *A Concise History of the Law of Nations.* New York, 1947.

Oakeshott, W. F. *Commerce and Society, a Short History of Trade and Its Effects on Civilisation.* Oxford, 1936.

Oates, Whitney J., and Eugene O'Neill, Jr., eds. *The Complete Greek Drama.* 2 vols. New York, 1938. (Plays by Aeschylus, Aristophanes, Euripides, and Sophocles.)

Ostrogorsky, Georg. *Geschichte des byzantinischen Staates.* Munich, 1940. (*History of the Byzantine State,* tr. Joan Jussey. New Brunswick, N.J., 1957.)

Panikkar, K. M. *A Survey of Indian History.* Bombay and Calcutta, 1954.

Pardessus, Jean Marie. *Collection de Lois Maritimes Antérieures au* XVIII*e Siècle.* 6 vols. Paris, 1828-45.

Pelliot, Paul. "Les Mongols et la Papauté," *Revue de l'Orient Chrétien,* XXIII (1922), XXIV (1924), XXVIII (1931).

Phillipson, Coleman. *The International Law and Custom of Ancient Greece and Rome.* 2 vols. London, 1911.

Pirenne, Henri. *Economic and Social History of Medieval Europe.* (Harvest Book) New York, 1937.

——. *Mahomet et Charlemagne.* Paris and Brussels, 1937. (*Mohammed and Charlemagne,* tr. from 10th French ed. by Bernard Miall. New York, 1939.)

——. *Medieval Cities: Their Origins and the Revival of Trade.* Princeton, 1939.

Plato. *The Works of Plato,* selected and edited by Irwin Edman. New York, the Modern Library, 1930.

Plutarch. *Lives of Illustrious Men,* tr. John Dryden and others. 3 vols. New York, n.d.

Poebel, A. "Der Konflikt zwischen Lagas und Umma zur Zeit Enannatums I und Entemenas," in *Oriental Studies, Published in Commemoration of the Fortieth Anniversary (1883-1923) of Paul Haupt as Director of the Oriental Seminary of The Johns Hopkins University.* Baltimore, 1926.

Pollock, Sir Frederick, and Frederic William Maitland. *The History of English Law.* 2 vols. Cambridge, 1923.

Polybius. *The Histories,* tr. W. R. Paton. 6 vols. London and New York, 1922.

Potiemkine, M., ed. *Histoire de la Diplomatie.* 3 vols. Paris, 1947.

Prasad, Beni. *Theory of Government in Ancient India.* Allahabad, 1927.

Prestage, Edgar, ed. *Chivalry.* New York, 1928.

Radin, Max. *The Jews among the Greeks and Romans*. Philadelphia, 1915.

Raeder, A. H. *L'Arbitrage International chez les Hellènes*. New York, 1912.

Rahman, F. "Internal Religious Developments in the Present Century Islam," *Cahiers d'Histoire Mondiale*, II (No. 4, 1955).

Ralston, J. H. *International Arbitration from Athens to Locarno*. Stanford University, Calif., 1929.

Rashdall, Hastings. *The Universities of Europe in the Middle Ages*. New ed. by F. M. Powicke and A. B. Emden. 3 vols. Oxford, 1936.

Rawlinson, G. *The Sixth Great Oriental Monarchy*. London, 1873.

———. *History of Phoenicia*. London and New York, 1889.

Rawlinson, H. G. *India, a Short Cultural History*. London, 1952.

———. *Intercourse between India and the Western World from the Earliest Times to the Fall of Rome*. Cambridge, 1916.

Robinson, C. A. *Alexander the Great: the Meeting of East and West in World Government and Brotherhood*. New York, 1947.

Robson, W. A. *Civilisation and the Growth of Law*. New York, 1935.

Roby, Henry John. *An Introduction to the Study of Justinian's Digest, together with a Full Commentary on One Title*. Cambridge, 1884.

Rörig, Fritz. "Hanseatic League," in *Encyclopaedia of the Social Sciences*, Vol. VII.

Ross, James Bruce, and Mary Martin McLaughlin, eds. *The Portable Renaissance Reader*. New York, 1953.

Rostovtzeff, M. *Caravan Cities*. Oxford, 1932.

———. *A History of the Ancient World*. 2 vols. Oxford, 1926.

———. *The Social and Economic History of the Hellenistic World*. 3 vols. Oxford, 1941.

Rougemont, Denis de. "Tableau du phénomène courtois," *La Table Ronde*, No. 97, January, 1956.

Runciman, Steven. *Byzantine Civilisation*. London, 1948.

———. *A History of the Crusades*. 3 vols. Cambridge, 1952-53.

Ruville, Albert von. *Die Kreuzzüge*. Bonn, 1920.

Sabine. George H. *A History of Political Theory*. Rev. ed. New York, 1950.

Sarton, George. *A History of Science*. 2 vols. Cambridge, 1952-59.

Schacht, Joseph. *The Origins of Muhammadan Jurisprudence*. Oxford, 1950.

Schevill, Ferdinand. *History of Florence from the Founding of the City through the Renaissance*. New York, 1936.

Schulz, Fritz. *History of Roman Legal Science*. Oxford, 1946.

Scott, E. F. "Gnosticism," in *Encyclopaedia of Religion and Ethics*, ed. James Hastings, Vol. VI.

Scott, James Brown. *The Spanish Origin of International Law*. Oxford, 1934.

Seagle, William. *The Quest for Law*. New York, 1941.

Selfridge, H. Gordon. *The Romance of Commerce*. New York, 1923.

Shahan, Thomas J. "Constance, Council of," in *The Catholic Encyclopaedia*, Vol. IV.

Sherwani, Haroon Khan. *Studies in Muslim Political Thought and Administration*. Lahore, 1945.

Shorter, Alan W. *An Introduction to Egyptian Religion*. London, 1932.

Sigerist, Henry E. *A History of Medicine*, Vol. i. Oxford, 1951.

Sinor, Denis. "Les Relations entre les Mongols et l'Europe jusqu'à la Mort d'Arghoum et de Bela IV," *Cahiers d'Histoire Mondiale*, iii (No. 1, 1956).

Smith, L. M. *Cluny in the Eleventh and Twelfth Centuries*. London, 1930.

Smith, Vincent A. *The Early History of India*. Oxford, 1924.

————. *History of India from the Sixth Century* B.C. *to the Mohammedan Conquest*, London, 1906 (being Vol. ii in A. V. Williams Jackson, ed., *History of India*, 9 vols., London.)

Spengler, Oswald. *Der Untergang des Abendlandes*. 2 vols. Munich, 1923. (*The Decline of the West*, tr. Charles Francis Atkinson. 1 vol. ed. New York, 1932.)

Stawell, F. M. *The Growth of International Thought*. London, 1929.

Stephenson, W. B. *The Crusaders in the East*. Cambridge, 1907.

Stubbs, William. *Seventeen Lectures on the Study of Mediaeval and Modern History and Kindred Subjects*. Oxford, 1900.

Suzuki, Daisetz Teitaro. *Essays in Zen Buddhism*. Series 1-3. Boston, London, and Tokyo. 1927-34.

Sykes, Sir Percy. *A History of Persia*. 2 vols. London, 1921.

————. *The Quest for Cathay*. London, 1936.

Tarn, W. W. *The Greeks in Bactria and India*. Cambridge, 1938.

————. *Hellenistic Civilisation*. 3d ed. London, 1952.

Taylor, Lily Ross. *The Divinity of the Roman Emperor*. Middletown, Conn., 1931.

Teggart, Frederick J. *Rome and China, a Study of Correlations in Historical Events*. Berkeley, 1939.

Thomas, Elbert D. *Chinese Political Thought*. New York, 1927.

Thompson, James Westfall. *Feudal Germany*. Chicago, 1928.

Thorndike, Lynn. *University Records and Life in the Middle Ages*. New York, 1944.

Thucydides. *The Peloponnesian War*, tr. Benjamin Jowett, in *The Greek Historians*, ed. F. R. B. Godolphin, Vol. i. New York, 1942.

Tod, M. Niebuhr. *International Arbitration amongst the Greeks*. Oxford, 1913.

Toynbee, Arnold J. *A Study of History*. 11 vols. London and New York, 1940-59.

————. *The World after the Peace Conference*. London, 1926.

Twiss, Sir Travers, ed. *The Black Book of the Admiralty*. 4 vols. London, 1871-76.

————. "Sea Laws," in *Encyclopaedia Britannica* (14th ed.), Vol. xx.

United Nations. *Charter of the United Nations and Statute of the International Court of Justice*. 2 vols. San Francisco, 1945.

————. *Demographic Yearbook, 1955*. New York, 1955.

————. General Assembly. *Special Report of the Trusteeship Council*, Supplement No. 9 (A.1286), Annex ii, "Statute for the City of Jerusalem," approved by the Trusteeship Council at its 81st meeting, April 4, 1950.

United Nations Educational, Scientific and Cultural Organization (UNESCO). *Humanism and Education in East and West*. Paris, 1953.

Vagts, Alfred. "The Balance of Power: Growth of an Idea," *World Politics*, I (No. 1, October, 1948).

Vasiliev, A. A. *Byzance et les Arabes*. 3 vols. Brussels, 1935-50.

——. *History of the Byzantine Empire, 324-1453*. 2d English ed., rev. Madison, Wis., 1952.

——. *The Russian Attack on Constantinople in 860*. Cambridge, Mass., 1946.

——. "Was Old Russia a Vassal State of Byzantium?" *Speculum*, VII, July 1932, number 31.

Vernadsky, George, and Michael Karpovich. *A History of Russia*. 3 vols. New Haven, 1943-53.

Villard, Henry Serrano. *Libya, the New Arab Kingdom of North Africa*. Ithaca, N.Y., 1956.

Vinogradoff, Sir Paul. *Outlines of Historical Jurisprudence*. Vol. II, *The Jurisprudence of the Greek City*. Oxford, 1922.

——. *Roman Law in Mediaeval Europe*. London and New York, 1909.

Vipper, R. *Ivan Grozny*. Moscow, 1947.

Viswanatha, S. V. *International Law in Ancient India*. London, 1925.

Voltaire, François Marie Arouet de. *The Age of Louis XIV*. (Everyman's Library) New York, 1926.

Von Grunebaum, Gustave E. *Medieval Islam, a Study in Cultural Orientation*. Chicago, 1946.

Waddell, Helen. *The Wandering Scholars*. London, 1927.

Waley, Arthur. *Three Ways of Thought in Ancient China*. New York, 1940.

Walker, Richard L. *The Multi-State System in Ancient China*. New Haven, 1953.

Walsh, E. A., ed. *The History and Nature of International Relations*. New York, 1922.

Walsh, James J. *The Thirteenth Greatest of Centuries*. New York, 1929.

Warmington, E. H. *The Commerce between the Roman Empire and India*. Cambridge, 1928.

Wei Yang. *The Book of Lord Shang, a Classic of the Chinese School of Law*, tr. J. J. L. Duyvendak. London, 1928.

Weigall, Arthur. *Alexander the Great*. London, 1933.

Westerman, W. Linn. "Greek Culture and Thought," in *Encyclopaedia of the Social Sciences*, Vol. I, Introduction I.

Whitehead, Alfred N. *The Aims of Education and Other Essays*. New York, 1929.

Wiet, Gaston. "L'Empire Neo-Byzantin des Omayyades et l'Empire Neo-Sassanide des Abbasides," *Cahiers d'Histoire Mondiale*, I (No. 1, July, 1953).

Wigmore, John Henry. *A Panorama of the World's Legal Systems*. Washington, 1936.

Wilber, Donald N. *Iran, Past and Present*. 4th ed. Princeton, 1958.

Williams, T. G. *The History of Commerce*. London, 1926.

536

Winternitz, M. *Geschichte der Indischen Litteratur*. 3 vols. Leipzig, 1920.

Wolff, Hans Julius. *Roman Law, an Historical Introduction*. Norman, Okla., 1951.

Wolfson, Henry Anstryn. *Philo: Foundations of Religious Philosophy in Judaism, Christianity and Islam*. 2 vols. Cambridge, 1947.

Wright, Arthur F. "Buddhism and Chinese Culture: Phases of Interaction," *The Journal of Asian Studies*, XVII (No. 11, November, 1957).

————. "Fo-t'u-teng, a Biography," *Harvard Journal of Asiatic Studies*, December 1948, vol. 11, nos. 3 and 4.

————. "Fu I and the Rejection of Buddhism," *Journal of the History of Ideas*, Vol. XII (No. 1, January, 1951).

————. "The Indianization of China" (a paper read at the Annual Meeting of the Far Eastern Association, Spring, 1949).

————, ed. *Studies in Chinese Thought*. Chicago, 1953.

————, Hellmut Wilhelm, and Benjamin Schwartz. "Chinese Reactions to Imported Ideas" (symposium), *Journal of the History of Ideas*, XII (No. 1, January, 1951).

Wright, Edwin M. "Conflicting Political Forces and Emerging Patterns," in Academy of Political Science, *Proceedings*, XXIV (No. 4, January, 1952), *International Tensions in the Middle East*.

Wright, Quincy. *A Study of War*. 2 vols. Chicago, 1941.

Wright, R. F. *Medieval Internationalism, the Contribution of the Medieval Church to International Law and Peace*. London, 1930.

Zimmer, Heinrich. *Philosophies of India*, ed. Joseph Campbell. New York, 1951.

Zimmern, Sir Alfred. *The Greek Commonwealth: Politics and Economics in Fifth Century Athens*. 5th ed., rev. Oxford, 1931.

Zimmern, Helen. *The Hansa Towns*. London, 1889.

308, 315, 324-56, 465, 471-77 passim; China's, 168; congressional, 499-504, 516 (*See also* congresses; councils); defined, 324; in the East, 392; Greek, 78; Hanseatic League and, 511; Indian, 118-26; Italian, 326; in modern European states system, 204, 267, 457-98, 518; Persian, 50, 68-69; profession of, 30, 464-77, 481-82; Roman, 172, 176, 204, 211; Russian, 340-56, 458-59; science and, 474-75; of Venice, 392, 464-77; war and, 276. *See also* ambassadors; balance of power; *and specific countries*

disputes, adjustment of, 267. *See also* arbitration; conciliation

Dominicans, 289

Dorpat, 507n, 509

Dortmund, 507

dualism: constitutional, 241-42; Greek, 63-64; in Holy Roman Empire, 301; in religion, 46-47; in Roman Empire, 221, 225; in Venetian approach to diplomacy, 472-73

Dubois, Pierre, 247-48, 515n

Duns Scotus, John, 434n

East, beginnings of relations with West, 57-89. *See also* Far East; Middle East; Near East

Eastern Rome, *see* Byzantium

ecclesiastical community, 241, 261-63, 499. *See also* religion; *and specific culture realms*

economic activities, 18, 22, 33, 39. *See also* industry; merchants; trade

economic cooperation: in ancient Near East, 30, 42; influence of Hanse on modern form of, 513, 518; among Mediterranean nations, 401-12. *See also* merchants

Edessa, 223, 280-81

Edict of Eternal Pacification, 271

education and learning: Alexander's approach to, 93, 101; differing views in East and West, 428-29; internationalization of, 421; in Mesopotamia, 20-21; missionaries and, 334-35; Roman, 179-81; in sixth and seventh centuries, A.D., 223. *See also* elite; literacy; universities

Edward I, 452

Egypt, 18-41 passim, 45; Byzantium and, 315; in empire of Alexander the Great, 65 (map), 90, 96; ethics, 25; foreign policy of, 361; Greece and, 62n; and historiography, 217; Islam in, 227,

358n; law of ancient, 25; Persian Empire, 43; politics in ancient, 24-27 passim; Ptolemaic, example of, for Roman rulers, 178; religion in ancient, 24-27 passim; right of asylum in, 76; Roman legal system in, 208; ruler cult in, 182-83; trade, 26, 27; Venetians and, 461

Elam, 26, 28

Eleanor of Aquitaine, 302-3, 398, 410n

Electoral College, 252, 442n

elite, 13, 164, 429, 431; Buddhist, 157; Byzantine, 311, 313-14, 318-19, 322; Chinese, 151, 154, 156n, 157, 164, 413; Communist, 4; Greek, 64; Hellenistic, 64, 100; Indian, 119, 121, 164; medieval Mediterranean, 398, 399-437; Muslim, 368, 371-81 passim, 385; priestly, 20; in Renaissance Italy, 487; Rhodian, 164, 411; Roman, 195-200 passim, 211, 380; Russian, 4, 348-49; Sicilian, 449; in Spain, 292; urbanization and, 404; in Western Europe, 411-12, 425-32. *See also specific types*, e.g., scholars

empire, as one of three great "virtues," 437, 505. *See also specific empires*, e.g., Byzantium

empire-in-motion, Islamic, 366-67

England: at Council of Constance, 501-4 passim; development as modern state, 451-54 passim; Eastern trade with, 506; as part of Holy Roman Empire, 442; politics in, 454n; Rolls of Oleron in, 411; Roman law in, 445n

English Model Parliament of 1295, 263

Enlil, 21-22, 89

eparchy, 116n

Ephesus, 66

Epicureans, 103

Epirus, 96

Eppstein, John, 256n

equality: Chinese attitude toward, 135-36, 138, 143; in European relations with American Indians, 294-95; Greek attitude toward, 78, 80, 94; in Indian society of states, 122; Islamic attitude toward, 362, 366, 385; in Near Eastern state system, 32; Roman attitude toward, 178, 179; Stoic philosophy, 103, 196; Western attitude toward, 521. *See also* values

Escarra, Jean, quoted, 137n

espionage: in Italy, 467, 479; in Persian Empire, 54-55

ethics and morality: in international relations, 47-48; law and, 201, 266; poli-